W9-ADK-728

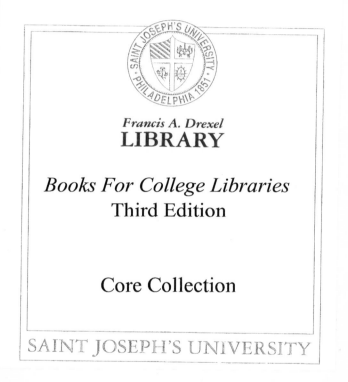

Francis A. Drexel
LIBRARY

Books For College Libraries
Third Edition

Core Collection

SAINT JOSEPH'S UNIVERSITY

UNITED STATES ARMY IN WORLD WAR II

The War in the Pacific

CARTWHEEL:
THE REDUCTION OF RABAUL

by

John Miller, jr.

ST. JOSEPH'S UNIVERSITY

D769.A533 vol. 2., pt. 13   STX

Cartwheel:

3 9353 00099 0844

118991

MILITARY INSTRVCTION

OFFICE OF THE CHIEF OF MILITARY HISTORY

DEPARTMENT OF THE ARMY

WASHINGTON, D. C., 1959

This volume, one of the series UNITED STATES ARMY IN WORLD WAR II, is the eighth to be published in the subseries THE WAR IN THE PACIFIC. All the volumes will be closely related, and the series will present a comprehensive account of the activities of the Military Establishment during World War II. A tentative list of subseries is appended at the end of this volume.

Library of Congress Catalog Card Number: 59–60004

Reprinted 1970

For sale by the Superintendent of Documents, U.S. Government Printing Office
Washington, D.C. 20402 - Price $6.75

UNITED STATES ARMY IN WORLD WAR II

Kent Roberts Greenfield, General Editor

Advisory Committee

(As of 30 May 1958)

Elmer Ellis
University of Missouri

Samuel Flagg Bemis
Yale University

Gordon A. Craig
Princeton University

Oron J. Hale
University of Virginia

W. Stull Holt
University of Washington

Brig. Gen. John B. Sullivan
U.S. Continental Army Command

Brig. Gen. Edgar C. Doleman
Army War College

Brig. Gen. Frederick R. Zierath
Command and General Staff College

Brig. Gen. Kenneth F. Zitzman
Industrial College of the Armed Forces

Col. Vincent J. Esposito
United States Military Academy

T. Harry Williams
Louisiana State University

Office of the Chief of Military History

Maj. Gen. Richard W. Stephens, Chief

Chief Historian	Kent Roberts Greenfield
Chief, Histories Division	Col. Seneca W. Foote
Chief, Editorial and Publication Division	Lt. Col. E. E. Steck
Editor in Chief	Joseph R. Friedman
Chief, Cartographic Branch	Elliot Dunay
Chief, Photographic Branch	Margaret E. Tackley

The History of

THE WAR IN THE PACIFIC

prepared under the direction of Louis Morton

. . . to Those Who Served

Foreword

The campaign described in the present volume was important to the Army as an experience in amphibious warfare and combined operations against a formidable and still resourceful enemy. It was also of critical importance in the evolution of American strategy in the Pacific. CARTWHEEL began as an uphill fight with means that seemed inadequate to the ends proposed, even though these were limited. But it swiftly brought our forces to a crest from which we were able to launch the two powerful drives, through the Southwest and Central Pacific, that crushed Japan before we redeployed the forces directed against Germany. The campaign put to the test the principle of unity of command, and also the capacity for co-operation between two theaters, one under Army, the other under Navy command, and both under forceful and dominant commanders. By ingenious and aggressive use of the ground, sea, and air forces at their disposal they made these suffice to achieve more than had been foreseen as possible, and opened up a new vista of strategy. They took a heavy toll of the enemy's resources, established the technique of bypassing his strongholds, including finally Rabaul itself, and threw him on the defensive. This book will be of interest not only to professional officers, but also to a wide variety of other readers and students.

Washington, D. C.
30 May 1958

R. W. STEPHENS
Maj. Gen., U. S. A.
Chief of Military History

The Author

Born in Scotland and a U.S. citizen since 1928, John Miller, jr., was awarded the degree of Doctor of Philosophy in History by the State University of Iowa in 1942. In World War II he saw service overseas with the U.S. Marine Corps in New Zealand and in the Solomon Islands, where he participated in the Bougainville operations described in this volume. A member of the historical staff of the Department of the Army since 1945, Dr. Miller is the author of *Guadalcanal: The First Offensive* in the present series, coauthor of *Korea: 1951–1953,* and contributor of several chapters to the 1956 edition of ROTC Manual 145–20, *American Military History, 1607–1953*. He has written articles and reviews for historical and military journals, and has taught history at the University of Omaha, the State University of Iowa, the Graduate School of the U.S. Department of Agriculture, and The American University in Washington, D.C.

Preface

The reduction of Rabaul was accomplished by a gigantic double envelopment which required closely co-ordinated land, sea, and air operations by the armed forces of the United States and her Pacific allies. This volume, like the others in the series, attempts to explain in detail the part played by the U.S. Army ground forces and to make clear, by summary, the contributions of all forces and nations.

The CARTWHEEL battles differed from those of the two earlier campaigns, Guadalcanal and Papua, that were directed toward the reduction of Rabaul. In Guadalcanal and Papua the antagonists, more evenly matched than in later campaigns, strained themselves to bring relatively small ground forces to bear on narrow fronts, so that great issues hinged on the outcome of regimental and battalion actions. A study of those campaigns, therefore, quite properly focuses on tactics. During the period covered by this book the Allied commanders could employ superior forces over a vast area while the Japanese had no recourse but to entrench themselves in an effort to hold out and inflict as many casualties as possible. This volume attempts to analyze the techniques by which the Allies employed their strength to bypass fortified positions and seize weakly defended but strategically important areas, or, in the apt baseball parlance used by General MacArthur, to "hit 'em where they ain't." It is, therefore, a study in strategy and high command as well as in tactics.

The willing, able counsel and assistance I have received in preparing this book have greatly eased my task. Dr. Louis Morton, Chief of the Pacific Section of the Office of Military History during the period of research and writing, and my other friends and colleagues in this Office have aided unstintingly. Dr. Kent Roberts Greenfield, Chief Historian of the Army, has been a constant source of wise and kindly help. The successive Chiefs of Military History—Maj. Gens. Orlando Ward, Albert C. Smith, John H. Stokes, and Richard W. Stephens—and Cols. Thomas J. Sands, George G. O'Connor, Ridgway P. Smith, Jr., and Seneca W. Foote have appreciated the nature and worth of history and provided encouragement and powerful support.

For locating and furnishing to me, without restriction, all the necessary records I wish to make public my gratitude to the efficient records staff of this Office and of the Military Records Branch, Federal Records Center, of the U.S. General Services Administration; the Historical Branch, G–3, Headquarters, U.S. Marine Corps; and the Naval History Division of the Office of the Chief of Naval Operations. I also owe thanks to Messrs. Stanley L. Falk and Thomas G. Wilds for performing research and translation in Japanese records, to Mrs. Marguerite Bartz for typing the manuscript, and to the participants named on pp. 386–87 who generously read all or parts of the manuscript and sent in helpful comments and additional information.

Final editing was the responsibility of Mrs. Gay Morenus Hammerman, who also prepared the index. Mrs. Nancy Easterling Payne was copy editor. Maps were prepared under the supervision of Maj. James F. Holly and Mr. Elliot Dunay. Miss Margaret E. Tackley selected the photographs and wrote the captions. To these capable and friendly colleagues who contributed so much—many thanks.

Responsibility for any deficiencies in this book is mine alone.

Washington, D. C.   JOHN MILLER, JR.
30 May 1958

Contents

Tables

Charts

Maps

Illustrations

All illustrations are from Department of Defense files.

CHAPTER I

The Strategic Background

The great Japanese bastion at Rabaul on New Britain in the Bismarck Archipelago posed a double threat to the Allies from 1942 through the early months of 1944. Bristling with warships and airplanes, it menaced the line of communications from the United States to Australia, and it blocked any Allied advance along the north coast of New Guinea to the Philippines. Reduction of Rabaul was therefore the primary mission, during this period, of the Allied forces of the South and Southwest Pacific Areas. In executing this mission these forces fought a long series of ground, air, and naval battles spaced across a vast region. (*Map 1—inside back cover*)

Early Pacific Strategy

Before the Allies could move effectively against Rabaul itself, they had to clear the way by seizing Guadalcanal and driving the Japanese out of the Papuan Peninsula. With the successful conclusion of these two campaigns in early 1943, the South and Southwest Pacific forces completed the first phase of a series of offensive operations against Rabaul that had been ordered by the U.S. Joint Chiefs of Staff in July 1942. The strategic purpose of this series was defensive, the scale limited. The immediate aim of the Joint Chiefs was, not to defeat the Japa-

nese nation, but to protect Australia and New Zealand by halting the Japanese southward advance from Rabaul toward the air and sea lines of communication that joined the United States and Hawaii to Australia and New Zealand.

These orders stemmed from earlier, more fundamental decisions by President Franklin D. Roosevelt, Prime Minister Winston S. Churchill, and the U.S.-British Combined Chiefs of Staff, who from the very outset had agreed to defeat Germany first and then to concentrate against Japan. Pending Germany's defeat, the Allies decided on a defensive attitude in the Pacific. But within this framework they firmly resolved that Australia, New Zealand, the Hawaiian Islands, and Midway were not to be allowed to fall into Japanese hands.[1]

Throughout the early months of 1942 the Japanese threat to the Allied line of communications had mounted stead-

---

[1] For complete discussions on the development of this strategy see Maurice Matloff and Edwin M. Snell, *Strategic Planning for Coalition Warfare: 1941–1942* (Washington, 1953), Chs. I–VIII; Louis Morton, *The Fall of the Philippines* (Washington, 1953), Chs. II–IV, IX; and Mark Skinner Watson, *Chief of Staff: Prewar Plans and Preparations* (Washington, 1950), pp. 367-521. All are in the series, UNITED STATES ARMY IN WORLD WAR II. See also Louis Morton's volumes on strategy, command, and logistics in the Pacific, now in preparation for the same series.

ily. The enemy's capture of Rabaul in January placed him in an excellent position to move south. Well situated in relation to Truk and the Palau Islands, Rabaul possessed a magnificent harbor as well as sites for several airfields. Only 440 nautical miles southwest of Rabaul lies the New Guinea coast, while Guadalcanal is but 565 nautical miles to the southeast. Thus the Japanese could advance southward covered all the way by land-based bombers. And since none of the islands in the Bismarck Archipelago–New Guinea–Solomons area lay beyond fighter-plane range of its neighbors, the Japanese could also cover their advance with fighters by building airstrips as they moved along. By May 1942 they had completed the occupation of the Bismarck Archipelago. They pushed south to establish bases at Lae and Salamaua on the northeast coast of New Guinea, and built airfields in the northern Solomons.

With the Japanese seemingly able to advance at will, the Joint Chiefs had been making all possible efforts to protect Hawaii, Midway, New Zealand, and Australia by holding the lines of communication. Troops to reinforce existing Allied bases and to establish new bases were rushed overseas in early 1942. The 32d and 41st Divisions went to Australia. The 37th Division was dispatched to the Fijis, the Americal Division to New Caledonia, and the 147th Infantry to Tongatabu. Troops of the Americal Division, plus Navy and Marine units, occupied posts in the New Hebrides beginning in March. A Navy and Marine force held Samoa.

At this time the Japanese planned to cut the line of communications and isolate Australia by seizing the Fijis, Samoa, New Caledonia, and Port Moresby in New Guinea. But even before they were turned back from Port Moresby by the Allies during May, in the naval battle of the Coral Sea, the Japanese had postponed the attacks against the Fijis, New Caledonia, and Samoa and had planned instead the June attempt against Midway. Although they managed to seize a foothold in the Aleutians, they failed disastrously at Midway. With four aircraft carriers sunk and hundreds of planes and pilots lost, the Japanese could no longer continue their offensives. The Allies were thus able to take the initiative in the Pacific.

To conduct operations, the Joint Chiefs organized the Pacific theater along lines which prevailed for the rest of the period of active hostilities. By agreement in March 1942 among the Allied nations concerned, they set up two huge commands, the Southwest Pacific Area and the Pacific Ocean Area.[2] (*Map 2*) The Southwest Pacific included Australia and adjacent waters, all the Netherlands Indies except Sumatra, and the Philippine Islands.

The vast Pacific Ocean Areas embraced nearly all the remainder of the Pacific Ocean. Unlike the Southwest Pacific, which was one unit, the Pacific Ocean Areas were divided into three parts—the South, Central, and North Pacific Areas. The North Pacific included the ocean reaches north of latitude 42°

---

[2] The plural is customarily employed for the Pacific Ocean Areas, although the JCS directive establishing the command used "Area." See CCS 57/1, Memo, JCS for President, 30 Mar 42, title: Dirs to CINCPOA and to the Supreme Comdr SWPA, with Incls.

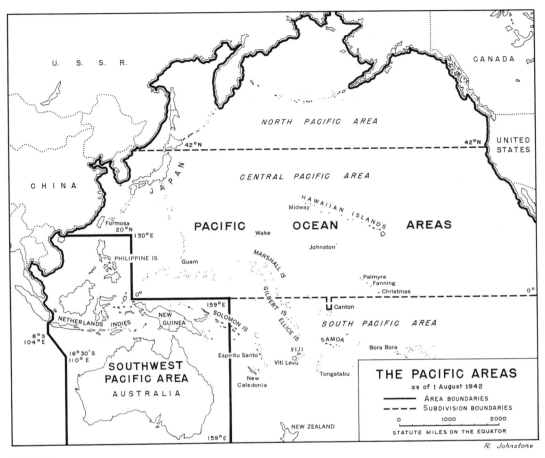

MAP 2

north; the Central Pacific lay between 42° north and the Equator.

The South Pacific Area, which lay south of the Equator, east of longitude 159° east, and west of longitude 110° west, was an enormous stretch of water and islands that included but one modern sovereign nation, the Dominion of New Zealand. Among the islands, many of them well known to readers of romantic fiction, were the French colony of New Caledonia, the British-French Condominium of the New Hebrides, and the Santa Cruz, Fiji, Samoa, Tonga, Cook, Society, and Marquesas Islands. The boundary separating the South and Southwest Pacific Areas (longitude 159° east) split the Solomon Islands.

General Douglas MacArthur, Supreme Commander or, as he came to be called, Commander in Chief of the Southwest Pacific Area, with headquarters at Brisbane, Australia, in early 1943, commanded all land, air, and sea forces

GENERAL DOUGLAS MACARTHUR, *Commander in Chief of the Southwest Pacific Area, with Admiral Chester W. Nimitz, Commander in Chief of the Pacific Ocean Areas. Photograph taken in Brisbane, Australia, March 1944.*

assigned by the several Allied governments.[3] This famous and controversial general was enjoined from directly commanding any national force. In contrast Admiral Chester W. Nimitz, who was concurrently Commander in Chief of the Pacific Ocean Areas, with authority over all Allied forces assigned, was also Commander in Chief of the Pacific Fleet. He exercised direct control over the North and Central Pacific Areas but in accordance with the Joint Chiefs' instructions appointed a subordinate as commander of the South Pacific Area with headquarters first at Auckland, New Zealand, and later at Nouméa, New Caledonia. Like MacArthur, this officer was ineligible to command any national force directly. Admiral William F. Halsey, Jr., the incumbent at the close of the Guadalcanal Campaign, replaced the original commander, Vice Adm. Robert L. Ghormley, on 18 October while the campaign was reaching its climax.

At the time of the Coral Sea engagement in May, a small Japanese force had garrisoned Tulagi in the Solomons, and shortly afterward the Japanese began

---

[3] "Supreme Commander" was the title used by CCS 57/1, 30 Mar 42. MacArthur seems to have preferred "Commander in Chief" and "Supreme Commander" fell into disuse.

building an airfield at nearby Lunga Point on Guadalcanal. Just before they learned of the Japanese airfield under construction on Guadalcanal, the Joint Chiefs capitalized on the Midway victory by ordering the South and Southwest Pacific Areas to begin the advance against Rabaul. The operations, as set forth in the Joint Chiefs' orders of 2 July 1942, were divided into three phases. The first, or "Task One," was the seizure of Tulagi and Guadalcanal in the Solomons, and of the Santa Cruz Islands. Since possession of the Santa Cruz Islands did not prove necessary, they were never taken. Task Two included the capture of the remainder of the Japanese-held Solomons and of Lae, Salamaua, and other points on the northeast coast of New Guinea in the Southwest Pacific Area. Task Three was the seizure and occupation of Rabaul itself, and of adjacent positions.[4]

Command during Task One, which would be executed in the South Pacific Area, was entrusted to the South Pacific commander. Tasks Two and Three, to be carried out by South and Southwest Pacific Area forces entirely within the Southwest Pacific Area, were to be conducted under MacArthur's command.

When they received the Joint Chiefs' directive, the commanders of the South and Southwest Pacific Areas met in Melbourne, Australia, to discuss the three tasks. They agreed that the advance should be governed by two basic concepts: the progressive forward movement of air forces and the isolation of Rabaul before the final assault. After the initial lunge into Guadalcanal, there would follow a series of advances to seize air and naval bases in New Guinea, New Britain, and the northern Solomons. With these bases Allied fighter planes and bombers would be in position to cover the entire Bismarck Archipelago–eastern New Guinea–Solomons area and isolate Rabaul from the east, west, north, and south before troops were put ashore to capture the great base.[5]

The Joint Chiefs of Staff assigned the reinforced 1st Marine Division as the landing force for Task One. That unit, landing on Guadalcanal and Tulagi on 7 August 1942, quickly captured its major objectives. The Japanese reaction to the invasion was so violent and resolute, and Allied control over the air and sea routes so tenuous, that the campaign did not end then but dragged on for six months. It was not until February 1943 —after two Army divisions and one more Marine division had been committed to the battle and six major naval engagements fought—that Guadalcanal was completely wrested from the enemy.[6]

---

[4] Jt Dir for Offen Opns in SWPA Agreed on by U.S. CsofS, 2 Jul 42, OPD 381, Sec 2, Case 83. Unlike other JCS directives, this paper bore no JCS number. It is also reproduced in JCS 112, 21 Sep 42, title: Mil Sit in the Pac.

[5] Dispatch, CINCSWPA and COMSOPAC to CofS USA, COMINCH, and CINCPAC, 8 Jul 42, CCR 82s, ABC 370.26 (7–8–42), Sec 1.

[6] For the history of the Guadalcanal Campaign see John Miller, jr., *Guadalcanal: The First Offensive*, UNITED STATES ARMY IN WORLD WAR II (Washington, 1949); Samuel Eliot Morison, *History of United States Naval Operations in World War II,* Vol. IV, *Coral Sea, Midway, and Submarine Actions* (Boston: Little, Brown and Company, 1949), and Vol. V, *The Struggle for Guadalcanal* (Boston: Little, Brown and Company, 1949); Maj. John L. Zimmerman, USMCR, *The Guadalcanal Campaign* (Washington, 1949); and Wesley Frank Craven and James Lea Cate, eds., *The Army Air Forces in World War II,* Vol. IV, *The Pacific: Guadalcanal to Saipan—August 1942 to July 1944* (Chicago: The University of Chicago Press, 1950).

With the Guadalcanal victory, the Allies seized the initiative from the Japanese and halted their southward advance. The Japanese never attempted the assaults against the Fijis, Samoa, and New Caledonia.

Just as the Guadalcanal Campaign was opening, a Japanese force landed at Buna, on the northeast coast of New Guinea's Papuan peninsula, and attempted to capture the vital Allied base at Port Moresby by crossing the towering Owen Stanley Range. But the offensive stalled, and MacArthur was able to move the 32d U.S. Division, the 7th Australian Division, and several additional American regimental combat teams and Australian infantry brigades against the Japanese beachheads at Buna, Gona, and Sanananda on the Papuan peninsula, as well as to establish bases at Milne Bay at Papua's tip and on Goodenough Island in the D'Entrecasteaux group.[7]

At the beginning of 1943, with both the Guadalcanal and Papuan campaigns drawing to a successful close, the Allies could look forward to using Guadalcanal and Papua as bases for continuing the advance against Rabaul. In the Central Pacific, Admiral Nimitz could not undertake any offensive westward from Pearl Harbor and Midway until the line of communications to Australia was absolutely secure. At this time both Halsey and MacArthur were preparing plans for their campaigns against Rabaul, but had not yet submitted them to the Joint Chiefs of Staff.

The Casablanca Conference

Although the Joint Chiefs of Staff had not yet received detailed plans for Rabaul, they were well aware of the importance of the operations in the South and Southwest Pacific Areas. These operations naturally had to be considered in the light of global strategy and reviewed by the U.S.-British Combined Chiefs of Staff.[8]

By the end of 1942, the Joint Chiefs were concluding their study of Allied objectives for the year 1943. President Roosevelt and the service chiefs were then preparing to meet at Casablanca in French Morocco with Prime Minister Churchill and the British Chiefs in order to explore the problem fully and determine Allied objectives for the year. No final plan for the defeat of Japan had been prepared but the subject was being studied in Washington.[9] Also under discussion were the question of advancing against Japan through the North Pacific

---

[7] For a detailed discussion of the war in the Southwest Pacific, 1942–43, see Samuel Milner, *Victory in Papua*, UNITED STATES ARMY IN WORLD WAR II (Washington, 1957).

[8] See Miller, *Guadalcanal: The First Offensive*, pp. 172–73; Min, JCS mtg, 22 Dec 42; Min, JPS mtg, 16 Sep 42; JCS 112/1, 14 Oct 42; title: Mil Sit in the Pac. For a more detailed discussion see Ray S. Cline, *Washington Command Post: The Operations Division*, UNITED STATES ARMY IN WORLD WAR II (Washington, 1951), pp. 215–19, and Robert E. Sherwood, *Roosevelt and Hopkins: An Intimate History* (New York: Harper & Brothers, 1948), Ch. XXVII. See also John Miller, jr., "The Casablanca Conference and Pacific strategy," *Military Affairs*, XIII (Winter 1949), 4.
Unless otherwise indicated, this section is based on the proceedings and papers of the Casablanca Conference which are filed in regular sequence with the CCS and JCS minutes and papers. They were also printed and bound, along with the proceedings of the meetings attended by the President and Prime Minister, in a useful separate volume—Casablanca Conference: Papers and Minutes of Meetings.

[9] JPS 67/2, 4 Jan 43, title: Proposed Dir for a Campaign Plan for the Defeat of Japan.

and the possibility of conducting operations in Burma to reopen the road to China.[10]

Pacific operations, and the emphasis and support that the advance on Rabaul would receive, were significantly affected by decisions made at Casablanca. During the ten-day conference that began on 14 January the President, the Prime Minister, and the Combined Chiefs of Staff carefully weighed their strategic ends, apportioned the limited means available to accomplish them, and so determined Allied courses of action for 1943.

The Americans and British who met at Casablanca agreed on general objectives, but their plans differed in several important respects. The Americans wished the Allies to conduct a strategic offensive directly against Germany and to aid the Soviet Union, but they also favored strong action in the Pacific and Far East. It was imperative, in their view, to guarantee the security of Allied lines of communication there and to break the enemy hold on positions that threatened them. Convinced that China had to be kept in the war, they recommended that the British, with the aid of American ships and landing craft, recapture Burma so that the Burma Road could be reopened and the Allies could send more supplies to bolster Generalissimo Chiang Kai-shek's armies. They wished to keep the initiative in the Southwest and South Pacific, to inflict heavy losses on the Japanese, and eventually to use Rabaul and nearby positions as bases for further advances. Admiral Ernest J. King, Chief of Naval Operations, expressed the hope

that 30 percent of Allied military power could be deployed against the Japanese instead of the 15 percent which he estimated was then being used.

The British understandably shied away from enlarging the scope of Allied action in the Pacific. With the Germans right across the Channel from England, the British stressed the importance of concentrating against Germany first. While admitting the necessity for retaking Burma, they strongly emphasized the importance of aiding the Soviet Union. They promised to deploy their entire strength against Japan after the defeat of Germany, and suggested that the Japanese should meanwhile be contained by limited offensives. At the same time the British desired to extend the scope of Allied operations in the Mediterranean.

General George C. Marshall, Chief of Staff, and Admiral King opposed what Marshall called "interminable operations in the Mediterranean." They advocated maintaining constant, unremitting pressure against the Japanese to prevent them from digging in and consolidating their gains. Warning that the American people would not stand for another Bataan, Marshall argued that sufficient resources must be kept in the Pacific; otherwise "a situation might arise in the Pacific at any time that would necessitate the United States regretfully withdrawing from the commitments in the European Theatre." [11] Admiral King, pointing out the strategic importance of an advance across the Central Pacific to the Philippines, raised the question of where to go after Rabaul was captured. The British did not wish to make spe-

---

[10] Min, JPS mtgs, 2 and 9 Dec 42; Min, JCS mtgs, 25 Aug, 15 Sep, and 15 Dec 42, and 5 Jan 43; Min, CCS mtg, 6 Nov 42.

[11] Min, CCS mtg, 17 Jan 43.

cific commitments for operations beyond Rabaul but suggested a meeting after its capture to decide the question.

By 23 January Americans and British had reconciled their differences over strategic objectives for 1943. They agreed to secure the sea communications in the Atlantic, to move supplies to the Soviet Union, to take Sicily, to continue their build-up of forces in Britain for the invasion of northern France, and—a decision that was to have a marked effect on Pacific operations—to bomb Germany heavily in the Combined Bomber Offensive that was to be launched by midsummer 1943. To make sure that none of these undertakings would be jeopardized by the need for diverting strength to prevent disaster in the Pacific, adequate forces would be maintained in the Pacific and Far East. What was considered "adequate" was not defined.

The Combined Chiefs agreed in principle that Burma was to be recaptured by the British and that they would meet later in the year to make final decisions. In the Pacific the Allies were to maintain constant pressure on Japan with the purpose of retaining the initiative and getting into position for a full-scale offensive once Germany had surrendered. Specifically, the Allies intended to capture Rabaul, make secure the Aleutians, and advance west through the Gilberts and Marshalls in the Central Pacific toward Truk and the Marianas. The Central Pacific advances were supposed to follow the capture of Rabaul.

CHAPTER II

Selecting Objectives

With Allied strategic objectives for 1943 determined at Casablanca, the next task facing the Army and Navy commanders in Washington and in the Pacific was the selection of exact tactical objectives. Two considerations would be paramount in making a choice: the military value of the objectives, and the resources that would be available. The process of selection was not completed until a full-dress conference involving the Joint Chiefs of Staff, the Joint Staff Planners, and representatives of all the Pacific commands had met in Washington.[1] Such a conference was made necessary by the large disparity between the size of the forces General MacArthur asked for to take his objectives and the size of the forces that were actually available.

Preliminary Theater Planning

General MacArthur's Plans

In the Southwest Pacific, General MacArthur had begun planning for the offensive against Rabaul at an early date. His plans for Tasks Two and Three—mutually supporting advances along two axes, culminating in a converging attack against Rabaul—were the same in early January 1943 as those outlined in July of the previous year. But his forces could not start Task Two until the Allies had successfully completed the Guadalcanal and Papuan campaigns in the first two months of 1943. There were not enough ground troops to undertake any offensive moves immediately, MacArthur reported, and there were far from enough air forces to conduct the campaigns.[2]

In order to advance against Rabaul in one continuous movement, MacArthur wished to assemble all the necessary forces before starting the offensive, and substantial reinforcements would be required. In both South and Southwest Pacific Areas there were troops equivalent to fifteen and two-thirds American, New Zealand, and Australian divisions, but not all were trained and equipped for offensive action. Of the six trained Southwest Pacific divisions, five would be resting and reorganizing for some time to come, after fighting in Guadalcanal, Papua, and the Middle East. There were seven trained divisions—six American and one New Zealand—as well as some separate infantry and cavalry regiments in the South Pacific. Three of the divisions and one regiment had seen service on Guadalcanal and were enjoying

---

[1] See below, pp. 11–15.

[2] Rad to MacArthur, 7 Jan 43, CM–OUT 2273; Rad to MacArthur, 8 Jan 43, CM–OUT 2833; Rad from MacArthur, 10 Jan 43, CM–IN 4574.

a well-deserved rest. The equivalent therefore of only five divisions plus several separate regiments could be counted as ready for immediate use.

In naval strength, MacArthur was limited to cruisers, destroyers, and submarines. He had no carriers, no battleships, and few cargo ships, transports, and landing craft. The greater part of the Pacific Fleet, including aircraft carriers, battleships, cruisers, and destroyers, was operating in the South Pacific Area.

Both areas boasted a total air strength of about 1,850 land-based planes of all types—bombers, fighters, and cargo planes. These planes came from the U.S. Army Air Forces, the U.S. Navy, the U.S. Marine Corps, the Royal New Zealand Air Force, and the Royal Australian Air Force.[3]

At this time General MacArthur was looking forward to targets well beyond Rabaul; he had set his sights on the Philippine Islands. In February 1943 he and his staff concluded that the completion of the campaign against Rabaul could secure for the Allies "important, but not decisive advantages." These advantages would certainly aid future operations but, except for the destruction of precious shipping, would do little damage to Japan's main economic structure. Since the Netherlands Indies contained the great economic wealth, especially oil, taken by Japan in 1941 and 1942, a

decisive blow could be struck, MacArthur reasoned, by cutting the lines of communication between Japan and the Indies. As the Philippine Islands lay squarely athwart all sea and air routes between Japan and the Indies, the Allies could cut them by establishing air and naval bases in the Philippines. General MacArthur concluded that he should move to the Philippines by advancing westward along New Guinea's north coast, then swinging northwest through the intermediate islands into the Philippines. The advance along the New Guinea coast might be started about the time that the siege of Rabaul began, but could not safely start until Rabaul was neutralized lest ships and planes based there harry or obstruct the advance.[4]

This plan for advancing to the Philippines, called RENO, had not yet been transmitted to Washington. It looked far into the future. There were not enough forces to inaugurate the Rabaul plan, ELKTON. Certainly not enough were available to begin RENO.

Admiral Halsey's Plan

In the South Pacific, Admiral Halsey looked on Munda Point in New Georgia as the most likely first objective for his forces under Task Two.[5] The Japanese had started an airfield at the Australian Methodist Mission on Munda in November 1942 when their attempts to recapture Henderson Field on Guadalcanal had faltered. The new field was intended to serve as an advanced air base in an-

[3] Information on strength and plans at this time is drawn from GHQ SWPA, ELKTON Plan for the Seizure and Occupation of the New Britain–New Guinea–New Ireland Area, 12 and 28 Feb 43, and from U.S. Strategic Bombing Survey, *The Employment of Forces Under the Southwest Pacific Command* (Washington, 1947), p. 18. The latter is an almost verbatim copy of a series of monographs prepared during and immediately after the war by the Historical Section, G–3, GHQ, SWPA.

[4] GHQ SWPA, Estimate of the Situation and Rough Draft, RENO Plan, 25 Feb 43, OCMH.

[5] The name "Munda" is apparently a phonetic rendition of a native term rather than a reflection of Caesar's glory.

other attempt to retake Henderson Field in 1943.

The Japanese exhibited skill and cunning in concealing their activities at Munda. Even though the Allies had long known that Munda Point was being used as a staging area, they were not sure that an airfield was under construction until 3 December. The Japanese had rigged cables to the tops of the palm trees, then cut the trunks away and left the cables holding up the treetops. Thus hidden from aerial observation, they built their runway and then cut down the camouflage. The day they completed the runway, 15 December 1942, the Japanese decided to build a second airfield at Vila on nearby Kolombangara.[6] The airfields at Munda and Vila, only 180 nautical miles from Henderson Field, presented a serious threat to the Allied positions in the Solomons and New Hebrides.

In Allied hands, Munda would be invaluable for continuing the advance against Rabaul, and Admiral Halsey's forces pressed on. They capped their success on Guadalcanal with the bloodless seizure of the Russell Islands on 21 February 1943. This shortened the airline distance to Munda by sixty-five miles and provided torpedo boat and landing craft bases to assist in the capture of all New Georgia, an operation then being planned by Halsey and his subordinates.

Munda Point was, physically, one of the best sites for an air base in the Solomon Islands. Strategically, it was well situated to support an advance to Bougainville, which would be necessary if South Pacific aircraft were to strike Rabaul effectively.[7] South Pacific forces would have to use aircraft carriers to advance directly from Henderson Field to Bougainville, but possession of Munda Point would enable them to advance progressively under cover of land-based fighter planes and bombers and obviate the need to use precious carriers close to islands that were studded with enemy airfields.[8]

The Pacific Military Conference

Neither MacArthur nor Halsey could start his offensive yet. They had not yet agreed on a co-ordinated plan, and they lacked enough forces to begin. Allotment of forces would depend on decisions by the Joint and Combined Chiefs of Staff, who at Casablanca had decided on the program for 1943 without knowing how many troops, planes, and ships would be needed for Rabaul.

Shortly before leaving Washington for Casablanca, the Joint Chiefs had instructed MacArthur to submit detailed plans for carrying out their directive of 2 July 1942 and authorized him to exchange views with Nimitz and Halsey. They suggested personal meetings by the

[6] Southeast Area Naval Operations, I, Japanese Monogr No. 48 (OCMH) in the series Japanese Studies in World War II, 47, 52; ONI USN, Combat Narratives: Solomon Islands Campaign, X, Operations in the New Georgia Area, 21 June–5 August 1943 [Washington, 1944], 1–2.

[7] From Henderson Field to the Shortland Islands is 285 nautical miles, to Kahili, 300 miles, to Buka Passage, 363 miles. From Munda, which is within fighter range of Henderson and the Russells, to the Shortlands is 100 nautical miles, to Kahili, 125 miles, to Buka Passage, 234 miles, and to Rabaul, 394 miles.

[8] Adm William F. Halsey, Jr., Narrative Account of the South Pacific Campaign, 3 Sep 44, OCMH; Lt Gen Millard F. Harmon, The Army in the South Pacific, 6 Jun 44, p. 7, OCMH; Fleet Admiral William F. Halsey and Lt Comdr J. Bryan, III, *Admiral Halsey's Story* (New York: Whittlesey House, 1947), p. 154.

commanders or by their staffs to prepare a broad plan that would enable the Joint Chiefs to give careful consideration to such matters as timing, reinforcement, supply, and the transfer of command over Tasks Two and Three to Mac-Arthur.[9] Maintaining that it was inconvenient for high commanders to undertake long journeys away from their headquarters, MacArthur radioed his ideas for Tasks Two and Three to Nimitz and Halsey. On 11 February Halsey sent his deputy commander, Rear Adm. Theodore S. Wilkinson, to Brisbane to begin a co-ordinated plan.[10]

Shortly thereafter MacArthur asked the Joint Chiefs for permission to send his chief of staff and several other officers to Washington to explain his plans. The Joint Chiefs approved, but stipulated that representatives from Halsey's and Nimitz' areas should also come for a general discussion of Pacific problems.[11] The delegates reached Washington on 10 March and two days later met with Admiral King and various officers from the Army and Navy planning and logistical staffs.[12]

Thus began the series of meetings, generally known as the Pacific Military Conference, which were to produce a new directive for operations. This conference constituted an excellent example of the detailed and undramatic, but absolutely essential, spadework that had to precede major decisions affecting the course of the war in the Pacific.

The ELKTON Plan

After Admiral King opened the first session on 12 March with a strategic review of the world situation, Maj. Gen. Richard K. Sutherland, MacArthur's chief of staff, presented the ELKTON plan

---

[9] Rad to MacArthur, 8 Jan 43, CM–OUT 2833; Rad to Maj Gen Rush B. Lincoln, New Caledonia (to be passed to Halsey), 8 Jan 43, CM–OUT 2834; Rad to Lt Gen Delos C. Emmons, Hawaii (to be passed to Nimitz), 8 Jan 43, CM–OUT 2835; Rad to MacArthur, 11 Jan 43, CM–OUT 3664.

[10] Rad from MacArthur, 27 Jan 43, CM–IN 12553; Rad from MacArthur, 11 Feb 43, CM–IN 5610; Commander, South Pacific Area and South Pacific Force, War Diary: 1 January 1943–30 June 1944 (hereafter cited as COMSOPAC War Diary), 11–12, 14–15 Feb 43 entries.

[11] Rad from MacArthur, 15 Feb 43, CM–IN 7418; Rads to MacArthur, 16 Feb 43, CM–OUT 5656 and CM–OUT 5660; Rads to Harmon (for Halsey), 16 Feb 43, CM–OUT 5658 and CM–OUT 5661; Rads to Emmons (for Nimitz), 16 Feb 43, CM–OUT 5657 and CM–OUT 5659. The Pacific representatives timed their trip to accompany Brig. Gen. Albert C. Wedemeyer to Washington. Wedemeyer, a member of the Operations Division of the War Department General Staff and of the Joint and Combined Staff Planners, visited the Southwest Pacific to explain the Casablanca decisions to MacArthur and to become better acquainted with the area.

[12] To represent him, Halsey had selected General Harmon, Commanding General, U.S. Army Forces in the South Pacific Area; Maj. Gen. Nathan F. Twining, commanding the Thirteenth Air Force; and two staff officers, Brig. Gen. Dewitt Peck, USMC, his war plans officer, and Capt. Miles R. Browning, USN, his chief of staff. MacArthur sent Maj. Gen. Richard K. Sutherland, his chief of staff; Brig. Gen. Stephen J. Chamberlin, his operations officer; and Lt. Gen. George C. Kenney, Commander, Allied Air Forces, SWPA. Representing Nimitz were his deputy and chief of staff, Vice Adm. Raymond A. Spruance, General Emmons, and Capt. Forrest P. Sherman. Present at the first meeting, besides King and the Pacific delegates, were Lt. Gen. Joseph T. McNarney, Deputy Chief of Staff of the Army; Lt. Gen. Stanley D. Embick, of the Joint Strategic Survey Committee; Maj. Gen. George E. Stratemeyer, Chief of the Air Staff; Maj. Gen. Thomas T. Handy, Assistant Chief of Staff, Operations Division, War Department General Staff; Maj. Gens. LeRoy Lutes and Lucius D. Clay, of Headquarters, Army Service Forces; Vice Adm. Russell Willson, of the Joint Strategic Survey Committee; Rear Adm. Charles M. Cooke, Jr.; and Wedemeyer.

to the conference.[13] This plan, bearing the date 28 February 1943, was a revision of the first ELKTON plan, which was dated 12 February, and prescribed the same general scheme of maneuver as MacArthur's earlier plans for the reduction of Rabaul. MacArthur had prepared it on the assumption that he would control both the Southwest and South Pacific forces for Tasks Two and Three, for the Joint Chiefs' directive had stated explicitly that these would be conducted under his command. Halsey, according to MacArthur, had already assented to ELKTON.

ELKTON's intelligence estimate pointed out that the Japanese generally controlled the north coast of New Guinea northwest of Buna, as well as New Britain, New Ireland, and the Solomons northwest of Guadalcanal. Japanese defenses were concentrated, as were Allied holdings in the region, in the vicinity of airfields. Except for the perimeters around the airfields and naval bases, the land areas were pretty well unoccupied.

Between 79,000 and 94,000 Japanese troops were thought to be stationed in the New Guinea–Bismarck Archipelago–Solomons area. Enemy air strength was estimated at 383 land-based planes, while 4 battleships, 2 aircraft carriers, 14 cruisers, 11 seaplane tenders, about 40 destroyers, numerous auxiliaries, and about 50 merchant ships of 3,000 tons or over were on hand for operations. It was expected that the Japanese, if attacked, could be immediately reinforced by 10,000 to 12,000 troops and about 250 planes as well as major portions of the *Combined Fleet* from the Netherlands Indies, Japanese home waters, and the Philippines Islands. In six months, 615 more aircraft could be committed, and 10 or 15 divisions might be dispatched if shipping was available.

Having described the forbidding nature of the enemy stronghold, General Sutherland proceeded, in his presentation of the ELKTON plan, to outline the contemplated Allied moves. The execution of Tasks Two and Three would require mutually supporting, co-ordinated advances along two lines: one, by Southwest Pacific forces in the west, from New Guinea to New Britain; the other, by South Pacific forces in the east, through the Solomons. ELKTON broke Tasks Two and Three into five operations:

1. Seizure of airdromes on the Huon Peninsula of New Guinea to provide air support for operations against New Britain;

2. Seizure of Munda Point as well as other airdromes on New Georgia to cover operations against New Ireland in the Bismarck Archipelago and the remainder of the Solomons;

3. Seizure of airdromes on New Britain and Bougainville to support operations against Rabaul and Kavieng in New Ireland;

4. Capture of Kavieng and the isolation of Rabaul, although it was considered possible that Kavieng might be taken after Rabaul;

5. Capture of Rabaul.

The timing of these missions was not rigidly fixed, nor was there an estimate of the time required to carry them out.

---

[13] Notes on Pac Conf Held in Mar 43, 1st mtg, 12 Mar 43. George C. Kenney, *General Kenney Reports: A Personal History of the Pacific War* (New York: Duell, Sloan and Pearce, 1949), devotes one chapter (VIII) to this conference.

Large forces, assembled in advance, were required to execute the five operations of ELKTON—and there was the rub from the point of view of the Washington planners faced with global responsibilities. They listened as Sutherland read a detailed accounting of forces on hand and forces requested. The plan, in brief, called for five additional divisions, forty-five additional air groups, or about twice the 1,850 land-based planes then on hand, and an unspecified number of warships, transports, cargo ships, and landing craft sufficient to mount and support all the operations.[14]

The official records do not disclose with what emotions the officers from the various Washington agencies received the information about the necessary reinforcements, but it is not difficult to imagine that some were surprised. At Casablanca the Americans had assumed the capture of Rabaul in 1943 as a matter of course, and had confidently discussed the possibility of advancing beyond Rabaul.

The Pacific delegates learned immediately that there was virtually no chance for them to get all the reinforcements that they wanted.[15] It was possible to effect some increases in the number of aircraft, but to give General MacArthur everything he asked would have cut too deeply into the bomber offensive against Germany. There were several trained divisions available in the United States, but there were not enough transports to ship them overseas in time, or to supply them after their arrival. Everyone at the conference was convinced of the necessity for offensive operations, but it was recognized that the operations would be limited by the available means. Admiral Halsey's representatives, Lt. Gen. Millard F. Harmon of the Army, Brig. Gen. Dewitt Peck of the Marine Corps, and Capt. Miles R. Browning of the Navy, endorsed the ELKTON plan, but some of the Navy planners in Washington were dubious of its value. They believed it would tie up too many ships and too many troops for too long a time, and would not achieve decisive results. The Washington planners informed the Pacific representatives that only two or three more divisions and a few more planes could be sent overseas.[16]

The solution therefore was to replace the ambitious directive of 2 July 1942 with something more realistic. Before deciding on a new directive, the Joint Chiefs instructed the Pacific delegates to decide what offensive operations they thought could be undertaken in 1943 with the allotted forces. It was understood that the Pacific commanders would not be committed by their subordinates' recommendations.[17]

The Pacific delegates answered promptly. They stated that the South and Southwest Pacific forces would be able to advance as far as the southeast part of Bougainville, seize eastern New Guinea up to Madang, extend to Woodlark and Kiriwina in the Trobriand Islands, and advance to Cape Gloucester

[14] GHQ SWPA, ELKTON Plan . . . , 28 Feb 43.
[15] Rad, Sutherland to MacArthur, 12 Mar 43, CM–OUT 1930.

[16] For the detailed record of debate and discussion at the various meetings of the Pacific Military Conference, see Notes on Pac Conf Held in Mar 43, with Inclosures and Annexes. See below, Bibliographical Note.
[17] Min, JCS mtg, 19 Mar 43.

in western New Britain. These operations were essentially the second task of the directive of 2 July 1942.[18] With this statement, the Pacific Military Conference as such came to a close, although the Pacific representatives remained in Washington a few days longer at the request of the Joint Chiefs of Staff.

Preparation of the Directive of 28 March 1943

The Joint Chiefs of Staff, having approved the additional Pacific reinforcements and heard the opinions of the Pacific delegates, immediately accepted the proposal that South and Southwest Pacific operations in 1943 be limited to Task Two, and turned to consideration of new orders for Halsey and MacArthur.[19]

Neither the limitation of operations to Task Two nor the inclusion of Woodlark and Kiriwina was an entirely new idea. The Joint U.S. Strategic Committee, commissioned by the Joint Staff Planners to prepare a plan for the defeat of Japan, in February had considered the means for, and limiting factors affecting, the operations planned at Casablanca, and recommended that only Task Two be carried out in 1943. The committee felt that the capture of Rabaul, which could not be undertaken until fairly late in 1943, might interfere with the recapture of Burma, an operation which was considered to be on a priority with the advance through the Central Pacific and the support of China. The Strategic Committee had

also recommended capture of Woodlark and Kiriwina.[20]

Seizure of these islands would bring Rabaul and the northern Solomons within range of fighters and medium bombers, and would thus compensate for the absence of enough heavy bombers. The islands, which lie outside the bad weather belt that frequently blankets the southeast tip of New Guinea, would also serve as staging bases for the rapid switching of air units between the South and Southwest Pacific. In December of the previous year, Admiral Halsey had suggested to MacArthur the establishment of an air base at Woodlark or Kiriwina, and offered to furnish some of the necessary troops. This project had the approval of Marshall and King.[21] The seizure of Woodlark and Kiriwina was included as part of Plan ELKTON of 12 February, but had

---

[18] Memo by Reps of the Pac Areas, in JCS 238/2, 21 Mar 43.

[19] Min, JCS mtg, 21 Mar 43.

[20] Memo, Secretariat JUSSC for Secretariat JPS, 13 Feb 43, sub: Opns in S and SW Pac Areas During 1943 and Their Relation to the Concept of Mil Strategy for 1943 as Set Forth in the Anfa Papers, with Incls A and B, attached to JPS 67/2, 4 Jan 43, title: Proposed Dir for a Campaign Plan for the Defeat of Japan, ABC 381 Japan (8–27–42), Sec 1. This paper is also filed as JPS 67/3, 15 Feb 43, title: Opns in S and SW Pac in 1943. The Casablanca Conference was held at Anfa and is often referred to as the Anfa Conference, although its code name was SYMBOL. The Joint U.S. Strategic Committee was renamed the Joint War Plans Committee in March 1943, and should not be confused with the Joint Strategic Survey Committee, which was composed of senior officers who advised on broad strategic matters.

[21] See C O M S O P A C to C O M S O W E S P A C [C I N C S W P A], 17 Dec 42; C O M I N C H to COMSOPAC, 18 Dec 42; Memo, King for Marshall, 20 Feb 43, sub: Instal of Airstrips on Kiriwina Island or Woodlark Island; Memo, Marshall for King, 22 Feb 43, same sub. All in CNO File A 16–3 (4) No. 1, Warfare Opns, SWPA, 1943, and made available by Lt. Grace P. Hays, USN, of the Hist Sec, JCS. See also Halsey and Bryan, *Admiral Halsey's Story*, p. 154.

been omitted from the version of ELK-TON which Sutherland brought to Washington.

Timing

Although the Joint Chiefs had accepted the delegates' proposals in principle, they were concerned about the timing of operations. They brought the Pacific representatives and some of the Joint Planners into their meeting on Sunday morning, 21 March, to help settle matters.

The Southwest Pacific delegates argued that lack of adequate forces would keep the South Pacific from beginning operations against New Georgia and southern Bougainville until after the Southwest Pacific had seized the Huon Peninsula in New Guinea, an operation that would take place about August. This sequence was approximately that set forth in the ELKTON plan. The South Pacific delegates, especially Harmon, felt that it would be better to move against New Georgia before the capture of the Huon Peninsula. A reasonable margin of safety would require that enough strength be mustered for a drive right through to Bougainville after Munda's capture.

The views of the Southwest Pacific delegates on New Georgia are somewhat curious. At an early meeting of the conference, Rear Adm. Charles M. Cooke, Jr., of Admiral King's staff, had asked Sutherland for MacArthur's opinion on the operation against Munda for which the South Pacific was then preparing. Sutherland replied that his chief would be unable to make recommendations until he had been "apprised" of the operations, the forces involved, and the

amount of assistance he would be expected to contribute.[22]

Admiral King was disturbed by the idea of postponing action in the Solomons, for the Japanese fleet was no longer pinned down by the Guadalcanal Campaign. If the Solomon operations were to be postponed, he suggested, the American fleet units assigned to the South Pacific might be more profitably employed elsewhere, perhaps in the Central Pacific. The Joint Chiefs directed the Joint Planners to draft a plan, but did not immediately attempt to decide on the timing of operations.[23] In the message the Joint Chiefs sent to MacArthur, Nimitz, and Halsey about the additional reinforcements, they stated that "prevailing opinion" in Washington favored launching the invasion of Munda after the establishment of an air base at Woodlark and possibly after the conclusion of the planned advance in New Guinea.

MacArthur replied at once to express his vigorous opposition to what he, Sutherland, and Kenney called "divergent action," that is, concurrent operations

---

[22] Notes on Pac Conf Held in Mar 43, 3d mtg, 13 Mar 43. It is difficult to comprehend Sutherland's statement as reported in the official record. MacArthur's message regarding Wilkinson's visit to Brisbane indicated that an exchange of views had taken place. According to the COMSOPAC War Diary, 4 March 1943 entry, MacArthur was informed on 4 March that South Pacific headquarters hoped to seize New Georgia about 10 April. Halsey discussed the action with Sutherland and Kenney at his headquarters in Nouméa, New Caledonia, and made it clear that MacArthur would not be asked for any assistance except for limited air action against the Shortland Islands. Finally, the 28 February ELKTON, which Sutherland read to the conference, specifically called for an invasion of New Georgia and made an estimate of the forces that would be needed.

[23] Min, JCS mtg, 21 Mar 43.

Some Pacific Planners in Conference. *From left, Capt. Cato D. Glover, Jr., Maj. Gen. Richard J. Marshall, Lt. Gen. George C. Kenney, Lt. Gen. Richard K. Sutherland, Rear Adm. Forrest P. Sherman, and Maj. Gen. Stephen J. Chamberlin. Photograph taken in Brisbane, Australia, March 1944.*

against New Georgia and New Guinea by the South and Southwest Pacific Areas. Neither area, he asserted, would be strong enough for independent action. The South Pacific would need strong air support from its neighbor in the New Georgia action, and there simply were not enough planes. He therefore recommended that the New Georgia invasion be postponed at least until the seizure of the Lae–Madang area guaranteed control of the Vitiaz Strait between the Huon Peninsula and western New Britain, prevented the Japanese from moving reinforcements to Rabaul from the west, and enabled the Southwest Pacific to support and protect its neighbor by bombing Rabaul

heavily. Then New Georgia could be taken, and the South and Southwest Pacific Areas, now mutually supporting, could begin the reduction of Rabaul.[24]

The question of timing was never finally determined by the Joint Chiefs. Speaking at their meeting on 28 March when the Joint Planners' draft of a new directive for Halsey and MacArthur was considered, King again emphasized the dangers of allowing the South Pacific to stand idly by while waiting for the northeast New Guinea coast to be

---

[24] Rad from MacArthur, 25 Mar 43, CM–IN 13461; Comments by Gen Kenney on draft MS of this volume, attached to Ltr, Gen Kenney to Maj Gen Albert C. Smith, Chief of Mil Hist, 11 Nov 53, no sub, OCMH.

cleared. Marshall, whose talents included great skill at reconciling divergent points of view, offered the opinion that both MacArthur and Halsey would take every advantage to press forward whenever Japanese resistance was weak. The Japanese would find themselves in a difficult position. If they strengthened the Solomons at the expense of New Guinea MacArthur could move forward, and Halsey could take advantage of any shifts of troops to New Guinea. Halsey himself, although willing to postpone the advance against New Georgia until after Woodlark and Kiriwina were taken, had stated that he would not remain idle. He intended to hit the Japanese with land-based aircraft and to be prepared to move into New Georgia and southern Bougainville if the Japanese weakened their defenses to such an extent that he could advance without precipitating a major engagement. King withdrew his objections, subject to the proviso that MacArthur submit detailed plans showing timing and sequence of operations and the composition of task forces.[25]

Command

One final question, command, remained to be decided before the Joint Chiefs could issue a new directive. This question was settled fairly quickly.[26] The directive of 2 July 1942 had provided that Tasks Two and Three would be under MacArthur's direction. This principle continued to be accepted by the Joint Chiefs without serious challenge. Both the Army and the Navy had been arguing somewhat heatedly over the question of a unified command for the entire Pacific, but the warmth of their debate did not seriously interfere with the preparation of the new directive. The possibility of mutual co-operation by Halsey and MacArthur was rejected. Some naval officers, including King, suggested that since Halsey would be operating west of the line of demarcation (longitude 159° east), it should be moved westward again, but did not press the point.[27] It was agreed that MacArthur would command the operations by the Southwest Pacific forces, and that Halsey's operations with South Pacific forces in the Solomons would be under MacArthur's "general directives."

One particularly important aspect of the command question related to the Pacific Fleet units that would take part in the operations. Admiral King always opposed any tendency to break up the Pacific Fleet by permanently assigning its units to any particular area, for then the fleet would lose part of its striking power as well as strategic and tactical mobility. For these reasons King had previously proposed that Nimitz' authority be extended to include the waters of the Southwest Pacific Area, but had apparently never insisted on this as a solution. The Joint Chiefs settled the matter on 28 March by agreeing that all units of the Pacific Ocean Areas other than those assigned by the Joint Chiefs to task forces engaged in the operations would remain under Nimitz' general control. This meant that MacArthur

[25] Min, JCS mtg, 28 Mar 43; COMSOPAC War Diary, 28 Mar 43 entry.

[26] But see Rad, Sutherland to MacArthur, 25 Mar 43, CM–OUT 9499.

[27] Kenney, *General Kenney Reports*, p. 213, indicates that discussions of this point in and out of the conference room were heated. The minutes do not yield much information about the emotions of the protagonists.

would exercise strategic direction only over Halsey's forces that were engaged in the Solomons west of longitude 159° east, and that Halsey's other forces, as well as Pacific Fleet units not assigned by the Joint Chiefs, would remain under Nimitz.[28] With the question of command settled and the problem of timing left largely to the commanders' discretion, the Joint Chiefs on 28 March approved a directive providing for offensive operations by MacArthur and Halsey in 1943.[29]

The 28 March Directive

Brief crisp orders were dispatched to Halsey, Nimitz, and MacArthur on 28 March. The Joint Chiefs canceled their directive of 2 July 1942. They ordered

MacArthur and Halsey to establish airfields on Woodlark and Kiriwina, to seize the Lae–Salamaua–Finschhafen–Madang area of New Guinea and occupy western New Britain, and to seize and occupy the Solomon Islands as far as southern Bougainville. The operations were intended to inflict losses on the Japanese, to deny the target areas to the enemy, to contain Japanese forces in the Pacific by retaining the initiative, and to prepare for the ultimate seizure of the Bismarck Archipelago. As previously indicated, operations would be conducted under MacArthur's command. The advances in the Solomons were to be under the direct command of Halsey, who would operate under MacArthur's strategic direction. Except for those units assigned by the Joint Chiefs of Staff to task forces engaged in these campaigns, all elements of the Pacific Ocean Areas would remain under Nimitz. MacArthur was directed to submit detailed plans including the composition of task forces and sequence and timing of operations.[30]

With this directive, the Joint Chiefs set the program for 1943 in the South and Southwest Pacific. There can be no doubt that they were disappointed by their inability to approach the goals set so freely at Casablanca, but the 28 March directive possessed the virtue of being based on assumptions that were realistic, even pessimistic. The defined objectives were believed to be surely attainable.

---

[28] The command question is treated in the following documents: Ltr, COMINCH-CNO [King] to CofS USA [Marshall], 6 Jan 43, no sub, included in JCS 112/1, 14 Oct 42, title: Mil Sit in the Pac, ABC 370.26 (7–8–42), Sec 1; Memo, Gen Handy for Capt Connolly, Naval War Plans Div, 29 Dec 42, no sub, OPD 384 PTO (12–29–42), Sec 2, Case 43; Memo, Marshall for COMINCH, 8 Jan 43, sub: Strategic Dir of Opns in the SW Pac, same file; Memo, COMINCH for CofS USA, 18 Feb 43, sub: Opns in SOPAC-SWPA, OPD Exec Off File No. 10, Item 67c; Memo, CofS USA for CNO, 19 Feb 43, same sub, same file; JCS 238/3, 21 Mar 43, title: Plan of Opns for Seizure of Solomon Islands–New Guinea–New Britain–New Ireland Area; JCS 238/4, 27 Mar 43, title: Plan of Opns for Seizure of Solomon Islands–New Guinea–New Britain–New Ireland Area–Offen Opns in the S and SW Pac During 1943; JCS 238/5/D, 28 Mar 43, title: Dir–Plan of Opns for Seizure of Solomon Islands–New Guinea–New Britain–New Ireland Area; and Min JCS mtg, 28 Mar 43.

[29] Min, JCS mtg, 28 Mar 43.

[30] JCS 238/5/D, 28 Mar 43.

CHAPTER III

Elkton III: The Plan for Cartwheel

The Southwest Pacific Area

Command Structure

Most of the commands of the Southwest and South Pacific Areas which would execute the Joint Chiefs' orders were already in existence.[1] General MacArthur, as Allied Commander in Chief, had organized his General Headquarters (GHQ), Southwest Pacific Area, on U.S. Army lines. Directly under Sutherland, the Chief of Staff,[2] were the four standard general staff and three special staff sections. Each section was headed by an American Army officer. Officers from the American Navy and from the Australian, Netherlands, and Netherlands Indies armed forces served in the most important staff sections, but in comparatively junior positions.[3] On the surface GHQ was a U.S. Army headquarters, but its responsibilities and authority were joint and Allied in nature. It was an operational headquarters.

Under GHQ in Australia were three other tactical headquarters—Allied Land Forces, Allied Naval Forces, and Allied Air Forces, whose names indicate their functions. (*Chart 1*) Allied Land Forces was commanded by an Australian, General Sir Thomas Blamey, and was theoretically responsible for the tactical direction of all Allied ground troops, less certain antiaircraft units which were controlled by Allied Air Forces. Under Allied Land Forces was the U.S. Sixth Army, established in the area in February 1943 under command of Lt. Gen. Walter Krueger. Included in Sixth Army were Lt. Gen. Robert L. Eichelberger's I Corps, the 2d Engineer Special Brigade, and the 503d Parachute Infantry Regiment. The 1st Marine Division was under Krueger's operational control.[4] The First and Second Australian Armies, many of whose units were still in training, were part of Allied Land Forces. The main tactical headquarters which operated under Blamey

---

[1] For details see Louis Morton's forthcoming volumes on strategy, command, and logistics in the Pacific, and Milner, *Victory in Papua.* For South Pacific organization, see below, pp. 67–70.

[2] Sutherland, a lean, spare, dedicated man, and an exacting taskmaster, was somewhat less than popular with some of the officers who commanded forces directly under GHQ, apparently because they felt that he, personally, tried to take over part of their authority. But his worst enemies have never questioned his professional competence.

[3] G–3, for example, contained a substantial number of U.S. Navy and Allied officers, and such subordinate sections of G–2 as the Allied Intelligence Bureau, the Allied Translator and Interpreter Service, and the Allied Geographical Section had large numbers of Allied officers.

[4] GHQ SWPA GO 17, 16 Feb 43, in GHQ SWPA G–3 Jnl, 16 Feb 43. The antiaircraft units, two antiaircraft coast artillery brigades that were controlled by Allied Air Forces, were assigned to Sixth Army.

CHART 1—ORGANIZATION OF FORCES FOR CARTWHEEL

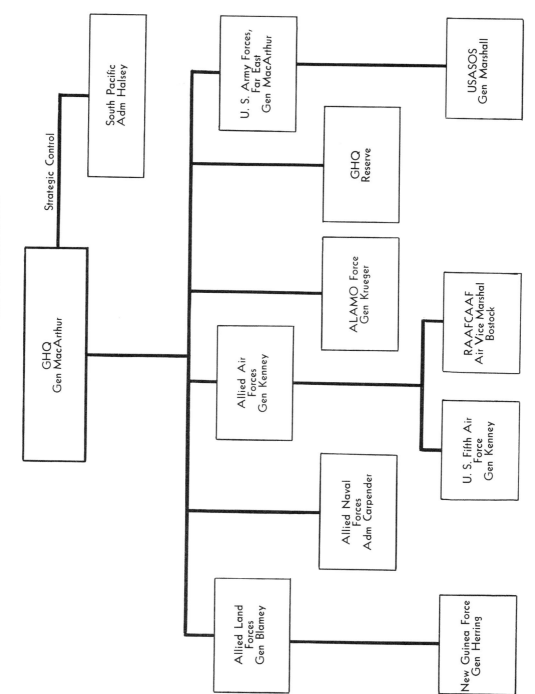

during early 1943 was New Guinea Force, a largely Australian headquarters responsible for the conduct of operations in New Guinea. GHQ usually established a temporary advanced echelon at Port Moresby, New Guinea, shortly before the beginning of each operation.

Allied Naval Forces was commanded by Vice Adm. Arthur S. Carpender (inevitably called "Chips") of the U.S. Navy, and included the U.S. Seventh Fleet (concurrently commanded by Carpender) and large parts of the Australian and Netherlands Navies. The most important component of Carpender's command was the VII Amphibious Force, organized under Rear Adm. Daniel E. Barbey in early 1943.

Lt. Gen. George C. Kenney, an American airman, led the Allied Air Forces which consisted of the U.S. Fifth Air Force and the Royal Australian Air Force Command, Allied Air Forces, under Air Vice Marshal William D. Bostock. Kenney also commanded the Fifth Air Force but for tactical purposes it was run by the Deputy Commander, Brig. Gen. Ennis C. Whitehead who led the Advanced Echelon at Port Moresby, New Guinea.[5]

All national forces serving under these tactical headquarters were administered and usually supplied by their own service elements. U.S. Army Forces, Far East, commanded by MacArthur, was responsible for administration of the Sixth Army, the Fifth Air Force, and U.S. Army Services of Supply, Southwest Pacific Area. This last, under Maj. Gen. Richard J. Marshall, had the responsibility for logistical support of American ground forces.[6] Australian Line of Communications units in Allied Land Forces supplied the Australian troops. Soldiers fighting in New Guinea under New Guinea Force were supplied by a U.S.-Australian organization known as the Combined Operational Service Command which had been created during the Papuan campaign.

Most echelons subordinate to GHQ had functioned during the Papuan campaign and by mid-1943 were operating with an efficiency born of this experience.

Geography

The forthcoming campaigns would be fought in New Guinea, the Solomon Islands, and the Bismarck Archipelago. Many places in these islands bear the names of outstanding figures in the history of exploration: Torres Strait, Dampier Strait, Bougainville, and D'Entrecasteaux Islands. Other names like New Britain and New Ireland are of more pedestrian origin, and the Bismarck and Solomon Seas were named during World War II.[7] Despite the familiarity of many place names, the area was one of the least known and least developed in all the world. Further, although there is perhaps no ideal place to fight a war, the New Guinea–Bismarcks–Solomons

---

[5] Craven and Cate, *The Pacific: Guadalcanal to Saipan*, p. 99.

[6] GHQ SWPA Stf Memo 3, 19 Feb 43; USAFFE GO 1, 26 Feb 43, adv copy. Both in GHQ SWPA G–3 Jnl, 19 Feb 43.

[7] Nothing is named for Meneses, who first visited New Guinea in 1526, nor for Mendaña who discovered the Solomons in 1568. But the whole group, the islands of Guadalcanal, San Cristobal, Santa Isabel, and Florida, and Point Cruz on Guadalcanal and Estrella Bay at Santa Isabel retain the names given by Mendaña.

area was one of the worst possible places. (*Map 3*)

All the islands have much in common, and much that is common is unpleasant. All have hot, wet, tropical climates. All are mountainous. All are heavily jungled. All are pest-ridden and full of tropical diseases, especially malaria. None has motor roads longer than a few miles. There are almost no ports with piers and quays to accommodate large ships.

The native inhabitants are Melanesians, most of them barely beyond the Stone Age. Cannibalism and headhunting were suppressed only recently in areas where British, German, Dutch, and Australian governments exerted their authority. During World War II there were rumors that some of the New Guinea natives, freed by the Japanese conquests from the white man's restraining influence, had reverted to their ancient practices.

New Guinea, the largest island in the area and after Greenland the largest island in the world, is about 1,600 statute miles long, 500 miles from north to south at its widest point, and has an area estimated at about 312,000 square miles. Its most distinctive geographic feature, aside from the jungle, is the great cordillera that runs the length of the island. This cordillera consists of a number of parallel east-west mountain ranges which narrow into the Owen Stanley Range in the Papuan peninsula. The highest peaks reach over sixteen thousand feet into the sky. The mountain valleys that are cut by such rivers as the Sepik, Ramu, Markham, and Bulolo are several thousand feet above sea level, and the climate is pleasant and relatively healthful. There are no really large rivers in New Guinea, but the Markham, which flows into Huon Gulf, and the Sepik and Ramu are several hundred miles long. The 600-mile Sepik, flowing between the Victor Emmanuel Range and the Torricelli Mountains, is navigable by steam launch for 300 miles above its mouth. Between the mountains and the sea are swampy lowlands and vast stretches of tropical rain forest so thick that the sun never penetrates the treetops to dry the ground and no underbrush ever grows.

At the outset of the war there were no motor roads of any significant length. There were short roads in and around the main ports and gold fields and innumerable native footpaths, or "tracks." As both Allied and Japanese forces had demonstrated during the Papuan campaign, overland travel was fantastically difficult. The best ways to travel were by water and by air. However, both the Australians and Japanese were, in the first part of 1943, engaged in ambitious transmontane road-building projects.

Before the war the Australians had exploited air travel to the utmost in developing the gold fields of the Bulolo Valley in the mountains southwest of Salamaua. They had avoided the difficulties of overland travel by cutting airstrips in the flatlands of the valley, then flying in gold-mining machinery, building materials, and, to add to the amenities of life in the attractive uplands, even race horses.

Across Vitiaz and Dampier Straits from New Guinea's Huon Peninsula lies Cape Gloucester, the western tip of New Britain, which curves northeasterly to culminate in Gazelle Peninsula and Rabaul. New Ireland, long and narrow, parallels the long axis of the Papuan peninsula so that it, the Admiralty Islands, part of New Guinea, and New Britain enclose the Bismarck Sea. New Britain, New Ireland, the Admiralties, and other islands form the Bismarck Archipelago.

Southeast of Rabaul, and northeast of the Papuan peninsula and the Louisiade Archipelago, lie the Solomon Islands. This 600-mile-long double-chained archipelago was found by Mendaña in 1568, but his calculations of longitude were so far wrong that two hundred years went by before white men found it again. Carteret, Bougainville, Surville, Shortland, and D'Entrecasteaux sighted or visited the archipelago between 1767 and 1793, and French geographers eventually concluded that these were the islands Mendaña had found.

The area was divided politically. That part of New Guinea west of longitude 141° east belonged to the Netherlands. Papua was an Australian possession with the status of Territory. Northeast New Guinea, the Admiralties, New Britain, New Ireland, Bougainville, and Buka made up the Australian Mandated Territory of New Guinea; Australia took them from Germany in World War I and was awarded a League of Nations mandate over them.[8] The Solomons southeast of Bougainville are, politically, the British Solomon Islands Protectorate, established by Great Britain in 1893 to suppress blackbirding.

---

[8] In 1947 the Mandated Territory and Papua were consolidated as a United Nations trusteeship.

A crude comparison may give a general idea of the size of the area. If a map of the New Guinea–Bismarck Archipelago–Solomon Islands area is superimposed on a map of the United States, with the western tip of New Guinea's Vogelkop Peninsula at Seattle, Washington, Milne Bay at southeastern New Guinea lies in Colorado, and the Solomon Islands lie in the Missouri and Mississippi Valleys.

Coastwatching

In early 1943 the key points of this huge area, except for Port Moresby, Milne Bay, Goodenough Island in the D'Entrecasteaux group, and the Guadalcanal–Russells–Florida area of the Solomons were in Japanese hands, but Allied intelligence agencies were able to keep a fairly close check on enemy troop, ship, and plane movements by means of radioed reports from observers operating behind the enemy lines. These observers were the coastwatchers, members of an organization, the Coastwatching Service, established before the war as part of the Directorate of Intelligence, Royal Australian Navy. Their territory originally embraced New Guinea, the Bismarck Archipelago, and the Solomons, but later islands of the Netherlands Indies were added to the network. Initially the coastwatchers were all British, Australian, or New Zealand civil servants or planters, commissioned in the Australian armed forces, but as the war progressed qualified men from the American forces were also assigned. The coastwatchers were part of the Allied Intelligence Bureau of the G–2 Section of GHQ. Those in the Solomons reported their observations directly to South Pacific agencies.[9]

These intrepid men were greatly aided in their work by the devotion and help of the natives. The Melanesians in general remained loyal to the Allied cause, and throughout the war rescued shot-down airmen and stranded sailors, worked as guides, bearers, and laborers, and a select few stayed with the various coastwatchers.

As the interior of the New Guinea–Bismarcks–Solomons area was little known and practically unmapped, the coastwatchers proved an invaluable source of information on terrain. In addition, their hideouts served as bases for the patrols that thrust behind the Japanese lines in advance of nearly every Allied operation.

The Plan of Maneuver

On receiving the instructions from the Joint Chiefs of Staff, General MacArthur and his subordinates turned to the job of preparing plans and issuing orders to carry out the directive of 28 March. The task was not difficult. All that was needed was a revamping of the two previous ELKTON plans.

MacArthur's headquarters issued its plan for South and Southwest Pacific Area operations for 1943 on 26 April, and followed it the next month with warning orders and operations instructions. The warning orders covered the

whole ELKTON plan; the operations instructions dealt specifically with the opening phases. The 26 April plan, designated ELKTON III, was issued after a personal conference in Brisbane between Admiral Halsey and General MacArthur.

This was the first meeting of the well-known admiral and the even more famous general. Halsey was deeply impressed by MacArthur; speaking of their wartime conferences, he wrote:

I have seldom seen a man who makes a quicker, stronger, more favorable impression. . . . On the few occasions when I disagreed with him, I told him so, and we discussed the issue until one of us changed his mind. My mental picture poses him against the background of these discussions; he is pacing his office, almost wearing a groove between his large, bare desk and the portrait of George Washington that faced it; his corncob pipe is in his hand (I rarely saw him smoke it); and he is making his points in a diction I have never heard surpassed.[10]

At this meeting, timing and co-ordination of the advance in New Guinea with the invasion of New Georgia were discussed.[11] Halsey carried some of his points with MacArthur; they agreed that the initial invasion of New Georgia would take place at the same time as the seizure of Woodlark and Kiriwina instead of after the establishment of Southwest Pacific forces on the Huon Peninsula, as the Southwest Pacific leaders had been advocating. ELKTON III specified that the New Georgia and Woodlark-Kiriwina operations would

---

[9] See Comdr. Eric A. Feldt, RAN, *The Coastwatchers* (Melbourne and New York: Oxford University Press, 1946); MIS GHQ FEC, The Intelligence Series, IV, Operations of the Allied Intelligence Bureau, GHQ, SWPA. The Royal New Zealand Navy also operated a coastwatching system east of the Solomons.

[10] Halsey and Bryan, *Admiral Halsey's Story*, p. 155.

[11] COMSOPAC War Diary, 25 Apr 43 entry; Halsey and Bryan, *Admiral Halsey's Story*, pp. 154–55.

be simultaneous, but that major forces were not to be committed.[12]

The CARTWHEEL Operations

The plan of maneuver decided on by MacArthur was the same as that set forth in previous plans—mutually supporting advances along two axes, converging finally on Rabaul. The general concept underlying these operations characterized most Allied operations in both South and Southwest Pacific Areas. Despite its stiff brand of English, the warning instruction that expressed this concept is worth noting:

The general scheme of maneuver is to advance our bomber line towards Rabaul; first by improvement of presently occupied forward bases; secondly, by the occupation and implementation of air bases which can be secured without committing large forces; and then, by the seizure and implementation of successive hostile airdromes.

By destructive air attack soften up and gain air superiority over each attack objective along the two axes of advance. Neutralize with appropriate aviation supporting hostile air bases and destroy hostile naval forces and shipping within range. Prevent reinforcement or supply of objectives under attack. Move land forces forward, covered by air and naval forces, to seize and consolidate each successive objective. Displace aviation forward onto captured airdromes. Repeat this process to successive objectives, neutralizing by air action, or by air, land, and sea action, intermediate hostile installations which are not objectives of immediate attack. The entire movement will be covered by air attack on Japanese air and sea bases along the general perimeter BUKA-RABAUL-

KAVIENG-WEWAK, with the object of denying supply and reinforcement of objectives under attack.[13]

The operations planned for ELKTON III were lumped under the code name CARTWHEEL, and were arranged according to a complicated but flexible schedule that provided for about thirteen invasions or captures in eight months, and also provided for maximum mutual support by South and Southwest Pacific Areas.

CARTWHEEL would start with amphibious movements by the Southwest Pacific into Woodlark and Kiriwina. Simultaneously the South Pacific, using "diversionary" and "aggressive" infiltration, would move into New Georgia "and/or" Santa Isabel without committing major forces to action.[14]

Woodlark and Kiriwina were not held by either belligerent. Kiriwina is 270 nautical miles from Rabaul, and southern Bougainville is 300 miles away. Thus Allied fighters and medium bombers would be brought within range of these enemy areas, and Allied control over the Solomon and Bismarck Seas would be intensified. During the seizure of Woodlark and Kiriwina (designated Operation I in ELKTON III), heavy bombers would strike southern Bougainville, Buka, and Rabaul. The South Pacific would support the move by its ground operations in the Solomons (Operation A) in addition to providing strategic naval support and pinning down Japanese aircraft in the Solomons. In

---

[12] Halsey and Bryan, *Admiral Halsey's Story,* p. 155; GHQ SWPA, ELKTON III, Plan for the Seizure of the Lae–Salamaua–New Britain–Solomons Areas, 26 Apr 43.

[13] GHQ SWPA Warning Instns 2, 6 May 43, in GHQ SWPA G–3 Jnl, 6 May 43.
[14] GHQ SWPA, ELKTON III . . . , 26 Apr. 43.

accordance with Halsey's original suggestion, the South Pacific would furnish the occupation force and an air squadron for Woodlark. The timetable included in ELKTON III allotted two months for Operations I and A. (*Chart 2*)

When Operation A ended, South Pacific forces would not undertake any large-scale movements, but would continue air and sea operations to support the Southwest Pacific. This area would execute Operation II, the seizure of Lae (IIa), Salamaua and Finschhafen (IIb), and Madang (IIc). Lae was to be seized two months after the initiation of the CARTWHEEL operations, Salamaua and Finschhafen six weeks after Lae, and Madang two weeks after Salamaua. The Madang operation, including the consolidation phase, would probably require two months. During Operation II aircraft from both areas would keep striking the Japanese in the Solomons, New Ireland, New Britain, and New Guinea. Airfields at Lae and in the Markham Valley behind Lae would support the advance against Madang as well as the South Pacific's thrust against southern Bougainville.

Five and one-half months after the start of CARTWHEEL, and one month after the move against Lae, the South Pacific would complete the seizure of New Georgia, and move forward to capture the Japanese bases at Faisi in the Shortland Islands and Buin in southern Bougainville (Operation B).[15] Allied aircraft

from Woodlark, Kiriwina, and the Huon Peninsula would support and cover these movements. It was expected that Operation B would require six weeks.

The next two sets of operations by the Southwest and South Pacific Areas would be practically concurrent. At the beginning of the seventh month, the South Pacific was to seize Kieta, a Japanese base on the east coast of Bougainville, and begin neutralizing the airfields on and near Buka (Operation C). In the middle of the sixth month, the Southwest Pacific would cross Vitiaz Strait to take Cape Gloucester and Arawe (Operation IIIa), then occupy Gasmata and neutralize Talasea (Operation IIIb). With the New Guinea and New Britain bases in Allied hands, Wewak could be neutralized, and the operations against western New Britain could be supported. Finally, with the execution of Operations III and C, light bombers and fighters could easily attack Rabaul and Kavieng, and the South and Southwest Pacific Areas could begin to neutralize them in advance of an amphibious assault on Rabaul. This entire set of operations, it was estimated, would last for eight months. For planning purposes, ELKTON III assumed that the CARTWHEEL operations would begin about the first of June.

The arrangements for mutual support of the two areas during these operations were more detailed and exact than those for the Guadalcanal and Papua Campaigns. ELKTON III and subsequent orders, besides specifying the time and place of the CARTWHEEL operations, also provided for direct communication between South and Southwest Pacific Areas. Starting on 15 May, daily operational

---

[15] This feature of ELKTON III was not closely followed by Halsey. References to the New Georgia operations in ELKTON III are rather vague. They probably were included after the Halsey-MacArthur conference.

CHART 2—ESTIMATED TIMING AND SEQUENCE OF CARTWHEEL OPERATIONS

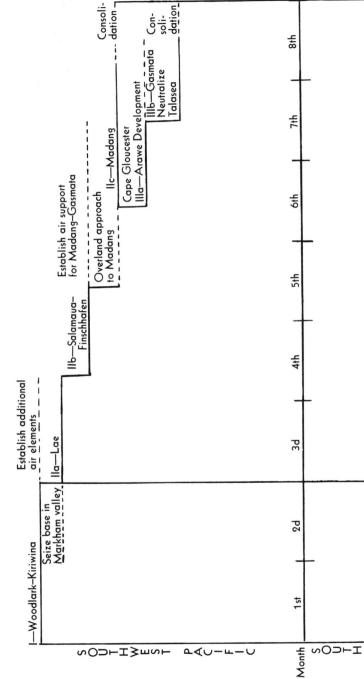

Source: Adapted from a chart in GHQ SWPA's ELKTON III, 26 Apr 43, Plan for the Seizure and Occupation of the Lae–Salamaua–Madang–Western New Britain–Solomons Areas.

and intelligence summaries would be exchanged. Instructions stressed particularly the necessity for a common radio frequency for fighter planes and a radio circuit connecting all major Allied air headquarters and bases. Beginning with Operations I and A, Southwest Pacific planes would conduct regular defensive reconnaissance over the Solomon and Bismarck Seas and the land areas west of longitude 155° east and southwest of the line Buka Passage–New Ireland. South Pacific aircraft would be responsible for defensive reconnaissance to the east and northeast of 155° east and the Buka Passage–New Ireland line, with a one-degree overlap granted to both areas. Offensive reconnaissance would be conducted without regard to any boundaries. MacArthur was to be notified well in advance of any movements by air or sea, and all further arrangements for co-ordination and mutual support would be made by him.[16]

Forces and Missions

MacArthur mainly used the existing headquarters in his area, but set up one new task force, primarily American, directly under GHQ. This organization, known at first as New Britain Force but from July on as ALAMO Force, was commanded by General Krueger, who retained his command of Sixth Army.[17] ALAMO Force headquarters was virtually the same as Sixth Army headquarters, and placing ALAMO Force directly under

GHQ had the effect of removing most American troops engaged in tactical operations from General Blamey's control. The plans called for New Guinea Force, with General Blamey in command, also to operate directly under GHQ. Roughly speaking, New Guinea Force would conduct the operations in New Guinea while ALAMO Force ran those in Woodlark, Kiriwina, and New Britain.[18] All operations would be supported and protected by Allied Air Forces and Allied Naval Forces.

Logistical responsibilities would be divided between American and Australian supply services. General Marshall's U.S. Army Services of Supply was assigned responsibility for the immediate movement of supplies for American ground forces by water (excluding naval movements) from rear bases in Australia to the intermediate bases at Port Moresby and Milne Bay, the advanced base at Oro Bay near Buna, and other bases when established. Marshall's command was to enlarge, stock, and operate ports and bases for the ALAMO Force, and would be responsible for completing airdromes then under construction on New Guinea and Goodenough Island. Australian Line of Communications units were to move supplies from rear bases to Cape York Peninsula, Port Moresby, and Milne Bay.

In amphibious assaults Allied Naval Forces would carry supplies forward from intermediate and advanced bases to the combat areas. When those areas were secured the regular American and Australian supply agencies would take over. In addition, Admiral Carpender's

---

[16] GHQ SWPA, ELKTON III . . . , 26 Apr 43; GHQ SWPA Warning Instns 2, 6 May 43, in GHQ SWPA G–3 Jnl, 6 May 43.

[17] ALAMO was the code name in clear; the secret code name was ESCALATOR Force.

[18] GHQ SWPA Warning Instns 2, 6 May 43, in GHQ SWPA G–3 Jnl, 6 May 43.

command would assist in the movement of supplies forward from Australia.

After some postponements caused by delays in assembling the troops for Kiriwina, D Day for Woodlark, Kiriwina, Nassau Bay in New Guinea, and New Georgia in the Solomons was set for 30 June.

The Intelligence Estimate

ELKTON III's estimate of Japanese strength in the Bismarck Archipelago, Solomons, and New Guinea reflected the recent changes in Japanese strength and like the 28 February estimate was fairly accurate. With the Japanese in control of all sea and air routes leading from their rearward island fortresses to Rabaul, MacArthur and his staff clearly recognized that the enemy might quickly strengthen his forces. They expected that strong naval units from Truk, including 6 battleships, 2 carriers, 3 auxiliary carriers, 8 seaplane tenders, 15 cruisers, about 40 destroyers, and 27 submarines as well as about 50 merchant vessels of over 3,000 tons displacement might be made available at once. Within thirty days, about four divisions could arrive, as well as 277 airplanes and fleet units from the Netherlands Indies and the Philippines. By the end of six months, the Japanese in the Bismarck Archipelago–Solomons–New Guinea area might be able to muster ten to fifteen divisions and 755 aircraft, but not much more in the way of fleet strength.

Just as on the Allied side, the crux of the matter would be shipping. The availability of troopships would govern the size of the ground combat forces that could be sent to and maintained in the area. About 300,000 gross tons of shipping, half consisting of ships over 3,000 tons, was immediately available, and to that 100,000 to 125,000 gross tons might be added.

No mention was made of possible Japanese offensives against positions held by the Allies. Enemy capabilities were considered to be entirely defensive. The Japanese were believed able to attempt the following: defense of Lae and Salamaua while reinforcing western New Britain and north New Guinea; air attacks against the Allied communication lines as well as in tactical support of ground defenses; naval interception of Allied amphibious movements; and diversions against northwest Australia and southeastern Papua.

Specifically, it was anticipated that the Japanese would attempt to hold Lae–Salamaua while rushing about 25,000 reinforcements to Madang and Finschhafen by sea. Once the Allied offensives got under way, reasoned MacArthur's planners, the Japanese would probably be unable to reinforce Lae or Salamaua. Enemy soldiers might be sent overland from Wewak through the Markham Valley to Lae, but would hardly be fit to fight on arrival. At the same time the Japanese could be expected to increase their garrisons at Cape Gloucester, Gasmata, and Arawe in western New Britain.

The enemy was expected to mount a maximum air effort in an attempt to defeat or delay the advancing Allies. Both daylight sorties and harassing night attacks would probably be used. If the Japanese could keep half their planes in serviceable condition, they could send out at least a hundred fighters and eighty-five bombers in the initial attacks. By draining the Solomons, they could attack on the second day with at least twenty-four fighters and ten bombers in addition to whatever aircraft were left from the first day, and by then more planes would be arriving from outside the area. The naval surface units at Rabaul could get to Lae in not more than eighteen hours, and strong forces could steam from Truk to Lae in a few days' time.[19]

---

[19] G–2 Estimate of Enemy Strength and Reinforcement Rate in the New Guinea–Bismarcks Area, Annex A to ELKTON III. A map showing enemy dispositions is appended to Annex A, and differs in certain minor respects from the order of battle data in the text of the annex.

CHAPTER IV

The Japanese

Just as the Allies were determined to advance against Rabaul, the Japanese were determined to hold it, and, indeed, to continue the advance that had been checked at Guadalcanal and Buna. The importance imparted to Rabaul by its airfield sites and harbor, as well as by its strategic location, had long been recognized by the Japanese. *Imperial General Headquarters'* instructions of November 1941 directed the capture of Rabaul at the earliest opportunity after the fall of Guam.[1] Rabaul supported the offensives against the Allied lines of communication, and defensively was a bastion which would help defend the Caroline Islands, the Netherlands Indies, and the Philippines against attack from the south. It was one of the most important bases in the semicircular string of island fortresses that stretched from Burma through the Indies and the Bismarck Archipelago to the Marshall Islands, thence north and northwest to the Kuriles.[2]

Japanese Command and Strategy

By late 1942 Rabaul had been developed into the major air and naval base in the Japanese Southeast Area, and was the site of the highest headquarters in that area. Although smaller than most Allied areas in the Pacific, the Southeast Area was huge. Its western boundary, as set on 2 April 1943, was longitude 140° east.[3] The northern boundary ran from 140° east just north of the Equator to a line drawn between Kapingamarangi in the Greenwich Islands to Nauru, thence southeast between the Fijis and Samoa. It thus embraced parts of both the South and Southwest Pacific Areas.

Unlike the Allied areas, the Southeast Area did not possess a unified command. The highest Army and Navy headquar-

---

[1] Unless otherwise indicated all data on the Japanese in this chapter are derived from the following monographs in the series Japanese Studies in World War II: 17th Army Operations, Vol. II, Monogr No. 40 (OCMH); 18th Army Operations, Vols. I, II, Monogrs No. 41, 42 (OCMH); Southeast Area Naval Operations, Vols. I–III, Monogrs No. 48–50 (OCMH); History of the Army Section, Imperial General Headquarters, 1941–45, Monogr No. 72 (OCMH); Outline of Southeast Area Naval Air Operations, November 1942–June 1943, Pt. III, Monogr No. 107 (OCMH); and 8th Area Army Operations, Monogr No. 110 (OCMH). Monograph No. 110 is a greatly improved revision of History of the 8th Area Army, 1942–44, Monograph No. 37 (OCMH).

[2] For early Japanese planning see Morton, *The Fall of the Philippines,* pp. 51–61; Milner, *Victory in Papua;* Miller, *Guadalcanal: The First Offensive,* pp. 4–7.

[3] From 7 January to 2 April 1943, the western boundary was the border of Dutch and Australian New Guinea—longitude 141° east. In addition to Japanese sources cited see U.S. Strategic Bombing Survey, *The Allied Campaign Against Rabaul* (Washington, 1946), pp. 10, 83.

CHART 3—ORGANIZATION OF JAPANESE FORCES, SOUTHEAST AREA, JUNE 1943

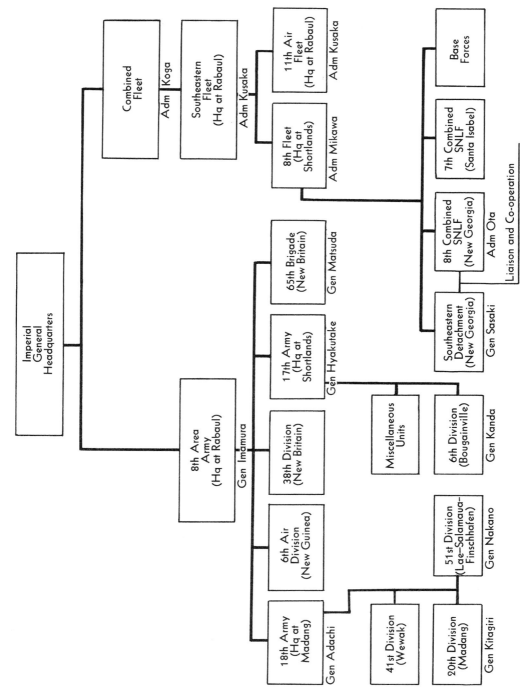

ters co-operated closely with one another, but were responsible to different higher authorities. (*Chart 3*) In charge of Army operations in eastern New Guinea, the Bismarck Archipelago, and the Solomons was General Hitoshi Imamura, commanding the *8th Area Army* with headquarters at Rabaul. Imamura was responsible to the *Army Section* of *Imperial General Headquarters*. The naval command was the *Southeast Area Fleet* or the *Southeastern Fleet* led by Vice Adm. Jinichi Kusaka. His immediate superior was the Commander in Chief of the *Combined Fleet* but on several occasions he seems to have dealt directly with Tokyo.

By the time the Guadalcanal and Papuan campaigns ended, the *8th Area Army* included two field armies and one air division. The *17th Army* operated in the Solomons; the *18th Army* was to be responsible for the campaigns in eastern New Guinea. The *6th Air Division*, with headquarters at Rabaul, generally operated in New Guinea under the tactical direction of the *18th Army*.

Under the *Southeastern Fleet* were the land-based *11th Air Fleet*, which operated principally in the Solomons, and the *8th Fleet* with bases at Rabaul and in the Shortlands–Buin area. The *8th Fleet*, whose strength and composition varied considerably, usually included cruisers, destroyers, submarines, transports, and naval base forces. An administrative rather than a battle fleet, its primary duties were patrol and escort. Large-scale combat operations were the mission of either the *3d* or the *Combined Fleet*, both then at Truk.[4]

Both the *8th Area Army* and the *Southeastern Fleet* had been set up in late 1942 when the Japanese, making their major offensive effort in the Solomons and still planning to drive the Americans from Guadalcanal, realized that they had to commit large forces to attain success. But *Imperial General Headquarters* then revised its strategy and decided to abandon Guadalcanal, evacuate the survivors, and withdraw to strong positions in front of Rabaul.

Under the revised strategy, *Imperial Headquarters* decided to shift its emphasis from the Solomons to New Guinea. A policy of "active defense" would be pursued in the Solomons in order to reinforce New Guinea and pursue an "aggressive offensive" there.[5] Lae, Salamaua, Wewak, and Madang on New Guinea's north coast were specifically mentioned as bases to be held. Imamura therefore ordered Lt. Gen. Hatazo Adachi, commander of the *18th Army*, to strengthen Lae, Salamaua, Wewak, and Madang. These points were valuable as harbors, airfield sites, or both. Lae and Salamaua were of great importance as their possessor could dominate Dampier and Vitiaz Straits and thus block any attempt to advance along the New Guinea coast to the Philippines or any other place in the Greater East Asia Co-Prosperity Sphere. The Japanese were determined not to yield "an operational route for the proclaimed enemy Philippines invasion."[6] These bases would also be necessary to the Japanese if they were

---

[4] USSBS, *The Allied Campaign Against Rabaul*, pp. 11, 43–44.

[5] Southeast Area Naval Operations, I, Japanese Monogr No. 48 (OCMH), 55.

[6] 18th Army Operations, I, Japanese Monogr No. 41 (OCMH), 55–56.

VICE ADM. JINICHI KUSAKA

GENERAL HITOSHI IMAMURA

to realize their hopes of capturing Port Moresby.

Thus the Japanese survivors of Buna were ordered to Salamaua, and on Imamura's orders Adachi directed more elements of his army to move from Rabaul to the New Guinea bases. The *20th Division* began moving to Wewak; the *41st* sent elements to Madang, and part of the *51st Division* was sent to Lae and Salamaua. The fixing of the west boundary of the Southeast Area on 7 January at the Dutch border apparently gladdened Adachi's heart. After being limited to the Buna region, "having suddenly obtained freedom of the operational area, it gave them [*the 18th Army*] bright and desirous hopes. . . ." [7]

At the same time, detachments of Field Marshal Count Hisaichi Terauchi's Netherlands Indies-based *Southern Army* were occupying areas along New Guinea's north coast from the Vogelkop Peninsula to Hollandia.

Imperial Headquarters' orders for the Solomons required the *8th Area Army,* in co-operation with the *Southeastern Fleet,* to hold the central and northern Solomons. Army and Navy authorities at Rabaul disagreed over exactly where the forward defense lines should be located. The Army favored the Bougainville area, holding that it would be too difficult to supply the islands farther south. The Navy insisted on New Georgia and Santa Isabel as outposts for Bougainville. Each service went its own way. The Army assumed responsibility for the defense of the northern Solomons. The Navy took over land defense of the central Solomons. Imamura gave to Lt. Gen.

[7] *Ibid.,* p. 110.

LT. GEN. HATAZO ADACHI

Haruyoshi Hyakutake's *17th Army,* then consisting chiefly of the *6th Division,* responsibility for Bougainville and adjacent islands.[8]

Having insisted on the necessity for holding New Georgia and Santa Isabel, naval authorities then complained that this responsibility placed an excessive demand on naval strength, and asked Imamura for some Army ground troops for New Georgia in addition to the few who were already there. The general, still invoking the difficulty of supply, was at first reluctant. In March the *Southeastern Fleet* sent the *8th Combined Special Naval Landing Force* to New Georgia, and another, the *7th,* to Santa

Isabel.[9] After a good deal of negotiation, and perhaps on orders from *Imperial Headquarters,* Imamura acceded to Kusaka's requests and sent more Army troops to New Georgia under their own headquarters, the *Southeastern Detachment,* and some additional units to Santa Isabel. Both the *8th Combined Special Naval Landing Force* and the *Southeastern Detachment,* as well as the Santa Isabel force, were under the tactical control of the *8th Fleet.*

Thus in early 1943 the Japanese were holding a network of mutually supporting air and naval bases arranged in depth, running in two converging arcs through New Guinea and the Solomons to Rabaul. From the defensive point of view, these positions would serve to protect Rabaul, the Netherlands Indies, and the Philippines. Offensively, these bases could support advances southward, and although the Japanese had decided on delaying action in the Solomons, they were determined to take the offensive in New Guinea.

Japanese Offensives, January–June 1943

The Attack Against Wau

The first offensive effort under the revised strategy was directed against Wau in the Bulolo Valley goldfields southeast of New Guinea's Huon Peninsula. Wau, the site of a prewar airfield, lies 145 air miles north by west of Port Moresby, and 25 air miles southwest of Salamaua. (*Map 4*) Since May 1942 Wau had been held by a small body of Australians, known as the KANGA Force, who operated

---

[8] Of the *17th Army* units which served on Guadalcanal, the *35th Brigade* (*Kawaguchi Force* or *Detachment*) went to Burma; the *2d Division,* to the Philippines; the *38th Division,* to New Britain under direct control of the *8th Area Army.*

[9] Composed of the *Kure 6th* and the *Yokosuka 7th Special Naval Landing Forces,* the *8th Combined* had been activated in Japan for service on Guadalcanal but did not get there before the evacuation.

under control of the New Guinea Force. As the Bulolo Valley could be reached overland from other Allied bases only over mountainous, jungled, and swampy routes, the KANGA Force was supplied largely by air. It had been ordered to keep watch over Lae and Salamaua and to hold the Bulolo Valley as a base for harrying the enemy until he could be driven out of the area.[10] If the Japanese had been able to establish themselves at Wau, they could have reaped great gains. They could have staged aircraft from Madang and Wewak through Wau, thus bringing Port Moresby within effective range of their fighters.[11] The *18th Army* entertained ambitious plans for capturing Wau and crossing the Owen Stanley Range to seize Port Moresby. It is not clear, however, whether Adachi intended to proceed from Wau over the rough trail that led from Wau to Bulldog on the Lakekamu River, or to move against Port Moresby via Kokoda. Either route would have outflanked the Allied Gona–Sanananda–Buna–Dobodura–Oro Bay positions that had been won in the arduous Papuan campaign.

When *18th Army* troops moved to New Guinea in early 1943, some went to Lae and Salamaua to strengthen naval forces already there.[12] The reinforced *102d Infantry Regiment* was sent in a convoy from Rabaul to Lae during the first week in January. But the Allies,

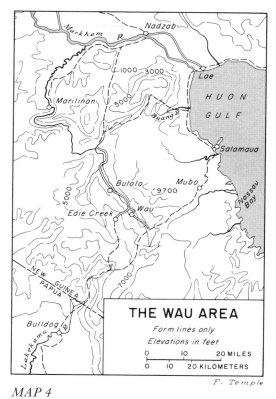

MAP 4

warned by the fact that the Japanese had given up their efforts to send troops to Buna, had anticipated that the Japanese might try to strengthen Lae and Salamaua and were therefore attempting to isolate that area by air action. Allied planes found the convoy, bombed it, and sank two transports. About three fourths of the *102d* went ashore at Lae, but half its supplies were lost.

Once at Lae, the *102d* was ordered by Adachi to seize Wau. This Allied enclave was connected to the north coast by several trails that could be traversed on foot. The Japanese commander at Lae, Maj. Gen. Toru Okabe, decided to begin his drive against Wau from Salamaua.

[10] Milner, *Victory in Papua*, Chs. I, III; ALF, Rpt on New Guinea Opns: 23 Sep 42–22 Jan 44.

[11] AAF Int Summary 74, 3 Feb 43, in GHQ SWPA G–3 Jnl, 2 Feb 43.

[12] Interrogation of Lt Gen Hatazo Adachi, Lt Gen Rimpei Kato (former CofS, *8th Area Army*), Lt Col Shoji Ota (former stf off, *8th Area Army*), and Capt Sadamu Sanagi (former Senior Stf Off, *Southeastern Fleet*), by members of the Mil Hist Sec, Australian Army Hq, at Rabaul, no date, OCMH.

LT. GEN. HARUYOSHI HYAKUTAKE

Brigade were flown from Milne Bay to Wau.[13]

After assembling at Salamaua, Okabe and the *102d Infantry* made their way laboriously upward to the Bulolo Valley. They struck at Wau in a dusk attack on 28 January and pushed through to the edge of the airfield. But there they were stopped. For the next three days Australian soldiers of the 17th Brigade, plus ammunition, supplies, and two 25-pounder guns, were flown in by air. In three days troop carriers of the Allied Air Forces flew in 194 planeloads, or one million pounds. So critical was the situation on the 29th that the first load of troops practically leaped from the planes firing their small arms. The Japanese pressed hard, but by 30 January acknowledged failure and began to withdraw.[14]

Having broken the enemy's attack, the Australians kept pressing him back toward Salamaua. In April the 3d Australian Division took over direction of operations and the KANGA Force was dissolved. The Australians then halted short of Salamaua to wait until other Allied troops could be made ready for a large-scale attack against the entire Finschhafen–Lae–Salamaua complex.[15]

The Australians' gallant defense of Wau thus frustrated the last Japanese attempt to attack Port Moresby overland, and kept for the Allies an advantageous

By 16 January he had gathered his attacking force there.

The Allies, determined to prevent the Japanese from capturing Wau and threatening Port Moresby, had meanwhile acted promptly. Headquarters, New Guinea Force, decided to reinforce Wau, and in mid-January advance elements of the 17th Australian Infantry

---

[13] ALF, Rpt on New Guinea Opns: 23 Sep 42–22 Jan 44; NGF OI 60, 13 Jan 43, in GHQ SWPA G–3 Jnl, 14 Jan 43.

[14] Craven and Cate, *The Pacific: Guadalcanal to Saipan*, pp. 136–37; Kenney, *General Kenney Reports*, pp. 186–87; ALF, Rpt on New Guinea Opns: 23 Sep 42–22 Jan 44.

[15] USSBS, *Employment of Forces*, p. 17; GHQ SWPA G–3 Opns Rpt 380, 21–22 Apr 43, in GHQ SWPA G–3 Jnl, 22 Apr 43.

position which would help support later offensives against the Huon Peninsula.

The Battle of the Bismarck Sea

The Australian defense of Wau had a third consequence that was more far-reaching than even the most ebullient Bulolo Valley veteran (if anyone was ebullient after fighting in the mud, mountains, and heat) realized at the time. It helped lead to the destruction of an entire Japanese convoy and the subsequent weakening of Lae.[16]

Okabe's attacks against Wau had so depleted his meager force that the Japanese at Rabaul, who were determined to hold Lae and Salamaua at all costs, became worried. The *20th* and *41st Divisions* could not be spared from Wewak and Madang. Thus Imamura, Adachi, and the naval commanders decided to send the rest of the *51st Division* in convoy to Lae. They planned very carefully.

They were well aware of the havoc that airplanes could wreak on troop transports. Guadalcanal had demonstrated that point, and if final proof was needed, Adachi had had it in the destruction of part of Okabe's shipment in January. Had it been possible for the convoy to sail from Rabaul to Madang and land the troops there to march to Lae, the ships could have stayed out of effective range of Allied fighters and medium bombers; heavy bombers, thus far relatively ineffective against ships, were

not greatly feared. But there was no overland or coastal route capable of getting large bodies of troops from Madang to Lae. It was therefore necessary to sail directly to Lae and thus come within range of fighters and medium bombers. The Japanese, employing almost two hundred planes based at Rabaul, Madang. Wewak, Cape Gloucester, Gasmata, and Kavieng, hoped to beat Allied planes down out of the air and to provide direct cover to the ships.

But the Allies had deduced Japanese intentions. Ship movements around New Britain in late February, though not part of the effort to reinforce Lae, were noted by Allied reconnaissance planes. As a result air search was intensified and air striking forces were alerted. On 25 February General Kenney and his subordinates came to the conclusion that the Japanese would probably try to put more troops ashore at Lae or Madang.[17]

Not only were the Allies warned; they were also ready. By the end of February airfields in Papua, with those at Dobodura near Buna carrying the biggest load, based 207 bombers and 129 fighters. The Southwest Pacific had no aircraft carriers and few if any carrier-type planes that were specifically designed for attacks against ships. But Kenney and his subordinates had redesigned the nose of the B–25 medium bomber and installed forward-firing .50-caliber machine guns so that the bomber could strafe the deck of a ship and thus neutralize all her exposed antiaircraft guns. Further, they had practiced the skip-bombing technique that proved particularly effective in sinking

---

[16] Unless otherwise indicated, this brief account is based on the Japanese monographs and on definitive accounts in Craven and Cate, *The Pacific: Guadalcanal to Saipan*, pp. 141–51, and Samuel Eliot Morison, *History of United States Naval Operations in World War II*, Vol. VI, *Breaking the Bismarcks Barrier: 22 July 1942–1 May 1944* (Boston: Little, Brown and Company, 1950), Ch. V.

[17] See Kenney, *General Kenney Reports*, p. 197. See also GHQ SWPA G–2 Est of Enemy Sit 343, 28 Feb–1 Mar 43, in GHQ SWPA G–3 Jnl, 1 Mar 43.

JAPANESE TROOP TRANSPORT UNDER ATTACK *by B–25's, Battle of the Bismarck Sea.*

ships.[18] Once warned, the Allied airmen prepared detailed plans for striking the convoy and executed a full-scale rehearsal off Port Moresby.

At Rabaul, 6,912 Japanese soldiers boarded eight ships. The ships weighed anchor about midnight of 28 February 1943 and, with eight destroyers as escort, sailed out of Rabaul and westward through the Bismarck Sea at seven knots. At first bad weather—winds, mist, and rain—hid them from the air, but soon the weather began to break and Allied patrol planes sighted the convoy first on 1

March and again the next morning off Cape Gloucester. As it was still beyond the reach of medium bombers, heavy bombers from Port Moresby attacked it in the Bismarck Sea. They sank one transport and damaged two others, a good score for heavy bombers. Survivors of the sunken ship, about 950 in number, were picked up by two of the destroyers which made a quick run to Lae to land the men after dark. The destroyers returned to the convoy on the morning of 3 March. During the night the convoy had sailed through Vitiaz Strait and into the Solomon Sea, tracked all the while by an Australian Catalina.

But now the ships entered the Huon Gulf in clear daylight, and were within range of medium bombers. The Allied planes that had organized and rehearsed

---

[18] For details see Craven and Cate, *The Pacific: Guadalcanal to Saipan,* pp. 140–41; Kenney, *General Kenney Reports,* pp. 21–22, 105, 144, 154–55, 162, 164. Maj. Gen. Henry H. Arnold had observed the RAF practicing skip-bombing in 1941 and introduced it to the AAF.

for the attack assembled over Cape Ward Hunt at 0930 and set forth for the kill. The Japanese had failed to destroy Allied air power in advance, and the convoy's air cover was ineffective. Starting about 1000 and continuing until nightfall, American and Australian airmen in P–38's, P–39's, P–40's, Beaufighters, A–20's, A–29's, Beaufort bombers, B–17's, B–24's and B–25's pounded the luckless Japanese from medium, low, and wavetop altitudes with resounding success. All remaining transports, along with four destroyers, sank on 3 and 4 March. After night fell motor torpedo boats from Buna and Tufi swept in to finish off crippled ships and shoot up survivors in the water.

Of the 6,912 troops on board, 3,664 were lost. Including those taken by destroyer to Lae, 3,248 were rescued by the Japanese. The sinking of eight transports and four destroyers in "the most devastating air attack on ships" since Pearl Harbor was a tremendous victory, and it was won at a cost of thirteen killed, twelve wounded, and four Allied planes shot down.[19]

The Japanese quickly changed their plans for future shipments. They decided to send no more convoys to Lae. Large slow ships would be sent only to Hansa Bay and Wewak; high-speed ships

and small craft would run to Finschhafen and Tuluvu on the north coast of New Britain. Small coastal craft would take men and supplies to Lae from Finschhafen and Cape Gloucester, and some men and supplies would be sent overland from Finschhafen to Lae. In emergencies supplies that were absolutely required at Lae would be sent in by high-speed ships or submarines. The main body of ground forces eventually intended for Lae would be sent overland after completion of a road, already under construction, from Wewak through Madang to Lae.

Road Building

Construction of the road had been started in January. This most ambitious project involved building a truck highway from Madang to Bogadjim, thence over the Finisterre Range and through the Ramu and Markham River Valleys to Lae. The *20th Division* was given this work.

In early February the Allies, having received reports from natives, were aware of enemy activity in the Ramu Valley. Allied intelligence deduced that the Japanese were interested in an inland route to Lae. Intelligence also minimized the danger of a serious threat, for it seemed unlikely that the road could

---

[19] Morison, *Breaking the Bismarcks Barrier*, p. 59. Allied casualty figures are from Kenney, *General Kenney Reports*, p. 206. Official communiques at the time, based on pilots' reports, claimed twenty-two ships and fifteen thousand men, and Kenney, in his book and in his comments on the draft manuscript of this volume, claimed six destroyers or light cruisers sunk, two destroyers or light cruisers damaged, and from eleven to fourteen merchant vessels in the convoy sunk; he also included, in his total for the Bismarck Sea, two small merchant ships that were sunk at Lae and Wide Bay. According to

Kenney a second enemy convoy joined the first, which explains the disparity. However, Craven and Cate, in *The Pacific: Guadalcanal to Saipan*, pp. 147–50, and Morison, in *Breaking the Bismarcks Barrier*, after surveying all available enemy records, maintained that the convoy consisted of eight transports and an equal number of destroyers, that there was no second convoy, and that eight transports and four destroyers were sunk. 8th Area Army Operations, Japanese Monogr No. 110 (OCMH) supports them.

be completed in time to be of much use.[20]

Allied intelligence was correct. The road-building projects were next to impossible for the Japanese to accomplish. Their maps were poor. The routes they selected, especially the inland route for the Madang–Lae road, led them through disease-ridden jungles and swamps, over towering mountains, and up and across canyons and gorges. They never had enough machinery and what they had was ineffective. Their trucks, for example, were not sufficiently powerful to climb steep slopes. Their horses fared poorly on jungle grasses. Bridges kept washing away on the Madang–Hansa Bay road. Combat troops were unhappy as laborers. Dense forests hid the road builders from air observation, but in the open stretches of the Finisterre Range they were constantly subject to air attack. By the end of June the Madang–Lae road had been pushed only through the Finisterre Range.

Lae therefore never did receive substantial reinforcements or supplies, despite the Japanese determination to hold it and dominate Dampier and Vitiaz Straits.

The I Operation

While Japanese Army troops were busy building roads in New Guinea, the Japanese Navy had also taken a hand in an effort to beat the Allies. Galled by the admittedly crushing defeat in the Bismarck Sea, fully aware of the threat that Allied air activity in the South Pacific presented to their shipments of troops and supplies to New Georgia and Santa Isabel, and concerned over their declining air strength, the Japanese decided to gather more planes, smash Allied air power, and attack Allied shipping in the Southeast Area.

Japanese air strength was somewhat less than substantial at this time. In March 1943 there were only about three hundred planes—one hundred Army and two hundred Navy—in the Southeast Area. Rabaul frequently complained that Tokyo never sent enough replacements to replace losses. Toward the end of March General Imamura asked *Imperial Headquarters* for more. *Headquarters* did send more, but not enough to satisfy Imamura, and some planes that were dispatched never arrived. For example, the *68th Air Regiment* navigated so badly while flying from Truk to Rabaul that many of its planes failed to find Rabaul and were lost at sea.

Admiral Isoroku Yamamoto, Commander in Chief of the *Combined Fleet,* decided to take a hand in the attempt to beat the Allies out of the air. For this effort, given the code name *I* Operation, he sent the planes from the *3d Fleet* carriers at Truk to join with *11th Air Fleet* planes at Rabaul, Kavieng, Buin, Buka, and Ballale. He took headquarters of both the *Combined* and *3d Fleets* from Truk to Rabaul to direct the *I* Operation, which involved more than three hundred aircraft.

Japanese aircraft had concentrated against the Allied New Guinea bases in March, and the month had been a quiet one on Guadalcanal. But that the Japanese had renewed their interest in the

---

[20] See GHQ G–2 Daily Summary of Enemy Int and G–2 Est of Enemy Sit 317, 2–3 Feb 43, in GHQ SWPA G–3 Jnl, 3 Feb 43. See also Australian Mil Forces Weekly Int Review 28, 5–12 Feb 43, in GHQ SWPA G–3 Jnl, 5 Feb 43.

Solomons was demonstrated to the Allies on 1 April when bombers and fighters struck at the Russells. Air combats raged for three hours as Allied fighters beat off the attackers, losing six of their number in the process.[21]

Six days later, 7 April, came the main phase of *I* Operation in the Solomons. It was a splendid opportunity for the Japanese, for there were many targets around Guadalcanal. A naval task force, having fueled at Tulagi, was steaming northwest en route to shell Vila and Munda that night. Including cargo ships, transports, and the task force, there were present about forty ships of corvette size or larger, and a larger number of smaller vessels. In addition much ammunition, fuel, and equipment were being stored on Guadalcanal in preparation for the invasion of New Georgia.

To attack these lucrative targets, Yamamoto dispatched 117 fighters and 71 bombers. Coastwatchers on New Georgia, counting more than 160 planes overhead, flashed warnings southward. Halsey canceled the scheduled bombardment; the task force rounded Florida and sped down Indispensable Strait. Other ships and craft started getting under way and most had reached open water when the Japanese arrived about 1500.

While Allied bombers flew to the southeast to avoid the Japanese, all available Allied fighters, seventy-six in number, took the air to intercept. P–38's (Lightnings) flew on top, and beneath them, at various altitudes, were F4U's (Corsairs), F6F's (Hellcats), and P–39's (Airacobras). As the Japanese planes broke up into separate flights, a general melee ensued. The skies above the Russells, Tulagi, and the waters between Guadalcanal and Florida saw violent combat. According to the Japanese, "resistance offered by the ten or so enemy Grummans [F6F's] and P–38's was beaten down and the attack on shipping was carried out." They reported seriously damaging most of the Allied ships, a claim that is as inaccurate as their statement that only ten Allied fighters tried to intercept.[22] They sank the New Zealand corvette *Moa*, the U.S. oiler *Kanawha*, and the U.S. destroyer *Aaron Ward*, and damaged one other oiler. They apparently never sighted the task force. Seven Allied fighters and one pilot were lost, but the Japanese lost many more.[23]

Yamamoto, apparently satisfied with the performance over Guadalcanal, then turned against the Allies in New Guinea. On 11 April 22 bombers and 72 fighters struck at Oro Bay. They sank one merchant ship, damaged another so badly that it had to be beached, and hit an Australian minesweeper. Next day 131 fighters and 43 bombers flew over the Owen Stanleys to hit Port Moresby. There were few Allied fighters on hand to oppose them. As he himself points out, General Kenney had expected the attack to hit Milne Bay and had sent most

---

[21] Craven and Cate, *The Pacific: Guadalcanal to Saipan*, p. 212.

[22] Southeast Area Naval Operations, II, Japanese Monogr No. 49 (OCMH), 13.

[23] Craven and Cate, *The Pacific: Guadalcanal to Saipan*, pp. 212–13; Morison, *Breaking the Bismarcks Barrier*, pp. 120–24. Allied airmen claimed thirty-nine Japanese planes downed in air combat, while surface ships claimed twenty-five. There were undoubtedly many duplications. The Japanese admit losing twenty-one.

of his fighter strength there.[24] Fortunately the damage was very light. Two days later the Japanese fulfilled Kenney's expectations by attacking Milne Bay, but they did little damage. One Dutch merchant ship was a total loss, and a British motorship and another Dutch ship were damaged. Yamamoto then concluded the *I* Operation, which he regarded as highly successful, and returned the carrier planes to their parent units at Truk. The Japanese, apparently misled by optimistic pilots' reports, boast of destroying 1 cruiser, 2 destroyers, 25 transports, and 134 planes, while losing 42 planes themselves. But actual Allied losses in the Solomons and New Guinea were 1 destroyer, 1 tanker, 1 corvette, 2 Dutch merchant ships, and about 25 planes.

Ambush Over Kahili

Yamamoto then decided to pay a morale-building visit to the Buin area. He, his chief of staff, and other officers left Rabaul on 18 April in two twin-engine bombers escorted by fighters. When the party reached a point thirty-five miles northwest of Kahili, the airdrome near Buin, they were jumped by eighteen P–38's from the South Pacific's Thirteenth Air Force, which had been sent there for that very purpose.

When Admiral Halsey returned to Nouméa after conferring with MacArthur in Brisbane, he learned that American intelligence officers had discovered the exact time on 18 April Yamamoto was due to reach the Buin area from Rabaul. Admiral Nimitz and his staff agreed that disposing of Yamamoto would advance the Allied cause, so the Commander, Aircraft, Solomons, was told to shoot him down. The eighteen P–38's, manned by picked pilots and led by Maj. John W. Mitchell, were sent on the mission. Taking off from Henderson Field on Guadalcanal, they flew low over the waves for 435 miles by a circuitous route to the interception point northwest of Kahili. Yamamoto's flight hove in sight just as its fighter escort was leaving. Mitchell's attack section, led by Capt. Thomas G. Lanphier, Jr., bored in and Lanphier made the kill. Yamamoto's plane crashed in the Bougainville jungle. He died. The other plane fell in the sea, but the chief of staff, whom it was carrying, survived. One American pilot was lost. This Lucifer-like descent of the aggressive, skillful Yamamoto, perhaps the brightest star in the Japanese military firmament, was a severe blow to the morale of the Japanese armed forces.[25]

The Big Raid

By early June, the Allies in the Solomons realized that the Japanese were again determined to accomplish what the *I* Operation had failed to do—cut the lines of communication to Guadalcanal by air action. Yamamoto fell from the skies believing that *I* had succeeded, but by June the enemy leaders at Rabaul knew that the Allies were freely building up supplies on Guadalcanal. On 7 June the Japanese inaugurated another series of fighter-escorted bombing attacks against Guadalcanal. Planes from the

---

[24] Kenney, *General Kenney Reports*, pp. 225, 228–29.

[25] Craven and Cate, *The Pacific: Guadalcanal to Saipan*, pp. 213–14; Halsey and Bryan, *Admiral Halsey's Story*, pp. 155–57; Morison, *Breaking the Bismarcks Barrier*, pp. 128–29. There are some differences in these accounts, chiefly regarding Yamamoto's destination and time of arrival. Halsey and Bryan, and Craven and Cate say he was to arrive at Ballale at 0945. Morison says he was due at Kahili at 1145.

Russells made the first interception that day. According to Allied accounts, the Japanese lost twenty-three fighters, four of them to P–40's of the No. 15 Royal New Zealand Air Force Fighter Squadron in its Solomons debut. Nine Allied planes were shot down but all pilots were recovered. In a second attack five days later, the Japanese are reported to have lost thirty-one planes, the Allies, six.

By mid-June Allied reconnaissance planes were reporting 245 planes at Rabaul, with the forward fields in the northern Solomons filled to capacity. What some Allied veterans of this period call "the big raid" on Guadalcanal came on 16 June when a large force of enemy bombers and fighters, numbering over 100 planes, flew down to attack Guadalcanal.[26] The coastwatchers again had sent their timely warnings, and 104 Allied fighters were ready. As in April, they intercepted promptly, the Japanese formations broke up into smaller flights, and air combats raged. Whenever possible ship- and shore-based antiaircraft took the enemy under fire. The Japanese hit three Allied ships, two of which had to be beached, and did some damage to shore installations before they were driven off. Six Allied fighters were shot down. The number of enemy planes destroyed was large, although the exact total cannot be determined. The Allies claimed 98. One Japanese account admits the loss of about 30 planes.[27]

Neither the *I* Operation nor "the big raid" achieved substantial results. The Japanese failed, partly because their efforts were brief and sporadic rather than long and sustained, and partly because Allied resistance had been vigorous and generally skillful.

Japanese Strength and Dispositions, 30 June 1943

In June Japanese strategy was still substantially what it had been in January.[28] Late in March Lt. Gen. Rimpei Kato, the *8th Area Army's* chief of staff, and other officers had gone to *Imperial Headquarters,* apparently to explain things after the Bismarck Sea debacle. The result of the visit was an Army-Navy "Central Agreement" which was really a reaffirmation of the policies laid down earlier. The Japanese still planned to defend the Solomons while strengthening the bases in New Guinea and the Bismarck Archipelago in preparation for future offensives, especially against Port Moresby. Ambitious plans for air supremacy were prepared, including one for maintaining 641 planes (284 Army and 357 Navy) in the Southeast Area, but, as has been shown above, these were destined to fail.

In April Imamura summoned his army commanders to Rabaul and gave them orders based on the Central Agreement. Instructions to Adachi emphasized holding Lae and Salamaua, building the Madang–Lae highway, and establishing coastal barge lines from western New Britain to Lae and Salamaua. In fulfillment of the policy of using naval air in

---

[26] USSBS, *The Allied Campaign Against Rabaul,* p. 46, says 150–60 planes attacked on 6 June, but 16 June is apparently intended.

[27] Craven and Cate, *The Pacific: Guadalcanal to Saipan,* pp. 218–19; U.S. Strategic Bombing Survey, *The Thirteenth Air Force in the War Against Japan* (Washington, 1946); Southeast Area Naval Operations, III, Japanese Monogr No. 50 (OCMH), 53.

[28] The basic research for this section was performed by Messrs. Stanley L. Falk and Burke C. Peterson.

the Solomons and Army air in New Guinea, the entire *6th Air Division* was told to move to New Guinea.

In June Imamura issued more orders, which restated the importance of Lae and Salamaua. The *18th Army* was told to strengthen them as well as Wewak, Madang, and Finschhafen. Adachi was to regroup his forces at Lae and Salamaua and prepare to capture the Allied outposts and patrol bases at Wau, Bena Bena, and Mount Hagen, and to infiltrate up the Ramu and Sepik River Valleys.

In anticipation of the operations against Bena Bena and Hagen, *Imperial Headquarters* transferred the *7th Air Division* from the Netherlands Indies to the *8th Area Army* about July, and shortly afterward placed *Headquarters, 4th Air Army* under Imamura to coordinate operations of the two air divisions.

Imamura also developed an ambitious airfield construction program which involved building new fields or enlarging old ones. By June, too, all divisions of the *18th Army*—the *20th, 41st,* and *51st*— were concentrated in New Guinea. The *17th Army*, still consisting chiefly of the *6th Division,* was in Bougainville. The *Southeastern Detachment* and the *8th Combined Special Naval Landing Force* were dug in deeply in New Georgia, and the *7th Combined Special Naval Landing Force* and Army elements still held Rekata Bay at Santa Isabel.

It is not possible, on the basis of existing information, to state positively just how many troops Imamura had under his command at this time. These figures, and those in the table of strength and dispositions, are guesses based on available enemy data: for the Solomons, 25,000; for the New Guinea coast east of the Dutch border, 55,000; for the Bismarck Archipelago, perhaps 43,000 ground troops, for a total of 123,000.[29]

In aircraft, the Japanese possessed a total of something over 500 planes in June, though some of them were usually

---

[29] Strength tables and reports do not seem to have survived the war, and available wartime and postwar documents and accounts are inexact, contradictory, or both. The most detailed figures on Japanese Army strength in the Southeast Area for June 1943 are contained in Southeast Area Naval Operations, Vol. II, Japanese Monograph No. 49 (OCMH), pp. 22–23, but this account gives no hint of the source of the figures that are not supported by the few strength figures in Army records. For example, the naval account states that there were 55,000 men holding Lae, Salamaua, Finschhafen, Madang, and Wewak—the *18th Army's* area of responsibility—in June 1943, but an *18th Army* statistical table indicates that the *18th Army* then contained 80,000 men. The office of Official War History, Department of the Interior, of the Commonwealth of Australia, believes that the figure of 80,000 for the *18th Army* is correct. Ltr, Mr. Gavin Long to Dr. Kent Roberts Greenfield (Chief Historian, OCMH), 7 Dec 55, OCMH. Japanese documents give no data on ground-troop strength in the Bismarck Archipelago for June 1943. The nearest date for which there are anything like valid figures is November 1943, and those figures are given in the U.S. Strategic Bombing Survey's *The Allied Campaign Against Rabaul.* Its text asserts that in November 1943 there were 97,870 (76,300 Army and the remainder Navy) in the Bismarck Archipelago, but this statement does not seem to be solidly supported by the interrogations upon which the text is based. General Imamura is quoted on pages 10, 11, and 82, as stating that of 90,000 troops in the Rabaul area in November, 55,000 belonged to his army. From whatever November figure is selected, the strength of the *17th Division,* which arrived in New Britain in September and October of 1943, must be subtracted. Unfortunately, there are no figures on that division's strength. The figure 43,000, given in the text above, for the Bismarcks was obtained by the arbitrary method of subtracting 12,000, a reasonable estimate of the strength of the *17th Division,* from Imamura's November figure of 55,000. There are fewer problems for the Solomons, which seem to have contained about 25,000 Japanese ground troops.

TABLE 1—COMPARISON OF ALLIED INTELLIGENCE ESTIMATES WITH JAPANESE STRENGTH AND DISPOSITIONS, SOUTHEAST AREA, 30 JUNE 1943

GROUND FORCES

Allied Estimates	Japanese Units and Approximate Strength
130,250/131,550	123,000
Bismarck Archipelago: 42,800	43,000
(Rabaul, Talasea, Gasmata,	8th Area Army Hq
Cape Gloucester, Tuluvu,	6th Air Div Hq
Kavieng, Lorengau)	38th Div
8th Area Army Hq	65th Brig
18th Army Hq	Naval Units
Elements 38th Div	
65th Brigade	
Naval Units	
New Guinea (east of Dutch	
border): 47,200/48,300	55,000
Lae–Salamaua–Finschhafen:	
9,000/9,100	15,000
51st Div	51st Div
SNLF	SNLF
Misc	Misc
Saidor: 500 unidentified	?
Madang: 12,000/13,000	20,000
Adv Hq, 18th Army	18th Army Hq
20th Div	20th Div
Hansa Bay: 5,000	?
Misc	
Wewak: 20,000	20,000
41st Div	41st Div
Misc	Naval Units

GROUND FORCES—Continued

Allied Estimates	Japanese Units and Approximate Strength
Aitape: 200 unidentified	?
Vanimo: 500 Misc	?
Solomons: 40,250/40,450	25,000
Buka: 4,000	1,130
6th Cav	6th Cav
SNLF	SNLF
Bougainville–Shortlands:	
26,700/26,900	8,480
17th Army Hq	17th Army Hq
6th Div	6th Div
SNLF	SNLF
New Georgia: 10,550	10,500
229th Inf	13th Inf
SNLF	229th Inf
	SNLF
Santa Isabel: 2,000	3,100
SNLF	SNLF
Misc	1 Army Inf Bn
Choiseul; none listed	1,500/2,200

NAVAL FORCES

1 light cruiser	1 cruiser
9/10 destroyers	8 destroyers
5 submarines	8 submarines

AIR FORCES

461 planes	540 planes (390 operational)

Source: Allied estimates are from GHQ SWPA G–2 Int Bulletin, Summary Enemy Dispositions, 30 Jun 43, in GHQ SWPA G–3 Jnl, 30 Jun 43; and CTF 31 Opn Plan A8–43, 4 Jun 43, Int Annex, Off of Naval Rcds and Library. Approximate strengths of Japanese units are from Japanese Monographs Nos. 37, 40–42, 48–50, 72, 110, and 107 (OCMH). The Australian Official War historians regard the postwar estimates as too low. See Ltr, Long to Green-field, 7 Dec 55. They are, however, admittedly conservative, and based on the best Japanese data available in Washington.

out of action. For example, of the 300 planes assigned to the *11th Air Fleet* on 30 June, only 225 were ready for combat operations. Of 240 belonging to the *6th Air Division*, 50 needed minor attention and 25 required major repairs.

Planes were given a high degree of tactical mobility by the large number of conveniently spaced air bases in the area. Kavieng had one field. Rabaul boasted four—Lakunai, Vunakanau, Ra-popo, and Keravat (which never amounted to much)—with one more under construction at nearby Tobera. In addition, the *8th Area Army* was improving fields, or building new ones, at Wewak, Hansa Bay, Alexishafen, Madang, Lae–Salamaua, Tuluvu, and Talasea. The same situation prevailed in the Solomons. Besides the New Georgia fields and the seaplane bases at Rekata Bay and Shortland-Faisi, there were fields at Kahili and Ballale in the Buin–Shortlands area, and another, Kara, soon to be built. There was one at Buka, with another, Bonis, under construction just across Buka Passage. On the east coast of Bougainville the Tenekau and Kieta strips were being built, apparently under orders of the *8th Area Army*.[30]

The *8th Fleet,* in June, had one cruiser, eight destroyers, and eight submarines. The potential of this fleet had been cut somewhat by Admiral Mineichi Koga, who had succeeded to command of the *Combined Fleet.* Because the recapture of Attu in May was regarded as a direct threat to the Japanese homeland, he diverted 20 percent of the forces (apparently including aircraft) "in the course of being assigned or available for assignment" in the Southeast Area to the Aleutians and to Saipan.[31]

Table 1 compares Allied estimates of enemy strength, and dispositions of that strength, with an approximation of enemy strength and dispositions based on available enemy records. It will be noted that Allied estimates for Japanese strength and dispositions throughout the Southeast Area were quite accurate.

In June 1943 the Japanese still cherished ambitions toward future offensives. It is clear in retrospect that their resources made them capable of defensive action only. But, as at Guadalcanal and Buna, the Japanese were so skillful in defensive operations that Allied troops were faced with a long series of hard battles.

---

[30] In addition to the Japanese monographs cited above, see USSBS, *The Allied Campaign Against Rabaul,* pp. 11–12, 46; USAFISPA Photo Int Unit Periodic Rpt, Airdromes and Seaplane Anchorages, Jul 43.

[31] Southeast Area Naval Operations, II, Japanese Monogr No. 49 (OCMH), 18.

CHAPTER V

CARTWHEEL Begins:
The Southwest Pacific

On 30 June 1943—D Day for CART-WHEEL—Allied air, sea, and ground forces facing the Japanese from New Guinea to the Solomons were ready to attack. The Japanese were expecting the offensive but did not know just when or where it would come. And the Allies had determined to compound their uncertainty by launching not one, but three invasions—in New Georgia, at Woodlark and Kiriwina, and at Nassau Bay in New Guinea in preparation for the Markham Valley–Lae–Salamaua operations.

CHRONICLE

Plans and Preparations

Planning for the seizure of Woodlark and Kiriwina (designated Operation CHRONICLE) had started at General Krueger's Sixth Army headquarters near Brisbane in early May. General MacArthur had directed Allied Air and Naval Forces to support ALAMO Force and had made Krueger responsible for the co-ordination of ground, air, and naval planning.[1] Krueger, Kenney, Carpender, Barbey,

and staff and liaison officers participated. Krueger's authority to co-ordinate planning gave him a pre-eminent position; he was first among equals.

Planning had not proceeded far before a hitch developed. When Admiral Halsey suggested the seizure of Woodlark and Kiriwina he offered to provide part of the invasion force, an offer that had been cheerfully accepted. Thus in midmonth Generals Harmon and Twining and Vice Adm. Aubrey W. Fitch, who commanded all South Pacific aircraft, flew to Brisbane to discuss details of the transfer of forces to the Southwest Pacific. On the way over from Nouméa Harmon and Twining made an air reconnaissance of Woodlark, and on arriving at Brisbane offered their opinion that Woodlark would be of little use in providing air support for the South Pacific's invasion of southern Bougainville. But Kenney, Carpender, Brig. Gen. Stephen J. Chamberlin, G–3 of GHQ, and Brig. Gen. Hugh J. Casey, the chief engineer of GHQ, explained how difficult it would be for Kenney's aircraft to support that invasion without the additional airfield that Woodlark would provide. The South Pacific repre-

---

[1] GHQ SWPA OI 33, 7 May 43, in GHQ SWPA G–3 Jnl, 8 May 43; CG Sixth Army, Hist of CHRONICLE Opn, in GHQ SWPA G–3 Jnl, 30 Aug 43.

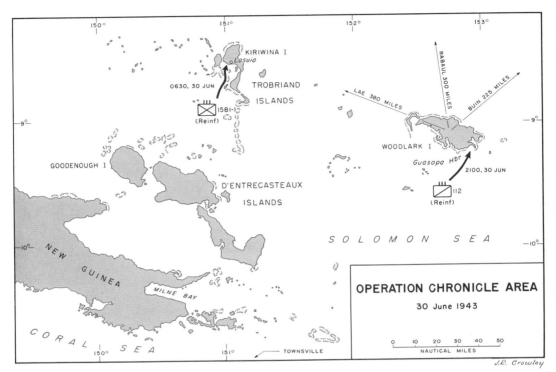

MAP 5

sentatives then agreed to go on with the operation, and the details whereby ground force units, a fighter squadron, naval construction units, and six motor torpedo boats would be transferred, and destroyer-transports (APD's) and tank landing ships (LST's) would be lent to the Southwest Pacific, were arranged.[2]

The invasion of the two islands was the first real amphibious movement undertaken in MacArthur's area. Planning was so thorough and comprehensive that the plans for movement of troops, sup-

plies, and equipment in amphibious shipping became standing operating procedure for future invasions.

Kiriwina, a narrow, north–south island twenty-five miles long, lies within fighter and medium bomber range of Rabaul, Buin in southern Bougainville, and Lae, and 60 miles from the nearest Allied base at Goodenough Island in the D'Entrecasteaux group. From Rabaul to 44-mile-long Woodlark is 300 nautical miles, from Buin 225, from Lae 380, and from Goodenough 160. Neither island was occupied by the Japanese. (*Map 5*)

MacArthur had ordered Allied Naval Forces to support the ALAMO Force by carrying troops and supplies, destroying Japanese forces, and protecting the lines

---

[2] Rad [apparently from Twining] to Comdr Ad-Von 5AF, 16 May 43, in GHQ SWPA G–3 Jnl, 16 May 43; Notes of Conf Between Reps of SOPAC and SWPA, Brisbane, 17 May 43, in GHQ SWPA G–3 Jnl, 17 May 43.

Brig. Gen. Nathan F. Twining, *left, Lt. Gen. Millard F. Harmon, and Col. Glen C. Jamison examining a map of the South Pacific area. Photograph taken October 1942.*

of communication. To carry out these orders Admiral Carpender organized several task forces of which the most important were Task Forces 74 and 76. (*Chart 4*) The first, commanded by Rear Adm. V. A. C. Crutchley, RN, and consisting of Australian and American cruisers and destroyers, was to destroy enemy ships in the Coral and Arafura Seas and be prepared to co-operate with South Pacific forces in the event of a major Japanese naval offensive. Task Force 76 was the Amphibious Force which had been organized in January 1943 under Admiral Barbey. Barbey's ships—4 APD's, 4 APC's, 12 LST's, 18 LCI's, and 18 LCT's with 10 destroyers, 8 subchasers, 4 minesweepers and 1 tug as escort— would transport and land the attacking troops. As ships at Kiriwina would be vulnerable to submarine attack, Barbey assigned 4 destroyers to cover Kiriwina until all defenses were in, and ordered PT boats to patrol at each island.[3]

Kenney's orders directed Air Vice Marshal Bostock's Royal Australian Air

[3] ANF Opn Plan 4–43, 19 May 43, in GHQ SWPA G–3 Jnl, 21 May 43; CTF 76 Opn Plan 1–43, 14 Jun 43, in GHQ SWPA G–3 Jnl, 16 June 43; CTF 74 Opn Order 2–43, 18 Jun 43, in GHQ SWPA G–3 Jnl, 24 Jun 43; Ltr, CTF 76 to COMINCH, 1 Oct 43, sub: Rpt on Opn CHRONICLE, in GHQ SWPA G–3 Jnl, 5 Aug 43.

CHART 4—SOUTHWEST PACIFIC ORGANIZATION FOR WOODLARK–KIRIWINA

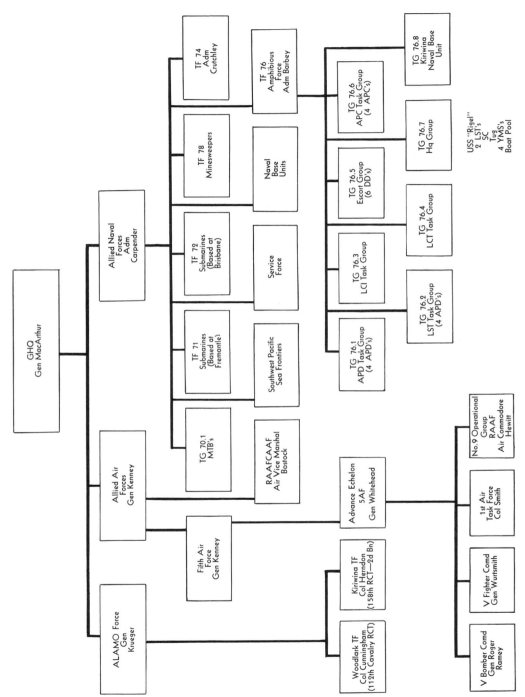

Force Command to protect the lines of communication along the east coast of Australia and to support the defense of forward bases, but assigned the support of the Woodlark–Kiriwina operation to the Fifth Air Force as a primary mission. The V Bomber Command, under Col. Roger M. Ramey, was to attempt the destruction of Japanese air power at Rabaul, using one heavy bomb group nightly from 25 through 30 June, weather permitting, and to attack Japanese ships, continue its reconnaissance missions, provide antisubmarine patrols during daylight within two hundred miles of the Allied bases in New Guinea, and render close support to the ground troops as needed. Since there were no Japanese on the islands support bombardment was not necessary. To Brig. Gen. Paul B. Wurtsmith's V Fighter Command went the main burden of providing fighter escort and cover for convoys and landing operations from the airfields at Dobodura, Port Moresby, and Goodenough Island. Wurtsmith was also directed to be prepared to station fighters on Woodlark and Kiriwina once the airstrips were ready.

The 1st Air Task Force and No. 9 Operational Group of the RAAF, respectively commanded by Col. Frederic H. Smith and Air Commodore J. E. Hewitt, were ordered to destroy Japanese ships and aircraft threatening the operation, and to provide antisubmarine escort and reconnaissance. No fighter umbrella was provided for the convoys, a lack which the naval commanders protested vigorously but unsuccessfully. Fighter squadrons were maintained on ground alert at Dobodura, Milne Bay, and Goodenough Island, ready to fly if

hostile aircraft attacked the shipping.[4]

The 112th Cavalry Regiment, Col. Julian W. Cunningham commanding, and the 158th Infantry, a separate regiment led by Col. J. Prugh Herndon, plus substantial supporting arms and services, had been allotted to the ALAMO Force. Krueger organized the troops that had come from the South Pacific—the 112th Cavalry (a dismounted two-squadron unit serving as infantry), the 134th Field Artillery Battalion (105-mm. howitzers), the 12th Marine Defense Battalion, plus quartermaster, port, ordnance, medical, and engineer units, a naval base unit and a construction battalion—into the Woodlark Task Force and ordered it to seize and defend Woodlark and build an airfield.[5] The Kiriwina Task Force, under Herndon's command, consisted of the 158th Infantry (less the 2d Battalion),

[4] AAF SWPA OI 36, 14 May 43, and Fifth AF OI 3, 15 May 43. Both in GHQ SWPA G–3 Jnl, 15 May 43. AdVon 5AF FO 83, 27 Jun 43; Ltr, CofS V Fighter Comd to CG ESCALATOR, 22 Jun 43, sub: Protection of Shipg; Rad, CTF 76 to Comdr Seventh Flt, 23 Jun 43; Rad, CG AdVon 5 to CG ESCALATOR, 24 Jun 43; Rad, CG ESCALATOR to CTF 76, 26 Jun 43. Last five in Sixth Army G–3 Jnl and File No. 4, 23 Jun–1 Jul 43. CG Sixth Army, Hist of CHRONICLE Opn, in GHQ SWPA G–3 Jnl, 30 Aug 43; Craven and Cate, The Pacific: Guadalcanal to Saipan, pp. 164–65.

The 1st Air Task Force consisted of a headquarters based at Dobodura which had operational control of units temporarily assigned by General Whitehead. The additional headquarters was considered necessary because the towering Owen Stanleys rendered radio communication between Port Moresby and Dobodura somewhat temperamental. The Fifth Air Force thus had three headquarters as well as those of the bomber and fighter commands. See Craven and Cate, The Pacific: Guadalcanal to Saipan, pp. 164–65.

[5] A Marine Corps defense battalion consisted of antiaircraft batteries (90-mm., 40-mm., and 20-mm. antiaircraft guns, and searchlights) and coast artillery (155-mm. guns). A few defense battalions also included tank platoons.

the 148th Field Artillery Battalion (105-mm. howitzers), plus additional 155-mm. gun units and engineer, ordnance, medical, antiaircraft, and quartermaster troops. It was to capture and hold Kiriwina and construct an airdrome. The first echelon of the Woodlark Force would be carried on 6 APD's, 6 LCI's, and 6 LST's, that of the Kiriwina Force on 2 APD's and 12 LCI's.[6]

Doctrine regarding unity of command and the passage of command from ground to naval officers on embarkation, and back to ground officers on landing, was not clearly set forth in the plans. For the relationship between naval and ground commanders, the principle of unity of command rather than co-operation seems to have been followed, but it would have been sounder to have prescribed the exact command relationships in the orders.

In contrast with the practice of the South Pacific Area, where naval doctrine prevailed, no air units were placed under naval or ground commanders. The ultimate authority common to air, naval, and ground units was GHQ itself. Air liaison and support parties, however, were set up at ALAMO Force headquarters and at Dobodura.

Krueger from the first had planned to establish ALAMO headquarters at Milne Bay. When reconnaissance showed that development of the bay into a satisfactory base would constitute a sizable operation, he and his staff pitched in to do the job.

Assembly of the invasion force was complicated by the fact that the Kiriwina Force was scattered from Port Moresby to Australia. (The Woodlark Force had come virtually intact from the South Pacific, and was, except for naval and air elements, concentrated at Townsville). Movement schedules were carefully worked out, and the first elements of the Kiriwina Force reached their staging area at Milne Bay in early June. It was soon apparent that assembly of the forces could not be completed before the third week in June. For this reason D Day for CHRONICLE, which would also be D Day for Nassau Bay and New Georgia, had been set for 30 June.[7]

On 20 June Krueger's ALAMO headquarters opened at Milne Bay, and Mac-Arthur and Barbey arrived shortly afterward. Within a few days all elements of Herndon's Kiriwina Force reached the bay. Final training of this regimental combat team in loading and unloading landing craft and in beach organization was inhibited by the necessity for unloading ships and developing the base. On the other hand the 112th Cavalrymen at Townsville were able to make good use of the opportunity to train uninterruptedly. Barbey's amphibious force, Task Force 76, was also able to train effectively, an activity that had begun in early May.[8]

At Townsville and Milne Bay, soldiers and sailors marked "loading slots" or

---

[6] ESCALATOR FO's 1 and 2, 2 Jun 43, in GHQ SWPA G-3 Jnl, 12 and 10 Jun 43. Like Task Force 76's plans these orders included so much detail as to constitute standing operating procedure.

[7] Rpt of Com Appointed by Gen Krueger, 25 May 43, in GHQ SWPA G-3 Jnl, 27 May 43; GHQ SWPA OI 33/10, 17 Jun 43, in GHQ SWPA G-3 Jnl, 8 May 43.
[8] CG Sixth Army, Hist of CHRONICLE Opn, in GHQ SWPA G-3 Jnl, 30 Aug 43; BYPRODUCT [Kiriwina] TF Jnl and Hist of Kiriwina TF; CTF 76 Rpt on CHRONICLE.

deck-plan layouts of LST's and LCT's on the beaches with tape, then assembled loads in the slots to test the cargo space allotted against the cargo assigned. All units agreed the technique worked very well.

During the last days of June bad weather prevented the planned air attacks against Rabaul, but B–25's and A–20's made about seventy sorties against Lae and Salamaua. On 30 June the weather cleared and eight B–17's and three B–24's attacked Vunakanau airstrip at Rabaul. Bombing on this small scale, which was all the resources in the area would permit, continued for the next few days while the ground troops consolidated themselves at Woodlark and Kiriwina.[9]

The Advance Parties

In early May two small engineer reconnaissance parties headed by the Sixth Army's deputy engineer had slipped ashore on Woodlark and Kiriwina to gather data on airfield sites, beach conditions, and defense positions.[10] Their reports, coupled with the fact that there

were no Japanese troops present, indicated that it would be advisable and possible to send in parties to prepare beaches and roads in advance of the main landings. Thus CHRONICLE was unusual among amphibious operations, for the shore party landed ahead of the assault troops.

At 0400, 21 June, the APD's Brooks and Humphreys left Townsville carrying almost two hundred men of the 112th Cavalry. They stopped at Milne Bay to pick up more men the next day, and at 1600 left Milne Bay at high speed to make the night run to Woodlark. The trip was timed to keep the ships within range of fighter cover until dusk on the outgoing trip, and after dawn on the return voyage. The APD's reached Woodlark without incident, and at 0032 of 23 June the advance party, under Maj. D. M. McMains, started landing at Guasopa Harbor in six LCP(R)'s. Rough seas and high winds slowed the landings, which were not completed until 0400, when the APD's shoved off for Milne Bay.

The Australian coastwatcher had not been informed before the landing. When told that troops were coming ashore he formed his native guerrillas in skirmish line and got ready to fight. Fortunately before anything tragic happened he heard the invaders speaking the American variety of English and joined them.

The Brooks and Humphreys reached Milne Bay during daylight of 23 June and took aboard the 158th Regimental Combat Team's shore party, a part of the 59th Combat Engineer Company and the 158th Infantry's communication platoon, under command of Lt. Col. Floyd G. Powell. Departing Milne Bay at 1810,

---

[9] Craven and Cate, *The Pacific: Guadalcanal to Saipan,* p. 166.

[10] This and the next two subsections are based on Morison, *Breaking the Bismarcks Barrier,* Ch. IX; Office of the Chief Engineer, General Headquarters Army Forces Pacific [GHQ AFPAC] *Engineers of the Southwest Pacific: 1941–1945,* I, *Engineers in Theater Operations* (Washington, 1947), 100–102; CG Sixth Army, Hist of CHRONICLE Opn, in GHQ SWPA G–3 Jnl, 30 Aug 43; Ltr, CTG 76.1 to CTF 76, 24 Jun 43, sub: Adv Landing LEATHERBACK [Woodlark], in Sixth Army G–3 Jnl and File No. 4, 23 Jun–1 Jul 43; Ltr, Col Cunningham to CG ESCALATOR, 3 Jul 42, sub: Current Opns LEATHERBACK TF, in Sixth Army G–3 Jnl and File No. 4, 2 Jul–10 Jul 43; CTF 76 Rpt on CHRONICLE; Sixth Army G–3 Jnl and File for the period covered; Woodlark TF [112th Cav RCT] Opns Diary; BY-PRODUCT TF Jnl and Hist of Kiriwina TF.

four hours behind schedule, they reached Kiriwina at midnight.[11] The island is almost entirely surrounded by a coral reef, with a five-mile-long channel winding through the reef to a 200-yard-wide beach at Losuia on the south coast of the main part of the island. Unloading of the APD's went very slowly as the LCP (R)'s threaded their way through the channel. The tide was low, and the landing craft ran aground several times in the darkness. Admiral Barbey also blamed the 158th's inadequate training for part of the delay. Daylight came before the ships were emptied; they departed with part of their loads still on board. Three nights later they returned to unload heavy communication and engineer equipment that had been left in their holds. This led Barbey to recommend that APD's carry no item of equipment that could not readily be carried by one man.

At Woodlark the advance party reconnoitered, established outposts and beach defenses, dug wells, blasted coral obstructions out of the channels, cleared trails and dispersal and bivouac areas, prepared six beaching points for LST's, and installed signs, markers, and lights to mark channels and beaches for the main body, which would be landing in darkness to avoid Japanese air attacks. Similar efforts by the Kiriwina party were not as successful, partly because of the delay in landing engineer equipment. A good deal of effort was expended in building a coral causeway, 7 feet high and 300 yards long, across the reef on

---

[11] Col Herndon's comments on draft MS of this volume, attached to his 1st Ind, 16 Nov 53, to Ltr, Gen Smith, Chief of Mil Hist, to Col Herndon, 6 Oct 53, no sub, OCMH.

the north coast to permit a landing there. Natives aided in this work by lugging basketloads of coral.

The Japanese were unaware of, or indifferent to, the advance parties; they launched neither surface nor air attacks against them.

The Landings

About half the Woodlark Force—units of the 112th Cavalry, the 134th Field Artillery Battalion, and the 12th Marine Defense Battalion—left Townsville on 25 June aboard six LST's, with one subchaser and two destroyers as escort. The voyage to the target was uneventful. Landing of the 2,600 troops began at 2100 of 30 June. Unloading of the LST's at their beaching points was rapid. Cunningham's force had borrowed extra trucks at Townsville to permit every item of equipment to be put aboard a truck which was driven aboard an LST at Townsville, then driven off at Woodlark. Emptied of their loads, the slow-moving LST's cleared Woodlark before daylight.

Two APD's, carrying part of the Woodlark Force from Milne Bay, arrived shortly before 0100, 1 July, but encountered trouble in navigating the channel with the result that landing craft were not put into the water until 0230. The landing craft coxswains had trouble finding the right beach, but by 0600 the APD's were emptied and ready to leave. Some confusion had existed on the beach, but not enough to prevent its being cleared by the same time.

Additional echelons arrived in LCI's and LST's on 1 July, and all these were unloaded quickly and easily. The LST's took 310 instead of the 317 trucks, Cunningham explained, because one LST raised its bow ramp and closed its doors before all its trucks could be driven aboard.

On shore, defense positions were set up. Antiaircraft and coast artillery pieces of the 12th Defense Battalion were installed, and machine gun and 37-mm. beach positions were established. Cargo was moved inland, and work on the airfield began on 2 July.

Meanwhile Colonel Herndon's Kiriwina Force had been landing, but without the smoothness that characterized operations at Woodlark. Shortly after dawn on 30 June, twelve LCI's, which with six escorting destroyers had sailed from Milne Bay the previous noon, began landing their 2,250 troops. Trouble accompanied the landing from the start. The LCI's had great difficulty getting through the narrow, reef-filled channel to Red Beach near Losuia. And the water shallowed near shore so much that they grounded 200–300 yards from the shoreline. The landing went slowly.[12]

Sunset of 30 June saw the arrival of twelve LCT's and seven LCM's which had left Milne Bay on 29 June and stopped overnight at Goodenough Island. Again there were problems. Heavy rains were falling. The tide was out. Only one LCT was able to cross a sandbar which blocked the approach to the jetty at Losuia. Other LCT's hung up on the bar and were forced to wait for the tide to float them off. The remainder

TROOPS DISEMBARKING FROM LCI *at Kiriwina Island wade ashore, 30 June 1943.*

made for Red Beach but grounded offshore with the result that much of the gear on board had to be hand-carried ashore. Some of the vehicles were driven ashore, but several drowned out in the salt water.

LCT's in subsequent echelons avoided some of the difficulties by landing on the north shore of Kiriwina where the coral causeway had been built. Here trucks could back right up onto the bow ramps of the LCT's, but several were damaged by sliding off the causeway.

In the absence of enemy interference Admiral Barbey approved a change in the original plan to move part of the supplies to Goodenough aboard LST's, then transship them to LCT's for the trip to Kiriwina. After 12 July LST's

---

[12] Colonel Herndon stated on 16 November 1953 that part of the trouble arose from a navigational error that caused the ships to sail past Kiriwina and made them late. He also stated that, originally, the main body was to land on the north coast, but that for some reason the plan was changed and Red Beach and Losuia Jetty were used.

NATIVES CARRYING LUGGAGE *which had been deposited on the coral causeway, north shore of Kiriwina Island, 1 July 1943.*

sailed directly from Milne Bay to the north shore of Kiriwina.

Unloading on the north shore, while easier than at Losuia, complicated matters further for the troops ashore. Heavy equipment was landed some distance from the proposed airfield near Losuia. Building the necessary roads was slowed by heavy rains and lack of enough heavy engineer equipment.

Base Development

Meanwhile the construction program at Woodlark went forward. By 14 July the airfield was near enough completion to accommodate C–47's. One week later 5,200 feet of runway were surfaced with coral, and on 23 July the air garrison—the 67th Fighter Squadron which had served on Guadalcanal in the grim days of 1942—arrived for duty.

On Kiriwina heavy rains continued and added to the engineers' troubles in building and maintaining roads. All construction equipment was used on the roads until about 10 July; during that time the airfield site was partly cleared with hand tools. General Krueger visited the island on 11 July and expressed his dissatisfaction with the progress of road and airfield construction. Three days later he placed Col. John T. Murray, formerly of the 41st Division, in command of the Kiriwina Task Force and returned Colonel Herndon to command of the 158th Infantry. Herndon had asked for more engineers and machinery. These arrived after Murray took com-

JEEP AND TRAILER LEAVING AN LST *anchored off north shore of Kiriwina Island, July 1943.*

mand and thereafter the work went faster. By D plus 20 the first airstrip, 1,500 feet long, was cleared, roughly graded, and ready for surfacing. By the month's end the strip was 5,000 feet long and ready for coral. No. 79 Squadron of the RAAF flew in and began operations on 18 August.

Except for reconnaissance and two small bombing attacks against Woodlark, the enemy did not react to the invasions, so that Barbey was able to transport twenty echelons to Kiriwina and seven to Woodlark without losing a ship or a man. By mid-August transport of supplies and men to the two islands was no longer a tactical mission. U.S. Army Services of Supply was ready to relieve Barbey of logistical responsibility.

Thus the Southwest Pacific Area, using small forces, was able to secure two more airfields to further the Allies' control over the Solomon Sea.

Nassau Bay

Plans and Preparations

The invasion of Nassau Bay was designed to ease the problem of supplying the troops that were to attack Salamaua and Lae. They could not be wholly supplied by ship, by landing craft, by airplane, or by land. The threat of Japanese air attacks in the restricted waters of Huon Gulf and Vitiaz Strait, coupled with the prevailing shortage of troop and cargo ships, rendered the use of large ships impractical if not impossible. The

CLEARING AIRFIELD SITE WITH HAND TOOLS, *Kiriwina Island, July 1943.*

shortage of landing craft and the distance limited the extent of any shore-to-shore operations. The Australian troops operating out of Wau against Salamaua were still being supplied by air, and this placed a heavy burden on Southwest Pacific air transport and limited the number of ground troops that could be employed. In order to supplement air transport the Australians had begun their road from Edie Creek at the south end of the Bulolo Valley to the headwaters of the Lakekamu River on the southwest coast of the Papuan peninsula, but the tremendous difficulties inherent in pushing roads through New Guinea mountains slowed the Australians as they had the Japanese. It was clear that the opening of the Markham Valley–Huon Peninsula campaign would be delayed beyond August if it had to await

completion of the mountain highway.[13]

The seizure of Nassau Bay offered a possibility of at least partially solving these problems, a possibility which fitted neatly into the pattern of plans already being prepared. Nassau Bay lies less than sixty miles from Lae, or within range of the landing craft of the 2d Engineer Special Brigade which GHQ expected to employ, and it is just a short distance down the Papuan coast from Salamaua. Troops of the 3d Australian Division were operating inland from Nassau Bay at this time. Seizure of the bay by a shore-to-shore movement from Morobe, then held by the U.S. 162d Infantry

---

[13] USSBS, *Employment of Forces,* pp. 21–22; ALF, Rpt on New Guinea Opns: Wau–Salamaua, 22 Jan–13 Sep 43; Memo, Comdr ALF for GHQ SWPA, 5 May 43, sub: Warning Instns, in GHQ SWPA G–3 Jnl, 6 May 43.

of the 41st Division, would provide a means by which the Australians getting ready to attack Salamaua could be supplied by water to supplement the air drops, and would also provide a staging point for the shore-to-shore movement of an entire Australian division to a point east of Lae. Therefore GHQ and New Guinea Force headquarters decided to seize Nassau Bay on the same day that Woodlark, Kiriwina, and New Georgia were invaded. The troops seizing Nassau Bay would then join forces with 3d Australian Division and press against Salamaua in order to keep the Japanese from deducing that the Allies were planning a major assault against Lae.[14]

General Blamey was supposed to assume personal command of the New Guinea Force for the Markham Valley–Huon Peninsula operations but the pressure of his duties kept him in Australia until August. Pending his arrival in New Guinea Lt. Gen. E. F. Herring of the Australian Army retained command of the New Guinea Force and operated under Blamey's headquarters instead of GHQ as originally planned. Maj. Gen. Stanley G. Savige, General Officer Commanding the 3d Australian Division, had tactical command of the operations against Salamaua. Troops of the U.S. 162d Regimental Combat Team, which was assigned to Nassau Bay and subsequent operations against Salamaua, would come under General Savige's control once they were ashore.

When the Australians had defeated the Japanese attempt to capture Wau, they pursued the retreating enemy out of the Bulolo Valley and down through the mountains to a point inland from Nassau Bay. In preparation for Nassau Bay and the attack on Salamaua, Savige ordered his division to push against Salamaua from the west and south. He directed the MacKechnie Force, essentially a battalion combat team of the 162d Infantry, to make the initial landing at Nassau Bay and operate on the right (east) flank of his 17th Brigade. At the same time the 24th Australian Infantry Battalion would create a diversion by operating against the Japanese detachments in the Markham Valley and establishing an ambush on the Huon Gulf at the mouth of the Buang River, halfway between Lae and Salamaua. (*Map 6*)

From 20 through 23 June the Japanese counterattacked the 17th Brigade's positions in the vicinity of Mubo and Lababia Ridge, a 3,000-foot eminence that is surrounded by the Bitoi and Buyawim Rivers and has a commanding view of Nassau Bay to the southeast, Bitoi Ridge to the north, and the Komiatum Track which served as the line of communications from Salamaua to the Japanese facing the Australians. The Japanese fought hard but failed to budge the 17th Brigade. Starting on 23 June they retired a short distance to the north. On 30 June Savige's 15th Brigade was attacking Bobdubi and the 17th Brigade, facing north, was holding Mubo and Lababia Ridge.[15]

---

[14] GHQ SWPA OI 33, 7 May 43, in GHQ SWPA G–3 Jnl, 8 May 43; Ltr, Land Hq [ALF] to Gen Off Commanding NGF, 17 May 43, sub: POSTERN—Seizure Lae–Salamaua–Finschhafen–Madang Area, in GHQ SWPA G–3 Jnl, 7 Jun 43; GHQ SWPA OI 34, 13 Jun 43, in GHQ SWPA G–3 Jnl, 14 Jun 43.

[15] ALF, Rpt on New Guinea Opns: Wau–Salamaua, 22 Jan–13 Sep 43; Incl 1, Tactical Sit to 1630, 30 Jun 43, to GHQ SWPA G–2 Daily Summary of Enemy Int and G–2 Est of Enemy Sit 465, 30 Jun–1 Jul 43, in GHQ SWPA G–3 Jnl, 1 Jul 43.

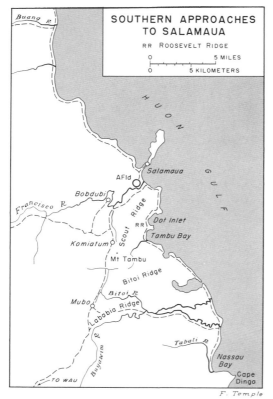

SOUTHERN APPROACHES
TO SALAMAUA

RR ROOSEVELT RIDGE

0   5 MILES

0   5 KILOMETERS

F. Temple

MAP 6

mented by American and Australian units.[16]

By late June the 3d Battalion, 162d, had relieved the MacKechnie Force of the mission of defending Morobe. Thirty days' supply and ten units of fire had been assembled. The troops trained for the landing by boarding PT boats, then transferring at sea to LCVP's, and debarking on beaches from the landing craft. On the night of 28 June the Intelligence and Reconnaissance Platoon, 162d, outposted the islands lying offshore between Nassau Bay and Mageri Point about ten miles north-northwest of Morobe, where the invasion was to be mounted, in order to install lights to guide the invasion flotilla. Colonel MacKechnie flew to the Bulolo Valley for a conference with General Savige, and at his request Savige dispatched one of his companies from Lababia Ridge to the mouth of the Bitoi River to divert Japanese attention from Nassau Bay. As

The MacKechnie Force, designated to land at Nassau Bay on 30 June, consisted of the reinforced 1st Battalion, 162d Infantry. In command was Col. Archibald R. MacKechnie, commander of the 162d. This regiment had arrived in New Guinea from Australia in February 1943. Organized in March, the MacKechnie Force moved by land marches and seaborne movements in landing craft and trawlers from the Buna-Sanananda area to Morobe, where it set up defensive positions to protect an advanced PT boat base. For Nassau Bay the force was aug-

---

[16] 162d Inf Rpt of Opns, 29 Jun–12 Sep 43, in Morobe–Nassau–Bitoi Ridge–Mt. Tambu–Tambu Bay-Salamaua Area of New Guinea; William F. McCartney, *The Jungleers: A History of the 41st Infantry Division* (Washington: Infantry Journal Press, 1948), p. 51; Ltr, Col MacKechnie to Gen Smith, Chief of Mil Hist, 20 Oct 53, no sub, OCMH.

The augmented MacKechnie Force consisted of Lt. Col. Harold R. Taylor's 1st Battalion, 162d; one platoon of the regimental Antitank Company; part of the regimental Service Company; one company of the 116th Engineer Battalion; elements of the 116th Medical Battalion and a portable surgical hospital; the 218th Field Artillery Battalion (75-mm. pack howitzers), less A Battery; detachments from the 41st Division signal, quartermaster, and ordnance companies; detachments of the Combined Operational Service Command and the Australian New Guinea Administrative Unit, a military organization in charge of native affairs; a detachment of C Battery, 209th Coast Artillery Battalion (Antiaircraft); A Company, Papuan Infantry Battalion (native enlisted men and Australian officers); and A and D Companies of the 532d Engineer Boat and Shore Regiment, 2d Engineer Special Brigade.

the landing was to be made in darkness, one platoon of this company was sent to the landing beach to set up lights to guide the landing craft. Company A, Papuan Infantry Battalion, of the Mac-Kechnie Force, reconnoitered to Cape Dinga just south of Nassau Bay, and one of its scouts even sneaked into the enemy camp at Cape Dinga and spent the night with the Japanese. On the basis of the Papuan Infantry Battalion's reports it was estimated 300–400 Japanese were in the vicinity of Nassau Bay, and about 75 more near the south arm of the Bitoi River.[17]

The Enemy

This estimate was somewhat exaggerated. Present at Cape Dinga were about a hundred men of the *102d Infantry, 51st Division,* and about fifty sailors of a naval guard unit.[18] The Japanese were expecting an Allied landing to come in Huon Gulf rather than at Nassau Bay, and had made their dispositions accordingly.

General Adachi, commanding the *18th Army* from his headquarters at Madang, had been carrying out the *8th Area Army* commander's orders to strengthen Wewak, Madang, Finschhafen, and especially Lae and Salamaua to protect Vitiaz Strait while preparing to attack Wau, Bena Bena, and Mount Hagen and infil-

trate the Ramu and Sepik River Valleys. (*See below, Map 12.*) The Madang–Lae Highway was still under construction but had been pushed only to the Finisterre Range which parallels the north coast of the Huon Peninsula. The Japanese correctly estimated that the Allies planned to use the air base sites in the mountain valleys to support their advances along the coast. Therefore they planned the moves against Wau and against Bena Bena and Mount Hagen, two outposts that had been used since 1942. The *6th Air Division,* based in the Wewak area, was ordered to attack these points daily.

In command at Lae was Maj. Gen. Ryoichi Shoge, infantry group commander of the *41st Division.* His command at this time was largely transient, as the *18th Army* was sending troops through Lae to strengthen Salamaua. Since the March disaster in the Bismarck Sea, some troops had been landed at Lae from submarines, forty men per boat; others came in barges and destroyers to Cape Gloucester from Rabaul, thence to Finschhafen by barge and overland or by barge to Lae. In April and May the *66th Infantry* (less the *3d Battalion*), *51st Division,* had been transferred to Salamaua from Lae, and elements of the *115th Infantry,* the *14th Artillery Regiment,* and the *51st Engineer Regiment,* all of the *51st Division,* staged through Lae for Salamaua. At Salamaua Lt. Gen. Hidemitsu Nakano, commander of the *51st Division,* was directing operations.

The third infantry regiment of Nakano's division, the *102d,* had made the January attack against Wau and had been almost continuously in action since that time.

---

[17] 162d Inf Rpt of Opns; McCartney, *The Jungleers,* p. 52.

[18] This subsection is based on 8th Area Army Operations, Japanese Monogr No. 110 (OCMH), pp. 43–45; 18th Army Operations, II, Japanese Monogr No. 42 (OCMH), 1–22; 18th Army Operations, Annex B (Maps), Japanese Monogr No. 47 (OCMH); Hist Div MIS GHQ FEC, Statements of Japanese Officials on World War II (English Translations), IV, 119–20, OCMH; Interrogation of Adachi *et al.,* by Mil Hist Sec, Australian Army Hq, OCMH.

By the end of June Nakano had six thousand men under his command. The Japanese defensive positions included the high ground inland from the shore—Mount Tambu, Komiatum, and Bobdubi.

Landing of the MacKechnie Force

As dusk fell at Morobe on 29 June three PT boats of the Seventh Fleet took aboard 210 men of the MacKechnie Force. A fourth PT, without passengers, escorted.[19] At the same time twenty-nine LCVP's, two Japanese barges, and one LCM of the 532d Engineer Boat and Shore Regiment took the other 770 men of the MacKechnie Force on board at Mageri Point. The landing craft were organized in three waves which departed Mageri at twenty-minute intervals. The night was dark, the sea heavy; rain was falling.

The first two waves rendezvoused with the two PT boats from Morobe which were to guide them to the target but the third missed and proceeded on the forty-mile run to Nassau Bay without a guide.

Thus far things had gone fairly well but the remainder of the night was full

of troubles. The rain obscured the guide lights on the offshore islands. The escorting PT lost the convoy. The lead PT overshot Nassau Bay. Some of the landing craft of the first wave followed it, then lost time turning around and finding the convoy again.

The landing began, in rainy darkness, shortly after midnight. The Australian platoon on shore had lost its way and arrived at Nassau Bay in time to install only two instead of three lights. Thus the first two waves of landing craft intermingled and landed together on the same stretch of beach. And a ten- to twelve-foot surf, a rare occurrence at Nassau Bay, was pounding. It rammed the landing craft so far up on the beach that seventeen of them could not back off but promptly broached and filled with water, almost complete wrecks. The LCM, after unloading a bulldozer, was able to retract; it proceeded out to sea and got the troops off the lead PT boat, and then returned to the beach where it swamped.

There was no enemy opposition, nor any casualties. Japanese in an outpost at the beach had fled into the jungle, believing, prisoners reported later, that the bulldozer was a tank. Except for the landing craft, there were no serious losses of equipment, but most of the radios were damaged by salt water.

Seven hundred and seventy men were landed that night.[20] The leader of the third wave, which arrived hours after the first two, realized that his craft were the only ones immediately available for resupply and decided not to land until the surf abated. He took the barge and the rest of the LCVP's, with B Company

---

[19] This subsection is based on McCartney, *The Jungleers,* pp. 52–55; Morison, *Breaking the Bismarcks Barrier,* pp. 136–37; Office of the Chief Engineer, GHQ AFPAC, *Engineers of the Southwest Pacific: 1941–1945,* VIII, *Critique* (Washington, 1951), 84–85; ALF, Rpt on New Guinea Opns: Wau–Salamaua, 22 Jan–13 Sep 43; Ltr, Brig Gen William F. Heavey, CO 2d ESB, to Chief Engr SWPA, 13 Jul 43, sub: Rpt on Nassau Bay Opns, in GHQ SWPA G–3 Jnl, 19 Jul 43; GHQ SWPA G–3 Jnl for period covered; 41st Div G–3 Jnl and File for period covered; 162d Inf Rpt of Opns, and Jnl and Files for period covered; Ltr, Gen Heavey to CofEngrs USA, 30 Jun 44, sub: Rpt of Combat Opns, DRB AGO; MacKechnie, Notes on Nassau Bay–Mubo–Tambu Bay–Salamaua Opns, 29 Jun–12 Sep 43, no date, DRB AGO.

[20] The first report gave 740 but was soon corrected. See msgs in 41st Div G–3 Jnl, 30 Jun 43.

on board, to shelter in a cove down the coast. When the storm subsided they returned to Nassau Bay but failed to make contact with the troops, who were beating off a Japanese attack. The wave returned to Mageri Point, then went back to Nassau Bay and landed on the afternoon of 2 July.

Once on shore A and C Companies, 162d Infantry, established defense lines three hundred yards north and south, respectively, of the landing beach. The Australian platoon defended the west (inland) flank. There was no contact with the enemy that night. By daybreak of 30 June the beach was cleared of all ammunition, equipment, and supplies. Beach defenses, employing machine guns salvaged from the wrecked landing craft, were set up. Communication with higher headquarters was a problem. Most of the water-soaked radios would not work, and during the first few days Colonel MacKechnie was out of contact with New Guinea Force, 41st Division headquarters, and Morobe at one time or another. Nothing was heard from the Papuan Infantry Battalion elements on the other side of Cape Dinga for several days. All the SCR's 511 and 536, the small hand radios used for tactical communication within infantry battalions, had been soaked and were never usable during the subsequent operations against Salamaua.

After daylight of 30 June C Company marched south to the Tabali River just west of Cape Dinga. Company A started north from its night positions to clear the area as far as the south arm of the Bitoi River but soon ran into enemy mortar and machine gun fire (its first such experience) and halted. Patrols went out and reported the enemy as present in some strength. Then A Company, reinforced by a platoon of D Company, 2/6th Australian Infantry Battalion of the 17th Brigade, which had flashed the landing lights, attempted to strike the Japanese right (west) flank but was stopped. When the Australian platoon ran out of ammunition it was relieved by a detachment of engineers from the crews of the wrecked landing craft. Two of the C Company platoons came up from the south to join A Company. At 1500 the force started forward and by 1650 had brushed away scattered Japanese opposition to reach the south arm of the Bitoi River.

When General Adachi received word of the invasion his first thought was to destroy the MacKechnie Force before it had a chance to consolidate. But General Nakano persuaded him that it would be better to "delay the enemy advance in NASSAU from a distance" and to concentrate on the Australian threat at Bobdubi.[21] So no more enemy troops were sent against MacKechnie. Meanwhile the Papuan Infantry Battalion troops began pressing against the rear of the Japanese detachment at Cape Dinga. This detachment began moving toward the American beachhead.

About 1630 the C Company platoon defending the left (south) flank reported that Japanese troops were crossing the Tabali River just south of its position, whereupon it was ordered to withdraw to the south flank of the landing beach proper to hold a line between the beach and a swamp which began a short dis-

[21] 18th Army Operations, II, Japanese Monogr No. 42 (OCMH), 14.

tance inland. Before the platoon could move, Japanese troops attacked its rear and flank. The platoon fought its way north, losing its commander and four enlisted men killed on the way.

While the platoon was withdrawing, Capt. Paul A. Cawlfield, MacKechnie Force S–3, organized a defense line at the beach using engineers, part of D Company, and men from force headquarters. At dusk the harassed platoon reached this line, and then the enemy struck in a series of attacks that lasted all night. Machine gun, mortar, and rifle fire and grenades hit the American positions, and small parties attempted to infiltrate. But the American units, in action for the first time, beat off the attackers who, except for scattered riflemen that were hunted down and killed, pulled out just before sunrise. The MacKechnie Force estimated that it had killed fifty Japanese. Its own casualties were eighteen killed, twenty-seven wounded. Colonel MacKechnie later asserted that in his opinion several of the American casual-ties were caused by American troops firing at each other in the excitement of the night action.

By 2 July, with the landing of B Company and other elements of the third wave, the Nassau Bay beachhead was considered secure. On that date the Americans made contact with the 17th Brigade, and the MacKechnie Force made ready to execute its missions in the northward drive against Salamaua.

Thus with the landings at Woodlark, Kiriwina, and Nassau Bay, General MacArthur's Southwest Pacific Area inaugurated CARTWHEEL. Compared with the massive strokes of 1944 and 1945, the operations were small, but they gave invaluable amphibious experience to soldiers and sailors and they began a forward movement that was not halted until final victory.

Meanwhile, on the other side of the Solomon Sea, Admiral Halsey's South Pacific forces had executed their first CARTWHEEL missions by invading New Georgia.

CHAPTER VI

Toenails: The Landings in New Georgia

The South Pacific's tactical and logistical planning for the invasion of New Georgia (Toenails, or Operation A) involved all the major echelons of the complex command that was Admiral Halsey's. Halsey's position was somewhat unusual. As he phrased it, the Joint Chiefs' orders of 28 March "had the curious effect of giving me two 'hats' in the same echelon." [1] His immediate superior in the chain of command was Admiral Nimitz, who was responsible, subject to decisions by the Joint Chiefs, for supplying him with the means of war. For the strategic direction of the war in the Solomons, MacArthur was Halsey's superior.

South Pacific Organization

Whereas MacArthur's headquarters followed U.S. Army organization, Halsey's followed that of the Navy. [2] There were many more subordinates, such as island commanders, reporting directly to Halsey than reporting to MacArthur, and the South Pacific was never organized as simply as the Southwest Pacific. Halsey, by the device of not appointing a single tactical commander of all naval forces, retained personal control of them. There was a single commander of land-based aircraft, but there was never a single ground force commander with complete tactical authority. (*Chart 5*)

Naval forces, designated the Third Fleet in March 1943, came generally from the U.S. Navy and the Royal New Zealand Navy. Except for New Zealand ships, no warships were ever permanently assigned; as need arose Nimitz dispatched warships to the South Pacific. The South Pacific Amphibious Force (Task Force 32), on the other hand, was a permanent organization to which landing forces were attached for amphibious operations. In command was Rear Adm. Richmond K. Turner who had led the Amphibious Force in the invasion of Guadalcanal the year before.

Land-based air units from all Allied services in the South Pacific were under the operational control of the Commander, Aircraft, South Pacific, Admiral Fitch. Fitch's command, Task Force 33, was made up of Royal New Zealand and U.S. Army, Navy, and Marine Corps air units. Principal administrative organizations within Task Force 33 were General Twining's Thirteenth Air Force and the

---

[1] Halsey and Bryan, *Admiral Halsey's Story*, p. 154.

[2] Unless otherwise indicated this section is based on The History of the United States Army Forces in the South Pacific Area [USAFISPA] During World War II: 30 March 1942–1 August 1944, MS, Pt. II, Chs. I–II, IV, and Pt. III, Vol. I, Ch. I, OCMH.

CHART 5—ORGANIZATION OF PRINCIPAL SOUTH PACIFIC FORCES, JUNE 1943

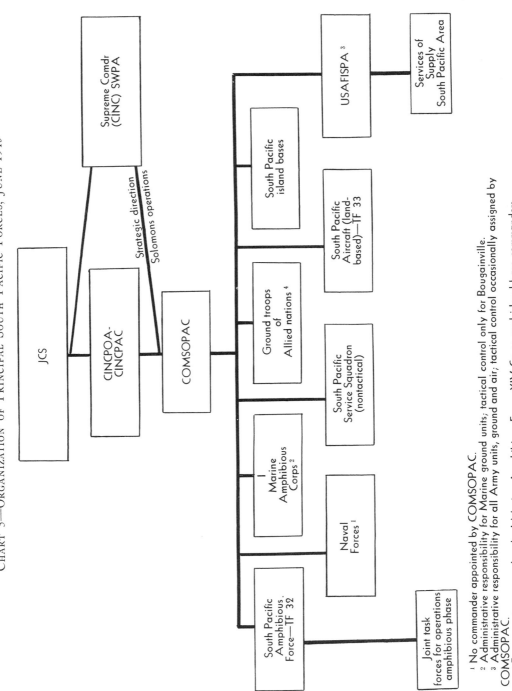

1 No commander appointed by COMSOPAC.
2 Administrative responsibility for Marine ground units; tactical control only for Bougainville.
3 Administrative responsibility for all Army units, ground and air; tactical control occasionally assigned by COMSOPAC.
4 For operations, served under I Marine Amphibious Force, XIV Corps, and island base commanders.

1st and 2d Marine Air Wings. The most important tactical organization in Fitch's force was the interservice, international outfit known as Air Command, Solomons, that had grown out of the exigencies of the Guadalcanal Campaign.[3] Fitch issued general directives which were executed under the tactical direction of the Commander, Aircraft, Solomons, who until 25 July 1943 was Rear Adm. Marc A. Mitscher.

There were two principal ground force commanders in early 1943. The first, General Harmon, an experienced airman who had served as Chief of Air Staff in Washington, was the commanding general of U.S. Army Forces in the South Pacific Area; his command embraced air as well as ground troops. His authority was largely administrative and logistical, but he also advised the area commander on tactical matters and Halsey throughout the period of active operations relied heavily on him. Under Harmon, in early 1943, were four infantry divisions, the American, 25th, 37th, and 43d, as well as the Thirteenth Air Force. The American and 25th Divisions had fought in the Guadalcanal Campaign. The 43d Division had seen no fighting but had received valuable experience when elements of the division took part in the invasion of the Russells. The 37th, which had gone out the year before to garrison the Fijis, was as yet untried. In addition to these divisions, which usually fought under the tactical command of the XIV Corps, there were, in Harmon's command, the Army garrison troops in the island bases and a growing number, but never enough to satisfy the local commanders, of service units. By mid-1943 Harmon's command embraced about 275,000 men.

The Marine Corps counterpart to Harmon's command, as far as ground forces were concerned, was the I Marine Amphibious Corps. This organization, under Maj. Gen. Clayton B. Vogel, USMC, had administrative responsibility over all Marine Corps units, except ships' detachments and certain air units, in the South Pacific—two Marine divisions, one raider regiment, six defense battalions, one parachute regiment, and service troops. The 1st Marine Division in the Southwest Pacific was nominally administered by the I Marine Amphibious Corps but drew its supplies from Southwest Pacific agencies.

The highest logistic agency, the Service Squadron, South Pacific Force, operated directly under Halsey. It controlled all ships, distributed all supplies locally procured, assigned shipping space, designated ports, and handled all naval procurement. An equally important logistic agency was the Army's Services of Supply, South Pacific Area. In early 1943 under Maj. Gen. Robert G. Breene it was an expanding organization which was playing an important part in South Pacific affairs.

The organization of the South Pacific, as set forth on paper, seems complicated and unwieldy. Perhaps it could have functioned awkwardly, but the personalities and abilities of the senior commanders were such that they made it work. There is ample testimony in various reports to attest to the high regard in which the aggressive, forceful Halsey and his subordinates held one another, and

---

[3] During the Guadalcanal Campaign the senior naval aviator on the island commanded all aircraft there, with the informal title of COMAIR CACTUS.

events showed that the South Pacific was able to plan and conduct offensive operations involving units from all Allied armed services with skill and success.

Preparations and Plans

Admiral Halsey and his officers had begun planning and preparing for New Georgia in January 1943, before the end of the Guadalcanal Campaign. This process, which involved air and naval bombardments, the assembly of supplies, and reconnaissance of the target area, as well as the preparation and issuance of operation plans and field orders, continued right up to D Day, 30 June.

The Target

In climate, topography, and development, the Solomons are much like New Guinea and the Bismarcks. Their interiors were virtually unexplored. They are hot, jungled, wet, swampy, mountainous, and unhealthful.[4]

New Georgia is the name for a large group in the central Solomons which includes Vella Lavella, Gizo, Kolombangara, New Georgia (the main island of the group), Rendova, and Vangunu, Simbo, Ganonnga, Wana Wana, Arundel, Bangga, Mbulo, Gatukai, Tetipari (or Montgomery), and a host of islets and reefs. (Map 7) From Vella Lavella to Gatukai, the cluster is 125 nautical miles in length. Several of the islands have symmetrical volcanic cones rising over 3,000 feet above sea level.

In addition to the multitude of small channels, narrows, and passages, navi-

gable only by small craft, there are several large bodies of water in the group. The Slot, the channel sailed so frequently by the Japanese during the Guadalcanal Campaign, lies between New Georgia on one side and Choiseul and Santa Isabel on the other. Marovo Lagoon on New Georgia's northeast side is one of the largest in the world. Vella Gulf separates Vella Lavella from Kolombangara, which is set off from New Georgia by Kula Gulf. Blanche Channel divides New Georgia from Rendova and Tetipari.

The island of New Georgia proper, the sixth largest in the Solomons, is about forty-five statute miles long on its northwest–southeast axis, and about thirty miles from southwest to northeast. It is mountainous in the interior, low but very rough in the vicinity of Munda Point.

New Georgia proper was difficult to get to by sea except in a few places. Reefs and a chain of barrier islands blocked much of the coast line, which in any event was frequently covered by mangrove swamps with tough aerial prop roots. The best deepwater approach was the Kula Gulf which boasted a few inlets, but Japanese warships and seacoast guns defended much of the shore line of the gulf. There were protected anchorages in the southeast part of the island at Wickham Anchorage, Viru Harbor, and Segi Point. Munda Point, the airfield site, was inaccessible to large vessels. East and west of the point visible islets and reefs, and also invisible ones, barred Roviana and Wana Wana lagoons to large ships. Rounding the lagoons like a crude fence on the seaward side is a tangled string of islands, rocks, and coral reefs—Roviana, Sasavele, Baraulu, and

---

[4] Data for this subsection are taken from U.S. Navy hydrographic charts; military maps; MIS WDGS, Survey of the Solomon Islands; a terrain study in 37th Div records.

others, some with names, some without. These all have cliffs facing the sea (south) and slope down to sea level on the lagoon side. The channels between the barrier islands were too shallow for ships. Nor could ships reach Munda Point from Kula Gulf and Hathorn Sound. Diamond Narrows, running from Kula Gulf to the lagoons, was deep but too narrow for large vessels.

Across Blanche Channel from Munda and her guardian islands lies mountainous Rendova, which could be reached from the Solomon Sea. Rendova Harbor, though by no means a port, offered an anchorage to ocean-going ships.

During the first months of 1943 coastwatchers covered the Solomons thoroughly. Buka Passage, between Bougainville and Buka, and Buin on southern Bougainville had been the sites of coastwatching stations for several months, and in October 1942 flying boats and submarines took watchers to Vella Lavella, Choiseul, and Santa Isabel.[5]

At Segi Point on New Georgia was Donald G. Kennedy, a New Zealander who was District Officer in the Protectorate Government. Like Resident Commissioner William S. Marchant, the Anglican Bishop of Melanesia, and various other officials and members of religious orders, Kennedy remained in the Solomons when the Japanese came.[6] At Segi Point Kennedy organized a network of white and Melanesian watchers covering Kolombangara, Rendova, Vangunu, Santa Isabel, and Roviana. A Euronesian medical practitioner was posted on Santa Isabel. On Roviana Sgt. Harry Wickham of the British Solomon Islands Defense Force organized the natives to keep watch over Munda Point.

Kennedy raised a guerrilla band to protect his hideout at Segi Point, for the Japanese occasionally sent out punitive expeditions to hunt him down. The primary mission of the coastwatchers was watching, not fighting, but Kennedy and his band were strong enough to wipe out several patrols that came too close. On one occasion Kennedy and his men, aboard the ten-ton schooner *Dadavata,* saw a Japanese whaleboat systematically reconnoitering the islets in Marovo Lagoon. They attacked with rifles, rammed the whaleboat, sank it, and killed or drowned its company.[7]

In addition to gaining information from terrain studies, interrogation of former residents, and coastwatchers' reports, South Pacific headquarters was able to augment its knowledge of New Georgia by a series of ground patrols. The first such expedition was directed by General Vogel. Four officers and eight enlisted men from each of the four battalions of the 1st Marine Raider Regiment assembled on Guadalcanal on 17 March, then sailed to Florida to board amphibian patrol planes (PBY's) which took them to Segi Point. After Kennedy furnished them with native scouts and bearers, patrols went out to reconnoiter Kolombangara, Viru Harbor, Munda Point, and other areas. Traveling overland and by canoe, they carefully exam-

[5] By July, unfortunately, the Japanese were hunting the Bougainville coastwatchers so resolutely that the stations there had to be abandoned. See Feldt, *The Coastwatchers,* Ch. XI.

[6] [British] Central Office of Information, *Among Those Present: The Official Story of the Pacific Islands at War* (London: His Majesty's Stationery Office, 1946), pp. 11, 43.

[7] *Ibid.,* p. 52.

ined caves, anchorages, and passages. Their mission completed, all parties reassembled at Segi Point on 9 April.

The raiders' reports indicated that troops in small craft could be taken through Onaiavisi Entrance to a 200-yard-long beach at Zanana, east of the Barike River. From there they could strike westward toward Munda.[8] Before D Day, additional patrols from the invading forces went to New Georgia and stayed.

From November 1942 until D Day, Munda and Vila airfields were continuously subjected to air and naval bombardments. Vila, located in a swampy region, was practically never used by the enemy. From January until D Day, Allied cruisers and destroyers shelled Munda four times at night, Vila three times. The net result of the continuous air bombardment and the sporadic naval shelling was that the Japanese could not base planes permanently at Munda. It was used, and only occasionally, as a forward staging field.[9]

Logistic Preparations

On Halsey's orders South Pacific agencies had begun assembling supplies and developing bases and anchorages for the invasion of New Georgia as early as Jan-

uary 1943. Admiral Turner, remembering his experiences in the Guadalcanal Campaign, suggested that supplies for the invasion be stockpiled on Guadalcanal, and in February movement of supplies to Guadalcanal (under the appropriate code name DRYGOODS) began. In spite of the fact that the port of Nouméa, New Caledonia, was jammed with ships waiting to be unloaded, in spite of the fact that port facilities at Guadalcanal were so poor, and in spite of a bad storm at Guadalcanal in May that destroyed all the floating quays, washed out bridges, and created general havoc, enough supplies for the invasion were ready on Guadalcanal by June. This was accomplished by Herculean labor at Nouméa, by routing some ships directly to Guadalcanal, and by selective discharge of cargo from other ships. The effects of the storm at Guadalcanal were alleviated by using the ungainly-looking 2½-ton, six-wheel amphibian truck (DUKW) to haul supplies from ships to inland dumps over open beaches. By June 54,274 tons of supplies, exclusive of organization equipment, maintenance supplies, and petroleum products discharged from tankers, had been put ashore. In addition many loaded vehicles, 13,085 tons of assorted gear, and 23,775 drums of fuel and lubricants were moved from Guadalcanal. to the Russells in June. Bulk gasoline storage tanks with a capacity of nearly 80,000 barrels were available on Guadalcanal.[10] Although

---

[8] I Mar Amphib Corps, Report on New Georgia Ground Reconnaissance: 21 March–9 April 43, 18 Apr 43.

[9] Morison, *The Struggle for Guadalcanal,* pp. 322–47; Morison, *Breaking the Bismarcks Barrier,* pp. 106–10; U.S. Strategic Bombing Survey, *Interrogations of Japanese Officials* (Washington, 1946), I, 142, 192; USSBS, *The Allied Campaign Against Rabaul,* p. 43; USSBS, *The Thirteenth Air Force in the War Against Japan,* p. 6; Southeast Area Naval Operations, II, Japanese Monogr No. 49 (OCMH), 19; Southeast Area Air Operations, 1942–44, Japanese Monogr No. 38 (OCMH), pp. 7–11.

[10] COMSOPAC War Diary, 1 Jan 43 entry; Extract of recommendations submitted by COMAMPHIBFORSOPAC, Incl F to memo, Gen Peck for Gen Breene *et al.,* 16 Jan 43, sub: Notes on Mtg Held in War Plans See COMSOPAC, 14 Jan 43, in USAFISPA File No. 381, Preliminary Plng COMSOPAC and COMGENSOPAC, Jan–June 43, KCRC;

Nouméa and Espiritu Santo in the New Hebrides were still the main South Pacific bases, Guadalcanal was ready to play an important role. The South Pacific commanders had insured that haphazard supply methods would not characterize TOENAILS.

Tactical Plans

Final plans and orders for TOENAILS were ready in June.[11] Halsey had hoped to invade New Georgia in April, but could not move before the Southwest Pacific was ready to move into the Trobriands and Nassau Bay. The general concept of the operation was worked out by Admiral Halsey, a planning committee, and members of Halsey's staff. The committee consisted of General Harmon, the Army commander; Admiral Fitch, the land-based air commander; Admiral Turner, the amphibious commander; and General Vogel of the I Marine Amphibious Corps. The principal staff officers concerned were Admiral Wilkinson; Captain Browning, Halsey's chief of staff;

and General Peck, Halsey's war plans officer. By May agreement was reached on the general plan. It called for the simultaneous seizure of Rendova, Viru Harbor, Wickham Anchorage, and Segi Point. A fighter field would be built at Segi Point. After the initial landings small craft from Guadalcanal and the Russells would stage through Wickham Anchorage and Viru Harbor to build up Rendova's garrison. Munda's field would be harassed and neutralized by 155-mm. guns and 105-mm. howitzers emplaced on Rendova and the nearer barrier islands. These moves were preparatory to the full-scale assaults against Munda and Vila, and later against southern Bougainville.

Assigned to the operation were South Pacific aircraft, warships, the South Pacific Amphibious Force, and the heavily reinforced 43d Division with its commander, Maj. Gen. John H. Hester, in command of the landing forces. The 37th Division, less elements, was in area reserve to be committed only on Halsey's orders.

Final plans and tactical organization were complicated, as TOENAILS called for four separate simultaneous invasions (Rendova, Wickham Anchorage, Segi Point, and Viru Harbor) with the Rendova landing to be followed by two more on the same island.

Admiral Halsey's basic plan, issued on 3 June, organized the task forces, prescribed their general missions, and directed Admiral Turner to co-ordinate the planning of the participating forces. Four task forces were assigned to the operation: Task Force 33, the Aircraft, South Pacific, under Admiral Fitch; Task Force 72, a group of Seventh Fleet submarines

---

Ltr, COMSOPAC to COMGENSOPAC *et al.,* 24 Feb 43, sub: Assembly of Sups for Future Opns, in USAFISPA G–2 Hist Sec File, Plng for New Georgia Opn, OCMH; The History of USAFISPA, Pt. I, Vol. I, p. 178, and Pt. III, pp. 649–51, 661, 669, 673–74, OCMH; ONI USN, Operations in the New Georgia Area, p. 3.

[11] Two files previously cited, USAFISPA G–2 Hist Sec File, Plng for New Georgia Opn, and USAFISPA File No. 381, Preliminary Plng COMSOPAC and COMGENSOPAC, contain valuable material for the student interested in the genesis and development of tactical plans. This subsection is based on these two files and on Hq NGOF FO 1, 16 Jun 43, and Addendum 1, 24 Jun 43; 43d Div FO 1, 17 Jun 43; COMSOPAC Opn Plan 14–43, 3 Jun 43, with annexes; CTF 31 Opn Plan A8–43, 4 Jun 43, with annexes; CTG 31.3 Opn Order AL 10–43, 21 Jun 43; CTG 31.1 Loading Order 1–43, 13 Jun 43; CTG 31.3 Loading Order 1–43, 16 Jun 43. Last five in Off of Naval Rcds and Library.

CHART 6—ORGANIZATION OF SOUTH PACIFIC FORCES FOR TOENAILS

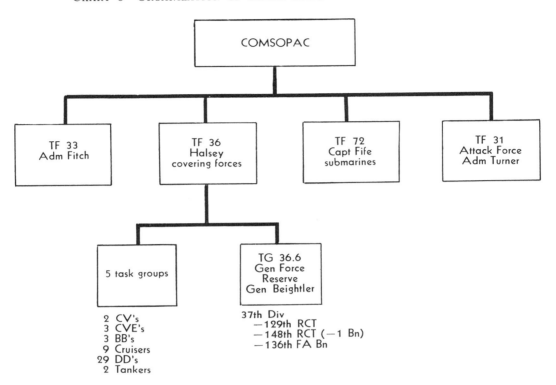

commanded by Capt. James F. Fife and now under Halsey's operational control; Task Force 36, the naval covering force commanded, in effect, by Halsey himself; and Task Force 31, the attack force. (*Chart 6*)

Task Force 33, to which Halsey temporarily assigned planes from Carrier Division 22 (three escort carriers), was to provide defensive reconnaissance for New Georgia operations and the Southwest Pacific's seizure of Woodlark and Kiriwina, and to cover the area northeast of the Solomons (Southwest Pacific planes were responsible for the Bismarcks). It was to destroy enemy units which threatened South and Southwest

Pacific forces, especially Japanese planes operating from New Georgia and southern Bougainville. Fitch's planes were also to provide fighter cover, direct air support, and liaison and spotting planes for the attack force. Starting D minus 5, Task Force 33 would attempt to isolate the battlefield by attacking the Japanese air bases at Munda, Ballale, Kahili, Kieta, and Vila, and by striking at surface vessels in the Bougainville and Munda areas. During daylight, fighters would cover ships and ground troops, and antisubmarine patrols would be maintained for convoys. Black Cats (PBY's) would cover all night movements. Striking forces at all times were to be prepared to hit enemy surface ships. Beginning on D Day, eighteen dive bombers would remain on stand-by alert in the Russells. Medium bombers were to be prepared to support the ground troops. Finally, arrangements were made for air dropping supplies and equipment to the ground troops in New Georgia.

One innovation in the command of supporting planes had apparently arisen from Maj. Gen. Alexander A. Vandegrift's recommendations based on his experiences in invading Guadalcanal.[12] Halsey directed that on take-off from Guadalcanal and Russells fields planes assigned to missions in the immediate area of operations would come under control of the local air commander (the Commander, New Georgia Air Force). Direction of fighters over Task Force 31 was to be conducted by a group aboard a destroyer until direction could be conducted ashore on Rendova. Similarly, bomber direction for direct air support would be handled aboard Turner's flagship *McCawley* until bomber director groups could establish themselves ashore. In early June, Fitch issued orders concentrating most of his strength in the Guadalcanal area under Admiral Mitscher.[13] Totals for aircraft involved were fairly impressive. On 30 June Fitch had on hand for the operation 533 planes, of which 213 fighters, 170 light bombers,

and 72 heavy bombers were ready to fly.[14]

Task Force 36 included part of the 37th Division on Guadalcanal in area reserve, besides all Halsey's naval strength except that assigned to the attack force. Naval units, including aircraft carriers (two CV's and three CVE's), battleships, cruisers, and destroyers, would operate out of Nouméa, New Caledonia, and the New Hebrides into the Coral and Solomon Seas to intercept and destroy any Japanese forces which ventured out. The reserve 37th Division forces were to be committed, on five days' notice, on orders from Halsey.

Captain Fife's submarines would at first conduct offensive reconnaissance from about latitude one degree north southward to the prevailing equatorial weather front. Once the Japanese were aware of the invasions, Fife's boats were either to concentrate on locating enemy vessels or to withdraw south to cover Bougainville Strait and the waters between New Ireland and Buka. This reconnaissance would be in addition to patrols by Central Pacific submarines, which would keep watch over any Japanese surface forces approaching the South from the Central Pacific.

Admiral Turner's attack force (Task Force 31) consisted of ships and landing craft from the South Pacific or III Amphibious Force (Task Force 32), plus the ground troops. These troops, designated the New Georgia Occupation Force, initially included the following units:

---

[12] See Jeter A. Isely and Philip A. Crowl, *The U.S. Marines and Amphibious War: Its Theory, and Its Practice in the Pacific* (Princeton, N.J.: Princeton University Press, 1951), p. 172, and Miller, *Guadalcanal: The First Offensive*, p. 71.

[13] Ltr, COMAIRSOPAC to COMSOPAC, 4 Jun 43, sub: Availability of Aircraft at MAINYARD [Guadalcanal] for TOENAILS Opn, in USAFISPA G–2 Hist Sec File, Plng for New Georgia Opn, OCMH.

[14] ONI USN, Operations in the New Georgia Area, p. 62.

43d Division

9th Marine Defense Battalion

1st Marine Raider Regiment (less two battalions)

136th Field Artillery Battalion (155-mm. howitzers), 37th Division

Elements of the 70th Coast Artillery Battalion (Antiaircraft)

One and one-half naval construction battalions

Elements of the 1st Commando, Fiji Guerrillas[15]

Radar units

Naval base detachments

A boat pool

Creating the New Georgia Occupation Force, and attaching all ground troops to it (instead of attaching the supporting units to the 43d Division), made another headquarters necessary, and threw a heavy burden on 43d Division headquarters. General Hester commanded both force and division, and the 43d Division staff was, in effect, split into two staffs. The 43d Division's staff section chiefs (the Assistant Chiefs of Staff, G–1, G–2, G–3, and G–4), as well as officers from Harmon's headquarters, served on the Occupation Force staff sections, and their assistants directed the division's staff sections. Brig. Gen. Harold R. Barker, 43d Division artillery commander, commanded all Occupation Force artillery—field, seacoast, and antiaircraft.

From the start General Harmon was dubious about the effectiveness of this arrangement. He was "somewhat concerned that Hester did not have enough command and staff to properly conduct his operation in its augmented concept."[16] On 10 June, with Halsey's concurrence, he therefore told Maj. Gen. Oscar W. Griswold, commanding the XIV Corps and the Guadalcanal Island Base, to keep himself informed regarding Hester's plans in order to be prepared to take over if need be.[17]

The general plan of maneuver called for assault troops from Guadalcanal and the Russells to move to Rendova, Segi Point, Wickham Anchorage, and Viru Harbor on APD's, transports, cargo ships, minesweepers, and minelayers. Segi, Wickham, and Viru would be taken by small forces to secure the line of communications to Rendova while the main body of ground forces captured Rendova. Artillery on Rendova and the barrier islands was to bombard Munda, an activity in which ships' gunfire would also be employed. On several days following D Day, slow vessels such as LST's and LCT's would bring in more troops and supplies. They would travel at night and in daylight hours hide away, protected from Japanese planes by shore-based antiaircraft, in Wickham Anchorage and Viru Harbor. About D plus 4, when enough men and supplies would be on hand, landing craft were to ferry assault troops from Rendova across Roviana Lagoon to New Georgia to begin the march

---

[15] This unit included besides the Fijians some Tongans and a few Solomon Islanders. See [British] Central Office of Information, *Among Those Present*, pp. 53–56. American documents list this unit variously as "1st South Seas Scout Company," "South Pacific Scouts," "native troops," and erroneously, as "1st Company, 1st Fiji Infantry," which was a different unit serving at Port Purvis on Florida.

[16] Ltr, Harmon to Handy, 15 Jul 43, quoted in part in Hq SOPACBACOM File, Suppl New Georgia Material, OCMH.

[17] Rad, COMGENSOPAC to COMGEN MAINYARD, 10 Jun 43, Hq SOPACBACOM File, Suppl New Georgia Material, OCMH.

CHART 7—ORGANIZATION OF ATTACK FORCE, D DAY[1]

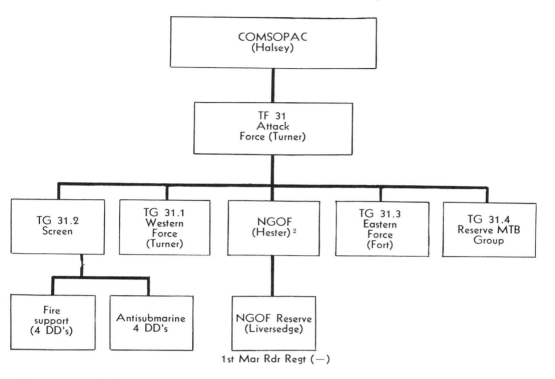

[1] This chart shows D-Day organization only. Second and third echelons were organized along similar lines.
[2] To assume control of all assigned land, sea, and air forces in New Georgia on orders from Admiral Halsey.

against Munda. Coupled with this advance would be the amphibious seizure of Enogai Inlet in the Kula Gulf to cut the Japanese reinforcement, supply, and evacuation trail between Munda and Enogai, and thus prevent the Japanese on Kolombangara from strengthening their compatriots on New Georgia. Once Munda and Enogai were secured, it was planned, Vila on Kolombangara would be seized and further advances up the Solomons chain would follow.

Turner organized his force into five groups. (*Chart 7*) The Western Force (Task Group 31.1), which Turner commanded in person, would seize Rendova and make subsequent assaults against Munda, Enogai, and Kolombangara. The Eastern Force, under Rear Adm. George H. Fort, was to take Segi, Viru, and Wickham. Task Group 31.2, consisting of eight destroyers, would cover the transports. No ships' gunfire support was planned in advance, but all ships, including transports, were ordered to be ready to deliver supporting and counterbattery fire if necessary.

The New Georgia Occupation Force, under General Hester, included the Western Landing Force (under Hester), which during the amphibious phase would function as part of Turner's Western Force; the Eastern Landing Force (under Col. Daniel H. Hundley), which during the amphibious phase would be part of Fort's Eastern Force; naval base forces for all points to be captured; the reserve under Col. Harry B. Liversedge, USMC; and two more whose designations are not self-explanatory—the New Georgia Air Force and the Assault Flotillas. (*Charts 8 and 9*)

The New Georgia Air Force, led by Brig. Gen. Francis P. Mulcahy, USMC, consisted initially of Headquarters, 2d Marine Air Wing. In contrast with the system in the Southwest Pacific, this air headquarters was under the landing force commander. Mulcahy was to take over control of New Georgia air operations during the amphibious phase once that control was relinquished by Turner; he would take command of the planes from Guadalcanal and the Russells that would be supporting the attack, once they were airborne. He was eventually to command the air squadrons to be based at Munda and Segi Point. The Assault Flotillas consisted of landing craft to be used to ferry the assault troops from Rendova to New Georgia proper when the attack against Munda was ready to begin.

Two ground force units which Turner retained temporarily under his direct control were small forces designated to make covering landings. The Onaiavisi Occupation Unit, composed of A and B Companies, 169th Infantry, was to land from two APD's and one minesweeper on Sasavele and Baraulu Islands on either side of Onaiavisi Entrance to hold it until the day of the assault against the mainland through the entrance. The

landing of the occupation unit was scheduled for 0330, 30 June. The Rendova Advance Unit, C and G Companies (each less one rifle platoon), was to land from two APD's on Rendova at 0540 to cover the landing of the main body of the Western Landing Force. The latter, about 6,300 strong, was to start landing on Rendova at 0640, 30 June.

Command over all air, sea, and ground forces in New Georgia would pass from Turner to Hester on orders from Halsey.

The presence of the DRYGOODS stockpiles on Guadalcanal greatly simplified logistical problems. Three Army units of fire and thirty days' supplies were to be put ashore at Rendova, and five units of fire and thirty days' supplies at Viru, Segi, and Wickham. Supply levels were to be built to a sixty-day level out of the DRYGOODS stocks. General Griswold was told to make the necessary quantities available to Turner. Turner was responsible for the actual movement of supplies to New Georgia.

Directions for unloading during the assault phase were simple and clear. Turner instructed all vessels to be ready for quick unloading. All ships were to square away before reaching the transport areas offshore, and if possible to work all hatches from both sides. Unloading parties included 150 men for each cargo ship and transport, 150 men per LST, 50 men per LCT, and 25 men per LCI. The shore party totaled 300 men. Once ashore, cargo was to be moved off the beaches and into inland dumps as fast as possible.

Secondary Landings

With tactical plans for TOENAILS largely ready by mid-June, the invasion

CHART 8—WESTERN FORCE ON D DAY

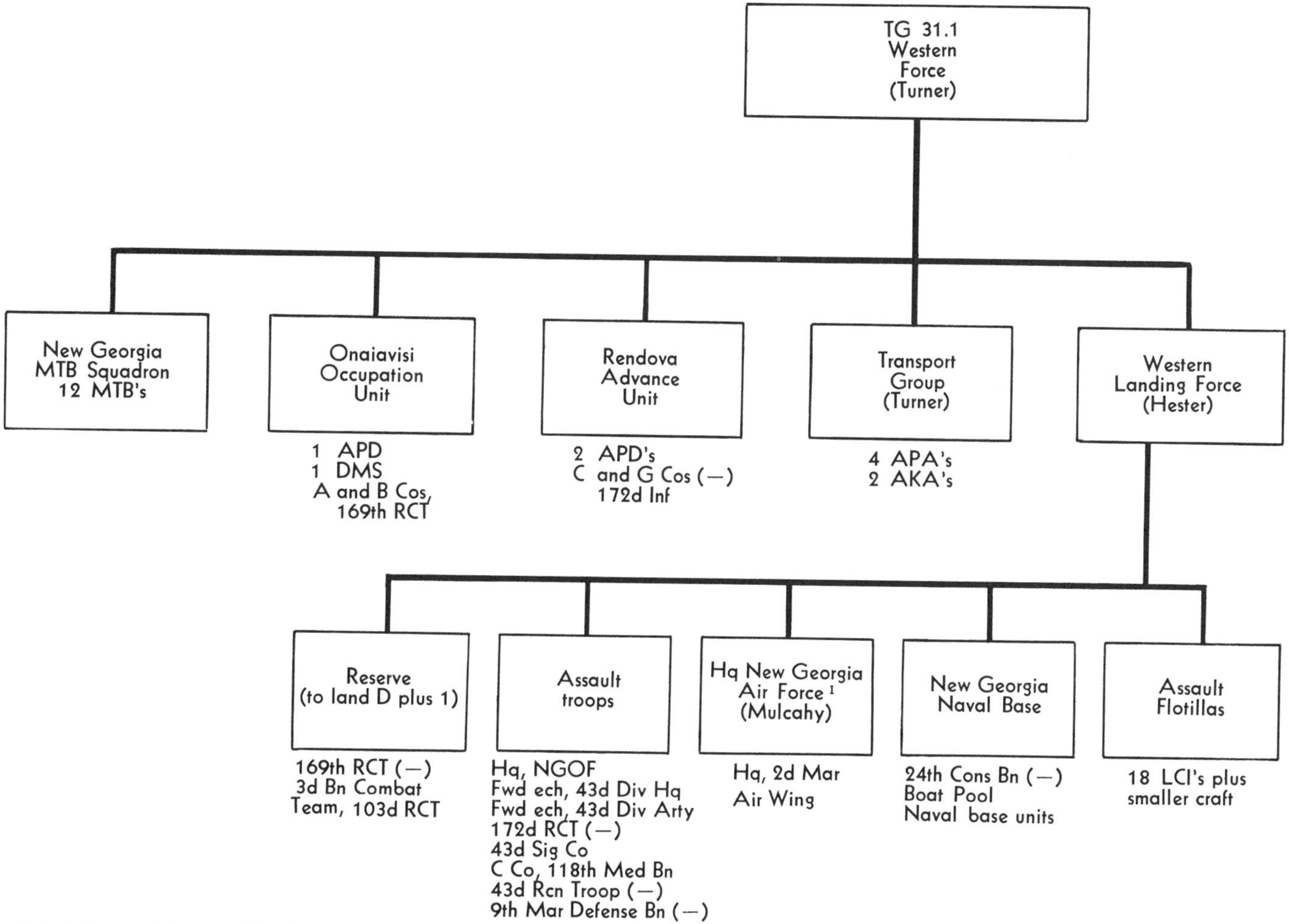

```
                                    TG 31.1
                                    Western
                                     Force
                                    (Turner)
                                       |
     ┌──────────────┬──────────────┬──┴───────────┬──────────────┐
     │              │              │              │              │
New Georgia    Onaiavisi      Rendova        Transport      Western
MTB Squadron   Occupation     Advance        Group          Landing Force
12 MTB's       Unit           Unit           (Turner)       (Hester)

               1 APD          2 APD's        4 APA's
               1 DMS          C and G Cos (—) 2 AKA's
               A and B Cos,   172d Inf
               169th RCT

     ┌───────────┬────────────┬────────────┬────────────┬────────────┐
     │           │            │            │            │            │
Reserve      Assault     Hq New Georgia  New Georgia  Assault
(to land     troops      Air Force¹      Naval Base   Flotillas
D plus 1)                (Mulcahy)

169th RCT (—) Hq, NGOF    Hq, 2d Mar      24th Cons Bn (—)  18 LCI's plus
3d Bn Combat  Fwd ech, 43d Div Hq  Air Wing  Boat Pool   smaller craft
Team, 103d RCT Fwd ech, 43d Div Arty          Naval base units
              172d RCT (—)
              43d Sig Co
              C Co, 118th Med Bn
              43d Rcn Troop (—)
              9th Mar Defense Bn (—)
```

¹ To include naval forces at Segi Point, Wickham Anchorage, and Viru Harbor after establishment ashore.

CHART 9—EASTERN FORCE ON D DAY

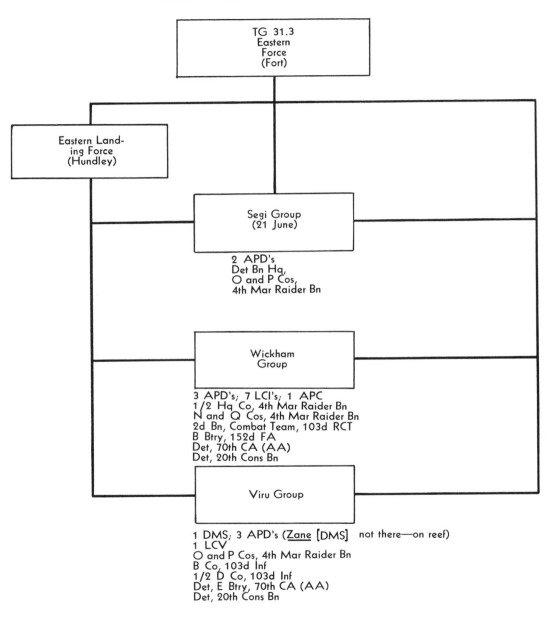

TG 31.3
Eastern
Force
(Fort)

Eastern Land-
ing Force
(Hundley)

Segi Group
(21 June)

2 APD's
Det Bn Hq,
O and P Cos,
4th Mar Raider Bn

Wickham
Group

3 APD's; 7 LCI's; 1 APC
1/2 Hq Co, 4th Mar Raider Bn
N and Q Cos, 4th Mar Raider Bn
2d Bn, Combat Team, 103d RCT
B Btry, 152d FA
Det, 70th CA (AA)
Det, 20th Cons Bn

Viru Group

1 DMS; 3 APD's (Zane [DMS] not there—on reef)
1 LCV
O and P Cos, 4th Mar Raider Bn
B Co, 103d Inf
1/2 D Co, 103d Inf
Det, E Btry, 70th CA (AA)
Det, 20th Cons Bn

forces spent the rest of the month making final preparations—checking weapons and supplies, conducting rehearsals in the New Hebrides, and studying orders, maps, and photographs. South Pacific aircraft pounded Vila, Munda, and the Shortlands–Bougainville bases while Southwest Pacific planes continued their long-range strikes against Rabaul.

Segi Point

In the midst of these preparations, Admiral Turner received disquieting news about Segi Point, which was scheduled to furnish the Allies with an airfield. Coastwatcher Donald Kennedy reported on 20 June that the Japanese were moving against his hideout and that he was heading for the hills. He requested help.[18]

Kennedy's report was correct. In early June a small Japanese force had gone to the southeast part of Vangunu to deal summarily with disaffected natives, and on 17 June half the *1st Battalion, 229th Infantry,* under a Major Nagahara or

Hara had moved from Viru Harbor southeast toward Segi Point.

As loss of Segi Point prior to D Day would deprive the Allies of a potential air base, Turner, a man of fiery energy and quick decision, abruptly changed his plans. He had originally intended to land the heavily reinforced 1st Battalion, 103d Infantry, at Segi on 30 June to build the fighter field and establish a small naval base. But on receipt of Kennedy's call for aid, he hurriedly dispatched the handiest force available, the 4th Marine Raider Battalion (less N and Q Companies), from Guadalcanal in the fast destroyer-transports *Dent* and *Waters* to seize Segi and hold it. Ships and marines wasted no time. By 2030 of the same day—20 June—the ships were loaded and under way. Before dawn next morning they had safely worked their way through Panga Bay, though both vessels scraped bottom in the reef- and rock-filled waters. Kennedy, still safe, had lit bonfires on the beach and when the marines started ashore at 0550 he was there to meet them. There were no Japanese. The major and his men were still in the vicinity of Lambeti Village.

Next morning the APD's *Schley* and *Crosby* brought A and D Companies of the 103d Infantry and an airfield survey section to Segi Point. Though alerted several times against enemy attack, the Segi garrison was undisturbed until 30 June, when a series of Japanese air attacks made things lively. Construction of the airfield began on 30 June. Using bulldozers and power shovels, and working under floodlights at night, the Seabees of the 20th Naval Construction Battalion had the strip ready for limited

---

[18] The remainder of this chapter is based on Halsey and Bryan, *Admiral Halsey's Story,* pp. 158–61; Craven and Cate, *The Pacific: Guadalcanal to Saipan,* pp. 221–29; Morison, *Breaking the Bismarcks Barrier,* pp. 138–60; ONI USN, Operations in the New Georgia Area, pp. 9–23; History of the New Georgia Campaign, MS, 13 Aug 45, prepared by Hist Sec, G–2 SOPACBACOM, Vol. I, Chs. II–III, V, OCMH; after action rpts, jnls, int rpts, and hists of USAFISPA, NGOF, COMAIR New Georgia (2d Mar Air Wing), XIV Corps, I Mar Amphib Corps, 43d and 37th Divs, and subordinate units, and 1st Mar Raider Regt; COMSOPAC, TF 31, and TF 33 War Diaries; 17th Army Operations, Vol. II, Japanese Monogr No. 40 (OCMH); 17th Army Operations, Map Supplement, Japanese Monogr No. 40A (OCMH); Southeast Area Naval Operations, Vol. II, Japanese Monogr No. 49 (OCMH); Outline of Southeast Area Naval Air Operations, Pt. IV, Japanese Monogr No. 108 (OCMH).

AIRFIELD AT SEGI POINT, *New Georgia.*

operations as a fighter staging field by 11 July.[19]

Wickham Anchorage

The force selected for the seizure of Wickham Anchorage by Vangunu Island was ready to sail from the Russells on 29 June. Commanded by Lt. Col. Lester E. Brown, the force included Colonel Brown's 2d Battalion, 103d Infantry, reinforced, and N and P Companies, plus a headquarters detachment, of the 4th Marine Raider Battalion. Under Admiral Fort aboard the *Trever,* the convoy consisted of the destroyer-transports *Schley* and *McKean,* carrying ma-

rines, and seven LCI's which bore soldiers. The ships cast off shortly after 1800 and set course for Oleana Bay, about two and one-half miles west by south from Vura village.

Allied scouting parties had reported that the main Japanese concentration at Wickham Anchorage—one platoon of the *229th Infantry* and a company of the *Kure 6th Special Naval Landing Force*— was near Vura, and had also reported that on the east shore of Oleana Bay a 500-yard-long strip of solid sand offered a good landing beach. It had therefore been decided to land the troops at Oleana Bay and then march overland and outflank the enemy positions from the west. There were two trails from Oleana Bay to Wickham Anchorage. One, which followed the shore line, was believed used by the Japanese, but a shorter one had been cut farther inland in April by Ken-

[19] "The lighting of the airstrip at night was a carefully figured risk. We calculated we could get sufficient warning from our radar to turn off the lights before the attackers arrived." Ltr, Col Hundley to Gen Smith, Chief of Mil Hist, 19 Oct 53, no sub, OCMH.

nedy's men in order to get scouts into the Vura area. This trail was thought to be unknown to the Japanese, and troops following native guides could be expected to cover it in five or six hours.

Visibility was practically nonexistent for the Wickham-bound convoy on the night of 29–30 June. Rain, lashed by a stiff wind, fell throughout the night, and continued as the vessels threaded their cautious way through the shoals and reefs into Oleana Bay. At 0335, 30 June, the ships hove to. Shortly afterward the first wave of marines began to debark from the destroyer-transports into LCVP's, a task complicated by darkness, rain, high wind, and heavy seas. Two LCVP's were almost loaded when the APD commanders discovered they were lying off the west rather than the east shore of the bay. The marines reboarded the destroyer-transports which then moved a thousand yards eastward.

Again the marines loaded into LCVP's and started for the beach, which was obscured by rain and mist. Beach flares which had been set by members of the scouting party were invisible. Only the noise of the breakers indicated the direction of the shore. But things got worse. As the first wave of LCVP's blindly made their way shoreward, the LCI's broke into the formation and scattered it. Unable to re-form, or even to see anything, the LCVP coxswains proceeded on their own. The result was exactly what might be expected from a night landing in bad weather. The assault wave of marines landed in impressive disorganization. Six LCVP's smashed up in the heavy surf that boiled over coral reefs. Fortunately, the Japanese were not present to oppose the landing. There were no casualties.

The LCI's, landing in daylight, found the proper beach, and by 0720 the Army troops were ashore. More marines had begun landing at 0630 at the correct beach. With all landing operations concluded by 1000, the ships departed.

Three officers of the reconnaissance party had met the landing force and informed Colonel Brown that the Japanese main strength was at Kaeruka rather than Vura. Once the scattered troops had been collected, the overland advance began with a small column moving toward Vura along the coastal trail while the main column marched against Kaeruka over Kennedy's trail. The marines and soldiers first met the enemy in early afternoon. Then ensued four days of fighting in the sodden jungles, with the Americans receiving support from dive bombers and warships, from their own heavy weapons, and from the 105-mm. howitzers of the 152d Field Artillery Battalion on the beach at Oleana Bay. By the end of 3 July the Americans, having blasted the Japanese out of their entrenchments, were in complete possession of Wickham Anchorage. Many of the Japanese garrison had been killed; some escaped by barge, canoe, or on foot. In the seizure of this future staging point for landing craft, the marines lost twelve killed, twenty-one wounded. Army casualties are not listed.

Viru Harbor

When the Viru Occupation Force, the reinforced B Company, 103d Infantry, on board three destroyer-transports, sailed into Viru Harbor before daylight on 30 June, lookouts vainly scanned the shore line for a white parachute flare. This was to have signaled that the ma-

MEN OF 152D FIELD ARTILLERY BATTALION *firing a 105-mm. howitzer in support of Colonel Brown's 2d Battalion, 103d Infantry.*

rine raider companies that landed at Segi Point had moved against Viru from inland and seized positions flanking the harbor, for it had been agreed that attempting to land the infantry in frontal assault against the high cliffs surrounding the harbor would be too risky. But Lt. Col. Michael S. Currin, commanding the 4th Marine Raider Battalion, had warned that his overland march was going slowly and that he might not arrive and take the harbor by 30 June. Thus the destroyer-transports waited just outside the harbor, beyond range of a Japanese shore battery (Major Hara had left part of his battalion at Viru) and at noon went to Segi Point where with Turner's approval the troops went ashore. The at-

tack force commander agreed that in view of the delay B Company should follow the marine raiders in their overland march.

Currin's men had begun the first leg of their twelve-mile advance from Segi Point to Viru Harbor in rubber boats on 27 June. They landed near Lambeti Plantation that night, and the next morning set out on their overland march. Skirmishes with the Japanese, coupled with the difficulty of walking through the jungle, slowed them down. They forded streams, knee-deep in mud and shoulder-high in water. The leading elements of the column churned the trail into slippery ooze, so that the rear elements floundered and stumbled along. Thus it was evening of 30 June before the marines reached Viru Harbor, which they took handily the next day by a double envelopment supported by dive bombers that knocked out the Japanese shore battery.[20] On 4 July B Company, 103d, which had come up from Segi Point, took over the defenses of Viru Harbor from the marines.

Thus were the operations of the Eastern Force conducted, separately from each other and separately from those of the Western Force, but under Admiral Turner's general supervision in his capacity of attack force commander. They had provided one airfield and two staging bases. While important, they were undertaken only to support the seizure of Rendova by a substantial force, which was then to assault Munda and Vila.

Rendova

Admiral Turner's ships that were assigned to Rendova arrived off Guadalcanal in the morning of 29 June.[21] They had come up from Efate bearing the assault troops of the Western Landing Force's first echelon. They weighed anchor late that afternoon and made an uneventful journey through the mist and rain to Blanche Channel between Rendova and New Georgia.

No enemy warships were there to oppose them. Their absence had been ensured by a group of cruisers, destroyers, and minelayers from Halsey's Task Force 36 under Rear Adm. Aaron Stanton Merrill. Merrill's ships, on the night of 29–30 June, had bombarded Munda and Vila, then ventured northwest to the Shortlands to shell enemy bases and lay mines. This action inflicted damage to the Japanese while placing a surface force in position to cover Turner's landings. The bad weather canceled the air strikes against the Bougainville–Shortland bases, but Allied planes—dive and torpedo bombers—were able to hit Munda and Vila on 30 June.

The night of 29–30 June was short for the six-thousand-odd troops aboard Turner's ships. Reveille sounded at 0200, more than four hours before the ships hove to off Renard Entrance, the channel leading to Rendova Harbor.

First landings were made by the Onaiavisi Occupation Unit—A and B Companies, 169th Infantry. These had come from the Russells in the destroyer-transport *Ralph Talbot* and the minesweeper *Zane* to land on Sasavele and Baraulu Islands before daylight in order to hold Onaiavisi Entrance against the day that the New Georgia Occupation Force made its water-borne movement against the mainland. Later in the morning B Company's 2d Platoon outposted Roviana Island and the next day wiped out a Japanese lookout station. These landings were not opposed. The Japanese had maintained observation posts on the barrier islands but had not fortified them. The only mishap in this phase of TOENAILS occurred early in the morning of 30 June, when the *Zane* ran on a reef while maneuvering in the badly charted waters in the rain. She was pulled free by the tug *Rail* in the afternoon.

The landing of the 172d Infantry on

---

[20] According to Colonel Hundley, some naval vessels, apparently unaware of the postponement, sailed into Viru Harbor just as the bombing began. The Japanese manned the shore defenses, which were promptly knocked out, and were completely surprised by the marine attack. *Ibid.*

[21] There were six transports, two destroyer-transports, and eight destroyers.

SHIPS MOVING TOWARD RENDOVA, *late afternoon, 29 June 1943.*

Rendova was somewhat disorderly. C and G Companies, guided by Maj. Martin Clemens and Lt. F. A. Rhoades, RAN, of the coastwatchers, and by native pilots, were to have landed from the destroyer-transports *Dent* and *Waters* on East and West Beaches of Rendova Harbor at 0540 to cover the main body of the 172d Infantry when it came ashore.[22] But again the weather played the Allies foul. The mist and rain obscured the Renard Entrance markers and the white signal light on Bau Island that the reconnaissance party, present on Rendova since 16 June, had set up. As a result the APD's first landed C and G Companies several miles away, then had to re-embark them and go to the proper place.

Meanwhile, the six transports took their stations north of Renard Entrance as the destroyers took screening positions to the east and west. By now the clouds had begun to clear away, and visibility improved. The troops gathered on the transport decks, and the first wave climbed into the landing craft at the rails, carrying their barracks bags with them. The order "All boats away, all troops away" was given aboard Turner's flagship, the transport *McCawley*, as the sun rose at 0642. Four minutes later

---

[22] C and G Companies, 172d Infantry, and A Company, 169th Infantry, had received special physical conditioning and training in jungle fighting and small boat handling. They were given the somewhat romantic title of "Barracudas." Clemens, a former district officer in the government of the British Solomon Islands Protectorate, was a major in the British Solomon Islands Defense Force, and had been a great help during the Guadalcanal Campaign. Rhoades had been a plantation manager before the war.

ABOARD THE TRANSPORT McCAWLEY, *Admiral Turner's flagship, 29 June 1943. From left, Brig. Gen. Leonard F. Wing, Rear Adm. Theodore S. Wilkinson, Rear Adm. Richmond Kelly Turner, and Maj. Gen. John H. Hester.*

Turner warned the first boats as they headed for shore, some three thousand yards to the south: "You are the first to land, you are the first to land—expect opposition." [23]

As the landing craft moved shoreward the waves became disorganized. When the craft reached Renard Entrance between Bau and Kokorana Islands, there was confusion and milling about until they began going through the entrance two abreast toward the narrow East and West Beaches that fronted Lever Brothers' 584-acre plantation.

As the first landing craft touched down about 0700, the troops sprang out and

ran across the beaches into the cover of the jungle. C and G Companies reached Rendova Harbor about ten minutes after the troops from the transports, and they joined with the main body and moved inland toward the Japanese. [24]

[24] 43d Division documents give no data on the planned composition and timing of assault waves. They are at variance regarding the time of landing. The 43d Division and New Georgia Occupation Force reports (which are virtually identical) state that C and G Companies landed at 0630 and that the main body began landing at 0745. These assertions are undoubtedly incorrect. The 172d report states that C and G Companies went astray but landed along with the main body about 0700. And the 43d Division's time of 0745 is contradicted by that division's G–3 Journal which states that the division command post opened on Rendova at 0730. CTF 31 War Diary states that the first troops hit the beach at 0656.

[23] CTF 31 War Diary, 30 Jun 43 entry.

The Japanese Rendova detachment—about 120 troops from the *229th Infantry* and the *Kure 6th Special Naval Landing Force*—had been alerted early during the morning of 30 June. The alert proved to be a false alarm and they went back to sleep. The next alert—their first realization that they were being attacked—came when the American assault craft hit the beach. As it was too late for the Japanese to man their beach defense positions, they posted themselves in the coconut plantation about one hundred yards behind East Beach. Radiomen tried to warn Munda but could not get the message through. A lookout at Banieta Point fired four blue flares and signaled headquarters by blinker.

The Japanese could not hope to do more than harass the Americans. The special naval landing force commander, hit in the face by a burst from a BAR, was an early casualty. When about a dozen men were dead, the disorganized Japanese fell back into the jungle. They are reported to have lost some fifty or sixty men, while killing four Americans and wounding five, including Col. David M. N. Ross, the 172d's commander. By the end of the day the Americans had pushed inland one thousand yards. The 105-mm. howitzers of the 103d Field Artillery Battalion were in position to cover Renard Entrance, the north coast of Rendova, and the barrier islands.

All troops except working parties on board ship were ashore within thirty minutes after the landing of the first wave. This number included General Harmon who went along to observe operations. In the absence of strong enemy resistance on Rendova, the chief problem that confronted the invaders was unloading supplies, getting them ashore, and moving them inland. Less than half an hour after they had been lowered into the water, the first landing craft returned to the ships for cargo. No landing waves were formed; each craft moved cargo ashore as soon as it was loaded by its mother ship.

The first real delay in unloading was caused by shallow water. Many tank lighters (LCM's) grounded on reefs in the harbor and lost time refloating and finding passages through deeper water. Many lighters, grounding about fifty feet offshore, had to lower their ramps in water while the troops waded ashore with cargo in their hands or on their shoulders. In consequence, disorderly stacks of gear began piling up near the shore line. The beachmaster attempted, with only partial success, to prevent this.

During most of the morning the Japanese did little. The Rendova garrison had not amounted to much; after the war the Japanese explained that the Munda and Rabaul commanders had not expected the Americans to land on the offshore islands. "Therefore," a postwar report states, "the landing on RENDOVA Island completely baffled our forces." [25] When it became clear that the Americans were indeed landing on Rendova, 120-mm. and 140-mm. naval coast defense batteries at Munda and Baanga Island opened up on the ships, and they immediately replied with 5-inch fire. The destroyer *Gwin* was soon hit. She was the only casualty in the exchange of fire between ships and shore batteries that continued all day. But Turner and General Hester were operating very close

---

[25] Southeast Area Naval Operations, II, Japanese Monogr No. 49 (OCMH), 36.

MEN OF 43D SIGNAL COMPANY WADING ASHORE *from LCM's with signal equipment, 30 June 1943.*

to the Japanese air bases in southern Bougainville and the Shortlands, and these presented the greatest danger. Fortunately for the Americans, the Japanese were not prepared to counterattack at once.

The commanders at New Georgia were not the only Japanese surprised by the invasion. Those at Rabaul were taken equally unaware. They had, of course, known that some form of Allied activity was impending in late June. The move to help Kennedy, the increasing tempo of Allied air and naval action, and intercepted Allied radio traffic told them as much. So Admiral Kusaka gathered air attack forces together and sent them to the airfields around Buin. But after 26 June, when Allied movements seemed

to slow down (Turner's task force was then rehearsing in the New Hebrides), the Japanese command concluded that the Allies had been simply reinforcing Guadalcanal on a grand scale. Kusaka pulled his air units back to Rabaul. Thus it was that although a submarine had sighted Turner's ships south of New Georgia about midnight, Kusaka, with sixty-six bombers, eighty-three fighters, and twenty reconnaissance seaplanes at his disposal, could do nothing about the invasion for several hours.

Turner, whose plans called for unloading to be completed by 1130, was first interrupted by a false air raid alarm at 0856. The ships stopped unloading and steamed around in Blanche Channel while the thirty-two fighter planes covering the landing got ready to intercept. The reported enemy planes failed to appear, and unloading was resumed.

The first real enemy air attack, a sweep by twenty-seven fighters, came just after 1100. The Allied fighter cover shot most of them down before they could do any damage, but Turner's schedule was further delayed by the necessity for going to general quarters and getting under way.

By about 1500 all but about fifty tons of gear had been unloaded. Turner ordered the transports and screening destroyers back to Guadalcanal and they speedily took their departure. Shortly afterward twenty-five Japanese bombers, escorted by twenty-four fighters, came down from Rabaul. The majority of the bombers were shot down, but one managed to put a torpedo into the flagship *McCawley*. At 1715 eight more bombers struck at the retiring task force but failed to score. That evening overeager American PT boats, mistaking the crippled *McCawley* for an enemy, put two more torpedoes into her sides and she sank in Blanche Channel, fortunately without loss of life.

Meanwhile the landing and handling of supplies on Rendova had been less than satisfactory. The invading forces had hoped to use Rendova Plantation to store supplies, although the preinvasion patrols had not been able to investigate it thoroughly because the Japanese were there. As the rain continued, the streams flooded, and the red clay of the plantation turned into mud. The mile-long prewar road that linked East and West Beaches served well early in the day, but soon heavy truck traffic

ground it into a muddy mess. Seabee drivers of the 24th Naval Construction Battalion had to hook their truck cables to trees and winch their 2½-ton, 6 x 6 trucks along in order to haul supplies from the heaped beaches to the cover and safety of high ground farther inland. They cut hundreds of coconut logs into twelve-foot lengths and tried to corduroy the roadbed, but the mud seemed to be bottomless. One bulldozer sank almost out of sight. To add to the supply difficulties, many containers were inadequately marked and medical supplies became mixed among rations, fuel, and ammunition. The Rendova naval base force could not find all its radios, and little was known regarding the progress of operations at Wickham and Viru. The clutter and confusion caused by bogged trucks on the muddy roads and trails finally became so bad that the next day General Hester requested Turner to stop further shipments of trucks until the beachhead could be better organized.

Despite the confusion ashore and the loss of the *McCawley*, operations on 30 June were largely successful. Six thousand men of the 43d Division, the 24th Naval Construction Battalion and other naval units, and the 9th Marine Defense Battalion had come ashore with weapons, rations, fuel, ammunition, construction equipment, and personal baggage. The Japanese had lost Rendova and several planes, and although they enthusiastically reported inflicting heavy damage to Turner's ships, they admitted that, "due to tenacious interference by enemy fighter planes, a decisive blow could not be struck against the enemy landing convoy." "The speedy disembarkation of the enemy," they felt, "was absolutely miraculous." [26]

With the capture of the beachhead, General Hester dissolved the 172d Regimental Combat Team and returned the field artillery, engineers, and medical and communications men to divisional control. The build-up of troops and supplies for the attack against Munda and Vila was ready to begin.

The second echelon of the Western Force came in on LST's the next day. This echelon included the 155-mm. howitzers of the 192d Field Artillery Battalion and the 155-mm. guns of A Battery, 9th Marine Defense Battalion. Succeeding reinforcements continued to arrive at Rendova, Segi Point, Viru, and Wickham through 5 July until virtually the entire New Georgia Occupation Force as then constituted was present in New Georgia, with the main body at Rendova.

The Japanese were unable to do anything to prevent these movements, and did little damage to the beachhead. Only Japanese aircraft made anything like a sustained effort. Storms and poor visibility continued to prevent Allied planes from striking at the Shortlands-Bougainville fields, although they were able to hit the Munda and Vila airfields as well as Bairoko. The Japanese reinforced their air strength at Rabaul and sent planes forward to southern Bougainville and the Shortlands. On 2 July Admiral Kusaka had under his command 11 fighters and 13 dive bombers from the carrier *Ryuho*, 11 land-based twin-engine bombers, 20 fighters, 2 reconnaissance planes, and a number of Army bombers that were temporarily assigned. The same day foul weather began closing in the rearward Allied bases. About noon the Commander, Aircraft, Solomons, from his post on Guadalcanal, ordered all Allied planes back. This left New Georgia without air cover. To make matters worse, the 9th Marine Defense Battalion's SCR 602 (a search radar designed for immediate use on beachheads) broke down that morning, and the SCR 270 (a long-range radar designed for relatively permanent emplacement) was not yet set up.

Kusaka sent all his planes to New Georgia. They reached the Rendova area in the afternoon, circled behind the clouded 3,448-foot twin peaks of Rendova Peak, then pounced to the attack. Many soldiers saw the planes but thought they were American until fragmentation clusters dropped by the bombers began exploding among them. The Rendova beachhead, with its dense concentrations of men and matériel, was an excellent target. At least thirty men were killed and over two hundred were wounded. Many bombs struck the fuel dumps, the resulting fires caused fuel drums to explode, and these started more fires. Three 155-mm. guns of the 9th Marine Defense Battalion were damaged. Much of the equipment of the 125-bed clearing station set up by the 118th Medical Battalion was destroyed; for a time only emergency medical treatment could be rendered. The wounded had to wait at least twenty-four hours before they could receive full treatment at Guadalcanal.

That night nine Japanese destroyers and one light cruiser shelled Rendova but hit nothing except jungle. The Jap-

---

[26] *Ibid.*, pp. 29, 37.

anese, it was clear, did not intend to land troops on Rendova, but they did not intend to allow the Americans to remain there unmolested. The air attacks, while serious, did not disrupt preparations for the next phase of TOENAILS.

The Move to Zanana

After the occupation of Rendova, the next tasks facing the invaders were the movement to the New Georgia mainland and the assault against Munda airfield. On 2 July Admiral Halsey, doubtless encouraged by the lack of effective Japanese opposition, directed Turner to proceed with plans for the move against Munda. To carry out these plans, Turner on 28 June had reorganized the Western Force into five units: the transport unit consisting of destroyer-transports and high-speed minesweepers; a destroyer screen; a fire support group, eventually consisting of three light cruisers and four destroyers; two tugs; and the Munda-Bairoko Occupation Force under General Hester.

The Munda-Bairoko Occupation Force was further divided into five components. The Northern Landing Group, under Colonel Liversedge, was to operate against Bairoko. The Southern Landing Group (the 43d Division less the 1st Battalion of the 103d Infantry, the 136th Field Artillery Battalion, the 9th Marine Defense Battalion less elements, and the South Pacific Scouts) under Brig. Gen. Leonard F. Wing, assistant commander of the 43d Division, was to attack Munda. The New Georgia Air Force, the Assault Flotillas (twelve LCI's, four LCT's, and native canoes), and a naval base group comprised the remaining three components. The Southern

Landing Group was to land at Zanana Beach about five air-line miles east of Munda and attack westward to capture Munda while the Northern Group landed at Rice Anchorage in the Kula Gulf and advanced southward to capture or destroy the enemy in the Bairoko–Enogai area, block all trails from there to Munda, and cut off the Japanese route of reinforcement, supply, and escape.[27]

The troops on Rendova had been making ready since 30 June, but some of their efforts were marked by less than complete success. Hester had ordered aggressive reconnaissance of the entire area east and north of Munda. Starting on the night of 30 June–1 July, patrols from the 172d Infantry were to pass through Onaiavisi Entrance and Roviana Lagoon, land at Zanana, and begin reconnoitering, while Marine patrols pushed south from Rice Anchorage. The 43d Division patrols were to operate from a base camp west of Zanana established on the afternoon of 30 June by Capt. E. C. D. Sherrer, assistant intelligence officer of the New Georgia Occupation Force.

At 2330, 30 June, despite a false rumor that Onaiavisi Entrance was impassable for small boats, patrols left Rendova on the eight-mile run to the mainland. The next morning regimental headquarters discovered that the patrols, unable to find the entrance in the dark, had landed on one of the barrier islands. The next evening the 1st Battalion, accompanied by Colonel Ross, shoved off for the mainland but could not find its way. Thus it was concluded that the move should

---

[27] Rice Anchorage lies about fifteen statute miles north by east of Munda Point. The other beach near Munda, Laiana Beach, lay within range of the Japanese artillery at Munda and would have been a risky place to land.

TRUCK TOWING A 155-MM. HOWITZER OVER MUDDY TRAIL, *Rendova, 7 July 1943.*

be made in daylight. Accordingly A Company, 169th Infantry, and the 1st Battalion, 172d Infantry, moved out for Zanana on the afternoon of 2 July. Native guides in canoes marked the channel. Everything went well except that about 150 men returned to Rendova at 2330. Questioned about their startling reversal of course, they are reported to have stated that the coxswain of the leading craft had received a note dropped by a B–24 which ordered them to turn back.[28] By the next morning, however, the entire 1st Battalion was on the mainland.

The build-up of supplies on Rendova continued to be difficult; the rain and

mud partially thwarted the efforts of the 118th Engineer and the 24th Naval Construction Battalions to drain the flat areas. East Beach was finally abandoned. The Occupation Force supply officers, after examining the solid coral subsurfaces under the sandy loam of the barrier islands, began using the islands as staging points for supplies eventually intended for the mainland.

On the other hand, the artillery picture was bright. General Barker, the artillery commander, had never planned to make extensive use of Rendova for artillery positions, as the range from Rendova to Munda was too great for all weapons except 155-mm. guns. Such barrier islands as Bau, Kokorana, Sasavele, and Baraulu could well support artillery, and these islands, open on their

---

[28] There seem to be no further available data regarding this interesting but absurd excuse.

north shores, possessed natural fields of fire. The field artillery could cover the entire area from Zanana to Munda, and initially would be firing at right angles to the axis of infantry advance and parallel to the infantry front. This would enable the artillery to deliver extremely accurate supporting fire, since the dispersion in artillery fire is greater in range than in deflection. On the other hand, it would increase the difficulty of co-ordination between artillery and infantry, for each artillery unit would require exact information regarding not only the front line of the unit it was supporting, but also the front line of the unit's neighbors. Three battalions of artillery were in place in time to cover the move of the 1st Battalion, 172d Infantry, to Zanana, and by 6 July two battalions of 105-mm. howitzers (the 103d and 169th), two battalions of 155-mm. howitzers (the 136th and 192d), and two batteries of 155-mm. guns (9th Marine Defense Battalion) were in place, registered, and ready to fire in support of the infantry.

Antiaircraft managed to make a tremendous improvement over its performance of 2 July, and celebrated Independence Day in signal fashion when a close formation of sixteen unescorted enemy bombers flew over Rendova. This time radars were working, the warning had been given, and fire control men and gunners of the 9th Marine Defense Battalion's 90-mm. and 40-mm. batteries were ready. The Japanese flew into a concentration of fire from these weapons, and twelve immediately plunged earthward in return for the expenditure of eighty-eight rounds. The fighter cover

from the Russells knocked down the remaining four.

Meanwhile, at Zanana, the 1st Battalion, 172d Infantry, established a perimeter of 400 yards' radius, wired in and protected by machine guns, 37-mm. antitank guns, and antiaircraft guns. Here General Wing set up the 43d Division command post, and to this perimeter came the remaining troops of the 172d and 169th Infantry Regiments in echelons until 6 July when both regiments had been completely assembled. Ground reconnaissance by 43d Division soldiers, marines, and coastwatchers, aided after 3 July by the 1st Company, South Pacific Scouts, under Capt. Charles W. H. Tripp of the New Zealand Army, was still being carried on. The advance westward was ready to begin.

Rice Anchorage

While 43d Division troops were establishing themselves at Zanana, Colonel Liversedge's Northern Landing Group was boarding ships at Guadalcanal and making ready to cut the Japanese communications north of Munda. The Northern Landing Group was originally to have landed on 4 July, but the delays in getting a foothold at Zanana forced Turner to postpone the landing, and all other operations, for twenty-four hours.

Because the Bairoko–Enogai area, the New Georgia terminus of the Japanese seaborne line of communications, was strongly held, and because preinvasion patrols had reported the Wharton River to be unfordable from the coast to a point about six thousand yards inland, Turner and Liversedge had decided to land at Rice Anchorage on the south bank of the river about six hundred yards inland.[29] Supervised by Capt. Clay A. Boyd, USMC, and Flight Officer J. A. Corrigan of the RAAF and the coastwatchers, native New Georgians cleared the landing beach and bivouac areas inland, and began hacking two trails from Rice Anchorage to Enogai to supplement the one track already in existence.

The organization of Liversedge's Northern Landing Group was somewhat odd; the group consisted of three battalions from three different regiments. The 3d Battalions of the 145th and 148th Infantry.Regiments of the 37th Division and the 1st Raider Battalion, 1st Marine Raider Regiment, made up the force.[30] And the force was lightly equipped. In order to permit rapid movement through the thick jungles and swamps of the area north of Munda, the troops took no artillery of any kind. Machine guns and mortars were their heaviest organic supporting weapons.

The battalions boarded the APD's, destroyers, and minesweepers at Guadalcanal on the afternoon of 4 July. The troops carried one unit of fire and rations for three days; five days' rations and one unit of fire were stowed as cargo. Escorted by Rear Adm. Walden L. Ainsworth's three light cruisers and nine destroyers, the speedy convoy started up the Slot at dusk. Shortly before midnight of a dark, rainy night, the ships rounded Visuvisu Point and entered Kula Gulf. Ainsworth bombarded Vila and then Bairoko Harbour with 6-inch and 5-inch shells, while the transport group headed for Rice Anchorage.

As the cruisers and destroyers were concluding their bombardment, the destroyer *Ralph Talbot's* radar picked up two surface targets as they were leaving the gulf. These were two of three Japanese destroyers which had brought the first echelon of four thousand Japanese Army reinforcements down from the Shortland Islands.[31] The Japanese ships had entered Kula at the same time as Ainsworth; warned by his bombardment, they were clearing out, but fired torpedoes at long range. One scored a fatal hit on the destroyer *Strong*. As two other destroyers were taking off her crew, four 140-mm. Japanese seacoast guns at Enogai opened fire, joined soon by the Bairoko batteries, but did no damage.[32]

Liversedge's landing started about 0130, just after Ainsworth's bombardment ceased. The APD's unloaded first, then destroyers, finally minesweepers. Each LCP (R) towed one ten-man rubber boat to shore. The way was marked by native canoes and shore beacons. The Japanese batteries harassed the troops but did not hit anything. There were no Japanese on the landing beach.

Nonetheless the landing was attended by troubles. A shallow bar obstructed the mouth of the Wharton River so effectively that many boats were grounded and later craft got over the bar only by coming in with lighter loads. The landing beach was too small to accommo-

---

[29] The patrols had left Segi on 14 June by boat. Turner had also considered landing the force at Roviana Lagoon and having it march overland to Bairoko but decided against it because the terrain was too rugged.

[30] Turner had originally planned to use the 4th Raider Battalion but when it was delayed at Viru Harbor the 3d Battalion, 145th, was substituted.

---

[31] See below, p. 98.

[32] Ainsworth had first wanted to bombard Enogai but did not because air reconnaissance showed no evidence of shore batteries there.

date more than four boats at once, and the river mouth was thus continually jammed with loaded boats waiting their turns at the beach. Also, about two hundred men of the 3d Battalion, 148th Infantry, were landed at Kobukobu Inlet, several hundred yards north of Rice Anchorage, a mishap which may have occurred because of the darkness of the night. Some days elapsed before the two hundred men made their way through the jungle to catch up with their battalion.

As dawn of 5 July was breaking, the volume of fire from the Enogai batteries against the ships was increasing, and it seemed unwise to risk this fire in daylight as well as to invite air attack. All but seventy-two troops and 2 percent of the cargo had been put ashore. Therefore, the convoy commander withdrew. Liversedge, with nearly all his three battalions ashore and under his control, made ready to move south.

Thus by 5 July TOENAILS was over. Throughout the complicated series of operations certain characteristics stood out. The weather had been consistently foul. The Japanese had not been able to resist effectively. The American performance, in spite of several instances of confusion, was very good, in that six landings in all had been carried out according to a complicated schedule that called for the most careful co-ordination of all forces. Clearly, Admiral Turner's reputation as an amphibious commander was well founded.

The Americans had now established themselves in New Georgia. Viru Harbor and Wickham Anchorage were secure points on the line of communications. The airfield at Segi Point was nearing completion. And at Rice Anchorage and Zanana General Hester's Munda-Bairoko Occupation Force was making ready to strike against Munda airfield.

CHAPTER VII

The Offensive Stalls

Although enemy resistance had been ineffective, and casualties in TOENAILS were relatively few, the Japanese were not finished. They planned to hold New Georgia. The New Georgia Occupation Force had had difficulties, but greater troubles were in store for it.

Japanese Plans

On 2 July, with the Americans in possession of Rendova, Segi Point, and Viru Harbor, the Japanese altered their command on New Georgia.[1] By mutual agreement Maj. Gen. Noboru Sasaki, commander of the *Southeastern Detachment,* took over direction of all Army and Navy forces in New Georgia. This action brought Rear Adm. Minoru Ota's *8th Combined Special Naval Landing Force* under Sasaki, who was under the tactical control of the *8th Fleet.* Except for small detachments on Vella Lavella, Gizo, and other islands, the 10,500 men in Sasaki's joint force were about evenly divided between Kolombangara and Munda. At Kolombangara, under Col. Satoshi Tomonari, were two battalions of the *13th Infantry,* most of the *3d Battalion, 229th Infantry,* the *Yokosuka 7th Special Naval Landing Force* (less elements), and artillery and engineer units. Guarding Munda, where Sasaki and Ota maintained their headquarters, were Col. Genjiro Hirata's *229th Infantry* (less two battalions) and artillery, engineer, communication, and medical units. The main body of the *Kure 6th Special Naval Landing Force* was concentrated at Bairoko.

Sasaki was well aware that the Americans would attack Munda. He could see the troops moving from Rendova to the mainland. Munda field was receiving shellfire from the American 155's. If further proof was needed, Japanese patrols had brushed with the Allies near Zanana on 3 July, and the next day the *229th Infantry* reported a clash with about five

---

[1] Unless otherwise indicated this chapter is based on SOPACBACOM, History of the New Georgia Campaign, Vol. I, Ch. III, OCMH; the jnls, diaries, and after action rpts of COMSOPAC, CTF 31, NGOF, XIV Corps, 43d Div, 43d Div Arty, 1st Raider Regt, 145th Inf, 148th Inf, 169th Inf, and 172d Inf; 8th Area Army Operations, Japanese Monogr No. 110 (OCMH); 17th Army Operations, Vol. II, Japanese Monogr No. 40 (OCMH); Southeast Area Naval Operations, Vol. II, Japanese Monogr No. 49 (OCMH); Outline of Southeast Area Naval Air Operations, Pt. IV, Japanese Monogr No. 108 (OCMH); Operations of the 1st Battalion, 169th Infantry (43d Infantry Division) in the New Georgia Campaign: 30 June–18 July 1943 (Northern Solomons Campaign), a monograph relating the personal experience of a battalion intelligence officer, prepared by Maj. Jack Swaim; Ltr, Lt Col Marvin D. Girardeau to Chief of Military History, sub: Comments Re Hist Monogr, Marines in Central Solomons, 6 Feb 57, with inclosures, OCMH.

MAJ. GEN. NOBORU SASAKI

hundred Americans in the same place. Immediately after the invasion of Rendova Sasaki had instructed Tomonari to alert his units for possible transfer to Munda and directed that two 140-mm. naval guns and two mountain guns be moved from the Bairoko area to Munda. After receiving the *229th*'s report he brought the *3d Battalion, 229th Infantry*, from Kolombangara through Bairoko to Munda to rejoin the regiment on 4 July.

On the same day, Sasaki proposed a counterlanding against Rendova. As their artillery pieces lacked the range to hit Rendova, the Japanese on Munda could not retaliate when shells from American 155's crashed on Munda field. Sasaki therefore suggested that the main body of the Munda garrison board landing craft, avoid recognition by mingling with American craft, and assault Rendova amid the resulting confusion. This interesting plan might have succeeded and caused a disaster to the Allies. More probably, by removing the Munda troops from their strong defense positions, it would have saved the Americans a lot of fighting. *8th Fleet Headquarters* apparently vetoed the proposal.

Also on Independence Day General Imamura and Admiral Kusaka, who wished to hold New Georgia at all costs as a key outpost for Bougainville, considered the problem of holding the island in relation to the general defense of the Southeast Area. They decided to strengthen New Georgia and to hold New Guinea with the troops already there. Imamura agreed to give four thousand more *17th Army* troops to Sasaki. These, including additional units from the *13th* and *229th Infantry Regiments* plus artillerymen, engineers, and medical men, were to be shipped in echelons from Erventa in the Shortlands to Kolombangara. Warships would transport them. It was the first echelon of these troops that Admiral Ainsworth's task force kept from landing on the night of 4–5 July.

On 5 July the Japanese naval officers' worries regarding New Georgia were increased by Hester's build-up at Zanana and Liversedge's landing at Rice Anchorage. The Japanese assigned ten destroyers to transport the second echelon, which was to be put ashore at Vila in the early morning hours of 6 July. Informed that Japanese warships were getting ready to sail from the Shortlands, Halsey ordered Ainsworth's task group to intercept, reinforced by two destroyers to replace the *Strong* and the damaged destroyer *Chevalier*. Ainsworth, retiring from the Kula Gulf, was in Indispensable Strait when Halsey's orders reached him. He reversed course and entered Kula Gulf about midnight, a few minutes behind the Japanese destroyers. In the ensuing Battle of Kula Gulf, the veteran cruiser *Helena* was sunk. The Japanese lost the destroyers *Niizuki* and *Nagatsuki,* but put 850 soldiers ashore at Vila.[2] This addition of 850 men enabled Sasaki to send part of another battalion from Kolombangara to Munda that same day.

Admiral Kusaka, who moved his headquarters from Rabaul to Buin "to alter the grave situation and raise the morale of all the forces," wanted still more troops for New Georgia.[3] On 7 July he asked Imamura for 11,000 more soldiers. The general, who had just approved sending 4,000 men to New Georgia, now stated that he doubted that even Bougainville could be made secure. Although willing to consider sending another division to Bougainville, he refused to provide 11,000 more troops for New Georgia.

It was well for the Americans that Imamura refused the 11,000 men. Blasting the existing garrisons out of Munda and Bairoko was to prove sufficiently difficult and bloody.

Operations of the Northern Landing Group

The March to Dragons Peninsula

At 0600 of 5 July, with nearly all his

Northern Landing Group ashore and in hand, Colonel Liversedge ordered his troops to move out. The 1st Marine Raider Battalion, the 3d Battalion, 148th Infantry, and K and L Companies of the 145th Infantry were to advance southward toward Dragons Peninsula, the piece of land lying between Enogai Inlet and Bairoko Harbour. (*Map 8*) Once they had reached the head of Enogai Inlet, the Raiders and K and I Companies, 145th, were to swing right to take the west shore of Enogai Inlet prior to assaulting Bairoko, while the 3d Battalion, 148th, advanced southwest to block the Munda–Bairoko trail. M, L, and Headquarters Companies of the 3d Battalion, 145th Infantry, were ordered to stay and defend Rice Anchorage under Lt. Col. George C. Freer, the battalion commander.

The preinvasion reconnaissance parties, after examining the ground between Rice Anchorage and Dragons Peninsula to determine whether an overland attack would be practicable, had reported the country generally level with sparse undergrowth. There were no swamps. Enogai Inlet, with a good anchorage, had a mangrove-covered shore line except at its head where firm ground rose steeply to an elevation of about five hundred feet. Dragons Peninsula itself was hilly, swampy, and jungled, but on the inland shore of Leland Lagoon a ridge ran from Enogai to Bairoko village. Bairoko Harbour was deep, and was backed by swamplands.

The advance to Dragons Peninsula began immediately after Liversedge issued his orders. Guided by natives, the troops moved along the three parallel trails—the original track and the two cut by

---

[2] For a full account see Morison, *Breaking the Bismarcks Barrier*, pp. 160–75.
[3] Southeast Area Naval Operations, II, Japanese Monogr No. 49 (OCMH), 32.

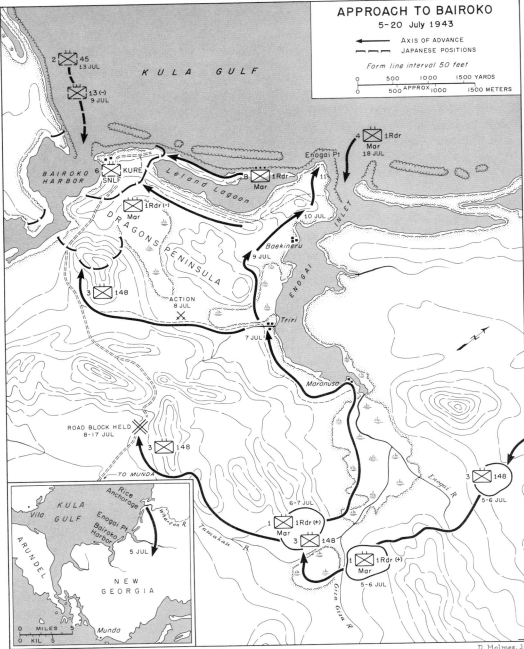

APPROACH TO BAIROKO
5-20 July 1943

◄───── AXIS OF ADVANCE
▭ ▭ ▭ JAPANESE POSITIONS

Form line interval 50 feet

0   500   1000   1500 YARDS
0   500 APPROX 1000   1500 METERS

KULA GULF

2 ⊠ 45
13 JUL

⊠ 13 (-)
9 JUL

BAIROKO
HARBOR

6 ⊠ KURE
SNLF

Leland Lagoon

DRAGONS PENINSULA

3 ⊠ 148

ACTION
8 JUL

⊠ 1Rdr (-)
Mar

B ⊠ 1Rdr
Mar

Enogai Pt

4 ⊠ 1Rdr
Mar
18 JUL

11

10 JUL

ENOGAI INLET

Baekineru

9 JUL

Triri

7 JUL

ENOGAI R

Maranusa

ROAD BLOCK HELD
8-17 JUL

3 ⊠ 148

─ TO MUNDA ─

Enogai R

3 ⊙ 148
5-6 JUL

6-7 JUL

1 ⊠ 1Rdr (+)
Mar

3 ⊠ 148

1 ⊙ 1Rdr (+)
Mar
5-6 JUL

Tamakau R.

Giza Giza R.

Rice
Anchorage

Wharton R.

5 JUL

KULA GULF

Vila

Enogai Pt
Bairoko
Harbor

ARUNDEL

NEW
GEORGIA

Munda

0 MILES 5
0 KIL 5

D. Holmes, Jr.

MAP 8

Corrigan's natives. The 1st Marine Raider Battalion, Lt. Col. Samuel B. Griffith, III, commanding, led the way, followed in order by K and L Companies, 145th, under Maj. Marvin D. Girardeau, and Lt. Col. Delbert E. Schultz's 3d Battalion, 148th Infantry. The patrols' reports had implied that the going would be easy, but the march proved difficult. The rough trails, winding over hills and ridges, were obstructed by branches, roots, and coral outcroppings. Rain wet the troops all day. The Raiders, whose heaviest weapon was the 60-mm. mortar, made fairly steady progress, but the soldiers of M Company, 148th Infantry, fell behind as they floundered through the mud with their heavy machine guns, 81-mm. mortars, and ammunition.

At 1300 part of D Company of the Raiders, the advance guard, was sent on ahead to secure a bridgehead on the far bank of the Giza Giza river.[4] Three hours later the Raiders' main body and the companies of the 145th Infantry arrived at the river and bivouacked there overnight. They had covered five and one-half miles in the day's march without meeting a single Japanese. Colonel Schultz's battalion camped for the night about one and one-half miles to the north.

Next morning, 6 July, the Raiders led out again, and D Company pushed ahead to secure a crossing over the Tamakau River. The rains had flooded the river; it was now nine feet deep. Without tools or time to build a proper bridge, the Raiders threw a log over the stream, and improvised rafts from poles and ponchos

to ferry over their heavy equipment. After several rafts had capsized, they gave up and carried everything over on the log. Several men slipped off the log and fell into the swollen river; a few had to be rescued from drowning. The crossing had started before noon, but not until dusk did the last man cross the river. Schultz's battalion, also delayed by high water, caught up with the Raiders and bivouacked near them for the night.

On the morning of 7 July the Raiders and Girardeau's companies set out for Enogai, while Schultz's battalion pushed south toward the Munda–Bairoko trail. The country was rough, the going hard for both forces. The Raiders took five hours to cover the 2,500 yards between their bivouac and the east end of Enogai Inlet.

The 3d Battalion, 148th, reached the trail at 1700. In the afternoon the two hundred men who had been landed astray on 5 July caught up with the main body. There had been no opposition from the Japanese; a patrol was observed but kept its distance.

Capture of Enogai Inlet

When the Marine Raiders and Girardeau's two companies reached Enogai Inlet, one platoon, again from D Company, pushed forward to secure the deserted village called Maranusa. From there a patrol marched toward Triri, another village which was hardly more than a clearing. Up to now the marines had not seen any Japanese, but as the patrol approached Triri its point detected five Japanese ahead. The marines ambushed the party and killed two of its members. They belonged to the *Kure 6th Special Naval Landing Force.* The

---

[4] At this time the lettered companies of the 1st Raider Battalion were all rifle companies; there was no heavy weapons company.

other three fled. When Liversedge heard about this action, which made it obvious that his force had been discovered, he ordered Griffith to secure Triri at once in order to prepare to repel a counterattack. Griffith dispatched the demolition platoon from battalion Headquarters Company with orders to pass through D Company and seize Triri. On the way up, the platoon ran into a strong enemy patrol which opened fire. The marines retired to a defensive position on the bank of a stream and kept the enemy in place with fire. At this point D Company appeared on the scene, swung to the left, struck the Japanese on their inland (right) flank, and drove them off. Three marines and ten Japanese were killed in this skirmish. One of the dead Japanese had on his person a defense plan which showed the exact location of the heavy guns at Enogai. By 1600 all elements of the Enogai attacking force were installed at Triri.

At dawn the following morning—8 July, the day on which Schultz's battalion completed its block on the Munda–Bairoko trail—two Raider combat patrols went out of Triri. B Company sent one out to ambush a trail which led northwesterly to Enogai, and a D Company patrol advanced south along a cross-country track leading to Bairoko to lay another ambush. This patrol had advanced a short distance by 0700, when it ran into an enemy force of about company strength. A fire fight broke out, and at 1000 Griffith sent C Company to drive the enemy back a short distance.

In the meantime, the patrol which had advanced toward Enogai reported no contact with the enemy. In order to assemble all companies of the 1st Raider Battalion for the attack against Enogai, Griffith sent K and L Companies of the 145th south to take over from C Company. C Company then disengaged, moved back to Triri, and in the early afternoon the 1st Raider Battalion marched northwest toward Enogai. But the trail led the marines into an impassable mangrove swamp. The battalion therefore retired to Triri, while scouts hunted for a better route to use the next day.

In the south sector, the fight between the Japanese and K and L Companies had continued. The Japanese in repeated assaults struck hard at K Company which was on the right (west). Capt. Donald W. Fouse, commanding K Company, was wounded early in the action but stayed with his company until the fight was over. When the Raider battalion retired to Triri, the Demolition Platoon was committed to the line, and when K Company was hard hit a platoon from B Company of the Raiders swung wide around the Japanese left flank and struck them in the rear. This maneuver succeeded. The enemy scattered.[5]

The 1st Raider Battalion resumed its advance against Enogai the next morning, using a good trail, apparently unknown to the Japanese, that led over high ground west of the swamp. K and L Companies remained to hold Triri, the site of Liversedge's command post. Griffith's battalion, meeting no opposition, made good time. By 1100 the marines were in sight of Leland Lagoon. They swung slightly to the right toward

---

[5] K Company reported killing a hundred Japanese; the marine platoon is reported to have killed twenty.

Enogai Point and at 1500 ran into two Japanese light machine guns which opened fire and halted the advance. Griffith deployed, with A Company on the left, C in the center, B on the right, and D in reserve. The companies then assaulted, but the Japanese defended so resolutely that no further progress was made that day.

Patrols reconnoitered vigorously so that by 0700, 10 July, Griffith had been informed that the Japanese were strongest in front of his center and left, and that there were no Japanese directly in front of B Company. The battalion resumed the attack at 0700. C and A Companies advanced slowly against rifle and machine gun fire. Supported by 60-mm. mortars, B Company drove forward rapidly, cleared the village of Baekineru, and captured two machine guns. Then A Company, strengthened by one platoon from battalion reserve, pushed over Enogai Point to the sea. By 1500 all organized resistance had ended except for a pocket in front of A Company. When D Company started establishing beach defenses, it was troubled by three machine guns from another enemy pocket. Mopping up these two groups of Japanese took until 11 July.

The Raiders had run out of food and water by midafternoon of 10 July, but were succored by L Company, 145th, which brought rations and water up from Triri. These had been dropped, at Liversedge's urgent request, by C–47's from Guadalcanal.

By 12 July Enogai was organized for defense against land or seaborne attacks. Estimates of Japanese casualties ranged from 150 to 350. Postwar Japanese accounts assert that Enogai was defended by one platoon of soldiers and 81 men of the *Kure 6th Special Naval Landing Force*. The marines lost 47 killed, 4 missing, and 74 wounded. They captured 3 .50-caliber antiaircraft machine guns, 4 heavy and 14 light machine guns, a searchlight, rifles, mortars, ammunition, 2 tractors, some stores and documents, and the 4 140-mm. coastal guns that had harassed the landing at Rice Anchorage. The guns were intact except that their breechblocks had been removed. Luckily, a marine digging a foxhole uncovered one, and a hasty search of the area turned up the other three. The marines used these guns to help guard the seaward approaches to the newly won position.[6]

Roadblock North of Munda

While the Raiders were thus engaged, the soldiers of the 3d Battalion, 148th Infantry, were deep in the jungle holding their block. The block, completed on 8 July, was set up on a well-used trail some two miles southeast of Enogai Inlet and eight miles north of Munda. I Company, with one M Company platoon attached, faced toward Bairoko; K Company faced Munda. L Company covered the flanks of I and K, and extended its lines back to protect the battalion command post. M Company, with the Antitank Platoon attached, was in a supporting position to the rear. Each rifle company held one platoon in reserve under battalion control. All positions were camouflaged. Colonel Schultz ordered his men to fire at enemy groups larger than four men; smaller parties were to be killed with bayonets.

---

[6] Sasaki apparently had ordered two of these guns to Munda.

The battalion held the block from 8 through 17 July. Patrols went out regularly. General Hester had ordered patrols to push far enough to the south to make contact with the 43d Division's right flank as it advanced westward against Munda, but this was never done.

Schultz was strengthened on 11 July by the addition of I Company, 145th Infantry, after a group of Japanese had overrun part of L Company's positions in a series of attacks starting 10 July. Except for this, the Japanese made no effort to dislodge Schultz's men, whose greatest enemy proved to be hunger. The troops had left Rice Anchorage carrying rations for three days on the assumption that Enogai Inlet would be taken in two days and that American vessels could then land stores there. These could be delivered to the troops after a relatively short overland haul. But Enogai was not secured until 11 July. The 120 native carriers thus had to carry food all the way from Rice Anchorage. Although, according to Colonel Liversedge, the natives "accomplished an almost superhuman task," they could not carry supplies fast enough to keep the troops fed.[7]

By 9 July the food shortage was serious. Only 2,200 D rations had been delivered. Late that evening, with food for the next day reduced to one ninth of a D and one ninth of a K ration per man, Schultz radioed to Liversedge an urgent request that food be brought in by carrier. He also hoped the natives could carry out two badly wounded men who were being cared for in the battalion aid station. But as there were not enough natives, C–47's dropped food, as well as ammunition, to the battalion the next afternoon. Much of the food fell far beyond the 3d Battalion's lines, and some of the ammunition was defective. Schultz was forced to cut the food allowance for the next twenty-four hours to one twelfth of a K ration. Fortunately Enogai had now fallen, and on 13 July Flight Officer Corrigan's natives carried in three hundred pounds of rice which the men cooked in their helmets, using salt tablets for seasoning. The next day, though, was another hungry one; one D and one K ration was the allowance for each eighteen men. Thereafter, until the block was abandoned, carrying parties and air drops kept food stocks high enough.

During the nine days it held the block, the 3d Battalion lost 11 men killed and 29 wounded; it estimated it had killed 250 Japanese.

At the time it was believed that the blockers had cut off Munda from reinforcement via Bairoko, and that they held the Japanese Bairoko force in place, prevented Enogai from being reinforced from either Munda or Bairoko, and protected Griffith's right flank and rear.[8] Knowledge gained after the event indicates that none of these beliefs was warranted.

That Munda was not isolated is demonstrated by the fact that the Japanese reinforcement of Munda was in full swing, and all the reinforcements seem to have reached Munda without much trouble. The enemy obviously stopped using the blocked trail after 8 July and shifted to another one farther west.

Meanwhile, reinforcement by water

---

[7] 1st Mar Raider Regt [NLG], Combat Rpt and War Diary, 4 Jul–29 Aug 43 entries.

[8] NGOF, Report of Operations on New Georgia; 1st Mar Raider Regt, Special Action Rpt, New Georgia, 6 Oct 43.

continued. On 9 July, when 1,200 Japanese from the Shortlands landed on Kolombangara, 1,300 of the *13th Infantry* transferred by barge to Bairoko. Three days later, on 12 July, a Japanese ten-ship force left Rabaul to carry 1,200 more soldiers to Kolombangara, and Halsey sent Ainsworth's task force to intercept again. The two forces collided early on 13 July northeast of Kolombangara in a battle named for that island. The Allies lost the destroyer *Gwin;* the New Zealand light cruiser *Leander* and the American light cruisers *St. Louis* and *Honolulu* suffered damage. The Japanese flagship, the light cruiser *Jintsu,* was sunk, but 1,200 enemy soldiers were landed on the west coast of Kolombangara.[9]

At Bairoko, during this period, the *13th Infantry* made ready to go to Munda. It was part of this regiment which attacked the trail block on 10 July.[10] On 13 July, when the Bairoko garrison was strengthened by the *2d Battalion, 45th Infantry,* and a battery of artillery, the *13th Infantry* marched south to the Munda front.

As far as pinning down the Bairoko troops was concerned, the block lay more than two miles from Bairoko, and thus could not have affected the Bairoko garrison very much. And surely, had the Japanese desired to reinforce Enogai from Bairoko, they would have used the direct trail along the shore of Leland Lagoon rather than going over the more roundabout route which was blocked.

In view of the American strength at Rendova and Zanana, the thesis that the Japanese might have sent troops from Munda to Enogai is equally untenable, even if it were not known that the Japanese were reinforcing Munda, not Enogai. Finally, Schultz's battalion was too far from Griffith's to render much flank protection in that dense, dark jungle.[11] It is clear that the trail block failed to achieve results proportionate to the effort expended. So far, the principal effect of the entire Rice Anchorage–Enogai–Bairoko operation had been to employ troops that could have been better used at Munda.

By 11 July, with Enogai secured, Liversedge was five days behind schedule. Casualties, illness, and physical exhaustion had reduced the 1st Raider Battalion to one-half its effective strength. Considering that two fresh battalions could reduce Bairoko in three days, he asked Admiral Turner, with Hester's approval, for additional troops. There were not two more battalions to be had, Turner replied, but he promised to land the 4th Raider Battalion at Enogai by 18 July, and authorized a delay in the assault against Bairoko until then. Thus short one battalion, Liversedge directed Schultz to abandon his block and march to Triri on 17 July. The 3d Battalion, 148th, was to join the Raiders and part of the 3d Battalion, 145th, in the Bairoko attack.

The Northern Landing Group had accomplished the first phase of its mission by capturing Enogai, but was behind schedule. On the Munda front, General

---

[9] For a full account of the battle see Morison, *Breaking the Bismarcks Barrier,* pp. 180–91.

[10] An enemy account claims that the Americans were "annihilated." See 17th Army Operations, Vol. II, Japanese Monogr No. 40 (OCMH).

[11] On 10 July General Hester explicitly directed Colonel Liversedge to keep his battalions within supporting distance of one another.

Wing's Southern Landing Group was also behind schedule.

Operations of the Southern Landing Group

From Zanana to the Barike River

Once the 169th and 172d Regiments had landed at Zanana, General Hester had originally planned, the two regiments were to march overland about two and one-half to three miles to a line of departure lying generally along the Barike River, then deploy and attack west to capture Munda airfield. (Map 9) The regiments were directed to reach the line of departure and attack by 7 July, but by the time the two regiments had reached Zanana all operations were postponed one day.

The overland approach to Munda involved a march through the rough, jungled, swampy ground typical of New Georgia. The terrain between Zanana and Munda was rugged, tangled, and patternless. Rocky hills thrust upward from two to three hundred feet above sea level, with valleys, draws, and stream beds in between. The hills and ridges sprawled and bent in all directions. The map used for the operation was a photomap based on air photography. It showed the coast line and Munda airfield clearly, but did not give any accurate indication of ground contour. About all the troops could tell by looking at it was that the ground was covered by jungle.

The difficulty of travel in this rough country was greatly increased by heat, mud, undergrowth, and hills. Visibility was limited to a few yards. There were no roads, but a short distance north of Zanana lay Munda Trail, a narrow foot track that hit the coast at Lambeti Plan-

tation. Engineers were making ready to build a road from Zanana to Munda Trail, and to improve the latter so that it could carry motor traffic.

Having made their way from Zanana to the line of departure on the Barike, the two regiments would, according to Hester's orders, deliver a co-ordinated attack against Munda airfield, which lay about two and one-half miles westward. The 172d Infantry on the left (south) would be responsible for a front extending inland from the coast. The 169th Infantry's zone of action lay north of the 172d's; its right flank would be in the air except for protection given it by South Pacific Scout patrols operating to the north. The attack would be supported by General Barker's artillery and by air and naval bombardments.

Two days after the beginning of the two-regiment attack, a heavy naval bombardment would prepare the way for an assault landing by the 3d Battalion, 103d Infantry, and the 9th Marine Defense Battalion's Tank Platoon at 0420, 9 July, at the west tip of Munda Point.

Hester and Wing did not expect to meet any serious opposition between Zanana and the Barike River, and their expectations must have been confirmed by the experience of the 1st Battalion, 172d. On 3 July Colonel Ross had ordered this battalion to remain at Zanana, making every effort at concealment. The message was apparently not received, for on 4 July the battalion, accompanied by A Company, 169th Infantry, easily marched to the Barike River, meeting only small Japanese patrols on the way. It was this premature move that helped to alert Sasaki.

Next morning Captain Sherrer of the

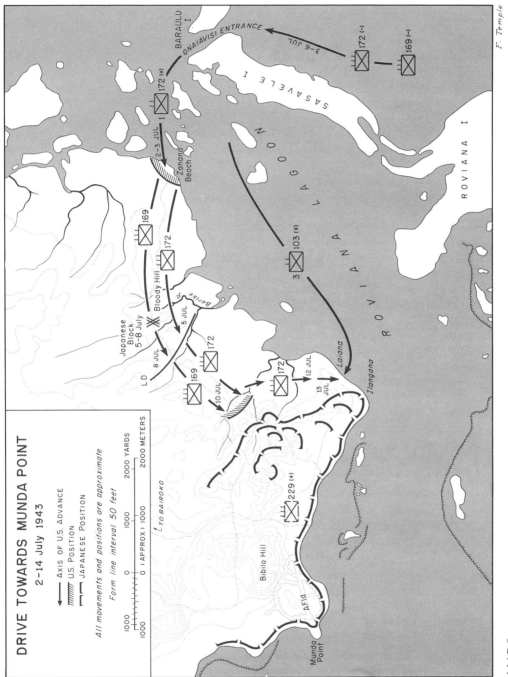

DRIVE TOWARDS MUNDA POINT

2–14 July 1943

Axis of U.S. Advance
U.S. Position
Japanese Position

All movements and positions are approximate

Form line interval 50 feet

1000   0 (APPROX) 1000   2000 YARDS
1000   0   1000   2000 METERS

BARAULU I

ONAIAVISI ENTRANCE

3–6 JUL

172 (-)

169 (-)

SASAVELE I

172 (+)

2–3 JUL

Zanana Beach

169

172

Bloody Hill

Barike R.

5 JUL

Japanese Block 5–8 July

8 JUL

LD

169

10 JUL

172

172

12 JUL

13 JUL

Laiana

Ilangana

103 (+)

ROVIANA LAGOON

ROVIANA I

L. TO BAIROKO

229 (+)

Bibilo Hill

Afid

Munda Point

F. Temple

MAP 9

G–2 Section led a patrol of six New Zealanders, twelve Americans, and eighteen Fijians from his base camp toward the upper reaches of the Barike River. They intended to set up a patrol base on high ground suitable for good radio transmission and reception. Normally they would have avoided detection by moving off the trails and striking out through the wilderness, but, laden with radio gear, they followed Munda Trail. As they approached a small rise that lay about two miles from Zanana, and about eleven hundred yards east of the line of departure, they met enemy machine gun fire. They replied with small arms, and the fire fight lasted until dusk when Sherrer's group disengaged and went south to the bivouac of the 1st Battalion, 172d, near the mouth of the Barike. B Company, 172d, went out to investigate the situation the next morning and found the Japanese still occupying the high ground, astride the trail. Attacks by B Company and by A Company, 169th, failed to dislodge the Japanese. By afternoon of 6 July, however, the three battalions of the 172d Infantry were safely in place on the Barike, the 1st and 3d on the left and right, the 2d in regimental reserve.

But the 169th Infantry, commanded by Col. John D. Eason, was not so fortunate. That regiment's 3d Battalion, under Lt. Col. William A. Stebbins, set out along the trail from Zanana to the line of departure on the morning of 6 July. Natives guided the battalion as it moved in column of companies, each company in column of platoons, along the narrow trail. The men hacked vines and undergrowth to make their way more easily. Shortly after noon, General

Wing ordered Stebbins' battalion to destroy the point of Japanese resistance that Sherrer had run into.

It was estimated, correctly, that about one platoon was trying to block the trail. General Sasaki, aware of the Allied activity east of him, had ordered part of the *11th Company, 229th Infantry*, to reconnoiter the Barike area, clear fire lanes, and establish this trail block with felled trees and barbed wire.

The 3d Battalion, 169th, apparently did not run into the block on 6 July. It dug in for the night somewhere east of the block, but does not seem to have established the sort of perimeter defense that was necessary in fighting the Japanese in the jungle. Foxholes were more than six feet apart. The battalion laid no barbed wire or trip wire with hanging tin cans that rattled when struck by a man's foot or leg and warned of the approach of the enemy. Thus, when darkness fell and the Japanese began their night harassing tactics—moving around, shouting, and occasionally firing—the imaginations of the tired and inexperienced American soldiers began to work. They thought the Japanese were all around them, infiltrating their perimeter with ease. One soldier reported that Japanese troops approached I Company, calling, in English, the code names of the companies of the 3d Battalion, such stereotypes as "come out and fight," and references to the Louisiana maneuvers.[12]

The men of the battalion, which had landed in the Russells the previous March, must have been familiar with the sights and sounds of a jungle night, but affected by weariness and the presence of the enemy, they apparently forgot. In

---

[12] 169th Inf Hist, 20 Jun–30 Sep 43, p. 5.

their minds, the phosphorescence of rotten logs became Japanese signals. The smell of the jungle became poison gas; some men reported that the Japanese were using a gas which when inhaled caused men to jump up in their foxholes. The slithering of the many land crabs was interpreted as the sound of approaching Japanese. Men of the 169th are reported to have told each other that Japanese nocturnal raiders wore long black robes, and that some came with hooks and ropes to drag Americans from their foxholes. In consequence the men of the battalion spent their nights nervously and sleeplessly, and apparently violated orders by shooting indiscriminately at imaginary targets.

Next day, the shaken 3d Battalion advanced with I Company leading followed by L, M, Battalion Headquarters, and K Companies. It ran into machine gun fire from the Japanese trail block at 1055. I Company deployed astride Munda Trail, L Company maneuvered to the left, K was initially in reserve. M Company brought up its 81-mm. mortars and heavy machine guns but could not use them profitably at first as banyan trees and undergrowth blocked shells and bullets. The mortar platoon then began clearing fields of fire by cutting down trees. B Company of the 172d also attacked the block from the south.

I Company launched a series of frontal assaults but was beaten back by machine gun fire. Three platoon leaders were wounded in these attacks. K Company came out of reserve to deliver a frontal assault; its commander was soon killed. Neither it nor any of the other companies made progress. The Japanese were well dug in and camouflaged. Riflemen

covered the automatic weapons. Fire lanes had been cut. The enemy weapons had little if any muzzle blast, and the Americans had trouble seeing targets. Some tried to grenade the enemy but were driven back before they could get close enough to throw accurately. At length the 81-mm. mortars got into action; observers operating thirty yards from the Japanese position brought down fire on it. Some Japanese are reported to have evacuated "Bloody Hill," as the Americans called it, that afternoon. At 1550 the 3d Battalion withdrew to dig in for the night.[13] After dark the Japanese harassed the 3d Battalion again. According to the 169th Infantry, "a sleepless night was spent by all under continued harassing from enemy patrols speaking English, making horror noises, firing weapons, throwing hand grenades, swinging machetes and jumping into foxholes with knives."[14]

On 8 July, the 1st Battalion, 169th Infantry, which had been behind the 3d within supporting distance, was ordered to bypass the 3d and move to the Barike while the 3d Battalion reduced the block. On 7 July General Wing had ordered Colonel Ross to use part of the 172d against the block, but apparently by the afternoon of 8 July no elements of the 172d except B Company had gone into action against it. On 8 July the 3d Battalion, 169th, and B Company, 172d, struck the block after a mortar preparation and overran it. The 3d Battalion

---

[13] The 169th Infantry History (p. 4) claims that the block was destroyed on 7 July, and that a day was lost when the 1st Battalion, 169th, moved ahead of the 3d on 8 July. But messages in the 43d Division G–3 Journal indicate that the block was still active on 8 July.

[14] 169th Inf Hist, p. 4.

lost six men killed and thirty wounded, and suffered one case diagnosed as war neurosis, in reducing the block. The trail from Zanana to the Barike was open again, but the attack against Munda had been delayed by another full day.

By late afternoon of 8 July, the 1st Battalion, 169th, had reached the Barike River and made contact on its left with the 3d Battalion, 172d; A Company, 169th, had been returned to its parent regiment; the 3d Battalion, 169th, was behind and to the right of the 1st Battalion. With the two regiments on the line of departure, Hester and Wing were ready to start the attack toward Munda early on 9 July. Hester told Wing: "I wish you success." [15]

The Approach to the Main Defenses

By 7 July General Hester, after conferences with General Wing and Colonels Ross and Eason, had abandoned the idea of the amphibious assault against Munda by the 3d Battalion, 103d Infantry, and the 9th Marine Defense Battalion's tank platoon. He was probably influenced in his decision by the strength of the Munda shore defenses. The plan for the attack on 9 July called for the 169th and 172d Regiments to advance from the Barike, seize the high ground southwest of the river, and capture the airfield. On the high ground—a complex of ridges that ran from Ilangana on the beach inland in a northwesterly direction for about three thousand yards—were the main Japanese defenses. The 172d Infantry was to move out astride the Munda Trail with the 1st and 3d Battalions abreast. Each bat-

talion zone would be three hundred yards wide. Battalions would advance in column of companies; each rifle company would put two platoons in line. The 169th Infantry, maintaining contact on its left with the 3d Battalion, 172d, would advance echeloned to the right rear to protect the divisional right flank. The 1st Battalion was to advance abreast of the 172d; the 3d Battalion would move to the right and rear of the 1st.

The regimental commanders planned to advance by 200-yard bounds. After each bound, they intended to halt for five minutes, establish contact, and move out again. They hoped to gain from one to two thousand yards before 1600.

The division reserve consisted of the 2d Battalion, 169th, which was to advance behind the assault units. Antitank companies from the two regiments, plus Marine antiaircraft artillerymen, were defending the Zanana beachhead. In Occupation Force reserve, under Hester, was the 3d Battalion, 103d Infantry, on Rendova. H Hour for the attack was set for 0630.

General Barker's artillery on the offshore islands inaugurated the first major attack against Munda at 0500 of 9 July with a preparation directed against rear areas, lines of communication, and suspected bivouac areas and command posts. After thirty minutes, fire was shifted to suspected centers of resistance near the line of departure. In one hour the 105-mm. howitzers of the 103d and 169th Field Artillery Battalions, the 155-mm. howitzers of the 136th Field Artillery Battalion, and the 155-mm. guns of the 9th Marine Defense Battalion fired over 5,800 rounds of high explosive. Starting at 0512, four destroy-

---

[15] 43d Div G–3 Jnl, 8 Jul 43.

Troops of the 172d Infantry Wading Across a Creek *on the Munda Trail.*

ers from Admiral Merrill's task force, standing offshore in the Solomon Sea, opened fire at the area in the immediate vicinity of the airfield in accordance with plans prepared in consultation with General Barker. Naval authorities had originally wanted to fire at targets close to the line of departure as well, but the 43d Division, fearing that the direction of fire (northeast to east) might bring shells down on its own troops, rejected the proposal.[16] Between 0512 and 0608, the destroyers fired 2,344 5-inch rounds. At 0608, four minutes before the bombardment was scheduled to end, some Japanese planes dropped bombs and strafed one ship; the destroyers retired.

Then Allied planes from Guadalcanal and the Russells took over. Fifty-two torpedo bombers and thirty-six dive bombers dropped seventy tons of high explosive bombs and fragmentation clusters on Munda. Now it was the infantry's turn.

H Hour, 0630, came and went, but not a great deal happened. The 1st Battalion, 169th Infantry, reported that it was ready to move but could not understand why the 172d Infantry had not advanced. At 0930, General Wing was informed that no unit had yet crossed the line of departure. Several factors seem to have caused the delay. Movement as usual was an ordeal. The Barike was flooded. Soldiers, weighted with weapons, ammunition, and packs, had to wade through waist-to-shoulder-deep water.

---

[16] Merrill thought the 43d Division was generally too cautious. See Morison, *Breaking the Bismarcks Barrier*, p. 179.

The river, which had several tributaries, wound and twisted to the sea. It crossed the Munda Trail three times; the spaces between were swampy. The men, sweating in the humid heat, struggled to keep their footing, and pulled their way along by grabbing at roots and undergrowth. Leading platoons had to cut the wrist-thick rattan vines.

Although patrols of New Georgians, Fijians, Tongans, New Zealanders, and Americans had reconnoitered the area, their information could not always be put to good use. There was no accurate map on which to record data, nor were there any known landmarks.

In the jungle, orthodox skirmish lines proved impractical. As men dispersed they could not be seen and their leaders lost control. At any rate, movement off the trails was so difficult that most units moved in columns of files, the whole unit bound to one trail. Thus one or two Japanese, by firing on the leading elements, could halt an entire battalion.

The Occupation Force intelligence officer had estimated that the main Japanese defenses lay 1,600 yards from the Barike, anchored on Roviana Lagoon and extending inland to the northwest. This was correct, except that the defense line on the ridges was actually about 2,500 yards from the Barike's mouth. Beyond the main defenses, the Japanese outposts, using rifles, machine guns, and sometimes mortars and grenade dischargers, were well able to delay the advance.

At 1030 General Barker returned to the 43d Division command post from a tour of the front and reported that at 1000 the 172d Infantry was a hundred yards beyond the Barike, but that the 169th was still east of the river. The only opposition had come from the outpost riflemen that the Americans usually called "snipers." At the time these were believed, probably erroneously, to be operating in the treetops.[17]

Japanese fighter aircraft appeared over New Georgia during the day; the Allied air power prevented any from getting close enough to strafe the attacking troops.

By 1630, when it dug in for the night, the 172d had gained some eleven hundred yards.[18] The 169th had made no progress to speak of. The 1st Battalion got one hundred yards west of the Barike; the other two apparently remained east of the river.

The 169th was facing about the same obstacles as the 172d, but it is possible that the 169th was a badly shaken regiment before the attack began.[19] The night before the attack, 8–9 July, the 3d Battalion was bivouacked near Bloody Hill, and the other two lay to the west. When the Japanese made their presence known to the three battalions, or when the Americans thought there were Japanese within their bivouacs, there was a great deal of confusion, shooting, and

---

[17] Whereas the Japanese, like the Allies, used trees whenever possible for observation posts, it is doubtful that "snipers" used many trees in the jungle. See Miller, *Guadalcanal: The First Offensive*, p. 318. Anyone who has ever climbed a tree in the jungle can testify to the difficulties a man with a rifle would encounter—lack of visibility, tree limbs in the way, and the innumerable little red ants whose bite is like the prick of needles.

[18] From 1100, 8 July, to 1300, 9 July, this regiment was commanded by Lt. Col. Charles W. Capron. Colonel Ross, wounded on 30 June, had apparently been ordered to Rendova for medical treatment.

[19] The 172d was either not subjected to night harassing or was not sufficiently bothered by it to report it.

EVACUATING CASUALTIES, 12 JULY 1943. *Jeep, converted into an ambulance, could carry three litters and one sitting patient.*

stabbing. Some men knifed each other. Men threw grenades blindly in the dark. Some of the grenades hit trees, bounced back, and exploded among the Americans. Some soldiers fired round after round to little avail. In the morning no trace remained of Japanese dead or wounded. But there were American casualties; some had been stabbed to death, some wounded by knives. Many suffered grenade fragment wounds, and 50 percent of these were caused by fragments from American grenades. These were the men who had been harassed by Japanese nocturnal tactics on the two preceding nights, and there now appeared the first large number of cases diagnosed as neuroses. The regiment was to suffer seven hundred by 31 July.

The 43d Division resumed the attack on 10 July. The 172d Infantry, reporting only light opposition, advanced a considerable distance. The 169th Infantry, with the 1st Battalion in the lead and the 2d Battalion to its right rear, advanced successfully until it reached the point where the Munda Trail was intersected by a trail which ran southeast to the beach, then circled to the southwest to the native villages of Laiana and Ilangana. Reaching this junction about 1330 after crossing a small creek on two felled tree trunks, the leading battalion was halted by machine gun fire. This fire came from rising ground dominating the trail junction, where Capt. Bunzo Kojima, commanding the *9th Company, 229th Infantry,* had established a camouflaged trail block. He employed one rifle platoon, reinforced by a machine gun section, some 90-mm. mortars, and elements of a 75-mm. mountain artillery battalion. When the 1st Battalion was stopped, Colonel Eason decided to blast the strong point. While the infantry pulled back a hundred yards, the 169th's mortars and the Occupation Force artillery opened fire. Barker's guns fired over four thousand rounds of 105-mm. and 155-mm. high explosive, shattering trees, stripping the vegetation, and digging craters.[20] Coincident with this bombardment, eighty-six Allied bombers (SBD's and TBF's) unloaded sixty-seven tons of bombs on Lambeti Plantation and Munda. During the artillery bombardment Kojima's men lay quiet but when the fire ceased they immediately stood to their guns and halted the American infantrymen when they attacked. At the day's end, the Japanese were still on the high ground; the 169th Infantry, after advancing about fifteen hundred yards, was forced to bivouac in a low swampy area. The American commanders concluded that they were nearing a main defensive line. They were right. The high ground to their front contained the main Japanese defenses that were to resist them for weeks.

Laiana Beachhead

By 11 July the advancing regiments were still in trouble. Progress had been slowed by the enemy, and also by the supply problems arising from the fact that the troops had landed five miles east of their objective and thus committed themselves to a long march through heavy jungle. Now the regiments, in spite of their slow advance, had outdistanced their overextended supply line.

The 118th Engineer Battalion had made good progress in building a jeep trail from Zanana to the Barike River. Using data obtained from native scouts, the engineers had built their trail over high, dry ground, averaging one half to three quarters of a mile per day. There was little need for corduroying with logs, a time-consuming process. When they ran into trees too big to knock down with their light D–3 bulldozers, the engineers blasted them with dynamite. Lacking heavy road-graders, the 118th could not make a two-lane, amply ditched road, but it managed to clear a one-lane track widened at regular intervals to permit two-way traffic. Near a five-foot-deep, fast-running stream east of the Barike the engineers hit soft mud. To get to ground firm enough to permit construction of footbridges and two thirty-foot trestle bridges, they were forced to swing the road northward parallel to the river for two and one-half miles to get to a firm crossing. The advancing regiments crossed the Barike on 9 July, but several days were to elapse before the bridges were completed.

Thus there was a gap between the end of the road and the front. To bridge the gap, nearly half the combat troops were required to carry forward ammunition, food, water, and other supplies, and to evacuate casualties. Allied cargo planes

---

[20] One fortunate concomitant of artillery fire was better visibility as the heavy shellings tore the jungle apart.

were used to parachute supplies to the infantry, but there were never enough planes to keep the troops properly supplied.

With fighting strength reduced by the necessity for hand carry, with his right flank virtually exposed, and his extended supply line open to harassment by the enemy, Hester decided, on 10 July, to change his plan of attack in order to shorten the supply line. If a new beachhead could be established at Laiana (a native village about two miles east by south from Munda airfield), some five thousand yards would be cut off the supply line. Patrols, operating overland and in canoes, examined Laiana beach at night and reported that it was narrow but suitable, with a coral base under the sand. Unfavorable aspects included a mangrove swamp back of the beach and the fact that the Japanese main defenses appeared to start at Ilangana, only five hundred yards southwest of Laiana, and arch northwest toward the Munda Trail.

But the advantages outweighed the disadvantages. Hester ordered the 172d Infantry to swing southward to Laiana, seize and hold a beachhead from the land side, then advance on Munda. The 169th Infantry was to continue its attempt to drive along the Munda Trail. Hester ordered the reinforced 3d Battalion, 103d Infantry, at Rendova, to be prepared to land at Laiana after the 172d had arrived.

At 1000, 11 July, the 172d Infantry disengaged from the attack, turned south, and started moving toward shore through knee-deep mud. The regiment tried to keep its move a secret, but Japanese patrols quickly observed it, and

JEEP TRAIL FROM ZANANA, *built through heavy jungle by 118th Engineer Battalion, 13 July 1943.*

mortar fire soon began hitting it. The wounded were carried along with the regiment. The advance was halted about midafternoon after a gain of some 450 yards. Both 1st and 3d Battalions (the 2d had remained behind to block the trail and thus cover the rear until the 169th could come up) reported running into pillboxes. Aside from the mortar shelling and some infiltration by patrols between the 172d and the 169th, the Japanese appeared to have stayed fairly still.

The march was resumed on 12 July with the hope of reaching Laiana before dark, for the regiment had not re-

INFANTRYMEN LOADING ON LCP (R)'s *for the trip to Laiana, New Georgia, 14 July 1943. Men are from the 3d Battalion of the 103d Infantry, 43d Division.*

ceived any supplies for two days. Colonel Ross reported that the carrying parties equaled the strength of three and one-half rifle companies. Despite this fact, and although food and water were exhausted, the regiment kept moving until late afternoon when leading elements were within five hundred yards of Laiana. There machine gun and mortar fire halted the advance. At this time scouts confirmed the existence of pillboxes, connected by trenches, extending northwest from Ilangana. The pillboxes, which the Americans feared might be made of concrete, housed heavy machine guns, and were supported by light machine guns and mortars.

That night (12–13 July) Japanese mortars registered on the 172d's bivouac, and the troops could hear the Japanese felling trees, presumably to clear fields of fire.

His hungry, thirsty regiment was without a line of communications, and Colonel Ross, concerned over the Japanese patrols in his rear, had to get to Laiana on 13 July. With the artillery putting fire ahead, the 172d started out through mangrove swamp on the last five hundred yards to Laiana. The enemy fire continued. The advance was slow, but late afternoon found the 172d in possession of Laiana. It organized the area for defense while patrols sought out the

LCM's Approaching Laiana, New Georgia, *under Japanese artillery fire, 14 July 1943. The Tank Platoon of the 9th Marine Defense Battalion is aboard these landing craft.*

Japanese line to the west. That night twelve landing craft left Rendova to carry food and water to Laiana and evacuate the wounded. For some reason the 172d failed to display any signals. The landing craft, unable to find the right beach, returned to Rendova.

When the 172d was nearing Laiana on 13 July, General Hester ordered the 3d Battalion, 103d Infantry, 43d Division, to be prepared to land at 0900 the following morning. The Tank Platoon of the 9th Marine Defense Battalion was attached; to help the tanks and to aid in the reduction of fixed positions, engineers (bridge builders, demolitions

men, flame thrower operators, and mine detector men) were also attached.

The reinforced battalion, loaded in LCP(R)'s and LCM's, rendezvoused at daybreak of 14 July in Blanche Channel. When the daily fighter cover arrived from the Russells, the landing craft started for Laiana. With the 172d already holding the beachhead, the first wave landed peacefully at 0900. Reefs forced some craft to ground in waist-deep water, but the hungry soldiers of the 172d helped unload them. As the LCM's neared shore Japanese artillery shells began falling on the water route and on the landing beach. To blind the Japanese observers, the field artillery fired more than five hundred white phosphorous rounds as well as high explosive at suspected Japanese gun positions and observation posts on Munda Point and on the high ground (Bibilo Hill) northeast of Munda field. The Japanese artillery did no damage.

General Sasaki reported that he had repulsed the landing, and that the Americans had lost, of seventy landing craft, thirteen sunk and twenty damaged. Nevertheless, *8th Area Army* headquarters appears to have learned that the landing had succeeded.

Once ashore, 43d Division engineers began building a jeep trail from Laiana north to the 169th Infantry. Supplies came in for the 172d, and its wounded men were evacuated. Telephone crews laid an underwater cable between Zanana, Laiana, and General Barker's artillery fire direction center.

The 3d Battalion, 103d, was still in division reserve, but Colonel Ross was authorized to use it in case of dire need. He committed L Company to fill a gap between the 2d and 3d Battalions of the 172d on the morning of 15 July when the 172d was making an unsuccessful attack toward Ilangana. Soldiers of the Antitank Platoon of the 3d Battalion, 103d, disassembled a 37-mm. gun, carried it forward, reassembled it on the front line, and destroyed three pillboxes with direct fire. This was the only success; the day's end found the 172d still facing the main enemy defense line.

The Seizure of Reincke Ridge

While the 172d had been driving to Laiana and getting ready to attack westward, the 169th Infantry was pushing against the high ground to the north. On 10 July, the day before the 172d turned southward, the 169th had been halted. It faced Japanese positions on the high ground which dominated the Munda–Lambeti trail junction. The Munda Trail at this point led up to a draw, with hills to the north (right) and south (left). The Japanese held the draw and the hills.

The regiment renewed the attack on 11 July just before General Hester replaced Colonel Eason with Col. Temple G. Holland, but made no gains. When Holland took over the regiment, he ordered the advance postponed until the next morning. The exact nature of the Japanese defenses was not yet completely clear, but it was evident that the Japanese had built mutually supporting pillboxes on the hills.

Holland's plan for 12 July called for the 1st Battalion to deliver the attack from its present position while the 2d Battalion enveloped the Japanese left (north) flank.[21] The 3d Battalion, temporarily in division reserve, would be released to the regiment when the trail junction was secure. The 169th attacked as ordered but bogged down at once, partly because it became intermingled with elements of the 172d, which was starting for Laiana. When the units were disentangled the two battalions attacked again. The 1st Battalion ran head on into Japanese opposition but reported a gain of three hundred yards. The 2d Battalion received enfilading fire from the northernmost ridge but kept its position. A

---

[21] Ltr, Col Holland to Gen Smith, Chief of Mil Hist, 12 Oct 53, no sub, OCMH.

second attack, supported by a rolling barrage, was attempted in the afternoon. The infantry, unable to keep pace with the barrage which moved forward at the rate of ten yards a minute, fell behind and halted. At the day's end, Holland, who reported to Hester that his regiment was badly disorganized, asked General Mulcahy for air support the following day.

Next morning, 13 July, after thirty minutes of artillery fire and a twelve-plane dive-bombing attack against the south ridge, the 169th attacked again. All three battalions were committed. The 2d Battalion, in the center, was to assault frontally up the draw while the 1st Battalion, on the right, and the 3d Battalion on the left, moved against the north and south ridges with orders to envelop the Japanese.

The 3d Battalion, with I and L Companies in line and M in support, struggled forward for four hours.[22] It pushed four hundred to five hundred yards into the Japanese lines and managed to secure its objective, the south ridge, which it named Reincke Ridge for Lt. Col. Frederick D. Reincke, who had replaced Stebbins in command on 8 July.

The other two battalions were not as successful. The 2d Battalion, with E and F Companies in line and G in support, met machine gun fire in the draw, halted, was hit by what it believed to be American artillery fire, and pulled back. The 1st Battalion, attacking the north ridge, found it obstructed by fallen limbs from blasted trees and by shell

and bomb craters. The Japanese who had survived the bombardments opened fire from their pillboxes and halted the assaulting companies. The battalion, now operating without artillery or mortar support, tried to assault with rifle and bayonet. Some men started to climb to the ridge crest but were killed or wounded by machine gun fire. B Company lost three of its four officers in the attempt. Japanese artillery and mortar fire cut communication to the rear. The battalion returned to its original position.

The 1st and 2d Battalions took positions on the flanks and rear of the 3d Battalion, which held Reincke Ridge. The Japanese held the north ridge and the draw. To the west they held the higher ground called Horseshoe Hill. To the south was the gap left by the 172d when it turned south. In spite of the 3d Battalion's exposed situation Holland and Reincke decided to hold the hard-won position which was the only high ground the 169th possessed. Its possession was obviously vital to the success of an attack against the main enemy defenses.

All that night and all the next day (14 July) the Japanese tried to push the 3d Battalion from Reincke Ridge. I Company was hit hard but held its ground with the loss of two men killed and nineteen wounded. Artillery and mortar shells kept exploding on the ridge top, while Japanese machine guns covered the supply route to the rear. During its first twenty-four hours on the ridge, Reincke's battalion suffered 101 casualties; L Company consisted of just fifty-one enlisted men by the end of 14 July.

---

[22] K Company had been detached to guard the regimental command post.

During part of the time no medical officer was present, but the battalion medical section under S/Sgt. Louis Gullitti carried on its duties of first aid and evacuation.

On the same day Holland reorganized the other two battalions. The regimental Antitank Company had landed at Zanana on 13 July and been assigned the task of carrying supplies forward from the trail's end. This task had eased, because the engineers finished bridging the Barike on 12 July and by 14 July had extended the trail to within five hundred yards of the 169th's front lines. Rations, water, and ammunition were parachuted to the regiment on 14 July. Colonel Holland relieved part of the Antitank Company of its supply duties and assigned sixty of its men to the 2d Battalion, twenty to the 1st. He also sent patrols south to cover the gap to his left. Late in the afternoon he reported to Hester that morale in his regiment had improved.

Next day the 1st Battalion, 145th Infantry, landed at Zanana and was immediately attached to the 43d Division with orders to advance west and relieve part of the 169th on the line. The battalion reached the regiment at 1700. Colonel Holland put it in regimental reserve pending the completion of the operations against the hills in front of him.

Operations against Munda airfield had gone very slowly but by 15 July had achieved some success. Liversedge had captured Enogai and while waiting for another battalion was getting ready to attack Bairoko. The 169th Infantry had some high ground and was in contact with the main enemy defense line. The 172d Infantry was also in contact with the main Japanese defenses, and the new beachhead at Laiana would soon shorten the supply line.

Casualties

While Hester's men had been attaining limited tactical successes, unusual medical problems had appeared within his division.

Enemy resistance was not great at first. Some 90 men of the 43d Division were killed up to 17 July; 636 were wounded. Other men had been injured by vehicle collisions, falling trees, accidental explosions, and the like. Disease had put over 1,000 men out of action.[23]

Diarrhea and dysentery, ailments helped along by improper field sanitation, were prevalent in early July. They put men on the sick list for several days. Skin fungus infected about one quarter of the men. And there was always malaria. Although malaria control measures seem to have been carried out so conscientiously that few new cases broke out in the Occupation Force, all the troops had been in the Solomons for some time and there were always recurrent cases.

An especially large number of casualties was caused not by wounds or infectious disease but by mental disturbance. Between fifty and a hundred men were leaving the line every day with troubles which were diagnosed as "war neuroses." Col. Franklin T. Hallam, surgeon of the XIV Corps, arrived in New Georgia on 14 July when mental troubles were at their height. In Hallam's opinion, "war neurosis" was a "misnomer in most instances," because men suffering simply

---

[23] XIV Corps G-3 Jnl, 17 Jul 43.

from physical exhaustion "were erroneously directed or gravitated through medical channels along with the true psychoneurotics and those suffering with a temporary mental disturbance currently termed 'WAR NEUROSIS.' " [24]

These unfortunate men "who had not changed clothes or had two continuous hours of sleep all had the same expression. Their hair was matted and muddy, and beards were ½ inch in length, eyes were sunk in, dark, and had a strained expression. Gait was plodding and methodical, no spring or bounce. When they stopped walking they fell in their tracks, until it was time to proceed again." [25] Colonel Hallam's description is even more graphic:

At least 50% of these individuals requiring medical attention or entering medical installations were the picture of utter exhaustion, face expressionless, knees sagging, body bent forward, arms slightly flexed and hanging loosely, hands with palms slightly cupped, marked coarse tremor of fingers . . ., feet dragging, and an over-all appearance of apathy and physical exhaustion. About 20% of the total group were highly excited, crying, wringing their hands, mumbling incoherently, an expression of utter fright or fear, trembling all over, startled at the least sound or unusual commotion, having the appearance of trying to escape impending disaster. Another 15% showed manifestations of the various types of true psychoneurotic complexes. The remaining 15% included the anxiety states, and those with various bizarre somatic disturbances. These were the individuals whose symptoms were of insidious onset, starting with insomnia, vague digestive symptoms, bad dreams, frequency of urination, irritability, diminished ability to concentrate, and a generally reduced efficiency in the performance of assigned duties. [26]

Of about 2,500 men in the New Georgia Occupation Force whose troubles were diagnosed as "war neuroses" between 30 June and 30 September, the 43d Division contributed 62 percent during the period 30 June–31 July. About 1,500 cases came from the three infantry regiments of the 43d Division: 700 from the 169th Infantry, 450 from the 172d Infantry, and 350 from the 103d Infantry. [27]

Attempting to explain this mental trouble, Hallam divided the causes into two groups he termed "basic causative factors" and "precipitating causative factors." Basic causes involved leadership, orientation, discipline, and physical fitness. Units with poor leaders were more apt to have trouble than those in which the standard of leadership was high. In some units there was a direct correlation between the incidence of mental troubles among the leaders and among the led. When soldiers were not adequately oriented—not told what was going on, what their objectives were, and what they were expected to do—they were more apt to become excited by loose talk and

---

[24] Ltr, Col Hallam to The Surgeon, USAFISPA, 31 Oct 43, sub: Med Service, New Georgia Campaign, p. 31.

[25] This description comes from a personal account, "Medic on Munda," by Capt. Joseph Risman (Medical Corps), 169th Infantry, and is quoted in SOPACBACOM, History of the New Georgia Campaign, Vol. I, Ch III, p. 26, OCMH.

[26] Ltr, Hallam to The Surgeon, USAFISPA, 31 Oct 43, sub: Med Service, New Georgia Campaign, pp. 36–37.

[27] Ibid., p. 32. Of the 2,500 cases occurring from 30 June to 30 September, the 43d Division had about 1,950 or 79 percent; the 37th Division, 200 or 8 percent; the 25th Division, 150 or 6 percent; Navy and Marine Corps units, 200 or 8 percent. In July, the New Georgia Occupation Force had 1,750 cases or 70 percent, in August, 650 or 26 percent, and in September, 100 or 4 percent.

wild rumors. The significance of lack of proper discipline and physical fitness in any military organization, but especially in one engaged in battle, is perfectly obvious. Interestingly enough, however, Hallam noted that men "with borderline physical defects, consisting principally of eye, teeth, joint, weight, and feet defects, did not break, but did some of the best fighting." [28] Remarkably few men wounded in action became neurosis cases, perhaps because their knowledge that they would be evacuated eased their mental strain.

The basic causes, of course, were present in some units when they came to New Georgia. It was Hallam's opinion that men affected by any of the basic causes were triggered into mental disturbance by the precipitating factors, which were combat fatigue, enemy action, noise, and mass hysteria. Combat fatigue, the almost unutterable physical and mental weariness that comes from long stress and strain in battle, probably accounted for half the diagnoses of war neuroses. The most effective enemy action was the kind which so seriously disturbed the 169th Infantry—the real, and occasionally the wholly imaginary, nocturnal harassing tactics of the Japanese. Although aerial bombardment was also effective, the noises to which Hallam referred were not the sounds of guns firing and shells bursting, but the natural sounds of a jungle night, the breezes, branches, birds, and land crabs. These caused great anxiety among men to whom they were unfamiliar. On occasion mass hysteria took over; mental breaks spread like infection among troops.

Most of the mental cases, and especially those caused by fatigue, Hallam believed, could have been cured by a few days in a rest camp in the combat area. Sedatives, sleep, clean clothes, baths, shaves, good food, relief from duties, and recreation would soon have enabled the men to return to their units. But up to mid-July there were no rest camps, nor even any real hospital facilities, in New Georgia. The 43d Division, about 30–35 percent understrength in medical officers and enlisted men, had only a 125-bred clearing station to care for casualties. [29] Men requiring more than twenty-four hours of medical treatment were being evacuated, usually by water, to Guadalcanal, with the result that casualties frequently did not reach hospitals until three days after they had been taken out of the line.

These medical problems, coupled with the slow progress of ground operations up to mid-July, caused serious concern to all the responsible higher commanders.

Command and Reinforcements

As early as 10 July, Generals Hester and Wing were far from pleased with the performance of all units and commanders. On 10 July Wing, who had visited the command post of the 3d Battalion, 169th Infantry, on 8 July, directly ordered the regimental commander to relieve the 3d Battalion's commander and put Colonel Reincke in his place.

Three days prior to this relief, the 145th Infantry Regiment (less the 3d Battalion, serving under Liversedge) of the 37th Division, which had been stand-

---

[28] *Ibid.,* p. 35.

[29] The 17th Field Hospital came up from Guadalcanal and opened on New Georgia on 28 July.

ing by on Guadalcanal in area reserve, had been dispatched to Rendova. The first echelon sailed on 7 July, the second two days later. The regimental commander, Colonel Holland, had hardly arrived on Rendova when Hester relieved the commander of the 169th Infantry and ordered Colonel Holland to take over the regiment temporarily. Also relieved were the executive, intelligence, and operations officers of the 169th. Leaving Lt. Col. Theodore L. Parker in command of his old regiment, Holland took his own executive, intelligence, and operations officers and eighteen enlisted men from the 145th to headquarters of the 169th.

Meanwhile problems of higher command for New Georgia had not ceased to concern Admirals Halsey and Turner and especially General Harmon. On 5 July Harmon was on Guadalcanal, as were Turner and General Griswold. After informing Turner and Griswold of his views, he radioed to Halsey a recommendation that the forward echelon of the XIV Corps staff be sent to New Georgia about 8 July to prepare, under Hester, to take over supply, administration, and planning. Once Munda airfield fell, Harmon urged, Griswold should become commander of the New Georgia Occupation Force. This would free Hester to reorganize his main striking force and directly command the attack against Vila in Kolombangara. Such a change was necessary, Harmon explained, because Hester's small staff was not capable of bearing the responsibilities that would soon be thrust on it.[30]

Admiral Turner was not a man given to avoiding responsibility or yielding authority. Harmon wrote later, in explaining his reasons for urging a change in command, that Turner was "inclined more and more to take active control of land operations." [31] In his message to Halsey, he did not make this point. The South Pacific commander replied to Harmon the next day, telling him to augment Hester's 43d Division staff as he saw fit. Halsey wished to discuss with Harmon the recommendations on superseding Hester before reaching a decision. On the same day Halsey directed Turner to prepare plans for Kolombangara in consultation with Hester.[32]

The next day the irascible Turner presented his views to Halsey in very mild terms. Expressing regret over the necessity for disagreeing with Harmon, he strongly urged that Hester retain command of the New Georgia Occupation Force. Griswold and his staff were excellent, Turner agreed, but Hester was conducting operations "in a manner much to be admired." Superseding him would hamper the operation "by inducing a severe blow to morale." [33]

At this point Harmon, a peppery, wiry man, grew impatient. He boarded his B-17 and flew to Halsey in Nouméa. ". . . before nightfall," he later related,

---

[30] Rad, Harmon to COMSOPAC, 5 Jul 43, Hq SOPACBACOM File, Suppl New Georgia Material, OCMH.

[31] Ltr, Harmon to Handy, 15 Jul 43, quoted in part in Hq SOPACBACOM File, Suppl New Georgia Material, OCMH.

[32] Rad, COMSOPAC to Harmon, 6 Jul 43, Hq SOPACBACOM File, Suppl New Georgia Material, OCMH; COMSOPAC War Diary, 6 Jul 43.

[33] Rad, CTF 31 to COMSOPAC, 7 Jul 43, Hq SOPACBACOM File, Suppl New Georgia Material, OCMH.

"Admiral Halsey approved the course of procedure I had recommended." [34]

Griswold received instructions on 10 July to take six officers from his staff and fly to New Georgia on 11 July in an amphibian plane. The remainder of the XIV Corps staff would follow by water on 12 July. On orders from Halsey, which the admiral expected to issue after the capture of Munda airfield, Griswold would assume command of the New Georgia Occupation Force. Turner's authority over the Occupation Force would cease, but he was to continue to support the operation. Halsey repeated to Turner his instructions regarding plans for taking Kolombangara, and told him that, if Griswold approved the idea, Hester would command the ground forces in the attack.[35]

Griswold arrived at Rendova on 11 July just as Hester and Wing were changing their plan of attack against Munda and sending the 172d Infantry to seize the Laiana beachhead. The XIV Corps commander was not long in reaching a judgment regarding operations to date.

General Harmon, at his headquarters in Nouméa, wrote an optimistic letter to Washington on the morning of 13 July. He reported that operations in New Georgia seemed to be progressing favorably. He did not send the letter, for later in the morning he received a radio-gram from General Griswold, who said, "From an observer point of view things are going badly." Griswold urged that the 25th Division and the remainder of the 37th Division be sent into the battle at once. Although he reported, "Enemy resistance to date not great," he did not think the 43d Division would ever take Munda. It was, he declared, "about to fold up." [36]

This message had an immediate effect. Halsey met with Harmon and informally appointed him as his deputy. He ordered Harmon to "assume full charge of and responsibility for ground operations in New Georgia," and "to take whatever steps were deemed necessary to facilitate the capture of the airfield." [37]

Before leaving for Koli Point on Guadalcanal to be nearer the scene of action, Harmon ordered Griswold to hasten his preparations for assuming command on New Georgia. All ground forces assigned for the operation, he told Griswold, would be available by the time he assumed command. Harmon promised to alert one regimental combat team of the veteran 25th Division for movement, but it would be dispatched to New Georgia only if he specifically approved.

Of the assigned 37th Division forces, the 145th Infantry, like the 136th Field Artillery Battalion, was already on hand in New Georgia, the 1st and 2d Battalions at Rendova and the 3d Battalion under Liversedge along with 3d Battalion, 148th Infantry. Admiral Turner at once

---

[34] Ltr, Harmon to Handy, 15 Jul 43, quoted in part in Hq SOPACBACOM File, Suppl New Georgia Material, OCMH; COMSOPAC War Diary, 9 Jul 43.

[35] Rad, COMSOPAC to CTF 31, 9 Jul 43; and Rad, COMGENSOPAC to CG XIV Corps, 10 Jul 43, in Hq SOPACBACOM File, Suppl New Georgia Material, OCMH; XIV Corps G-3 Jnl, 10–11 Jul 43.

[36] Rad, Griswold to Harmon, 13 Jul 43, quoted in SOPACBACOM, History of the New Georgia Campaign, Vol. I, Ch. III, p. 39, OCMH.

[37] Harmon, The Army in the South Pacific, p. 8; Halsey, Narrative Account of the South Pacific Campaign, p. 7. Both in OCMH.

REAR ADM. THEODORE S. WILKINSON *(left) and Lt. Gen. Millard F. Harmon in the chart room of the transport* McCawley.

ordered Col. Stuart A. Baxter, commanding the 148th Infantry in the Russell Islands, to alert Headquarters, the 1st and 2d Battalions, and the Antitank Company of his regiment for immediate movement to New Georgia. These movements would put two full infantry regiments of the 37th Division in New Georgia.

On the 16th, Griswold proposed that the 37th Division units operate under control of their division commander, Maj. Gen. Robert S. Beightler, and that Beightler and his senior staff officers fly to New Georgia for conferences and personal reconnaissance. Harmon agreed, and Beightler left for New Georgia in a PBY on 19 July.

On arriving at Guadalcanal, Harmon ordered Maj. Gen. J. Lawton Collins, commanding the 25th Division, to get one regimental combat team ready for transfer to New Georgia. Collins, who on Griswold's departure had become island commander and as such responsible for Guadalcanal's defense, decided that the 161st Regimental Combat Team could most easily be spared from its defense missions. On 14 July he directed Col. James L. Dalton, II, regimental and combat team commander, to be ready to move on twelve hours' notice.[38]

The next day Admiral Turner was relieved of his posts of Commander, South Pacific Amphibious Force (III Amphibious Force and Task Force 32), and Commander, New Georgia Attack Force (Task Force 31). This relief apparently had nothing to do with recent events on New Georgia. Admiral Nimitz, then preparing for the great Central Pacific drive that was to start with the invasion of the Gilberts in November 1943, had directed Halsey to send Turner to Hawaii. Turner departed on the 15th, and during the next two years commanded the V Amphibious Force in the invasions of the Gilberts, the Marshalls, the Marianas, Iwo Jima, and Okinawa. His posts in the South Pacific were taken over by Admiral Wilkinson, until then Halsey's deputy commander.

On the day Turner left, Harmon ordered Griswold to assume command of the New Georgia Occupation Force at midnight of 15–16 July, and to seize Munda and join forces with Liversedge as soon as possible. Griswold took over

command as ordered. Hester reverted to command of the 43d Division.

Thus by mid-July Turner and Hester, the two officers most responsible for the execution of the New Georgia tactical plans, had been replaced. With the offensive stalling, General Griswold was facing his first experience in commanding a corps in combat. His problems were formidable, although some progress had been made. Liversedge's three battalions were behind schedule but had taken Enogai and were preparing to attack Bairoko. On the Munda front the 169th and 172d Infantry Regiments, also behind their schedule, had laboriously made their way from Zanana across the Barike to Laiana and the vicinity of Reincke Ridge and were in contact with the main Japanese defenses. These forces were obviously not adequate to break through and capture the airfield, but additional regiments were on their way. Aside from the difficulties presented by the enemy and the terrain, Griswold was confronted by an abnormally high rate of mental illness, and by the need to improve the Occupation Force supply system so that the regiments would be taken care of in the normal manner instead of by emergency air drop. Obviously, it was a case calling for generalship of a high order.

---

[38] The regimental combat team consisted of the 161st Infantry; the 89th Field Artillery Battalion; A Company, 65th Engineer Battalion; and A Company, 25th Medical Battalion.

CHAPTER VIII

Griswold Takes Over

General Griswold at once concluded that he could not mount a large-scale offensive against Munda until he had received reinforcements and reorganized the Occupation Force. Estimating that four battalions of "Munda moles well dug in" faced him, he planned to keep "pressure on slant-eye," and to gain more advantageous ground for an offensive, by using the 43d Division in a series of local attacks. At the same time he would be getting ready for a full corps offensive to "crack Munda nut and allow speedy junction with Liversedge." [1] In the rear areas, Griswold and his staff set to work to improve the system of supply and medical treatment.

The Attack on Bairoko

Meanwhile Colonel Liversedge, after taking Enogai and abandoning the trail block, was making ready to assault Bairoko. (See Map 8.) Liversedge's opera-

tions against Bairoko were not closely co-ordinated with action on the Munda front. Upon assuming command Griswold directed Liversedge to submit daily reports, but radio communication between Liversedge and Occupation Force headquarters on Rendova had been poor. Curiously enough Liversedge's signals from his Navy TBX radio could barely be picked up at Rendova, although the radio at Segi Point was able to receive them without much difficulty. As a result Liversedge had to send many messages through Segi Point to headquarters of Task Force 31 at Guadalcanal, from there to be relayed to Rendova, a slow process at best.

In the days following the fall of Enogai, Liversedge sent patrols out to cover Dragons Peninsula. They made contact with the Japanese only once between 12 and 17 July. Little information was obtained. "Ground reconnaissance," wrote Liversedge, ". . . was by no means all it should have been." Most patrols, he felt, were not aggressive enough, had not been adequately instructed by unit commanders, and were not properly conducted. ". . . some patrols were sent out in which the individual riflemen had no idea of where they were going and what they were setting out to find."

[1] Rad, Griswold to Harmon, 16 Jul 43, in XIV Corps G-3 Jnl, 16 Jul 43. Unless otherwise indicated this chapter is based on SOPACBACOM, History of the New Georgia Campaign, Vol. I, OCMH; the orders, action rpts, jnls and jnl files of NGOF, XIV Corps, 43d Div, 37th Div, 25th Div, NLG, and their component units; USAFISPA's Daily Int Summaries and Periodic Int Rpts; 17th Army Operations, Vol. II, Japanese Monogr No. 40 (OCMH); Southeast Area Naval Operations, Vol. II, Japanese Monogr No. 49 (OCMH); the published naval and air histories previously cited.

JAPANESE PRISONERS CAPTURED NEAR LAIANA BEACH *are escorted to division headquarters for interrogation.*

There was always the problem of "gold-bricking on the part of patrols who are inclined to keep their activity fairly close to their camp area. . . ." Patrols made "grave errors in distance and direction" and frequently were unobservant. Many returned from their missions unable to tell in what direction the streams flowed, whether there were fresh enemy tracks around a given stream, and the approximate dimensions of swamps they had passed through.[2]

Prisoners might have supplied a good deal of information, but only two had been captured. Air photography, too, might have furnished Liversedge with data on strongpoints, gun emplacements, stores, and bivouac areas, but he complained that he had received practically no photos. One group of obliques received just before the landing at Rice Anchorage turned out to be pictures of marines landing at Segi Point. Thus, except for the map captured on 7 July, Liversedge had no sound information on the installations at Bairoko. He was aware only that the Japanese were digging in and preparing to resist. The Americans could only guess at Japanese strength at Bairoko, whither the survivors of the Japanese garrison at Enogai

---

[2] NLG War Diary and Combat Rpt, pp. 9–10.

had gone. Harmon's headquarters estimated that one Army infantry battalion
plus two companies, some artillerymen,
and part of the *Kure 6th Special Naval
Landing Force* were defending Bairoko.
The actual strength of the garrison is
not clear. It consisted, however, of the
2d Battalion, 45th Infantry, the *8th Battery, 6th Field Artillery* (both of the *6th
Division*), and elements of the *Kure 6th
Special Naval Landing Force*.[3]

Liversedge had few more than three
thousand men to use in the attack. The
move of Colonel Schultz's 3d Battalion,
148th Infantry, to Triri and the 18 July
landing of the 4th Marine Raider Battalion at Enogai gave him a force almost
four battalions strong, although casualties and disease had reduced the three
battalions that made the initial landing.
M Company and the Antitank Platoon
of the 3d Battalion, 145th Infantry, were
holding Rice Anchorage. The 1st and 4th
Raider Battalions and L Company,
145th, were at Enogai. Schultz's battalion
and the remainder of the 3d Battalion,
145th, were at Triri.

Liversedge called his battalion commanders together at 1500, 19 July, and
issued oral orders for the Bairoko attack,
which was to take place early next morning. The Raider battalions, advancing
some three thousand yards southwest
from Enogai along the Enogai-Bairoko
trail, would make the main effort. One
platoon of B Company, 1st Raider Battalion, was to create a diversion by advancing down the fifty-yard-wide sandspit forming the west shore of Leland

Lagoon. The 3d Battalion, 148th, was
to make a separate enveloping movement. Advancing southwest from Triri
to the trail junction southeast of Bairoko, it was to swing north against the
Japanese right flank. A and C Companies, 1st Marine Raider Battalion, and
elements of the 3d Battalion, 145th,
formed the reserve at Enogai.

Late in the day the B Company platoon took landing craft from Enogai to
the tip of the sandspit, went ashore, and
moved into position for the next morning's attack. The remainder of the attacking force stayed in bivouac. From
2000, 19 July, to 0500, 20 July, Japanese
aircraft bombed and strafed Enogai,
which as yet had no antiaircraft guns.
No one was killed, but the troops had
little rest.

The two Raider battalions started out
of Enogai at 0800, 20 July, and within
thirty minutes all units had cleared the
village and were marching down the
trail toward Bairoko. The 1st Raider
Battalion (less two companies) led, followed by the 4th Battalion and regimental Headquarters. At 0730 Schultz's
battalion had left Triri on its enveloping
march.

The Northern Landing Group was attacking a fortified position. A force delivering such an attack normally makes
full use of all supporting services, arms,
and weapons, but Liversedge's men had
little to support them. No one seems to
have asked for naval gunfire. Liversedge,
who had been receiving fairly heavy air
support in the form of bombardments
of Bairoko, is reported to have requested
a heavy air strike to support his assault.
His message reached the Guadalcanal
headquarters of Admiral Mitscher, the

---

[3] Japanese sources give no strength figures for
these units. SOPACBACOM, History of the New
Georgia Campaign, Vol. I, Ch. V, gives approximately two thousand, a figure which may be high.

Commander, Aircraft, Solomons, too late on the 19th for action next day.[4]

The marines definitely expected air support. The 4th Raider Battalion noted at 0900: "Heavy air strike failed to materialize."[5] Artillery support was precluded by the fact that there was no artillery. Hindsight indicates that the six 81-mm. mortars of the 3d Battalion, 145th Infantry, might have been used in general support of the attack, but these weapons remained with their parent battalion.

The Raiders advanced without meeting an enemy until 0955 when the 1st Battalion's point sighted four Japanese. When the first shot was fired at 1015, B and D Companies, 1st Raider Battalion, deployed and moved forward. Heavy firing broke out at 1045. By noon the battalion had penetrated the enemy outpost line of resistance and was in the outskirts of Bairoko. When D Company, on the left, was halted by machine gun fire, Liversedge began committing the 4th Raider Battalion to the left of the 1st. Then D Company started moving again. Driving slowly but steadily against machine gun fire, it advanced with its flanks in the air beyond B Company until by 1430 it had seized a ridge about three hundred yards short of the shore of Bairoko Harbour. Liversedge ordered more units forward to cover D Company's flank. These advances were made with rifle, grenade, and bayonet against Japanese pillboxes constructed of logs and coral, housing machine guns. The jungle overhead was so heavy that the Raiders' 60-mm. mortars were not used. The platoon on the sandspit, meanwhile, was held up by a number of machine guns and was unable to reach the mainland to make contact with the main body.

So far the marines, by attacking resolutely, had made good progress in spite of the absence of proper support, but now 90-mm. mortar fire from Japanese positions on the opposite (west) shore of Bairoko Harbour began bursting around the battalion command posts and on D Company's ridge. With casualties mounting, D Company was forced off the ridge. By 1500 practically the entire force that Liversedge had led out of Enogai was committed and engaged in the fire fight, but was unable to move farther under the 90-mm. mortar fire. Colonel Griffith, commanding the 1st Raider Battalion, regretted the absence of heavy mortars in the Marine battalions. Liversedge, at 1315, sent another urgent request for an air strike against the positions on the west shore of Bairoko Harbour, but, as Griswold told him, there could be no air strikes by Guadalcanal-based planes on such short notice. With all marine units in action, the attack stalled, and casualties increasing, Liversedge telephoned Schultz to ask if his battalion could make contact with the marines before dark.[6] Other-

---

[4] Maj. John N. Rentz, USMCR, *Marines in the Central Solomons* (Washington, 1952), p. 111. The XIV Corps G-3 Journal for 19 July contains a message from Liversedge, sent at 2235, 18 July, requesting a twelve-plane strike on 19 July, and a "large strike to stand by for July 20 A M and SBD's to stand by for immediate call remainder of day." XIV Corps headquarters replied that a "large strike stand by" for 20 July was "impracticable."

[5] 4th Mar Raider Bn Special Action Rpt, Bairoko Harbor, New Georgia Opn, p. 3.

[6] All men of Headquarters Company, 4th Raider Battalion, were engaged in carrying litter cases to the rear.

wise, he warned, the attack on Bairoko would fail.

Schultz's battalion had marched out of Triri that morning in column of companies. Except for two small swamps, the trail was easy. By 1330 the battalion had traveled about 3,000 yards, passing some Japanese corpses and abandoned positions on the way, and reached the point where the Triri trail joined one of the Munda–Bairoko tracks. Here, about 2,500 yards south of Bairoko, the battalion swung north and had moved a short distance when the advance guard ran into an enemy position on high ground. Patrols went out to try to determine the location and strength of the Japanese; by 1530 Schultz was ready to attack. M Company's 81-mm. mortars opened fire, but the rifle companies, attempting to move against machine guns, were not able to advance. One officer and one enlisted man of K Company were killed; two men were wounded. This was the situation at 1600 when Schultz received Liversedge's call.

Schultz immediately told Liversedge that he could not reach the main body before dark. A few minutes later, the 1st Marine Raider Regiment's executive officer, having been dispatched to Schultz to tell him to push harder, arrived at the battalion command post. According to the 3d Battalion's report, the executive agreed that contact could not be made before dark and he so informed Liversedge.

The group commander concluded that he had but one choice: to withdraw. He issued the order, and the marine battalions began retiring at 1700. Starting from the left of the line, they pulled back company by company. Machine gun and mortar fire still hit them, but the withdrawal was orderly. All uninjured men helped carry the wounded. The battalion retired about five hundred yards and set up a perimeter defense on the shore of Leland Lagoon. When L Company of the 145th came up from Enogai carrying water, ammunition, and blood plasma, it was committed to the perimeter. Construction of the defenses was impeded by darkness, but the task was completed and the hasty defenses were adequate to withstand some harassing Japanese that night.

Some of the walking wounded had been sent to Enogai in the late afternoon of the 20th, and at 0615 of the 21st more were dispatched. Evacuation of litter cases began at 0830, and an hour later a group of Corrigan's natives came from Enogai to help. Carrying the stricken men in litters over the primitive trail in the heat was hard on the men and on the litter bearers. Liversedge therefore ordered that landing craft from Enogai come up Leland Lagoon and take the wounded back from a point about midway between Bairoko and Enogai. This evacuation was carried out, and by late afternoon, the withdrawal, which was covered by Allied air attacks against Bairoko, had been completed. All the marines were at Enogai, where they were joined by Schultz's battalion, which had retired to Triri and come to Enogai by boat. The Raider battalions lost 46 men killed, 161 wounded. They reported counting 33 enemy corpses, but estimated that the total number of enemy dead was much higher.

Once again at Enogai, the Northern Landing Group resumed daily patrols over Dragons Peninsula.

Pressure on the Japanese

On the Munda front, meanwhile, the 169th and 172d Regiments were engaged in their limited offensive to hold the Japanese in position and secure more high ground from which to launch the corps offensive that was to start on 25 July. (*See below, Map 10.*)

The 172d Infantry

From 16 through 24 July the 172d Infantry expanded the Laiana beachhead. It moved west about six hundred yards and established a front line that ran for about fifteen hundred yards inland from the beach near Ilangana. During this period it had the support of tanks for the first time. Reconnaissance had revealed some trails in front of the 172d that the tanks could use. Therefore three M3 light tanks of the 9th Marine Defense Battalion were assigned to each of the 172d's battalions, and six riflemen were ordered to advance with and cover each tank.

In the zone of the 2d Battalion, 172d, on the beach, the tanks made good progress along a jeep trail on 16 July. But when they reached the trail's end, their rate of advance slowed to about one mile an hour as logs, stumps, and trees caused constant backing, towing, and rerouting. About seventy-five yards beyond the 2d Battalion's front lines, in an area where artillery fire had partly cleared the vegetation, the tanks sighted Japanese pillboxes. They deployed into a wedge formation, then fired 37-mm. high explosive shells. As this fire cut down the underbrush other pillboxes became visible. Japanese machine gunners manning positions in grass shacks opened fire, but were immediately blasted by canister from the tanks. Such heavy fire then struck the tanks that they were forced to close their turret hatches, but they found the source of much of the fire—a machine gun position at the base of a banyan tree. The marines shot at this position for some time, but as they killed one gunner, his replacement would bound forward from the rear, man the gun, and keep shooting until he was killed. At length the tanks destroyed the gun, drove the surviving crew members into a nearby pillbox, pulled up close, and demolished three pillboxes with short-range fire. Troops of the 2d Battalion then moved forward to grenade the wreckage.

The three tanks operating with the 3d Battalion, to the right of the 2d, had less success, as the ridges in that zone were so steep that the tanks could not elevate or depress their guns enough to hit the enemy positions.

The destruction of the pillboxes near the shore gave the troops an opportunity to inspect the type of defenses they would have to overcome before they could take Munda. The pillboxes were not concrete, as had been feared, but were made of coconut logs and coral. From ten to twelve feet square, they had three or four layers of logs banked with six to eight feet of weathered coral. About ten feet from floor to ceiling, they were dug into the earth so that only two or three feet of pillbox projected above the ground. Each had several firing slits for riflemen as well as a firing platform for a heavy machine gun. Outside were foxholes among banyan and mahogany trees. Trenches connected all positions, which were well camouflaged. Besides employing terrain contours for concealment, the Japanese used earth, grass,

PILLBOX MADE OF COCONUT LOGS AND CORAL *near Munda Airfield.*

vines, palm fronds, and leaves to such good effect that the American soldiers might receive fire from a pillbox and still not be able to see it. Soldiers of the 43d Division remarked that the Japanese positions were easier to smell than see. As usual, the Americans reported the presence of many snipers in trees, but these reports had little basis in fact. No one ever seems to have actually seen one.

The tanks attacked again on the 17th, but lack of tank-infantry co-ordination hampered their efforts. The Marine tanks and the Army infantry had not trained together. Foot soldiers had no sure means of communicating with the tanks when they were closed up for action. Tank crews, with hatches closed, could see very little in the jungle. The tankers uttered the classic complaint that the riflemen did not give them proper support and protection, while the infantrymen claimed that the tanks did not always press forward to support them. Doubtless both accusations were based on truth.

Japanese antitank tactics, practically nonexistent at first, improved each day, for staff officers had hurried down from Rabaul to instruct Sasaki's men in methods of dealing with tanks. The Japanese used mines, flame throwers, Molotov cocktails, and fuzed charges of TNT against the tanks, but apparently had no antitank guns. After two tanks were permanently disabled on 17–

18 July, General Griswold withdrew the other tanks from the front to permit repairs. He ordered the 9th Marine Defense Battalion tank commander to reconnoiter for terrain suitable for tank action, and at the same time requested that the Tank Platoon of the 10th Marine Defense Battalion, then in the Russells, be sent to New Georgia.

Kelley Hill

In the 169th Infantry's zone farther north, the 3d Battalion's seizure of Reincke Ridge was being exploited. The 2d Battalion was able to capture the hill immediately north of Reincke Ridge, and on 15 July Maj. Joseph E. Zimmer, commanding the 1st Battalion, reconnoitered the high ground (Kelley Hill) four hundred yards southwest of Reincke Ridge in preparation for an attack.

At 0830 the next day, 16 July, the 155-mm. howitzers of the 136th Field Artillery Battalion and the 3d Battalion's mortars put fire on the objective. At the same time the 1st Battalion, fortified by hot coffee and doughnuts, passed through the 3d Battalion's lines and advanced to the attack. One platoon from C Company, carrying .30-caliber light machine guns, struck out down the west slope of Reincke Ridge and up the east slope of Kelley Hill, seized the crest, and set up machine guns to cover the advance of the battalion's main body, which was to envelop Kelley Hill from the south. The whole effort was bloodless. The battalion's advance elements climbed the hill without meeting any opposition. They found only empty pillboxes and abandoned foxholes. By 1530 the entire battalion was on the ridge top. The men found they could

look west and see the waters south of Munda Point, although the airfield was hidden from view. Because natives had formerly dug yam gardens on the ridge, there was an open area about 75 by 150 yards. Zimmer's men, using Japanese positions when possible, started building an all-round defense in the clearing. Automatic rifles, machine guns, and M1903 and M1 rifles were posted on the line, with mortars in supporting positions in rear.

There was a brush with a Japanese patrol at 1650, and before dark, when the emplacements were still incomplete, Japanese artillery and mortar fire struck the battalion. Fourteen men died, including 1st Lt. John R. Kelley, in whose memory the hill was named. Just fifteen minutes after midnight part of the *3d Battalion, 229th Infantry,* now commanded by Captain Kojima, assaulted the hill from positions on Horseshoe Hill. Beaten off, Kojima tried twice more against the right (north) and rear (east) but failed to dislodge Zimmer's battalion.

The 1st Battalion held to the ridge, but as day broke on 17 July the troops realized that their situation was not enviable. That the Japanese were still active was indicated by their resistance to an attempt by the 2d Battalion to drive into the draw between Reincke Ridge and Kelley Hill. This attempt was beaten back. The 1st Battalion's rations and ammunition were running low; the battalion surgeon had no medical supplies. And when Japanese machine guns fired on a party carrying twenty wounded men to the rear and forced it to return west to Kelley Hill, the men of the battalion knew that they were virtually isolated. Fortunately the telephone line to the regimental command post was still operating, and Major Zimmer was able to keep Colonel Holland informed on his situation. As the hot day wore on, the supply of water dwindled. Some men left their positions to drink from puddles in shell holes. Eight of those who thus exposed themselves were wounded by Japanese riflemen. In midafternoon succor came. A party of South Pacific Scouts, accompanied by Capt. Dudley H. Burr, the regimental chaplain, escorted a supply party through to Kelley Hill. The party brought ammunition, rations, water, blood plasma, litters, and orders from Holland to hold the hill. The wounded were carried out. The unwounded on Kelley Hill, securely dug in, made ready to meet the Japanese night attack which they had reason to expect.

The Enemy Counterattacks

Up to now, Japanese ground troops had harried the Americans at night with local attacks, but had not attempted any large co-ordinated offensives. They had manned their defensive positions, fired at the American infantry, and had received bombs, shells, and infantry assaults without retaliating very actively. This quiescence, so different from enemy reactions during the Guadalcanal Campaign, puzzled the American commanders. General Sasaki was well aware that only offensive action would destroy the Allied forces on New Georgia, and he had brought the *13th Infantry* to Munda from Kolombangara for that purpose.

Sasaki ordered the *13th*, acting in concert with as much of the *229th Infantry* as he could spare from the defenses east

of Munda, to assemble on the upper reaches of the Barike, fall upon the Allied flank and rear, and destroy the whole force.[7] The *13th Infantry*, having completed its march from Bairoko, assembled on the upper Barike on 15 July. It claims to have attacked the 43d Division's right flank on that date, a claim that is not supported by the 43d Division records. Two days later the *13th* made ready to attack from the upper Barike.

In the afternoon of the 17th American patrols operating on the practically open right flank reported that an enemy column, 250–300 men strong, was moving eastward. A platoon from the 43d Cavalry Reconnaissance Troop went out to ambush the column but failed to intercept it. It was obvious that the Japanese had some sort of offensive action in mind.

It was equally obvious that the Allied forces in front of Munda were in a vulnerable position. Their right flank was in the air; the front line positions were exposed to envelopment from the north. The Japanese reinforcement route from Bairoko was still open, and 43d Division -rear installations, strung out from Zanana to the front, were unguarded except for local security detachments. Movement was slow along the Munda Trail; the track north from Laiana was not yet completed. It would thus be difficult to send speedy reinforcement to any beleaguered unit. A resolute, skillful attack by the *13th Infantry*, such as Sasaki had planned, could destroy the 43d Division's rear installations, cut the line of communications from Zanana to the front, and if co-ordinated with the

---

[7] This order probably accounts for the withdrawal of part of the *229th* from Kelley Hill.

efforts of the *229th Infantry* might surround the American regiments on the front lines.

Captain Kojima was ready to do his part. He had prepared another attack against Kelley Hill. At 0015, 18 July, Japanese machine guns north of Kelley opened fire. They covered the advance of riflemen who were attempting an assault against the west slope of Kelley Hill. The 1st Battalion fired at the Japanese infantry with all weapons that would bear, including two captured Japanese machine guns. Tracers from Kojima's machine guns revealed their location, and 3d and 1st Battalion mortar crews put their fire on the Japanese positions to the north. Kojima's first attack failed. His men pulled back, regrouped, and tried again, this time from the north. They succeeded in seriously threatening the line. The broken ground on the north slope of Kelley Hill provided some cover from the fire of one of the machine guns that was supposed to sweep the area. The Japanese, taking advantage of the dead space, crawled within grenade-throwing range of the northern line of the 1st Battalion. But mortar fire killed some of them and forced the others to withdraw. The 1st Battalion reported counting 102 Japanese bodies on the slopes of Kelley Hill after daybreak.

A predawn attack by the *2d Battalion, 229th Infantry*, against the beach positions of the 3d Battalion, 103d Infantry, in the 172d's sector, was readily repulsed.[8]

Elsewhere on the night of 17–18

July the Japanese caused alarms and uproar. They launched simultaneous raids against the engineer and medical bivouacs and the 43d Division command post at Zanana. Near one of the Barike bridges they ambushed a party taking wounded of the 169th to the rear, then attacked the hasty perimeter set up by the party and killed several of the wounded.

The attacks against the engineer and medical bivouacs were easily beaten off, but at the command post the raiders' first onslaught carried them through the security detachment's perimeter and into the communication center where they ripped up telephone wires and damaged the switchboard before being chased off. The division artillery liaison officer, Capt. James Ruhlen, called for supporting fire from the 136th Field Artillery Battalion. Adjusting by sound, he put fire on a nearby hill where the Japanese were thought to be emplacing mortars and laid a tight box barrage around the command post. This fire was continued throughout the night. During the action Lt. Col. Elmer S. Watson, 43d Division G–3, was wounded. Maj. Sidney P. Marland, Jr., his assistant, took his place.

Shortly after receiving word of the attack, General Griswold ordered a battery of artillerymen from Kokorana to Zanana to protect the command post, and on his orders Colonel Baxter selected the 1st Battalion of his 148th Infantry to move from Rendova to Zanana at daybreak.

The *13th Infantry* then withdrew to the north. It had caused a few casualties but accomplished very little, certainly not enough to justify its trip from Kolombangara. As might be expected, Gen-

---

[8] The 3d Battalion, 103d, was attached to the 172d Infantry.

eral Sasaki was disappointed.[9] Reincke Ridge, Kelley Hill, and Laiana beachhead remained in American hands.

Preparations for the Corps Offensive

Commitment of the 37th Division

General Griswold, preparing for his corps offensive, needed fresh troops at the front. On 18 July he ordered Colonel Baxter to advance west with the 2d Battalion of his 148th Infantry and relieve the 169th Infantry as soon as possible. Baxter, whose 1st and 2d Battalions had arrived at Zanana that morning, effected the relief by 21 July after being delayed by Japanese detachments at the Barike.

After the 169th's relief, regimental command changed again. Colonel Holland took over his old regiment, the 145th, while Lt. Col. Bernard J. Lindauer succeeded to command of the 169th. Lindauer's regiment returned to Rendova for rest and reorganization. Its 3d Battalion, after receiving 212 replacements, was sent into reserve at Laiana on 24 July.

By 23 July the major part of the 37th Division had arrived at New Georgia and was either in action or ready to be committed. Present were Division and Division Artillery Headquarters; the 145th and 148th Infantry Regiments less their 3d Battalions, which were under

Liversedge; the 135th and 136th Field Artillery Battalions; the 37th Cavalry Reconnaissance Troop; and the signal, quartermaster, ordnance, engineer, and medical units (except B Company, 117th Engineer Battalion, and B Company, 112th Medical Battalion).

General Griswold, on 22 July, directed General Beightler to resume command at noon of all his units then on New Georgia except the 136th Field Artillery Battalion. To the 37th Griswold attached the 161st Regimental Combat Team less its artillery, and the 169th and 192d Field Artillery Battalions of the 43d Division. The 136th Field Artillery Battalion was serving as part of corps artillery. The other three organic and attached artillery battalions were under the 37th Division for direct fire support missions only; for all others they would be controlled by corps artillery, now commanded by General Barker.

Griswold, reshuffling units for the offensive, set the boundary between divisions along an east-by-south–west-by-north line approximately thirteen hundred yards north of Ilangana. The 43d Division was on the left (south), with the 103d and 172d Regiments in line from south to north.[10] The 172d moved right to establish contact with the 37th Division's left.

The 37th Division, assigned an indefinite frontage north of the 43d Division, gave the 145th Infantry a narrow front of 300 yards on the left, because only the 2d Battalion, 145th, which had been covering the gap north of the 172d Infantry, was immediately available. The

---

[9] Japanese records do not indicate just what the main body of the *13th* actually did during the period 17–19 July. The various raids could not have been the work of the entire unit. The main body apparently never got into action at all. The 170 hungry survivors of Major Hara's Viru garrison may have caused some of the trouble to the Americans, for on 18 or 19 July they reached Munda after marching overland from Viru and infiltrating the American lines from the rear.

[10] The 2d Battalion, 103d, having been relieved by the 1st Battalion, had come up from Wickham Anchorage.

SOLDIERS OF THE 161ST INFANTRY *debarking from an LCI, New Georgia, 22 July 1943.*

1st Battalion was still holding the high ground taken over from the 169th Infantry. The 161st Infantry was given a 500-yard front in the center. One of its battalions constituted the corps reserve. The 148th Infantry was put on the right, with no definite frontage, and assigned the responsibility for protecting the corps' right flank and rear.

All units had moved into position by 24 July. The 161st Infantry, whose transfer had been approved by General Harmon, had arrived at Baraulu Island on 21 July, moved to New Georgia the next day, and suffered its first casualties of the campaign when two captains of the regimental staff were killed on reconnaissance. On 23 July the regiment moved to assembly areas in preparation for the offensive. Most of the 161st's zone of action lay north of the high ground taken by the 169th Infantry.

The corps line of departure ran northwest from a point near Ilangana. In the 161st's zone, it lay about three hundred yards west of the assembly areas, and ran over Horseshoe Hill. Colonel Dalton, who had taken over command of the regiment in the closing days of the Guadalcanal Campaign, sent out patrols to reconnoiter for the line of departure. These patrols were stopped short of the line by Japanese on a ridge that formed part of the northeast slope of Horseshoe Hill, and returned to report to Dalton that there were two pillboxes on the ridge. A reinforced platoon went out to deal with the enemy. This platoon came back and claimed the destruction of two positions but reported the presence of several more. Because Beightler did not want to commit the regiment to general action before 25 July, he ordered Dalton

to use one rifle company to clear the ridge on 24 July. I Company, supported by M Company's 81-mm. mortars, attacked and reported knocking out two more pillboxes, apparently by killing the occupants. But I Company also reported the presence of a dozen more pillboxes. Before nightfall, patrols reported that the Japanese had reoccupied the two positions I Company had attacked. Thus just before D Day the 161st Infantry was aware that a strong enemy position lay camouflaged between it and the line of departure.

Reorganization

In the days following his assumption of command, General Griswold and his staff were deeply occupied with administrative as well as tactical matters. Reinforcements from the 25th and 37th Divisions had to be received and assigned. The supply system was overhauled; medical services were improved.

General Griswold immediately designated Barabuni Island as supply dump for the 43d Division, Kokorana for the 37th. Ships from Guadalcanal would land equipment and supplies in these islands, whence landing craft would transport them through the barrier islands to Laiana or to other positions on the barrier islands.

Hester's move to Laiana was paying dividends. Although low, swampy ground had at first slowed construction of the trail from Laiana north to the Munda Trail, six hundred yards had been built by 17 July, and on 20 July the whole trail was opened to motor traffic. As a result, Hester reported, his regiments would no longer need to be supplied from the air. The 43d Division command post moved from Zanana to Laiana on 21 July. At the same time most of the 43d Division's service installations moved to Laiana. Two-lane roads were built within the dump areas, and additional trails out of Laiana, plus more trails to the various regiments, were also built. Bulldozer operators working inland received fire from enemy riflemen on occasion. After one driver was wounded, the engineers fashioned shields for the bulldozers with steel salvaged from wrecked enemy landing craft. A D–4 and a much heavier D–7 bulldozer that came in with A Company, 65th Engineer Battalion, on 23 July, speeded construction of a trail to the 161st Infantry and of lateral trails in the 37th Division's area. With the roads built it was possible to assemble supplies close behind the infantry regiments and to plan their systematic delivery in the future.

The XIV Corps and its assigned units also undertook the improvement of medical care. Several hours after he assumed command Griswold asked Harmon to send the 250-bed 17th Field Hospital from Guadalcanal to Rendova at once. Harmon approved. Because of physical frailty some medical officers had become casualties themselves, and the resulting shortage prevented careful supervision and handling of casualties. Griswold asked Harmon for fifteen medical officers physically able to stand the rigors of field service. To make sure that casualties being evacuated from New Georgia received proper medical attention during the trip to Guadalcanal, the corps surgeon arranged with naval authorities for a naval medical officer to travel on each LST carrying patients.

Finally, all units benefited by the 43d Division's experience in dealing with war neurosis. Rest camps, providing hot food, baths, clean clothes, and cots, were established on the barrier islands, and Colonel Hallam tried to see to it that more accurate diagnoses were made so that men suffering from combat fatigue were separated from true neurotics and sent to the camps.

Air Support

Air support of the New Georgia operation had been generally good, and the scale of bombing was increasing. Completion of the Segi Point field on 10 July and full employment of the Russells fields made it possible for fighters to escort all bombing missions. These missions could therefore be executed in daylight with resulting increases in accuracy. South Pacific air units were able to put more planes in the air at one time than ever before. Regular strikes against the Shortlands and southern Bougainville were intensified.

Allied fighters providing the 0700 to 1630 cover for the New Georgia Occupation Force also escorted the almost daily bombing attacks against Munda, Bairoko, and Vila. Fighter operations were proving especially effective in protecting the beachheads and shipping. On 15 July some seventy-five Japanese bombers and fighters were intercepted by thirty-one Allied fighters, who reported knocking down forty-five enemy craft at a cost of three American planes. Thereafter Japanese aircraft virtually abandoned daylight attacks against Rendova and New Georgia and confined their efforts to nocturnal harassment.

Bombing and strafing missions in sup-

BOMBING OF MUNDA AIRFIELD, EARLY MORNING, *12 July 1943. Photograph taken from Kokorana Island.*

port of the ground troops were numerous and heavy, considering the number of aircraft in the South Pacific. On 16 July 37 torpedo bombers and an equal number of dive bombers struck at Lambeti with thirty-six 1,000-pound, eighteen 2,000-pound, and eighty-eight 500-pound bombs at 0905. The strike was followed by another against Munda by 36 SBD's and TBF's. These dropped twelve 1,000-pound and twelve 2,000-pound bombs at 1555. On 19 July 20 TBF's and 18 SBD's hit at positions north of Munda, and the next day 36 SBD's dropped 1,000-pound bombs at suspected gun positions north of Lambeti. Two days later 36 SBD's and 18 TBF's again bombed the Munda gun positions, which were struck once more by 16 SBD's on 23 July. On 24 July, the day before the corps offensive began, 37 TBF's and 36 SBD's with a screen of 48 fighters dropped thirty-seven 2,000-pound and thirty-six 1,000-pound bombs on Bairoko in the morning. In late afternoon 18 SBD's and 16 TBF's hit Munda and Bibilo Hill.

Most of the aircraft flying these missions were piloted by marines. It will be noted that this air support was, according to then current Army doctrine, direct air support. Most of these missions were flown as part of "a combined effort of the air and ground forces, in the battle area, to gain objectives on the immediate front of the ground forces." [11] But

---

[11] See FM 100–20, Command and Employment of Air Power (1943), p. 16. See also TM 20–205, Dictionary of United States Army Terms (1944), p. 90.

as most of the targets were several thousand yards from the front lines, this was not close air support, which was defined after the war as "attack by aircraft on hostile ground or naval targets which are so close to friendly forces as to require detailed integration of each air mission with the fire and movement of these forces." [12] South Pacific commanders, including General Harmon, had hoped to make extensive use of close air support on New Georgia, and a few close air support missions such as that requested by Colonel Holland had been executed, but they were difficult for the air forces to execute and dangerous to the ground troops. There was, at that time, no systematized target marking system nor any good means of radio communication between the front lines and the aircraft. The Thirteenth Air Force had no tactical air communications squadron. The dense jungle and rolling terrain where the troops were operating had so few landmarks that pilots could not easily orient themselves. Nor could the ground troops orient themselves any more easily. Panels marking the front lines could scarcely be seen from the air. Enemy positions could rarely be identified by spotters in observation planes or by air liaison parties on the ground. Because maps were inexact, and the troops had difficulty in locating themselves precisely, bombing missions executed close to the front lines resulted in casualties to American troops. Three soldiers of the 172d Infantry were killed in that way on 16 July. For these reasons close air support was seldom used in any of the CARTWHEEL operations. The direct air support on New Georgia was, however, of great value, and General Griswold had every intention of following Harmon's order that the New Georgia operation employ air support to the maximum degree.

Griswold, in the nine days following his assumption of command, had improved supply and evacuation on New Georgia. In spite of the failure at Bairoko, the tactical position, too, had improved. The tired 169th had been relieved, and fresh 25th and 37th Division regiments were ready to enter the fight. The troops had repulsed a counterattack, improved their position by seizing high ground, and now held a southeast-northwest line about three thousand yards from the east end of Munda field. The XIV Corps could look forward to receiving the same resolute, effective air and naval support that had aided the 43d Division. With the logistic and tactical situations of his troops thus improved, and sure of ample air and naval support, Griswold was ready to attack Munda.

---

[12] SR 320–5–1, Dictionary of United States Army Terms, (Aug 50), p. 48.

CHAPTER IX

XIV Corps Offensive

The plan for the XIV Corps' drive against Munda was completed shortly after Griswold took over.[1] Col. Eugene W. Ridings, Griswold's assistant chief of staff, G–3, flew to Koli Point to confer with General Harmon and Admiral Wilkinson on naval gunfire and air support. Ridings also asked for, and obtained, a better radio (SCR 193) for Liversedge, to improve communications between him and Griswold. Harmon stressed the importance of submitting a precise plan for air support to Admiral Mitscher. Dive bombers would naturally be the best for close work, while mediums and heavies should be used for area bombing, he asserted. Harmon agreed to send in more tanks at Griswold's request.[2]

Plans

The American Plan

Naval support plans called for a seven-destroyer bombardment of Lambeti Plantation shortly before the infantry's advance. Comdr. Arleigh A. Burke, the destroyer division commander, came to Rendova on 23 July to view Roviana La-goon and select visual check points. Air support for the offensive would include, besides the normal fighter cover, pattern bombing by multiengine planes in front of the 43d Division about halfway between Ilangana and Lambeti Plantation. Single-engine planes would strike at positions north and northeast of Munda field. Artillery spotting planes and liaison planes would be on station continuously.

Artillery support would be provided by Barker's artillery from its island positions. Plans called for fairly standard employment of the field artillery, providing for direct and general support of the attack, massing of fires in each infantry's zone of advance, counterbattery fire, and the defense of Rendova against seaborne and air attack. One 105-mm. howitzer battalion was assigned to direct support of each regiment, one 155-mm. howitzer battalion to general support of each division. Except for specific direct and general support missions, all artillery would operate as the corps artillery under Barker. The XIV Corps had neither organic artillery nor an artillery commander.[3]

Griswold's field order, issued on 22

---

[1] Unless otherwise indicated this chapter is based on the same sources as Chapter VIII.

[2] It was at this conference that he approved the transfer of the 161st Regimental Combat Team to New Georgia.

---

[3] See Miller, *Guadalcanal: The First Offensive,* pp. 218–19.

July, directed his corps to attack vigorously to seize Munda airfield and Bibilo Hill from its present positions which ran from Ilangana northwest for about three thousand yards. (*Map 10*) The 37th Division was to make the corps' main effort. Beightler's division was to attack to its front, envelop the enemy's left (north) flank, seize Bibilo Hill, and drive the enemy into the sea. At the same time it would protect the corps' right flank and rear. The 43d Division was ordered to make its main effort on the right. Its objectives were Lambeti Plantation and the airfield. Liversedge's force, depleted by the abortive attack on Bairoko, was to continue patrolling and give timely information regarding any Japanese move to send overland reinforcements to Munda. The 9th Defense Battalion's Tank Platoon would assemble at Laiana under corps control. The 1st and 2d Battalions, 169th Infantry, at Rendova, constituted the corps reserve.[4]

All units were ordered to exert unceasing pressure on the enemy. Isolated points of resistance were not to be allowed to halt the advance, but were to be bypassed, contained, and reduced later. Griswold ordered maximum use of infantry heavy weapons to supplement artillery. Roads would be pushed forward with all possible speed.

D Day was set for 25 July. The thirty-minute naval bombardment was to start at 0610, the air bombing at 0635. The line of departure, running northwest from Ilangana, was practically identical with the American front lines except in the zone of the 161st Infantry where the existence of the Japanese strongpoint east of the line had been determined on 24 July.

The XIV Corps was thus attempting a frontal assault on a two-division front, with the hope of effecting an evelopment on the north. In the initial attack it would employ two three-battalion regiments (the 161st and the 172d) and three two-battalion regiments (the 103d, the 145th, and the 148th).

Enemy Positions and Plans

On 22 July the Japanese front line ran inland in a northwesterly direction for some 3,200 yards. This line was manned by the entire *229th Infantry*, and at the month's end the *2d Battalion, 230th Infantry*, was also assigned to it. In support were various mountain artillery, antitank, antiaircraft, and automatic weapons units.[5] The positions were the same complex of camouflaged and mutually supporting pillboxes, trenches, and foxholes that had halted Hester in midmonth. The pillboxes started near the beach at Ilangana and ran over the hills in front of the 103d, 172d, 145th, and 161st Regiments.

---

[4] Griswold issued his attack order as NGOF FO 1, 22 July 43, although Hester had issued NGOF FO 1 in June.

The 37th Division was less the 129th Regimental Combat Team and the 3d Battalions, 145th and 148th Infantry Regiments, and was reinforced by the 161st Regimental Combat Team (less its artillery) and a detachment of South Pacific Scouts.

The 43d Division was less nearly all its headquarters, whose officers were filling most of the posts in Occupation Force headquarters, and less two battalions of the 169th Infantry and the 1st Battalion, 103d Infantry.

[5] These included the *Antitank Battalion, 38th Division; 2d Independent Antitank Battalion;* a detachment of the *2d Battalion, 90th Independent Mountain Artillery Regiment;* thirteen 7.7-mm. machine guns, and two 75-mm. antiaircraft units.

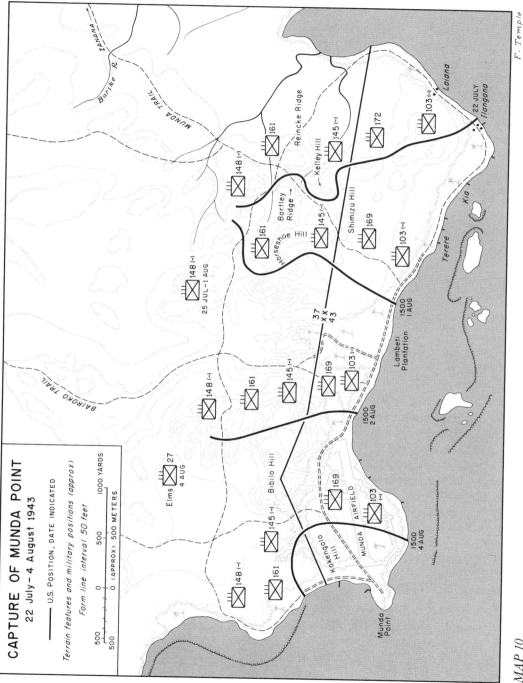

CAPTURE OF MUNDA POINT
22 July – 4 August 1943

U.S. POSITION, DATE INDICATED

Terrain features and military positions (approx)

Form line interval 50 feet

500   0   500   1000 YARDS

500   0   (APPROX) 500 METERS

MAP 10

F. Temple

A particularly strong series lay on a tangled set of jungled hills: Shimizu Hill in front of the 172d Infantry, and Horseshoe Hill (so named from its configuration) in front of the 145th and 161st Regiments. Horseshoe Hill lay northwest of Kelley Hill and west of Reincke Ridge. East of Horseshoe Hill lay the Japanese pocket discovered by the 161st. The pocket lay on a north-south ridge that was joined to Horseshoe Hill by a rough saddle. The pillbox line terminated at about the northern boundary of the 161st Infantry. When the *2d Battalion, 230th Infantry,* was committed it did not occupy carefully prepared positions. From the end of the pillboxes the line ran west to the beach, and this north flank does not seem to have been strongly held.

XIV Corps headquarters still estimated that four enemy battalions faced it; three at Munda and one at Bairoko. This was a fairly accurate estimate of strength on the enemy line, but Sasaki had an ace up his sleeve—the *13th Infantry.* This regiment, which was not in full strength, was stationed on the American right flank about 4,900 yards west by north from Ilangana. Sasaki's plans to use his ace were similar to his earlier plans. On the same day that Griswold issued his field order, Sasaki directed Colonel Tomonari to attack the American right flank in the vicinity of Horseshoe Hill on 23 July, then drive east along the Munda Trail. But the Americans struck before Tomonari made his move.

Ilangana and Shimizu Hill: The 43d Division

In the 43d Division's zone, the offensive began as scheduled on the morning of 25 July. For once the weather was favorable. D Day dawned fair and clear, with visibility as good as could be expected in the jungle.

Naval gunfire, air, and artillery preparations went off as scheduled. Commander Burke's seven destroyers had sailed up from Tulagi. At 0609 the two screening destroyers fired the first of four thousand 5-inch shells at Lambeti Plantation; these were followed by the main group at 0614. Visibility to seaward was good, but the morning haze still hung over Lambeti Plantation. Fifteen minutes later visibility had improved but now the target area was partly obscured by smoke and dust raised by the bombardment.[6] Firing ceased at 0644.

From 0630 to 0700, 254 aircraft unloaded 500,800 pounds of fragmentation and high explosive bombs on their target area, a 1,500-by-250-yard strip beginning about 500 yards west of the 103d Infantry's front lines. No corps artillery concentrations were fired on 25 July, but the 43d Division's supporting artillery began before 0700 the first of more than 100 preparations that were fired

---

[6] When the infantrymen later reached Lambeti Plantation they found that although the bombardment had done extensive damage many positions, which could have been destroyed only by direct hits, remained intact. The theoretical density of this shelling was 70 rounds per 100 square yards. Admiral Wilkinson, who thought the target area was too far west of the front lines, later observed that 200 rounds per 100 square yards would be required to achieve complete destruction. Because of the difficulty in distinguishing targets in morning haze, Commander Burke recommended that shore bombardments should not start earlier than twenty minutes before sunrise. See CTF 31 (Com III AMPHFOR) Action Rpt for Morning 25 Jul 43, The Bombardment of Munda, 3 Sep 43, in Off of Naval Rcds and Library; and ONI USN, Operations in the New Georgia Area, pp. 53–54.

that day. The 103d and 152d Field Artillery Battalions fired more than 2,150 105-mm. howitzer shells; the 155-mm. howitzers of the 136th Field Artillery Battalion threw 1,182 rounds at the enemy.

With the din subsiding as the artillery shifted its fire to positions farther west, the infantrymen of the 43d Division moved to the attack at 0700. In the 172d Infantry's zone the 2d and 3d Battalions on the left and right attacked westward against Shimizu Hill. But by 1000 they had run into the enemy pillbox line and halted. Colonel Ross then requested tanks, got some from the corps reserve, and attacked again. By 1430 three tanks were disabled, and the attack stalled. A little ground had been gained on the regimental left.

The 103d Infantry, now commanded by Colonel Brown, attacked alongside the 172d with little more success.[7] The 3d Battalion, on the left, pushed forward against machine gun and mortar fire, but immediately hit the Japanese line and stopped. The battalion attempted to move around the pillboxes but found that this maneuver took its men into other machine gun fire lanes.

The 2d Battalion, 103d, in the center of the 43d's zone, did better. It moved forward two or three hundred yards against light opposition. By 1040 E Company's leading elements had advanced five hundred yards. The company kept moving until noon, when it had reached the beach near Terere. Here it set up a hasty defense position. But the companies on either flank had not been able to keep up, and the Japanese moved in behind E Company to cut the telephone line to battalion headquarters.

To exploit E Company's breakthrough, General Hester took the 3d Battalion, 169th Infantry, out of division reserve and ordered it to push through the same hole E Company had found. But the Japanese had obviously become aware of the gap, and as the 3d Battalion marched to the line of departure it was enfiladed by fire from the south part of Shimizu Hill and from the pillboxes to the south. It halted. Five Marine tanks were then ordered to push over Shimizu Hill but could not get up the steep slopes. When three of them developed vapor lock all were pulled back to Laiana. In late afternoon the E Company commander decided to abandon his exposed, solitary position, and E Company came safely back through the Japanese line to the 2d Battalion.

North of the 43d Division the 37th Division had made scant progress.[8] Thus the first day of General Griswold's offensive found the XIV Corps held for little gain except in the center of the 43d Division's line.

The 43d Division was weakened by almost a month's combat, and its reduced strength was spread over a long, irregular, slanting front. It was obvious that combat efficiency would be increased by narrowing the front, and this could be done by advancing the left and straightening the line. Consequently Hester's plan for 26 July called for the 172d to stay in place while the 103d Infantry attempted to advance the eight

---

[7] Colonel Brown, formerly commander of the 2d Battalion, took over regimental command when Colonel Hundley replaced the 43d Division chief of staff on 22 July.

[8] See below, pp. 149–52.

hundred yards from Ilangana to Terere.

Strong combat patrols went out in the morning of 26 July to fix the location of the Japanese pillboxes as accurately as possible. After their return, the artillery began firing at 1115, one hour before the infantry was to attack. At 1145 the 103d's front was covered with smoke and under its cover the front-line companies withdrew a hundred yards. At noon the artillery put its fire on the Japanese positions directly in front. As the tanks were not quite ready at H Hour, 1215, the artillery kept firing for ten more minutes. It lifted fire one hundred yards at 1225, and the 103d started forward. The tanks led the advance in the center; behind them was the infantry. Attached to the 103d for the attack were 2d Lt. James F. Olds, Jr., the acting corps chemical officer, and six volunteers from the 118th Engineer Battalion. Each carried a flame thrower, a weapon which the 43d Division had brought to New Georgia but had not used up to now.[9] Griswold, whose headquarters had conducted flame thrower schools on Guadalcanal, was aware of the weapon's possibilities. That morning the six engineers had received one hour of training in the use of the M1A1 flame thrower.

The flame throwers went forward with the infantry, which halted about twenty yards in front of the pillbox line and covered it with small arms fire. Under cover of this fire the flame thrower operators, their faces camouflaged with dirt, crawled forward. Operating in teams of two and three, they sprayed flame over three barely visible pillboxes in front of the center of the 103d's line. Vegetation was instantly burned off. In sixty seconds the three pillboxes were knocked out and their four occupants were dead.[10]

Operations of the infantry, tanks, flame throwers, and supporting heavy weapons and artillery met with almost complete success. The 103d Infantry encountered seventy-four pillboxes on a 600-yard front, but by midafternoon, spurred on by pressure from General Wing, it had reduced enemy resistance at Ilangana. From there it continued its advance through underbrush and vines and gained almost 800 yards. By 1700 the left flank rested on the coastal village of Kia. The 43d Division's line, formerly 1,700 yards long, was now much straighter by 300 yards.

From 28 through 31 July, the 43d Division inched slowly forward, a few yards on the right flank and about five hundred yards along the coast. This was accomplished by "aggressive action and small unit maneuver, combined with constant artillery and mortar action [which] gradually forced the enemy back from his high ground defenses."[11] The 172d ground its way over Shimizu Hill, the last real ridge between it and Munda airfield, and in doing so it helped unhinge the main Japanese defense system in its zone, just as the 103d's drive

---

[9] On 19 July Griswold radioed Guadalcanal to state his urgent need for more M1A1 flame throwers.

[10] Capt. James F. Olds, Jr., "Flamethrowers Front and Center," *Chemical Warfare Bulletin*, Vol. 30, No. 3 (June–July 1944), pp. 5–9. This account, while valuable, seems to have telescoped two situations and actions into one, for Olds asserts that the 103d was at Lambeti Plantation on 26 July. From the fact that three pillboxes had only four occupants, it would seem that this part of the Japanese line was lightly manned.

[11] 43d Div Rpt of Opns, Munda Campaign, p. 13.

through Ilangana had broken the enemy line on the left.[12]

Major Zimmer's 1st Battalion, 169th Infantry, was brought over from Rendova on 29 July; the 3d Battalion, now commanded by Maj. Ignatius M. Ramsey, was taken out of division reserve and the 169th (less the 2d Battalion) was assigned a zone between the 172d and the 103d.[13] As the month ended the 169th (less its 2d Battalion in corps reserve) was in the process of extending to the northwest to pinch out the 172d.

Command of the 43d Division changed hands on 29 July when Maj. Gen. John R. Hodge, the tough, blunt commander of the Americal Division, came up from the Fijis to take over from Hester. This change was ordered by General Harmon who felt that Hester had exhausted himself. General Hodge had served as assistant commander of the 25th Division during the Guadalcanal Campaign, and thus had had more experience in jungle warfare than any other general then in New Georgia. Hodge, Harmon wrote, was the "best Div Comdr I have in area for this particular job." [14]

The 43d Division, having cracked through the Shimizu Hill–Ilangana positions, was in a favorable position to drive against Munda under its new commander, while the 37th Division on its right fought its way through the enemy positions in its hilly, jungled zone.

The Attack Against the Ridges: The 37th Division

The dawn of D Day, 25 July, found the 43d Division committed to a general attack, but the 37th Division was forced to postpone its advance. General Beightler had issued a field order on 23 July calling for a general attack by his three regiments, to start at 0700, 25 July. The 145th, 161st, and 148th Infantry Regiments were to attack due west, toward Bibilo Hill, on the division's left, center, and right, with the 145th maintaining contact with the 172d Infantry on its left and the 148th Infantry covering the corps' right flank and rear. But the discovery of the strong Japanese position east of the 161st Infantry's line of departure altered the plans.

On 24 July Beightler ordered Colonel Holland not to advance his 145th Infantry, but to stay in place. He told Colonel Baxter to move the 148th Infantry only up to the line of departure. The two regiments would hold while part of the 161st contained the Japanese position and the rest of the regiment bypassed it and came up on a line with the 145th and 148th.

After Baxter received the commanding general's orders, he suggested that his regiment could perhaps help the 161st reduce the pocket by making a limited advance. Baxter hoped to establish an observation post on high ground from which both Munda airfield and the pocket in front of the 161st could be

---

[12] Unfortunately the records are too scanty to provide details showing just how the 172d took this position. During the attack 1st Lt. Robert S. Scott almost singlehandedly halted a Japanese counterattack and for his gallantry was awarded the Medal of Honor. WD GO 81, 14 Oct 44.

[13] Colonel Reincke was now regimental executive officer.

[14] See Ltr, Harmon to Griswold, quoted in SOPACBACOM, History of the New Georgia Campaign, I, 25, OCMH. See also Halsey and Bryan, *Admiral Halsey's Story*, p. 161; Rad 2027, COMGENSOPAC to CofS USA, 10 Aug 43, in Marshall's IN Log.

seen. Beightler assented to this request at 0910, 25 July. Patrols went out, and on their return the direct support artillery battalion laid a ten-minute preparation 400 yards in front of the line of departure while mortars covered the 400-yard gap. The 2d Battalion, 148th, commanded by Lt. Col. Herbert Radcliffe, started forward, met no Japanese, and gained 500–600 yards.[15] The 1st Battalion, Lt. Col. Vernor E. Hydaker commanding, moved up to the 2d Battalion's old positions.

Bartley Ridge and Horseshoe Hill

When I Company, 161st Infantry, had been unable to reduce the Japanese strongpoint on Bartley Ridge on 24 July, Colonel Dalton issued orders for its seizure on D Day.[16] I Company was to contain the Japanese pocket by attacking to its front while the 1st Battalion and the rest of the 3d Battalion executed a double envelopment.[17] The 1st Battalion was to move around the Japanese left (north) flank while the 3d Battalion went around the right, after which the two battalions would drive southward and northward for two hundred yards. Fifteen minutes of mortar fire would precede these moves. Beightler arranged for the 145th and 148th Regiments to support the 161st with heavy

weapons fire. He also asked corps headquarters for tanks to help the 161st, but the 43d Division had been given the tanks for the D-Day attack.

From positions near the Laiana Trail eight 81-mm. mortars opened fire at 0745, 25 July, in support of Dalton's attack. Heavy weapons of the adjoining regiments attempted to deliver their supporting fires, but the denseness of the jungle prevented forward observers' controlling the fire. The unobserved fire began obstructing rather than helping the 161st, and that part of the plan was abandoned.

The 3d Battalion, commanded by Lt. Col. David H. Buchanan, was unable to gain. Shortly after 0800, when the attack began, I Company reported that its attack against the ridge strongpoint had stalled. A knob projecting east from Bartley Ridge and the heavy undergrowth provided enough cover and concealment to let the infantrymen reach the base of the ridge, but uphill from the knob, where the growth was thinner, all movement was halted by fire from the crest. The 161st Infantry had made plans to use flame throwers, and an operator carrying his sixty-five pounds of equipment made two laborious climbs and silenced an enemy machine gun, but many other Japanese positions remained in action. The main body of the 3d Battalion, attempting to get around the south end of Bartley Ridge, was also halted.

The 1st Battalion was more successful. At 1035 its commander, Lt. Col. Slaftcho Katsarsky, radioed Dalton that he had found the north flank of the Japanese position on Bartley Ridge, and

---

[15] Because of the inaccurate maps and densely jungled, rough ground, all units had difficulty in determining distances and exact locations. Nearly all reports warn that distances and locations are only estimates, and all give widely varying figures.

[16] Bartley Ridge was named in memory of 2d Lt. Martin E. Bartley, an I Company platoon leader killed on 25 July.

[17] The 2d Battalion was in division reserve along with the 37th Cavalry Reconnaissance Troop.

that he was moving his battalion around it. Shortly afterward Beightler, Dalton, and staff officers conferred and decided that the 3d Battalion should contain the strongpoint while the 1st Battalion pushed westward with orders to develop enemy positions but not to engage in full-scale combat. The 37th Division could not advance westward in force until Bartley Ridge had been cleared.

The 3d Battalion established itself in containing positions north, east, and south of Bartley Ridge. E Company was released from reserve and sent into line on high ground just north of Bartley to secure the right flank in the 161st's zone. The 1st Battalion advanced to a point about four hundred yards west of Bartley and halted on a small rise northeast of Horseshoe Hill. Tanks of the newly arrived 10th Marine Defense Battalion were to be committed to support the 37th Division the next day, and in the afternoon the tank commander made a personal reconnaissance of Colonel Buchanan's zone in preparation for the attack.

Six light Marine tanks were to lead out in the attack at 0900, 26 July, after preparatory fire by machine guns and 81-mm. mortars. L and K Companies, in column, would move behind the tanks, which were supported by infantrymen armed with .30-caliber M1 rifles, .30-caliber Browning Automatic Rifles (BAR's), and two flame throwers. Tank-infantry communication was indirect. The tank radios formed a net within the Tank Platoon, and a 161st radio car maintained radio contact between the Tank Platoon commander and Colonel Buchanan.

When the tanks, with their hatches closed, got off the approach trail that had been bulldozed by members of the 65th Engineer Battalion, Colonel Buchanan directed the infantrymen to lead them forward. It was 0925 before the attack got started. In two lines of three vehicles each, the tanks lumbered over the littered undergrowth, steep slopes, and felled logs toward the southeast slope of Bartley Ridge. The Japanese quickly responded with fire from anti-tank and 70-mm. battalion guns, machine guns, and mortars.

The attack went well at first. About a dozen pillboxes were reported knocked out by 1110, and Buchanan ordered his men to occupy them to keep the Japanese from moving in again at night. Unfortunately, the tanks had encountered exactly the sort of difficulties that might be expected in tangled terrain with communications uncertain. In their lurches and frequent changes of direction they injured some of the accompanying foot troops. Poor visibility caused them to get into untenable positions from which they had to be extricated with consequent delays to the attack. During the morning a Japanese soldier stole out of the tangled brush and planted a magnetic mine that disabled one tank. A second tank was halted by a ruptured fuel line. The remaining four withdrew at 1110 to reorganize.

The flame thrower operators, carrying their bulky, heavy fuel tanks on their backs, were not properly protected by the riflemen and were soon killed.

In the course of the day's fighting some fourteen pillboxes and a number of machine gun positions were knocked out, and the 3d Battalion advanced about two hundred yards up Bartley Ridge.[18] But it met such heavy fire from Bartley and Horseshoe Hill that its position clearly could not be held. Attempts to pull out the disabled tanks were unsuccessful. The battalion withdrew to its previous positions. The attack had disclosed the existence of so many more positions that Dalton received Beightler's permission to make a thorough reconnaissance before attacking again.

While the 161st was attacking Bartley Ridge on 25 and 26 July, Colonel Holland's 145th Infantry stayed in its forward positions on Reincke Ridge and Kelley Hill. During this period it sent out patrols to the north and west to try to find the source of the 90-mm. mortar fire that had been hitting the regiment since 22 July. It received no artillery support at this time because its front line was considered too close to enemy targets for the artillery to fire without hitting American infantry. By the end of 26 July the 1st Battalion, 161st, had fought its way forward to come up on line north of the 145th, but near the regimental boundary the line sagged eastward in the shape of a great U. Colonel Parker's 2d Battalion, 145th, was occupying positions in rear of the 1st Battalion, 145th, commanded by Lt. Col. Richard D. Crooks.

General Beightler ordered Holland to commit his 2d Battalion, in order to reduce the Japanese positions on Horseshoe Hill that had fired on the 3d Bat-

talion, 161st, during its 26 July attack against Bartley Ridge. Doubtless because troops of the 161st had not been able to get past the south end of Bartley, Colonel Parker's battalion was to march northward right around the 3d Battalion, 161st, push west around the north of the enemy positions on Bartley Ridge, then attack to the southwest. This maneuver would entail a march of about one and one-half miles to the assembly area.

Parker's battalion moved out in the early morning of 27 July. It reached its assembly area on the north flank of Bartley Ridge without incident. After a preparation of one hundred rounds by the division artillery, which cleared some of the foliage, the battalion advanced to the attack in column of companies. "Having to fight every foot of the way," it gained about three hundred yards before 1300, when E Company in the lead moved south off slopes of a ridge and started up a small knob projecting from Horseshoe Hill.[19] As the company ascended the hill it was struck by fire from pillboxes. Among the first men killed was Capt. Gardner B. Wing, E Company's commander, in whose honor the 145th christened the knob.

On the same day, while American mortars fired intermittently at Bartley Ridge, patrols from the 3d Battalion, 161st Infantry, examined the Japanese lines to procure data for a preparation by the corps artillery. In the course of the reconnaissance Colonels Dalton and Buchanan observed enemy pillboxes on the right flank of the 1st Battalion, 145th

---

[18] In the course of the day's action Capt. Paul K. Mellichamp, battalion executive officer, picked up a radio from a wounded operator and directed mortar fire. He was wounded, but continued to direct the fire until he collapsed. He died shortly afterward, and was awarded the Distinguished Service Cross.

[19] 37th Div G–3 Jnl, 27 Jul 43.

Infantry, and recommended that the attack be delayed until 29 July.[20] General Beightler gave his assent. Dalton and Buchanan also decided to attack from the northwest instead of the southeast. Reconnaissance and pressure were to continue on the 28th.

On the morning of the 28th a ten-man patrol from I Company, led by Lt. Walter Tymniak, set out in a southerly direction toward the top of Bartley Ridge. To their surprise and satisfaction, the Americans met no fire, got safely to the top, and found several abandoned pillboxes. They occupied them, and I Company followed to the crest and began infiltrating the pillboxes. Not all were vacant, but the task of the attackers was eased as each pillbox was taken, for its fire could then no longer be used with that of its neighbors to make crossfire or interlocking bands of fire. Because the Japanese appeared to be evacuating and the American front was intermingled with the enemy front, the artillery preparation was called off. The 3d Battalion continued its infiltration on 29 July. At the end of the day it was relieved by Maj. Francis P. Carberry's 2d Battalion and went into division reserve.

The 145th Infantry's zone was shifted farther north on 30 July as part of a general shift in boundaries that General Griswold was making in order to widen the 43d Division's front. This move placed the southern half of Bartley Ridge within the 145th's zone. Colonel Parker's 2d Battalion, 145th, had just completed its move around the 161st's north flank, thence southwest against Horseshoe Hill. On 30 July it was attached to the 161st for the completion of the reduction of Bartley Ridge and Horseshoe Hill.

Carberry's and Parker's battalions pushed their attacks on 30 July. In contrast with Carberry's battalion, which met little resistance, Parker's men engaged in sharp fighting in the west. The Japanese who had evacuated the position facing Carberry had apparently moved into positions facing Parker. With grenade, rifle, machine gun, mortar, and flame thrower the two battalions fought all day and part of the next, until by midafternoon of 31 July the Japanese rear guards on Bartley Ridge were either dead or in flight, and the 2d Battalion, 161st, had advanced west and was on a line with the 1st. Bartley Ridge had contained forty-six log and coral pillboxes and thirty-two other lighter positions. First attacked by a company, it fell only after seven days' fighting by two battalions.

On Horseshoe Hill the Japanese resisted from their pillboxes and foxholes with equal skill and enthusiasm. The Americans used small arms, grenades, automatic weapons, mortars, flame throwers, and field artillery as they systematically reduced the enemy positions, almost pillbox by pillbox.[21] On 1 August Parker's battalion received orders to attack in late afternoon, obeyed, and took Horseshoe Hill without firing a shot or losing a man. The Japanese had gone.

---

[20] It is not clear whether these pillboxes were on Horseshoe Hill or were on the saddle connecting Bartley Ridge with Horseshoe Hill.

[21] During these operations Pfc. Frank J. Petrarca, a medical aid man, so distinguished himself by gallant, selfless devotion to duty that he was posthumously awarded the Medal of Honor. WD GO 86, 23 Dec 43.

Advance and Withdrawal of the 148th Infantry

On 1 August, the day on which the Americans completely occupied the ridge positions, the 148th Infantry returned eastward to the 37th Division's lines after an advance which had taken it almost to Bibilo Hill. The 148th Infantry was the only regiment not confronted by prepared enemy positions, and it had made comparatively rapid progress from the first. When Colonel Baxter moved his regiment forward on 25 July, it went around the north flank of the Japanese defense line and met no resistance. However, none of the Americans then knew that the major part of the enemy *13th Infantry* lay to the north of Baxter's right flank. Patrols, accompanied by Fiji scouts, went out and reported the presence of a few Japanese to the west, none to the south. Generals Griswold and Beightler had emphasized the importance of maintaining lateral contact and Beightler had expressly directed that the 148th was to maintain contact with the 161st, and that all units were to inform their neighbors and the next higher unit of their locations. The 148th, however, was not able to make contact on its left with the 161st Infantry.

Baxter's two-battalion regiment advanced regularly for the next three days. Colonel Radcliffe's 2d Battalion led on 26 and 27 July; on 28 July Colonel Hydaker's 1st Battalion bypassed the 2d and led the advance to a point somewhere east of Bibilo Hill.[22] Patrols went out regularly and at no time reported the presence of a sizable body of the enemy. On 27 July Baxter reported that he had established "contact with Whiskers." Colonel Dalton, the "guest artist" regimental commander of the attached 161st Infantry, sported a beard and was dubbed "Whiskers" and "Goatbeard" in the 37th Division's telephone code. But the 148th's front was almost a thousand yards west of Whiskers' 1st Battalion, and the contact must have been tenuous. Next day G Company was ordered to move to the left to close a gap between the two regiments, but the gap stayed open.

During the move troops of the 117th Engineer Battalion labored to push a supply trail behind the advancing battalions. The rate of march was in part geared to the construction of the supply trail. As Baxter told Radcliffe over the telephone on 27 July, "I am advancing behind you as fast as bulldozer goes."[23]

Next day, however, there occurred a disturbing event. A platoon from A Company, 117th Engineer Battalion, was using a bulldozer to build the trail somewhere north of Horseshoe Hill when it was ambushed by the enemy. Three engineers were killed and two were wounded before elements of the Antitank Company and of the 1st Battalion rescued the platoon and extricated the bulldozer.

Japanese movements during this period are obscure, but this and subsequent attacks were made by the *13th Infantry* coming south at last in accordance with Sasaki's orders.

The situation became more serious on 28 July, the day on which Baxter's ag-

---

[22] The total of daily yardage reported in the journals, if correct, would have placed the 148th west of Bibilo Hill on 28 July, but the 148th soldiers, like almost everyone else in the jungle, overestimated the distances they had traveled.

[23] 148th Inf Jnl, 27 Jul 43.

gressive movement took him almost to Bibilo Hill. At this time the regiment was spread thinly about fifteen hundred yards beyond the 161st; its front lay some twelve hundred yards west of the regimental ration dump and eighteen hundred yards from the point on the supply line "which could be said to be adequately secured by other division units." [24] There was still no contact with the 161st, and in the afternoon a group of the *13th Infantry* fell upon the ration dump. From high ground commanding it the enemy fired with machine guns, rifles, and grenade discharges at men of the regimental Service Company. The Service Company soldiers took cover among ration and ammunition boxes and returned the fire. The dump, under command of Maj. Frank Hipp, 148th S-4, held out until relieved by two squads of the Antitank Company and one platoon from F Company. East of the dump, troops of the *13th Infantry* also forced the 148th's supply trucks to turn back. Baxter, stating "I now find my CP in the front line," asked Beightler to use divisional units to guard the trail up to the dump.[25]

All the 148th's troubles with the Japanese were in the rear areas. The westward push, which took the leading battalion as far as one of the Munda–Bairoko trails, had been practically unopposed. But early on the morning of 29 July General Beightler, unaware of the *13th*'s position, telephoned Baxter to say that as the Japanese seemed to be moving from the southwest through the gap between the 148th and 161st Regi-

ments, and around the 148th's right, Baxter was to close up his battalions and consolidate his positions. At 0710 Beightler told Baxter to withdraw his battalions to the east, to establish contact with the 161st, and to protect his supply route. Baxter, who had sent patrols out in all directions early in the morning, at 0800 ordered one company of the 2d Battalion to clear out the supply trail to the east. At 0941, with Japanese machine guns still dominating the supply trail, Beightler sent Baxter more orders similar to those of 0710, and also ordered forward a detachment of the 37th Cavalry Reconnaissance Troop to help clear the east end of the supply trail. The telephone, so busy with conversations between Beightler and Baxter on 29 July, was then quiet for an hour.

Meanwhile Beightler had been conferring with Dalton, Holland, and members of the divisional general staff. As a result he had decided that the 161st should continue reducing Bartley Ridge, that the 145th should stay in place, and that the 148th would have to withdraw. So at 1055 Baxter ordered his regiment to turn around and pull back to the east. The 2d Battalion, 148th, was to use at least one company to establish contact with the 161st while the rest of the battalion withdrew toward the ration dump. The 1st Battalion would move back to the 2d Battalion's positions. At 1150 Baxter reported the 2d Battalion in contact with the 161st, and shortly afterward Beightler ordered Baxter to move the 1st Battalion farther east, putting it in position to deliver an attack the next morning against the rear of the Japanese holding up Dalton's regiment. The division commander again empha-

---

[24] 37th Div Opn Rpt, p. 6.
[25] 37th Div G-3 Jnl, 28 Jul 43.

sized the necessity for maintaining firm contact with the 161st.[26] At 1305, with the 148th moving east, Colonel Katsarsky reported that his 1st Battalion, 161st, had as yet no contact with the 148th. Beightler at once told Baxter that, as Japanese machine gunners were operating between the two regiments, the gap must be closed before dark. An hour later Baxter called Beightler to say that he was too far west to close with the 161st before dark. When Beightler ordered him to close up anyway, Baxter demurred. Asking his general to reconsider the order, he stated that he could almost, but not quite, close the gap. Beightler thereupon told Baxter to comply with his orders as far as was physically possible.

The 2d Battalion had meanwhile been pushing east, except for F Company's main body, which was advancing west toward the ration dump. Both bodies were encountering enemy resistance, and the day ended before the Japanese were cleared out. The Reconnaissance Troop cleared some Japanese from the eastern part of the supply trail, but at 1758 Baxter reported that the trail had been closed by raiding Japanese.

The 148th Infantry, in examining the personal effects of some of the dead Japanese, found that the men belonged to the *13th Infantry*. Some of them had been carrying booty taken in the raids east of the Barike several days earlier. Colonel Baxter later estimated that the enemy harrying his regiment numbered no more than 250, operating "in multi-

ple small light machine gun and mortar detachments and . . . [moving] from position to position utilizing the jungle to its maximum advantage. You can well imagine what we could do with our M-1's, BAR's and Machine Guns if all we had to do was dig in and wait for the Jap to come at us." [27]

General Beightler, a National Guardsman most of his life, was an affable man, but he was far from satisfied with the outcome of the day's action.[28] At 1832 he radioed Baxter that General Griswold had ordered the 148th to establish contact with the 161st early the next morning and to protect the supply route. "Use an entire battalion to accomplish latter if necessary. At no time have you been in contact on your left although you have repeatedly assured me that this was accomplished . . . Confirmation of thorough understanding of this order desired." Baxter thereupon telephoned division headquarters and put his case before a staff officer. General Beightler's criticism, he felt, was not justified. "Please attempt to explain to the General that I have had patrols in contact with the 161 and have documentary evidence to substantiate this. I have not, however, been able to maintain contact and close the gap by actual physical contact due to the fact that the 161st had been echeloned 600 to 800 yards to my left rear. I have been trying and will continue tomorrow

---

[26] As the Americans still did not know the *13th Infantry's* location, they thought the attack had originated from the southwest rather than from the north.

[27] Opns of the 148th Inf in New Georgia, 18 Jul– 5 Aug 43, p. 21.

[28] General Beightler's record as a division commander was somewhat unusual in that he was in command of the 37th at the outbreak of war, led it overseas in 1942, and retained command of it through the Solomons and Philippines campaigns until the end of the war.

morning to establish this contact. It is a difficult problem as I have had Japs between my left flank and the 161st." [29]

Rain and mud added to Baxter's troubles on 30 July. Still harried by enemy machine guns and mortars, the 2d Battalion pushed east and south toward the 161st as the 1st Battalion covered the left (north) flank. Elements of the 37th Cavalry Reconnaissance Troop, C Company, 117th Engineer Battalion, and the 3d Battalion, 161st Infantry, pushed north to give additional protection to the division's right (north) flank and to protect the east end of Baxter's supply route. Baxter attempted to cut a new trail directly into the 161st's lines, but Japanese rifle fire forced the bulldozer back. Some of the 148th's advance elements sideslipped to the south and got through to the 161st that day, but the main body was still cut off.[30] Some of the Japanese who were following the 148th attacked the 1st Battalion, 161st, but were halted. This action then settled down into a nocturnal fire fight.

The plight of the rest of the regiment was still serious. Water was running low. Part of the Reconnaissance Troop tried to take water forward to the 148th on 30 July. It was stopped by Japanese fire. But rain fell throughout the night of 30–31 July and the thirsty men were able to catch it in helmets and fill their canteens.

On 31 July Beightler suggested that

Baxter destroy heavy equipment and break his regiment into small groups to slip northward through the jungle around the enemy. The 148th blew up all the supplies it could not carry but it had to fight its way along the trail. It had over a hundred wounded men and could not infiltrate through the jungle without abandoning them.

Toward the end of the day B Company, which had been trying to clear the Japanese north of the supply trail, was ordered to disengage and withdraw slightly for the night. One of B Company's platoons, however, had come under fire from a Japanese machine gun about seventy-five yards to its front and found that it could not safely move. Pvt. Rodger Young, who had been wounded in the shoulder at the first attempt to withdraw, told his platoon leader that he could see the enemy gun and started forward. Although a burst from the gun wounded him again and damaged his rifle, he kept crawling forward until he was within a few yards of the enemy weapon. As a grenade left his hand he was killed by a burst that struck him in the head. But he had gotten his grenade away, and it killed the Japanese gun crew. His platoon was able to withdraw in safety. For his gallantry and self-sacrifice Young was posthumously awarded the Medal of Honor.[31]

Colonel Baxter's radio fairly crackled the next morning, 1 August, with orders from General Beightler: "Time is precious, you must move." "Get going."

---

[29] The version of the radiogram quoted is taken from the 37th Div G–3 Jnl File, 29 Jul 43; the telephone message is from the 37th Div G–3 Jnl, 29 Jul 43.

[30] F and H Companies, part of E Company, and the 2d Battalion Headquarters Company were the elements that got through to the 161st.

---

[31] Stanley A. Frankel, *The 37th Infantry Division in World War II* (Washington: Infantry Journal Press, 1948), p. 101; WD GO 3, 6 Jan 44. Mr. Frank Loesser commemorated this exploit in a popular song, "Rodger Young," copyright 1945.

"Haste essential." [32] Thus urged on, Baxter ordered an assault by every man who could carry a rifle. He formed all his command—A, E, B, and G Companies—in a skirmish line with bayonets fixed, and assaulted by fire and movement at 0850. The attack succeeded. By 0930 the leading elements, ragged, weary, and muddy, reached Katsarsky's area. The 148th was given fresh water and hot food, then passed into division reserve. As the men struggled in after their ordeal, all available ambulances, trucks, and jeeps were rushed up to transport the 128 wounded men to the 37th Division's clearing station at Laiana.

Capture of the Airfield

The first day of August had broken bright and clear after a night of intermittent showers. It is likely that the spirits of the top commanders were also bright, for things were looking better. With Ilangana and Shimizu Hill reduced, the 43d Division was in possession of the last piece of high ground between it and Munda airfield. Bartley Ridge had fallen; Horseshoe Hill was about to fall, and the 148th was completing its retirement.

General Griswold had issued no special orders for the day; the field order that had started the corps offensive was still in effect. In the 37th Division's zone the most significant development was the return of Baxter's men. The 145th Infantry was patrolling; the 161st was mopping up. In the 43d Division's area of responsibility, General Hodge had ordered an advance designed to bring his division up on line with the 145th Infantry.

The 103d Infantry began its attack at 1100. E, G, and F Companies advanced in line behind patrols. Meeting practically no opposition, they gained ground rapidly and by 1500 were nearing Lambeti Plantation. The 2d Battalion, 169th Infantry, then in process of pinching out the 172d, attacked northwest across the front of the 172d and established contact with the 145th Infantry. The 172d completed a limited advance before going into division reserve. The 3d Battalion, 169th, on the left of the 2d, attacked in its zone and at 1500 was still advancing. For the first time since it had landed on New Georgia, the 43d Division could announce that the going was easy.

The day before, Generals Hodge and Wing, accompanied by Colonel Ross, had visited the command and observation posts of the 1st Battalion, 145th Infantry, from where they could see part of Munda airfield. They detected evidence of a Japanese withdrawal, which seemed to be covered by fire from the enemy still on Horseshoe Hill.

Thus at 1500, 1 August, with the 43d Division still moving forward, General Griswold ordered all units to send out patrols immediately to discover whether the Japanese were withdrawing. "Smack Japs wherever found, even if late." [33] If the patrols found little resistance, a general advance would be undertaken in late afternoon. Colonel Ridings telephoned the orders to 37th Division headquarters, and within minutes patrols went out. They found no enemy. At 1624 Ridings called Beightler's head-

---

[32] 37th Div G–3 Jnl, 1 Aug 43.

[33] XIV Corps G–3 Jnl, 1 Aug 43.

quarters again with orders to advance aggressively until solid resistance was met, in which case its location, strength, and composition were to be developed. The 148th Infantry was to have been placed in corps reserve with orders to protect the right flank, patrol vigorously to the north, northeast, and northwest, and cut the Munda–Bairoko trail if possible. Since the 27th Infantry of the 25th Division was arriving and moving into position on the 37th Division's right flank, Beightler persuaded corps headquarters to let him use the 148th Infantry.[34] Ridings required, however, that the 148th be given the mission of protecting the right flank because the 27th Infantry would not have enough strength for a day or two.

All went well for the rest of the day. The 103d Infantry reached the outer taxiways of Munda airfield; the 169th pulled up just short of Bibilo Hill. The 37th Division's regiments plunged forward past Horseshoe Hill, which was free of Japanese, and gained almost seven hundred yards.

The Japanese Withdrawal

The Japanese positions facing the XIV Corps had been formidable, and the Americans had been held in place for long periods. But the Americans had wrought more destruction than they knew. The cumulative effect of continuous air and artillery bombardment and constant infantry action had done tremendous damage to Japanese installations and caused large numbers of casualties. By late July most of the Japanese emplacements near Munda were in shambles. The front lines were crumbling. Rifle companies, 160–170 men strong at the outset, were starkly reduced. Some had only 20 men left at the end of July. The 229th Infantry numbered only 1,245 effectives. Major Hara, Captain Kojima, and many staff officers of the 229th had been killed by artillery fire. Hospitals were not adequate to care for the wounded and sick. The constant shelling and bombing prevented men from sleeping and caused many nervous disorders.

To compensate for the diminution of his regiment's strength, Colonel Hirata ordered the soldiers of his 229th Infantry to kill ten Americans for each Japanese killed, and to fight until death.

Higher headquarters, however, took a less romantic view of the situation. On 29 July a staff officer from the 8th Fleet visited Sasaki's headquarters and ordered him to withdraw to a line extending from Munda Point northeast about 3,800 yards inland. The positions facing the XIV Corps, and Munda airfield itself, were to be abandoned. Sasaki and his subordinates thought that it would be better to withdraw even farther, but the views of the 8th Fleet prevailed over those of the responsible men on the spot. The withdrawal, which was deduced by XIV Corps headquarters on 1 August, was accomplished promptly, and except for detachments at Munda and in the hills the main body of Sasaki's troops was in its new position by the first day of August.

Jungle Techniques and Problems

The Americans did not yet know it, but the worst was over. All regiments began making steady progress each day

---

[34] See below, pp. 167–69.

MUNDA AIRFIELD

against light, though determined and skillful, opposition.[35]

By now all regiments, though depleted by battle casualties and disease, had become veterans. Pockets that once would have halted an entire battalion or even a regiment were now usually reduced with speed and skill. The flame thrower, receiving its most extensive use in the Pacific up to this time, was coming into

its own as an offensive weapon. All regiments employed it against enemy positions, both in assault and in mopping up. The flame thrower did have several important disadvantages. The equipment was large and heavy, and required the operator to get very close to enemy positions, then expose his head and body in order to use his weapon. He needed to be protected by several riflemen. But even with its disadvantages, it was useful in destroying enemy positions.

Tanks, too, were of great value. General Griswold felt that, despite the difficulties inherent in operations over hilly jungle, the actions of the Tank Platoons

[35] Unless otherwise indicated all lessons-learned data are from CG XIV Corps, Informal Report on Combat Operations in the New Georgia Campaign. This document is not a narrative report. It contains data on tactics, weapons, logistics, and special jungle problems as compiled by the corps, division, and special headquarters participating in the operation.

of the 9th and 10th Marine Defense Battalions had been successful. On 29 July, looking forward to fighting over easier terrain around Munda airfield, he asked General Harmon for more tanks. Corps headquarters, he also announced, was preparing to mount flame throwers on tanks.[36] The operation ended before flame throwing tanks could be used, but the idea was successfully carried out in later campaigns.

The technique of reducing a pillbox, whether isolated or part of a defensive system, was now mastered. The official records unfortunately do not give much exact information on the reduction of specific pillboxes, but after the battle the 37th Division gave a valuable general description of the methods employed. The first essential was a complete reconnaissance to develop the position, intention, and strength of the enemy. This was quite difficult in the jungle. "To one unskilled in jungle fighting, it is inconceivable that well trained reconnaissance patrols in sufficient numbers cannot develop the situation in front of the advancing forces."[37] Because they could not see far enough, because they could not always get close enough, and because Japanese fire discipline was sometimes so good that a given position would not fire until actually attacked, reconnaissance patrols could not always develop positions. The next step was a recon-

naissance in force by a reinforced platoon. This often uncovered a portion of the enemy position but not all of it. Usually the complete extent of a center of resistance was determined only by the attack.

The attack itself consisted of three parts: artillery preparation, 81-mm. mortar fire, and assault.

The artillery preparation had a threefold effect. It improved visibility by clearing away brush and foliage. It destroyed or damaged enemy positions. And it killed, wounded, and demoralized enemy soldiers.

The 81-mm. mortars, using heavy shell that had a delay fuze, fired on observed positions and usually covered the area between the American infantry and the artillery's targets. They frequently drove the Japanese soldiers out of their pillboxes into the open where they became targets for rifle and machine gun fire. The 60-mm. mortars, though more mobile than the 81-mm.'s, threw too light a shell to be very effective in these attacks. Their shells usually burst in the trees, but the 81-mm. heavy shells penetrated the treetops and often the tops of the pillboxes themselves before exploding.

The assault consisted of a holding attack by a company or platoon delivering assault fire to cover a close-in single or double envelopment. BAR's, M1's, and grenades were used extensively, and flame throwers were employed whenever possible. Units of the 25th Division, which later drove northward from Munda to Zieta, encountered pillbox positions that were too shallow, and in country too dense, for artillery and mortars to be used without endangering the

---

[36] Rad, Griswold to Harmon, 29 Jul 43, in XIV Corps G-3 Jnl, 30 Jul 43. Part of the 754th Army Tank Battalion was alerted at Nouméa for transfer to Guadalcanal to be equipped with flame throwers for employment in New Georgia but Munda airfield had fallen before it was moved.

The Tank Platoon of the 11th Marine Defense Battalion arrived in early August.

[37] 37th Div Rpt, G-3 Narrative, Jungle Tactics and Opns, p. 3.

REDUCING AN ENEMY PILLBOX WITH A FLAME THROWER. *Pillbox is along the beach near Munda Airfield.*

attacking infantry. Men of this division therefore advocated flame throwers, infantry cannon, and tanks for pillbox reduction.

These techniques, which simply represented the application of established tactical principles, were being applied well in early August, but several problems remained. Because the infantry units did not advance at the same rate, the front line became irregular and the supporting artillery was thus unable to capitalize on the advantages of firing at right angles to the axis of advance. All unit commanders were eager to employ artillery and mortar support to the utmost, but they frequently complained that neighboring units' supporting artillery and

mortar fires were falling in their areas and endangering their troops. They had a tendency to forget that the enemy also used artillery and mortars and, when receiving American artillery fire, frequently lobbed 90-mm. mortar shells into the American front lines to convince the American infantrymen that they were being fired on by their own artillery. In most cases the complaints were probably caused by Japanese rather than American fire.

Because maps were inaccurate and reconnaissance was inhibited by poor visibility, it was extremely difficult to determine the exact location of friendly units. In the 37th Division's zone several artillery preparations were called off because of uncertainty about the position of the 148th Infantry. Flares and smoke pots, and sometimes flame throwers, were used to mark flanks, but usually could not be seen by anyone not in the immediate vicinity. Griswold had ordered the front line battalions to mark their flanks daily with white panels twenty-five feet long by six feet wide. These were to be photographed from the air. Reconnaissance planes made daily photographic flights, but there were no clearings in the New Georgia jungle large enough to permit the panels to be spread out, and this effort failed. By plotting close-in defensive artillery fires, forward observers were able to provide some reliable information on the location of front lines. When the 37th Division rolled forward after 1 August, it estimated positions and distances on the basis of speedometer readings from locations that had been plotted by air photography and interpolated on maps.

The difficulties of scouting and patrolling naturally affected nearly every aspect of the operation. Because enemy positions could not be fixed in advance, the troops often attacked terrain rather than the enemy. This procedure resulted in slow advances and in a high expenditure of mortar ammunition on areas actually free of the enemy. And mortar ammunition supply was laborious; shells had to be hand-carried from trail-end to the mortar positions. Poor scouting caused battalions to advance on narrow fronts and thus be halted by small enemy positions. One regimental operations officer asserted that inadequate reconnaissance was due in part to the fact that "higher commanders" did not issue orders until the late afternoon preced-

ing an attack. Thus battalions did not have time for full reconnaissance:

"Many times, units were committed in an area which had not been reconnoitered. This fact resulted in commanders having to make decisions concerning a zone of advance in which he knew little or nothing about the enemy positions. Enemy strong points encountered in this fashion often times resulted in hasty withdrawals which were costly both in men and weapons." [38]

"Munda is yours"

The XIV Corps maintained the momentum of its advance against the enemy delaying forces. On 2, 3, 4, and 5 August the advance continued all across the corps' front. The 103d and 169th Infantry Regiments, which had gained the outer taxiways of the airfield on 1 August, kept going. The 3d Battalion, 172d, was committed on the 169th's right on 4 August. In the more open terrain around the airstrip the troops were able to use 60-mm. mortars effectively, and their advance was consequently speeded. Kokengolo Hill, the rise in the center of the airfield where a Methodist mission had once stood, held up the advance temporarily. Bibilo Hill, whose fortifications included six 75-mm. antiaircraft guns that the Japanese had been using as dual-purpose weapons, was reduced in three days of action by elements of the 169th, 172d, 145th, and 161st Regiments, supported by Marine tanks. The 148th Infantry, on the north flank, established blocks and ambushes on a north—south track

[38] Rpt, Maj Carl H. Coleman, S–3 145th Inf, to G–3 37th Div, 1 Sep 43, sub: Informal Rpt on New Georgia Campaign.

LIGHT TANKS M3 OF THE 9TH MARINE DEFENSE BATTALION *supporting infantry action near the base of Bibilo Hill.*

that was presumed to be the Munda–Bairoko trail.

On 5 August, with Bibilo Hill cleared, the units of the 37th Division crossed the narrow strip of land between the hill and the water. This tactical success had one effect of great personal importance to the soldiers: many had their first bath in weeks.

In the 43d Division's zone on 5 August, the infantry, with tank and mortar support, killed or drove the last Japanese from the tunnels, bunkers, and pillboxes of Kokengolo Hill. Here were found caves stocked with rice, bales of clothing and blankets, and occupation currency. Crossing the western part of the runway, with its craters, grass, and wrecked Japanese planes, the infantry-

men secured it in early afternoon. General Wing telephoned General Hodge from Bibilo Hill: "Munda is yours at 1410 today." [39] Griswold radioed the good news to Admiral Halsey: ". . . Our ground forces today wrested Munda from the Japs and present it to you . . . as the sole owner. . . ." Halsey responded with "a custody receipt for Munda . . . . Keep 'em dying." [40]

The major objective was in Allied hands. The hardest part of the long New Georgia battle was over.

---

[39] 43d Div G–3 Jnl, 5 Aug 43.

[40] Rad, CG NGOF to COMSOPAC, 5 Aug 43, in XIV Corps G–3 Jnl, 5 Aug 43; Rad, COMSOPAC to CG NGOF, 6 Aug 43, in XIV Corps G–3 Jnl, 7 Aug 43.

CHAPTER X

After Munda

The hardest slugging was over, at least on New Georgia. But several tasks faced the troops. The airfield had to be put into shape at once and the remaining Japanese had to be cleaned out of New Georgia and several of the offshore islands. (*Map 11*)

The Airfield

Repair and enlargement of the battered airstrip began immediately after its capture.[1] ". . . Munda airfield looked like a slash of white coral in a Doré drawing of hell. It lay like a dead thing, between the torn, coffee-colored hills of Bibilo and Kokengolo."[2] Seabees of the 73d and 24th Naval Construction Battalions began the work of widening, resurfacing, and regrading the field. On 9 August additional naval construction battalions added their tools and men to the task. Power shovels dug coral out of Kokengolo Hill, and bulldozers, earthmovers, graders, and rollers spread and flattened it. Good coral was plentiful, as were men and tools, and the work moved rapidly forward. By 7 August the field, although rough, was suitable for emergency wheels-up landings.

Advance parties from General Mulcahy's air headquarters moved from Rendova to Munda during the second week of August. On the 14th, the day after the first Allied plane landed, General Mulcahy flew from Rendova to Munda in his amphibian plane and opened Headquarters, Air Command, New Georgia, in a Japanese-dug tunnel in Kokengolo Hill.

Two Marine fighter squadrons (VMF 123 and VMF 124), with twelve Corsairs (F4U's) each, arrived on the 14th and began operations at once. Together with the fighters based at Segi Point,

---

[1] Unless otherwise indicated this chapter is based on Craven and Cate, *The Pacific: Guadalcanal to Saipan*, pp. 237–44; Morison, *Breaking the Bismarcks Barrier*, pp. 225–39; ONI USN, Combat Narratives: Solomon Islands Campaign, XI, Kolombangara and Vella Lavella, 6 August–7 October 1943 [Washington, 1944]; SOPACBACOM, History of the New Georgia Campaign, Vol. I, Chs. VII–VIII; the rpts, jnls, and jnl files of NGOF, COMAIR New Georgia, XIV Corps, 25th Div, 43d Div, northern landing force, and component units; History of the 8th Area Army, 1942–44, Japanese Monogr No. 37 (OCMH); 17th Army Operations, Vol. II, Japanese Monogr No. 40 (OCMH); Southeast Area Naval Operations, Vol. II, Japanese Monogr No. 49 (OCMH); outline of Southeast Area Naval Air Operations, August 1942–October 1942, Pt. II, Japanese Monogr No. 106 (OCMH). This section is also based on *Building the Navy's Bases in World War II: History of the Bureau of Yards and Docks and the Civil Engineer Corps, 1940–1946*, II (Washington, 1947), 265–66.

[2] John A. DeChant, *Devilbirds: The Story of United States Marine Corps Aviation in World War II* (New York: Harper & Brothers, 1947), p. 109.

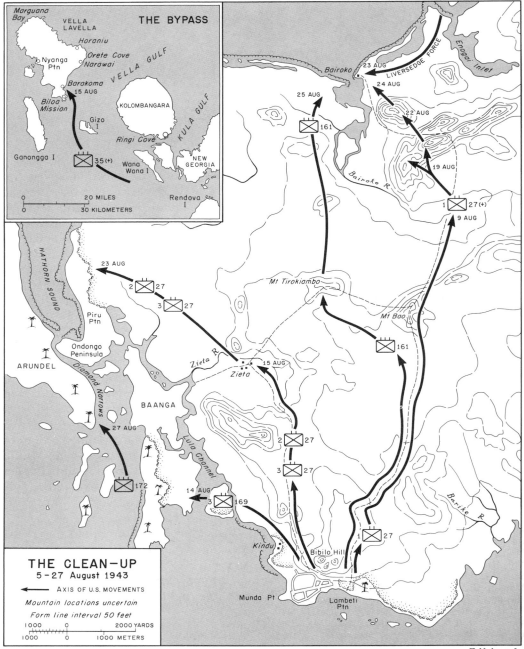

THE BYPASS

Marguana Bay
VELLA LAVELLA
Horaniu
Orete Cove
Narawai
Nyanga Ptn
Barakoma
15 AUG
Biloa Mission
Gizo I
Ganongga I
35 (+)
Wana Wana I
VELLA GULF
KOLOMBANGARA
Ringi Cove
KULA GULF
NEW GEORGIA
Rendova I

0   20 MILES
0   30 KILOMETERS

Bairoko
23 AUG
LIVERSEDGE FORCE
24 AUG
Enogai Inlet
22 AUG
25 AUG
161
19 AUG
Bairoko R
1   27 (+)
9 AUG

HATHORN SOUND
23 AUG
2   27
3   27
Piru Ptn
Ondongo Peninsula
ARUNDEL
Diamond Narrows
BAANGA
Zieta R
Zieta
15 AUG
Mt Tirokiambo
Mt Bao
161
27 AUG
172
2   27
3   27
14 AUG
3   169
Lula Channel
Kindu
Bibilo Hill
1   27
Barike R
Munda Pt
Lambeti Ptn

THE CLEAN-UP
5-27 August 1943

  AXIS OF U.S. MOVEMENTS

Mountain locations uncertain

Form line interval 50 feet

1000   0   2000 YARDS
1000   0   1000 METERS

D. Holmes, Jr

MAP 11

which were also under Mulcahy, they and other Allied squadrons covered the Allied landing at Vella Lavella on 15 August.[3] There were some difficulties at first. Maintenance crews were inexperienced, there were not enough spare parts, the field was not complete, and taxiways and dispersal areas were small and in poor condition. Japanese naval guns, promptly nicknamed "Pistol Pete," shelled the airfield from the nearby islet of Baanga intermittently from 16 through 19 August. But conditions quickly improved, and Pistol Pete, which had not done much damage, was captured by elements of the 43d Division on 19 August.

As the field was enlarged, more planes and units continued to arrive. Operations intensified, and as the Japanese were cleared from the central Solomons Mulcahy's planes began to strike targets in the northern Solomons. For this reason his command was removed from the New Georgia Occupation Force on 23 September and assigned as part of the Air Command, Solomons. Mulcahy's fighters escorted bombers to the Bougainville bases, and Munda-based bombers soon began dropping loads there too.

Munda airfield, which by mid-October had a 6,000-foot coral-covered runway and thus was suitable for bombers, became the best and most-used airfield in the Solomons. The rotation of Navy, Marine Corps, and Army Air Forces commanders that was standard in the South Pacific had brought about the relief of Admiral Mitscher as Commander, Aircraft, Solomons, by General Twining, the Thirteenth Air Force commander. General Twining moved his headquarters on 20 October from Guadalcanal to Munda and made the most intensive possible use of the new base.

Reinforcements

Airfield development, though of primary importance, could be of only minor interest to the ground troops who had the dreary task of slogging northward from Bibilo Hill in an attempt to trap the retreating Japanese. The job had been assigned to the 27th and 161st Infantry Regiments, both operating under their parent command, the 25th Division.

Addition of the 27th Infantry to the New Georgia Occupation Force had come about because of General Griswold's urgent requests for more men. During July the Western Force of Task Force 31 had carried fully 26,748 men to Rendova,[4] but by the month's end not that many men were available for combat. Many of the arrivals were service troops. Further, casualties and disease had weakened the infantry regiments. The three infantry regiments in the 37th Division (less the two battalions with Liversedge) had an authorized total strength of about 7,000 men. But the 161st Infantry, which entered the campaign below strength, was short 1,350 men. The two-battalion regiments were short too, so that the 37th Division's rifle regiments had only 5,200 men. And the 43d Division was in worse shape. With an authorized strength of 8,000 men, its three rifle regiments had but

---

[3] See below, pp. 179–80.

[4] CTF 31 War Diary, 31 Jul 43 entry. Also transported were: 4,800 tons of rations; 17,431 drums of fuel, or 3,486 tons; 2,281 vehicles weighing 6,895 tons; 9,961 tons of ammunition; and 5,323 tons of other freight.

MUNDA AIRFIELD IN OPERATION. *C–47 transport taking off is evacuating wounded men.*

4,536 men. Griswold had asked Liversedge if he could release two infantry battalions for the Munda drive but Liversedge replied that that would be possible only if Enogai and Rice Anchorage were abandoned. His raider battalions were then only 60 percent effective.[5]

On 28 July Griswold asked Harmon for replacements or for a regimental combat team less artillery. This request posed a grave problem for Harmon and Admiral Halsey. The injunction against committing major forces to New Georgia was still in effect; at least it was theoretically in effect, for in small island warfare, especially in 1943, 26,000 men constituted a major force. The only immediately available division was the 25th, and one of its regiments, the 161st, had been sent in fairly early. Further, Halsey and Harmon had planned to use the 25th for the invasion of the Buin–Faisi area of Bougainville.

Yet as long as the high command retained confidence in Griswold, there could be but one answer. As Harmon wrote to his chief of staff, Brig. Gen. Allison J. Barnett, ". . . we *have* to make this Munda-Bairoko business go— and as quickly as possible. It is the job 'in hand' and whatever we use we have to get it done before we go on to the next step." One of the major difficulties,

---

[5] See XIV Corps G–3 Jnl File, 28–29, 31 Jul 43. By 14 August sickness and casualties had rendered the 4th Marine Raider Battalion practically unfit for fighting. The battalion surgeon, Lt. J. C. Lockhart, USNR, reported that out of 453 men present only 137 were fit for duty. Memo, 4th Mar Raider Bn Surgeon for CO 4th Mar Raider Bn, 14 Aug 43, sub: Health of Personnel of 4th Raider Bn, in XIV Corps G–3 Jnl File, 23 Aug 43.

according to Harmon, was the fact that the Americans had underestimated the job in hand. "Munda is a tough nut—much tougher in terrain, organization of the ground and determination of the Jap than we had thought. . . . In both Guadalcanal and New Georgia we greatly underestimated the force require to do the job." [6] Thus Harmon alerted the 27th Infantry of the 25th Division for transfer to New Georgia and recommended to Halsey that the 25th Division be taken off the list for Bougainville. [7] As soon as he received Halsey's approval Harmon ordered up the 27th Infantry. On 29 July Col. Thomas D. Roberts of Harmon's staff arrived at Griswold's headquarters to announce the imminent arrival of the 27th Infantry and some replacements.

At this time the Japanese were still holding the Ilangana–Shimizu Hill–Horseshoe Hill–Bartley Ridge defense line, and no one was anticipating the rapid advances that characterized the first days of August. Thus on 30 July with Colonel Roberts' concurrence Griswold asked for more 25th Division troops and Harmon promptly promised the 35th Infantry.

Advance elements of the 27th Infantry, and Headquarters, 25th Division, landed on the barrier island of Sasavele on 1 August, and in the next few days the regiment was moved to the right (north) flank of the Munda front to protect the XIV Corps' right flank and rear.

The Cleanup

North to Bairoko

The Japanese withdrawal from Munda released a sizable body of American troops to attempt the cleanup of the Japanese between Munda and Dragons Peninsula. After the rapid advances began on 1 August the 27th Infantry, temporarily commanded by Lt. Col. George E. Bush, sent out patrols to the north before advancing to clear out the Japanese and make contact with Liversedge. [8]

Meanwhile General Griswold decided that mopping-up operations would have to include a drive from Bibilo Hill northwest to Zieta, a village on the west coast about four crow's-flight miles northwest of Bibilo, to cut off the retreating Japanese. On 2 August the 37th Division had reported that Fijian patrols had cut the Munda–Bairoko trail but found no evidence of any Japanese traffic. Lt. Col. Demas L. Sears, Assistant Chief of Staff, G–2, 37th Division, offered the opinion that if the Japanese were evacuating New Georgia they were moving along the coast to Zieta rather than to Bairoko. This opinion was buttressed by reports from Colonel Griffith of the Raiders who radioed on 2 August that there had been no traffic in or out of Bairoko.

Next day, on orders from Griswold, the 3d Battalion, 148th Infantry, left Enogai on a cross-country trek toward Zieta, a trek that was halted short of there on 5 August by additional orders

---

[6] Ltr, Harmon to Barnett, 28 Jul 43, quoted in SOPACBACOM, History of the New Georgia Campaign, Vol. I, Ch. IV, p. 35, OCMH.
[7] He suggested substituting the 2d Marine Division or the 3d New Zealand Division.

[8] Col. Douglas Sugg had commanded the regiment until a few days before the move to New Georgia. He fell ill and was hospitalized, and his place was taken by Colonel Bush, the executive. Sugg resumed command of his regiment on 12 August.

4-TON TRUCK STUCK IN THE MUD *on a jeep trail, New Georgia.*

from Griswold. He had decided to use the two 25th Division regiments under General Collins, the commander who had led the division on Guadalcanal, to drive to Zieta and Bairoko.

From then until 25 August, the 25th Division units slogged painfully along the swampy jungle trails in pursuit of the elusive enemy. The Japanese occasionally established roadblocks, ambushes, and defenses in depth to delay the Americans, but the worst enemy was the jungle. The terrain was, if anything, worse than that encountered on the Munda front. The maps were incorrect, inexact, or both. For example, Mount Tirokiamba, a 1,500-foot eminence reported to lie about 9,000 yards north-west of Bibilo Hill, was found to be 4,500 yards south by west of its reported position. Mount Bao, thought to be 6,000 yards east-northeast of Bibilo Hill, was actually 2,500 yards farther on.

As the regiments advanced, bulldozers of the 65th Engineer Battalion attempted to build jeep trails behind them. But the rain fell regularly and the trails became morasses so deep that even the bulldozers foundered. General Collins ordered the trail building stopped in mid-August. Now supplies were carried by hand and on men's backs to the front, and when these methods failed to provide enough food and ammunition the regiments were supplied from the air.

37TH DIVISION TROOPS CARRYING WEAPONS AND AMMUNITION *forward, 5 August 1943.*

The 1st Battalion, 27th Infantry, trekked north on the Munda–Bairoko trail and made contact on 9 August with Liversedge. The 2d and 3d Battalions, 27th Infantry, after some sharp fighting took Zieta on 15 August, then pushed northwest to Piru Plantation. The plantation lay about seven and one-half airline miles northwest of Bibilo Hill, but the regiment's advance on the ground required a 22-mile march. The 161st Infantry, following the 1st Battalion, 27th, moved up the trail and after mid-August began patrolling to the west short of Bairoko Harbour. On 25 August, after Griffith had reported two nights of busy enemy barge activity in and out of Bairoko Harbour, the Americans bloodlessly occupied its shores.

The Japanese Evacuation

But the main body of Japanese survivors had slipped out of Zieta and Bairoko. Traveling light, they had evaded the slower-moving, more heavily encumbered Americans. On 5 August General Sasaki had decided that he could defend New Georgia no longer. He therefore sent the *13th Infantry* and most of the Bairoko-based special naval landing force units to Kolombangara, the *229th Infantry,* the *3d Battalion, 230th Infantry,* and the *3d Battalion, 23d Infantry,* to Baanga, a long narrow island which lay across Lulu Channel from Zieta. These units, plus two 120-mm. naval guns, were ordered to defend Baanga, and the naval guns were to shell Munda airfield.

Sasaki's headquarters, having moved out of Munda, was established on Baanga until 7 August, and the next day he moved to Kolombangara.

Baanga

The islet of Baanga, 6,500 yards long and some 4,000 yards west of Kindu Point on New Georgia, was captured to extend Allied control over Diamond Narrows and to stop the shelling of Munda by the two 120-mm. guns nicknamed "Pistol Pete" by the American troops.

Seizure of Baanga was entrusted to the 43d Division, briefly commanded by General Barker after 10 August, when General Hodge returned to the Americal Division.[9] Patrolling started on 11 August, but the Japanese on Baanga fought back hard, and the 169th Infantry, which Barker initially assigned to Baanga, gave a "shaky performance."[10] The 172d Infantry (less one battalion) joined in, and the southern part of the island was secured by 21 August. The 43d Division lost 52 men killed, 110 wounded, and 486 nonbattle casualties in this operation.

The Japanese, meanwhile, had decided to get off Baanga. General Sasaki had evolved a plan to use the *13th Infantry,* then on Kolombangara, to attack

New Georgia, and dispatched his naval liaison officer to *8th Fleet* headquarters to arrange for air and fleet support. But he was to get none. Moreover, no more ground reinforcements were to be sent to New Georgia. The last attempted shipment consisted of two mixed battalions from the *6th* and *38th Divisions,* to be carried to Kolombangara on destroyers.[11] But Comdr. Frederick Moosbrugger with six destroyers surprised the Japanese force in Vella Gulf on the night of 6–7 August and quickly sank three Japanese destroyers. The fourth enemy ship, which carried no troops, escaped. Moosbrugger's force got off virtually scot free, while the Japanese lost over fifteen hundred soldiers and sailors as well as the ships. About three hundred survivors reached Vella Lavella.[12] When Sasaki's request reached the *8th Fleet,* Vice Adm. Gunichi Mikawa, basing his decision on instructions from *Imperial General Headquarters,* ordered Sasaki to cancel his plan for attacking New Georgia and to concentrate the Baanga troops on Arundel to forestall further Allied advances. So the Japanese left on barges for Arundel, completing the movement by 22 August.

Vella Lavella: The Bypass

Meanwhile an Allied force had made a landing at Barakoma on Vella Lavella, which lay about thirty-five nautical miles northwest of Munda. This landing represented a major and completely successful departure from the original TOENAILS plan. The plan had called for the attack against Munda to be followed by

---

[9] Barker was replaced several days later, on orders from the War Department, by General Wing, who was senior to him.

[10] See Ltr, Griswold to Harmon, 24 Aug 43, quoted in SOPACBACOM, History of the New Georgia Campaign, Vol. I, Ch. VII, p. 7, OCMH.

[11] Each battalion consisted of four rifle companies, a machine gun platoon, and a small artillery unit.

[12] For a complete account see Morison, *Breaking the Bismarcks Barrier,* pp. 212–22.

the seizure of Vila airfield on Kolombangara, but the Japanese were now correctly believed to be established on Kolombangara in considerable strength. Some estimates placed the enemy garrison at ten thousand, a little under the actual total. And Admiral Halsey did not want a repetition of the Munda campaign. As he later put it, "The undue length of the Munda operation and our heavy casualties made me wary of another slugging match, but I didn't know how to avoid it." [13]

There was a way to avoid a slugging match, and that way was to bypass Kolombangara completely and land instead on Vella Lavella. The advantages were obvious: the airfield at Vila was poorly drained and thus no good while Vella Lavella looked more promising. Also, Vella Lavella was correctly reported to contain few Japanese. Vella Lavella, northwesternmost island in the New Georgia group, lay less than a hundred miles from the Japanese bases in the Shortlands and southern Bougainville, but a landing there could be protected by American fighter planes based at Munda and Segi Point.

The technique of bypassing, which General MacArthur has characterized as "as old as warfare itself," was well understood in the U.S. Army and Navy long before Vella Lavella, but successful bypassing requires a preponderance of strength that Allied forces had not hitherto possessed.[14] The first instance of an amphibious bypass in the Pacific occurred in May 1943 when the Allied capture of Attu caused the Japanese to evacuate Kiska.

When members of Halsey's staff proposed that South Pacific forces bypass Kolombangara and jump to Vella Lavella of the more euphonious name, the admiral was enthusiastic.[15] On 11 July he radioed the proposal to Admirals Turner and Fitch. "Our natural route of approach from Munda to Bougainville," he asserted, "lies south of Gizo and Vella Lavella Islands." He asked them to consider whether it would be practicable to emplace artillery in the Munda–Enogai and Arundel areas to interdict Vila; cut the supply lines to Vila by artillery and surface craft, particularly PT boats; "by-pass Vila area and allow it to die on the vine"; and seize Vella Lavella and build a fighter field there. The decision on this plan would depend on the possibility of building a fighter field on Vella Lavella to give close fighter support for the invasion of Bougainville.[16] Both Turner and Fitch liked the idea.

Reconnaissance

Reconnaissance was necessary first.

---

[13] Halsey and Bryan, *Admiral Halsey's Story*, p. 170.

[14] Ltr, MacArthur to Smith, Chief of Mil Hist, 5 Mar 53, no sub, OCMH.

In ground operations field orders usually specify that isolated pockets of resistance are to be bypassed, contained, and reduced later, so that the advance will not be held up.

[15] Ltrs, Adm Halsey to Maj Gen Orlando Ward, Chief of Mil Hist, 27 May and 27 Aug 52, no subs, OCMH. The second letter contains as inclosures letters from Admiral Robert B. Carney, formerly Chief of Staff, South Pacific Area, and Lt. Gen. William E. Riley, USMC (Ret.), formerly Halsey's war plans officer, to Admiral Halsey. Other former staff officers credit Wilkinson and Comdr. William F. Riggs, Jr., with the idea. See Ltr, Vice Adm D. B. Duncan to Gen Smith, Chief of Mil Hist, 10 Nov 53, no sub, OCMH.

[16] Rad, COMSOPAC to CTF 31 and COMAIRSOPAC, 11 Jul 43, in GHQ SWPA G–3 Jnl, 12 Jul 43.

Allied knowledge of Vella Lavella was limited. Coastwatchers, plantation managers, and such members of the clergy as the Rev. A. W. E. Silvester, the New Zealand Methodist missionary bishop whose see included New Georgia and Vella Lavella, provided some information but not enough to form the basis for the selection of an airfield site or an invasion beach. Col. Frank L. Beadle, Harmon's engineer, therefore took command of a reconnaissance party consisting of six Army, Navy, and Marine officers. Beadle was ordered to concentrate his reconnaissance in the coastal plain region of Barakoma and Biloa Mission on the southeast tip of Vella Lavella because it was closest to Munda, the natives were friendly, coastwatcher Lt. Henry Josselyn of the Australian Navy and Bishop Silvester were there, and the terrain seemed favorable. The Japanese had already surveyed the Barakoma area for a fighter strip.

Beadle's party boarded a torpedo boat at Rendova on the night of 21–22 July and slipped through the darkness to land at Barakoma. Silvester, Josselyn, and two natives were on hand to meet the American officers. For six days Beadle's party, the bishop, the coastwatcher, and several natives explored the southeast part of the island, and ventured up the west coast to Nyanga Plantation, about twelve crow's-flight miles northwest of Barakoma. Returning to Rendova on 28 July, Beadle reported that the vicinity of Barakoma met all requirements, and that there were no Japanese on the southeast coast of the island. Beadle recommended that the landing be made on beaches extending some 750 yards south from the mouth of the Bara-

koma River, and suggested that an advance detachment be sent to Barakoma to mark beaches. These recommendations were accepted.

Admiral Wilkinson, Turner's successor, chose an advance party of fourteen officers and enlisted men from the various units in the Vella Lavella invasion force and placed it under Capt. G. C. Kriner, USN, who was to command the Vella Lavella naval base. This group proceeded from Guadalcanal to Rendova, then prepared to change to PT boats for the run through the night of 12–13 August toward Barakoma. The work of the advance party was of a highly secret nature. If the Japanese became aware of its presence, they could kill or capture the men and certainly would deduce that an Allied invasion was imminent.

On 11 August coastwatcher Josselyn radioed Guadalcanal to report the presence of forty Japanese. (Japanese survivors of the Battle of Vella Gulf, 6–7 August, had landed on Vella Lavella.) His message indicated that pro-Allied natives had taken them prisoner. From Koli Point General Harmon radioed General Griswold to ask for more men to accompany the advance party and take the prisoners into custody. Accordingly one officer and twenty-five enlisted men from E and G Companies, 103d Infantry, were detailed to go along.

The whole party left Rendova at 1730 on 12 August. En route Japanese planes bombed and strafed the four torpedo boats for two hours. One was hit and four men were wounded but the other three made it safely. During the hours of darkness they hove to off Barakoma. Rubber boats had been provided to get the party from the torpedo boats to shore, but no one was able to inflate the rubber boats from the carbon dioxide containers that were provided. So natives paddled out in canoes and took the Americans ashore.

Meanwhile Josselyn had radioed Wilkinson again to the effect that there were 140 Japanese in the area; 40 at Biloa and 100 about five miles north of Barakoma. They were, he declared, under surveillance but were not prisoners. Once ashore Captain Kriner discovered there were many starving, ragged, poorly armed stragglers but no prisoners. He requested reinforcements, and in the early morning hours of 14 August seventy-two officers and enlisted men of F Company, 103d Infantry, sailed for Barakoma in four torpedo boats. This time the rubber boats inflated properly and the men paddled ashore from three hundred yards off the beach.

The advance party with the secret mission of marking beaches and the combat party with the prisoner-catching mission set about their respective jobs. Beach marking proceeded in a satisfactory manner although the infantrymen in that party were not completely happy about the presence of the 103d troops. They felt that the two missions were mutually exclusive and that the prisoner-catching mission destroyed all hope of secrecy. Only seven Japanese were captured.[17] F Company, 103d, held the beachhead at Barakoma against the arrival of the main invasion force.

Plans

Once Colonel Beadle had made his recommendations the various South Pacific headquarters began laying their plans. This task was fairly simple, for Admiral Halsey and his subordinates were now old hands at planning invasions. Actual launching of the invasion would have to await the capture and development of Munda airfield.

It was on 11 August that Halsey issued his orders. He organized his forces much as he had for the invasion of New Georgia. (*Chart 10*) The Northern Force (Task Force 31) under Admiral Wilkinson was to capture Vella Lavella, build an airfield, and establish a small naval base. Griswold's New Georgia Occupation Force would meanwhile move into position on Arundel and shell Vila airfield on bypassed Kolombangara. New Georgia-based planes would cover and support the invasion. South Pacific Aircraft (Task Force 33) was to provide air support by striking at the Shortlands–Bougainville fields. As strikes against these areas were being carried out regularly, the intensified air operations would not necessarily alert the enemy. Three naval task forces of aircraft carriers, battleships, cruisers, and destroyers, and the submarines of Task Force 72, would be in position to protect and support Wilkinson. On Wilkinson's recommendation, Halsey set 15 August as D Day.[18]

Admiral Wilkinson also issued his orders on 11 August. The Northern Force was organized into three invasion echelons (the main body and the second

---

[17] SOPACBACOM's History of the New Georgia Campaign, Vol. I, Ch. VIII, pp. 20–21, OCMH, contains some fanciful data concerning the sinking of one PT boat and the killing of about fifty Japanese.

[18] COMSOPAC Opn Plan 14A–43, 11 Aug 43, in Off of Naval Rcds and Library.

CHART 10—SOUTH PACIFIC ORGANIZATION FOR VELLA LAVELLA INVASION

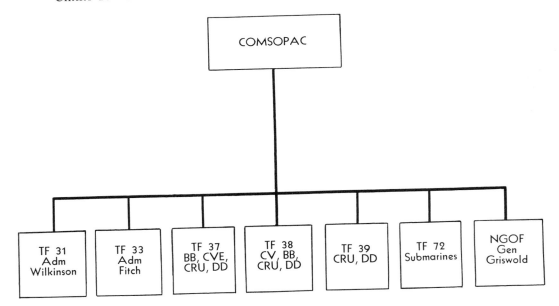

and third echelons) and the motor torpedo boat flotillas. (*Chart 11*) Under Wilkinson's direct command, the main body consisted of three transport groups, the destroyer screen, and the northern landing force. Each transport group, screened by destroyers, was to move independently from Guadalcanal to Vella Lavella; departure from Guadalcanal would be so timed that each group would arrive off Barakoma just before it was scheduled to begin unloading. Three slow LST's, each towing an LCM, would leave at 0300, 14 August, six LCI's at 0800, and seven fast APD's at 1600. The motor torpedo boat flotilla would cover the movement of the main body on D minus 1 by patrolling the waters east and west of Rendova, but would retire to Rendova early on D Day to be out of the way. Preliminary naval bombardment would in all probability not be

necessary, but Wilkinson told off two destroyers to be prepared to support the landing if need be. Two fighter-director groups were put aboard two destroyers. Once unloaded, each transport group would steam for Guadalcanal. The second echelon, composed of three LST's and three of the destroyers that would escort the main body, was to arrive at Barakoma on D plus 2, beach overnight, and return to Guadalcanal. The third echelon consisted of three destroyers and three LST's from the main body. Wilkinson ordered it to arrive on D plus 5, beach throughout the night, and depart for Guadalcanal the next morning.[19]

The northern landing force, 5,888 men in all, consisted of the 35th Regimental Combat Team of the 25th Di-

---

[19] CTF 31 Opn Plan A12–43, 11 Aug 43, in Off of Naval Rcds and Library.

CHART 11—ORGANIZATION OF NORTHERN FORCE [TF 31], VELLA LAVELLA

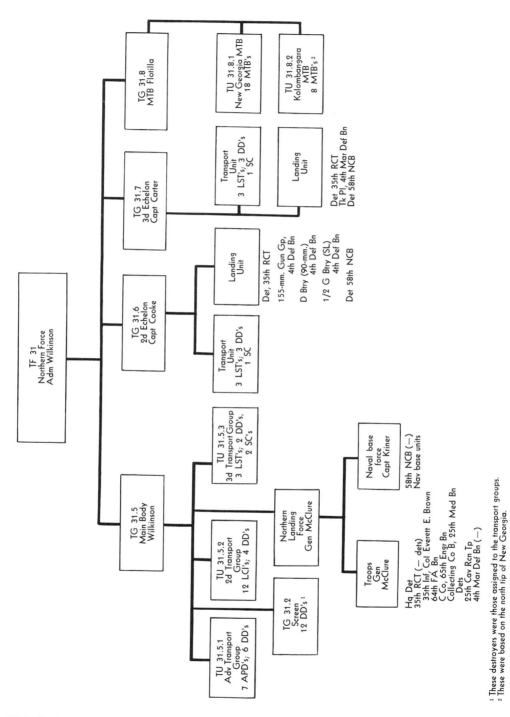

¹ These destroyers were those assigned to the transport groups.
² These were based on the north tip of New Georgia.

vision; the 4th Marine Defense Battalion; the 25th Cavalry Reconnaissance Troop; the 58th Naval Construction Battalion; and a naval base group.[20] Command of the landing force was entrusted to Brig. Gen. Robert B. McClure, assistant commander of the 25th Division, who as a colonel had commanded the 35th Infantry during the Guadalcanal Campaign. General McClure would be under Wilkinson's control until he was well established ashore. He would then come under General Griswold.

The Japanese on Vella Lavella (no garrison at all but only a group of stragglers) were estimated to total about 250, with 100 more on nearby Ganongga and 250 at Gizo. Wilkinson warned that enemy air strength in southern Bougainville, less than a hundred miles away, and at Rabaul was considerable, and that naval surface forces were based at both places.

To carry off such a stroke almost literally under the enemy's aircraft would require, besides fighter cover, considerable speed in unloading. Wilkinson planned to unload the main body in twelve hours. Troops debarking from APD's were to go ashore in LCVP's, forty to a boat. At the beach ten of each forty would unload the boat while the

thirty pushed inland. Once emptied, LCVP's were to return to their mother ships for the rest of the men and supplies. Sixty minutes were allotted for unloading the APD's and clearing the beach. The LCI's would then come in to the beach and drop their ramps. Passenger troops would debark via both ramps, ground their equipment, then reboard by the starboard ramps, pick up gear, and go ashore down the port ramps. One hour was allotted for the LCI's. Then the LST's, bearing artillery, trucks, and bulldozers, would ground. Trucks were to be loaded in advance to help insure the prompt unloading of the LST's.

The 35th Infantry, commanded by Col. Everett E. Brown, had been making ready for several days. It had been alerted for movement to Munda on 1 August, and on 9 August had received orders from Harmon's headquarters to prepare for an invasion. The 1st and 2d Battalions on Guadalcanal and the 3d Battalion and the 64th Field Artillery Battalion in the Russells then began rehearsing landings. In the week preceding the invasion South Pacific Aircraft struck regularly at Kolombangara, Buin, Kahili, and Rekata Bay.

By 14 August the landing force and its supplies were stowed aboard ship, and all transport groups of the main body shoved off for Barakoma on schedule. Once on board, the men were informed of their destination. Japanese planes were reported over Guadalcanal, the Russells, and New Georgia, but Wilkinson's ships had an uneventful voyage up the Slot and through Blanche Channel and Gizo Strait. The sea was calm, and a bright moon shone in the

---

[20] The 35th Regimental Combat Team consisted of the 35th Infantry; the 64th Field Artillery Battalion (105-mm. howitzer); C Company, 65th Engineer Battalion; Collecting Company B, 25th Medical Battalion, and detachments from other divisional services. Harmon, who had promised the 35th Infantry for New Georgia on 1 August, later considered using the 145th Infantry, but concluded that it could not be pulled out of New Georgia and brought back to Guadalcanal in time. Rads, Harmon to Griswold, 1 Aug and 6 Aug 43, in XIV Corps G–3 Jnl.

clear night sky. Northwest of Rendova the LCI's overhauled the LST's while the APD's passed both slower groups.

Seizure of Barakoma

As first light gave way to daylight in the morning of 15 August, the APD's carrying the 1st and 2d Battalions of the 35th Infantry arrived off Barakoma and hove to. General Mulcahy's combat air patrol from Munda and Segi Point turned up on schedule at 0605. With part of the 103d Infantry and the secret advance party already on shore and in possession of the landing beach, there was no need for support bombardment. The APD's swung landing craft into the water, troops of the 2d Battalion climbed down the cargo nets and into the boats, and the first wave, with rifle companies abreast, departed. The 2d Battalion hit the beach at 0624 and at once pushed south toward the coconut plantation around Biloa Mission, about four thousand yards from the beach. The 1st Battalion, having left the APD's at 0615, landed with companies abreast at 0630 and pushed northward across the waist-deep Barakoma River. Thus quickly unloaded, the APD's cleared the area and with four escorting destroyers proceeded toward Guadalcanal.

The twelve LCI's arrived on schedule and sailed in to the beach, but quickly found there was room for but eight at one time. Coral reefs a few yards from shore rendered the northern portion of the beach unusable. The remaining four LCI's had to stand by offshore awaiting their turn. The 3d Battalion started unloading but had barely gotten started when enemy aircraft pounced at the invasion force.

This time the Japanese were not caught so completely asleep as they had been on 30 June. In early August Japanese radio intelligence reported a good deal of Allied radio traffic, and the commanders at Rabaul were aware that ships were again concentrating around Guadalcanal. They concluded that a new invasion was impending but failed to guess the target. At 0300 of the 15th a land-based bomber spotted part of Wilkinson's force off Gatukai. Six dive bombers and forty-eight fighters were sent out on armed reconnaissance, and these found the Americans shortly before 0800. Mulcahy's planes and ships' antiaircraft guns promptly engaged them. The Japanese planes that broke through went for the destroyers, which steamed on evasive courses and escaped harm. The Japanese caused some casualties ashore by strafing, but did not attack the LST's and LCI's. They ebulliently reported repulsing fifty Allied planes.

This attack, together with the limitations of the beach, delayed the unloading of the LCI's, which did not pull out until 0915.[21] The three LST's then beached and began discharging men and heavy cargo. Unloading continued all day.

The Japanese struck again at 1227; eleven bombers and forty-eight fighters came down from the north. Some attacked the LST's but these "Large, Slow Targets" had mounted extra antiaircraft guns and brought down several Japanese planes.

At 1724, some thirty-six minutes before the LST's departed, the enemy came again. Forty-five fighters and eight bomb-

---

[21] The 35th Infantry later reported the existence of a longer beach eight hundred yards north of Barakoma.

ers attacked without success. The Japanese pilots who flew against the Northern Force on that August day showed a talent for making unwarranted claims. A postwar account soberly admits the loss of seventeen planes, but claims the sinking of four large transports, one cruiser, and one destroyer. It states that twenty-nine Allied planes were shot down and that four large transports were damaged.[22] The ships retiring from Vella Lavella were harried from the air almost all the way, fortunately without suffering damage.

D Day, a resounding success, had proceeded with the efficiency that characterized all Admiral Wilkinson's operations. Landed were 4,600 troops (700 of whom were naval personnel) and 2,300 tons of gear including eight 90-mm. antiaircraft guns, fifteen days' supplies, and three units of fire for all weapons except antiaircraft guns, for which one unit was landed. The 35th Regimental Combat Team established a perimeter defense. Field artillery was in position by 1700, and by 1530 the 4th Marine Defense Battalion had sixteen .50-caliber, eight 20-mm., and eight 40-mm. antiaircraft guns and two searchlights in place. The guns engaged the last flight of enemy planes. There were some problems, of course. The LST's had been unloaded slowly, but supplies came ashore faster than the shore party could clear them off the beach. Boxes of equipment, ammunition, and rations were scattered about. The troops had brought their barracks bags and these lay rain-soaked in the mud. Unused field stoves stood in the way for several days.

The bypass to Vella Lavella was easier and cheaper than an assault on Kolombangara. Twelve men were killed and forty wounded by air bombing and strafing, but D Day saw no fighting on the ground.

There was never any real ground combat on Vella Lavella, because Japanese stragglers were mainly interested in escape rather than fighting. When it became known that Wilkinson was landing on Vella Lavella officers of the *8th Fleet* and the *17th Army* went into conference. They estimated, with an accuracy unusual for Japanese Intelligence, that the landing force was about a brigade in strength. With blithe sanguinity someone proposed sending a battalion to effect a counterlanding. General Imamura's headquarters took a calmer view and pointed out that sending one battalion against a brigade would be "pouring water on a hot stone."[23] The *8th Area Army* stated that two brigades would be needed to achieve success, but that not enough transports were available. In view of the general Japanese strategy of slow retreat in the central Solomons in order to build up the defenses of Bougainville and hold Rabaul, it was decided to send two rifle companies and one naval platoon to Horaniu at Kokolope Bay on the northeast corner of Vella Lavella to establish a barge staging base between the Shortlands and Kolombangara.

The real struggle for Vella Lavella took place in the air and on the sea. Japanese naval aircraft made a resolute effort to destroy the American ships bearing supplies and equipment to Vella.

---

[22] Southeast Area Naval Operations, II, Japanese Monogr No. 49 (OCMH), 47–48.

[23] *Ibid.*, p. 48.

Fighters and bombers delivered daylight attacks and seaplanes delivered a series of nocturnal harassing attacks that were all too familiar to Allied troops who served in the Solomons in 1942, 1943, and early 1944.

The combat air patrol from Mulcahy's command made valiant efforts to keep the Japanese away during daylight, but as radar-equipped night-fighters did not reach the New Georgia area until late September shore- and ship-based antiaircraft provided the defense at night.[24] For daylight cover Mulcahy had planned to maintain a 32-plane umbrella over Barakoma, but the limited operational facilities at Munda made this impossible at first. On 17 August only eight fighters could be sent up at once to guard Barakoma. To add to the difficulties, the weather over New Georgia was bad for a week, the fighter-director teams on Vella Lavella were new to their task, and one of the 4th Defense Battalion's radars was hit by a bomb on 17 August.

The Northern Force's second echelon, under Capt. William R. Cooke, having departed Guadalcanal on 16 August, beached at Barakoma at 1626 the next day. The fighter cover soon left for Munda and at 1850, and again at 1910, Japanese planes came over to bomb and strafe. General McClure ordered Cooke not to stay beached overnight but to put to sea. Escorted by three destroyers, the LST's went down Gizo Strait where they received an air attack of two hours and seventeen minutes' duration. The convoy sailed toward Rendova until 0143, then reversed and headed for Barakoma.

One LST caught fire, probably as a result of a gasoline vapor explosion, and was abandoned without loss of life. The other two reached Barakoma, suffered another air attack, unloaded, and returned safely to Guadalcanal.

Capt. Grayson B. Carter led the third echelon to Vella Lavella. It was attacked by enemy planes in Gizo Strait at 0540 on 21 August; one destroyer was slightly damaged and two men were killed. Planes struck off and on all day at the beached LST's, but men of the 58th Naval Construction Battalion showed such zeal in unloading that the LST's were emptied by 1600. The next convoys, on 26 and 31 August, had less exciting trips. The weather had cleared and the air cover was more effective. During the first month they were there, the Americans on Vella Lavella received 108 enemy air attacks, but none caused much damage. In the period between 15 August and 3 September, the day on which Wilkinson relinquished control of the forces ashore, Task Force 31 carried 6,505 men and 8,626 tons of supplies and vehicles to Vella Lavella.

During that period General McClure's troops had strengthened the defenses of Barakoma, established outposts and radar stations, and patrolled northward on both coasts. On 28 August a thirty-man patrol from the 25th Cavalry Reconnaissance Troop that had accompanied radar specialists of the 4th Marine Defense Battalion in search of a new radar site reported considerable enemy activity at Kokolope Bay.

Capture of Horaniu

Having decided to establish the barge base at Horaniu, the Japanese sent the

---

[24] Robert Sherrod, *History of Marine Corps Aviation in World War II* (Washington: Combat Forces Press, 1952), p. 163.

WARSHIP FIRING AT JAPANESE DESTROYERS *near the coast of Vella Lavella, early morning, 18 August.*

two Army companies and the naval platoon, 390 men in all, out of Erventa on 17 August. Four torpedo boats, 13 troop-carrying *daihatsu* barges,[25] 2 armored barges, 2 submarine chasers, 1 armored boat, 4 destroyers, and 1 naval air group from the Shortlands were involved. The destroyers were intercepted north of Vella Lavella in the early morning hours of 18 August. The *daihatsus* dispersed. The Americans sank the 2 submarine chasers, 2 motor torpedo boats, and 1 barge. The Japanese destroyers, two of which received light damage, broke off the action and headed for Rabaul.[26] Harried by Allied planes, the *daihatsus* hunted for and found Horaniu, and the troops were ashore by nightfall on 19 August. About the same time, General Sasaki took alarm at the seizure of Barakoma and sent the *2d Battalion, 45th Infantry,* and one battery of the *6th Field Artillery Regiment* from Kolombangara to defend Gizo.

When General McClure received the

---

[25] *Daihatsu* is an abbreviation for *Ogata Hatsudokitei* which means a large landing barge. The *daihatsu* was 41–44 feet long; it could carry 100–120 men for short distances, 40–50 on long trips. The sides were usually armored, and it carried machine guns.

[26] For a complete account see Morison, *Breaking the Bismarcks Barrier,* pp. 234–37.

report from the reconnaissance troop patrol on 28 August, he ordered Maj. Delbert Munson's 1st Battalion to advance up the east coast and take the shore of Kokolope Bay for a radar site. To take the 1st Battalion's place in the perimeter defense, McClure asked Griswold for a battalion from New Georgia. The 1st Battalion, 145th Infantry, was selected.

On the morning of 30 August Major Munson dispatched A Company up the east coast ahead of his battalion, and next day, after the arrival of the 1st Battalion, 145th Infantry, the main body of the 1st Battalion, 35th, started north. Josselyn and Bishop Silvester had provided native guides and the bishop gave Munson a letter instructing the natives to help the American soldiers haul supplies. C Company, 65th Engineer Battalion, was to build a supply road behind Munson.

By afternoon of 1 September A Company had reached the vicinity of Orete Cove, about fourteen miles northeast of Barakoma. The main body of the battalion was at Narowai, a village about seven thousand yards southwest of Orete Cove. The coastal track, which had been fairly good at first, narrowed to a trail that required the battalion to march in single file. Inland were the jungled mountains of the interior. Supply by hand-carry was impossible, and McClure and Colonel Brown, who had been informed that higher headquarters expected the Japanese to evacuate, decided to use landing craft to take supplies to Munson. On 2 September supplies arrived at Orete Cove along with seventeen Fiji scouts under Tripp, who had recently been promoted to major.

From that day until 14 September Munson's battalion, supported by the 3d Battalion, 35th, and C Battery, 64th Field Artillery Battalion, moved forward in a series of patrol actions and skirmishes.

Horaniu fell on 14 September. The Japanese did not seriously contest the advance. Instead they withdrew steadily, then moved overland to the northwest corner of the island.

Up to now troops of the United States had borne the brunt of ground combat in the Solomons, but Admiral Halsey had decided to give the 3d New Zealand Division a chance to show its mettle. He had earlier moved the division from New Caledonia to Guadalcanal. On 18 September Maj. Gen. H. E. Barrowclough, general officer commanding the division, took over command of Vella Lavella from General McClure. On the same day the 14th New Zealand Brigade Group under Brigadier Leslie Potter landed and began the task of pursuing the retreating enemy.[27] Battalion combat teams advanced up the east and west coasts, moving by land and by water in an attempt to pocket the enemy. But the Japanese eluded them and got safely off the island.

The Seabees had gone to work on the airfield at once. As at Munda, good coral was abundant. By the end of August they had surveyed and cleared a strip four thousand feet long by two hundred feet wide. They then began work on a control tower, operations shack, and fuel tanks.

---

[27] A brigade group was similar in strength and composition to a U.S. regimental combat team. For details of Potter's operations see Oliver A. Gillespie, *The Pacific,* "The Official History of New Zealand in the Second World War, 1939–1945" (Wellington, New Zealand, 1952), pp. 125–42.

The first plane to use the field landed on 24 September, and within two months after the invasion the field could accommodate almost a hundred aircraft.

The decision to bypass Kolombangara yielded this airfield in return for a low casualty rate. Of the Americans in the northern landing force, 19 men were killed by bombs, 7 died from enemy gunfire, and 108 were wounded. Thirty-two New Zealanders died, and 32 were wounded.

Final Operations

Arundel

About the time that Vella Lavella was being secured, General Griswold's forces on New Georgia were carrying out their part of Admiral Halsey's plan by seizing Arundel and by shelling Kolombangara to seal it off. The attack on Arundel, which is separated from the west coast of New Georgia by Hathorn Sound and Diamond Narrows, proved again that it was all too easy to underestimate the Japanese capacity for resolute defense. The 172d Infantry invaded it on 27 August, but the Japanese fought so fiercely that the 27th Infantry, two battalions of the 169th Infantry, one company of the 103d Infantry, B Company of the 82d Chemical Battalion (4.2-inch mortars, in their South Pacific debut), the 43d Reconnaissance Troop, and six Marine tanks had to be committed to keep the offensive going.

Resistance proved more intense than expected in part because the indefatigable Sasaki had not yet abandoned his hope of launching an offensive that would recapture Munda. On 8 September he sent the *3d Battalion, 13th Infantry,* from Kolombangara to strengthen

his forces on Arundel, and five days later, when Allied air and naval forces had practically cut the supply lines between Bougainville and Kolombangara and his troops faced starvation, he decided to attack Munda or Bairoko via Arundel and seize the Americans' food. He therefore dispatched Colonel Tomonari (who was slain in the ensuing fight) and the rest of the *13th Infantry* to Arundel on 14 September.

Thus the battle for Arundel lasted until 21 September, and ended then, with the Americans in control, only because Sasaki ordered all his Arundel troops to withdraw to Kolombangara.

The Japanese Evacuation

Sasaki had ordered the evacuation of Arundel because *Imperial General Headquarters* had decided to abandon the New Georgia Islands completely. While the Americans were seizing Munda airfield, the Japanese naval authorities in the Southeast Area realized that their hold on the central Solomons was tenuous. But they resolved to maintain the line of communications to Kolombangara, so that Sasaki's troops could hold out as long as possible. If Sasaki could not hold out, the next best thing would be a slow, fighting withdrawal to buy time to build up defenses for a final stand on Bougainville.

Such events in early August as the fall of Munda and the Japanese defeat in Vella Gulf on 6–7 August precipitated another argument between Japanese Army and Navy officers over the relative strategic merits of New Guinea and the Solomons. This argument was resolved in Tokyo by the *Imperial General Headquarters* which decided to give equal

14TH NEW ZEALAND BRIGADE GROUP *landing on Vella Lavella, 18 September 1943.*

priority to both areas. Tokyo sent orders to Rabaul on 13 August directing that the central Solomons hold out while Bougainville was strengthened, and that the central Solomons were to be abandoned in late September and early October. The decision to abandon New Georgia was not made known at once to General Sasaki.

Sasaki, with about twelve thousand men concentrated on Kolombangara, prepared elaborate defenses along the southern beaches and, as shown above, prepared plans for counterattacks. Finally on 15 September, after Sasaki had sent the *13th Infantry* to Arundel, an *8th Fleet* staff officer passed the word to get his troops out.

Southeastern Fleet, 8th Fleet, and

Sasaki's headquarters prepared the plans for the evacuation. A total of 12,435 men were to be moved. Eighteen torpedo boats, thirty-eight large landing craft, and seventy or eighty Army barges (*daihatsus*) were to be used.[28] Destroyers were to screen the movement, aircraft would cover it, and cruisers at Rabaul would stand by in support.

The decision to use the *daihatsus* was logical, considering the destroyer losses in Vella Gulf and the success the nocturnal *daihatsus* had enjoyed. American

---

[28] 17th Army Operations, II, Japanese Monogr No. 40 (OCMH), 54, says 138 "large motor boats" were to be used; Southeast Area Naval Operations, II, Japanese Monogr No. 49 (OCMH), 52, lists 18 torpedo boats, 38 large landing barges, and about 70 Army craft.

PT boat squadrons, four in all, had been operating nightly against the enemy barges in New Georgian waters since late July, and had sunk several, but only a small percentage of the total. Destroyers and planes had also operated against them without complete success. The Japanese put heavier armor and weapons on their barges for defense against torpedo boats, which in turn replaced their torpedoes—useless against the shallow-draft barges—with 37-mm. antitank and 40-mm. antiaircraft guns. The barges were too evasive to be suitable targets for the destroyers' 5-inch guns. Planes of all types, even heavy bombers, hunted them at sea, but the barges hid out in the daytime in carefully selected staging points. Those traveling by day covered themselves with palm trees and foliage so that from the air they resembled islets.

Sasaki ordered his troops off Gizo and Arundel; those on Arundel completed movement to Kolombangara by 21 September. The seaplane base at Rekata Bay on Santa Isabel and the outpost on Ganongga Island were also abandoned at this time. The evacuation of Kolombangara was carried out on the nights of 28–29 September, 1–2 October, and 2–3 October. Admiral Wilkinson had anticipated that the enemy might try to escape during this period, the dark of the moon. Starting 22 September American cruisers and destroyers made nightly reconnaissance of the Slot north of Vella Lavella, but when Japanese submarines became active the cruisers were withdrawn. The destroyers attempted to break up the evacuation but failed because enemy planes and destroyers interfered. The Japanese managed to get some 9,400 men, or some 3,600 less than they had evacu-

ated from Guadalcanal in February, safely off the island. Most of them were sent to southern Bougainville. Twenty-nine landing craft and torpedo boats were sunk, one destroyer was damaged, and sixty-six men were killed.[29]

The final action in the New Georgia area was the Battle of Vella Lavella on the night of 6–7 October, when ten Japanese destroyers and twelve destroyer-transports and smaller craft came down to Vella Lavella to rescue the six hundred stranded men there. Facing odds of three to one, American destroyers engaged the Japanese warships northwest of Vella Lavella. One Japanese destroyer was sunk; one American destroyer was badly damaged and sank, and two more suffered damage. During the engagement the transports slipped in to Marquana Bay on northwest Vella Lavella and got the troops out safely.[30] The last organized bodies of Japanese had left the New Georgia area.

When the 1st Battalion, 27th Infantry, landed at Ringi Cove on southern Kolombangara on the morning of 6 October, it found only forty-nine abandoned artillery pieces and some scattered Japanese who had been left behind.[31] The long campaign—more than four months had elapsed since the Marines landed at Segi Point—was over.

---

[29] Southeast Area Naval Operations, II, Japanese Monogr No. 49 (OCMH), 54–55. At the time the Americans greatly overestimated their success against barges. See for example Halsey and Bryan, *Admiral Halsey's Story*, p. 172.

[30] See Morison, *Breaking the Bismarcks Barrier*, pp. 243–52, for a more complete account.

[31] ACofS G–2 XIV Corps to CG XIV Corps, 29 Oct 43, sub: Photo Int Rpt, Kolombangara, with incls, Exhibit 6, List of Guns Abandoned by Enemy in the Vila Area.

TABLE 2—AMERICAN CASUALTIES ON NEW GEORGIA

	25th Division	37th Division	43d Division	Others	Total
Killed in action and died of wounds..	141	220	538	196	1,094
Wounded	550	887	1942	494	3,873
Missing	1	5	17		23
Accidental death	2	2			4

Source: NGOF, Narrative Account of the Campaigns in the New Georgia Group, p. 29.

Conclusion

New Georgia had been lengthy and costly. Planned as a one-division affair, it had used up elements of four divisions. It would be months before the 25th and 43d Divisions were ready to fight again. American casualties totaled 1,094 dead, 3,873 wounded. (*Table 2*) These figures do not tell the complete story, for they count only men killed or wounded by enemy fire. They do not include casualties resulting from disease or from combat fatigue or war neuroses. For example the 172d Infantry reported 1,550 men wounded *or* sick; the 169th Infantry, up to 5 August, suffered 958 nonbattle casualties. The 103d Infantry had 364 "shelled-shocked" and 83 non-battle casualties.[32]

Japanese casualties are not known, but XIV Corps headquarters reported a count of enemy dead, exclusive of Vella Lavella, of 2,483.

The Allied soldiers, airmen, marines, and sailors who suffered death, wounds, or illness, and those who fought in the campaign without injury, had served their cause well. New Georgia was a success. The bypassing of Kolombangara, though overshadowed by later bypasses and clouded by the fact that the bypassed troops escaped, was a satisfactory demonstration of the technique; the seizure of Vella Lavella provided Halsey's forces with a good airfield for a much lower price in blood than an assault on Kolombangara. The Allies swiftly built another airfield at Ondonga Peninsula on New Georgia. This gave them four—Munda, Barakoma, Ondonga, and Segi. The first three, the most used, brought all Bougainville within range of Allied fighters. When South Pacific forces invaded the island, they could pick an undefended place and frustrate the Japanese efforts to build up Bougainville's defenses and delay the Allies in New Georgia.

The New Georgia operation is also significant as a truly joint operation, and it clearly illustrates the interdependence of air, sea, and ground forces in oceanic warfare. Victory was made possible only by the close co-ordination of air, sea, and ground operations. Air and sea forces fought hard and finally successfully to cut the enemy lines of communication while the ground troops clawed their way forward to seize objectives intended for use by the air and sea forces in the next advance. Unity of command, established

---

[32] 172d Inf Rpt of Opns, New Georgia; 169th Inf Jnl, 5 Aug 43; 103d Inf Rpt of Opns, New Georgia.

MAJ. GEN. J. LAWTON COLLINS *talking to Maj. Charles W. Davis, Commanding Officer, 3d Battalion, 27th Infantry (left), New Georgia, August 1943.*

from the very start, was continued throughout with obvious wholeheartedness by all responsible commanders.

No account of the operation should be brought to a close without praising the skill, tenacity, and valor of the heavily outnumbered Japanese who stood off nearly four Allied divisions in the course of the action, and then successfully evacuated 9,400 men to fight again. The obstinate General Sasaki, who disappears from these pages at this point, deserved his country's gratitude for his gallant and able conduct of the defense.

CHAPTER XI

The Markham Valley and the Huon Peninsula

While South Pacific troops had been so heavily engaged in New Georgia, General MacArthur's Southwest Pacific forces were executing Operation II of the ELKTON plan—the seizure of the Markham Valley and the Huon Peninsula of New Guinea—aimed at increasing the Southwest Pacific Area's degree of control over Vitiaz and Dampier Straits. (*Map 12*) This operation had actually started in January 1943 with the Australian defense of Wau in the Bulolo Valley, and was furthered by the Australian advance from the Bulolo Valley toward Salamaua and the 30 June landing of the MacKechnie Force at Nassau Bay.

Plans

The Allies

The ground forces in Operation II (or POSTERN) were under command of the New Guinea Force.[1] General Blamey arrived at Port Moresby and assumed command of the New Guinea Force on 20 August 1943, and General Herring went to Dobodura, where as general officer commanding the I Australian Corps he exercised control over tactical operations. General Blamey was responsible for co-ordination of ground, air, and naval planning. In the actual conduct of ground, air, and naval operations, the principle of co-operation rather than unity of command appears to have been followed.

---

[1] The subsection is based on ALF, Rpt on New Guinea Opns: 4 Sep 43–26 Apr 44; GHQ SWPA Warning Instns 2, 6 May 43, in GHQ SWPA G–3 Jnl, 6 May 43; GHQ SWPA OI 34, 13 Jun 43, and subsequent amendments, in GHQ SWPA G–3 Jnl, 14 Jun 43; Craven and Cate, *The Pacific: Guadalcanal to Saipan*, pp. 183–86; Kenney, *General Kenney Reports*, pp. 273–87; Morison, *Breaking the*

Bismarcks Barrier, Ch. XIV; Memo, ACofS G–3 GHQ SWPA for CofS GHQ SWPA, 14 Jul 43, no sub, in GHQ SWPA G–3 Jnl, 14 Jul 43; Ltr, Adv Hq ALF to GHQ SWPA, 16 Jul 43, sub: Opns CARTWHEEL, in GHQ SWPA G–3 Jnl, 16 Jul 43; Ltr, Brig Gen Donald Wilson, CofS AAF SWPA, to CINCSWPA, 20 Jul 43, sub: Supporting Plan, GHQ OI 34, same file; LHQ [ALF] OI 54, 30 Jul 43, in GHQ SWPA G–3 Jnl, 31 Jul 43; NGF OI 95, 25 Aug 43, in GHQ SWPA G–3 Jnl, 25 Aug 43; Memo, Gen Chamberlin, ACofS G–3 GHQ SWPA, for CofS GHQ SWPA, 25 May 43, sub: Control of Opns of 2d ESB, in GHQ SWPA G–3 Jnl, 25 May 43; ANF Opn Plan 5–43, 19 Jul 43, in GHQ SWPA G–3 Jnl, 20 Jul 43; AAF SWPA OI 37, 18 Jun 43, in GHQ SWPA G–3 Jnl, 19 Jun 43; Ltr, Comdr ANF to CINCSWPA, 16 Aug 43, sub: Air Support for Troop and Sup Overwater Movements During POSTERN Opn, in GHQ SWPA G–3 Jnl, 16 Aug 43; Memo, Gen Kenney for Gen Chamberlin, 25 Aug 43, sub: Opn Plan, Adv Ech 5th AF, POSTERN Opn, same file; G–2 Est POSTERN, 20 Aug 43, in GHQ SWPA G–3 Jnl, 20 Aug 43.

The operations involved in the seizure of the Huon Peninsula and the Markham Valley were complex. The Southwest Pacific lacked enough ships for a completely amphibious assault, and had too few aircraft for a completely airborne attack; there were enough ground troops, but New Guinea terrain precluded large-scale overland movements. To bring sufficient power to bear General MacArthur and his subordinates and staff therefore employed all available means—amphibious assault, an assault by parachute troops, an airlift of an entire division, and the shore-to-shore operation already executed at Nassau Bay.

MacArthur, in operations instructions issued before the invasions of Woodlark, Kiriwina, and Nassau Bay, and followed by a series of amendments, ordered the New Guinea Force to seize the Lae–Markham Valley area by co-ordinated airborne and overland operations through the Markham Valley and amphibious operations (including Nassau Bay) along the north coast of New Guinea. The Markham Valley operations were to be based on Port Moresby; the north coast operations on Buna and Milne Bay. MacArthur directed the seizure of the coastal areas of the Huon Gulf, including Salamaua and Finschhafen, and initially ordered the New Guinea Force to be prepared for airborne-overland and shore-to-shore operations along the north coast of New Guinea as far as Madang on Astrolabe Bay. The immediate objectives were Lae and the Markham and Ramu Valleys.

The two river valleys form a tremendous trough between the Finisterre and Kratke Ranges. Starting at the mouth of the Markham River at Lae and running northwesterly for 380 miles to the mouth of the Ramu, the trough varies from 5 to 25 miles in width. The rivers flow in opposite directions from a plain in the level uplands of the trough some 80 miles northwest of Lae. Both valleys contain extensive flats of grass-covered sand and gravel, and thus there were many excellent sites for air bases. Already in existence were several emergency strips that had been used by Australian civil aviation before the war.

Lae, a prewar sea terminal for air service to the Bulolo Valley, had a developed harbor and airfield, and was the key to successful employment of airfields in the valleys. Once it was captured, ships could carry supplies to Lae, and roads could be pushed up the Markham Valley to carry supplies to the airfields. The New Guinea Force was ordered to construct airfields in the Lae–Markham Valley area as specified by General Kenney. They were eventually to include facilities for two fighter groups, some night fighters, two medium and two light bombardment groups, one observation squadron, one photo-reconnaissance squadron, and four transport squadrons. MacArthur wanted Madang taken in order to protect the Southwest Pacific's left flank during the subsequent landings on New Britain. Salamaua was not an important objective, but MacArthur and Blamey ordered the 3d Australian Division with the MacKechnie Force attached to press against it for purposes of deception. They wanted the Japanese to believe that Salamaua and not Lae was the real objective, and so to strengthen Salamaua at Lae's expense.

The commander in chief ordered Kenney and Carpender to support the New Guinea Force with their Allied Air and Allied Naval Forces. Allied Land Forces could make the necessary troops available.

U.S. Army Services of Supply and Line of Communications units of Allied Land Forces would provide logistical support. From thirty to ninety days of various classes of supply was to be stocked at intermediate and advance bases. General Marshall's U.S. Army Services of Supply would be responsible for supply of American forces in the Huon Peninsula and Markham Valley, and would provide all items to the Army and Navy. MacArthur ordered Marshall's command to aid Allied Naval Forces in transporting the 2d Engineer Special Brigade to the combat zone, and to prepare to relieve Allied Naval Forces of the responsibility for transporting supplies to Lae and to Woodlark and Kiriwina.

Some of the plan's outstanding features were the ways it proposed to use air power. The impending assault by parachute would be the first tactical employment of parachute troops as such by Allied forces in the Pacific.[2] The combination of airlifted troops and parachute troops in co-ordination with amphibious assault had also not been used hitherto by the Allies in the Pacific. The year before, General Whitehead had "sold the Aussies on the scheme of an airborne show at Nadzab to take Lae out from the back," and General MacArthur had liked the idea too, but there were not enough transport planes in the area

to carry it out at that time.[3] Generals MacArthur and Blamey had planned to operate overland from the Lakekamu River to the Bulolo Valley and thence to the Markham Valley in conjunction with a parachute assault by one battalion. Delays in building the mountain road from the Lakekamu to the Bulolo Valley made necessary a decision to land an entire parachute regiment at Nadzab, a superb airfield site in the Markham Valley where a prewar Australian airstrip already existed, and to fly an entire division from Port Moresby to Nadzab immediately afterward.

The third unusual feature of the POSTERN air operations was made possible by General Kenney's enthusiastic willingness to try any experiment that offered a hope of success and by the fact that both Allied and Japanese forces were concentrated in small enclaves on the New Guinea coast, with the highlands and hinterland available to whichever force could maintain patrols there. On General Kenney's recommendation, MacArthur ordered the development of two grass strips, one in the Watut Valley west of Salamaua and the other in the grassy plateau south of Madang where the Markham and Ramu Rivers rise. These strips could serve as staging bases that would enable Kenney to send fighters from Port Moresby and Dobodura as far as the expanding enemy base at Wewak or over the western part of New Britain, and to give fighter cover to Allied bombers in the vicinity of Lae. Thus the Allied Air Forces would be using inland airfields to support and protect a seaborne invasion of a coastal area.

---

[2] The 1st Marine Parachute Battalion fought well at Guadalcanal and Tulagi in 1942, but it fought on foot as an infantry battalion. It made no tactical jumps.

[3] Kenney, *General Kenney Reports,* p. 128.

D Day was set for planning purposes as 1 August, but was postponed to 27 August and finally to 4 September to permit the assembly of enough C–47's, more training for the 7th Australian Division, and the relief of the VII Amphibious Force of its responsibilities for Woodlark and Kiriwina. The precise date was picked by General Kenney on the basis of weather forecasts. He wanted fog over western New Britain and Vitiaz and Dampier Straits that would keep Japanese aircraft away while bright clear weather over New Guinea—a fairly common condition—permitted the flight to and jump into the Markham Valley. The fourth of September promised to be such a date and was selected.[4]

The final tactical plans were prepared by New Guinea Force and by the various higher headquarters in the Allied Air and Allied Naval Forces under the supervision of General MacArthur, General Sutherland, MacArthur's chief of staff, and such subordinates as General Chamberlin, the G–3 of GHQ.[5]

Final plans, issued in August, called for the employment of two veteran Australian divisions, the 7th and the 9th, the U.S. 503d Parachute Infantry Regiment, and elements of the U.S. 2d Engineer Special Brigade, as well as the American and Australian troops already pressing against Salamaua in their deception maneuver. The 9th Australian Division was to be carried by the VII Amphibious Force, with elements of the 2d Engineer Special Brigade, attached, from Milne Bay to beaches far enough east of Lae to be beyond range of enemy artillery.

Early plans had called for the 2d Engineer Special Brigade to carry the 9th Australian Division to Lae and support it thereafter. But closer study showed that an engineer special brigade could carry and support but one brigade in reduced strength—about 3,000 men, or not nearly enough to attack Lae. Therefore the VII Amphibious Force was ordered to carry the 9th Division, and the 2d Engineer Special Brigade was attached to Barbey's command for the initial phases. Two brigade groups, totaling 7,800 men, plus elements of the amphibian engineers, were to land starting at 0630, 4 September.[6] That evening 2,400 more Australians would land, and on the night of 5–6 September the VII Amphibious Force, having retired to Buna after unloading on 4 September, was to bring in the 3,800 men of the reserve brigade group. The time for H Hour, 0630, was selected because it came thirty minutes past sunrise, by which time the light would be suitable for the preliminary naval bombardment.

---

[4] In his book Kenney tells how the American and Australian weather teams kept altering their forecasts and disagreeing with one another. Finally the American team picked 5 September; the Australians decided on 3 September. General Kenney "decided that neither one of them knew anything about weather, split the difference between the two forecasts, and told General MacArthur we would be ready to go on the morning of the 4th for the amphibious movement. . . ." *General Kenney Reports*, p. 288.

[5] GHQ supervised the preparation of the plans for Operation II more closely than, for example, those for Woodlark–Kiriwina. The staff at GHQ felt that New Guinea Force and subordinate headquarters were slow in preparing plans, tended to prepare plans for initiating operations rather than for carrying them through completely, failed to provide for co-ordination of forces, and did not thoroughly appreciate logistics. See Memo, Chamberlin for CofS GHQ SWPA, 28 Aug 43, no sub, in GHQ SWPA G–3 Jnl, 16 Jul 43.

[6] A brigade group was similar in strength and composition to a U.S. regimental combat team.

Admiral Carpender organized his Allied Naval Forces into almost the same task forces that he had set up for Woodlark and Kiriwina and assigned them similar missions. Admiral Barbey organized his VII Amphibious Force into a transport group of 2 destroyers, 4 APD's, 13 LST's, 20 LCI's, 14 LCT's and 1 AP; a cover group of 4 destroyers; an escort group of 2 destroyers; an APC group of 13 APC's, 9 LST's, and 2 subchasers; and a service group of 1 tender, 3 LST's, 10 subchasers, 5 minesweepers, 1 oiler, and 1 tug. The attached engineer special brigade elements possessed 10 LCM's and 40 LCVP's.

Allied Air Forces' plans for support of the invasion called for General Whitehead to provide close support to ground troops, to provide escort and cover for the amphibious movements, to establish an air blockade over Huon Peninsula, to specify to General Blamey the air facilities to be constructed in the target areas, and to prepare to move forward to the new bases.

But again there was an argument over the method by which the air forces would cover the VII Amphibious Force. Admirals Carpender and Barbey had no aircraft carriers and thus were completely dependent upon the Allied Air Forces for air support. They pointed out that the amphibious movement to Lae would involve over forty ships, 7,800 soldiers and 3,260 sailors. This represented all suitable vessels available, with none retained in reserve. Losses to Japanese air attacks would seriously jeopardize the success of future operations, and therefore they argued that only a fighter umbrella providing continuous cover for the VII Amphibious Force would be adequate. The airmen, who were planning to use over three hundred planes in the Markham Valley parachute jump, were willing to provide air cover for Barbey's ships over Lae itself on D Day, but argued that the movement of the convoys would be amply protected by maintaining fighter squadrons on ground alert at Dobodura and the staging airfield in the Watut Valley. The argument, a heated one, went up the chain of command to General MacArthur himself, and was finally settled by Kenney's agreement to use a total of thirty-two planes to give as much cover as possible over the VII Amphibious Force during daylight and to maintain fighter squadrons on ground alert.

There remained the problem of fighter control. One fighter control unit was stationed at Dobodura, and another at the staging field in the Watut Valley, but radar coverage over the area was far from complete. Japanese aircraft from Wewak or Madang could fly south of the mountains to Lae, or from New Britain across Dampier and Vitiaz Straits, and radar would not pick them up until they were almost over Lae. And as Brig. Gen. Charles A. Willoughby, MacArthur's G–2, pointed out, Allied experience at New Georgia showed that the Japanese air reaction might be violent. An Australian airman suggested that the difficulty be alleviated by posting a radar-equipped destroyer between Lae and Finschhafen. This was accepted, and the U.S. destroyer *Reid*, which was part of Barbey's antisubmarine screen, was selected as picket with orders to steam in Vitiaz Strait some forty-five miles southeast of Finschhafen.

Markham Valley plans called for the

503d Parachute Infantry Regiment, flying from Port Moresby in C–47's, to jump onto Nadzab airstrip on the north bank of the Markham River on 5 September, the day after the amphibious assault. Nadzab was not believed to be occupied by the Japanese, but this seizure would block the valley and prevent the enemy's sending troops overland from Wewak. Once captured, Nadzab airstrip was to be quickly readied for airplanes by the 503d and by a force of Australian engineers and pioneers. The Australians were to paddle in boats from the staging airfield in the Watut Valley down the Watut River to Nadzab—a distance of about thirty-two air miles, but actually twice that far for anything but crows and airplanes. Then one brigade of the 7th Australian Division, plus engineers and antiaircraft units, having been flown to the Watut Valley previously, would fly in. The next brigade would come in directly by air from Port Moresby. Once adequate strength had been assembled, the 7th Australian Division would march eastward down the Markham River against Lae, and at the same time the 9th Australian Division would drive westward from the landing beaches.

Seizure of Nadzab would have a threefold effect: it would provide Allied forces with one more air base with which to increase their control over the Huon Peninsula, the straits, and western New Britain; it would provide a base for the 7th Division's eastward march against Lae; and an Allied force at Nadzab could forestall any attempt by the Japanese to reinforce Lae from Wewak by marching through the Ramu and Markham Valleys.

The Enemy

Japanese strategic intentions were not changed by the invasion of the Trobriands or of Nassau Bay. In August 1943 Generals Imamura and Adachi were still resolved to hold Lae and Salamaua as parts of the outer defenses of Wewak and Madang, and were still planning to move into Bena Bena south of the Ramu Valley.[7] There were about ten thousand men in the Lae–Salamaua area, with somewhat more than half of these defending Salamaua. Many of the ten thousand, reported the Japanese after the war, were sick. Some estimates run as high as 50 percent. At Lae, General Shoge, temporarily detached from his post as infantry group commander of the *41st Division,* led a force consisting of a naval guard unit, elements of the *21st, 102d,* and *115th Infantry Regiments,* and artillerymen and engineers. In addition to defending Lae, Shoge was responsible for patrolling up the Markham River and for protecting the southern approaches to Finschhafen on the east coast of the Huon Peninsula.

In the months following the Bismarck Sea disaster the supply systems for Lae and Salamaua had almost broken down. The Allied aerial blockade of the Huon Peninsula prevented the use of large ships to carry supplies forward to Lae. Until June, six submarines helped carry supplies, but then the number was cut to three and the bulk of supplies had to be carried on barges. Supply of the ten

---

[7] This subsection is based upon 8th Area Army Operations, Japanese Monogr No. 110 (OCMH), pp. 22–34, 36–85; 18th Army Operations, II, Japanese Monogr No. 42 (OCMH), 27–54; USSBS, *Allied Campaign Against Rabaul,* p. 84.

thousand men for the five months preceding September would have required 150 bargeloads per month, while 200 more barges were needed for transport of reinforcements and ammunition. But there were far too few barges. Only 40, for example, were making the run to Lae from the staging base at Tuluvu on the north shore of Cape Gloucester. The sea and the tides in Dampier Strait damaged many, and several fell victim to Allied aircraft and to nocturnal PT's which, like their sister boats in the Solomons, prowled the barge lanes.

Imperial General Headquarters, meanwhile, had paid heed to Imamura's request for more planes. On 27 July *Imperial Headquarters* ordered the *4th Air Army,* commanded by Lt. Gen. Kumaichi Teramoto, from the Netherlands Indies to the Southeast Area. Teramoto's army would include the *7th Air Division,* the *14th Air Brigade,* some miscellaneous squadrons, and the *6th Air Division,* which was already based at Wewak.

The *4th Air Army* headquarters arrived at Rabaul on 6 August, whereupon Imamura ordered Teramoto and his planes to proceed to Wewak with the mission of escorting convoys, destroying Allied planes and ships, and co-operating with the *18th Army.* The move was made at once; the Allies were well aware that the Japanese were building up strength on the four Wewak airfields.

Allied Air and Naval Preparations

Increases in Air Strength

The increases in Allied strength that had been promised to the Southwest Pacific Area at the Pacific Military Conference in March had been coming through practically on schedule.[8] P-47's of the 348th Fighter Group began arriving in Australia in June, and before the end of July the whole group had been deployed to New Guinea. The 475th Fighter Group, flying P-38's, was ready for combat by the middle of the next month.

Bomber strength, too, was increasing. Newly arrived B-24's of the 380th Heavy Bombardment Group went into action from Darwin, Australia, in mid-July. One of the 380th's first large-scale operations was a spectacular raid on the oil center at Balikpapan, Borneo, on 13 August, a feat that required a 1,200-mile round trip. Port Moresby saw the arrival of new B-25's of the 345th Medium Bombardment Group in July. And the C-47's were also increasing in number. By September the 54th Troop Carrier Wing could boast fourteen full squadrons of transport planes.

By the end of August the Southwest Pacific Area had on hand nearly all its authorized plane strength—197 heavy bombers and 598 fighters. Keeping this number in flying condition, however, was next to impossible. Many of the planes were old, and with the air forces constantly in action there were always battle casualties. Kenney was always short of manpower; he could never obtain enough replacement pilots to keep all his new and veteran squadrons up to strength, a condition that was probably duplicated in every active theater.

Operations

The first important action of Kenney's

---

[8] This section is based on Craven and Cate, *The Pacific: Guadalcanal to Saipan,* pp. 168–86; Morison, *Breaking the Bismarcks Barrier,* pp. 257–61; Kenney, *General Kenney Reports,* pp. 251–79.

Allied Air Forces in preparation for the Markham Valley–Huon Peninsula operation was the development of the staging fields in the Watut Valley and in the Ramu–Markham trough. Ever since the Buna campaign Kenney had been anxious for a good fighter field near Lae to use in covering the invasion. He hoped to fly troops into an existing emergency strip and seize it, as he had done during the Buna campaign. Kokoda and Wau had been surveyed but found unsuitable. Then in May an aviation engineer officer, with orders to find a field farther forward than Wau, trekked from the Bulolo Valley almost to Salamaua, found nothing suitable, and thereupon backtracked and went down the Watut River where he found and recommended an emergency landing strip at Marilinan. But Marilinan was not perfect; it was feared the September rains would render its clay too muddy to be usable. At this point General Wurtsmith of the V Fighter Command took a hand. Looking over the ground himself, he picked a site at Tsili Tsili four miles down the Watut River from Marilinan. Kenney and Whitehead agreed with his choice.

Meanwhile Kenney and Herring arranged to build the second staging field, using a few Australian troops and native labor, at Bena Bena south of the Ramu Valley. This emergency strip had long served as a New Guinea Force patrol base, and the Japanese at this time were hoping to capture it eventually. The Allies decided to build a grass strip suitable for fighters at Bena Bena (C–47's carrying supplies to the Australian patrols had been using Bena Bena for some time), and to burn off the grass in fashion so obvious as to distract the enemy's attention from Tsili Tsili.

In June and July, C–47's flew Australian troops and the U.S. 871st Airborne Engineer Battalion to Marilinan. The troops moved down the river to Tsili Tsili, cleared the strips, and C–47's flew in specially designed bulldozers and other earth-moving equipment. Some gear, including trucks sawed in half so they could be loaded into C–47's, was also flown to Tsili Tsili, where the trucks were welded together. Two strips at Tsili Tsili were soon ready, and by mid-August three thousand troops, including a fighter squadron, were based there. Japanese aircraft failed to molest the Allies until the fields were all built; they raided Tsili Tsili on 15 and 16 August without doing much damage and thereafter left it alone.

While General Kenney had liked the prospects of Tsili Tsili from a technical point of view, he had felt that *Tsili Tsili* had an unfortunate sound. He therefore officially directed that the base be given the more attractive name of Marilinan.[9]

During this period the Fifth Air Force had been supporting the Allied diversionary attacks against Salamaua. Nearly every day of July saw some form of air attack against the Lae–Salamaua area. Sorties during the month totaled 400 by B–25's, 100 by B–24's, 45 by RAAF Bostons, 35 by A–20's, 30 by B–17's, and 7 by B–26's. The Japanese supply point at Madang was also raided during the period 20–23 July by B–25's and heavy bombers.

But these raids were secondary to Kenney's main air effort, which was di-

---

[9] Craven and Cate in *The Pacific: Guadalcanal to Saipan,* however, use the name Tsili Tsili.

B-24 OVER SALAMAUA, *13 August 1943. Note smoke from bomb bursts.*

ENEMY AIRCRAFT DESTROYED ON THE GROUND *by Allied planes near Lae.*

rected against Wewak. Aware of the increase in Japanese air strength at Wewak, and lacking enough strength to hit both Wewak and Rabaul, Kenney had decided to concentrate against Wewak rather than Rabaul up to the day of the landing at Lae, and to rely in part on the weather for protection against Rabaul-based planes. There were too many Japanese fighter planes at Wewak, however, for Kenney to risk sending unescorted bombers there. Raids against Wewak had to await completion of the Marilinan staging field, which would extend the range of Allied fighters as far as Wewak. Meanwhile Kenney ordered his bombers not to go as far as Wewak, thus leading the Japanese to believe that Wewak lay beyond bomber range and to send planes there with a false sense of security.

On 13 August photographs taken by Allied reconnaissance planes showed a total of 199 Japanese airplanes on the four fields at Wewak. The *4th Air Army* was now due for a surprise. Marilinan was ready by midmonth and so was the Fifth Air Force. General Whitehead had four bombardment groups with enough range to hit Wewak from Port Moresby —two heavy groups with 64 planes in commission and two medium groups totaling 58 B–25's. With Marilinan in commission the bombers would have fighter protection all the way.

B–25 MEDIUM BOMBERS *leaving installations aflame in the Wewak area.*

Heavy and medium bombers and fighters struck the four Wewak fields on 17 August and achieved excellent results. Taking the Japanese by surprise, they caught most of the enemy planes on the ground. Next day they were back in strength, and the Wewak offensive continued throughout the rest of August. The planes struck at Hansa Bay and Alexishafen during the same period.

Damage inflicted by these raids was heavy, though less than estimated at the time. Kenney's headquarters claimed over 200 Japanese aircraft destroyed on the ground, a claim that Army Air Forces headquarters scaled down to 175. Postwar Japanese reports, however, give

losses as about half what the Allies initially claimed.[10] But despite the efforts of Imamura and Teramoto, strength of the *4th Air Army* thereafter averaged but 100 planes, and "the prospect of the New Guinea operation [was] much gloomier." [11]

The Allied Naval Forces, which had not played a decisive part in the Buna campaign because it lacked enough ships

---

[10] 8th Area Army Operations, Japanese Monogr No. 110 (OCMH), p. 83, states that one hundred planes were lost; 18th Army Operations, II, Japanese Monogr No. 42 (OCMH), 29, asserts that sixty to seventy were destroyed.

[11] 8th Area Army Operations, Japanese Monogr No. 110 (OCMH), p. 84.

and because hydrographic information on the waters of New Guinea's north coast was almost nonexistent, was also taking a hand. PT boats based at Morobe were stalking the enemy barge routes at night and making the transport of men and munitions to Lae increasingly difficult. The Fifth Air Force's successful strike against Wewak encouraged Admiral Carpender to send warships as far up the coast as Finschhafen. Thus on 22 August four destroyers under Capt. Jesse H. Carter left Milne Bay, stopped at Buna to discuss air cover and obtain target information, and sailed for Finschhafen. Starting at 0121, 23 August, Carter's ships bombarded Finschhafen with 540 rounds of 5-inch shells and returned safely to Milne Bay. This operation was small in itself, but it was significant because this was the first time Allied warships had ventured so far up the New Guinea coast.

During the first three days of September Allied planes executed preparatory bombardments in support of the Lae invasion. They launched heavy attacks against airfields, supply points, and shipping lanes on 1 September, the same day on which medium and heavy bombers raided Alexishafen and Madang. Next day B–25's and P–38's delivered a low-level attack against Wewak. Gasmata and Borgen Bay on New Britain, and Lae itself, were struck on 3 September, and eleven nocturnal RAAF Catalinas raided Rabaul.

The Salamaua Attack,
1 July–12 September 1943

During July and August, while the various headquarters of the Southwest Pacific Area were preparing plans and assembling troops and supplies for the Lae–Markham Valley invasions, and while the air and naval forces were attacking Japanese aircraft, bases, and lines of communication, the troops in front of Salamaua were carrying out their part of the plan by the diversionary attack against that port.[12] Starting from the arc-shaped positions they held in early July, the 3d Australian Division and the MacKechnie Force, soon joined by the remainder of the 162d Infantry, fought their way forward until by the end of August they were closing in on the town and airfield of Salamaua. (*See Map 6.*)

At first the reinforced 1st Battalion, 162d Infantry, fighting on the right of the 3d Australian Division, was the only American unit present, but this force was enlarged in July, after the capture of Bitoi Ridge, when other elements of the 41st Division were attached to the 3d Australian Division. This attachment came about because more U.S. infantrymen and artillerymen were needed to secure the Tambu Bay–Dot Inlet area northwest of Nassau Bay, and because a supply base for Australians and Americans in the combat area was required. Consequently the Coane Force, commanded by Brig. Gen. Ralph W. Coane who was also 41st Division artillery commander, was organized during the second

---

[12] Unless otherwise indicated this section is based on McCartney, *The Jungleers,* Ch. VII; ALF, Rpt on New Guinea Opns: 1 Mar–13 Sep 43; 162d Inf Rpt of Opns, and Jnl; 41st Div Arty, Hist of Salamaua Campaign, 23 Apr–4 Oct 43; Combined Operational Int Center GHQ SWPA, Resume of Allied Mil Opns and Int Leading to the Capture of Lae and Salamaua From the Enemy: Jun–Sep 43, 20 Sep 43, in GHQ SWPA Jnl, 20 Sep 43.

week in July.[13] The MacKechnie Force, then fighting forward from Bitoi Ridge, was not a part of the Coane Force. Some units assigned to the Coane Force were already in the Nassau Bay area; others soon came up from Morobe.[14]

Both Coane and MacKechnie Forces fought under command of General Savige, commanding the 3d Australian Division, and after Savige's headquarters was relieved on 24 August by Headquarters, 5th Australian Division, under command of Maj. Gen. E. J. Milford, the Americans served under Milford. At the same time Col. William D. Jackson, 41st Division artillery executive officer, was appointed as Commander, Royal Artillery, of the 3d and then the 5th Australian Divisions. Jackson, using a com-

posite Australian and American staff, served as artillery commander until the end of hostilities in that area.

On 17 July the Coane Force moved forward from Nassau Bay, and by the end of the next day had secured the southern headland of Tambu Bay, where a supply base was set up. Starting on 20 July, the Americans launched a series of attacks with strong artillery support which resulted on 13 August in the capture of the high ground—Roosevelt Ridge, Scout Ridge, and Mount Tambu —overlooking Tambu Bay and Dot Inlet. On 12 August the Coane Force was dissolved and the entire 162d Infantry reverted to Colonel MacKechnie's control.

At the same time the Australians pressed forward so that by the first week in September they had reached the Francisco River, which flows in an west-east direction just south of the Salamaua airfield. All advances were made up and down precipitous ridges varying from eight hundred to three thousand feet in height. With characteristic skill the Japanese had established strong defensive positions on the ridges; there were many automatic weapons emplacements, with earth-and-log pillboxes predominating, that gave each other mutual support with interlocking bands of fire. Trenches and tunnels connected the emplacements.

Early September saw Japanese resistance slackening. On 11 September the Australians and the 162d Infantry Reconnaissance Platoon crossed the rain-swollen Francisco River and by the end of 12 September the airfield, the town, and the entire isthmus, which had been held by the Japanese for eighteen months, was back in Allied hands.

The cost was not cheap. On 29 June

---

[13] It consisted at first of the 2d and 3d Battalions, 162d Infantry; the 162d Infantry Cannon Company; 3d Platoon, Antitank Company, 162d Infantry; C Battery, 209th Coast Artillery Battalion; A Battery, 218th Field Artillery Battalion; A Company, 116th Medical Battalion; A and D Companies, 532d Engineer Boat and Shore Regiment, 2d Engineer Special Brigade; A Company, Papuan Infantry Battalion; a Combined Operational Service Command detachment; Troop D, 2/6th Royal Australian Artillery Regiment; and signal and quartermaster troops.

[14] Problems involving command over the mixed Australian-American units appear to have been additional factors in the decision to create the Coane Force rather than to turn all American troops over to Colonel MacKechnie. The MacKechnie Force was attached to the 3d Australian Division, but Maj. Gen. Horace H. Fuller, commanding the 41st U.S. Division, retained control over the American troops at the actual beachhead. Thus, as he put it later, Colonel MacKechnie was "placed in the unenviable position of trying to obey two masters" who kept giving him conflicting orders. The impossibility of obeying them both finally led MacKechnie to request relief as commanding officer of the 162d. He was reassigned as Coane Force S–3, and later as liaison officer with the 3d Australian Division, but returned to command the 162d on the dissolution of the Coane Force. See Ltr, Col MacKechnie to Gen Smith, Chief of Mil Hist, 2 Nov 53, no sub, OCMH.

SALAMAUA, *objective of the attack.*

there were 2,554 men in the 162d Infantry. By 12 September battle casualties and disease had reduced the regiment to 1,763 men. One hundred and two had been killed, 447 wounded. The 162d estimated it had killed 1,272 Japanese and reported the capture of 6 prisoners.

The Japanese had lost Salamaua after a stiff fight and the very strength of their defense had played into Allied hands, for of the ten thousand enemy soldiers in the Lae–Salamaua area, the majority had been moved to Salamaua. The Allied ruse had succeeded.

Lae: The Seaborne Invasion

The Landing

The unit slated to invade Lae, Maj. Gen. G. F. Wootten's 9th Australian Division, embarked on the ships of Admiral Barbey's Task Force 76 at Milne

CROSSING RAIN-SWOLLEN FRANCISCO RIVER

Bay on 1 September.[15] Next day Barbey's ships sailed to Buna and to Morobe, where they were joined by fifty-seven landing craft of the 2d Engineer Special

Brigade that had assembled there in the latter part of August. On the night of 3–4 September the armada set out for Lae, eighty miles distant; it arrived at the landing beaches east of Lae at sunrise of 4 September. (*Map 13*)

At 0618, eighteen minutes after the sun rose, five destroyers fired a ten-minute bombardment on the beaches. Then sixteen landing craft from the APD's started for the beaches carrying

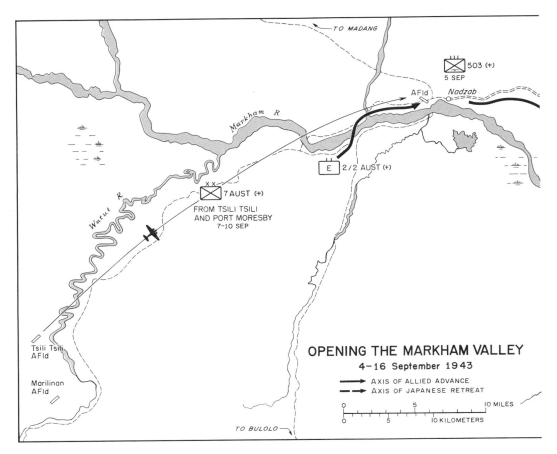

MAP 13

the assault waves. At 0631 the 20th Australian Infantry Brigade began going
ashore at Red Beach, near Bulu Plantation and some eighteen miles east of Lae.
This landing was unopposed. Two
minutes later troops of the 26th Australian Infantry Brigade landed at
Yellow Beach, eighteen miles east of
Lae, east of the Bulu River. A small
group of Japanese on Yellow Beach ran
away at the approach of the Australians.
Scouts of the 2d Engineer Special Brigade landed with the Australian infantry.

Fifteen minutes after the assault waves
beached, LCI's pushed their bows onto
the beaches and put more riflemen
ashore. They were followed by LCT's
and LST's. All assault troops had landed
by 0830, and by 1030 fifteen hundred
tons of supplies had been landed. By
the end of the day the beachheads were
secure, 2,400 more Australians had
landed, and the 26th Brigade and the
2/17th Australian Infantry Battalion had
crossed the Buso and begun the advance
westward against Lae.

There was no resistance on the

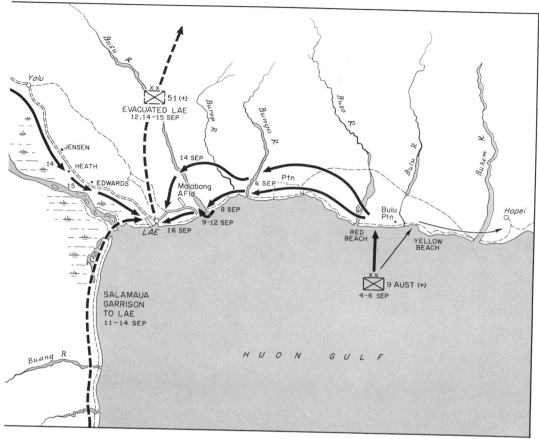

D. Holmes, Jr.

ground, but Japanese aircraft attempted to break up the invasion. About 0700, before fighter cover had arrived, a few two-engine bombers with fighter escort attacked Task Force 76 and damaged two LCI's. Imamura dispatched eighty planes from Rabaul to attack Barbey but these were delayed by the fog over New Britain that Kenney's weathermen had predicted. The picket destroyer *Reid's* radar located them over Gasmata in the afternoon just as Task Force 76 was making ready to sail for Milne Bay. The *Reid* vectored out forty P–38's and twenty P–47's which intercepted the flight and broke it up. Some planes got through, however, and attacked a group of six LST's off Cape Ward Hunt. They damaged two and killed over a hundred Australian soldiers and American sailors. The Japanese did not attack the jammed landing beaches at this time, but returned in the evening to blow up an ammunition dump, damage two beached LCI's, and kill two men.[16]

---

[16] They claimed to have sunk 14 transports, 2 barges, 1 PT boat, 3 destroyers, and to have shot down 38 planes.

AUSTRALIAN TROOPS DEBARKING FROM LST's *for the occupation of Lae.*

The Advance Westward

Once the assault troops had landed control of the 2d Engineer Special Brigade elements—thirteen hundred men of a reinforced boat company, a boat control section, a shore battalion, a medical detachment, scouts, and a headquarters detachment—passed from Admiral Barbey to General Wootten. A salvage boat, ten LCVP's, and two additional LCVP's mounting machine guns for support of landings remained at Red Beach. Eventually, twenty-one LCM's and twenty-one LCVP's were sent to Red Beach. Because of breakdowns, these replacements were necessary if ten craft of each type were to be kept in operation. All these craft were used to support the 9th Division's march against Lae.

The 2/13th Australian Infantry Battalion, once landed, pushed east from Bulu Plantation and secured the east flank by seizing Hopoi. The reserve 24th Infantry Brigade landed on schedule on the night of 5–6 September, and at daylight started west behind the 26th Brigade. On 6 September, after a ten-mile march, the 26th Brigade met its first opposition at the Bunga River.

The 24th Brigade advanced along the coast while the 26th Brigade moved some distance inland in an effort to get behind Lae and cut off the enemy garrison. The 24th's advance was rendered difficult, not so much by the enemy as by the terrain. The heavy September rains flooded the creeks and turned the trails into deep mud that was virtually impassable for vehicles. Fortunately the boats of the 2d Engineer Special Brigade were available to ferry supplies by water to coastal dumps and enable the advance to continue. The leading Australian battalions reached the Busu (not to be confused with the Buso farther east) on the morning of 8 September. This swollen river, five feet deep and sixty feet wide at the mouth, and flowing at twelve knots, was a severe obstacle in itself, and the west bank was held by the Japanese.

Patrols attempted to force a crossing on the morning of 9 September but the combination of Japanese bullets and the swift current forced them back. In the late afternoon elements of four rifle companies got across in rubber boats and by wading and swimming. Several men were drowned and many weapons lost in this act of gallantry, but the four companies seized a bridgehead on the west bank and held it against enemy counterattacks.

Meanwhile the troops on the east bank loaded men, weapons, and ammunition onto the 2d Engineer Special Brigade's landing craft and sent them to the west bank. For the next sixty hours, the landing craft plied back and forth until the entire 24th Brigade had been transferred to the west bank. Rain, mist, and darkness helped hide the boats from the Japanese, who tried to hit them with artillery, machine guns, and rifles. During the same period a box girder bridge was moved in pieces by landing craft from Bulu Plantation to the mouth of the Burep River, then laboriously hauled inland to the 26th Brigade's zone over a jeep track built by the 2d Engineer Special Brigade. The bridge was installed over the Busu under enemy fire on the morning of the 14th. The 26th Brigade crossed over that night. Both brigades

were then on the west bank of the Busu and were ready to resume the advance against Lae and effect a junction with the troops of the 7th Australian Division that were advancing east out of Nadzab.

Nadzab: The Airborne Invasion

The Jump

Capture of Nadzab had been spectacularly effected on 5 September. This mission, assigned to Col. Kenneth H. Kinsler's 503d Parachute Infantry Regiment, was coupled with the additional mission of preparing the airstrip for C–47's carrying Maj. Gen. George A. Vasey's 7th Australian Division from Marilinan and Port Moresby.[17]

Reveille for the men of the 503d sounded early at Port Moresby on the morning of 5 September. The weather promised to be fair, although bad flying weather over the Owen Stanleys delayed take off until 0825. New Guinea Force had prepared its plans flexibly so that the seaborne invasion on 4 September would not be slowed or altered if any threat of bad weather on 5 September delayed the parachute jump, but Kenney's weathermen had forecast accurately.

The paratroopers and a detachment of

[17] Unless otherwise indicated this section is based on Craven and Cate, *The Pacific: Guadalcanal to Saipan;* pp. 184–86; Morison, *Breaking the Bismarcks Barrier,* pp. 266–69; Kenney, *General Kenney Reports,* pp. 292–96; ALF, Rpt on New Guinea Opns: 4 Sep 43–26 Apr 44; Combined Operational Int Center GHQ SWPA, Resume . . . Lae and Salamaua, in GHQ SWPA G–3 Jnl, 20 Sep 43; 503d Parachute Inf Rpt of Opns, Markham Valley, 5–19 Sep 43; Japanese Operations in the Southwest Pacific Area, MS (Vol. II of the MacArthur hist), Ch. VII, OCMH; 8th Area Army Operations, Japanese Monogr No. 110 (OCMH), pp. 81–85; 18th Army Operations, II, Japanese Monogr No. 42 (OCMH), 18–80; Interrogation of Adachi *et al.,* by Mil Hist Sec, Australian Army Hq, OCMH.

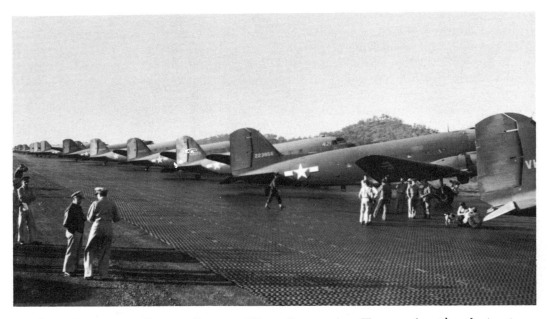

C–47 Transport Planes Loaded With Parachute Troops *for the drop at Nadzab. Two men at left are General Kenney and General MacArthur.*

2/4th Australian Field Regiment which was to jump with its 25-pounder guns reached the airfield two hours before take off.[18] There they put on parachutes and equipment. The 54th Troop Carrier Wing had ninety-six C–47's ready, and the troops boarded these fifteen minutes before take-off time.

The first C–47 roared down the runway at 0825; by 0840 all transports were aloft. They crossed the Owen Stanleys, then organized into three battalion flights abreast, with each flight in six-plane elements in step-up right echelon.

An hour later bombers, fighters, and weather planes joined the formation over Marilinan, on time to the minute. All together 302 aircraft from eight different fields were involved. The air armada then flew down the Watut Valley, swung to the right over the Markham River, and headed for Nadzab. The C–47's dropped from 3,000 feet to 400–500 feet. The parachutists had stood in their planes and checked their equipment over Marilinan, and twelve minutes later they formed by the plane doors ready to jump.

In the lead six squadrons of B–25 strafers with eight .50-caliber machine guns in their noses and six parachute fragmentation bombs in their bays worked over the Nadzab field. Six A–20's laid smoke after the last bomb had exploded. Then came the C–47's, closely covered by fighters.

The paratroopers began jumping from the three columns of C–47's onto separate jump areas about 1020. Eighty-one C–47's carrying the 503d were emptied

---

[18] The 503d had trained this detachment.

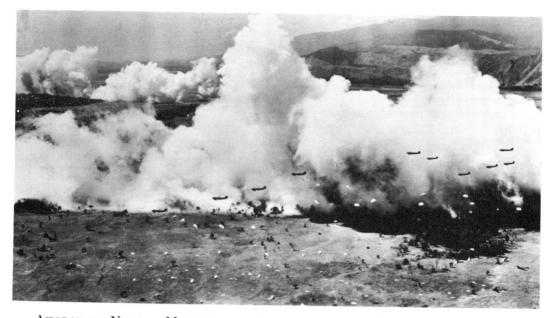

AIRDROP AT NADZAB, MORNING OF 5 SEPTEMBER 1943. *The paratroopers began jumping from C–47's onto separate jump areas about 1020.*

in four and one-half minutes. All men of the 503d but one, who fainted while getting ready, left the planes. Two men were killed instantly when their chutes failed to open, and a third landed in a tree, fell sixty feet to the ground, and died. Thirty-three men were injured. There was no opposition from the enemy, either on the ground or in the air. Once they reached the ground, the 503d battalions laboriously moved through high kunai grass from landing grounds to assembly areas.

Five B–17's carrying supply parachutes stayed over Nadzab all day. They dropped a total of fifteen tons of supplies on ground panel signals laid by the 503d. The Australian artillerymen and their guns parachuted down in the afternoon. The whole splendid sight was witnessed by Generals MacArthur and Ken-

ney from what Kenney called a "brass-hat" flight of three B–17's high above. MacArthur was in one, Kenney in another, and the third B–17 was there to provide added fire power in case the Japanese turned up.

The 503d's 1st Battalion seized the Nadzab airstrip and began to prepare it to receive C–47's. The 2d and 3d Battalions blocked the approaches from the north and east. As soon as the parachutists had begun landing, the Australian units that had come down the Watut River—the 2/2d Pioneer Battalion, the 2/6th Field Company, and one company of the Papuan Infantry Battalion—began landing on the north bank of the Markham. They made contact with the 503d in late afternoon and worked through the night in preparing the airstrip.

The next morning the first C–47 arrived. It brought in advance elements of the U.S. 871st Airborne Engineer Battalion.

Twenty-four hours later C–47's brought in General Vasey's 7th Division headquarters and part of the 25th Australian Infantry Brigade Group from Marilinan, where they had staged from Port Moresby. Thereafter the transports flew the Australian infantry and the American engineers directly from Port Moresby. By 10 September the well-timed, smoothly run operation had proceeded fast enough that 7th Division troops at Nadzab were able to relieve the 503d of its defensive missions. Enough American engineers had arrived to take over construction of new airstrips.

The 503d's only contact with the enemy came in mid-September when the 3d Battalion ran into a Japanese column at Yalu, east of Nadzab. The parachute regiment was withdrawn on 17 September. It had lost 3 men killed jumping, 8 men killed by enemy action, 33 injured jumping, 12 wounded by the enemy, and 26 sick.[19]

This was, comparatively, small cost for the seizure of a major airbase with a parachute jump. Nadzab paid rich dividends. Within two weeks the engineers had completed two parallel airstrips six thousand feet long and had started six others.

The Advance Against Lae

The 25th Australian Infantry Brigade

Group moved eastward out of Nadzab toward Lae on 10 September while General Wootten's 9th Division troops were forcing a crossing over the Busu River east of Lae. The Markham Valley narrows near Lae, with the Atzera Range on the northeast and the wide river on the southwest. A prewar road in the Atzera foothills connected Nadzab with Lae, and a rough trail on the other side of the Atzeras paralleled this road from Lae to Yalu, where it intersected the road. Thus while some troops blocked the trail at Yalu, and the 2/33d Australian Infantry Battalion guarded the line of communications, the 2/25th Australian Infantry Battalion advanced down the road and part of the 2/2d Australian Pioneer Battalion moved down the north bank of the river.

When a small group of Japanese offered resistance to the advance at Jensen's Plantation, toward the lower end of the valley, the 2/25th Battalion drove it back and on 14 September captured Heath's Plantation farther on. The 2/33d Australian Infantry Battalion then took over and pushed on toward Lae. By now the Australians had come within range of Japanese 75-mm. guns and found the going harder. But an assault the next day cleared Edward's Plantation and enemy resistance ended.

The advance elements of the 25th Brigade entered Lae from the west the next morning, 16 September. In the afternoon the 24th Brigade, which had advanced from the east and captured Malahang Airdrome on 15 September, pushed into Lae and made contact with the 25th Brigade. Lae had fallen easily and speedily. The Japanese had vanished.

---

[19] These figures are taken from a table of casualties attached to the 503d's report and differ slightly from casualty figures in the body of the report.

The Japanese Evacuation

Throughout July and August the Salamaua Japanese were reinforced at Lae's expense, but were continually forced back. On 24 August General Nakano, reflecting the importance which his superior had attached to Salamaua, addressed his troops thus: "Holding Salamaua is the Division's responsibility. This position is our last defense line, and we will withdraw no further. If we are unable to hold, we will die fighting. I will burn our Divisional flag and even the patients will rise to fight in close combat. No one will be taken a prisoner." [20]

Imperial Headquarters, however, did not order a suicidal last stand. Nakano was ordered to hold out as long as possible, but to withdraw if he could not hold Salamaua. The Australian landing between Lae and Finschhafen and the 503d's seizure of Nadzab, coupled with Allied air and PT boat activity in the Huon Gulf and the straits, caused General Adachi on 8 September to order Nakano to abandon Salamaua and pull back to Lae. Nakano's hospital patients and artillery had already been sent to Lae, and on 11 September withdrawal of the main body began.

Meanwhile, after considerable discussion *Imperial Headquarters,* Imamura, and Adachi abandoned their plans to take Bena Bena and Mount Hagen. Adachi saw that the Allied operations at Salamaua, Nadzab, and Lae threatened to cut off the *51st Division.* He now decided that he would have to withdraw from Lae, but determined to hold the Finisterre Range, the Ramu Valley, and

Finschhafen. Therefore he ordered Nakano and Shoge to withdraw overland from Lae to the north coast of the Huon Peninsula, and directed the *20th Division* to move from Madang to Finschhafen and to dispatch a regiment to the Ramu Valley to assist the *51st.*

Thus the Allied troops pushing toward both Lae and Salamaua in early September met only delaying forces. The Salamaua garrison had assembled at Lae by the 14th, two days after the first echelon of the Lae garrison had started north. Another echelon left that day, and the last slipped out on the 15th. The day before, General Vasey had learned from a captured document and from interrogation of a prisoner that the Japanese were leaving Lae. He dispatched troops northward to reinforce the 2/4th Australian Independent Company, which was operating in the wilds north of Lae, but the Japanese eluded their pursuers. It was a band of retreating enemy that the 3d Battalion, 503d, encountered at Yalu, and when Australian forces rushed there the Japanese hastily altered their route to avoid interception.

Once out of Lae, the *51st Division* and the Lae naval garrison executed one of the difficult overland marches that were to characterize so many future Japanese operations in New Guinea. There was little fighting, but Australian patrols harried the retreat. The Japanese moved north out of Lae and avoided Nadzab and the obvious Markham–Ramu trough that Adachi had originally planned to use for the withdrawal. They moved in a generally north-northeasterly direction, crossed the Busu River by means of a rough-hewn bridge on 20–22 September, and skirted the west ends of

[20] 18th Army Operations, II, Japanese Monogr No. 42 (OCMH), 37.

the Rawlinson Range and Cromwell Mountains in the vicinity of Mount Salawaket about 25 September.

They had started with food for ten days, but this was exhausted by the time they reached Salawaket. Thereafter they lived by looting native gardens and by eating roots and grasses. Dysentery and malaria made their appearance, but as there were plenty of suppressive drugs the malaria rate was low.

The *51st Division* had already abandoned most of its heavy equipment before the retreat. Along the way mountain artillerymen, unable to drag their guns over the precipitous slopes, were forced to abandon them. Many soldiers threw away their rifles. This was in strong contrast to the behavior of the *1st Battalion, 20th Division,* which had reinforced the *51st Division* at Salamaua. The commander, a Major Shintani, had threatened death to any soldier who abandoned his arms. Shintani died on the road, but his battalion rigorously adhered to his orders. Each soldier who completed the march carried his rifle and his helmet.

By mid-October the troops reached the north coast of the Huon Peninsula. The Army troops went to Kiari, naval personnel to nearby Sio. Slightly over 9,000 men had left Lae; 600 were march casualties. Nearly 5,000 soldiers arrived at Kiari, and some 1,500 sailors went to Lio. Many others were taken to the hospital at Madang. The defense of Lae–Salamaua and the subsequent retreat cost almost 2,600 lives.

Strategic Reconsiderations

The Japanese Pull Back

The fall of Lae and Salamaua, coming hard on the heels of defeat in the central

Solomons, had a profound effect upon Japanese strategic plans, an effect that went far beyond the immediate importance of Lae and Salamaua. Although the twin losses of Guadalcanal and Buna were severe, *Imperial General Headquarters* had not regarded these as irretrievable. It had continued to prepare plans for offensives in the Southeast Area.[21] Now the war leaders in Tokyo reassessed the situation and determined on a drastic retrenchment.

The fall of the central Solomons and of Lae–Salamaua closely followed the loss of Attu and the evacuation of Kiska in the Aleutians, and came at a time when *Imperial Headquarters* entertained well-justified fears about the opening of an Allied offensive through the Central Pacific.[22] The Japanese in September decided that they were overextended. They determined to withdraw their perimeter in order to set up a defense line that would hold back the Allies while they themselves marshaled their strength for decisive battle. This perimeter would be strongly manned and fortified. It was hoped that the defensive preparations behind it would be completed by the early part of 1944.

So *Imperial Headquarters* drew its main perimeter line from western New Guinea through the Carolines to the Marianas. This was "the absolute national defense line to be held by all

---

[21] This subsection is based upon: 8th Area Army Operations, Japanese Monogr No. 110 (OCMH), pp. 80–87; and 18th Army Operations, II, Japanese Monogr No. 42 (OCMH), 19–22, 48–53, 58–64, 84–86, 151–54.

[22] The offensive began in November 1943. See Philip A. Crowl and Edmund G. Love, *The Seizure of the Gilberts and Marshalls,* UNITED STATES ARMY IN WORLD WAR II (Washington, 1955).

means." [23] The Southeast Area, including Rabaul, once the focus of such great but elusive hopes for victory, was now on the outpost line.

But the war was far from over for MacArthur's and Halsey's troops. General Imamura and Admiral Kusaka were no longer counted on to win decisively, but they were ordered to hold out as long as possible, and so delay the Allied advance. To strengthen the Southeast Area, *Imperial Headquarters* in September ordered the *17th Division* from Shanghai to Rabaul "to reinforce the troops manning the forward wall." [24]

Imamura and Kusaka determined to hold Bougainville, whose defenses they had been trying to build up during the long fight on New Georgia, to develop and strengthen Madang and Wewak, to develop the transport system connecting the main bases of the Southeast Area, and to hold Dampier and Vitiaz Straits. Control of these straits had been essential to nearly all Japanese movements to New Guinea and, as before, the Japanese were resolved to hold them in order to block any Allied westward advance. (*See Map 12*.)

To this end Imamura, who kept the *38th Division* under his control to defend Rabaul, had previously dispatched the reinforced *65th Brigade* to Tuluvu on the north coast of Cape Gloucester with orders to develop a shipping point there and to maintain the airfield. On 5 September he sent Maj. Gen. Iwao Matsuda to Tuluvu to take command of the *65th Brigade,* some elements of the *51st Division,* and the *4th Shipping Group.* To Matsuda's responsibility for handling shipping he added that of defending the coasts of western New Britain.

On the New Guinea side of the straits, the Japanese regarded Finschhafen as the key defensive position. Possessed of two good harbors—Finschhafen itself and Langemak Bay—and a small airfield, it had long been used as a barge staging point. In early August Adachi had been concerned about a possible attack against Finschhafen, but he did not have enough troops to strengthen its small garrison substantially while the *41st Division* was defending Wewak, the *51st Division* was defending the Lae–Salamaua area, and the *20th Division* was working on the Madang–Lae road. He did, however, send the *80th Infantry* and one battalion of the *21st Field Artillery Regiment* of the *20th Division* from Madang to Finschhafen. By the end of August Maj. Gen. Eizo Yamada, commanding the *1st Shipping Group* and the combat troops at Finschhafen, had about one thousand men.

When the 9th Australian Division landed east of Lae on 5 September, Adachi foresaw the danger to Finschhafen. He suspended construction of the Madang–Lae road, which was now a twenty-foot-wide all-weather road running along the coast from Madang to Bogadjim, thence over the Finisterre Range at a defile named Kankirei and into the Ramu Valley to a point ten miles north of Dumpu. This decision freed the *20th Division* for combat duty. Adachi ordered a small force of the *20th*

---

[23] 8th Area Army Operations, Japanese Monogr No. 110 (OCMH), p. 87.
[24] Japanese Operations in the Southwest Pacific Area (Vol. II of MacArthur hist), Ch. VII, p. 26, OCMH.

Division, under Maj. Gen. Masutaro Nakai, the divisional infantry commander, to advance to Kaiapit, which is on the uplands near the sources of the Markham and Ramu Rivers. The move was intended to keep the Allies from advancing through the Ramu Valley, over Kankirei to the coast, and on against Madang and Wewak, and was also to help cover the retreat of the *51st Division* from Lae up the trough to Madang. When Adachi decided not to use the Markham and Ramu Valleys for the retreat he ordered Nakai north to hold the Kankirei defile.

Adachi ordered the main body of the *20th Division,* commanded by Lt. Gen. Shigeru Kitagiri, to march to Finschhafen. The division departed Bogadjim on 10 September on its march of nearly two hundred miles, but was still far from its destination when the Allies struck the next blow.

Allied Decisions

General MacArthur's ELKTON III called for the capture of Finschhafen as a step toward gaining control of Vitiaz and Dampier Straits. The plan had set the tentative date for the move against Finschhafen at six weeks after the invasion of Lae. At least two factors, however, impelled a speed-up in the timetable. The first was the quick fall of Lae and Salamaua after the landing on 4 September. The second was the *20th Division's* move toward Finschhafen. But before orders could be sent out for the capture of Finschhafen, it was necessary to consider this operation in relation to the larger problems involved in capturing Madang, an operation considered necessary to protect the left flank during

the seizure of Cape Gloucester. Seizure of Finschhafen, Madang, and Cape Gloucester would of course give physical control of both sides of the straits to the Allies.[25]

Capture of Madang was bound to be a large operation. Allied intelligence estimated that in late August a total of 55,000 Japanese held the regions between Lae and Wewak. At this time General Blamey, in a letter to MacArthur, held that the Japanese would exert every effort to defend the Markham and Ramu Valleys, Bogadjim (near the defile into the Ramu), Lae, Salamaua, and Finschhafen. Capture of Madang, which had been assigned to his New Guinea Force, would require as preliminary conditions complete air and naval superiority, support by the VII Amphibious Force, physical possession of Lae, the Markham Valley, Salamaua, and Finschhafen, and the neutralization of the Japanese in western New Britain.

Blamey set forth three steps to be followed after the capture of Lae. The first was the capture of Finschhafen by a seaborne assault. Blamey recommended as the second step seizure of an intermediate objective between Finschhafen and Bogadjim, because 256 miles of water separated Lae from Bogadjim,

---

[25] See above pp. 27, 190 and Chart 2. This subsection is based on ALF, Rpt on New Guinea Opns: 4 Sep 43–26 Apr 44; Ltr, Blamey to MacArthur, 31 Aug 43, no sub, in GHQ SWPA G–3 Jnl, 31 Aug 43; Memo, Chamberlin for CofS GHQ SWPA, 3 Sep 43, sub: Comment on Ltr From Cmdr ALF, 31 Aug 43, Opns for Capture of Madang, same file; Chamberlin's Memo for File, 3 Sep 43, same file; and GHQ SWPA OI 34/12, 15 Sep 43, in GHQ SWPA G–3 Jnl, 14 Jul 43; GHQ SWPA OI 34/14, 17 Sep 43, same file.

178 separated Finschhafen and Bogadjim, and these were long distances to travel with a flank exposed. The third and final step would be the capture of Madang by a combination of airborne invasion and amphibious assault coupled with pressure from troops advancing northwestward out of the Ramu Valley. To avoid exposing the right flank, he strongly urged capturing Cape Gloucester (which had been assigned to the ALAMO Force) before taking Madang. This would be feasible, he argued, because Madang was so much farther from Finschhafen than was Cape Gloucester.

These proposals received close study at the advanced echelon of GHQ, which had moved to Port Moresby during the planning for Lae and the Markham Valley. General Chamberlin looked on them as generally sound. Regarding Blamey's concern over control of Cape Gloucester as well as the coasts of the Huon Peninsula, however, he pointed out to General Sutherland that "G–3 believes that a physical occupation of areas has little bearing on the control of Vitiaz Strait but considers that airfields strategically placed which cover the water areas north of Vitiaz Strait are the controlling considerations." [26]

As to the intermediate objective between Finschhafen and Bogadjim, which Chamberlin placed at Saidor (with a harbor and prewar airfield) on the north coast of the Huon Peninsula, he felt that little would be gained by seizing it as well as Madang. On the other hand it appeared that Saidor might prove a satisfactory substitute for Madang.

Timing of operations would be tricky, largely because the VII Amphibious Force lacked enough ships to conduct two operations at once. It would be committed to operations on the Huon Peninsula until mid-November. Therefore the Cape Gloucester invasion could not take place until about 1 December, but the attack against the north coast of the Huon Peninsula would also have to be launched about the same time if the New Britain offensive was to be protected effectively. For these reasons Chamberlin recommended deferring the decision on whether to move to New Britain before or after invading the north coast of the Huon Peninsula. For this latter operation, he proposed two alternatives: seizure of a prewar airfield at Dumpu in the Ramu Valley without operating on the coast at all, or seizure of the Saidor airfield without operating in the Ramu Valley.

The questions were threshed out at a conference at Port Moresby on 3 September. MacArthur, Sutherland, Chamberlin, Kenney, Whitehead, Blamey, Carpender, and others attended. Blamey spoke strongly in favor of his recommendations. Kenney urged a deep penetration of the Ramu Valley all the way to Hansa Bay, which lies between Madang and Wewak. After Hansa Bay, he recommended, the advance could turn southward in co-ordination with the Cape Gloucester attack. Admiral Carpender wanted an operation somewhere

---

[26] Memo, Chamberlin for CofS GHQ SWPA, 3 Sep 43, sub: Comment on Ltr From Comdr ALF, 31 Aug 43, Opns for Capture of Madang, in GHQ SWPA G–3 Jnl, 31 Aug 43. Japanese sources often use "Dampier Strait" to mean both Vitiaz and Dampier Straits; Allied sources often use "Vitiaz Strait" for both.

between Madang and Saidor to precede Cape Gloucester. He received some support in his view from MacArthur, who asserted the necessity for seizing an area between Finschhafen and Madang before capturing Cape Gloucester, so as to assure the safe movement of supplies to support the latter operation. After a good deal of discussion, opinion crystallized in favor of covering the move to Gloucester by seizing the line Dumpu–Saidor. Dumpu would be seized at once by airborne and overland advances, and would then be used to cover simultaneous moves against Saidor and Gloucester. These moves, Chamberlin estimated on 3 September, would take place about 1 November at the earliest, but 1 December was more probable.

Thus it was that on 15 September MacArthur ordered Blamey's New Guinea Force, supported by Kenney's forces, to seize Kaiapit at the head of the Markham Valley and Dumpu about thirty miles south of Bogadjim. Two days later he ordered the New Guinea Force, with naval support, to capture Finschhafen. It would serve as an advanced air base, and Allied Naval Forces, basing light naval craft there, would use it to cut off the Japanese from Cape Gloucester and Saidor. The attack on Madang was postponed.

Advance Through the Ramu Valley

With his forces converging on Lae from east and west General Blamey completed plans for Kaiapit and Dumpu. Tactically the initial phases of the task appeared fairly simple; patrols had reported the area between Nadzab and the Leron River, a tributary of the

Markham, to be free of the enemy.[27] Logistics would present the greatest difficulty. No overland line of communications existed, and until roads were built all supplies for the advancing troops would have to be flown in. This fact limited the attacking force to one division (the 7th) of but two brigade groups.

The 2/6th Australian Independent Company began the drive in September when Kenney's transport planes landed it on a prewar airstrip in the Markham Valley some thirty miles northwest of Nadzab near the Leron River. The 2/6th then made its way eight miles up the river to Kaiapit, after a sharp encounter on 19 September, captured the village from a small group of Japanese, and held it against their repeated counterattacks. Two days later the Kaiapit strip saw the arrival, after a flight up from Nadzab, of the 21st and 25th Brigade Groups of General Vasey's 7th Australian Division.

At the month's end the 21st Brigade, followed by the 25th, left Kaiapit and entered the Ramu Valley. By 6 October the 21st was in possession of Dumpu, where 7th Division headquarters was established. The great Markham–Ramu trough had fallen with an ease that the Allies had not expected, an ease brought about by the hasty Japanese decision not to retreat through the trough.

Behind the lines engineers set to work building a truck highway from Lae to Nadzab along the prewar road, but rain fell during forty-six of the final sixty

---

[27] This section is based on ALF, Rpt on New Guinea Opns: 4 Sep 43–26 Apr 44; Craven and Cate, *The Pacific: Guadalcanal to Saipan,* pp. 190–93.

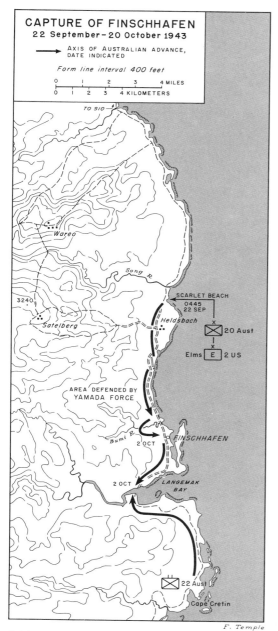

CAPTURE OF FINSCHHAFEN
22 September – 20 October 1943

→ AXIS OF AUSTRALIAN ADVANCE, DATE INDICATED

Form line interval 400 feet

0 1 2 3 4 MILES
0 1 2 3 4 KILOMETERS

TO SIO

Wareo

Song R.

SCARLET BEACH
0445
22 SEP

3240

Heldsbach

20 Aust

Satelberg

Elms E 2 US

AREA DEFENDED BY
YAMADA FORCE

Bumi R.   FINSCHHAFEN
2 OCT

2 OCT   LANGEMAK BAY

22 Aust

Cape Cretin

F. Temple

MAP 14

days of the project and it was December before the task was finally finished and large amounts of supplies could be sent to Nadzab. Nadzab and the other sites in the Markham and Ramu Valleys received all their supplies and equipment by airlift during the period the road was under construction.

By the end of December Allied Air Forces possessed three first-class air bases in full-scale operation in the Markham and Ramu Valleys: one at Nadzab, one at Lae, and one at the juncture of the Gusap and Ramu Rivers. The last site was selected in preference to Kaiapit, which proved too swampy and malarious for extensive development. Dumpu served as a staging field for fighter planes.

After establishing strong positions at Dumpu, the 7th Australian Division continued its part in seizing the Huon Peninsula. Marching north-northwest from Dumpu, it attacked Nakai's positions in the defiles of the Finisterres. The defiles were secured in February after almost three months of the most arduous kind of fighting. Nakai retreated toward Madang while Vasey's division broke out to the coast east of Madang.

The Coastal Advance

Finschhafen

Vasey's operations through the Ramu Valley were co-ordinated with those of Wootten's 9th Australian Division, which was operating on the coasts of the Huon Peninsula in a series of operations that began with Finschhafen. Before leaving Milne Bay for Lae, Wootten had been alerted to the possibility that he might have to send a brigade to Finschhafen. (*Map 14*) Thus GHQ's decision on 17 September to invade Finschhafen at once was no surprise to the veteran Australian commander.[28] Admiral Barbey had just time enough, and no more, to assemble 8 LST's, 16 LCI's, 10 destroyers, and 4 APD's for the invasion on 22 September, but "Uncle Dan" was now an old amphibious hand and he met the deadline. The LST's loaded at Buna, and the whole task group assembled in the harbor at Lae on 21 September. General Wootten meanwhile had selected the 20th Infantry Brigade Group of his division to make the landing, and had ordered the 22d Infantry Battalion to advance east along the coast to threaten Langemak Bay, just south of Finschhafen. Elements of the 2d Engineer Special Brigade had been attached to Wootten, and these units also made ready. No close air support was planned for the invasion, but in the days preceding 22 September B–24's and B–25's bombed the Gasmata airfield on the south coast of New Britain. Daytime A–20's and B–25's struck at Japanese lines of communication to Finschhafen, and PT's took over the work at night.

Troops of the 20th Brigade boarded their convoy on the afternoon of 21 September. The force included, besides the Australians and Barbey's American

sailors, one boat company, half the shore battalion of the 532d Engineer Boat and Shore Regiment, and medical and signal troops, or 575 men, 10 LCM's, and 15 LCVP's. The 22d Battalion marched out of Lae en route to Langemak Bay on the 21st, and the same day the amphibious force sailed for Finschhafen, eighty-two miles distant.

The beach selected for the landing, designated Scarlet, lay six miles north of Finschhafen at the mouth of the Song River. It was nine hundred yards long (north to south), thirty feet wide, and was marked by coral headlands to the north and south.

Destroyers bombarded Scarlet Beach on the morning of 22 September, and during darkness, at 0445, the first Australian assault wave touched down. Coxswains had difficulty finding the right beach in the dark with the result that most landing craft carrying the first two waves lost direction and landed in a small cove south of Scarlet Beach. First light aided the LCI's carrying the third wave; they landed at the right place. The waves that landed at the cove met some scattered but ineffective fire from enemy posts in the fringe of the jungle. The third wave met better organized opposition from log-and-earth pillboxes, but by 0930 all resistance had been overcome, all troops and supplies were ashore, and the landing craft retracted. The Japanese survivors retired to rising ground about a half mile inland and some sharp fighting ensued before the 2/17th Battalion was in complete possession of the beachhead. The 2/13 Battalion meanwhile swung left (south) toward the village of Heldsbach, which was just north of the Finschhafen airstrip.

---

[28] This section is based on Craven and Cate, *The Pacific: Guadalcanal to Saipan,* pp. 187–89; Morison, *Breaking the Bismarcks Barrier,* pp. 269–74; Off of Chief Engr, GHQ AFPAC, *Engineers in Theater Operations,* p. 112, and *Critique,* pp. 106–09; ALF, Rpt on New Guinea Opns: 4 Sep 43–26 Apr 44; 2d ESB Rpt; GHQ SWPA Check Sheet, Chief Engr SWPA to CINC, CofS, and G–3 SWPA, 23 Oct 43 [a rpt of 2d ESB action], in GHQ SWPA G–3 Jnl, 23 Oct 43; Japanese Operations in the Southwest Pacific Area (Vol. II of MacArthur hist), Ch. VII, OCMH; 8th Area Army Operations, Japanese Monogr No. 110 (OCMH), pp. 82–83; 18th Army Operations, III, Japanese Monogr No. 43 (OCMH), 84–117.

General Yamada had posted only a small part of his force at Scarlet Beach. He was keeping the rest of his 4,000-man command at Hanisch Harbor on the south coast of the peninsula and on Satelberg, a 3,240-foot peak which was about six miles west of Scarlet Beach, dominated the entire coastal region, and overlooked both Finschhafen and Langemak Bay. When General Adachi received news of the Allied landing he ordered Yamada to concentrate his force at Satelberg and attack at once. This attack was designed to hold or destroy the Australians pending the arrival of General Kitagiri's *20th Division*. By 21 September the *20th Division*, advancing overland and hauling its heavy matériel on barges, had reached Gali, one hundred miles from Finschhafen; it expected to arrive at Finschhafen on 10 October. Adachi ordered Kitagiri to hurry.

Admiral Barbey's retiring ships offered a tempting target to Japanese airmen, but the *7th Air Division*, under orders to cover a Wewak-bound convoy, hesitated to leave it unprotected. The *4th Air Army* headquarters ended this indecision by ordering the *7th* out against Barbey, but bad weather over central New Guinea kept the Army planes on the ground. Those of the naval *11th Air Fleet* at Rabaul went up and fiercely attacked the amphibious force on 22 and 24 September. But the vigilant destroyer *Reid* had given warning and Allied fighters, the ships' own antiaircraft, and "good luck in addition to good ship maneuvering" kept the ships from harm.[29]

At the beachhead the American engineers built roads and dumps and un-loaded naval craft. The larger engineer craft carried additional supplies from Lae to Scarlet Beach, while the LCVP's hauled supplies at night from Scarlet Beach to the Australians who were pushing south toward Finschhafen.

The 20th Brigade continued its move toward Finschhafen on the 23d. It captured Heldsbach, the airfield, and part of the shore of the harbor before meeting stiff resistance at the Bumi River, where three hundred enemy sailors and one company of the *2d Battalion, 238th Infantry*, defended the south bank. Two companies of the 2/15th Battalion moved inland (right) to outflank the enemy, and the next morning the Australians forced their way over the river in the face of stalwart resistance. The brigade commander, who was becoming increasingly aware of the Japanese concentration at Satelberg, asked Wootten for one more battalion with which to hold Scarlet Beach while he concentrated his brigade against Finschhafen. Wootten assented. The 2/43d Battalion landed at Scarlet Beach on the night of 29–30 September to relieve the 2/17th, and the latter moved out at once for Finschhafen. Following air and artillery bombardment, the three Australian battalions—the 2/13th, 2/15th, and 2/17th—attacked on 1 October, fought all day, and overwhelmed the defenders. The next morning they occupied the village and harbor of Finschhafen and made contact south of Langemak Bay with patrols of the 22d Battalion, which had advanced overland from Lae.

The Counterattack

To gain complete control of the New Guinea side of Vitiaz Strait, Generals

---

[29] Ltr, Adm Barbey to Gen Smith, Chief of Mil Hist, 20 Nov 53, no sub, OCMH.

MacArthur and Blamey had ordered that the capture of Finschhafen be followed by an advance along the coast to Sio, fifty land miles distant. But the advance could not be undertaken until the Japanese were driven from their dominating positions at Satelberg and on Wareo spur, a lower spur which lay north of the Song River from Satelberg.

On 26 September Yamada had launched an unsuccessful attack with the *80th Infantry* against the Australian beachhead. After Finschhafen fell on 2 October, the 20th Brigade moved back to Scarlet Beach in preparation for an assault against Satelberg. Two battalions attacked but met stout resistance.

When General Wootten's headquarters and the 24th Brigade arrived, Wootten decided that all signs indicated the Japanese would counterattack immediately, before he could complete his preparations for advancing to Sio. He decided to go on the defensive for the time being.

Meanwhile the *20th Division* was on its way; advance elements totaling 2,354 men had reached Sio by 30 September. General Kitagiri decided to advance by an inland route rather than use the coastal track to Satelberg. Like so many other Japanese generals in similar circumstances during World War II, he decided not to concentrate all his forces before attacking but ordered his units to attack the Australians upon arriving. Japanese tactical doctrine warns of the dangers of such piecemeal commitment but Japanese generals frequently aided the Allied cause by putting aside their doctrine in favor of pell-mell, piecemeal attack.

For his main attack against Scarlet Beach Kitagiri decided to drive eastward from Satelberg with most of his forces while a small detachment aboard four landing craft attempted an amphibious assault. But his division was no better at safeguarding important documents than was any other Japanese unit. On 15 October General Wootten received a captured Japanese order which warned him to expect a two-regiment attack from Satelberg, coupled with a seaborne assault. The Australians made ready.

Next day the 9th Division, though suffering some local reverses, repulsed the *20th's* attack from Satelberg. At 0300, 17 October, Japanese planes bombed the Allies, whereupon 155 men of the *10th Company, 79th Infantry,* attempted to land from their four craft. Two barges were sunk, one departed in haste, and the other reached shore in the vicinity of a .50-caliber machine gun position manned by Pvt. Nathan Van Noy, Jr., of the 532d Engineer Boat and Shore Regiment, and one other American engineer. As the enemy soldiers disembarked they hurled grenades, one of which wounded Van Noy before he opened fire. But Van Noy held his fire until the Japanese were visible, then opened up and killed about thirty of them. He died of his wounds, and for his gallant devotion was awarded the Medal of Honor.[30] Though the Japanese claim that the few men who reached the shore wrought great damage, in actuality they were all quickly killed.

Later in the morning came another major attack from Satelberg. Wootten,

---

[30] See *The Medal of Honor of the United States Army* (Washington, 1948), pp. 283–84. Van Noy's loader, who was wounded, received the Silver Star.

who had no reserve brigade, asked for the 26th and Barbey's ships transported it to Scarlet Beach on 20 October. The Japanese attacks continued through 25 October, but all failed. As his food supplies were exhausted, Kitagiri suspended the attacks and regrouped for another try. The Australians, losing 49 dead in these actions, reported killing 679 of the enemy.

General Adachi, who had often been in and out of Salamaua during the fighting there, traveled from Madang via Kiari and Sio to Satelberg. He arrived on 31 October, and stayed for four days. During this period Kitagiri made some hopeful estimates on the success of future, more gradual offensives.

Satelberg to Sio

But Wootten was now ready to assume the offensive. By 17 November one more brigade, the 4th, had arrived to hold the beachhead while the three infantry brigades of the 9th Division attacked. Meanwhile work on the airstrip and advanced naval base at Finschhafen had gone forward so quickly that PT boats from Finschhafen were now harrying enemy sea communications at night in consort with PBY's ("Black Cats"). With the support of tanks and artillery, and rocket-equipped LCVP's lying offshore, the 9th Division fought a major

action starting on 17 November. By 8 December it had captured Satelberg and Wareo spur and was ready to push up the coast to Sio, whence the *20th Division* was retreating on orders from General Imamura himself.

Wootten's men advanced slowly but steadily against the retreating enemy, supported all the while by the 2d Engineer Special Brigade craft.[31] The Australians found many sick, wounded, and dead Japanese who had fallen by the way as the weakened *20th Division*, which numbered 12,526 men on 10 September and only 6,949 men by December, laboriously marched along. On 15 January 1944 the 9th Division entered Sio, on the north coast of the Huon Peninsula.

Fighting on the peninsula was not yet over, but the main strategic objectives—the airfield sites and the coast of Vitiaz Strait—were now in Allied hands. When the Lae–Nadzab road and the airfields were completed, the Allies could control the air over the straits and bring a heavier weight of metal to bear on Japanese bases to the north and to the west.

---

[31] In the Nassau Bay–Lae–Finschhafen operation the 2d Engineer Special Brigade lost twenty-one dead, ninety-four wounded, and sixty evacuated sick. On the pursuit to Sio four LCVP's were lost to enemy action, four more to surf and reefs.

CHAPTER XII

The Invasion of Bougainville

While MacArthur's and Halsey's troops were gaining the Trobriands, the Markham Valley, the Huon Peninsula, and the New Georgia group for the Allied cause, the Joint Chiefs of Staff and their subordinate committees in Washington had been making a series of decisions affecting the course of the war in the Pacific. These decisions related not so much to CARTWHEEL itself as to General MacArthur's desire to make the main effort in the Pacific along the north coast of New Guinea into the Philippines. But, since they called for troops to support the offensives in Admiral Nimitz' Central Pacific Area, they had an immediate impact upon CARTWHEEL, especially on the Bougainville invasion (Operation B of ELKTON III) and on MacArthur's plans to seize Rabaul and Kavieng after CARTWHEEL.

The Decision To Bypass Rabaul

Once the Combined Chiefs at Casablanca had approved an advance through the Central Pacific, the Joint Chiefs put their subordinates to work preparing a general strategic plan for the defeat of Japan. An outline plan was submitted at the meeting of the Combined Chiefs in Washington, 12–15 May 1943. The Combined Chiefs approved the plan as a basis for further study.[1]

The plan, which governed in a general way the operations of Nimitz' and MacArthur's forces until the end of the war, aimed at securing the unconditional surrender of Japan by air and naval blockade of the Japanese homeland, by air bombardment, and, if necessary, by invasion. The American leaders agreed that naval control of the western Pacific might bring about surrender without invasion, and even without air bombardment. But if air bombardment, invasion, or both proved necessary, air and naval bases in the western Pacific would be required. Therefore, the United States forces were to fight their way westward across the Pacific along two axes of advance: a main effort through the Central Pacific and a subsidiary effort through the South and Southwest Pacific Areas.[2] (See Map 1.)

The Washington commanders and

---

[1] Cline, *Washington Command Post*, pp. 219–22.
[2] In point of fact the terms "main effort" and "subsidiary effort," though used constantly, bore so little relation to the number of troops, aircraft, and ships engaged as to be almost without meaning. In general, the Central Pacific had the preponderance of fleet (included carrier-based air) strength; MacArthur had the greater number of divisions and land-based aircraft.

planners preferred the Central Pacific route for the main effort because it was shorter and more healthful than the South–Southwest Pacific route; it would require fewer ships, troops, and supplies; success would cut off Japan from her overseas empire; destruction of the Japanese fleet, which would probably come out fighting to oppose the advance, would enable naval forces to strike directly at Japan; and it would outflank and cut off the Japanese in the Southeast Area. The main effort should not be made through the South and Southwest Pacific Areas, it was argued, because a drive from New Guinea to the Philippines would be a frontal assault against large islands with positions closely arranged in depth for mutual support. The Central Pacific route, in contrast, permitted the continuously expanding U.S. Pacific Fleet to strike at small, vulnerable positions too widely separated for mutual support.

The Joint Chiefs decided on the two axes, rather than the Central Pacific alone, because the Japanese conquests in the first phase of the war had compelled the establishment of comparatively large Allied forces in the South and Southwest Pacific Areas; to shift all these to the Central Pacific would take too much time and too many ships, and would probably intensify the already strong and almost open disagreement between MacArthur and King over Pacific strategy. Further, the Joint Chiefs hoped to use the oilfields on the Vogelkop Peninsula.[3] Twin drives, co-ordinated and timed for mutual support, would

give the U.S. forces great strategic advantages, for the Japanese would never know where the next blow would fall.[4]

At Washington in May the Combined Chiefs, as they had at Casablanca, approved plans for seizure of the Gilbert and Marshall Islands as the opening phase of the Central Pacific advance. They also approved the existing plans for CARTWHEEL, which the Joint Chiefs estimated would be ended by April 1944.

Next month, the Joint Chiefs, concerned with the problem of co-ordinating Nimitz' and MacArthur's operations, asked MacArthur for specific information on organization of forces and dates for future operations and informed him that they were planning to start the Central Pacific drive in mid-November. They planned to use the 1st and 2d Marine Divisions, then in the Southwest and South Pacific Areas, respectively, all the South Pacific's assault transports and cargo ships (APA's and AKA's), and the major portion of naval forces from Halsey's area.[5]

Faced with the possibility of a rival offensive, using divisions and ships that he had planned to employ, General MacArthur hurled back a vigorous reply. Arguing against the Central Pacific (he

---

[3] This hope came to nothing. Robert Ross Smith, *The Approach to the Philippines,* UNITED STATES ARMY IN WORLD WAR II (Washington, 1953), pp. 425–28.

[4] See JSSC 40/2, 3 Apr 43; JPS 67/4, 28 Apr 43; JCS 287, 7 May 43; JCS 287/1, 8 May 43; CCS 220, 14 May 43. All these papers are entitled "Strategic Plan for Defeat of Japan" or something very similar. See also Crowl and Love, *The Seizure of the Gilberts and Marshalls,* Ch. I; Smith, *The Approach to the Philippines,* Ch. I; Cline, *Washington Command Post,* Ch. XVII; relevant chapters in Morton's forthcoming volumes on strategy, command, and logistics in the Pacific, and in Maurice Matloff, Strategic Planning for Coalition Warfare: 1943–1944, also in preparation for the series UNITED STATES ARMY IN WORLD WAR II.

[5] Min, JCS mtg, 15 Jun 43; Rad, JCS to MacArthur, 15 Jun 43, CM–OUT 6093.

called the prospective invasion of the Marshalls a "diversionary attack"), he set forth the virtues of advancing through New Guinea to the Philippines. Withdrawal of the two Marine divisions, he maintained, would prevent the ultimate assault against Rabaul. He concluded his message with the information on target dates and forces that the Joint Chiefs had requested.[6] Two days later, 22 June, Admiral Halsey protested the proposed removal of the 2d Marine Division and most of his ships.[7]

Although General MacArthur may not have known it at the time, his argument that transfer of the two divisions would jeopardize the Rabaul invasion was being vitiated. In 1942 there had been general agreement that Rabaul should be captured, but in June 1943 members of Washington planning committees held that a considerable economy of force would result if Rabaul was neutralized rather than captured.[8] The Joint Strategic Survey Committee, in expressing itself in favor of giving the Central Pacific offensive priority over CARTWHEEL, also argued that the Allied drive northward against Rabaul was merely a reversal of the Japanese strategy of the year before and held "small promise of reasonable success in the near future."[9]

On the other hand Admiral William D. Leahy, chief of staff to the President and senior member of the Joint Chiefs, was always a strong supporter of MacArthur's views.[10] He argued strongly against any curtailment of CARTWHEEL. Admiral King, however, was far from pleased (in June 1943) with the rate of "inch by inch" progress in the South and Southwest Pacific. He wanted to see Rabaul "cleaned up" so the Allies could "shoot for Luzon," and seemed to imply that if CARTWHEEL did not move faster he would favor a curtailment.[11]

The immediate question on the transfer of the Marine divisions was compromised. The 1st Marine Division would remain in the Southwest Pacific. The 2d Marine Division, heretofore slated for the invasion of Rabaul, was transferred from New Zealand to the Central Pacific, where it made its bloody, valorous assault on Tarawa in November 1943. Assured by King that the Central Pacific offensive would assist rather than curtail CARTWHEEL, Leahy withdrew his objections.[12]

By 21 July the arguments against capturing Rabaul had so impressed General Marshall that he radioed MacArthur to suggest that CARTWHEEL be followed by the seizure of Kavieng on New Ireland and Manus in the Admiralties, with the

---

[6] Rad, MacArthur to Marshall, 20 Jun 43, CM–IN 13149.

[7] Rad, MacArthur to Marshall, 22 Jun 43, CM–IN 13605. Halsey sent his views to MacArthur who relayed them.

[8] Incl B, Jt War Plans Com 58/D, 24 Jun 43, title: Memo for RAINBOW Team, in OPD 384 Marshall Islands (10 Jun 43) Sec 1.

[9] JSSC 386, 28 Jun 43, title: Strategy of the Pac.

[10] See Fleet Admiral William D. Leahy, *I Was There* (New York: Whittlesey House, 1950), *passim*.

[11] Min, JCS mtg, 29 Jun 43. At this time King wanted to go to Luzon by way of the Marianas, which he always regarded as the key to the Pacific because he believed that an attack there would smoke out the Japanese fleet.

[12] Min, JCS mtg, 20 Jul 43; JCS 386/1, 19 Jul 43, Strategy in the Pac; JPS 205/3, 10 Jul 43, title: Opns Against Marshall Islands; Draft Memo, JPS for JCS, 12 Jul 43, sub: Strategy in the Pac, OPD 381 Security 195; OPD Draft Memo, 14 Jul 43, no sub, same file; JPS draft paper, 19 Jul 43, title: Strategy in the Pac, and attached papers, with JPS 219/D in ABC 384 Pac (28 Jun 43); OPD Brief, Notes on JWPC 58/2, in OPD 384 Marshall Islands (10 Jun 43) Sec 1.

purpose of isolating Rabaul, and by the capture of Wewak. But MacArthur saw it otherwise. Marshall's plan, he stated, involved too many hazards. Wewak, too strong for direct assault, should be isolated by seizing a base farther west. Rabaul would have to be captured rather than just neutralized, he insisted, because its strategic location and excellent harbor made it an ideal naval base with which to support an advance westward along New Guinea's north coast.[13]

Marshall and King were not convinced. Thus the Combined Chiefs, meeting with President Roosevelt and Prime Minister Churchill in Quebec during August, received and approved the Joint Chiefs' recommendation that Rabaul be neutralized, not captured. They further agreed that after CARTWHEEL MacArthur and Halsey should neutralize New Guinea as far west as Wewak, and should capture Manus and Kavieng to use as naval bases for supporting additional advances westward. Once these operations were concluded, MacArthur was to move west along the north coast of New Guinea to the Vogelkop Peninsula. Subsequently MacArthur was informed that his cherished ambition to return to the Philippines would be realized; Marshall radioed him that once the Vogelkop was reached, the Southwest Pacific's next logical objective would be Mindanao.[14]

Papers containing the Combined Chiefs decisions were delivered to General MacArthur by Col. William L. Ritchie of the Operations Division, War Department General Staff, who reached GHQ on 17 September.[15]

From then on MacArthur did not raise the question of Rabaul with the Joint Chiefs; his radiograms dealt instead with broader questions relating to the Philippines and the relative importance of the Central and Southwest Pacific offensives.[16] Although the evidence is not conclusive, the general course of events and certain opinions MacArthur gave during the planning for Bougainville seem to indicate that he knew of the decision to neutralize rather than capture Rabaul, or else had reached the same decision independently, some time before Colonel Ritchie reached the Southwest Pacific.

The General Plan

If ever a series of offensives was conducted according to plan, it was the extremely systematic Allied moves in the Pacific that started in 1943. At the time that Allied forces were fighting in New Guinea and New Georgia, the Joint Chiefs were considering the wisdom of neutralizing Rabaul, and General MacArthur and Admiral Halsey were preparing for the invasion of Bougainville.

ELKTON III had initially provided that the southern Bougainville area (Buin and Faisi) was to be invaded during the

---

[13] Rad 8604, Marshall to MacArthur, 21 Jul 43, in Marshall's OUT Log; Rad 16419, MacArthur to Marshall, 23 Jul 43, in Marshall's IN Log.

[14] See Cline, *Washington Command Post*, p. 225; CCS 319/5, 24 Aug 43, title: Final Rpt to the President and Prime Minister; CCS 301/3, 27 Aug 43, title: Specific Opns in Pac and Far East, 1943–44; Rad 8679, Marshal to MacArthur, 2 Oct 43, in Marshall's OUT Log. See also Smith, *The Approach to the Philippines*, Ch. I.

[15] Rad, Ritchie to Handy, 18 Sep 43, CM–IN 13521.

[16] MacArthur's subsequent plans called for the neutralization of Rabaul, followed by its possible capture. See GHQ SWPA, RENO III, 20 Oct 43, in ABC 384 Pac, Sec 3–A.

fifth month after the beginning of CART-
WHEEL, simultaneously with the con-
quest of New Georgia, and one month
before the invasion of Cape Gloucester.
(*See Chart 2.*) Admiral Halsey had altered the plan by managing to start his
invasion of New Georgia on 30 June. In
June General MacArthur, in ordering
the Markham Valley–Huon Peninsula
attack, directed Admiral Halsey to be
ready to take southern Bougainville on
orders from GHQ.[17] At this time Admiral Halsey, planning in accordance
with ELKTON III, intended to use the 3d
Marine Division and the 25th Division
against southern Bougainville, the 2d
Marine and 3d New Zealand Divisions
against Rabaul.[18] Before long, however,
the 25th Division, sent into New Georgia, was too worn for further combat
and the 2d Marine Division was ordered
to invade the Gilberts instead of Rabaul.[19]

Tactical planning for Bougainville began in the South Pacific in July when
Halsey assigned the Commanding General, I Marine Amphibious Corps, to
command the ground forces. (*Map 15*)

His mission was the seizure of Buin,
Kahili, and Tonolei Harbor on southern Bougainville and of the nearby islands in Bougainville Strait—the Shortlands, Faisi, and Ballale, where there
were then an estimated twenty thousand
Japanese soldiers and sailors.

Near the end of July Admiral Halsey
suggested a change in plan to General
MacArthur. It was based on two assumptions: first, that the objectives of the
operation were denying the use of airfields and anchorage to the Japanese
and securing airfields and anchorages
for the Allies, as a step toward the capture of Rabaul; and second, that because
terrain, strategic position, and Japanese
dispositions indicated that southern Bougainville was extremely important to
the Japanese, the operation would be
a major one. With the difficulties of the
then bogged-down New Georgia invasion and the success of the artillery on
the offshore islands against Munda both
obviously in mind, he suggested that
he could save men, matériel, and time
by avoiding the Bougainville mainland
completely. He proposed to seize the
Shortlands and Ballale, to emplace artillery on the former with the mission of
interdicting Kahili, to build one or more
airfields in the Shortlands, and to use
the anchorages there that the Japanese
8th Fleet then employed regularly. Mac-
Arthur heartily approved the scheme.[20]

By early September, however, Admiral
Halsey had decided on a further change

[17] GHQ SWPA OI 34, 13 Jun 43, in GHQ SWPA
G–3 Jnl, 14 Jun 43. This section is based in part on
Craven and Cate, *The Pacific: Guadalcanal to
Saipan*, pp. 245–51; Halsey and Bryan, *Admiral
Halsey's Story*, pp. 173–74; Morison, *Breaking the
Bismarcks Barrier*, pp. 279–84; Maj. John N. Rentz,
USMCR, *Bougainville and the Northern Solomons*
(Washington, 1948), Ch. I; The Bougainville Cam-
paign, MS, prepared by Hist Sec G–2, SOPACBA-
COM, Vol. I, Ch. I, OCMH. None of these, how-
ever, is entirely satisfactory for they do not employ
Southwest Pacific Area sources.

[18] Rad, Comdr Third Flt to CINCSWPA, 21 Jun
43, in GHQ SWPA G–3 Jnl, 23 Jun 43.

[19] The 25th Division stayed on Guadalcanal after
the conclusion of the campaign there. It had little
opportunity for rest and reorganization before
moving to New Georgia.

[20] Ltr, COMSOPAC to CINCSWPA, 26 Jul 43,
sub: Bougainville Opn, in GHQ SWPA G–3 Jnl,
31 Jul 43; Rad, CINCSWPA to Comdr Third Flt,
4 Aug 43, in GHQ SWPA G–3 Jnl, 4 Aug 43;
COMSOPAC War Diary, 26 Jul and 4 Aug 43
entries.

in plan. Several factors influenced his decision. The impressive and inexpensive success on Vella Lavella had demonstrated once more the validity of the old principle of striking soft spots, when possible, in preference to headlong assault against fixed positions. Further, reconnaissance had indicated that airdrome sites on the Shortlands were not very good. Landing in the Shortlands, which the Japanese were believed to be reinforcing, would entail heavy losses; poor beaches would impede the landing of heavy construction equipment and artillery for the neutralization of Kahili. It was also estimated that assaulting the Shortlands–Ballale–Faisi area would require two divisions, while two more would be needed to operate on southern Bougainville proper. As the South Pacific had but four divisions—the 37th and American Divisions of the U.S. Army, the 3d Marine Division, and the 3d New Zealand Division—that were considered fit to fight, no more advances would be possible for months.[21]

Looking for a method of neutralizing the southern Bougainville–Shortlands area without capturing it, a method that would retain enough troops for a major forward move later, Halsey acted on the advice of his principal subordinate commanders. He decided in favor of increased air effort from the New Georgia fields against southern Bougainville and Buka. Starting about 1 November, he proposed to capture the Treasury Islands and Choiseul Bay as airfield, radar, and PT base sites from which to "contain and strangle" southern Bougainville and the Shortlands. He proposed that after the mainland of Bougainville had been reconnoitered he and MacArthur could decide whether to advance from Choiseul to Kieta on the east coast or from the Treasuries to Empress Augusta Bay on the west if post-CARTWHEEL plans required the establishment of positions on the mainland of Bougainville.[22]

This plan was consistent with ELKTON III, and varied only slightly from the July schemes approved by MacArthur. But by now, MacArthur, perhaps aware of the decision to neutralize rather than capture Rabaul, and obviously anxious to hurry up CARTWHEEL and get started on the drive toward the Philippines, had changed his mind about the scope and nature of the operation. Thus when Halsey's chief of staff, Rear Adm. Robert B. Carney, and his new war plans officer, Col. William E. Riley, USMC, presented the Treasuries–Choiseul plan to MacArthur at GHQ on 10 September, MacArthur was against it. With the successful airborne move to Nabzab in mind, he expressed his agreement with the principle of the bypass, but maintained that Halsey's plan would make it impossible for South Pacific aircraft to hit at Rabaul effectively before 1 March

---

[21] The 2d Marine Division was due to leave; the 25th and 43d Divisions were due for rest and rehabilitation.

[22] Ltr, Halsey to CINCSWPA, 9 Sep 43, sub: ELKTON III–S Bougainville Objectives, in GHQ SWPA G–3 Jnl, 10 Sep 43; Memo, Adm Fitch, Gen Harmon, Maj Gen Charles D. Barrett [CG I Mar Amphib Corps], and Adm Wilkinson for COMSOPAC, 7 Sep 43, no sub, ABC 384 (1–17–43) Sec 2; Halsey, Narrative Account of the South Pacific Campaign, p. 8, OCMH; Harmon, The Army in the South Pacific, p. 9, OCMH. Some advocated bypassing Bougainville completely in favor of a jump to Emirau in the Saint Matthias group northwest of Kavieng.

1944. He wanted Halsey's aircraft established within fighter range of Rabaul in time to assist with the neutralization of Rabaul that would cover the Southwest Pacific's invasion of Cape Gloucester. This would be necessary, MacArthur held, because Southwest Pacific air forces could not attack all the objectives (including Madang and Wewak) that would have to be neutralized in order to protect the invasions of Cape Gloucester and of Saidor, on the north coast of the Huon Peninsula. Southwest Pacific headquarters hoped to start Operation III (chiefly Cape Gloucester) shortly after 1 December; Cape Gloucester itself would probably be invaded between 25 December 1943 and 1 January 1944. Therefore it would be necessary for South Pacific forces to establish themselves on the mainland of Bougainville about 1 November. So important was the operation that MacArthur tacitly approved commitment of the major part of South Pacific ground forces.

Specifically, he proposed the following outline plan:

1. 15 October–1 November, Southwest Pacific air forces would make heavy attacks against Japanese aircraft, air installations, and shipping at Rabaul;

2. 20–25 October, South Pacific forces would occupy the Treasuries and positions on northern Choiseul in order to establish radar positions and PT boat bases;

3. 1 November, South Pacific forces would occupy Empress Augusta Bay on the west coast of Bougainville in order to establish airfields within fighter range of Rabaul;

4. 1–6 November, the Southwest Pacific would continue air attacks on Rabaul and would assist in the neutralization of Buka;

5. 25 December 1943–1 January 1944, Southwest Pacific forces would seize Cape Gloucester and Saidor in order to gain control of Vitiaz and Dampier Straits and to secure airdromes for the neutralization of Kavieng. During this period South Pacific forces would neutralize Rabaul.[23]

General MacArthur stressed the importance of a landing on the mainland at another meeting on 17 September attended by General Harmon and Colonel Riley. Asked if he preferred a landing on the east or the west coast of Bougainville, he put the decision entirely in Admiral Halsey's hands.

And so on 22 September, Halsey issued warning orders which canceled all his earlier plans and assigned the units to constitute the invasion force. Admiral Wilkinson would lead it. The landing forces, under Wilkinson, were still to be under the commanding general of the I Marine Amphibious Corps. Halsey instructed Wilkinson and his units to be ready to carry out one of two plans: either they were to seize and hold the Treasury Islands and the airfield sites in the Empress Augusta Bay region on the west coast of Bougainville; or they were to seize the Treasuries and Choiseul Bay, build airfields, PT boat bases, and landing craft staging points, and in late December seize the Japanese

---

[23] Ltr, MacArthur to Halsey, 11 Sep 43, no sub, and Notes for Memo on Conf Between Reps of SWPA and SOPAC, GHQ SWPA, 10 Sep 43. Both in GHQ SWPA G–3 Jnl, 11 Sep 43.

airfield at Tenekau on the east coast of Bougainville.[24]

Submarines took patrols to the east coast and to Empress Augusta Bay to gather data, and South Pacific intelligence officers interviewed missionaries, traders, planters, coastwatchers, and fliers who had been shot down over Bougainville. The east coast patrol, carried by the submarine *Gato,* delivered an unfavorable report. The west coast patrol, composed of marines, debarked from the submarine *Guardfish* about ten miles northwest of Cape Torokina in Empress Augusta Bay. The marines were unable to examine Cape Torokina because it was occupied by the Japanese, but they took samples of soil similar to that at Torokina. When tested, it showed that Cape Torokina was suitable for airfields.

Between the sea and the mountains at Cape Torokina, which lay within fighter range of Munda, was a coastal plain of about seven square miles. It was lightly defended; Halsey estimated that there were about one thousand Japanese in the area. So forbidding were the surrounding mountains that the area was almost isolated from the strong Japanese garrisons in southern Bougainville. Halsey and his planners estimated that if Allied forces seized Torokina the

Japanese would require three or four months to bring enough heavy equipment over the mountains to launch an effective counterattack. But there were disadvantages. The heavy surf in Empress Augusta Bay, which had no protected anchorages, would make landing operations difficult. No more than 65 miles separated the cape from all the Japanese air bases on Bougainville, and Rabaul was only 215 miles to the northwest.

Admiral Halsey calculated the chances and decided on Torokina. In his words: "The conception was bold and the probability of provoking a violent air-land-surface action was accepted and welcomed on the premise that the by-products of enemy destruction would, in themselves, greatly further the over-all Pacific plan. Enthusiasm for the plan was far from unanimous, even in the South Pacific, but, the decision having been made, all hands were told to 'Get going.'"[25]

Halsey informed MacArthur of his decision on 1 October. Expressing his complete agreement, MacArthur promised maximum air support from the Southwest Pacific. The invasion would be launched on 1 November.[26]

Air Operations in October

The Fifth Air Force

By October the Fifth Air Force in the Southwest Pacific Area was well situ-

---

[24] Ltr, COMSOPAC to CG 1 Mar Amphib Corps, CTF 31, and CTF 33, 22 Sep 43, sub: Warning Order, in GHQ SWPA G-3 Jnl, 24 Sep 43. During this period Admiral Halsey received communications from Admiral King's office which seemed to require him to seize southern Bougainville and then Kieta and Buka. This confused the issue until Admiral Nimitz assured Halsey that the messages from King were estimates and not directives, and that Halsey was to operate under the provisions of the 28 March 1943 directive.

[25] Halsey, Narrative Account of the South Pacific Campaign, p. 8, OCMH.
[26] Rad, Halsey to MacArthur, 1 Oct 43, and Rad, MacArthur to Halsey, 1 Oct 43, in GHQ SWPA G-3 Jnl, 1 Oct 43.

ated to carry the fight against Rabaul.[27] Nearly all its warplanes had been displaced to forward bases. Port Moresby, an outpost in 1942, was now a rear base. Dobodura was the main staging base for heavy bombers, and Nadzab was being readied as the main base for future operations. P-38's from New Guinea could stage through Kiriwina and escort the bombers all the way to Rabaul.

Rabaul was ripe for air attack. Transports, cargo ships, and smaller craft, together with some warships, crowded Simpson Harbor. Supply depots were fully stocked. Four all-weather airfields —Lakunai, Vunakanau, Rapopo, and Tobera—were in operation in and near Rabaul.[28]

Southwest Pacific aircraft had been harrying Rabaul with small raids since January 1942, but now the Allies were ready to attack this bastion on a large scale. General Kenney was ready for the first big attack on 12 October. All together, 349 planes took part: 87 heavy bombers, 114 B–25's, 12 Beaufighters, and 125 P–38's, plus some weather and photo reconnaissance planes—or, as he put it, "Everything that I owned that was in commission, and could fly that far."[29] B–25's and Beaufighters made sweeps over Vunakanau, Rapopo, and Tobera while the heavy bombers struck at shipping. The Allies lost four planes and estimated a great deal of damage to Japanese aircraft and ships. Their estimates were somewhat exaggerated, especially those on shipping damage, but some Japanese planes were destroyed. The Japanese, taken by surprise and unable to send up fighters to intercept, later reported that this and later raids in October were "a great obstacle to the execution of operations."[30]

Bad weather over New Guinea halted Kenney's operations against Rabaul for the next few days. The Japanese used the respite to send out attacks against Oro Bay on 15 and 17 October, and Finschhafen on 17 and 19 October. The Allied planes did not sit idle while Rabaul was inaccessible, but struck at Wewak on the 16th and again the next day.

Kenney planned and sent out another big raid against Rabaul on 18 October, but when the air armada was over the Solomon Sea the weather closed in. Fifty-four B–25's went on to Rabaul anyway. Kenney followed this attack with three successive daylight raids on 23, 24, and 25 October before the weather again imposed a delay, this time until the 29th, when B–24's and P–38's bombed Vunakanau.

The weather intervened again, so that it was not until 2 November, the day after South Pacific forces landed at Em-

[27] This section is based on Craven and Cate, *The Pacific: Guadalcanal to Saipan,* pp. 251–55, 317–26; Kenney, *General Kenney Reports,* 313–20; Morison, *Breaking the Bismarcks Barrier,* pp. 275–88, 271–92; Thomas C. Wilds, "The Admiral Who Lost His Fleet," *United States Naval Institute Proceedings,* Vol. 77, No. 11 (November 1951); CTF 33 War Diary, Oct 43 entries; Southeast Area Naval Operations, Vol. III, Japanese Monogr No. 50 (OCMH), pp. 5–11; Outline of Southeast Area Naval Air Operations, Pt. IV, Japanese Monogr No. 108 (OCMH), pp. 42–44.

[28] Lakunai had a sand and volcanic ash surface; the other three were concrete. Keravat field on the west coast of Gazelle Peninsula had never been used.

[29] Kenney, *General Kenney Reports,* p. 313.

[30] Outline of Southeast Area Naval Air Operations, Pt. IV, Japanese Monogr No. 108 (OCMH), p. 44.

BOMBING RABAUL. *Top left and right: Japanese corvette off the coast of New Britain near Rabaul suffers a direct hit from a B–25. Bottom: Vunakanau airfield is attacked by low-flying bombers dropping parachute bombs.*

press Augusta Bay, that Southwest Pacific aircraft again struck at Rabaul. On that day seventy-five B–25's escorted by P–38's attacked and ran into the fiercest opposition the Fifth Air Force encountered during World War II. A large number of carrier planes and pilots from the *Combined Fleet* at Truk had just been transferred to Rabaul, and they put up a stiff fight.

Although it is clear that these raids failed to wreak as much havoc at Rabaul as Kenney's fliers claimed, it is also clear that they caused a good deal of damage to aircraft and prevented the Japanese planes at Rabaul from undertaking any purely offensive missions. In short, the Southwest Pacific's air support for the Bougainville invasion, though not as devastating as was thought at the time, was effective.

Certainly American pilots, like the Japanese, and like soldiers and sailors on the ground and in ships, tended to exaggerate the damage they inflicted. But there were two important differences between American and Japanese claims. First, Japanese claims were wildly exaggerated whereas American claims were merely exaggerated. Second, Japanese commanders apparently took the claims seriously, so that nonexistent victories often served as the bases for decision. On the other hand American commanders, taking human frailty into account, evaluated and usually scaled down claims so that decisions were normally based on more realistic estimates of damage.

Air Command, Solomons

General Twining's composite force, Air Command, Solomons, had been striking hard at the northern Solomons bases during the same period and for the same purpose—to knock out the Bougainville bases so that Wilkinson's convoys could sail past in safety. Twining's available air strength had been displaced forward to bases within range of south Bougainville targets. At the start of operations in October, Twining had 614 Army, Navy, Marine Corps, and Royal New Zealand Air Force planes. Of these, 264 fighters and 223 medium, dive, torpedo, and patrol bombers were at New Georgia and the Russells, and 127 heavy bombers and patrol planes were at Guadalcanal.

Ever since 1942 South Pacific planes had been battering at the Japanese bases at Kahili, the Shortlands, Ballale, Kieta, and Buka, and now the process was intensified in an effort to put them out of commission.[31] Starting on 18 October, Twining—whose high professional qualifications were matched by a physical appearance so striking that he looked like Hollywood's idea of a diplomat—drove his interservice, international force hard in a continuous series of high-level, low-level, dive, glide, and torpedo bombing attacks and fighter sweeps, all made with escorting fighters from the four air services in the command. The primary mission was accomplished. The hard-hit enemy showed skill and determination in keeping his airfields in repair, but these qualities were not enough. By 1 November all his Bougainville airfields had been knocked out of commission, and the continuous attacks kept them that way.

---

[31] Kenney offered to include Buka in his attacks, but Halsey asked him to concentrate on Rabaul and leave Buka to Twining.

MATCHIN BAY

B–25's LEAVING BOUGAINVILLE *after an attack on airfields and supply areas.*

The Japanese

Of Admiral Kusaka's *11th Air Fleet,* a substantial portion was based at Rabaul in early October, the remainder in southern Bougainville. When Air Command, Solomons, intensified its operations, Kusaka withdrew his planes to Rabaul, and to avoid being completely destroyed by Kenney's heavy raids he frequently pulled his planes back to Kavieng in New Ireland. Despite these attacks Kusaka was usually able to maintain about two hundred planes in operating condition at Rabaul throughout October.

Now Admiral Koga, like the late Yamamoto, decided to use his carrier planes jointly with the land-based planes of Kusaka's air fleet in an effort to improve the situation in the Southeast Area. As a result of the September decision to withdraw the main defensive perimeter, Koga developed a plan to cut the Allied lines of communication in the Southeast Area and so delay the Allies and buy time for the Japanese to build up the defenses along the main perimeter. This plan, called Operation *RO,* was to be executed by the operational carrier air groups of the *Combined Fleet,* transferred from Truk to Rabaul, and by the *11th Air Fleet.* Vice Adm. Tokusaburo Ozawa, commander of the *3d Fleet,* and Kusaka would conduct the operation jointly from Rabaul. Koga decided on this course of action fully aware that his surface strength would be immobilized while his carrier planes were at Rabaul.

He had planned to transfer the planes in mid-October, but delayed the move because he received a false report that the U.S. Pacific Fleet was out against the Marshalls. On 20 October, now aware that Nimitz' forces were not moving against the Marshalls, Koga ordered the carrier planes dispatched. By the beginning of November, 173 carrier planes— 82 fighters, 45 dive bombers, 40 torpedo bombers, and 6 patrol planes—had reached Rabaul to team with Kusaka's 200. It was Ozawa's carrier pilots who gave Kenney's men such a hard fight on 2 November. Koga had first planned to deliver his main stroke against New Guinea but the increased tempo of Allied activity in the Solomons made him decide to strike in the Solomons.

Koga's decision to execute Operation *RO* was to have far-reaching results, results that were the precise opposite of what he expected. The transfer of the carrier planes coincided with the South Pacific's invasion of Bougainville.

Forces and Tactical Plans
The Allies

Bougainville, the largest of the Solomon Islands, is 125 miles long on its northwest-to-southeast axis, and 30 to 48 miles wide.[32] Its mountainous spine com-

prises two ranges, the Emperor and the Crown Prince. Two active volcanoes, 10,000-foot Mount Balbi and 8,000-foot Mount Bagana, send continual clouds of steam and smoke into the skies. Mount Bagana, a stark and symmetrical cone, overlooks Empress Augusta Bay and is the most outstanding feature of the region's dramatic beauty.

The mountain range ends toward the southern part of the island, and there, on the coastal plain near Buin, the Japanese had built the airfields of Kahili and Kara. On the western coast the mountains slope down through rugged foothills and flatten out into a narrow and swampy coastal plain that is cut by many small rivers. These silt-laden streams constantly build bars across their own mouths and thus frequently change their courses.

Good harbors in varying stages of development were to be found at Buka, Numa Numa, Tenekau, Tonolei, and in the islands off the south coast. Empress Augusta Bay, exposed as it was to the open sea, was a poor anchorage. The Japanese had airfields at Buka and Bonis on either side of Buka Passage, at Tenekau, Kieta, Kara, and Kahili on the mainland, and at Ballale near the Shortlands, and had seaplane anchorages and naval bases in the Shortlands. As on all the other islands, there were no real motor roads, only native trails near the coasts plus a few that led through the mountains.

The native population consisted of over forty thousand nominally Christian Melanesians, who were slightly darker in color than their fellows in the southern Solomons. Before the war about a hundred white missionaries, planters,

---

[32] This section is based on Morison, *Breaking the Bismarcks Barrier,* pp. 279–89; Halsey and Bryan, *Admiral Halsey's Story,* pp. 173–76; SOPACBACOM, The Bougainville Campaign, Vol. I, Ch. I, OCMH; Japanese Operations in the Southwest Pacific Area (Vol. II of MacArthur hist), Ch. IX, p. 216, OCMH; Southeast Area Naval Operations, III, Japanese Monogr No. 50 (OCMH), 7–8; 8th Area Army Operations, Japanese Monogr No. 110 (OCMH) pp. 85–103; 17th Army Operations, II, Japanese Monogr No. 40 (OCMH), 95–99; COMSOPAC Opn Plan 16–43, 12 Oct 43, in GHQ SWPA G–3 Jnl, 17 Oct 43.

traders, and government officials had lived on the island. Some of the natives, it was known, were pro-Japanese and had aided the enemy in rooting out the coastwatchers earlier in the year.

Allied intelligence agencies estimated enemy strength at about 37,500 soldiers and 20,000 sailors, and correctly reported that the Army troops belonged to the *17th Army,* commanded by General Hyakutake, who had been responsible for the direction of the Guadalcanal Campaign.[33] Over 25,000 of Hyakutake's men were thought to be in the Buin–Shortlands area, with an additional 5,000 on the east coast of Bougainville, 5,000 more at Buka and Bonis, and light forces at Empress Augusta Bay. Air reconnaissance enabled the Allies to keep a fairly accurate count of Japanese warships and planes in the New Guinea–Bismarcks–Solomons area.

Admiral Halsey, in preparing his attack, was not embarrassed by too many ships. Admiral Nimitz was getting ready to launch his great Central Pacific advance in November and had removed many of Halsey's ships, leaving him but eight transports and four cargo ships, or enough shipping to carry one reinforced division in the assault. Because South Pacific commanders expected the Japanese to oppose the invasion with vigorous air attacks, they decided not to use the slow LST's for the assault. The South Pacific had one carrier force, Task Force 38 under Rear Adm. Frederick C. Sherman, consisting of the 910-foot air-

craft carrier *Saratoga,* the light carrier *Princeton,* two antiaircraft cruisers, and ten destroyers. Nimitz, in response to Halsey's requests for additional cruiser-destroyer and carrier task forces, assured Halsey that Central Pacific forces would be within reach to assist if necessary, and agreed to send Halsey another carrier task force on or about 7 November.[34]

Halsey issued the basic orders for the operation on 12 October. He organized five task forces similar to those that had made up the New Georgia attack forces. They were: Task Force 31 (the attack force), under Admiral Wilkinson; Task Force 33 (South Pacific land-based aircraft), under Admiral Fitch; Sherman's Task Force 38; the cruisers and destroyers of Admiral Merrill's Task Force 39; and Captain Fife's submarines in Task Force 72.

The submarines were to carry out offensive reconnaissance in the waters of the Bismarck Archipelago, and would be supplemented in their work by Central Pacific submarines operating out of Pearl Harbor. Merrill's ships would support the invasion by operating against enemy surface ships and by bombarding Buka and the Shortlands. Halsey also planned to employ Sherman's Task Force 38 in a raid against Buka and Bonis, which lay beyond effective fighter range of the New Georgia airfields. Task Force 33 was ordered to carry out its usual missions of reconnaissance, destruction of enemy ships and aircraft, and air cover and support of the invasion force. Air

---

[33] "Harukichi," listed in Miller, *Guadalcanal: The First Offensive* as Hyakutake's given name, is a mistranslation.

[34] Ltr, Adm Duncan to Gen Smith, Chief of Mil Hist, 16 Nov 53, no sub, OCMH.

Command, Solomons, which was part of Task Force 33, was making its intensive effort during October against the Japanese airfields in southern Bougainville and the outlying islands, so that these areas could safely be bypassed. Arrangements for local air support were the same as for New Georgia. The local air commander with the invasion force was designated, as a subordinate of Twining's, Commander, Aircraft, Northern Solomons, and would take command of all support aircraft as they took off from their bases.

Admiral Wilkinson's invasion force, Task Force 31, consisted of eight transports, four cargo ships, two destroyer squadrons, mine craft, almost all the South Pacific's PT squadrons, and a large force of ground troops under the Commanding General, I Marine Amphibious Corps (IMAC).

The ground commander was General Vandegrift, USMC, an apple-cheeked, deceptively soft-spoken Virginia gentleman, who had won distinction by his conduct of operations on Guadalcanal from 7 August 1942 until December of that year. Vandegrift was at this time slated to become commandant of the Marine Corps in Washington, but was given the Bougainville command temporarily because Maj. Gen. Charles D. Barrett, who had replaced Vogel in command of the I Marine Amphibious Corps, had met accidental death in Nouméa. Halsey's choice for the corps command fell upon Maj. Gen. Roy S. Geiger, USMC, another hero of Guadalcanal, who was then in Washington as Director of Marine Corps Aviation. Vandegrift was to exercise the command until Geiger could arrive.

Ground forces assigned to the attack included the following: I Marine Amphibious Corps headquarters and corps troops; 3d Marine Division; 37th Division; 8th Brigade Group, 3d New Zealand Division; 3d Marine Defense Battalion; 198th Coast Artillery Regiment (Antiaircraft); 2d Provisional Marine Raider Battalion; 1st Marine Parachute Battalion; naval construction and communications units, and a boat pool.

In area reserve, to be committed on orders from Admiral Halsey, were the American Division in the Fijis; the 2d Battalion, 54th Coast Artillery (Harbor Defense) Regiment at Espiritu Santo; and the 251st Coast Artillery (Antiaircraft) Regiment in the Fijis.

Naming D Day as 1 November, the date for the invasion of Empress Augusta Bay, Halsey ordered Task Force 31 to seize and hold the Treasury Islands on D minus 5 (27 October) and establish radar positions and a small naval base. Wilkinson's main attack would be the seizure of Empress Augusta Bay on 1 November, which would be followed by the speedy construction of two airfields on sites to be determined by ground reconnaissance after the troops had landed. Task Force 31 was initially ordered to be ready to establish a PT base on northern Choiseul. This part of the plan was changed on the recommendation of Vandegrift, who argued that the Treasury landings might reveal to the Japanese the intention to invade Empress Augusta Bay. Halsey, Wilkinson, and Vandegrift decided instead to use the 2d Marine Parachute Battalion in a twelve-day raid on Choiseul which they hoped would mislead the enemy into believing that the real objective lay on Bougainville's east coast.[35]

Halsey made Wilkinson, whose headquarters was then at Guadalcanal, responsible for co-ordination of all amphibious plans. Wilkinson was to command all elements of Task Force 31 until, at a time agreed upon by him and the ground commander, direction of all air, ground, and naval forces at Empress Augusta Bay would be transferred to the latter.

Wilkinson divided Task Force 31 into a northern force, which he commanded himself, for the main attack and a southern force, led by Admiral Fort, for the Choiseul raid and the seizure of the Treasuries. The assault echelon of the northern force, scheduled to land at Empress Augusta Bay on D Day, included destroyers, the transports and cargo ships, and Maj. Gen. Allen H. Turnage's 3d Marine Division, less one regimental combat team and plus supporting units. The Treasuries echelon of the southern force was made up of 8 APD's, 2 LST's, 8 LCI's, 4 LCT's, 2 APC's, the 8th Brigade Group of the 3d New Zealand Division, the 198th Coast Artillery, A Company of the 87th Naval Construction Battalion, and communications and naval base detachments. The parachute battalion would be transported by four APD's escorted by destroyers. The 37th Division, in corps reserve, would be picked up at Guadalcanal by the northern force transports and would start ar-

LT. GEN. ALEXANDER A. VANDEGRIFT

riving at Bougainville soon after D Day to help hold the beachhead.

Guadalcanal and the Russells were to serve as the main staging and supply bases. However, the shortage of shipping led the I Marine Amphibious Corps to shorten the lines by establishing a supply base at Vella Lavella. Plans called for

---

[35] General Geiger described the plan of maneuver as "a series of short right jabs designed to throw the enemy off balance and conceal the real power of the left hook to his midriff at Empress Augusta Bay." He must have boxed left-handed.

the Vella depot to be stocked with a thirty-day supply of rations and petroleum products, but so strained was South Pacific shipping that only a ten-day supply had been stocked at Vella Lavella by 1 November.

During the last half of October the ground units completed their training and conducted final rehearsals. The 3d Marine Division, part of which had served in Samoa in 1942 before joining the main body in New Zealand, had recently transferred from New Zealand to Guadalcanal. It completed its amphibious and jungle training there and rehearsed for Empress Augusta Bay in the New Hebrides from 16 to 20 October. The 37th Division, returned from New Georgia to Guadalcanal in September, likewise conducted amphibious and jungle training at Guadalcanal. The 3d Marine Defense Battalion, which after serving in the Guadalcanal Campaign had been sent to New Zealand and from there back to Guadalcanal, rehearsed there. The 8th Brigade practiced landings at Efate en route to Guadalcanal from New Caledonia, and from 14 to 17 October rehearsed at Florida.

The Japanese

The Japanese fully expected Halsey to attack Bougainville and were busy preparing to meet the invasion. *Imperial Headquarters'* orders in September had stressed the importance of Bougainville as an outpost for Rabaul, and General Imamura had instructed General Hyakutake to make ready. This the *17th Army* commander did, acting in conjunction with the commander of the *8th Fleet.* The Japanese planned to use

air and surface strength to smash any Allied attempt at invasion before the assault troops could get off their transports. But if troops did succeed in getting ashore, the Japanese hoped to attack and destroy their beachheads.

Hyakutake's army consisted mainly of the *6th Division,* Lt. Gen. Masatane Kanda commanding. (This division had acquired an unsavory reputation for indiscipline by its sack of Nanking, China, in 1937). Also assigned were the *4th South Seas Garrison Unit* (three infantry battalions and one field artillery battery), and field artillery, antiaircraft artillery, and service units. Imamura was sending four rifle battalions and one artillery battalion of the *17th Division* from New Britain to northern Bougainville; these were due in November.[36]

Hyakutake, whose headquarters was on tiny Erventa Island near Tonolei Harbor, had disposed most of his strength to cover the Shortlands, Buin, and Tonolei Harbor, the rest to protect Kieta and Buka. Some 26,800 men—20,000 of the *17th Army* and 6,800 of *8th Fleet* headquarters and naval base forces—and an impressive number of guns ranging from machine guns to 140-mm. naval rifles were stationed in southern Bougainville and the islands. Over 4,000 men were at Kieta, and the arrival of the *17th Division* units would bring the Buka Passage garrison to 6,000.[37]

---

[36] The units attached to the *Southeastern Detachment* had been returned to their parent organizations. The *Detachment* was inactivated in December.

[37] These figures are taken from Southeast Area Naval Operations, III, Japanese Monogr No. 50 (OCMH), 7–8. Army accounts do not give strength figures.

The unpromising nature of the terrain on the west coast of Bougainville had convinced Hyakutake that the Allies would not attempt to land there. Consequently only a small detachment was stationed at Empress Augusta Bay. Hyakutake was aware that he would be outnumbered and outgunned in any battle, but like most of his fellow Japanese generals he placed great faith in the superior morale he believed his troops possessed.

"The battle plan is to resist the enemy's material strength with perseverance, while at the same time displaying our spiritual strength and conducting raids and furious attacks against the enemy flanks and rear. On this basis we will secure the key to victory within the dead spaces produced in enemy strength, and, losing no opportunities, we will exploit successes and annihilate the enemy." [38] Pride goeth before destruction, and an haughty spirit before a fall.

Preliminary Landings

The Treasuries

The assault echelon of Admiral Fort's southern force consisted of five transport groups: the advance transport group with 8 APD's and 3 escorting destroyers; the second with 8 LCI(L)'s, 2 LCI(G)'s,[39] and 6 destroyers; the third with 2 LST's, 2 destroyers, and 2 minesweepers; the fourth with 1 APC, 3 LCT's, and 2 PT boats; the fifth with 1 APC, 6 LCM's,

and a rescue boat.[40] These ships loaded troops and supplies at Guadalcanal, Rendova, and Vella Lavella and departed for the Treasuries on 26 October. Their departures were timed for the five groups to arrive in Blanche Harbor, which is between Mono and Stirling Islands, between 0520 and 0830, 27 October.[41] All possible measures were taken to avoid detection, because the small forces had to get established in the Treasuries before the Japanese were able to send in reinforcements from their ample reserves in the nearby Shortlands. But detection was almost inevitable in an operation so close to enemy bases, and at 0420, 27 October, a reconnaissance seaplane sighted the ships near the Treasuries and reported their presence. Admiral Merrill's task force, covering the operation some distance westward, was also discovered.

Heavy rain fell as the leading APD's arrived off the western entrance to Blanche Harbor. Low-hanging clouds obscured the jungled hills of Mono Island. As Blanche Harbor was too nar-

---

[38] 17th Army Operations, II, Japanese Monogr No. 40 (OCMH), 95.

[39] The LCI (G) was a gunboat designed to give close fire support in landings. Two 20-mm., three 40-mm., and five .50-caliber machine guns were installed on an LCI (L).

[40] This section is based on Gillespie, *The Pacific*, pp. 142–59; Morison, *Breaking the Bismarcks Barrier*, pp. 293–96; Rentz, *Bougainville and the Northern Solomons*, pp. 92–114; ONI USN, Combat Narratives: Solomon Islands Campaign, XII, The Bougainville Landing and the Battle of Empress Augusta Bay, 27 October–2 November 1943 [Washington, 1945], 11–23; SOPACBACOM, The Bougainville Campaign, Ch. II, OCMH; 8th Area Army Operations, Japanese Monogr No. 110 (OCMH), p. 102; 17th Army Operations, II, Japanese Monogr No. 40 (OCMH), 100–103; Outline of Southeast Area Naval Air Operations, Pt. IV, Japanese Monogr No. 108 (OCMH), p. 44.

[41] In Samuel Eliot Morison's words, "The historian wishes that the exploring captains of H.M.S. *Blanche*, *Renard*, and *Gazelle* had not been so fond of their ships as to name several harbors, channels, and sounds after each one." *Breaking the Bismarcks Barrier*, p. 293, n. 1.

row to permit ships to maneuver safely, the fire support destroyers and seven APD's remained west of the harbor. While the troops boarded the landing craft, destroyers opened fire on the landing beaches on Mono's south shore, and the minesweepers checked Blanche Harbor. At the same time the APD *McKean* put a radar party ashore on Mono's north coast.

Covered by the destroyers' gunfire and accompanied by the LCI gunboats, the first wave of LCP(R)'s, carrying elements of two battalions of the 8th Brigade, moved through the channel in the wet, misty half-light. There were only a handful of Japanese on Mono, some 225 men of the special naval landing forces. The naval bombardment drove most of the defenders out of their beach positions, and as the New Zealand infantry went ashore they drove out or killed the Japanese in the vicinity of the beach. However, enemy mortars and machine guns from hidden positions in the jungle fired on the landing beaches and on the LST's of the fourth transport group, which beached at 0735. This fire caused some casualties, damaged some weapons and equipment, and delayed the unloading. But before noon the 8th Brigade troops captured two 75-mm. guns and one 90-mm. mortar and resistance to the landing ceased.

Stirling Island, which was not occupied by the enemy, was secured by a battalion during the morning. A total of 2,500 men—252 Americans of the 198th Coast Artillery and several detachments from other units, the rest New Zealanders—had been landed on the south shore of Mono. The radar detachment and accompanying combat troops that had landed on the north coast of Mono numbered 200.

Meanwhile the American destroyers were busy. In addition to providing fire support for the landings they escorted the unloaded transport groups back to Guadalcanal. Two picket destroyers with fighter director teams aboard were stationed east and west of the Treasuries to warn against enemy air attacks.

General Hyakutake had decided that the Treasury landings were a preliminary to a systematic operation, and that the Allies would build an airfield on the Treasuries, take Choiseul, and after intensified air and surface operations, would land three divisions on southern Bougainville in late November. He felt that they might possibly invade Buka. Warning that the recent decline in Japanese naval strength might cause the Allies to move faster, he stressed the importance of building up the south Bougainville defenses. In short, he believed just what the Allies hoped he would.

When Admiral Kusaka at Rabaul was notified of the Allied landing, he brought some planes forward from Kavieng and sent fighters and dive bombers against the Allies. Most of these were headed off by the New Georgia-based P-38's and P-40's that formed the southern force's air cover, but some got through to damage the picket destroyer *Cony* and harass the retiring LST's. The Japanese pilots reported that they had sunk two transports and two cruisers.

On shore, Brigadier R. A. Row of the New Zealand Army, the landing force commander, set up beach defenses. By 12 November his troops had killed or captured the enemy garrison which had fled into the hills of Mono. Two hundred and five Japanese corpses were counted; 40 New Zealanders and 12 Americans had been killed, 145 New Zealanders and 29 Americans wounded.

Succeeding transport echelons, thirteen in all, brought in more troops and equipment from 1 November 1943 through 15 January 1944. During this period the boat pool, an advanced naval base, and radars were established; these supported the main operation at Empress Augusta Bay. Seabees of the U.S. Navy built a 5,600-foot-long airstrip on Stirling that was ready to receive fighter planes on Christmas Day.

The Choiseul Raid

Four of the APD's that had carried Brigadier Row's troops to the Treasuries sailed to Vella Lavella on 27 October and there took aboard 725 men of Lt. Col. Victor H. Krulak's 2d Marine Parachute Battalion, plus fourteen days' rations and two units of fire. Escorted by the destroyer *Conway*, the APD's steamed for the village of Voza on Choiseul, and that night landed the parachutists and their gear.

General Vandegrift had ordered Krulak so to conduct operations that the Japanese would believe a large force was present. Krulak therefore raided a barge staging point at Sagigai, some eight miles from Voza, and then sent strong combat patrols to the western part of Choiseul. But by 2 November the Japanese appeared to be concentrating at Sagigai with the obvious intention of destroying the 2d Parachute Battalion. From eight hundred to one thousand enemy were reported to have moved into Sagigai from positions farther east,

with more on the way. By now the Empress Augusta Bay landing had been safely executed, and Vandegrift ordered Krulak to withdraw. The battalion embarked on three LCI's in the early morning hours of 4 November. The raid cost 11 Marines dead, 14 wounded; 143 Japanese were estimated to have been slain.

Japanese sources do not indicate what estimates Imamura and Hyakutake placed on the operation. However, since Hyakutake expected that Choiseul would be invaded after the Treasuries and before southern Bougainville, it is not unlikely that Krulak's diversion confirmed his belief that southern Bougainville was the main Allied objective.

Seizure of Empress Augusta Bay

Supporting Operations

In invading Empress Augusta Bay, Halsey's forces were bypassing formidable enemy positions in southern Bougainville and the Shortlands, and placing themselves within close range of all the other Bougainville bases, as well as within fighter range of Rabaul—thus the strong air attacks by the Fifth Air Force and the Air Command, Solomons. In addition, Halsey had planned to make sure that the Japanese bases on Bougainville were in no condition to launch air attacks during the main landings on 1 November.[42] Forces assigned to this

---

[42] This subsection is based on Halsey and Bryan, *Admiral Halsey's Story*, pp. 177–79; Morison, *Breaking the Bismarcks Barrier*, pp. 292–93; Admiral Frederick C. Sherman, *Combat Command: The American Aircraft Carriers in the Pacific War* (New York: E. P. Dutton & Co., Inc., 1950), pp. 199–200; ONI USN, The Bougainville Landing and the Battle of Empress Augusta Bay, pp. 25–37.

mission were the 2 carriers, 2 antiair-craft light cruisers, and 10 destroyers of Admiral Sherman's Task Force 38 and the 4 light cruisers and 8 destroyers of Admiral Merrill's Task Force 39.

Task Force 38 sortied from Espiritu Santo on 29 October, Task Force 39 from Purvis Bay on Florida Island on 31 October. Both were bound initially for Buka.

Merrill, sailing well south of the Russells and west of the Treasuries on his 537-mile voyage in pursuance of Halsey's tight schedule, got there first. He arrived off Buka Passage at 0021, 1 November, and fired 300 6-inch and 2,400 5-inch shells at Buka and Bonis fields. Shore batteries replied but without effect. Merrill then retired at thirty knots toward the Shortland Islands. Enemy planes harassed the task force but the only damage they did was to the admiral's typewriter. One fire started by the bombardment was visible from sixty miles away.

About four hours after the beginning of Merrill's bombardment Task Force 38 reached a launching position some sixty-five miles southeast of Buka. This was the first time since the outbreak of the war in the Pacific that an Allied aircraft carrier had ventured within fighter range of Rabaul, and the first tactical employment of an Allied carrier in the South Pacific since the desperate battles of the Guadalcanal Campaign. In Admiral Sherman's words:

"We on the carriers had begun to think we would never get any action. All the previous assignments had gone to the shore-based air. Admiral Halsey had told me that he had to hold us for use against the Japanese fleet in case it came down from Truk. . . ." [43]

The weather was bad for carrier operations as the planes detailed for the first strike, a force made up of eighteen fighters, fifteen dive bombers, and eleven torpedo bombers, prepared to take off in the darkness. The sea was glassy and calm; occasional rain squalls fell. There was no breeze blowing over the flight decks, and the planes had to be catapulted into the air, a slow process that, coupled with the planes' difficulties in forming up in the dark, delayed their arrival over Buka until daylight. Two torpedo bombers and one dive bomber hit the water upon take-off, doubtless because of the calm air. The rest of the planes dropped three 1,000-pound bombs on Buka's runway and seventy-two 100-pound bombs on supply dumps and dispersal areas.

The next strike—fourteen fighters, twenty-one dive bombers, and eleven torpedo bombers—was launched at 0930 without casualties. These planes struck Buka again and bombed several small ships offshore. At dawn the next morning, 2 November, forty-four planes attacked Bonis, and at 1036 forty-one more repeated the attack. Then Sherman, under orders from Halsey, headed for the vicinity of Rennell, due south of Guadalcanal, to refuel. In two days of action Task Force 38, operating within sixty-five miles of Buka, estimated that it had destroyed about thirty Japanese planes and hit several small ships. More important, it had guaranteed that the Buka and Bonis runways could not be used for air attacks against Admiral Wil-

---

[43] Sherman, *Combat Command*, p. 200.

MAJ. GEN. ALLEN H. TURNAGE *(right) and Commodore Laurence F. Reifsnider aboard a transport before the landings on Bougainville.*

kinson's ships. The Americans lost seven men and eleven planes in combat and operational crashes.

Meanwhile Merrill's ships had sped from Buka to the Shortlands in the early morning hours of 1 November to bombard Poporang, Ballale, Faisi, and smaller islands. Merrill had bombarded these before, on the night of 29–30 June, but in stormy darkness. Now the bombardment was in broad daylight; it started at 0631, seventeen minutes after sunrise. Japanese shore batteries replied with inaccurate fire. Only the destroyer *Dyson* was hit, and its casualties and

damage were minor. His mission completed, Merrill headed south.

Approach to the Target

The last days of October found Wilkinson's ships busy loading and rehearsing at Guadalcanal and the New Hebrides.[44] Wilkinson had organized his eight

---

[44] The rest of this chapter is based on Morison, *Breaking the Bismarcks Barrier*, pp. 296–305; Rentz, *Bougainville and the Northern Solomons*, pp. 21–39; ONI USN, The Bougainville Landing and the Battle of Empress Augusta Bay, pp. 37–49; SOPAC-BACOM, The Bougainville Campaign, Ch. III, OCMH; 8th Area Army Operations, Japanese Monogr No. 110 (OCMH), pp. 103–05; Southeast

transport and four cargo ships of Task Force 31's northern force into three transport divisions of four ships each. A reinforced regiment of marines was to be carried in each of two of the divisions, the reinforced 3d Marine Defense Battalion in the third. The four transports of Division A, carrying 6,421 men of the 3d Marines, reinforced, departed Espiritu Santo on 29 October and steamed for Koli Point on Guadalcanal. There Admiral Wilkinson and General Vandegrift boarded the *George Clymer*. General Turnage, 3d Marine Division commander, and Commodore Laurence F. Reifsnider, the transport group commander, had come up from the New Hebrides rehearsal in the *Hunter Liggett*. Transport Division B, after the rehearsal, took the 6,103 men of the reinforced 9th Marines from the New Hebrides and in the late afternoon of 30 October joined with the four cargo ships of Transport Division C south of San Cristobal. Division C carried the reinforced 3d Marine Defense Battalion, 1,400 men, and a good deal of heavy equipment.

All transport divisions, plus 11 destroyers, 4 destroyer-minesweepers, 4 small minesweepers, 7 minelayers, and 2 tugs, rendezvoused in the Solomon Sea west of Guadalcanal at 0740, 31 October. They sailed northwestward until 1800, then feinted toward the Shortlands, and after dark changed course again toward the northwest. During the night run to Empress Augusta Bay PB4Y4's (Navy

---

Area Naval Operations, III, Japanese Monogr No. 50 (OCMH), 11–13; Outline of Southeast Area Naval Air Operations, Pt. IV, Japanese Monogr No. 108 (OCMH), p. 46; observations of the author, who participated as a member of D Battery, 3d Marine Defense Battalion.

Liberators), PV–1's (Vega Ventura night fighters), and PBY's (Black Cats) covered the ships. Enemy planes were out that night and made contact with the covering planes but apparently did not spot the ships, for none was attacked and Japanese higher headquarters received no warnings.

Empress Augusta Bay was imperfectly charted and the presence of several uncharted shoals was rightly suspected. Consequently Wilkinson delayed arrival at the transport area until daylight so that masthead navigation could be used to avoid the shoals.

The Landings

At 0432 of 1 November, Wilkinson's ships changed course from northwest to northeast and approached Cape Torokina in Empress Augusta Bay. Speed was reduced from fifteen to twelve knots. The minesweepers went out ahead to check the area. General quarters sounded on all ships at 0500, and forty-five minutes later the ships reached the transport area. The transport *Crescent City* struck a reef but suffered no damage.

Sunrise did not come until 0614, but the morning was bright and clear enough for the warships to begin a slow, deliberate bombardment of Cape Torokina at 0547. As each transport passed the cape it too fired with its 3-inch and antiaircraft guns. Wilkinson set H Hour for the landing at 0730. At 0645 the eight transports anchored in a line pointing north-northwest about three thousand yards from shore; the cargo ships formed a similar line about five hundred yards to seaward of the transports.

Wilkinson, sure that the Japanese would launch heavy air attacks, had come

MOUNT BAGANA

so lightly loaded that four to five hours of unloading time would find his ships emptied. Vandegrift and Turnage, anticipating little opposition at the beach, had planned to speed unloading by sending more than seven thousand men ashore in the assault wave. They would land along beaches (eleven on the mainland and one on Puruata Island off Cape Torokina) with a total length of eight thousand yards.

The assault wave boarded landing craft at the ships' rails. The winchmen quickly lowered the craft into the water; and the first wave formed rapidly and started for shore.

The scene was one to be remembered, with torpedo bombers roaring overhead, trim gray destroyers firing at the beaches, the two lines of transports and cargo ships swinging on their anchors, and the landing craft full of marines churning toward the enemy. This scene was laid against a natural backdrop of awesome beauty. The early morning tropical sun shone in a bright blue sky. A moderately heavy sea was running, so that at the shore a white line showed where the surf pounded on the black and gray beaches, which were fringed for most of their length by the forbidding green of the jungle. Behind were the rugged hills, and Mount Bagana, towering skyward, emitting perpetual clouds of smoke and steam, dominated the entire scene.

The destroyers continued firing until 0731, when thirty-one torpedo bombers from New Georgia bombed and strafed the shore line for five minutes. The first troops reached the beach at 0726, and in the next few minutes all the assault wave came ashore. There was no opposition except at Puruata Island and at Cape Torokina and its immediate vicinity. There the Japanese, though few in numbers, fought with skill and ferocity.

Cape Torokina was held by 270 Japanese soldiers of the *2d Company, 1st Battalion,* and of the *Regimental Gun Company, 23d Infantry.* One platoon held Puruata. On Cape Torokina the enemy had built about eighteen log-and-sandbag pillboxes, each with two machine guns, mutually supporting, camouflaged, and arranged in depth. He had also emplaced a 75-mm. gun in an open-ended log-and-sand bunker to fire on landing craft nearing the beach.

Neither air bombardment nor naval gunfire had had any appreciable effect on these positions. Because air reconnaissance had shown that the enemy had built defense positions on Cape Torokina (a low, flat, sandy area covered with palm trees), it had been a target for naval bombardment. Two destroyers had fired at the cape from the south, but had done no damage. Exploding shells and bombs sent up smoke and dust that made observation difficult; some shells had burst prematurely in the palm trees. Poor gunnery was also a factor, for many shells were seen to hit the water.[45]

Thus when landing craft bearing the 3d Marines neared the cape the 75-mm. gun and the machine guns opened fire. The men were forced to disembark under fire and to start fighting the moment they put foot to the ground. Casualties were lighter than might have been expected—78 men were killed and 104 wounded in the day's action—but only after fierce fighting and much valor were the men of the 3d Marines able to establish themselves ashore. The pillboxes were reduced by three-man fire teams: one BAR man and two riflemen with M1's, all three using grenades whenever possible. The gun position was taken by Sgt. Robert A. Owens of A Company, 3d Marines, who rushed the position under cover of fire from four riflemen. He killed part of the Japanese crew and drove off the rest before he died of wounds received in his assault.[46]

By 1100 Cape Torokina was cleared. Most of its defenders were dead; the survivors retreated inland. Puruata Island was secured at about the same time, although some Japanese remained alive until the next day. Elsewhere the landing waves, though not opposed by the enemy, pushed inland slowly through dense jungle and a knee-deep swamp that ran two miles inland and backed most of the beach north and east of Cape Torokina. The swamp's existence had not previously been suspected.

Air Attacks and Unloading

The Allied air forces of the South and Southwest Pacific Areas had performed mightily in their effort to neutralize the Japanese air bases at Rabaul, Bougainville, and the Shortlands, but they

---

[45] See Rentz, *Bougainville and the Northern Solomons,* p. 34; Isely and Crowl, *The U.S. Marines and Amphibious War,* p. 180.

[46] Sergeant Owens received the Medal of Honor posthumously.

3D MARINES LANDING ON CAPE TOROKINA

had not been able to neutralize Rabaul completely. In planning the invasion of Empress Augusta Bay, the South Pacific commanders were aware that the Japanese would probably counterattack from the air. General Twining had arranged for thirty-two New Georgia-based fighter planes of all types then in use in the South Pacific—Army Air Forces P–38's, New Zealand P–40's, and Marine F4U's—to be overhead in the vicinity all day. These planes were vectored by a fighter director team aboard the destroyer *Conway*. Turning in an outstanding performance, they destroyed or drove off most of the planes that the Japanese sent against Wilkinson. But they could not keep them all away.

At 0718, as the last boats of the assault wave were leaving their transports, the destroyers' radars picked up a flight of approaching enemy planes then fifty miles distant. The covering fighters kept most of the planes away, but a few, perhaps twelve, dive bombers broke through to attack the ships.

These bombers had come from Rabaul, where the enemy commanders were making haste to organize counterattacks. On 30 October Vice Adm. Sentaro Omori, commanding a heavy cruiser division, had brought a convoy into Simpson Harbor at Rabaul. Next morning a search plane reported an Allied convoy of three cruisers, ten destroyers, and thirty transports near Gatukai in the

New Georgia group. This was probably Merrill's task force; it could not have been Wilkinson's. On receiving this report Admiral Kusaka ordered the planes of his *11th Air Fleet* to start attacks, and he and Koga, over the protests of the *8th Fleet* commander, who warned of the dangers of sending surface ships south of New Britain, directed Omori to take his force and all the *8th Fleet* ships out to attack. This Omori did, but he missed Merrill and returned to Rabaul on the morning of 1 November.

Then came the news of the landing at Empress Augusta Bay. General Hyakutake was still sure that the main Allied attack would be delivered against southern Bougainville, but General Imamura ordered him to destroy the forces that had landed. Imamura also arranged with Kusaka for a counterattacking force from the *17th Division*, made up of the *2d Battalion, 54th Infantry,* and the *6th Company, 2d Battalion, 53d Infantry,* to be transported to Empress Augusta Bay.[47] It would be carried on 6 destroyer-transports and escorted by 2 heavy cruisers, 2 light cruisers, and 6 destroyers, all under Omori.

Admirals Koga and Kusaka, just completing their preparations for Operation *RO,* also ordered out their planes. The weather had come to their assistance by halting the heavy raid General Kenney had planned for 1 November. Koga alerted the *12th Air Fleet* for transfer from Japan to Rabaul. Kusaka sent out planes of his *11th Air Fleet.* The carrier planes apparently did not take part on 1 November.

According to enemy accounts, Japanese planes delivered three separate attacks against Wilkinson on 1 November. The Japanese used a total of 16 dive bombers and 104 fighters, of which 19 were lost and 10 were damaged.[48]

When Wilkinson's ships received warning at 0718, the transports and cargo ships weighed anchor and steamed for the open sea. They escaped harm, and the dive bombers were able to inflict only light damage to the destroyers. Two sailors were killed. The transports returned and resumed unloading at 0930, having lost two hours.

Another enemy attack at 1248 succeeded in breaking through the fighter cover. Warned again by radar, the transports, with the exception of the *American Legion,* which stuck on an uncharted shoal, fled. The Japanese attacked the moving ships instead of the *Legion.* No damage was done, but the ships lost two more hours of unloading time.[49]

The halts in unloading caused by air attacks, coupled with beach and terrain conditions that Admiral Halsey described as "worse than any we had previously encountered," slowed the movement of supplies and equipment.[50] Fully one third of the landing force—5,700 men in all—had been assigned to the shore party, but nature and the Japanese

---

[47] This force had been standing by awaiting orders to move to western New Britain. It was separate from the *17th Division* units scheduled for Bougainville mentioned above, p. 238.

[48] Southeast Area Naval Operations, III, Japanese Monogr No. 50 (OCMH), p. 46; p. 13 states that twenty-two planes were lost.

[49] As usual the Japanese claims, like those of American pilots, were exaggerated. They said they sank two transports and a cruiser.

[50] Halsey and Bryan, *Admiral Halsey's Story,* p. 179.

LCVP's on the Beach at Empress Augusta Bay *damaged by the rough, driving surf.*

aircraft thwarted efforts to unload all the ships on D Day.

Even on quiet days the surf at Empress Augusta Bay was rough, and on 1 November a stiff breeze whipped it higher. The northernmost beaches were steep and narrow. The surf, and possibly the inexperience of some of the crews, took a heavy toll of landing craft. No less than sixty-four LCVP's and twenty-two LCM's broached on shore and were swamped by the driving surf. As surf conditions got worse, several beaches became completely unusable. Five ships were shifted to beaches farther south, with more delay and congestion at the southern beaches. It was during this move that the *American Legion* ran aground.

By 1730 the eight transports were empty and Wilkinson took them back to Guadalcanal. But the four cargo ships, which carried heavy guns and equipment, were still practically full. Vandegrift, who had had ample experience at Guadalcanal in being left stranded on a hostile shore while much of his equipment remained in the holds of departing ships, persuaded Wilkinson to allow the cargo ships to put out to sea for the night and return the next morning to unload.[51] Most of the troops aboard went ashore in LCVP's before Commodore Reifsnider led the cargo ships out to sea. D Battery of the 3d Defense Battalion, for example, its 90-mm. antiaircraft

---

[51] Miller, *Guadalcanal: The First Offensive,* pp. 79–81.

guns, fire control equipment, and radars deep in the holds of the *Alchiba,* which had lost all its LCM's in the raging surf, went ashore as infantry and occupied a support position in the sector of the 9th Marines.

Except for the full holds of the cargo ships, D Day had been thoroughly successful. All the landing force, including General Turnage, Brig. Gen. Alfred H. Noble, corps deputy commander, Col. Gerald C. Thomas, the corps chief of staff, and several other officers, were ashore. General Vandegrift returned to Guadalcanal on the *George Clymer,* leaving Turnage in command at Cape Torokina. By the day's end the division held a shallow beachhead from Torokina northward for about four thousand yards. Aside from unloading the cargo ships (a task that was expeditiously accomplished the next day), the main missions facing the amphibious and ground commanders and the troops were threefold: to bring in reinforcements; to organize a perimeter defense capable of beating off the inevitable Japanese counterattack; and to build the airfields that would put South Pacific fighter planes over Rabaul.

CHAPTER XIII

Exploiting the Beachhead

The ground troops at Cape Torokina could be expected to carry out their missions efficiently only if they were unhampered by Japanese aircraft and warships. Therefore the real battle for the beachhead was fought in the air and on the sea. The primary mission of South Pacific aircraft and warships during the first days of November was protection of the newly won beachhead. In this mission they fought hard and with excellent results.

Air and Surface Action, 1–11 November

When Admiral Omori led his task force out of Rabaul in late afternoon of 1 November, he had orders to escort Imamura's troops and to attack Wilkinson's transports in Empress Augusta Bay. But after joining with the troop-carrying destroyers in Saint George's Channel between New Britain and New Ireland, Omori was sighted by a U.S. submarine. Further, an unidentified plane dropped a bomb near the light cruiser *Sendai*. The Japanese, sure that their intentions had been deduced, postponed the troop movement, but Omori was allowed to take his task force of two heavy and two light cruisers and six destroyers to Empress Augusta Bay with the intention of destroying the

American transports and cargo ships which he thought would still be there.[1]

Meanwhile, Admiral Merrill's Task Force 39 had sailed to the vicinity of Vella Lavella after the two bombardments on 1 November. Four of his eight destroyers were refueling in the late afternoon of 1 November when General Twining's reconnaissance planes spotted Omori and flashed a warning. Halsey ordered Merrill out to intercept Omori. Receiving continuous, accurate plots of Omori's course and speed, Merrill set his course and speed so that his four light cruisers and eight destroyers would intercept west of Empress Augusta Bay.

At 0229, 2 November, a few miles from Cape Torokina, Task Force 39 made contact with Omori and attacked at once. In this engagement, the Battle of Empress Augusta Bay, Merrill sank one light cruiser and one destroyer; except for the destroyer *Foote*, which lost her stern to a Japanese torpedo, the

[1] This section is based on Craven and Cate, *The Pacific: Guadalcanal to Saipan*, pp. 257–61, 325–28; Halsey and Bryan, *Admiral Halsey's Story*, pp. 180–85; Morison, *Breaking the Bismarcks Barrier*, pp. 305–37; Sherman, *Combat Command*, 201–08; CTF 33 War Diary; Southeast Area Naval Operations, III, Japanese Monogr No. 50 (OCMH), 14–29; Outline of Southeast Area Naval Air Operations, Pt. IV, Japanese Monogr No. 108 (OCMH), pp. 48–68.

American ships received light damage. The flashes from gunfire and explosions were visible to Commodore Reifsnider's four cargo ships, which had put out to sea, and to the marines ashore. The engagement lasted until dawn, when Omori, tacitly acknowledging failure, took his surviving ships back to Rabaul.

Near as he was to Rabaul, Merrill expected to suffer air attack at dawn, and he was not wrong. When a Japanese patrol plane sighted him 18 dive bombers and 80 fighters promptly took off from Rabaul to the attack. Bad weather on the morning of 2 November had kept most of the Allied fighters on the New Georgia fields, but 8 F6F's, 1 F4U, 3 P-38's, and 4 New Zealand P-40's, vectored by a destroyer still in Empress Augusta Bay, hurled themselves at part of the Japanese formation and shot down several planes.

The remaining enemy planes came upon Task Force 39 shortly before 0800 and promptly attacked. The task force maneuvered rapidly, sailing clockwise in a great circle and shooting 5-inch, 40-mm., 20-mm., and even 6-inch guns at the diving Japanese with considerable success. The light cruiser *Montpelier* suffered two bomb hits which wounded several men, but the other ships went unscathed. The Japanese broke off the action, but on the way home lost more planes to Allied fighters. More planes from Rabaul would doubtless have come out after Merrill that day but for the Fifth Air Force's raid on the airfields, which the Japanese carrier pilots contested so hotly.

Merrill's ships, after two busy days that included two shore bombardments, the night action of Empress Augusta

Bay, and the morning air attack, now escorted Reifsnider's retiring cargo ships as far as Rendova, then steamed for Florida and concluded their eventful, successful cruise. On the other hand, the Japanese had lost two ships and numerous aircraft, and had not inflicted anything like equivalent damage to the Americans. But Admiral Koga had not given up. When he was informed of the landings at Empress Augusta Bay, he ordered Vice Adm. Takeo Kurita to take seven heavy cruisers, one light cruiser, four destroyers, and a fleet train from Truk to Rabaul. Kurita arrived safely on 4 November, although later ships were hit by Twining's B-24's.

This force of heavy cruisers at Rabaul posed a serious threat to the new beachhead at Empress Augusta Bay, and created, wrote Admiral Halsey, "the most desperate emergency that confronted me in my entire term as COMSOPAC." [2] He knew that he had to stop them, but he had only two naval task forces—Merrill's, which was exhausted after its performance of 1-2 November, and Sherman's carriers. Up to now carriers had been employed against land bases only in the most gingerly fashion. The South Pacific staff calculated that Sherman, from his refueling position near Rennell, could strike Kurita before Kurita would strike Empress Augusta Bay. So Halsey ordered Sherman to hit Rabaul. When he gave these orders the South Pacific commander expected the carrier air groups to be "cut to pieces" and the carriers "stricken." [3]

"I fully expected that they [Sherman's

---

[2] Halsey and Bryan, *Admiral Halsey's Story*, pp. 180–81.

[3] *Ibid.*, p. 181.

carriers] would be lost." [4] ". . . but we could not let the men at Torokina be wiped out while we stood by and wrung our hands." [5] Halsey was never a man to stand idly by and wring his hands, or to allow anyone else that emotional luxury.

Halsey directed South Pacific land-based air (Task Force 33) to provide cover for Sherman during his daylight approach and retirement. This job was done by Navy fighters from New Georgia, which of course were capable of landing on carrier decks. Thus Sherman was able to send all his aircraft against Rabaul instead of keeping some of them overhead for protection.

Task Force 38 reached its launching point in the Solomon Sea 57 miles southwest of Torokina and 230 miles southeast of Rabaul at 0900, 5 November. The weather was fine for carrier operations; a steady breeze was blowing, and there were frequent rain squalls where the ships could hide in case of air attack. The two carriers sent out 97 planes: 23 torpedo bombers, 22 dive bombers, and 52 fighters. They arrived over Rabaul and dived through a hole in the clouds to take the Japanese by surprise. Though faced by intense antiaircraft fire they bored in with resounding success. They did not sink any ships, but damaged three heavy cruisers, two light cruisers, and two destroyers so severely that months passed before any of them were fit to fight again. This was done at a cost of fifteen men killed or missing, ten

planes lost. Halsey's gloomy expectations were not fulfilled.

Twenty-seven B–24's and fifty-eight P–38's from the Fifth Air Force reached Rabaul in the afternoon. As practically all the Japanese planes were out after Task Force 38, Kenney's men bombed the wharves. The Japanese failed to find Sherman, but they attacked an LCI, an LCT, and a PT boat near the southern arm of Empress Augusta Bay, and claimed a tremendous but nonexistent victory.[6]

Sherman's victory, on the other hand, was real. Next day Koga decided to pull his heavy cruisers back to Truk, and the threat to Cape Torokina was ended. Thereafter no more heavy Japanese ships went to Rabaul.

Meanwhile Kusaka's *11th Air Fleet* and the carrier planes, besides attacking Merrill and Sherman, had been striking day and night against Cape Torokina, hammering at reinforcement convoys, and fighting almost constantly with Allied fighter planes. They damaged three ships and sank one, but kept losing planes to ship- and shore-based antiaircraft guns and to Twining's fighters.

Air Command, Solomons, made a maximum effort to keep the enemy's Bougainville bases out of action and to keep the Rabaul-based planes away from Cape Torokina and the reinforcement convoys. For example, on 10 November there were 712 take-offs and landings at Munda airfield alone.

Rabaul was still a primary target for General Kenney. The weather prevented an attack on 6 November, but 10 November saw a heavy attack, and next day

---

[4] Halsey's preface to Sherman's *Combat Command*, p. 8.

[5] Halsey and Bryan, *Admiral Halsey's Story*, p. 181.

[6] For details see Morison, *Breaking the Bismarcks Barrier*, p. 329.

AIRCREWMAN WOUNDED IN STRIKE ON RABAUL *is helped out of his plane on flight deck of aircraft carrier USS* Saratoga, *5 November 1943.*

RAAF Beauforts and Fifth Air Force planes struck in the morning before heavy clouds piled up over Rabaul.

The additional carrier task group of the Fifth Fleet that Admiral Nimitz had promised to Halsey reached the South Pacific on 7 November. Commanded by Rear Adm. Alfred L. Montgomery, it consisted of the carriers *Essex, Bunker Hill,* and *Independence.* Halsey planned to use Montgomery's ships as well as Task Force 38 in a double carrier strike against Rabaul on 11 November.

Sherman sailed to a point in the Pacific Ocean near Green Island, north-northwest of Bougainville, and launched planes. They reached Rabaul in bad weather about 0830, struck at ships, and returned to the carriers, which retired southward without being detected.

Montgomery launched his strike from a point in the Solomon Sea about 160 miles southeast of Rabaul. His planes hit at ships too, then returned to their mother carriers. The Japanese found Montgomery and delivered a series of furious though unsuccessful air attacks which inflicted only slight damage. They lost thirty-five planes to ships' antiaircraft guns and to Allied fighters from New Georgia.

In eleven days of the *RO* operations against the Allied lines of communication and the Torokina beachhead, the

Japanese pilots had reported enormous damage to Allied ships and planes, whereas in reality they had accomplished very little and had suffered the real damage themselves.[7] Koga had sent 173 planes and 192 men down from Truk, and by the end of 11 November 121 planes had been destroyed and 86 of the men were dead. The *11th Air Fleet* had lost about 70 planes. These losses ". . . had put the carrier air force in a position where further combat would rob it of even a skeleton force around which to rebuild. . . ."[8] Koga may have believed his pilots' claims, but he also recognized the significance of his own losses. On 12 November he withdrew the carrier planes to Truk. The withdrawal, first of the cruisers and then of the planes, ended Rabaul's offensive threat. Thereafter it was a formidable defense position only, and after Armistice Day Southwest Pacific planes were able to cease their attacks against it and concentrate against enemy bases to the west.

The damage that Sherman's pilots inflicted on the heavy cruisers and Koga's losses in carrier planes had repercussions that were felt far beyond Empress Augusta Bay. Koga had planned to use the *Combined Fleet* to seek out and destroy the U.S. Pacific Fleet if the Americans invaded the Gilberts or Marshalls, but when Admiral Nimitz' forces moved into the Gilberts on 21 November 1943, Koga did not stir out of Truk; the cruiser damage and aircraft losses had completely immobilized the *Combined*

Fleet.[9] This series of events, wherein the Japanese shifted forces back and forth to meet Allied threats from different parts of the Pacific, and lost as a result, was an advantage the Joint Chiefs of Staff had in mind when they ordered two advances rather than one. The series illustrates also the strategic importance of Rabaul, and the advantages that their interior lines gave to the Japanese.

Operations Ashore

Now landed and completely protected from Japanese surface attack, although subject to frequent air raids by day and by night, the 3d Marine Division was hampered as much by terrain as by the enemy. The swamps and dense forest slowed the movement of supplies and the building of roads and airfields. During their first five days on shore the marines patrolled, established antiaircraft and beach defenses, and extended the perimeter two thousand yards inland. (*Map 16*) Seventy-eight marines were killed or missing, 104 wounded.[10]

More Troops

The first reinforcements, one battalion of the 21st Marine Regiment, arrived on

---

[7] The Japanese reported sinking 5 battleships, 10 aircraft carriers, 19 cruisers, 7 destroyers, and 9 transports between 27 October and 10 December.

[8] Southeast Area Naval Operations, III, Japanese Monogr No. 50 (OCMH), 25–26.

[9] See Wilds, "The Admiral Who Lost His Fleet," *United States Naval Institute Proceedings,* Vol. 77, No. 11 (November 1951); Crowl and Love, *The Seizure of the Gilberts and Marshalls,* Ch. IV.

[10] This section is based on Morison, *Breaking the Bismarcks Barrier,* pp. 337-69; Rentz, *Bougainville and the Northern Solomons,* pp. 39–80; [British] Central Office of Information, *Among Those Present,* pp. 64–73; SOPACBACOM, The Bougainville Campaign, Chs. III–IV, V, OCMH; Halsey, Narrative Account of the South Pacific Campaign, OCMH; Harmon, The Army in the South Pacific, OCMH; I Mar Amphib Corps, Bougainville Beachhead; 8th Area Army Operations, Japanese Monogr No. 110 (OCMH), pp. 103–06; 17th Army Operations, II, Japanese Monogr No. 40 (OCMH), 104; the author's observations.

AMPHIBIAN TRACTORS LVT (1), *carrying supplies and ammunition, move inland over a muddy trail.*

eight LST's and eight APD's on 6 November. Escorted by six destroyers and covered by Task Force 39, these ships had sailed from Purvis Bay two days before. Japanese aircraft harried them during the night of 5–6 November but did no damage.

For speedy unloading, the LST cargoes had been packed on trailers at Purvis Bay. But Cape Torokina did not boast very many beaches suitable for the LST's (which in the South Pacific almost never carried tanks). One beach at Puruata Island had room for three LST's, but using this meant unloading gear at Puruata and then transshipping it to the mainland. At the beaches east of Cape Torokina the LST's grounded offshore.

Seabees improvised coconut log runways, which failed to stand up under the strain. The eventual answer to the problem lay in steel pontons.

On 8 November substantial reinforcements came in, some aboard six of the ships that had made the initial invasion and then returned to Guadalcanal to pick up the 148th Regimental Combat Team of the 37th Division. Japanese aircraft made the day exciting as the soldiers unloaded and went ashore. Over a hundred planes attacked at noon. Twenty-eight Allied fighters from New Georgia kept many of them off, but some got through and damaged the *President Jackson*. Once ashore, the 148th relieved the 3d Marines on the left flank, and

TRACTOR AND TRAILER IN MUD. *Marines are perched on load of artillery ammunition.*

the marine regiment was assigned a position in the middle of the inland side of the perimeter defense.

General Geiger, having flown out from Washington and relieved General Vandegrift as corps commander, arrived at Bougainville on the 9th. On 13 November Admiral Wilkinson relinquished his control and Geiger became directly responsible to Halsey. The amphibious commander retained responsibility for the transport of troops and supplies to the beachhead.

Other reinforcements from the 37th and 3d Marine Divisions came in promptly. The 129th Regimental Combat Team landed on 13 November, and was followed six days later by the 145th.

Except for miscellaneous units and detachments, this completed the movement of General Beightler's veteran division to the beachhead. The remaining units of the 21st Marines arrived on 11 and 17 November. During the latter shipment the APD *McKean* was fatally torpedoed by a Japanese plane. Thus by the end of the third week in November there were two full divisions at Empress Augusta Bay, plus substantial bodies of corps troops, naval construction battalions, and naval base forces. The I Marine Amphibious Corps held a perimeter about sixteen thousand yards in circumference, including seven thousand yards along the beach. The 37th Division held the left, the 3d Marine Division the

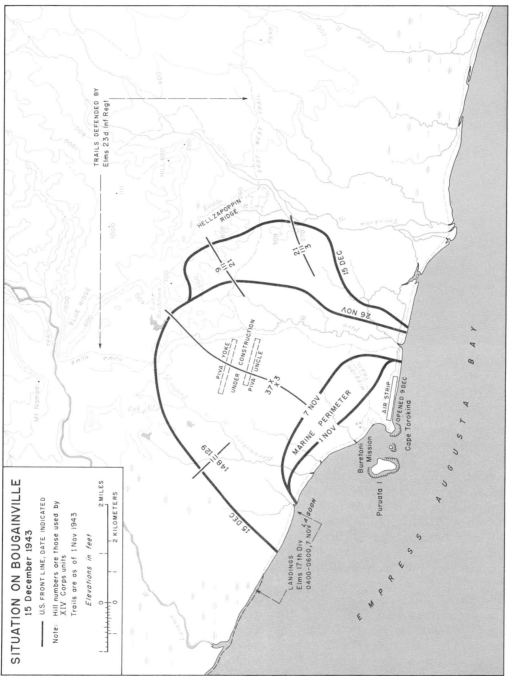

SITUATION ON BOUGAINVILLE
15 December 1943

U.S. FRONT LINE, DATE INDICATED

Note: Hill numbers are those used by
XIV Corps units
Trails are as of 1 Nov 1943

Elevations in feet

MILES
KILOMETERS

TRAILS DEFENDED BY
Elms 23d Inf Regt

HELLZAPOPPIN
RIDGE

EAST-WEST TRAIL

15 DEC

26 NOV

PIVA YOKE
UNDER CONSTRUCTION
PIVA UNCLE

37 × 3

7 NOV

MARINE PERIMETER

1 NOV

AIR STRIP

OPENED 9 DEC

Buretoni
Mission

Cape Torokina

Puruata I

148 │ 129

15 DEC

LANDINGS
Elms 17th Div
0400-0600, 7 NOV

EMPRESS   AUGUSTA   BAY

BLUE RIDGE

Mt Nampei

F. Temple

MAP 16

right. This perimeter was not attained without fighting, but the 37th Division was fortunate in that, except for patrol clashes, all the fighting occurred in the 3d Marine Division's zone.

Expansion of the Perimeter

Even after 1 November Japanese Army commanders continued to cherish the delusion that the main effort was yet to come, and that southern Bougainville or Buka was the real target. However, on orders from Imamura to destroy the wide, shallow Allied beachhead at Cape Torokina, Hyakutake dispatched the two battalions of the *23d Infantry* from the Buin area to the cape. Under command of Maj. Gen. Shun Iwasa, infantry group commander of the *6th Division,* the *23d* was to operate in conjunction with the *17th Division* troops whose transfer from Rabaul, first planned for 1 November, had been postponed. Aboard four destroyers, 475 men of this group finally got under way for Torokina on 6 November; 700 others sailed for Buka. The *17th Division* troops were to cover the movement of the *23d Infantry* by landing north of the cape near the Americans' left and creating a diversion. They would then move inland and join with the *23d.* Iwasa was to advance down a trail with the combined force and attack the beachhead.

The troop-carrying destroyers hove to off the beach between the Laruma and Koromokina Rivers in the predawn darkness on the morning of 7 November. Between 0400 and 0600, the 475 soldiers slipped ashore in twenty-one landing craft under the very noses of the American defenders. Patrolling PT boats missed the destroyers, and an antitank

SOLDIERS OF THE 148TH REGIMENTAL COMBAT TEAM *boarding the transport* President Jackson *for the run to Bougainville, 5 November 1943.*

platoon on shore saw the landing craft but thought they were American. The enemy soldiers landed so close to the American lines that they actually cut off several marines in an outpost, who were later rescued by two LCM's.

The Japanese attacked at once in the vicinity of a lagoon about fourteen hundred yards west of the Koromokina River. The sector was defended by troops of the 3d Marines who had just exchanged positions with the 9th Marines. General Turnage had ordered the transfer because the 3d had seen all the fighting on D Day, the 9th (which landed on the left) none, and there seemed to be no immediate prospect of fighting on the left. The enemy made some small local gains by infiltrating. The fighting, with rifles, machine guns, mortars, and grenades, was close work, but the marine lines held.

Next morning five field artillery batteries, plus mortars, antitank guns, and machine guns, fired a twenty-minute preparation into the Japanese position. Then the newly arrived 1st Battalion, 21st Marines, supported by light tanks, assaulted. It met only light opposition; the artillery preparation had come close to achieving perfection. Instead of engaging in a fierce fight, the 1st Battalion walked, cautiously but steadily, through the jungle. It found, in the small area where the Japanese had packed themselves, about three hundred men killed almost instantaneously, their dead bodies lying beside their smashed weapons. In this action at Koromokina Lagoon the marines suffered sixteen men killed, thirty wounded.

Meanwhile the *23d Infantry* had moved into position inland and had already begun attacking the trail blocks the marines had set up. Control of the trail system inland was of great importance to the security of the beachhead. It was clear that unless the Japanese had enough strength to deliver a major attack from the sea (and Admiral Sherman had settled that question on 5 November) any counteroffensives would be delivered along the axes of the trails. There were two important tracks at Cape Torokina, East–West Trail and the Numa Numa Trail. The latter ran from the shore near the mouth of the Piva River northward through the mountains to Numa Numa on the east coast. East–West Trail intersected the Numa Numa Trail about five thousand yards inland (north) of the Piva's mouth. It led eastward, then north through the mountains to Roravana Bay and intersected the several trails leading to Buin. A local track, Mission Trail, ran from a point about two thousand yards north of the Piva mouth southwestward to the Roman Catholic mission station at Buretoni just northwest of Torokina.

On 5 November the *23d Infantry* attacked a block on Mission Trail that was held by the 3d Raider Battalion. After the raider battalion beat off the *23d;* it and later the 3d Battalion, 9th Marines, counterattacked up Mission Trail and by Armistice Day had advanced to the junction of Mission and Numa Numa Trails. Losing 19 killed and 32 wounded, the marines estimated that they had accounted for 550 of the enemy.

Two days later the 21st Marines continued the fight, this time not only to keep control of the trails but also to secure an airfield site. Since landing the I Marine Amphibious Corps had also been hard at work pushing supply routes through the swamps, an extremely difficult and time-consuming task. At the same time patrols had found a good airfield site in a coconut grove by the right (west) bank of the Piva River near the junction of the Numa Numa and East-West Trails. This was some distance from the 3d Division's front, and the difficulties of pushing supplies so far prevented an immediate forward displacement of the 3d Division to include the site. Generals Geiger and Turnage therefore decided to establish a self-sustaining outpost at the trail junction in order to hold the airfield site. On 13 and 14 November troops of the 21st Marines, fighting hard against Japanese in prepared positions, made their way through the coconut grove and by 1600 of 14 November had seized the trail junction.

Because the building of roads and trails inside the beachhead eased the logistical situation, Geiger decided to move his whole front forward in the latter part of November. The 3d Division would advance on the east (right), the 37th Division on the west. Five artillery battalions, operating under the 37th Division artillery commander, Brig. Gen. Leo N. Kreber, would provide support, as would the Aircraft, Northern Solomons, under Brig. Gen. Field Harris, USMC. The 37th Division met no fighting in its advance but the 3d Marine Division continued to meet opposition from the *23d Infantry* along the trails, especially on the Numa Numa Trail north of the airfield site and in the region northeast of that site where the East-

West Trail crossed several tributary forks of the Piva River. Here, between 20 and 24 November, the Japanese resisted vigorously but vainly. By 26 November the 3d Marine Division, maintaining contact on the left with the 37th Division, had extended its lines as far north as the south shore of Lake Kathleen, about 7,500 yards north of the Piva's mouth. In the fighting in the Piva forks the 3d Marines took the first high ground in the beachhead. Along the shore line the I Corps held the beach from a point 6,000 yards northwest of Cape Torokina to a point 3,500 east of the cape. The inland lines of the perimeter were about 19,500 yards long.

During November the Japanese Army commanders still refused to believe that Halsey had made his main effort at Empress Augusta Bay and therefore undertook no counterattacks on a scale large enough to be effective. But Rabaul-based aircraft continued to raid the beachhead. Both division command posts were hit, as were several fuel and ammunition dumps, which blew skyward in impressive and expensive displays. On a few occasions the enemy planes swooped down suddenly over the mountains during daylight and caught the beachhead by surprise (the mountains blocked the radar beams), but most of the bombings were nocturnal, and the Japanese simplified the radar operators' problems by attacking from seaward where they were easy to locate in time for warning to be given and the antiaircraft guns to go into action. Puruata Island, with phosphorescent water outlining it clearly, was a favorite and profitable target, since it was nearly always packed with supplies

ADMIRAL WILLIAM F. HALSEY, JR., *center, with Maj. Gen. Roy S. Geiger, left, and Brig. Gen. Leo N. Kreber, Bougainville, 13 November 1943.*

37TH DIVISION TROOPS *moving inland from the beach over a slimy mud trail, 8 November 1943. These men are from the 148th Regimental Combat Team.*

Results of Japanese Bombing of Puruata Island, *20 November 1943. Top left, view from Bougainville. Note wrecked landing craft, foreground. Top right, damaged 90-mm. gun of F Battery, 3d Defense Battalion. Bottom, fuel dump on fire.*

awaiting transshipment to the mainland.[11]

These attacks did not jeopardize the security of the beachhead but they were a costly nuisance. Of ninety air alerts in November, twenty-two resulted in bombings and strafings that killed twenty-four men and wounded ninety-six. In addition to the antiaircraft guns a few PV-1 night fighters from New Georgia defended against Kusaka's fliers. Though their losses were lighter than in daylight attacks, the Japanese lost several planes to the night fighters and the antiaircraft batteries.

So sure were the Japanese that Buka was an ultimate target that they continued to send reinforcements there. Late in November 920 soldiers on board three destroyers with two more escorting attempted to get to Buka. They were intercepted in the Solomon Sea during the night of 25 November by Captain Burke's destroyer squadron, which chased them from near Buka almost to Cape Saint George, the southern tip of New Ireland. Burke's ships sank three destroyers without receiving as much as one hit themselves. This action, the Battle of Cape Saint George, was the last of the night surface engagements which had characterized the Solomons campaigns since the one off Savo Island on 8 August 1942.[12]

In November and December at Empress Augusta Bay the indefatigable Japanese had begun to emplace artillery of calibers as high as 150-mm. on the high ground around the beachhead, especially in a group of hills that lay east of the Numa Numa–East-West Trails' junction and paralleled the west bank of the Torokina River. With these guns they shelled the beachhead, especially the airstrips and the supply dumps. The 3d Marine Division reacted by extending its lines to include the hills in a series of operations that lasted from 9 December through 27 December. One eminence, Hellzapoppin Ridge, was a natural fortress three hundred feet long, with sharp slopes and a narrow crest. It overlooked much of the beachhead and was an excellent site for artillery. Here the Japanese had constructed extensive positions on the reverse slopes using natural and artificial camouflage. The 21st Marines attacked Hellzapoppin Ridge but were driven off on 18 December. Several air strikes missed the narrow ridge completely. Finally, co-ordinated air (TBF's dropped 100-pound bombs with delay fuzes), artillery, and infantry attacks resulted in the capture of Hellzapoppin on Christmas Day. In the air strikes success was finally attained by marking the American front lines with colored smoke and designating the enemy targets with white phosphorus.

By 15 December the Americans held their final defensive line, a perimeter defense that extended on its inland side for about 22,500 yards. Over 44,000 men were present. Construction of the defense perimeter had begun in some sectors on 25 November, and by 15 December the work was complete. The line consisted of two-man foxholes, trenches, emplacements for automatic weapons,

---

[11] In the early hours of 20 November a Japanese plane scored a direct hit on one of the 90-mm. guns of F Battery, 3d Defense Battalion, on Puruata that killed five and wounded eight of the crew as well as knocking the gun out of commission and blowing up a fuel dump.

[12] For details see Morison, *Breaking the Bismarcks Barrier*, pp. 352–59.

105-MM. HOWITZER *of the 135th Field Artillery Battalion in action.*

mortars, antitank guns, and artillery, with alternate positions for all weapons. Fields of fire were cleared for 100 yards in front of the lines but all possible foliage was left in place overhead. The field artillery, grouped under command of General Kreber, was sited to fire in support of any threatened sector, and all weapons were registered and adjusted for every possible avenue of approach. All trails were blocked, and the approaches to the swamps were mined. Whenever possible machine guns were posted in commanding positions on high ground. The 4.2-inch chemical mortars were so sited and adjusted that they could place their fire directly in front of the infantry. The whole front was wired in behind two rows of either double-apron or concertina barbed wire, and the wire was full of trip wires and of cans hung up to rattle when an enemy approached the wire. Several antiaircraft searchlights were set up to illuminate the front at night, either directly or by throwing up widely spread beams that would be reflected down from the clouds. The defenses were formidable, and it would be some time before the Japanese got around to testing them thoroughly. Meanwhile life inside the perimeter promised to be relatively agreeable.

The XIV Corps Takes Over

The 3d Marine Division had borne the brunt of operations thus far, but it was not to be allowed to settle down in comfort behind its defenses. Admiral Halsey had other plans. The American and 40th Divisions had at first been scheduled for the projected assault against Kavieng, but Halsey now wanted the I Marine Amphibious Corps, consisting of the 3d Marine Division and the 40th Infantry Division, to conduct the operation. He proposed sending General Griswold's XIV Corps headquarters to Bougainville to relieve General Geiger's headquarters, and transferring the American Division from the Fijis to relieve the 3d Marine Division.[13] When Halsey first announced his plan on 2 November General Harmon opposed it, but Halsey overrode his objections.

Thus on 15 December General Griswold relieved General Geiger of command of all Allied air, surface, and ground forces based at Empress Augusta Bay and in the Treasuries. Admiral Halsey also made Harmon his informal

---

[13] The 40th was then in Hawaii due for shipment to the South Pacific.

deputy for supervising operations of the
XIV Corps. On Christmas Day came
the first troops of the Americal Division,
the 164th Regimental Combat Team.
Bidden farewell by one of the area's frequent earthquakes, the battle-weary 3d
Marines departed on the ships that had
carried the 164th. On 28 December General Hodge arrived and took over command of the eastern sector from Turnage, and the 182d Regimental Combat
Team prepared to take over from the
21st Marines. The 132d Regimental
Combat Team took over its part of the
line on 9 February, and five days later
the Americal's field artillery battalions,
the 221st, 245th, 246th, and 247th, began
relieving the 3d Division's artillery regiment, the 12th Marines.[14] The 3d Defense Battalion and several Marine air
squadrons remained at Empress Augusta
Bay.

With the Japanese quiescent in December except for intermittent air attacks at night, the immediate problems
facing Griswold were logistical rather
than tactical. The road net had to be
finished; a good road net would not

4.2-INCH CHEMICAL MORTAR *firing in
support of infantry troops.*

only improve the supply situation but
would give Griswold all the benefits of
interior lines if and when the Japanese
attacked in strength. The inland airfields had to be completed, beach congestion ended, more dumps and depots
established. General Griswold stated the
problem thus:

Puruata Island was so heavily loaded
down it was about to sink. All beaches were
congested. No long range supply road system had been planned. Long hand carry
was the rule, particularly in the Marine Division sector (later the Americal) for the
front line troops. Forward ration dumps,
ammunition and bomb dumps, gasoline
dumps, hospital areas and bomb shelters for
the same, beach developments, interior supply roads, the Service Command area itself,
a central cemetery, refrigeration, sawmills,
drainage ditches, and a myriad of other

[14] Total casualties for the I Marine Amphibious
Corps to 15 December were:
1. Empress Augusta Bay, 293 killed, 1,071 wounded, 95 missing, and 1,161 sick and evacuated. (The
relatively large figure for missing was due to the
McKean's sinking and the loss of many of her
passengers.)
2. Treasuries, 53 killed, 174 wounded, and 1
missing.
3. Choiseul, 7 killed, 14 wounded, 4 missing. In
addition I Marine Amphibious Corps lost several
men at the base depot in Vella Lavella to aerial
bombardment. Of the total casualties, the 3d Marine
Division lost the most—186 killed, 624 wounded.
The 37th Division suffered 10 wounded during the
period. All these figures are taken from a casualty
report in I Marine Amphibious Corps' report, Phase
III. The 3d Marine Division reported that it had
counted 2,100 dead Japanese.

LT. GEN. MILLARD F. HARMON, *center, and Maj. Gen. Oscar W. Griswold, second from left, are briefed by a Marine officer.*

things were non-existent, and not even visualized. Space for all these things had to be carved out of the virgin jungle.[15]

Griswold, characterized by Halsey as "a farsighted and capable planner," set to work with his staff.[16] Harmon's headquarters contributed greatly to the solution of the logistical problems by activating, in New Caledonia on 15 December, a Provisional Service Command for Bougainville. This organization, specifically tailored for the particular mission of supporting the XIV Corps, began its operations on Bougainville on 6 January 1944. By 31 January its strength was slightly more than two thousand men.

Logistical development under Griswold was extensive and orderly. By now the swamp had been drained. Malaria was kept rigidly under control. The volcanic ash of the region made adequate roads, but the heavy rainstorms that fell almost daily tended to wash them away. Road maintenance was therefore one of the most difficult logistic problems. By 1 March forty-three miles of two-way and thirty-six miles of one-way roads had been built. The troops also cleared several acres for gardens. The hot sun and frequent rains gave them fair returns, and fresh vegetables, normally a rarity in that part of the world, improved the otherwise almost unvarying diet of C and K rations and dehydrated foods.

---

[15] Ltr, Griswold to Barnett, CofS USAFISPA, 15 Feb 44, quoted in SOPACBACOM, The Bougainville Campaign, Ch. 5, p. 239, OCMH.

[16] Halsey, Narrative Account of the South Pacific Campaign, p. 11, OCMH.

Green vegetables grew fairly well, but tomatoes and corn did not.[17] There were frequent distributions of books, movies, performances by motion picture and radio personalities, sports, and occasionally beer and soft drinks. Empress Augusta Bay was about as pleasant a beachhead as one could hope for.

During the first two and a half months following Griswold's assumption of command there was no heavy fighting. There were not enough troops to hold all the high ground inland, but combat and reconnaissance patrols went out to the east, the north, and the west to keep tab on all the possible routes of Japanese approach. Airplanes also reconnoitered trails, and PT boats, water routes.

One of the outstanding patrols was conducted by the 1st Battalion of the Fiji Infantry Regiment, which arrived in late December. This battalion, composed of 34 officers (some white, some Fijian) and 777 enlisted Fijians, was at first commanded by Lt. Col. J. B. K. Taylor of New Zealand. But Taylor was wounded his first night ashore and was replaced by Maj. Geoffrey T. Upton, also of New Zealand.[18] A detachment of the Fiji battalion left the beachhead on 28 December and walked through the mountains over the Numa Numa Trail to the village of Ibu, east of the mountains, where they set up an outpost on 30 December. From Ibu these natural jungle fighters kept watch over enemy movements on the east coast so that no Japanese could advance unsuspected along the Numa Numa Trail. They reported to corps headquarters by radio and were supplied by air drops from C-47's. They also hacked an airstrip suitable for L-4 planes (Piper Cubs) on the 1,700-foot-high shelf that Ibu rests on.

But during December 1943 all ground operations were of minor importance when compared with the air operations against Rabaul that were conducted by South Pacific aircraft.

December Attacks Against Rabaul

Eight Seabee battalions and one New Zealand engineer brigade had begun work on a fighter strip at Cape Torokina promptly after D Day. Because the area was one of the few relatively dry patches of ground at Empress Augusta Bay, there was some competition among other units to occupy it, but the squatters were evicted and the builders were able to work unimpeded.[19] The strip was ready for operations on 9 December, and the next day seventeen F4U's of Marine Fighting Squadron 216 (I Marine Aircraft Wing) flew in and set up at their new base.

Starting in mid-November B-24's of the Thirteenth Air Force had begun bombing Rabaul every few days, but

---

[17] Ltr, Hon. Hugh M. Milton, II (former CofS, XIV Corps), to author, 13 Jul 56, OCMH. Exceptions to the unvarying diet were: turkey for Thanksgiving and Christmas, steak early in 1944, and fresh (cold storage) eggs on Easter Sunday.

[18] The Fijians added more color to the beachhead than did any other unit. Immaculate in appearance, they were nearly all men of extraordinary physical stature. They obviously liked soldiering and their marching was impressive in its precision. They sang well and often, their repertoire ranging from their native songs through "Onward Christian Soldiers" to "Pistol Packin' Mama" in Fijian.

[19] This section is based on Craven and Cate, The Pacific: Guadalcanal to Saipan, pp. 350–52; Morison, Breaking the Bismarcks Barrier, pp. 392–98; USSBS, The Allied Campaign Against Rabaul, passim. See also Sherrod, History of Marine Corps Aviation in World War II, pp. 193–97.

C–47 AIR-DROPPING SUPPLIES *on a partially completed airstrip.*

now, with its new forward fighter fields at Torokina and in the Treasuries, Air Command, Solomons, was ready to start an intensive series of operations with the purpose of completely neutralizing Rabaul.

The Solomons air command now had a new commander. Maj. Gen. Ralph J. Mitchell of the Marine Corps relieved General Twining on 20 November. Twining returned to the United States, then went to Italy where he commanded the Fifteenth Air Force.[20] The strength of General Mitchell's command was formidable, even after the intensive operations of October and November. He had, in operating condition on 17 December, 199 fighters, 200 light and medium bombers, and 99 heavy bomb-

ers, or about twice what the Japanese had in the entire Southeast Area.[21]

The first time the Torokina field was used against Rabaul was 17 December, when fighters from New Georgia staged through it on a 76-plane sweep. From then on it was almost continuously in use. For the rest of December, except when the weather was too bad for flying, Mitchell continued the attacks, varying fighter sweeps with fighter-escorted raids by B–24's.[22]

But Mitchell's heavy bomber pilots,

---

[20] In the closing days of the war, Twining led the Twentieth Air Force.

[21] Total strength of Mitchell's command, including nonoperational planes, was 268 fighters, 252 light and medium bombers, and 111 heavy bombers.

[22] On Christmas Day Halsey sent a carrier raid against Kavieng. He ordered a surface bombardment of Buka in order to lure out enemy aircraft, whereupon Admiral Sherman's two carriers (*Bunker Hill* and *Monterey*) struck Kavieng soon after sunrise. But Sherman's pilots found few targets.

like Kenney's, were unable to knock out Rabaul, and toward the end of the year the Japanese sent in more planes. Medium, dive, and torpedo bombers would have to be used, and their employment would have to await completion of the strips near the Piva River. The first of these, termed Piva U or Piva Uncle, was started on 29 November and completed on 30 December. The second, Piva Yoke, was ready on 9 January 1944.[23]

---

[23] These dates are taken from *Building the Navy's Bases in World War II*, pp. 270–72.

It was clear that the reduction of Rabaul would not occur until 1944. Kenney's and Mitchell's attacks in 1943, however, were quite effective, if not completely successful. They caused enough damage to make the Japanese garrison start wholesale excavation in November in an effort to put everything possible under ground and so escape complete destruction.

Meanwhile, under partial cover of the invasion of Bougainville and Mitchell's attacks on Rabaul, General MacArthur's forces had crossed Vitiaz and Dampier Straits to invade New Britain.

CHAPTER XIV

Crossing the Straits

Plans and Preparations

By November 1943 CARTWHEEL was rolling along rapidly and smoothly. In just over five months Nassau Bay, Woodlark, Kiriwina, New Georgia, Vella Lavella, Salamaua, Nadzab, Lae, the Markham Valley, Finschhafen, the Treasuries, and Empress Augusta Bay had fallen to the Allies. At the newly won bases airfields were either in operation or under construction. Allied planes dominated the skies all the way to Rabaul, and Allied ships sailed the Solomon Sea and the Huon Gulf in comparative safety.

The capture of Finschhafen in Operation II was a step toward control of the straits between New Guinea and New Britain, a control that would help make possible the drive toward the Vogelkop Peninsula and the Philippines in 1944 and would be essential to any amphibious advance against Rabaul. The Southwest Pacific's next move (Operation III of ELKTON III) was first planned by GHQ on the assumption that Rabaul would be captured. Looking eastward rather than westward from the Huon Peninsula, it aimed at the establishment of air forces at Cape Gloucester on western New Britain and of PT boat bases on the south coast of New Britain. (*See Map 12.*) These were to increase Allied control over Rabaul and over Kavieng and Manus in the Admiralties, and to provide bases on the north side of the straits to insure the safe passage of convoys.

Selecting Targets

GHQ's orders for the operation, given the code name DEXTERITY, were published on 22 September.[1] They directed General Krueger's ALAMO Force, formerly the New Britain Force, supported by Allied Air and Allied Naval Forces, and by U.S. Army Services of Supply, Southwest Pacific, to seize Cape Gloucester by airborne and amphibious invasions and to neutralize the forward Japanese base at Gasmata on southern New Britain, to gain control over western New Britain as far east as the line Gasmata–Talasea, and to capture Vitu and Long Islands beyond the straits. General Blamey's New Guinea Force would meanwhile continue its operations in the Huon Peninsula and the valleys. Gasmata was to be neutralized by troops who would land at nearby Lindenhafen Plantation, establish an emergency airfield, and advance on Gasmata in a shore-to-shore movement. The

[1] GHQ SWPA OI 38, 22 Sep 43, and amendments, in GHQ SWPA G–3 Jnl, 22 Sep 43.

plan directed Krueger to prepare to participate with South Pacific forces in the capture of Rabaul but this order was canceled on 10 November.[2] Saidor was not specifically mentioned, although both MacArthur and Chamberlin had suggested it as a target earlier in the month.

D Day for the invasion of Cape Gloucester was initially set for 20 November but was postponed twice. The final date was 26 December.

This plan provoked a good deal of disagreement. The first to protest was General Kenney. With the decision to bypass Rabaul obviously in mind, he presented his objections to General MacArthur on 10 October. The original concept, he argued, called for an encircling ring of air bases, including Cape Gloucester, to be established around Rabaul in order to lay siege to it. But now that "faster action is contemplated" it would take too long to develop Gloucester into a useful air base. It would not be necessary to take either Gloucester or Lindenhafen, he told MacArthur: bases at Dobodura, Nadzab, and Kiriwina, plus the one at Finschhafen and perhaps a new one at Saidor, could provide support for invasions as far away as Kavieng.[3] In speaking of faster action, Kenney apparently was referring to the long-range plan RENO III, which was then being prepared. It called for completion of the

CARTWHEEL operations and then the move toward the Philippines, according to the following schedule: Hansa Bay, 1 February 1944; Kavieng (by the South Pacific), 1 March 1944; Admiralties, 1 March 1944; neutralization of Rabaul and perhaps, later, its occupation; Humboldt Bay and Arafura Sea, 1 June 1944; Geelvink Bay–Vogelkop Peninsula, 15 August–1 October, 1944; Halmahera, Amboina, the Palaus, 1 December 1944; Mindanao, 1 February 1945.

General Chamberlin, MacArthur's G–3, observed that the air general's plan differed from MacArthur's present plans.[4] There would be time, he asserted, to complete airdromes at Gloucester before undertaking the next operations. While he did not state that the Kavieng invasion could not be supported without Gloucester, he pointed out several advantages to be derived from the move to New Britain:

1. The Allies could better control Vitiaz Strait. (Here he reversed himself on the position he had taken on the point the month before.) Control from one side would be possible but it would be dangerous to leave the other side in Japanese hands.

2. Cape Gloucester would provide better support for the Kavieng and Admiralties attacks provided for in RENO III.

3. Cape Gloucester would provide better cover for convoys moving through Vitiaz Strait against the Admiralties. Even assuming the bypassing of Rabaul, Chamberlin concluded, a point on the south coast of New Britain would be needed to control Vitiaz Strait, neutralize

---

[2] GHQ SWPA OI 38/12, 10 Nov 43. Apparently there was a strategic lag at GHQ so that the impact of the Joint Chiefs' order to bypass Rabaul was not fully reflected at once in orders prepared by the GHQ staff.

[3] Ltr, Kenney to CINCSWPA, 10 Oct 43, sub: GHQ OI 38, 22 Sep 43, in GHQ SWPA G–3 Jnl, 11 Oct 43; Kenney, *General Kenney Reports*, pp. 326–27; General Kenney's comments on draft MS of this volume, OCMH.

[4] Chamberlin must also have been referring to RENO III.

Gasmata, and provide an emergency airfield for planes attacking Rabaul.[5]

Admirals Carpender and Barbey also seem to have favored holding both sides of the straits, as did General Krueger. The admirals did not favor the seizure of Gasmata, because they felt it would mean a reckless exposure of ships to Rabaul-based aircraft.[6]

Kenney was informed that MacArthur's plans, which encompassed the bypassing of Rabaul, required Cape Gloucester and Lindenhafen.[7] But Kenney's argument, coupled with the admirals' and added to the facts that Gasmata was swampy and that the Japanese were known to be sending more troops there, did have some effect. One month later MacArthur canceled Gasmata operations and directed the ALAMO Force to seize Cape Gloucester and to establish control over adjacent islands and "minimum portions" of western New Britain with the purpose of protecting Cape Gloucester.[8]

The matter did not end there. It was finally settled by a conference at GHQ in Brisbane on 21 November attended by Kenney, Carpender, and Barbey. The naval commanders opposed Gasmata and are reported to have wanted a PT boat base elsewhere on New Britain's south coast. Therefore Arawe, the name of a peninsula, a harbor, and an island west of Gasmata which had been listed as an objective in ELKTON III, was substituted for Gasmata with the intention of using it as a PT base and in the hope of diverting the enemy's attention from Cape Gloucester. Arawe had a fair anchorage and there were only a few Japanese in the area. General Kenney assured his fellow commanders that he could give better air cover to Arawe than to Gasmata. Cape Gloucester remained the main objective.[9] As the same ships had to be used for both invasions, the dates were staggered.

Setting Dates

The first dates selected, 14 November for Lindenhafen and 20 November for Cape Gloucester, proved impossible to meet and had to be postponed. The process of postponement and selection of new dates clearly illustrates some of the controlling factors in Southwest Pacific amphibious operations.

By 26 October Kenney, Sutherland, and Chamberlin realized that enough air cover would not be available to meet the first target dates. The Finschhafen airstrip would not be completed until about 5 December. Construction of the Lae–Nadzab road had fallen behind

[5] Memo, ACofS G–3 GHQ SWPA for CofS GHQ SWPA, 11 Oct 43, sub: Comments on Ltr From Comdr AAF, 10 Oct 43, in GHQ SWPA G–3 Jnl, 11 Oct 43; Craven and Cate, *The Pacific: Guadalcanal to Saipan,* pp. 330–31.

[6] Ltr, Adm Barbey to Gen Smith, Chief of Mil Hist, 20 Nov 53, no sub, OCMH.

[7] Ltr, GHQ SWPA to Comdr AAF, 16 Oct 43, sub: GHQ OI 38, in GHQ SWPA G–3 Jnl, 16 Oct 43.

[8] GHQ SWPA OI 38/12, 10 Nov 43. General Whitehead also disliked both Gasmata and Cape Gloucester. See his letter to Kenney, 11 November 1943, quoted in Craven and Cate, *The Pacific: Guadalcanal to Saipan,* pp. 329–30.

[9] Memo, SJC [Chamberlin] for MacArthur, 21 Nov 43, sub: Practicality of Establishing PT Base S Coast Western New Britain, in GHQ SWPA G–3 Jnl, 21 Nov 43; GHQ OI 38/15, 22 Nov 43; Ltr, Gen Krueger to Gen Smith, Chief of Mil Hist, 31 Oct 53, no sub, OCMH. For conflicting accounts see Kenney, *General Kenney Reports,* pp. 326–27, and Morison, *Breaking the Bismarcks Barrier,* p. 372. After the war Barbey expressed the view that the PT base was never an important factor.

schedule and it could not take heavy vehicles and machinery before 1 December; consequently the three airstrips in the lower Markham Valley would not be in shape to maintain air operations before 15 December. The VII Amphibious Force, which would carry the assault troops in DEXTERITY, could not be released from its responsibilities for supplying Lae and Finschhafen for some time. It was estimated that from 135,000 to 150,000 more tons of supplies would have to be sent to Lae, 60,000 to 70,000 more to Finschhafen, in order to support air operations. Shipments to Nadzab were slowed by the lack of enough men and docks at Lae, and movement of supplies to Finschhafen was slowed by the fact that until the airfield was finished the naval commanders would not risk sending heavy ships there.

Southwest Pacific invasions usually took place during the dark of the moon to help hide ships from nocturnal raiding planes. The last-quarter moon would come on 19 November, the first-quarter moon on 4 December. If the attack could not be mounted before 4 December it would have to be put off until after 19 December, the date of the next last-quarter moon. But this was the period of the northwest monsoon, and the longer the Southwest Pacific waited for ideal moon conditions the rougher would be the surf at Cape Gloucester. Chamberlin therefore recommended that DEXTERITY be put off until the earliest possible date in December, that the VII Amphibious Force keep on supplying Lae and Finschhafen a while longer, and that two engineer aviation battalions that were scheduled for Cape Gloucester be set to work at Lae and

Finschhafen for the time being.[10] MacArthur, accepting these recommendations, announced that he would delay the attack about fifteen days, and that the VII Amphibious Force would supply Lae and Finschhafen until about 20 November.[11]

This decision provoked the quiet, undramatic General Krueger to protest that the resulting schedule would be too tight. MacArthur's order meant that Gloucester would have to be invaded on 4 December. The subsidiary operation would have to be accomplished on 28 November. Since there was no reserve shipping, any losses on 28 November would hamper the main landing. Further, the VII Amphibious Force, once relieved at Lae and Finschhafen, could not be expected to get to Milne Bay until 26 or 27 November. Thus there would hardly be time for rehearsals. Krueger, asking for more ships or for more time, suggested that the first operation take place on 2 December, Gloucester on the 26th.[12] MacArthur agreed to another postponement and eventually set Z Day for Arawe at 15 December, D Day for Gloucester at 26 December.[13]

ALAMO Force Plans

Originally assigned to ALAMO Force for DEXTERITY were the 1st Marine Division; the 32d Division; the 632d Tank

[10] Memo, Chamberlin for CofS GHQ SWPA, 26 Oct 43, sub: Data of Attack on New Britain, in GHQ SWPA G–3 Jnl, 26 Oct 43.
[11] Rad, MacArthur to Comdrs NGF, ALAMO, et al., 28 Oct 43, in GHQ SWPA G–3 Jnl, 28 Oct 43.
[12] Ltr, Krueger to MacArthur, 12 Nov 43, no sub, in GHQ SWPA G–3 Jnl, 14 Nov 43.
[13] GHQ SWPA OI 38/17, 3 Dec 43; GHQ SWPA OI 38/18, 16 Dec 43.

Destroyer Battalion; the 503d Parachute Infantry Regiment, for Cape Gloucester only; and a number of quartermaster, medical, signal, engineer, and antiaircraft units. The 1st Cavalry and 24th Infantry Divisions, then in Australia but soon to move to New Guinea, and the 503d Parachute Infantry (which would be committed at Cape Gloucester) constituted GHQ's reserve. The 1st Marine and 32d Divisions moved from Australia to the forward area shortly before the invasions.[14]

As usual, MacArthur gave Krueger responsibility for co-ordinating the plans of supporting air and naval forces with those of the ALAMO Force. In contrast with the system of unity of command over all elements of an invasion force that prevailed in the South Pacific, the commander in chief specifically directed that Allied Air and Naval Forces would operate under GHQ through their respective commanders and exempted them from control by ALAMO or New Guinea Forces. However, if the Japanese attacked in any area the senior local commander was to control all Southwest Pacific forces in the threatened area.

General Krueger and the ALAMO Force staff had been planning for DEXTERITY since August.[15] In the beginning ALAMO headquarters was at Milne Bay, where it had been established at the opening of the CARTWHEEL offensives.

On 21 October Krueger moved it to Goodenough Island.[16]

During the planning period for DEXTERITY the Japanese were strengthening their garrisons in western New Britain in accordance with the orders issued by Imamura in September. Thus Allied estimates of Japanese strength in the area rose from 500 before September to 2,500 on the 26th. In December Krueger placed enemy strength at between 5,668 and 9,344, with the strongest concentration at Cape Gloucester. The 1st Marine Division, apparently deriving its information from the same sources as ALAMO Force, arrived at a higher figure—between 8,400 and 12,076.[17]

Little was known about the terrain of western New Britain, and Krueger ordered ground reconnaissance in addition to the extensive air photography that was undertaken by Allied Air Forces. Because PT boats were not allowed to operate off New Britain's north coast no patrols were able to examine Borgen Bay, where the main Cape Gloucester landings were to take place. Marine patrols landed from PT boats and reconnoitered the area south of Cape Gloucester from 24 September through

---

[14] The 32d Division went to Milne Bay and Goodenough, the 1st Division to Milne Bay, Oro Bay, and Goodenough.

[15] ELKTON III had provided for the invasion of Cape Gloucester, Arawe, and Gasmata, and in August and September GHQ had prepared general plans and specific orders that were superseded by RENO III and OI 38. See GHQ's MARFA Plans in ALAMO Force G–3 Jnl DEXTERITY No. 1.

[16] Sixth Army headquarters remained at Camp Columbia near Brisbane until 2 February 1944 when it moved to Cape Cretin on the southeast corner of the Huon Peninsula. ALAMO headquarters had moved from Goodenough to the cape on 24 December to be near the scene of operations. The advance echelon of GHQ remained at Port Moresby.

[17] ALAMO Force Rpt, DEXTERITY Opn, 15 Dec 43–10 Feb 44, and Incls, 17 May 44; ALAMO G–2 Periodic Rpt 18, 9 Dec 43, in ALAMO Force G–3 Jnl DEXTERITY No. 6; 1st Mar Div Order of Battle and Strength Est, New Britain, 13 Dec 43, in ALAMO Force G–3 Jnl DEXTERITY No. 7. The order of battle lists were nearly correct except that the Allies did not know that the *17th Division* was moving from Rabaul to western New Britain.

21 December in a series of patrols. A group of ALAMO Scouts, an informal reconnaissance organization operating directly under General Krueger, reconnoitered Gasmata from 6 through 27 October. On the night of 9–10 December one American officer and five natives disembarked from a PT boat east of Arawe, scouted the area, and concluded there were only a few Japanese present.[18]

More information was obtained from aerial photography. Missions were flown almost daily so that ALAMO and subordinate headquarters could be kept informed of gun positions, beach defenses, bridges, and trails. The VII Amphibious Force used air photos as the basis for its hydrographic charts, and the 1st Marine Division used them to pick the landing beaches.[19]

Krueger's first tactical plans, prepared in accordance with GHQ's orders, had called for the heavily reinforced 126th Regimental Combat Team, under Brig. Gen. Clarence A. Martin, of the 32d Division, to take Gasmata. Cape Gloucester was to have been captured by the BACKHANDER Task Force under Maj. Gen. William H. Rupertus, commander of the 1st Marine Division. The assault force was to have consisted of one regimental combat and one battalion landing team of Rupertus' division, the 503d Parachute Infantry Regiment, and the 12th Marine Defense Battalion. The marines were to have delivered an amphibious assault, coupled with a parachute jump by the 503d.[20] But this whole plan was drastically revised.

When on 22 November General MacArthur substituted Arawe for Gasmata, Krueger decided to use a smaller force than the 126th. He correctly believed Arawe to be weakly defended. For Arawe he formed the DIRECTOR Task Force under Brig. Gen. Julian W. Cunningham, who as a colonel had led the invasion of Woodlark. Its assault units included Col. Alexander M. Miller's two-squadron 112th Cavalry; the 148th Field Artillery Battalion; the 59th Engineer Company; Headquarters and Headquarters Battery, 236th Antiaircraft Artillery (Searchlight) Battalion; and C and D Batteries, 470th Antiaircraft Artillery (Automatic Weapons) Battalion. In reserve was the 2d Battalion, 158th Infantry. Supporting garrison units, to be moved to Arawe after 15 December (Z Day), consisted of several engineer, medical, ordnance, and other service detachments. All these units had been attached to the ALAMO Force for the invasion of the Trobriands in June, and were still occupying the islands.

The concept of the Cape Gloucester invasion was changed also; the parachute jump was canceled and the 503d removed from the troop list. Several factors contributed to this change. General Krueger's headquarters had never liked the idea. General Rupertus, too, had op-

[18] The patrols on western New Britain included Maj. John V. Mather, Australian Army; Sub-Lt. Andrew Kirkwell-Smith, a coastwatcher in the Australian Navy; and Sub-Lt. William G. Wiedeman, also of the Australian Navy but before the war a Church of England missionary at Sag Sag on western New Britain.

[19] ALAMO Force Rpt, DEXTERITY Opn; Craven and Cate, *The Pacific: Guadalcanal to Saipan*, p. 332.

[20] In reserve was Maj. Gen. William H. Gill's 32d Division less the 126th Regimental Combat Team. General Chamberlin doubted the wisdom of using the 503d as no suitable drop zone was to be found. ALAMO Force Rpt, DEXTERITY Opn; ALAMO Plan of Opn, DEXTERITY, 28 Sep 43, in GHQ SWPA G–3 Jnl, 28 Sep 43; Memo, ACofS G–3 GHQ SWPA for CofS GHQ SWPA, 10 Oct 43, sub: Plan of Opns DEXTERITY Submitted by ALAMO Force, same file.

posed the parachute jump from the start. He pointed out that bad weather, which had prevented several air attacks against Rabaul, might interfere with the parachute jump and thus deprive him of a substantial part of his assault force.[21] General Kenney's headquarters, in December, added its opposition. First, although ALAMO Force orders did not specify exactly how the jump was to be accomplished, it was understood at Allied Air Forces headquarters that a piecemeal and therefore dangerous drop was planned. Second, it seemed that the jump would be under way about the time that Japanese planes might be expected to turn up. Asking if the jump was necessary, Kenney's operations officer stated emphatically that the air commander wanted "no part" of it.[22]

General Rupertus' headquarters had disliked the whole scheme of maneuver as prescribed by ALAMO headquarters, as well as the parachute jump. ALAMO's first plans called for simultaneous, separated landings by two small forces, which were to converge on the airfield at Cape Gloucester in conjunction with the 503d's jump. But the 1st Marine Division, which had had ample experience with jungle warfare on Guadalcanal, felt that this plan was unsound because the rough and scarcely known terrain could easily delay either or both of the marching forces. Also, the Japanese could be expected to outnumber any one of the three landing forces. When Generals MacArthur and Krueger visited 1st

Marine Division headquarters at Goodenough on 14 December, Col. Edwin A. Pollock, divisional operations officer, frankly expressed the marines' objections to the parachute jump and the scheme of maneuver.

Krueger had included the parachute jump because MacArthur's headquarters had assigned the 503d Parachute Infantry to the operation, and he considered himself under orders to make his plans fit the forces assigned.[23] MacArthur, Krueger, and Kenney now discussed the matter further. It developed that Dobodura would not support the mounting of the 503d as well as all the planned bomber operations. To use the 503d would require moving one heavy bomber group from Dobodura to Port Moresby, and bad weather over the Owen Stanleys might keep the bomber group out of action. The jump was canceled.

ALAMO Force further revised its tactical plans for taking Cape Gloucester to meet the 1st Marine Division's objections. Final plans called for one regimental combat team to land on two beaches on the north coast of New Britain between Silimati Point in Borgen Bay and the airfield at Cape Gloucester, while a second (less a battalion landing team) landed immediately behind, passed through the first, and attacked toward Cape Gloucester to the airfields. One battalion landing team was to land near Tauali on the west coast of New Britain to block the coastal trail

---

[21] Memo, CG BACKHANDER TF for CG ALAMO, 3 Nov 43, no sub, in ALAMO Force G–3 Jnl DEXTERITY No. 3.

[22] Check Sheet, Dir Opns AAF for G–3 GHQ SWPA, 8 Dec 43, in GHQ SWPA G–3 Jnl, 8 Dec 43.

[23] Lt. Col. Frank O. Hough, USMCR, and Maj. John A. Crown, USMCR, *The Campaign on New Britain* (Washington, 1952), p. 19; Gen Krueger's comments on the draft MS of this volume, attached to his ltr to Maj Gen A. C. Smith, Chief Mil Hist, 31 Oct 53, no sub, OCMH.

and prevent reinforcement of the airdrome area from the south or retreat of the airdrome garrison to the south.

The assault units of Rupertus' BACKHANDER Task Force were two regimental combat teams of the 1st Marine Division; the 12th Marine Defense Battalion less its 155-mm. gun group; detachments, including LCM's and LCVP's, of the 2d Engineer Special Brigade; and the 913th Engineer Aviation Battalion. The reserve, supporting, and garrison units included the remainder of the 1st Marine Division, the 155-mm. gun group of the 12th Defense Battalion, and a large number of engineer, medical, quartermaster, and malaria control units, chiefly of the Army.

The Arawe (DIRECTOR) forces were to mount the invasion at Goodenough, the Gloucester (BACKHANDER) forces through Oro Bay, Goodenough, and Milne Bay. In ALAMO reserve was the 32d Division.[24]

Logistical plans called for the U.S. Army Services of Supply, Southwest Pacific Area, now commanded by Maj. Gen. James L. Frink, to establish and maintain at New Guinea bases sixty days' supply of all types except chemical and Air Force.[25] Thirty days' of the last two classes were to be maintained. Frink's command was to make building materials for ports and air bases available to the ALAMO Force by Z plus 5 and D plus 5, and was to furnish naval forces with supplies common to the Army and Navy pending establishment of the naval supply system, or in emergencies. The VII Amphibious Force would of course transport supplies to the beachheads until they were secured and Frink was ready to take over. Allied Air Forces was to transport supplies to the ground troops in emergencies.

All units in the task forces were to be stripped of equipment not needed for their combat missions. They would carry to Arawe and Cape Gloucester in the assault echelons thirty days' supply and three units of fire, which would be built up by succeeding shipments to sixty days' supply and six units of fire (ten for antiaircraft). Oro Bay was the main supply base, Milne Bay the secondary.[26] Cape Cretin, near Finschhafen on the southeast corner of the Huon Peninsula, which the ALAMO Force was preparing as a supply point and staging base, was to serve for resupply.

Krueger, on receiving data on Allied Air Forces' requirements, directed the BACKHANDER Task Force to build a small strip at Cape Gloucester for air supply at once, a 100-by-5,000-foot runway by D plus 10; a second 100-by-5,000-foot runway, capable of expansion to 6,000 feet, by D plus 30; and also overruns, parallel taxiways, roads, and airdrome facilities.[27]

---

[24] See ALAMO Force, Rpt, DEXTERITY Opn; ALAMO FO 5, and annexes, 30 Nov 43, in ALAMO Force G-3 Jnl DEXTERITY No. 5; Amendment 1 to ALAMO FO 5, 15 Dec 43, in ALAMO Force G-3 Jnl DEXTERITY No. 7; Craven and Cate, *The Pacific: Guadalcanal to Saipan*, p. 331; Hough and Crown, *The Campaign on New Britain*, p. 19. See also ACofS G-3 ALAMO, Revised G-3 Study, Gloucester, 2 Dec 43, in ALAMO Force G-3 Jnl DEXTERITY No. 5.

[25] General Marshall was Deputy Chief of Staff, GHQ.

[26] GHQ SWPA OI 38, 22 Sep 43, in GHQ SWPA G-3 Jnl, 22 Sep 43; ALAMO Administrative Order 4, 30 Nov 43, in ALAMO Force G-3 Jnl DEXTERITY No. 5.

[27] Appendix 4, Annex 4, Engr, to ALAMO FO 5, 17 Dec 43, in ALAMO Force G-3 Jnl DEXTERITY No. 8.

The Enemy

When the Allies landed on Cape Gloucester General Imamura could not have been surprised. He had anticipated such a move some time before. In October the *8th Area Army* staff had concluded that two lines of action were open to the Allies: capture of the New Britain side of the straits, invasion of Bougainville, and a direct assault upon Rabaul in February or March 1944; or the slower process of isolating Rabaul by seizing the Admiralties and Kavieng.[28] Considering the first course the more likely, he decided to send more troops to western New Britain in addition to those he had sent under General Matsuda in September. He would have liked to reinforce the Admiralties and Kavieng but felt he could not spare any more troops from the defenses of Rabaul.

Imamura therefore ordered the *17th Division,* less the battalions dispatched to Bougainville, to western New Britain. Reaching Rabaul from China between 4 October and 12 November, the *17th* went by echelons to its new posts by naval vessel and small boat. The movement began in October but was still under way in mid-December.

The *17th Division* commander was given operational control of the units already there, chiefly General Matsuda's *65th Brigade* and *4th Shipping Group* at Cape Gloucester and *2d Battalion, 228th Infantry,* and two naval guard

companies at Gasmata.[29] Final plans organized the entire force into three commands. The first and largest, under Matsuda, consisted of the *65th Brigade* (principally the *141st Infantry*), the *4th Shipping Group,* and a large number of field artillery, antiaircraft, automatic weapons, engineer, and communications units. Matsuda was charged with defense of the area from the emergency airstrip and barge staging point near Tuluvu around the coast to Cape Busching on the south. Under Matsuda Maj. Masamitsu Komori, with most of the *1st Battalion, 81st Infantry,* one company of the *54th Infantry,* and engineers plus detachments, was assigned responsibility for defense of Arawe. Col. Shuhei Hirashima, commanding the *54th Infantry,* less the *2d Battalion,* the *2d Battalion, 228th Infantry,* the *2d Battalion, 23d Field Artillery Regiment,* and the naval guard companies, was to hold the airfield at Gasmata.[30] The *17th Division* established its command post at Gavuvu, east of the Willaumez Peninsula and a long distance from the scene of operations.

The air strength available to the Japanese for the forthcoming fight had been reduced, not only by the Allied air attacks against Rabaul, but also by orders from Tokyo. The *2d Area Army* was established in the Netherlands Indies on 1 December 1943, and the boundary between it and Imamura's *8th Area Army* was set at longitude 140° east. But the

---

[28] This subsection is based on 8th Area Army Operations, Japanese Monogr No. 110 (OCMH), pp. 85–119; Southeast Area Air Operations, 1942–44, Japanese Monogr No. 38 (OCMH), pp. 25–29; Southeast Area Naval Operations, III, Japanese Monogr No. 50 (OCMH), pp. 36–39; 17th Division Operations in Western New Britain, Japanese Monogr No. 111 (OCMH), pp. 1–7.

[29] The *65th Brigade* had played an important part in the fighting on Luzon in the first Philippines campaign. See Morton, *The Fall of the Philippines.*

[30] A false report from natives in October that the Allies had landed east of Gasmata had caused the dispatch of the naval companies to Gasmata.

B–25's Over Wewak. *Three damaged enemy planes are visible on the ground.*

7th Air Division was transferred out of the *4th Air Army* and assigned to the *2d Area Army*.[31] This transfer seriously reduced Imamura's forces, but so far the *7th Air Division* had not operated effectively. Its most outstanding exploit had been the loss of planes on the ground at Wewak.

Air Operations

With the new fields in the Markham Valley and at Finschhafen in operation, Allied Air Forces' aerial preparations for DEXTERITY were the most extensive yet seen in the Southwest Pacific.[32] They included, besides daily P–38 photographic missions, long-range search missions by PBY's of the Seventh Fleet's Patrol Wing 10, RAAF Catalinas, and Fifth Air Force B–24's, and bombing and strafing.

Air attacks, which had been under way against New Britain since October, began on a large scale in late November. Cape Gloucester and Gasmata were the main targets. Arawe was avoided until 14 December in order to keep from warning the Japanese. During December Kenney's planes attacked Gasmata or Gloucester, or both, nearly every day and sometimes twice a day. As General Whitehead said, Cape Gloucester was "tailor made" for air operations. The target area lay along the beach and was long and narrow.[33] During December Kenney's planes flew 1,845 sorties over

Gloucester, dropped 3,926 tons of bombs, and fired 2,095,488 rounds of machine gun ammunition. The chief targets were Tuluvu airfield, antiaircraft guns, supply dumps, and the barge staging points. The airfield was knocked out of action early in the operation and stayed that way.

Arawe

Preliminaries

The 112th Cavalry, shipped aboard LST's, reached Goodenough Island from Woodlark on 1 and 2 December.[34] There General Cunningham gave Colonel Miller detailed orders for the landing of his regiment at Arawe on 15 December.

Arawe, which before the war had been a regular port of call for vessels of the

---

[31] Smith, *The Approach to the Philippines*, Ch. IV.

[32] This subsection is based on Craven and Cate, *The Pacific: Guadalcanal to Saipan*, pp. 332–38.

[33] Memo, Lt Col Paul Weyrauch, Asst Arty Off ALAMO, and Lt Col Carl A. Fields, Air Off ALAMO, for CofS ALAMO, 10 Nov 43, no sub, in ALAMO Force G–3 Jnl DEXTERITY No. 3.

[34] This section is based on Ltr, Comdr VII Amphib Force to COMINCH, 10 Jan 44, sub: Arawe Opn, and incls, in GHQ SWPA G–3 Jnl, 10 Jan 44; ALAMO Force Rpt, DEXTERITY Opn, and Incl 1, Lessons Learned; DIRECTOR TF, Hist Rpt, Arawe [in form of ltr, Gen Cunningham to CG Sixth Army, 6 June 44]; 112th Cav, Hist Rpt [Arawe], 24 Nov 43–10 Feb 44; 8th Area Army Operations, Japanese Monogr No. 110 (OCMH), pp. 119–22; 17th Division Operations in Western New Britain, Japanese Monogr No. 111 (OCMH), pp. 8–14; Southeast Area Air Operations, Japanese Monogr No. 38 (OCMH), pp. 29–30; Memo, Capt Joseph H. Baker for CO 592d Engr Boat and Shore Regt, 18 Dec 43, no sub, in ALAMO Force G–3 Jnl DEXTERITY No. 9; ALAMO Fragmentary FO's 1 and 2, 27 Dec 43, in ALAMO Force G–3 Jnl DEXTERITY No. 11; Capt T. H. Baker, USMC, Rpt Amphib Tractor Opn Arawe, 27 Dec 43, in ALAMO Force G–3 Jnl DEXTERITY No. 12; Ltr, Gen Cunningham to CG ALAMO, 6 Jan 44, sub: Opns DIRECTOR TF, in ALAMO Force G–3 Jnl DEXTERITY No. 15; Ltr, CG 2d ESB to CTF 76, 16 Dec 43, sub: Rpt Arawe Landing, and Log of Events as Seen From SC 742, both in ALAMO Force G–3 Jnl DEXTERITY No. 8; CTF 76 Opn Plan A3–43, 10 Dec 43, and Memo, JWC [Cunningham] for Gen Krueger, 18 Dec 43, no sub, and 2d ESB FO 1, 11 Dec 43, all in ALAMO Force G–3 Jnl DEXTERITY No. 7; G–2 ALAMO Ter-

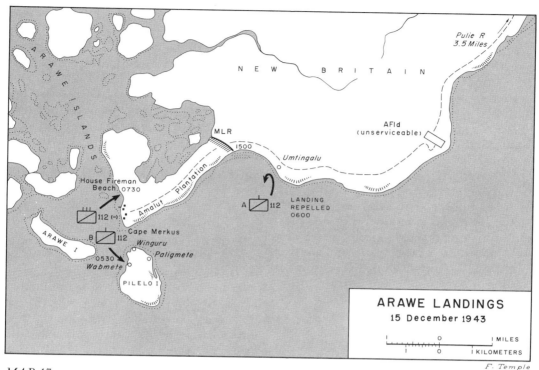

MAP 17

F. Temple

Burns-Philp South Seas Company, had a harbor suitable for large vessels. There were several beaches that landing craft could use, of which the two best were House Fireman on the west coast of the boot-shaped Arawe peninsula and the village of Umtingalu on the mainland, seventeen hundred yards east of the peninsula's base. The rest of the coast line consisted of stone cliffs about two hundred feet high, interspersed with low ground that was covered by mangrove swamp. Reefs fringed all the beaches, and it was clear that LCVP's could not get to the shore until detailed reconnaissance for passages was made. (*Map 17*) Therefore General Krueger arranged with Rupertus for one company of the 1st Marine Amphibian Tractor Battalion to be attached to the DIRECTOR Task Force to take the assault waves ashore. Krueger also attached part of the 592d Engineer Boat and Shore Regiment, 2d Engineer Special Brigade, with 17 LCVP's, 9 LCM's, 2 rocket-firing

rain Rpt, Arawe, 26 Nov 43, and Ltr, Hq ALAMO to CG BACKHANDER TF, 30 Nov 43, no sub, and DIRECTOR TF FO 1, 4 Dec 43, and Memo, DAA [Maj D. A. Alberti, ALAMO G–3 Sec] for G–3 ALAMO, 8 Dec 43, sub: Observation DIRECTOR Exercise, all in ALAMO Force G–3 Jnl DEXTERITY No. 5; Off of Chief Engr, GHQ AFPAC, *Critique*, pp. 109–17; Craven and Cate, *The Pacific: Guadalcanal to Saipan*, p. 335; Hough and Crown, *The Campaign on New Britain*, pp. 140–52; Isely and Crowl, *The U.S. Marines and Amphibious War*, pp. 186–88; Morison, *Breaking the Bismarcks Barrier*, pp. 373–77.

DUKW's, and 1 repair and salvage boat, to Task Force 76 for the landings.[35]

The 112th Cavalry stayed on Goodenough for ten days. During this period the troops received additional practice and training with all their weapons, including two new ones—the flame thrower and the 2.36-inch rocket launcher (bazooka). Before shoving off all men were informed of the general plan of attack and given aerial photographs and maps to study. The training period was topped by two landings. The first was intended to familiarize the troops with loading and unloading landing craft. The second was conducted under assumed combat conditions and involved the co-ordinated landing of all elements at proper intervals and their tactical deployment ashore. General Cunningham forcefully pointed out several major deficiencies. Units were not always under control of their commanders, intervals between landing waves were too long, and not all junior officers and noncommissioned officers knew their duties.

With Generals MacArthur and Krueger looking on, the DIRECTOR Task Force boarded the LSD Carter Hall, HMAS Westralia, and the APD's Sands and Humphreys on the afternoon of 13 December.[36] At midnight the ships departed for Buna, where General Cunningham left the Carter Hall and joined Admiral Barbey aboard the destroyer Conyngham, the flagship. The voyage to the target, which included a feint toward Finschhafen, was uneventful except for seas rough enough to cause the passenger troops some discomfort. Admiral Crutchley's cruisers and destroyers covered the move to the east while PT boats patrolled the straits to the westward.

The Landings

Barbey's convoy sighted the south coast of New Britain shortly after 0300, 15 December, and the troop ships soon hove to in the transport area about five miles east of Arawe.[37] By 0450 the Carter Hall had launched thirty-nine loaded amphibian tractors bearing the assault waves and the two rocket DUKW's out of her well deck.

Dawn was still one hour away when 150 men of A Troop, 112th, who had been aboard the APD Sands, started for the beach at Umtingalu in fifteen rubber boats. They had been ordered to make a surprise landing in darkness at H minus 1 hour and block the coastal trail that was the Japanese escape and reinforcement route to the east. About 0525, when the boats were nearing shore and in the moonlight were probably visible from the shore, they came under fire from machine guns, rifles, and a 25-mm. dual purpose gun, which promptly sank all but three of the rubber boats.

---

[35] The rocket DUKW, with 4.5-inch rockets, was an experimental craft that the engineer special brigades of the Southwest Pacific Area had developed in an effort to provide fire support for landings after naval gunfire had ceased or lifted. These DUKW's attempted, without much success, to carry out the function performed by the LCI gunboat in the South Pacific.

[36] The Westralia is listed variously as an APA and an LSI. TF 76, for Arawe, including supporting echelons, consisted of the ships listed above, ten escort and bombardment destroyers, an escort and mine group of patrol craft and subchasers, several LCT flotillas, and a service group of LST's plus landing craft attached from the 1st Marine Division and the 2d Engineer Special Brigade.

[37] All times are approximate. All sources employed give differing times for the same events.

The fire continued while the troops floundered in the water divesting themselves of their light combat packs and outer clothing. The destroyer *Shaw* then opened fire and quickly silenced the enemy.[38] Small boats picked up the survivors of A Troop, who later landed without arms and almost naked at House Fireman Beach. Twelve men were killed, four missing, and seventeen wounded in this repulse.

B Troop fared better. Ordered to land at H minus 1 hour on the islet of Pilelo, across Pilelo passage from the peninsula, its men were to take the Japanese by surprise and silence a radio station that was reported at the village of Paligmete. They left the APD *Humphreys* on fifteen rubber boats at the same time that A Troop left the *Sands*.

B Troop had planned to surprise the enemy by landing at Paligmete village, but when the Japanese started firing on A Troop it was obvious that surprise was lost. B Troop landed at Wabmete, on the west of Pilelo, instead. Once ashore the cavalrymen started on foot for Winguru.

The leading platoon reached Winguru at 0615 and met fire from Japanese in two caves on the rising ground south of the village. Leaving one squad to contain these Japanese, B Troop pushed on to Paligmete, found neither Japanese nor radio, and returned to Winguru to mop up. Bazooka fire closed one cave but the other was faced with logs which proved impervious to rockets and machine guns. Finally a flame thrower team, covered by machine gun fire, edged to within fifteen yards of the cave and let loose a blast of flame. B Troop then moved in, tossed grenades, and the action was over. One American soldier had been killed. Seven dead enemy were found. The action ended about 1130.

Meanwhile the main landing at House Fireman Beach had been accomplished successfully if not flawlessly. The assault waves came from Lt. Col. Clyde E. Grant's 2d Squadron, 112th Cavalry, organized into five landing waves: ten LVT (A) (2)'s (Buffaloes), carrying E and F Troops, in the first; eight LVT (1)'s (Alligators) each in the second, third, and fourth waves; and five Alligators in the fifth. The waves were scheduled to land at five-minute intervals. H Hour was set for 0630, after the conclusion of the air and naval bombardments. One and a half hours were allowed for the amphibian tractors to proceed from the ships to the beach, a move which would take place in poor light. Since dawn came at 0624 and sunrise at 0646, the landing itself would take place in daylight.

But someone along the line had become confused. Once boated, the first wave started directly for the shore in the dark. Brig. Gen. William F. Heavey, commanding the 2d Engineer Special Brigade, who had come along as an observer aboard the landing wave control craft, SC 742, saw the boats dimly about 0500. When radio communication with the flagship unaccountably failed, the

---

[38] General Cunningham was wroth at the *Shaw's* delay in opening fire, but Admiral Barbey and Brig. Gen. William F. Heavey [Commanding General, 2d Engineer Special Brigade], who observed the operation from the deck of SC 742, reported that the *Shaw* held her fire because she could not immediately locate any targets. The boats and the shore, viewed from the sea, blended into a dark blur. General Cunningham had tried the predawn landing against Admiral Barbey's advice.

subchaser's captain and Heavey headed off the errant amphibian tractors. There was much confusion and milling about in the darkness, and it was 0600 or later before the tractors regained their formation.

Destroyers bombarded House Fireman Beach with 1,800 5-inch rounds from 0610 to 0625, whereupon B–25's took over. Three squadrons had been assigned to air alert over Arawe under control of an air liaison party aboard the *Conyngham,* and the first of these bombed and strafed the peninsula and the beach. Under ideal conditions the interval between the cessation or lifting of support bombardment and the landing of troops is only long enough to prevent the troops from being hit by their own support fire, but the lead wave of tractors had been slowed by the confusion and by a stiff current in Pilelo passage. It did not land until after 0700. On the way in, the wave met machine gun fire that was quickly silenced by 4.5-inch rockets from the control craft and the two rocket DUKW's on the flanks. Otherwise there was no opposition.

This was fortunate, because the succeeding waves in the Alligators, which were slower craft than the Buffaloes, had not been able to keep up. Twenty-five minutes elapsed before the second wave landed, ample time for a resolute defending force to have inflicted heavy casualties on the first wave. When another fifteen minutes had passed the last three waves came ashore practically together.[39]

The 2d Squadron, once landed, reorganized, sent patrols to the toe of the peninsula, and pushed northwestward toward the base against slight opposition from scattered riflemen and rear guards. E Troop located twenty or more Japanese in caves in the cliff on the east side of the peninsula, killed several, and passed on. When others came out of their caves to snipe and harass, the 112th Cavalry Headquarters Troop sent out a patrol which disposed of them.

Only two companies of Japanese soldiers had been in the area, and when the 2d Squadron came ashore they retreated eastward. Major Komori and his force had not yet reached Arawe.

Meanwhile passages through the reefs had been found. The reserve 1st Squadron, under Maj. Harry E. Werner, had debarked from the *Westralia* while the *Carter Hall* was launching the tractors. Werner's squadron came ashore about 0800 in the 2d Engineer Special Brigade's 2 LCM's and 17 LCVP's. An hour later Barbey's second echelon, 5 LCT's carrying 150 tons of gear and 50 men per LCT, and 7 LCM's carrying 25 tons of gear per LCM, arrived from Cape Cretin and began unloading.

Operations at the beach were not smooth. The detachments forming the shore party had never worked together before, and although the beach was a good one it soon became congested. There was room for but two LCT's at one time; so unloading of beaching craft continued all day.

For DEXTERITY the admirals had won the air cover argument, and planes were assigned as combat air patrol over the

---

[39] After the event all units and observers reporting on the subject declared it a mistake to use vehicles with differing speeds in the assault waves.

ships instead of standing by on ground alert. The first fighter cover, in the form of 8 P–38's, took station overhead at 0715. This cover was subsequently increased and was maintained all day but it was not able to prevent an air attack at 0900. The *11th Air Fleet* at Rabaul had just received more planes and now totaled 50 bombers and 100 fighters. Both Kusaka's fleet and the *6th Air Division* sent out planes against Arawe. One flight of these, reported as consisting of 20 or 30 planes, eluded the P–38's and delivered the attack at 0900. The *Westralia* and *Carter Hall*, unloaded before dawn, had departed at 0500 to avoid air attack. The rest of Task Force 76, with the exception of craft actually at the beach and the flagship *Conyngham*, which remained to direct operations, sought the cover of clouds and rain squalls. The Japanese bombed and strafed the beached LCT's, the *Conyngham*, and the troops for about five minutes, scored no hits, and left with P–38's in pursuit.

By midafternoon the Director Task Force controlled the entire peninsula. The 2d Squadron had reached the base, and now began establishing a main line of resistance there. Over sixteen hundred men, five hundred from the attached units and the rest from the two squadrons of the 112th Cavalry, were ashore.

Operations, 16 December 1943–10 February 1944

During the next few days LCT's from Cape Cretin and APD's from Goodenough brought in heavy weapons, supplies, and more troops. There was no ground contact with the Japanese at Arawe, but in the air the enemy reacted with violence. Between 15 and 27 December naval planes delivered seven attacks against Arawe and against the 1st Marine Division at Cape Gloucester, and in about the same period the *6th Air Division* attacked four times. LCT's at Arawe on 16 December suffered almost continuous air attack. Resupply convoys lost one coastal transport sunk and another damaged, plus one minesweeper and six LST's damaged. Although General Cunningham's force had no 90-mm. antiaircraft guns to keep bombing planes away, damage ashore was fortunately light. Cunningham expressed his urgent need for the 90-mm.'s, but none was available for Arawe. By late December, however, the *11th Air Fleet* and the *6th Air Division* had lost so many planes to Allied fighters over New Britain, to Southwest Pacific attacks against Wewak, and to the South Pacific's raids on Rabaul that they were forced to stop daylight bombardment and confine their activities to the defense of Rabaul and Wewak. When Imamura asked Tokyo for more planes *Imperial Headquarters* responded by sending the *8th Air Brigade* to Hollandia under the *2d Area Army*.

The Japanese had not yet given up at Arawe. When the *17th Division* commander received word of Cunningham's landing he ordered Major Komori, who was then proceeding by boat and overland march to Arawe from Rabaul, to make haste. He also ordered the *1st Battalion, 141st Infantry*, to move from Cape Busching to Arawe and come under Komori's command. Komori was then to destroy the DIRECTOR Task Force.

The Americans soon became aware of the approaching Japanese. On 18 December two Japanese armed barges attacked a 112th Cavalry patrol on board two of the 2d Engineer Special Brigade's LCVP's (which had remained under Cunningham at Arawe). The Japanese scored hits; the patrol abandoned the LCVP's and made its way east to Arawe on foot. Komori's force reached the Pulie River east of Arawe on 20 December, advanced west, and on Christmas Day forced the 112th to abandon its observation posts and outposts east of Arawe.

Cunningham, correctly concluding that the Japanese were converging against him from two directions but erroneously concluding that Komori's command was but the advance guard of a stronger force from Gasmata, asked Krueger for reinforcements. The ALAMO commander hastily dispatched G Company, 158th Infantry, by PT boat.

Komori, with the *1st Battalion, 81st Infantry,* reached the area northwest of the main line of resistance on 26 December. Like the Americans, he had difficulty in getting any exact information on positions in the featureless, jungled terrain at the peninsula's base. Several of his night probing attacks were repulsed by mortar fire, as were daytime attacks on 28 and 29 December. The second of these took the lives of most of his men, but the *1st Battalion, 141st Infantry,* arrived in the late afternoon of 29 December. Several small attacks in early January 1944 by the 112th were beaten off, but the cavalrymen estab-

lished the fact that the Japanese were digging in about six hundred yards beyond their own perimeter. Komori had resolved to defend the prewar airstrip on the mainland east of the peninsula, which in any case the Allies did not want.[40]

On 6 January Cunningham reported to Krueger the existence of the Japanese positions. Cunningham's forces now totaled almost 4,750 men and his short front line—seven hundred yards—was a strong position with fields of fire cut, barbed wire emplaced, and artillery and mortar data computed.[41] The enemy positions he faced consisted largely of shallow trenches and foxholes and were practically invisible in the dense underbrush. There were only about 100 Japanese and half-a-dozen machine guns there, but lack of visibility and the fact that the Japanese moved their guns frequently made them almost impossible for artillery and mortars to hit. An assault would be further complicated by the fact that in the area there were no clearly defined terrain features which could serve to guide an attack and help it maintain its direction. Cunningham asked for tanks and more troops, and repeated his request for 90-mm. antiaircraft guns.

Krueger agreed that attacks by riflemen alone against Komori would result in a waste of lives and agreed to send

---

[40] For an amusing incident about this airstrip and the embarrassment caused by overenthusiasm on the part of public information officers, see Hough and Crown, *The Campaign on New Britain,* pp. 144–49.

[41] By 10 January Task Force 76 had carried 4,750 men and 8,165 tons of supplies to Arawe.

tanks as well as more troops. F Company, 158th Infantry, and B Company, 1st Tank Battalion, 1st Marine Division, reached Arawe from Cape Cretin on 10 and 12 January.

On the morning of 16 January attack and medium bombers struck at the Japanese positions, artillery and mortars shelled them, and the Marine light tanks, two companies of the 158th Infantry, and C Troop of the 112th Cavalry attacked. The tanks led, with infantrymen and cavalrymen following each tank. Direct communication between tanks and foot troops was successfully attained by a device which the tank company improvised; it installed an EE8 field telephone at the rear of each machine. The attack went well and carried forward for fifteen hundred yards. Next day B Troop and one tank platoon mopped up remaining pockets of resistance.

Thereafter Arawe was quiet. Casualties for all units in the DIRECTOR Task Force totaled 118 dead, 352 wounded, and 4 missing. Komori had actually withdrawn to defend the airstrip, and remained there until ordered to retreat to the east in February.

Ironically enough, no PT base was ever built at Arawe. Actually the final plans had never included any provision for one. Lt. Comdr. Morton C. Mumma, commanding Southwest Pacific PT's, successfully insisted that he did not want and did not need a PT base there to patrol the straits or to attack Japanese barges, which seldom used the south coast anyway. Arawe never became an air base either. The only airstrip ever used was one for artillery liaison planes

ALLIGATOR RETURNING TO BEACH ON ARAWE *for more supplies, 18 December 1943.*

that engineers hastily cleared on 13 January.

Cape Gloucester

Meanwhile the main event at Cape Gloucester had gotten under way. Elements of the 1st Marine Division scheduled for the main assault landings east of Cape Gloucester conducted final rehearsals at Cape Sudest on 21 December.[42] The heavily reinforced 7th Marines boarded ship at Oro Bay three days later and departed at 0600 on Christmas morning. En route ships carrying the reinforced 1st Marines (less one battalion landing team) from Cape Cretin joined up. The convoy then made its way peacefully through Vitiaz Strait, sailed between Rooke and Sakar Islands, and approached Cape Gloucester. The 2d Battalion Landing Team, 1st Marines, embarked at Cape Cretin and steamed through Dampier Strait for Tauali.[43] Admiral Crutchley's Task Force 74—the American cruisers *Phoenix* and *Nashville,* HMAS *Australia* and HMAS *Shropshire,* and eight destroyers—escorted Task Force 76 while PT boats patrolled the northern and western entrances to the straits.

The Landings

In the dim light of 0600 on 26 December Crutchley's ships opened their supporting bombardment on the landing beaches east of Cape Gloucester, a bombardment that continued for ninety

---

[42] This section is based on Craven and Cate, *The Pacific: Guadalcanal to Saipan,* pp. 337–45; Hough and Crown, *The Campaign on New Britain;* Morison, *Breaking the Bismarcks Barrier,* pp. 378–89; Office of the Chief Engineer, GHQ AFPAC, *Engineers of the Southwest Pacific: 1941–1945,* VI, *Airfield and Base Development* (Washington, 1951), 192–95; ALAMO Force Rpt, DEXTERITY Opn; 8th Area Army Operations, Japanese Monogr No. 110 (OCMH), pp. 119–22; 17th Division Operations in Western New Britain, Japanese Monogr No. 111 (OCMH), pp. 14–21.

[43] For Cape Gloucester Task Force 76 consisted of the flagship *Conyngham,* 10 APD's, 16 LCI's, 12 destroyers, 3 minesweepers, and 24 LST's; 14 LCM's, 12 LCT's, and 2 rocket DUKW's went to Tauali. In reserve were the *Westralia* and *Carter Hall.* Detachments of the 2d Engineer Special Brigade—181 men, 33 landing craft, and 2 rocket DUKW's—were attached to the 1st Marine Division.

minutes. Two new LCI's equipped with 4.5-inch rockets took station on the flanks as guide and fire support craft. After threading their way through a difficult channel, APD's, in the lead, lowered landing craft full of troops while behind them LCI's and LST's awaited their turns at the beaches. (*Map 18*)

The 1st Air Task Force of the Fifth Air Force had prepared extensive plans for all-day air cover and support that involved a total of five fighter squadrons and fourteen attack, medium, and heavy bomber squadrons. The first support bombers arrived from Dobodura about 0700 and B–24's, B–25's, and A–20's bombed and strafed the beaches and the airdrome. B–25's dropped smoke bombs on Target Hill, the 450-foot ridge just west of Silimati Point that gave clear observation of the beaches and airfields. A–20's strafed the landing beaches until the leading wave of landing craft was five hundred yards from shore. At that time the naval gunfire was moved inland and to the flanks.

An errant breeze blew so much smoke from Target Hill that some of the leading waves of landing craft carrying the 7th Marines could not easily identify the beaches. There was no opposition at the proper beaches, where most of two battalions of the 7th landed, but a detachment which wandered three hundred yards too far west had a brisk fire fight on shore.

The 7th Marines found that the landing beaches were good but very shallow. And as the assault waves crossed the beaches they were brought up sharply by jungle so dense they had to start hacking to get inland. Immediately behind the beach was a narrow shelf of relatively

EARLY MORNING BOMBARDMENT *of landing beaches east of Cape Gloucester,
26 December 1943.*

dry ground. Behind the shelf was a swamp which made anything like rapid movement or maneuver completely impossible. Men floundered through the mud, slipping into sinkholes up to their waists and even their armpits. And in the swamp giant trees, rotted by water and weakened by bombs and shells, toppled over easily. The first marine fatality on Cape Gloucester was caused by a falling tree.

The narrow beach and the swampy jungle behind it caused a good deal of congestion, especially when the LST's began discharging their cargo. As expected, Japanese planes from Rabaul attacked the ships and the beach during the day, although their first attacks were directed against Arawe in the belief that the convoy had been intended as reinforcement for Cunningham. They sank one destroyer, seriously damaged two more, and scored hits on two others, as well as on two LST's.

By the day's end the 7th Marines held the beachhead area. The artillery battalions of the 11th Marines had landed and emplaced their howitzers. The 1st Marines had come ashore, passed through the 7th, and begun the advance west toward the airdrome. The regiment first attempted to advance with battalions echeloned to the left rear, but the swamp forced movement in a long column with a narrow front along the coastal trail.

Also on 26 December the reinforced

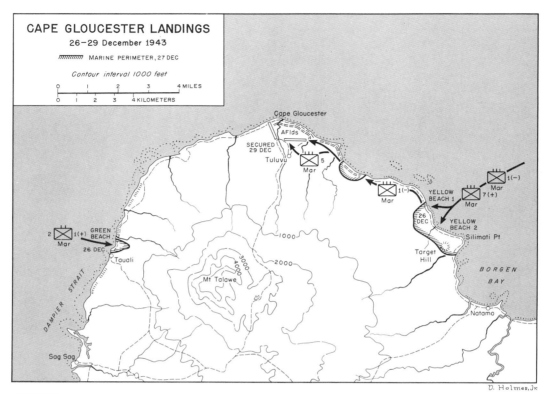

MAP 18

2d Battalion, 1st Marines, landed successfully at Tauali and D Company, 592d Engineer Boat and Shore Regiment, 2d Engineer Special Brigade, landed on Long Island to prepare a radar station there.

The first night ashore at Gloucester was miserable, and it was the first of many more that were just as bad. Drenching rains characteristic of the northwest monsoon poured down in torrents; more trees fell. The Japanese in the airdrome area, estimating that only 2,500 men had come ashore, counterattacked the 7th Marines, but they failed, as did a heterogeneous group that later struck at the Tauali positions.

Capture of the Airfield

The 1st Marines started westward along the coastal trail toward the cape and the airfield at 0730, 27 December. The swamp still forced the regiment to advance in column of battalions, with the rear battalion echeloned as much as possible to the left rear. Each battalion marched in column of companies and sent small patrols into the swamp to protect its flanks. General Sherman tanks of A Company, 1st Tank Battalion, supported. By 1615, when it dug in for the night, the regiment had gained three miles, and had become aware of the existence of a large Japanese block about a thousand yards east of the airfield.

7TH MARINES LANDING ON NARROW BEACH, *Cape Gloucester, 26 December 1943.*

Next day the 1st made deliberate preparations before attacking the block. The absence of Japanese resistance the day before had led to the conclusion that the enemy was concentrating his forces inside the block. The 1st Marines waited during the morning for more tanks to make their way up the trail, which by now was a veritable morass, and for artillery and aircraft to shell and bomb the block. The infantry and the tanks moved to the attack about noon and shortly ran into the block. This position was a strong point which originally had faced the sea for defense of the beach but which served alternately as a trail block. It consisted of camouflaged bunkers with many anti-tank and 75-mm. weapons. There was scarcely room for tanks and infantry to maneuver, but by the end of the after-noon the 1st Marines had reduced the block.

General Rupertus had been asking for his reserve, the reinforced 5th Marines, which had remained under Krueger's control, and on the 28th Krueger released the regiment. Rupertus then decided to hold up the advance on the airfield until the 5th arrived. It came on 29 December, but confusion over orders caused part of the 5th to land just behind the 1st, the rest at the D-Day beaches. When the 5th had been reassembled the drive began again. The 1st Marines continued the coastal advance and, because the swampland on the left had given way to jungle, the 5th was able to make a wide southwesterly sweep. There was almost no resistance. By the day's end most of the airdrome was in Allied hands and the major objective of the campaign had been achieved.

The Japanese Withdrawal

This phase of the operation had gone rapidly and at the cost of comparatively few casualties. But the absence of Japanese opposition made it clear that a large body of the enemy must be elsewhere in the vicinity. Thus in the first two weeks of 1944 the 7th Marines and the 3d Battalion, 5th Marines, under Brig. Gen. Lemuel C. Shepherd, the assistant division commander, attacked southward to clear Borgen Bay. Here waged the bitterest fighting of the campaign as the *141st Infantry* struggled to keep possession of the high ground.

Thereafter there was little combat. The marines patroled extensively in search of the enemy, who proved to be elusive. B Company, 1st Marines, landed on Rooke Island on 12 February but found it had been evacuated. Eventually elements of Rupertus' division advanced by shore-to-shore movements as far east as Talasea without encountering any large numbers of Japanese.[44]

The enemy garrison at Cape Gloucester, especially Matsuda's command, had been in poor physical condition before the invasion. The incessant air attacks against barge supply routes had forced it onto short rations, and malaria, dysentery, and fungus infections were rife.

The *17th Division* commander, Lt. Gen. Yasushi Sakai, seems to have had little heart for a resolute defense, for he urged General Imamura to approve a re-treat to the Willaumez Peninsula. Imamura at first refused, then assented in January. On 23 February he ordered Sakai's entire command—*17th Division, 65th Brigade, 4th Shipping Group,* and all attached units—to retreat all the way back to Rabaul and help defend it.

Base Development

Repair of the wrecked airdrome began in early January with the arrival of the 913th Engineer Aviation Battalion. The work was complicated and slowed by jungle, rain, and swampy ground, and by nocturnal air raids that prevented night work for nearly two weeks. GHQ and the Fifth Air Force revised their requirements and directed construction of a 5,000-foot strip and a second, parallel strip 6,000 feet long. The 864th and 141st Engineer Aviation Battalions arrived later in January and turned to on the strips and on roads and airdrome installations. By the end of the month 4,200 feet of the first airstrip had been covered with pierced steel matting, but it was 18 March before the strip was completed. By then Rabaul, Kavieng, and the Admiralties had been neutralized or captured and GHQ was planning the first giant step of its advance to the Philippines, a step which took it far beyond range of fighter planes based at Cape Gloucester.[45] The parallel 6,000-foot strip proved impossible to build and was never completed.

Cape Gloucester never became an important air base. It is clear that the Arawe and Cape Gloucester invasions were of less strategic importance than the other CARTWHEEL operations, and in the

---

[44] In April the 40th Division relieved the 1st Marine Division and the 112th Cavalry on New Britain.

[45] See Smith, *The Approach to the Philippines,* Ch. II.

light of hindsight were probably not essential to the reduction of Rabaul or the approach to the Philippines. Yet they were neither completely fruitless nor excessively high in casualties. The 1st Marine Division scored a striking tactical success at the cost of 310 killed, 1,083 wounded. And the Allied forces of the Southwest Pacific Area had, by means of these operations, broken out through the narrow straits.

Saidor

The first two DEXTERITY operations faced toward Rabaul, and as events later showed had much less effect on the course of the war than the other CARTWHEEL operations. But in December 1943 General MacArthur reversed his field and decided to exploit the tactical successes at Arawe and Cape Gloucester by moving west to seize Saidor, on the north coast of the Huon Peninsula. (*See Map 12.*) General Chamberlin had suggested Saidor in September, but it was 11 December before an outline plan was prepared.[46]

---

[46] This section is based on Craven and Cate, *The Pacific: Guadalcanal to Saipan*, pp. 345–49; Morison, *Breaking the Bismarcks Barrier*, pp. 389–91; Off of Chief Engr, GHQ AFPAC, *Engineers in Theater Operations*, pp. 118–19, and *Critique*, pp. 112–32; Smith, *The Approach to the Philippines*, pp. 90–93; ALAMO Force Rpt, DEXTERITY Opn; ALAMO Force G–3 Jnl, MICHAELMAS Opn, DEXTERITY; MICHAELMAS TF [126th RCT, reinforced], Rpt of MICHAELMAS Opn, 16 Dec 43–10 Feb 44; MICHAELMAS TF Opn Diary; CTF 76 Opn Plan 4–43, 29 Dec 43; CTF Rpt of Saidor Opn, 3 Feb 44; GHQ SWPA Outline Plan Saidor, 10 Dec 43, in ALAMO Force G–3 Jnl DEXTERITY No. 8; Memo, CAW [Gen Willoughby] for CofS GHQ SWPA, 21 Dec 43, no sub, in GHQ SWPA G–3 Jnl, 21 Dec 43; GHQ Ltr of Instns to Comdrs ALAMO Force, ANF, AAF, NGF, and USASOS, 17 Dec 43, sub: MICHAELMAS Opn, and GHQ SWPA OI 38/19, 31 Dec 43, both in GHQ SWPA G–3 Jnl, 22 Dec 43; ALF, Rpt on New Guinea Opns: 4 Sep 43–26 Apr 44; 8th Area Army Operations, Japanese Monogr No. 110 (OCMH), pp. 86–91; 18th Army Operations, II, Japanese Monogr No. 42 (OCMH), 125–80.

Saidor lay slightly northeast of Mounts Gladstone and Disraeli, which glower at each other from their 11,000-foot eminences. It had a prewar airstrip, and had been used as a barge staging point by the Japanese. Lying 110 nautical miles from Finschhafen, 52 from Madang, and 414 from Rabaul, it was well situated to support the advance westward toward the Vogelkop and the move northward against the Admiralties. In addition Allied seizure would cut the *18th Army* in two, for that army's main concentrations were at Madang–Wewak to the west, and at Sio–Gali to the east.

Preparations and Plans

The invasion of Saidor was not actually decided on until 17 December, two days after the invasion of Arawe and nine days before the invasion of Cape Gloucester. On that date General MacArthur ordered Krueger to prepare plans at once for an operation from Goodenough Island to seize Saidor and construct an advanced air and naval base there. Allied Air and Allied Naval Forces would support, and again MacArthur made Krueger responsible for co-ordination of planning by the ground forces and the commanders of close support air and naval forces. The New Guinea Force, whose troops were now advancing against Sio and patrolling in the Ramu Valley beyond Dumpu, would support by continuing the move against Sio and by vigorous demonstrations in the Ramu

Valley. U.S. Army Services of Supply was to haul supplies for the operation forward to Cape Cretin, where Krueger was to establish a temporary staging area and supply point pending the time that the U.S. Army Services of Supply base at Finschhafen began operating. Ground combat forces would come from the ALAMO reserve for Cape Gloucester, the U.S. 32d Division which had fought in the Papuan campaign. In addition Mac-Arthur assigned two engineer aviation battalions, an amphibian truck company, and an engineer boat and shore regiment.

Assignment of the mission to ALAMO Force instead of New Guinea Force represented a departure from the principle that New Guinea Force would command all operations in New Guinea. The change was probably made because nearly all trained Australian divisions were either committed to action or withdrawn for rest, and because it seemed clear that all the ALAMO reserve would not have to be committed to Arawe or Gloucester.

MacArthur gave Krueger and his air and naval colleagues little time to get ready. Actual initiation of the Saidor offensive, he announced, would depend on the progress of operations on Cape Gloucester, because landing craft for the former would have to come from the latter. It was expected, however, that D Day would be 2 January 1944, or shortly thereafter. Two days' notice would be given.

GHQ's first outline plan had envisaged a parachute assault to take Saidor, but that was decided against because there still were not enough forward airfields to support current bombing operations

and a parachute assault at the same time. The attack would have to be made by ground troops.

For the attack Krueger organized the MICHAELMAS [Saidor] Task Force under command of General Martin, assistant commander of the 32d Division, who had just reached Goodenough Island. Most combat troops of the task force came out of the force Krueger had originally organized for Gasmata. The rest were those assigned by General MacArthur. Martin's force was built around the 126th Regimental Combat Team of the 32d Division, which included the 120th Field Artillery Battalion (105-mm howitzers).[47] At the time of assignment the 32d Division units of the task force had just moved to Goodenough Island from Milne Bay. The rest of the force was scattered at such diverse points as Milne Bay, Kiriwina, and Lae.

Although time for planning and preparing was short, and the pressure of Admiral Barbey's duties prevented him from conferring frequently with Krueger in person, the reports of the participating units bear witness to the fact that the experience and state of training of the commanders and troops were so high that things went smoothly.

General Martin hastily organized a headquarters for his task force, taking as the nucleus Headquarters and Headquarters Company, 126th Infantry. To

---

[47] Other units were the 121st Field Artillery Battalion (75-mm. pack howitzers); Headquarters and Headquarters Battery, 191st Field Artillery Group; B and D Batteries, 209th Coast Artillery Battalion (AA, AW); A and D Batteries, 743d Coast Artillery Gun Battalion (AA); the Shore Battalion of the 542d Engineer Boat and Shore Regiment, 2d Engineer Special Brigade; the 808th and 863d Engineer Aviation Battalions; and a variety of service units.

REAR ADM. DANIEL E. BARBEY, *left, and Brig. Gen. Clarence A. Martin, center, observing landing operations at Saidor, 2 January 1944.*

this were added some officers from 32d Division headquarters. Col. Charles D. Blanchard, task force G–3, came from ALAMO Force as did a complete engineer section. Col. J. Sladen Bradley, commander of the 126th, also served as deputy commander and chief of staff of the MICHAELMAS Task Force.

Plans began to take shape on 20 December at a conference in ALAMO headquarters at Goodenough Island. Present were Admiral Barbey; Maj. Gen. William H. Gill of the 32d Division; General Heavey of the 2d Engineer Special Brigade; Brig. Gen. Edwin D. Patrick, ALAMO Force chief of staff; Col. Clyde D. Eddleman, G–3 of ALAMO

Force; General Whitehead; General Martin; and Colonel Blanchard. Whitehead, Patrick, and Eddleman presented their ideas, as did Barbey, who was just about to leave for Cape Gloucester. Both Barbey and Martin felt that, as Saidor was known to be lightly held by the enemy, preliminary air bombardment on the beaches on D Day would be of less value than a surprise landing at an early hour in the day. This conference was followed by two other brief ones during the next ten days.

As there was neither time nor opportunity for ground reconnaissance of Saidor, the landing beaches were chosen from aerial photographs. Three beaches, designated Red, White, and Blue from left (south) to right on the west shore of Dekays Bay just east of Saidor were selected. They were rough and stony but were chosen because they were close to the objective, because the beach gradient was steep enough to enable the troops to make a dry landing, because there was solid ground behind them, and because Dekays Bay could be expected to offer protection from the northwest monsoons prevailing at that time of year.

Formal orders were published in late December.[48] Admiral Barbey organized his force generally as follows:

APD's:
    Red Beach 3
    White Beach 2
    Blue Beach 4
LCI's:
    Red Beach 6
    White Beach 6
    Blue Beach 4
Destroyers:
    Escort 4
    Bombardment 6
    Cover 5
Control and rocket vessels:
    2 LCI's and 2 SC's.
Supply group:
    6 LST's.

These ships would carry the assault troops from Goodenough and land them at Saidor on D Day. Six more LST's would land additional troops and equipment on D plus 1, and LST shipments would continue to bring in troops and supplies from Goodenough and Cape Cretin for some time thereafter.

The assault waves of troops would land

from the APD's in thirty-six LCP(R)'s as follows: The 3d Battalion, 126th Infantry, was to land on Red Beach at H Hour with two companies abreast, while the 2d Battalion, 126th, put one company on White Beach and one company on Blue; the 1st Battalion, 126th, would land from LCI's on White Beach at H plus 30 minutes. All units would push inland and reconnoiter. Field and antiaircraft artillery were to land soon after the assault infantry. Forming the shore party would be A Company, 114th Engineer Battalion; the Antitank Company and part of the Cannon Company, 126th Infantry; and the Shore Battalion, 542d Engineer Boat and Shore Regiment. In all, seven thousand men and three thousand tons of gear were to be put ashore on D Day.

Plans for naval gunfire called for two destroyers to put 575 5-inch rounds of deep supporting fire at inland targets between H minus 20 minutes and H Hour. Four destroyers would fire 1,150 rounds at the beach from H minus 20 to H minus 3 minutes when the lead wave of landing craft would be nine hundred yards from shore. Fire from rocket-equipped LCI's would cover the landing craft during the last nine hundred yards. In accordance with Martin's and Barbey's desire for surprise, the air plans did not provide for a preliminary bombardment on D Day. Provisions were made, however, for bombers to strike at inland targets after H Hour, and for strafers and fighters to execute supporting missions on call.

H Hour was set for 0650, fifteen minutes before sunrise—the earliest possible minute that would allow adequate light for the earlier naval bombardment.

[48] See ALAMO [ESCALATOR] FO 7, 22 Dec 43, and MICHAELMAS TF FO 1, 29 Dec 43, both in ALAMO Force G-3 Jnl File, MICHAELMAS; CTF 76 Opn Plan 4-43, 29 Dec 43.

Weather could be expected to be either squally with rough surf or pleasant with smooth surf, and subject to sudden change from one extreme to the other.

Troops of General Martin's task force, aside from the 32d Division units, were arriving at Goodenough while the plans were being prepared. Some units arrived short of clothing and equipment, and these were supplied as well as possible.

Meanwhile General Krueger, concerned over the difficulties of supplying Arawe, Cape Gloucester, and Saidor simultaneously, argued in favor of postponing Saidor. But General MacArthur, Vice Adm. Thomas C. Kinkaid, and others, promising to make sure that enough supplies arrived at Saidor, and unwilling to lose momentum, agreed that the operation would be valueless if postponed. Preparations went forward.[49]

Admiral Kinkaid, a cool, soft-spoken, bushy-eyebrowed product of many years in the U.S. Navy, had relieved Admiral Carpender as commander of Allied Naval Forces and of the Seventh Fleet in November. A classmate of Admiral Turner at the Naval Academy, he had already had ample experience in the Pacific, having commanded carrier task forces during the Guadalcanal Campaign and led the invasion of the Aleutians.

On 28 December General Patrick notified Martin that the Cape Gloucester operation was proceeding successfully, and that his task force would probably invade Saidor on 2 January, the estimated date. As the LST's would have to sail from Goodenough on 31 December

in order to reach Saidor on D Day, Martin concluded that loading would have to start on 30 December, for the task force assembly area on Goodenough lay eighteen miles from the embarkation point. He ordered his force to move to the embarkation point at once. Movement and loading continued night and day, usually in rain which turned the roads into mud. On 30 December Martin received word officially that D Day would definitely be 2 January.

APD's and LCI's took aboard only troops, individual equipment, and individual or squad weapons. Heavy equipment, vehicles, motor-drawn weapons, bulk supplies, and some troops went aboard the LST's. Martin was forced to make a last-minute change in embarkation plans on 30 December when he found there would be nine APD's instead of the ten he had expected. The surplus infantrymen were ordered aboard an LCI, but since the units involved were then moving to the embarkation point some did not receive word of the change until they had reached the beach.

The difficulties were all overborne, and by 0830, 31 December, the six LST's had departed Goodenough. Their slots at the beach were promptly taken by the six that were to bring heavy equipment to Saidor on D plus 1. The LCI's left Goodenough in midafternoon, and the fast APD's completed loading at 1700. There had not been opportunity for a dress rehearsal, but the LCP(R)'s of the APD's practiced landing formations at Goodenough Bay.[50]

---

[49] Ltr, Krueger to CINCSWPA, 28 Dec 43, sub: Deferment of MICHAELMAS, and Rad, Gen R. J. Marshall to Gen Chamberlin, 28 Dec 43, both in GHQ SWPA G–3 Jnl, 29 Dec 43.

[50] The 126th Regimental Combat Team had received six weeks of amphibious training in Australia and three weeks training in LST's, LCI's, and APD's at Milne Bay.

For the soldiers and sailors aboard the APD's New Year's Eve passed quietly. Martin, the APD captains, Colonel Bradley, and the battalion commanders conferred aboard the destroyer *Stringham* and made minor last-minutes changes in landing plans. Some of the ships showed moving pictures. At 0600 on New Year's Day, 1944, the APD's sailed. They put in at Oro Bay en route, where they were joined by Admiral Barbey in his flagship, the destroyer *Conyngham*, to which General Martin transferred his command post afloat. During the ships' approach to Saidor on 1 January, sixty B–24's and forty-eight B–25's hit the Japanese installations with 218 tons of demolition bombs.

Barbey's final run through the straits to Saidor was unexciting. The early part of the night of 1–2 January was clear, with a quarter moon shining on the ships. After midnight the sky became overcast and rain fell.

Seizing Saidor

When the ships and landing craft hove to in Dekays Bay before sunrise of 2 January, heavy overcast and rain obscured the shore. Admiral Barbey postponed H Hour from 0650 to 0705 to provide more light for naval gunfire, loading and assembly of boats, and identification of beaches. There followed another delay of twenty minutes while LCP(R)'s formed up. The destroyers and rocket LCI's fired the scheduled 1,725 5-inch shells and 624 4.5-inch rockets at the beaches and inland areas. Troops aboard ship, one thousand yards offshore, felt the concussion of the explosives.

The assault waves meanwhile had boated and assembled, and were churning toward Red, White, and Blue Beaches. First craft touched down at 0725, and during the next seventeen minutes the four waves of thirty-six LCP(R)'s landed 1,440 troops. There was no opposition from the enemy. The sixteen LCI's, organized in three waves, grounded and put ashore more than 3,000 troops.

Each LST had towed an LCM of the 2d Engineer Special Brigade. The LST's cast loose their tows on arrival offshore, and three LCM's sailed to the beaches with the last wave of small craft. Thirty minutes before the LST's were scheduled to beach, an angledozer clanked out of each LCM and at once set to work grading landing points and beach exits to use in unloading the LST's. When the six LST's beached at about 0800, landing points and beach exits made of gravel and wire mesh were ready. This performance, plus the efficiency of the shore party, which Admiral Barbey praised highly, enabled cargo to come ashore in record time. Each LST rapidly unloaded three hundred tons of bulk supplies and two hundred tons of vehicles and equipment. By 1140 all LST's had unloaded and retracted. The bad weather delayed the scheduled air bombing, but later in the morning B–24's, B–25's, and A–20's bombed the Saidor airstrip and the high ground inland.[51]

---

[51] There was one hitch in the air plans. Martin did not receive the 1st Air Task Force's support plan until after he had left Goodenough and was aboard ship. There he discovered that one alternate target lay on the American side of the bomb safety line. As the ships were under radio silence he could not notify air headquarters. The air liaison party, after landing, radioed the necessary information directly to the bombers before any American casualties were incurred.

M10 MOTOR CARRIAGE MOUNTING 3-INCH GUN *on a rough and stony beach near Saidor, 2 January 1944.*

When they reached shore the rifle battalions began to push inland while the artillery established itself and the shore party moved supplies off the beach. Japanese resistance was limited to a few rifle shots. General Martin reported that only 15 enemy soldiers had been near the beaches at the time of the landing, and 11 of these were killed by the bombardments and by soldiers of the 126th. Saidor had a normal garrison of about 50, and on 2 January some 120–150 transients were present. All these promptly took to the hills. American casualties on D Day numbered 1 soldier killed and 5 wounded and 2 sailors drowned at Blue Beach. Forces ashore numbered 6,779:[52] 6,602 Army ground

troops, 129 from Army Air Forces units, and 48 sailors.

Admiral Crutchley's task force had performed its usual mission of covering the invasion against Japanese warships from Rabaul, but none appeared. Thirty-nine fighters and twenty-four bombers of the *4th Air Army* were based at Wewak but were unable to launch an attack until 1600. By then Barbey's ships were well out to sea, Martin's soldiers had dispersed their supplies, and little damage was done.

So ended the first day at Saidor. The speedy efficiency of Saidor operations, when compared, for example, with the Kiriwina invasion of the previous year, bears witness to the Southwest Pacific's improvement in amphibious technique. Yet the fact that there are flaws in even

[52] This figure comes from the MICHAELMAS Task Force report. CTF 76's report gives 7,200.

the best-executed operations was demonstrated the next morning. The MICHAELMAS Task Force expected six LST's (each towing an engineer LCM) carrying the 121st Field Artillery Battalion and A and D Batteries, 743d Coast Artillery Gun Battalion (Antiaircraft), to arrive at 0700, 3 January, which would be after daylight. When three vessels came dimly in view about a hundred yards from the north shore at 0510 and failed to identify themselves, the shore defenses opened fire. The vessels withdrew. After daylight they returned and were correctly identified as three of the six expected LST's.

Thereafter shipments of troops and supplies on the LST's were uneventful. The 808th Engineer Aviation Battalion arrived on 6 January; the larger part of the 128th Regimental Combat Team came in on 16 and 19 January in response to General Martin's request for more troops; the 863d Engineer Aviation Battalion was landed on 29 January. By 10 February, when General Krueger declared DEXTERITY over, and GHQ announced that U.S. Army Services of Supply, Southwest Pacific, would take over supplying Saidor, Arawe, and Gloucester on 1 March, the Saidor garrison numbered 14,979 in addition to a small naval detachment. Forty men had been killed, 111 wounded; 16 were missing.

Base Development

Construction missions assigned to the engineers included building or installing an airfield, roads, fuel storage tanks, docks, jetties, a PT boat base, and a hospital. Work on the airfield started promptly and in itself was not difficult, since the prewar field was in fair condition. The amphibian engineers unloaded ships and built roads, but continuous rainfall hindered their work and General Martin occasionally diverted the aviation engineers to assist the amphibians in their work. The Americans were assisted in all phases of construction work by native labor. A detachment of the Australian New Guinea Administrative Unit consisting of one officer, several enlisted men, and eleven native policemen had landed on 2 January to supervise the employment of New Guinea natives. Seven days later 100 native workers came up from Lae, and by 10 February there were 13 policemen, 200 Lae natives, and 406 local workers at Saidor. C–47's landed on the airfield on D plus 9, and by 10 February it was almost ready to receive warplanes.

Junction With the Australians

In the days immediately following D Day General Martin disposed one battalion in defensive positions on each flank, with the third patrolling in the mountains between the flanks. There were some fourteen miles of coast line between the flanks which were held by the coast artillery, supported by other units.

The MICHAELMAS Task Force was hardly ashore when General Krueger warned that, as the Japanese troops in the vicinity of Sio were preparing to move west to Madang, an attack against Saidor was to be expected. These warnings were repeated on 7 and 9 January. General Martin asked for more troops on 10 January and General Krueger sent him the 1st and 3d Battalion Combat Teams of the 128th Regimental Combat Team.

Meanwhile patrols went to the east, west, and south. There were occasional brushes with scattered Japanese patrols, but no pitched battles. January ended without an attack. The Japanese were known to be advancing west, but they had not yet touched Saidor.

Almost from the very outset General Martin had urged an advance to the east to hem in the Japanese between his forces and the advancing Australians, but, partly because it apparently did not wish to commit additional troops, and partly because of garbles in the transmission of messages, ALAMO headquarters did not at once accede to Martin's desires.[53]

Doubts regarding Japanese intentions were dispelled on 6 February when from a newly established observation post in the Finisterres American soldiers saw large numbers of Japanese troops marching along an inland trail that ran south of Saidor through the mountains and foothills. It was concluded that the Japanese were bypassing Saidor.

The conclusion was correct. In late December General Adachi, concerned over the state of things to the east, had flown from Madang to *51st Division* headquarters at Kiari. He received word of the American landing at Saidor just before he went overland to the *20th Division* at Sio. Opinion at General Imamura's Rabaul headquarters was divided over the best course of action. Some staff officers argued that the *20th and 51st Divisions* should attack Saidor. Others counseled that they slip peacefully past Saidor over an inland route and proceed

to Madang to join with the remainder of the *18th Army* to defend Wewak. Abandoning the attempt to hold the shores of the straits, Imamura decided in favor of bypassing Saidor. He sent orders to that effect to Adachi at Sio.

Adachi placed General Nakano of the *51st Division* in charge of the retreat and directed the *41st Division* to move from Wewak to defend Madang. Adachi left Sio by submarine "in a troubled state of mind because he would again have to force the two divisions to go through difficulties."[54] He later ordered General Nakai to send eight companies out of the Ramu Valley to Bogadjim. They were to advance down to the coast to harass Saidor while Nakano's force retreated.

Nakano, who first directed the *20th Division* to retreat along the coast while the *51st Division* and naval units moved inland, eventually decided to avoid enemy opposition by sending the whole force through the Finisterres.

The retreat began promptly. Sio was abandoned to the 9th Australian Division and the Japanese moved up the coast, then headed inland east of Saidor. The retreat to Madang, almost two hundred miles away by the coastal route, was another of the terrible Japanese marches in New Guinea. The troops struggled through jungles, across rivers, and over the awesome cliffs and mountains of the Finisterres. Fatigue, straggling, disease, and starvation characterized the retreat. "The men were no longer able to care for themselves and walked step after step looking ahead only a meter to see where

---

[53] Gen Martin, 1st Ind, 2 Nov 53, to Ltr, Gen Smith, Chief of Mil Hist, to Gen Martin, 6 Oct 53, no sub, OCMH. General Martin kindly attached to his indorsement several letters and papers and took the trouble to prepare an excellent narrative which clarified many obscure points.

[54] 18th Army Operations, II, Japanese Monogr No. 42 (OCMH), 132.

they were going." [55] The two divisions had totaled twenty thousand in December 1943; only ten thousand wearily entered Madang in mid-February.

Yet that the ten thousand made such a trip and that the Japanese could make such marches in retreat and in the advance are tribute and testimony to the patient fortitude and iron resolution of the Japanese soldier. They clearly illustrate that despite his baggy uniforms and bombastic phrases he was a formidable opponent.

After the fall of Sio the 5th Australian Division relieved the 9th and advanced up the coast. Its advance patrols made contact with those of the MICHAELMAS Task Force on the Yaut River about fourteen miles southeast of Saidor on 10 February 1944.

Because permission to move east was received too late, Martin could not block the Japanese in that direction. And the escape route to the south ran up and down such steep ravines and slopes that no heavy weapons could be carried there, and the Americans could not block that route either. General Martin decided to attack to the west. The move, executed by elements of the 1st and 3d Battalions, 126th Infantry, began at once.

General Gill and his staff reached Saidor on 18 February to assume command, and continued the westward move. By 24 February patrols of the 3d Battalion, 126th, had reached Biliau at Cape Iris, about twelve land miles from Saidor. On 5 March the 126th Infantry (less the 2d Battalion), the 121st Field Artillery Battalion, and B Battery, 120th

Field Artillery Battalion, disembarked from engineer landing craft at Yalau Plantation, twenty miles farther on. By now the 7th Australian Division had broken out of the Ramu Valley and General Nakai was retreating toward Madang. Patrols of the 32d U.S. and the 7th Australian Divisions made contact at Kul between the Sa and Kambara Rivers, about eight miles beyond Yalau Plantation, on 21 March. The Australians went on to take Bogadjim on 13 April.

Meanwhile *Imperial General Headquarters* had transferred the *18th Army* and the *4th Air Army* out of the *8th Area Army* and assigned them to control of the *2d Area Army* to pull Adachi's troops out of Madang and west to Wewak, Aitape, and Hollandia. Adachi's troops started west again, evacuating Madang just before the Australians entered from the east on 24 April.[56] So the large-scale attack on Madang envisaged in ELKTON III never came off. Saidor proved to be an effective and economical substitute.

Securing of the major objectives of Operation II of CARTWHEEL was completed by the seizure of Saidor, and subsequent operations on the Huon Peninsula were anticlimactic strategically, however bitter and tragic they were for those who fought and died in them. The Saidor landing completed the seizure of the Markham–Ramu trough and the Huon Peninsula for the Allies and obtained one more airfield to support operations against the Admiralties and enemy bases to the west.

---

[55] 18th Army Operations, II, Japanese Monogr No. 42 (OCMH), 180.

[56] For the *18th Army's* operations subsequent to the period embraced by this volume, see Smith, *The Approach to the Philippines*, Chs. V–VIII. The new boundary between the *8th Area* and the *2d Area Armies* was set at longitude 147° east.

Strictly speaking, Saidor was the last invasion of the CARTWHEEL operations. With it General MacArthur fulfilled the provisions of the Joint Chiefs' orders of 28 March 1943. But he and Admiral Halsey were not yet finished with the Japanese in the Southeast Area. By the end of 1943 Rabaul had not yet been completely neutralized, and before the approach to the Philippines could begin there remained a set of subsidiary, transitional operations to be accomplished. These, which the Joint Chiefs and MacArthur had discussed earlier in 1943, would complete the encirclement of Rabaul and would provide a naval base to substitute for Rabaul in the drive to the Philippines.

CHAPTER XV

Expanding Into the Bismarck Archipelago

General Plans

Further operations in the Bismarck Archipelago had been contemplated for nearly two years. The Joint Chiefs' directive which launched the campaigns against Rabaul in 1942 had authorized operations to follow Arawe and Cape Gloucester, and MacArthur's early plans called for the capture of Kavieng on northern New Ireland and of Manus in the Admiralty Islands as well as of Rabaul.[1] Further, when the Joint Chiefs were deciding to bypass Rabaul, General Marshall suggested that CARTWHEEL be extended to include seizure of Kavieng, Manus, and Wewak. MacArthur was less than enthusiastic about Wewak, which was a major enemy base. His plan for the drive to the Philippines, RENO III, called for the invasion of Hansa Bay on 1 February 1944, of Kavieng by the South Pacific on 1 March 1944, and of the Admiralties on 1 March 1944.[2]

Responsibility for base construction at Kavieng and at Seeadler Harbour at Manus was to be Admiral Halsey's, and he began planning these bases in November 1943. Kavieng was supposed to become a minor fleet base, a PT base, and a major air base with six airfields. Manus would serve as an air base (two airfields and a seaplane base) while Seeadler Harbour would be developed into a major fleet base whose complete repair facilities would include drydocks, and a main naval supply base. It would serve Admiral Nimitz' naval forces as well as the Seventh Fleet.[3]

Halsey, who conferred with MacArthur in Brisbane in late 1943 before departing on a trip to Hawaii and the continental United States, opposed the seizure of Kavieng. He wished to apply the bypass technique and seize Emirau in the Saint Matthias Islands, about ninety miles northwest of Kavieng, for this group had never been taken by the Japanese. Kavieng, on the other hand, was a major air and naval base and was reported to be strongly defended. In December MacArthur told members of Halsey's staff that an attack against Emi-

---

[1] See above, pp. 5, 13.
[2] See also GHQ SWPA Warning Instns 3, 23 Nov 43, in ALAMO ANCHORAGE Jnl 1, 23 Nov 43–12 Feb 44.

[3] File on Manus-Kavieng base development in GHQ SWPA G–3 Jnl, 5 Nov 43.

EXPANDING INTO THE BISMARCK ARCHIPELAGO

rau or Kavieng would serve equally well in the isolation of Rabaul.[4]

Halsey spent four days with Nimitz at Pearl Harbor and then, in early January, flew to San Francisco where he and Nimitz conferred with Admiral King. Here, and later in Washington, the South Pacific commander made known his views on Kavieng and Emirau.[5]

Halsey was not able to carry his point at this time. He did however discuss timing and the question of naval support for Manus and Kavieng. These were important because by now the Central Pacific offensives were well under way. Nimitz' forces, having invaded the Gilberts in November 1943, were planning their initial move into the Marshalls (Kwajalein and Roi-Namur) in late January. Kavieng, almost four hundred miles from Cape Torokina, lay beyond fighter-plane range of Halsey's most advanced air base. Thus aircraft carriers would have to provide cover for the invasion forces, and Admiral Nimitz agreed to furnish them. General Mac-Arthur wanted carriers to cover the invasion of Manus as well, in case bad weather kept the Fifth Air Force planes grounded in New Guinea and at Cape Gloucester. Nimitz pointed out, however, that such weather could also affect carrier operations.[6]

Admiral Carney, Halsey's chief of staff, had visited Pearl Harbor in December and reported that the ships for Kavieng would not be available until 1 May.[7] This would also put off the Admiralties operation.[8] But Admiral Nimitz then suggested that by delaying his second Marshalls invasion (Eniwetok) until 1 May he could provide support for Manus and Kavieng about 1 April. MacArthur was ready and willing to invade Manus and Kavieng in March before moving to Hansa Bay, but the Joint Chiefs ordered Nimitz to deliver a strong carrier strike against Truk during March. No direct naval supporting forces could be available for Manus and Kavieng until April.[9] Nimitz proposed that representatives of all the Pacific areas meet in Pearl Harbor to settle details of co-ordination and timing.[10]

The command question came up again in January when Marshall asked Mac-Arthur's opinion on a draft directive for the next operations. The draft, Marshall told him, had received the approval of General Kenney, who was also in Washington. Except for Kavieng it did not specify any particular localities to be attacked but authorized advances into the Bismarck Archipelago preparatory to the drive to the Philippines. South Pacific forces attacking Kavieng were to be placed under MacArthur's "general di-

---

[4] Memo, SJC [Chamberlin] for Jnl, 21 Dec 43, sub: Conf at GHQ, 20 Dec 43, in GHQ SWPA G-3 Jnl, 21 Dec 43.

[5] Halsey and Bryan, *Admiral Halsey's Story*, pp. 186-87; Ernest J. King and Walter Muir Whitehill, *Fleet Admiral King: A Naval Record* (New York: W. W. Norton & Company, Inc., 1952), pp. 533-34.

[6] Rad, CINCPOA to CINCSWPA, CNO, and COMSOPAC, 7 Jan 44, CM-IN 8330.

[7] Memo, Carney for Halsey, 12 Dec 43, sub: CINCPOA-SOPAC Stf Conf, 9-12 Dec 43, in GHQ SWPA G-3 Jnl, 21 Dec 43.

[8] Memo, B F [Brig Gen Bonner Fellers, G-3 Sec GHQ SWPA], no addressee, 22 Dec 43, sub: Conf G-3 Plng Sec, in GHQ SWPA G-3 Jnl, 22 Dec 43.

[9] Rad, CINCPAC to COMINCH, 22 Dec 43, in GHQ SWPA G-3 Jnl, 24 Dec 43; Rad, Halsey to MacArthur, 5 Jan 44, and Rad, MacArthur to Marshall and Halsey, 6 Jan 44, and Rad, COMSOPAC to COMSOPAC Administration, 9 Jan 44, all in Marshall's IN Log.

[10] Rad, CINCPAC to CINCSWPA, CNO, and COMSOPAC, 7 Jan 44, CM-IN 8330.

rection," and Nimitz was ordered to provide fleet support and more assault shipping for Manus and Kavieng after the approaching conference at Pearl Harbor.[11]

MacArthur objected strenuously. After reviewing the course of CARTWHEEL operations, which took place along two axes and for which, therefore, "loose co-ordination" sufficed, he argued that in the Bismarck Archipelago the South and Southwest Pacific forces would be converging in a fairly restricted area. South Pacific forces alone could not capture Kavieng, and elements of the forces might have to be mingled. Constant, complete co-ordination of air and surface units would be required. Unity of command, vested in himself, should be applied, urged MacArthur, with the South Pacific forces under Halsey's direct command. And, finally, the Joint Chiefs rather than Nimitz should determine the extent of fleet support and additional assault shipping.[12]

In their orders for the extension into the Bismarck Archipelago, dated 23 and 24 January, the Joint Chiefs acceded to MacArthur's suggestions on fleet support in a left-handed way. They directed Nimitz to provide fleet support and cover for the Manus–Kavieng invasions under his direct command, and to attach more warships and assault shipping to MacArthur's and Halsey's forces. The exact amounts were to be determined at the forthcoming Pearl Harbor conference, which would then forward recommendations to Washington for approval.

Control over South Pacific forces remained the same as for CARTWHEEL. Halsey was in direct command under MacArthur's direction.[13]

The conference at Pearl Harbor convened on 27 January. Halsey, flying out from Washington, had been grounded by bad weather in Fort Worth, Texas, and again in San Francisco, and so was not present. Carney, whom he had authorized to make preliminary arrangements with MacArthur, represented him, as did General Harmon. Representing MacArthur were Sutherland, Kenney, and Kinkaid. Nimitz, Rear Adm. Forrest P. Sherman, and others spoke for the Central Pacific.

Sutherland made it quite clear that MacArthur now definitely wanted the South Pacific to capture Kavieng for use as an air base, not Emirau. Halsey's proposal was shelved for the time being.

Besides discussing operations in the Bismarck Archipelago, the conference covered a wide range of topics—the value of the Marianas, B–29's, the possibility of bypassing Truk, and the comparative merits of the Central and Southwest Pacific routes to the Philippines. All agreed that whether Truk was bypassed or not, Seeadler Harbour was essential as a fleet base for the approach to the Philippines.

Nimitz proposed to give long-range support to the Manus-Kavieng invasions with a two-day strike against Truk by the main body of the Pacific Fleet starting about 26 March. In addition he agreed to send two divisions of fast car-

---

[11] Rad 3097, Marshall to MacArthur, 17 Jan 44, in Marshall's OUT Log.

[12] Rad, MacArthur to Marshall, 19 Jan 44, in Marshall's IN Log.

[13] JCS 679, 24 Jan 44, title: Dirs for Seizure of Control of Bismarck Archipelago; Rads, JCS to CINCPAC and CINCSWPA, 23 Jan 44, with JCS 679.

riers to operate under Halsey's command during the Manus–Kavieng invasions, while other carrier divisions and fast battleships operated in covering positions.[14]

These were large forces indeed. As originally planned the Bismarck operations would have been extensive. In addition to the naval forces, Halsey planned to use all his land-based aircraft and two divisions in assault, with one in reserve. However, not one of the operations approved by the Joint Chiefs and MacArthur was carried out according to the original plan.

Reducing Rabaul and Kavieng

All during the invasions of Arawe, Cape Gloucester, and Saidor, and during the discussions over the Bismarck Archipelago operations, the Solomons air command had been putting forth a maximum effort to reduce Rabaul. Completion of the Torokina fighter strip at Empress Augusta Bay, Bougainville, was a major step forward, for now New Georgia- and Guadalcanal-based bombers could have fighter escort in their attacks. But by the end of 1943 it was clear that high-level bombing would not suffice to neutralize Rabaul. Obviously, success depended on completion of the bomber strips by the Piva River (Piva Uncle and Piva Yoke).[15]

Piva Uncle, eight thousand feet by three hundred feet, was ready as a staging field on 30 December 1943. On 5 January 1944 SBD's and TBF's from Munda staged through to attack Rabaul, but by noon, when the bombers arrived over the target, Rabaul was as usual blanketed by heavy clouds. A similar attack two days later met the same difficulties, but on 9 January Piva Yoke was ready and from then on bombers could be permanently based at the Bougainville fields and could reach Rabaul in the morning, before it was covered by clouds.

Thereafter during January TBF's, SBD's, B–25's, and B–24's struck regularly at Rabaul. The Japanese lost many planes but occasionally received reinforcements from Truk, and continued to resist with fighter interception and antiaircraft fire. ". . . the skies overhead

---

[14] These forces were to include 3 aircraft carriers, 3 light carriers, 7 cruisers, and 18 destroyers. In addition 4 old battleships, 7 cruisers, 4 escort carriers, 48 destroyers, 30 destroyer-escorts, 1 command ship (AGC), 19 transports, 3 LSD's, 5 minesweepers, 36 LST's, and 36 LCI's would be assigned to Halsey's Third Fleet for Kavieng, while for Manus the Seventh Fleet was to receive 3 light cruisers, 4 escort carriers, 35 destroyers, 8 patrol frigates, 1 AGC, 1 transport, 1 cargo ship, 2 minesweepers, 1 LSD, 13 APD's, 30 LST's, 30 LCI's, 70 LCT's, and 30 submarines. Halsey and Bryan, *Admiral Halsey's Story,* p. 188; Craven and Cate, *The Pacific: Guadalcanal to Saipan,* pp. 551–52; Kenney, *General Kenney Reports,* p. 346; Smith, *The Approach to the Philippines,* pp. 7–8; Halsey, Narrative Account of the South Pacific Campaign, OCMH; Rad, CINCPAC to COMINCH-CNO, 29 Jan 44, in GHQ SWPA G–3 Jnl, 30 Jan 44; Ltr, CINCPOA to COMINCH, 30 Jan 44, sub: Assignment Naval Forces and Assault Shipg to Third and Seventh Flts for Opns Against Bismarck Archipelago, ABC 384 Pac (17 Jan 43) Sec 3–A.

[15] Unless otherwise indicated this section is based on Craven and Cate, *The Pacific: Guadalcanal to Saipan,* pp. 350–56; Morison, *Breaking the Bismarcks Barrier,* pp. 337–66, 392–410; Samuel Eliot Morison, *History of United States Naval Operations in World War II,* VII, *Aleutians, Gilberts and Marshalls: June 1942–April 1944* (Boston: Little, Brown and Company, 1951), 330; *Building the Navy's Bases in World War II,* II, 268–74; USSBS, *The Allied Campaign Against Rabaul,* Operations, Japanese Monogr No. 110 (OCMH), p. 123; Southeast Area Naval Operations, III, Japanese Monogr No. 50 (OCMH), 6, 58–63.

JAPANESE SHIPS BURNING AT RABAUL

were the scene of continuous annihilation battles. . . ." [16]

By the end of January heavy bombers had flown 263 sorties over Rabaul; B–25's, 180 sorties; SBD's, 368; TBF's, 227; fighters, 1,850. Losses totaled 8 B–24's, 14 B–25's, 8 SBD's, 5 TBF's, 19 P–38's, 37 F4U's, 5 F6F's, and 6 New Zealand P–40's.

Damage to Japanese equipment and weapons on the ground was relatively light, for in late November the enemy had begun the prodigious task of digging every possible item underground in Rabaul's volcanic rock, a task that was well along by January. But all buildings were knocked flat. Ships and grounded planes

were especially vulnerable to low-level bombing and dive-bombing. By February 1944 the Allies had won a signal victory; Japanese surface ships stopped using the harbor.

During the same period Kavieng received increased attention from both Allies and Japanese. Halsey, expecting to assault the base eventually, wanted to reduce Kavieng to help cut the Japanese lines of communication from rear bases to Rabaul. The Japanese, well aware of the threat to Rabaul, decided to strengthen Kavieng and the Admiralties to help protect Rabaul.

In October Imamura had sent the *230th Infantry* of the *38th Division* from Rabaul to New Ireland. Next month he sent an emissary to Tokyo to ask for one

[16] Southeast Area Naval Operations, III, Japanese Monogr No. 50 (OCMH), 58.

more division. *Imperial Headquarters* responded by sending the *1st Independent Mixed Regiment* to New Ireland. It reached its destination in late 1943 and early 1944. Imamura placed it, together with the *230th Infantry,* under Maj. Gen. Takeo Ito, infantry group commander of the *38th Division.* Ito's soldiers and the *14th Naval Base Force* were responsible for defense of New Ireland.

In December Halsey set a trap and ordered Buka bombarded to lure Japanese planes and ships away from Kavieng. Admiral Sherman, lying east of Kavieng with the carriers *Bunker Hill* and *Monterey* plus escorts, was then to strike at Kavieng in the hope of catching troopships and warships in the harbor. Before dawn on Christmas morning Sherman launched eighty-six planes, which bombed Kavieng at 0745 and were back aboard their carriers by 1015. But the results were disappointing as there were almost no ships in the harbor.

On New Year's day Sherman delivered another strike from 220 miles east of Kavieng. Outside the harbor his planes caught some of the ships that had just unloaded part of the *1st Independent Mixed Regiment* but the Japanese air cover of forty-two planes prevented the ships from suffering damage. Sherman struck Kavieng again three days later, again without doing much damage; no ships were present and the Japanese planes were out against Cape Gloucester.

In February the Fifth Air Force, using Finschhafen as a fighter base and Cape Gloucester as an emergency field, began to attack Kavieng with the aim of softening it before the projected invasion, cutting the line of communications to Rabaul, and supporting the South Pacific's invasion of the Green Islands. On the 11th forty-eight B–24's with P–38 escorts caught Kavieng's planes on the ground, and the next two days saw similar attacks.

During the first two weeks of February Rabaul's defenses grew obviously weaker as the Air Command, Solomons, maintained the intensity of its attack.[17] There were few attempts to intercept until 19 February. On that date twenty-eight SBD's, twenty-three TBF's, and sixty-eight fighters, finding no ships in the harbor, put bombs and rockets on Lakunai airfield. Twenty B–24's with thirty-five escorting fighters bombed from high altitudes. About fifty Japanese fighters attempted to break up the attack without success. This was the last attempted interception. Thereafter attacking Rabaul became a milk run. Allied pilots encountered antiaircraft fire but no planes. Rabaul no longer could threaten any Allied advance except one directed against itself.

Rabaul's impotence was of course largely brought about by the South and Southwest Pacific air and naval campaigns that had been under way for so long, but it was partly brought about by Admiral Nimitz' naval forces. The Central Pacific had invaded Kwajalein and Roi-Namur on 31 January and seized them so rapidly that the reserve and garrison forces did not have to be committed. When the Joint Chiefs told Nimitz that they were willing to delay the Manus–Kavieng invasions in order to proceed directly to Eniwetok, using the uncommitted troops, Nimitz decided to

---

[17] From 1 through 19 February fighters flew 1,579 sorties; B–24's, 256; B–25's, 263; TBF's, 244, and SBD's 573.

go there as quickly as possible. Accordingly he invaded Eniwetok on 17 February. In support of this move the main body of the Pacific Fleet, commanded by Vice Adm. Raymond A. Spruance, attacked Truk on 16 and 17 February, over one month ahead of schedule. Spruance's strike was an outstanding success. The *Combined Fleet* had already escaped toward home waters, but Spruance's pilots destroyed or damaged 250–275 planes as well as thousands of tons of shipping. Admiral Koga, thus almost bereft of planes, ordered all naval planes out of the Southeast Area at once. "... Rabaul, compelled to face the enemy with ground resources alone and completely isolated, was abandoned." [18]

The Allies dropped 20,584 tons of bombs on Rabaul throughout the war, and fired 383 tons of naval shells after Rabaul was reduced to the indignity of suffering destroyer and nocturnal PBY bombardment in March. Thirty naval vessels were sunk, 23 damaged. In addition 154 large cargo vessels and 517 barges were sunk; 70 small cargo vessels suffered damage. [19] "... The [Japanese] Navy lost the pick of its flight personnel at Rabaul, a fact which told heavily upon subsequent efforts to rebuild our air forces." [20]

Rabaul was abandoned only in the strategic sense, and it was impotent only for offensive action. It could have defended itself with bloody efficiency had

the Allies attacked. The garrison of New Britain numbered almost 98,000 men (76,300 in the *8th Area Army* and 21,570 in the naval forces). The rugged country of Gazelle Peninsula was well suited for defense. By the war's end some 350 miles of tunnels and caves had been excavated. At peak strength Rabaul had 367 antiaircraft guns (of which 73 were destroyed by air bombing), ranging in type and caliber from 13.2-mm. to 120.7-mm. dual purpose. There were 43 coast defense guns (1 destroyed) of calibers up to and including 150-mm. Of the 475 artillery guns and howitzers (37-mm. to 150-mm.), none was destroyed by bombing, nor were any of the 1,762 machine guns. Imamura's men also had tanks, mines, ditches, caves, bunkers, and concrete pillboxes, as well as rifles, grenades, bayonets, and ample ammunition.

Rabaul would not have been as valuable to the Allies as it was to the Japanese in their southward advance. It would have been useful to the Allies only in a northward move against Truk and the Marianas. Because the Joint Chiefs had decided to advance westward, and because Seeadler Harbour in the Admiralties was better than Rabaul's, the Japanese fortress was not worth the price the Japanese surely would have exacted.

Seizure of the Green Islands

Plans and Preparations

In December 1943 Admiral Halsey's planes were bombing Rabaul, his ships were patrolling the Solomon Sea, and his ground troops in Bougainville were either fighting the enemy or consolidating positions in anticipation of a fight.

---

[18] Southeast Area Naval Operations, III, Japanese Monogr No. 50 (OCMH), 6.

[19] These and subsequent statistics come from USSBS, *The Allied Campaign Against Rabaul*, pp. 11–36.

[20] Outline of Southeast Area Naval Air Operations, November 1942–June 1943, Pt. III, Japanese Monogr No. 107 (OCMH), p. 59.

But this was not enough to satisfy him. When he learned that Nimitz' plans, as they stood in December, would not permit the invasion of Manus and Kavieng for several months, he decided to seize an air base site within fighter range of Kavieng in the meantime.[21] At a conference in Port Moresby on 20 December attended by MacArthur, Kinkaid, Carney, Chamberlin, and others, the South Pacific representatives proposed that the Southwest Pacific attack Manus directly while South Pacific forces captured the Green Islands, some 37 miles northwest of Buka, and established there an airfield and PT boat base. Situated 117 miles east of Rabaul and 220 miles southeast of Kavieng, this circular coral atoll was not strongly held. The Japanese used it only as a barge staging base between Rabaul and Buka. Allied seizure of the atoll would put South Pacific fighter planes within range of Kavieng, extend the range of PT boat patrols as far as New Ireland, and cut the Japanese seaborne supply route to Buka.

MacArthur, deciding for the time being against a move to Manus in advance of the projected invasion of Hansa Bay, approved simultaneous attacks against Manus and Kavieng and told the South Pacific to go ahead with the plan to attack the Green Islands about 1 February.[22]

The island group consists of four flat, thickly wooded coral atolls which encircle a lagoon. The group is about nine miles long from north to south, five miles from east to west. Horseshoe-shaped Nissan, the main island, provided good landing beaches on its west shore inside the lagoon, but it was not known whether the passage between Barahun and Nissan would accommodate landing craft. Therefore Halsey sent four PT boats from Cape Torokina to examine the passage on the night of 10–11 January. They found seventeen feet of water there, or enough to float an LST.[23]

Admiral Halsey, who returned to Nouméa on 3 February, placed control of the operation and responsibility for the co-ordination of amphibious planning in Admiral Wilkinson's hands on 5 February.[24] This action confirmed warning orders which had been issued in early January.

Only destroyer-transports and landing craft were assigned to the attack force. Command of the landing force was given to General Barrowclough of the 3d New Zealand Division. Barrowclough's division (less the 8th Brigade Group), the 976th Antiaircraft Artillery Gun Battalion of the U.S. Army, a PT base unit, communications units, a boat pool, and a large naval base unit including an en-

---

[21] Unless otherwise indicated this section is based on Craven and Cate, *The Pacific: Guadalcanal to Saipan*, p. 355; Gillespie, *The Pacific*, pp. 168–95; Halsey and Bryan, *Admiral Halsey's Story*, p. 188; Morison, *Breaking the Bismarcks Barrier*, pp. 412–19; Rentz, *Bougainville and the Northern Solomons*, pp. 114–17; *Building the Navy's Bases in World War II*, II, 274–76; Halsey, Narrative Account of the South Pacific Campaign; Southeast Area Naval Operations, III, Japanese Monogr No. 50 (OCMH), 60–62.

[22] Memo, SJC [Chamberlin] for Jnl, 21 Dec 43, sub: Conf at GHQ, 20 Dec 43, in GHQ SWPA G–3 Jnl, 21 Dec 43.

[23] A fully loaded LST draws 14 feet 11¼ inches of water astern, 9 feet 9¼ inches when loaded for landing operations.

[24] Rad, Comdr Third Flt to CINCSWPA, CINCPAC, and all TF's SOPAC, 5 Feb 44, in GHQ SWPA G–3 Jnl, 7 Feb 44.

tire construction regiment, constituted the landing force. Halsey ordered the Solomons air command and Ainsworth's and Merrill's cruiser task forces to support and cover the invasion, and arranged with MacArthur for Kenney's air forces to deliver the attacks on Kavieng during the first fifteen days of February.[25]

As South Pacific headquarters estimated that Rabaul and Kavieng would be virtually neutralized by mid-February, D Day was set for the 15th. General Barrowclough, who had been island commander at Vella Lavella, moved his headquarters to Guadalcanal in January to be near Wilkinson during the planning. They decided to send a large reconnaissance party to Green in order to determine the strength of the enemy garrison and to examine possible airfield sites, beaches, and naval base sites, and the lagoon tides. The party was to spend twenty-four hours ashore.

Three hundred and twenty-two soldiers of the 30th New Zealand Battalion and twenty-seven American and eleven New Zealand hydrographic, air, small boat, communications, and intelligence specialists boarded three APD's on 29 January. The destroyer-transports hove to west of Barahun about midnight and launched landing craft. Two of the torpedo boats that had checked the passage led the landing craft through to the

beach. Once ashore the reconnaissance party waited for daylight while the APD's hauled clear. Guarded by the New Zealand soldiers, the specialists set to work and gathered their data. They found a good airfield site, and estimated that the enemy garrison numbered about a hundred. The twelve hundred native inhabitants proved so friendly and cooperative that preliminary naval bombardment to support the main landing was omitted. The specialists were not molested, but the enemy fired on one landing craft that went to the south part of the island where there was an abandoned Roman Catholic mission and killed three New Zealanders and one American. When Rabaul heard of the landing Kusaka sent six bomb-carrying fighters to Green. They attacked the landing boats but did no damage.

The APD's reclaimed the New Zealanders and Americans on 31 January and returned safely to Guadalcanal. On the way back two of the escorting destroyers sank a Japanese submarine near Buka Passage.

The Japanese Green Islands garrison reported it had suffered heavy losses, asked for reinforcements, and fled northwest in three landing craft to the Feni Islands. Kusaka put 123 men aboard a submarine on 1 February and sent them to Nissan. The submarine hove to off the northeast coast about midnight in a sea so rough that after 77 men had gone ashore, the submarine commander called off the operation and returned to Rabaul with 46 men still on board. The return of the original garrison to Nissan on 5 February brought total enemy strength to 102.

[25] Rad, Comdr Third Flt to CINCSWPA, 22 Jan 44, in GHQ SWPA G–3 Jnl, 23 Jan 44; Rad, MacArthur to Comdrs AAF, ANF, ALAMO, et al., 27 Jan 44, in GHQ SWPA G–3 Jnl, 27 Jan 44. Rear Adm. John F. Shafroth, Halsey's deputy commander, issued the warning orders on 3 January. Ltr, COMSOPAC to COMAIRSOPAC, COMGENSOPAC, et al., 3 Jan 44, sub: Warning Orders, in GHQ SWPA G–3 Jnl, 6 Jan 44.

The Landings

In the meantime the South Pacific's APD's returned from service in the Cape Gloucester operation. Shortly before 12 February the APD's, LST's, LCI's LCT's, LCM's, and patrol boats and coastal transports of the amphibious force took aboard the 5,806-man New Zealand-American landing force at Tulagi, Guadalcanal, the Russells, New Georgia, and Vella Lavella.[26] The ships, timing their departures so as to meet off Bougainville on 14 February, sailed from their various ports on the 12th and 13th.

A Japanese reconnaissance plane spotted them west of Bougainville on 14 February, reported their presence to Rabaul, and kept contact. Admiral Kusaka sent thirty-two planes against the ships throughout the moonlit night of 14–15 February. They did no damage to Wilkinson's ships but managed to hit the cruiser *Saint Louis* in Admiral Ainsworth's task force, which was operating south of Saint George's Channel. Twelve Japanese planes were lost.

The APD's arrived in the transport area west of Barahun shortly after 0600 on 15 February and promptly dispatched LCVP's toward the passage. Thirty-two fighters of the Solomons air command were on station overhead. But Kusaka did not yield easily. He sent out seven-

teen bombers and about fifteen of these attacked the landing craft. They scored no hits. At the same time Kenney's airmen, with four A–20 and seven B–25 squadrons, delivered a strong blow against Kavieng which kept that base from attacking the invaders at Green.

Within two hours all men of the New Zealand combat units went ashore on Nissan. During the day all ships and boats were completely unloaded and with the exception of the LCT's, all left for the south once they were emptied. The LCT's remained as part of the naval advanced base.

Between 15 and 20 February the New Zealand infantrymen hunted down and killed the Japanese garrison. Ten New Zealanders and 3 Americans were killed; 21 New Zealanders and 3 Americans were wounded.

By 17 March 16,448 men and 43,088 tons of supplies had been sent to the Green Islands. The 22d Naval Construction Regiment had begun work at once. Within two days of the landings a PT boat base opened. This extended the range of torpedo boat patrols to New Ireland and along the entire northeast coast of Bougainville. By 4 March a 5,000-foot fighter field was ready; in late March a 6,000-foot bomber field was opened. Kavieng now lay within range of fighters and light bombers as well as heavy bombers from Bougainville. But, stripped of its naval planes when Admiral Koga ordered their withdrawal in February, it had already ceased to menace the Allies.

---

[26] Eleven destroyers escorted; two aircraft rescue boats and two tugs were also in the amphibious force. There were 4,242 New Zealanders and 1,564 Americans in the landing force.

CHAPTER XVI

Action in the Admiralties

The Decision

First Plans

By the time Halsey's forces invaded the Green Islands, the Southwest Pacific's plans for moves to the Admiralties and Hansa Bay, which had been started in November 1943, were well developed.[1] On 13 February General MacArthur issued operations instructions to the South and Southwest Pacific Areas which called for these commands to gain control of the Bismarck Archipelago and to isolate Rabaul by seizing Manus and Kavieng about 1 April.[2] To General Krueger's ALAMO Force, supported by Allied Air and Allied Naval Forces, he assigned responsibility for the seizure of Seeadler Harbour and Manus, as well as Hansa Bay. Using naval construction battalions and Army service units furnished by Admiral Halsey, Krueger was to start building a major naval base at Seeadler Harbour and to develop the Japanese airfields at Lorengau on Manus and Momote Plantation on Los Negros. Mac-

Arthur also warned Krueger to make ready for the drive west along the New Guinea coast.

As in past and future operations, Krueger was responsible for the co-ordination of plans. But in these orders General MacArthur departed from the previous practice in his area and adopted principles similar to those prevailing in the South and Central Pacific areas. He specified that the amphibious (naval) commander would be in command of all assault forces, ships and troops but not aircraft, until the landing force was established ashore. Then the amphibious commander would pass the command to the landing force commander, who would become again responsible to his normal military superior—General Krueger in the case of units assigned to the ALAMO Force.[3]

The operations, as planned, differed from previous ones in another important respect. In one general area three separate naval forces would be operating: Halsey's, Kinkaid's, and the additional forces from Nimitz. Chamberlin therefore suggested that in the event of a major naval action command of these

---

[1] GHQ SWPA Warning Instns 3, 23 Nov 43, in ALAMO ANCHORAGE Jnl 1, 23 Nov 43–12 Feb 44.

[2] GHQ SWPA OI 44, 13 Feb 44, in GHQ SWPA G–3 Jnl, 13 Feb 44. Unless otherwise indicated this chapter is based on [Maj. William C. Frierson] *The Admiralties: Operations of the 1st Cavalry Division (29 February–18 May 1944)*, AMERICAN FORCES IN ACTION (Washington, 1946).

[3] This change was suggested by Chamberlin who felt that previous orders had, in this respect, been unsound. Note, SJC to CINC, 12 Feb 44, in GHQ SWPA G–3 Jnl, 13 Feb 44.

forces be vested in Halsey, who would be the senior admiral present.[4] This suggestion was accepted, although for some reason it was not followed in similar situations at Hollandia and Leyte.

Forces assigned to General Krueger for the Admiralties totaled 45,110 men. They included:

Forces	Number of Men
Southwest Pacific ground units	25,974
1st Cavalry Division	
Antiaircraft and coast artillery units	
592d Engineer Boat and Shore Regiment	
1st Marine Amphibian Tractor Battalion	
Engineer, medical, ordnance, quartermaster, signal, and naval base units	
Air units: No. 73 Wing, RAAF	2,488
South Pacific naval construction units	9,545
South Pacific Army service units	7,103

These were to be concentrated at Oro Bay and Cape Cretin. The 6th Division was designated as GHQ reserve.

Hansa Bay was supposed to be invaded on 26 April by the 24th and 32d Divisions. There an air and light naval base would assist in the isolation of Rabaul and the Madang–Alexishafen area and would support operations westward.[5]

The Target: Enemy Dispositions

The Admiralties, lying 200 miles northeast of New Guinea, 260 miles west of Kavieng, and 200 miles northeast of Wewak, were admirably situated to assist in isolating Rabaul and in supporting the approach to the Philippines.

They contained two airfields as well as a superb harbor. The Japanese had built and used the airfields but, possessing Rabaul, had never made extensive use of Seeadler. This harbor, formed by the horseshoe-shaped curvature of the two major islands, had a surveyed area 6 miles wide, 20 miles long, and 120 feet deep, ample for the fleets of World War II. Guarding the harbor entrance is a line of islets—Koruniat, Ndrilo, Hauwei, Pityilu, and others—which parallel Manus' north coast.[6] (*Map 19*)

Manus, the largest in the group, is separated from Los Negros by a narrow strait, Loniu Passage. Forty-nine miles from east to west and sixteen miles across, Manus is a heavily wooded island of volcanic origin. Mangrove swamps cover much of the shore line. A range of mountains, two thousand to three thousand feet in height, extends the east-west length. Many of the streams were navigable for small boats, and nearly all could be forded except when in spate. Principal overland routes consisted of four native tracks: three ran from the north coast over the high country; the fourth extended from Lorengau to the west part of Manus.

Los Negros, much smaller than Manus, is irregularly shaped and cut by several inlets. Papitalai Harbour, an extension of Seeadler Harbour, is separated from Hyane Harbour by a low spit only fifty yards across. Natives had built a skidway over the spit to drag their canoes from one harbor to the other.

---

[4] *Ibid.*

[5] Memo, Chamberlin for CINC, 9 Feb 44, sub: Outline Plan—Hansa Bay, and Memo, Chamberlin for Comdrs, 9 Feb 44, sub: Hansa Bay—SW Pac Forces, both in GHQ SWPA G–3 Jnl, 9 Feb 44.

[6] Data in this subsection are derived from [Frierson] *The Admiralties;* Morison, *Breaking the Bismarcks Barrier,* pp. 436–37; 8th Area Army Operations, Japanese Monogr No. 110 (OCMH), p. 133; Southeast Area Naval Operations, III, Japanese Monogr No. 50 (OCMH), 35–36.

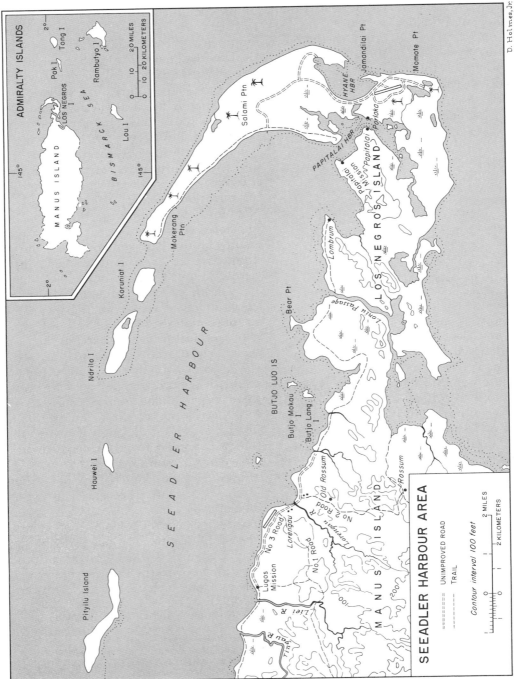

ADMIRALTY ISLANDS

2°

Pak I
Tong I

Los Negros I

MANUS ISLAND

BISMARCK SEA

Rambutyo I

Lou I

145°

145°

2°

0   10   20 MILES
0   10   20 KILOMETERS

Pityilu Island

Hauwei I

Ndrilo I

Koruniat I

SEEADLER HARBOUR

Mokerang Ptn

Salami Ptn

HYANE HBR

Jamondilai Pt

Porlaka

PAPITALAI HBR

Momote Pt

Papitalai

Papitalai Mission

Lombrum

LOS NEGROS ISLAND

Loniu Passage

Bear Pt

BUTJO LUO IS

Butjo Mokau

Butjo Long I

Old Rossum

Rossum

Lorengau R

No. 2 Road

MANUS ISLAND

No. 3 Road

No. 1 Road

Lorengau

Lugos Mission

Liei R

Tingau R

100

200

SEEADLER HARBOUR AREA

============ UNIMPROVED ROAD

----------- TRAIL

Contour interval 100 feet

0   1   2 MILES
0   1   2 KILOMETERS

D. Holmes, Jr.

MAP 19

The center part of Los Negros, in the vicinity of Momote, is flat and fertile. The swampy region north of the skidway had some coconut plantations. West of Momote are three jungled hill masses about two hundred feet high.

The thirteen thousand natives (Melanesian with some Micronesian admixture) lived largely in Los Negros and eastern Manus. Coconut was the standard commercial crop. The natives, who sailed their large canoes with skill, also dived for trochus shell and pearls. The climate—hot and wet—is about the same as that of the rest of the region.

Japanese troops had landed at Lorengau in April 1942 and developed an airfield there. The next year they built a 5,000-foot strip at Momote and improved the Lorengau field. Toward the end of the year, as the Allies advanced to the Markham Valley, the Huon Peninsula, and Cape Gloucester, the Japanese began using the Admiralties' fields as staging points for aircraft flying between Rabaul and Wewak and Hollandia.

Up to now the garrison had consisted of the *51st Transport Regiment,* but when the Japanese decided to strengthen Kavieng they also decided to reinforce the Admiralties. Elements of the *14th Naval Base Force,* the main body of which was stationed in New Ireland, were sent to Los Negros and Manus. On 9 December General Imamura directed Adachi to send one infantry regiment and an artillery battalion from New Guinea to be rehabilitated in the Palaus, from where they were to proceed to the Admiralties.[7] The *66th Infantry* reached the Palaus safely, but replacements and

reinforcing units en route from Japan were lost to a U.S. submarine. Then Imamura organized an infantry and an artillery battalion in the Palaus out of other replacements. These set out for the Admiralties in January, but their ships were so harried by submarines that they turned back. Imamura therefore arranged with Kusaka for destroyers to carry the *2d Battalion* of the *1st Independent Mixed Regiment* from Kavieng to the Admiralties. This movement was accomplished on 23–25 January, and at the month's end the *1st Battalion, 229th Infantry,* was dispatched. Though it suffered air attack on the way, it arrived safely.

By 2 February the Japanese garrison consisted of the two infantry battalions, the *51st Transport Regiment,* and several naval detachments. In command was Col. Yoshio Ezaki, who also led the *51st Transport Regiment.* He disposed his main strength on Los Negros to defend Seeadler Harbour and Momote airfield against attack from the north. An Allied attack through Hyane Harbour was not expected because it was small, with so narrow an entrance that landing craft would come under fire as they passed through.

"Prepare for Immediate Reconnaissance in Force"

General Kenney's Allied Air Forces had prepared elaborate plans for supporting the Admiralties invasion from Dobodura and Nadzab. During January and the first two weeks of February his planes bombed the Admiralties and Kavieng, and also continued their attacks against the Wewak airfields so as to keep them out of action and destroy the *4th*

---

[7] The Admiralties remained under Imamura's control after the reorganization in March 1944.

Air Army's planes. By 6 February Momote and Lorengau airfields were unserviceable, and no planes were present. Antiaircraft fire had stopped completely, not because the guns were destroyed but because Colonel Ezaki, to conceal his positions from the Allies, had ordered his troops neither to fire nor to move about in daylight.

At this time Kenney and Whitehead were eagerly seeking methods by which the whole advance could be made to move more rapidly. Whitehead wanted to get the Admiralties out of the way soon, so that he would have time to concentrate against Wewak and Hollandia in the westward advance. Kenney, who had experience in New Guinea with quick seizures of airfields by light forces, had a scheme in mind for another such operation. Some time before 23 February he told Whitehead to hit Los Negros hard but not to crater the runway. Hoping to force the Japanese to evacuate Los Negros and retire to Manus, he ordered frequent low-altitude photo-reconnaissance missions.[8]

The Allies were not yet fully aware that Japanese air resistance in the Southeast Area was almost a thing of the past, and that they had won. They knew, however, that the enemy was weakening. The runways at Rabaul were usually cratered. On 21 February Allied intelligence reasoned that Japanese aircraft were "absconding" from Rabaul, probably to Truk and other bases in the Carolines.[9] Further, five Seventh Fleet destroyers

sank a Japanese transport about one hundred miles east of Lorengau during a sweep on 22–23 February. Survivors testified that they were part of a 400-man detachment of air force ground crews that was being transferred to bases farther north. Three of the destroyers then sank a Japanese destroyer and a cargo ship south of New Hanover, skirted the southwest coast of New Ireland, and steamed safely past Rabaul through Saint George's Channel, which lies between New Britain and New Ireland, on the way back to base. The other two bombarded Kavieng. No Japanese aircraft opposed either group although these waters had formerly been dominated by Japanese air and surface forces.

On 23 February—shortly after the great Truk raid and the withdrawal of Japanese naval aircraft from the Southeast Area—Whitehead forwarded to Kenney a reconnaissance report from three B-25's that had just flown over Los Negros and Lorengau for ninety minutes. Although they flew as low as twenty feet, they were not fired on, saw no Japanese, no trucks, and no laundry hung out to dry. The airfields were pitted and overgrown with grass. The whole area looked "completely washed out." Whitehead recommended that a ground reconnaissance party go in at once to check.[10]

When Kenney received this message he was at his headquarters in Brisbane. Concluding, with Whitehead, that "Los Negros was ripe for the plucking," he hurried to MacArthur's office and proposed to MacArthur, Kinkaid, and part of MacArthur's staff that a few hundred troops carried on APD's seize Los Negros

---

[8] Kenney, *General Kenney Reports*, p. 358; Craven and Cate, *The Pacific: Guadalcanal to Saipan*, p. 559.

[9] GHQ SWPA G–2 Daily Summary of Enemy Int, and GHQ SWPA G–2 Est of Enemy Sit 700, 20–21 Feb 44, both in GHQ SWPA G–3 Jnl, 21 Feb 44.

[10] Rad, Comdr AdVon Fifth AF to Comdr AAF, 23 Feb 44, in GHQ SWPA G–3 Jnl, 23 Feb 44.

and repair Momote airfield at once, rather than capture Seeadler Harbour, so that they could be reinforced and supplied by air if need be. This should be a reconnaissance in force. If resistance proved too strong the invaders could withdraw. A quick seizure of the Admiralties, Kenney argued, might make possible the bypassing of Kavieng and Hansa Bay.[11]

General Willoughby, in contrast with the airmen, was convinced that the Japanese garrison was fairly strong. His estimate for 25 February placed enemy strength at 4,050.[12]

MacArthur quickly decided in favor of the reconnaissance in force. Next day he radioed orders to Krueger, Whitehead, and Barbey to "prepare for immediate reconnaissance in force." He directed Krueger and Barbey to send eight hundred men of the 1st Cavalry Division and other units aboard two APD's and one destroyer division from Oro Bay to Momote not later than 29 February. If successful the cavalrymen were to prepare the airfield for transport aircraft and hold their positions pending arrival of reinforcements.[13]

The Reconnaissance in Force

Preparations

With but five days between MacArthur's radiogram and D Day there was little time to make ready. But in accordance with GHQ's earlier orders, planning had begun in January when Krueger directed the 1st Cavalry Division to prepare terrain, logistical, and intelligence studies. Krueger, Whitehead, and Barbey had begun a series of planning conferences on 19 February.

Kinkaid's and Barbey's plans, issued on 26 February, provided for transporting and landing the reconnaissance force, then reinforcing it or withdrawing it if necessary. With the cruisers *Nashville* and *Phoenix* and four destroyers Rear Adm. Russell S. Berkey was to provide cover during the approach to the Admiralties and to deliver supporting gunfire against Los Negros, Lorengau, and Seeadler Harbour during the landings. The attack group, which Barbey placed under command of Rear Adm. William M. Fechteler, his deputy, consisted of eight destroyers and three APD's.[14]

The cruisers were added to the force because General MacArthur elected to accompany the expedition, and to invite Admiral Kinkaid to go with him, to judge from firsthand observation whether to evacuate or hold after the reconnaissance. The first plans had called for just one destroyer division and three APD's, but when Kinkaid learned of MacArthur's decision he added two cruisers and four destroyers. This was necessary because a destroyer had neither accommodations nor communications equipment suitable for a man of MacArthur's age and rank. A cruiser would serve better, but a single cruiser could not go to the Admiralties. Kinkaid's policy for-

---

[11] Kenney, *General Kenney Reports,* p. 359.

[12] Note, G–2 to G–3, 25 Feb 44, in GHQ SWPA G–3 Jnl, 25 Feb 44. GHQ SWPA G–3 Monthly Summary of Enemy Dispositions, 29 Feb 44, in GHQ SWPA G–3 Jnl, 29 Feb 44, gives the same figures.

[13] Rad, MacArthur to Comdr ALAMO, CG AdVon Fifth AF, and Comdr VII Amphib Force, 24 Feb 44, in GHQ SWPA G–3 Jnl, 24 Feb 44.

[14] Morison, *Breaking the Bismarcks Barrier,* pp. 435–36; Rad, Comdr Seventh Flt to CTF's 76 and 74, and CTG 74.2, 26 Feb 44, in GHQ SWPA G–3 Jnl, 28 Feb 44.

bade sending only one ship of any type on a tactical mission. Therefore he sent two cruisers, and the two cruisers required four additional destroyers as escorts.[15]

The air plans prescribed the usual missions but necessarily compressed them into a few days. Bad weather limited the air effort on 26 February, but next day four B–25 squadrons attacked Momote and Lorengau while seven squadrons of B–24's attacked the Wewak fields and B–25's struck at Hansa Bay. Heavy attacks against the Admiralties and Hansa Bay followed on 28 February, and that night seven B–24's attacked Hollandia, far to the west.[16]

Krueger had originally planned to send a preinvasion reconnaissance party to the western tip of Manus, from where it was to patrol eastward for several weeks and radio reports to his headquarters. But the new orders caused him to cancel this plan in favor of a reconnaissance on Los Negros. More data on Hyane Harbour and Japanese dispositions there and at Momote would have been useful, for there was still no agreement on enemy strength in that region. Willoughby's estimate of 4,050 conflicted sharply with that offered by Whitehead, who stated on 26 February that there were not more than 300 Japanese, mostly line of communications troops, on Los Negros and Manus.[17] And the 1st Cavalry Division's estimate placed Japanese strength at 4,900, despite an assertion

in its field order that "Recent air reconnaissance . . . results in no enemy action and no signs of enemy occupation." [18]

Because Krueger did not wish to risk betraying Allied plans by sending a patrol to Hyane Harbour and Momote, he decided to send one to examine the region about one mile south of the harbor. Accordingly, at 0645, 27 February, a PBY delivered a six-man party of ALAMO Scouts to a point five hundred yards off Los Negros' southeast shore under cover of air bombardment. The scouts took a rubber boat ashore, found a large bivouac area on southeastern Los Negros, and reported by radio that the area between the coast and Momote was "lousy with Japs." But when this report reached GHQ Kenney discounted it. He pointed out, with reason, that twenty-five enemy "in the woods at night" might give that impression and that the patrol had examined not the airdrome but only a part of the south end of Los Negros.[19]

This patrol did provide more data on which to base plans for naval gunfire support. Kinkaid and Barbey decided that one cruiser and two destroyers should fire on the bivouac area while the other cruiser and two more destroyers fired at Lorengau and Seeadler Harbour and other destroyers supported the landing itself.

The 1st Cavalry Division, which was

[15] Oral statement of Adm Kinkaid to the author et al., 16 Nov 53.

[16] Craven and Cate, *The Pacific: Guadalcanal to Saipan*, p. 563.

[17] Rad, Comdr AdVon Fifth AF to Comdr AAF, 26 Feb 44, in GHQ SWPA G–3 Jnl, 26 Feb 44.

[18] Cf par. 1a (2) of BREWER TF FO 2, 25 Feb 44, with Annex 1, Int, in ALAMO ANCHORAGE Jnl 3, 24–26 Feb 44. The reconnaissance forces estimated 1,500 on Los Negros, altogether 4,350 in the Admiralties. ALAMO FO 9 and BREWER TF FO 1 are orders prepared for the one-division invasion of the Admiralties scheduled for 1 April.

[19] Kenney, *General Kenney Reports*, p. 361.

to provide the landing force, was unique in the U.S. Army in World War II. Dismounted and serving as infantry, it was a square division of two brigades plus division artillery. Each brigade consisted of two cavalry regiments of about two thousand men each. Each regiment was composed of headquarters, service, and weapons troops, and two squadrons. The squadrons contained a headquarters troop, three rifle troops, and a weapons troop. The weapons troop, using the organization of the infantry heavy weapons company, had been added in 1943.[20] Division artillery had a headquarters battery, two 75-mm. pack howitzer battalions, and two 105-mm. howitzer battalions.

MacArthur's orders of 24 February specified that the landing force should number eight hundred men, including five hundred men of one squadron with additional artillery and service troops, but the next day he recommended that a slightly stronger force be used.[21]

On 26 February Krueger established the occupation force for the Admiralties as the BREWER Task Force. He placed it under Maj. Gen. Innis P. Swift, commanding the 1st Cavalry Division, and assigned to it the ground force units previously allotted by GHQ.

For the D-Day landing Krueger and Swift organized the BREWER reconnaissance force under Brig. Gen. William C. Chase, commander of the 1st Cavalry Brigade. It consisted of detachments from 1st Cavalry Brigade Headquarters and Headquarters Troop; the 2d Squadron, 5th Cavalry; two 75-mm. howitzers of B Battery, 99th Field Artillery Battalion; the 673d Antiaircraft Artillery Battery (.50-caliber machine guns); the 1st Platoon, B Troop, 1st Medical Squadron; the 30th Portable Surgical Hospital; air and naval liaison officers and a shore fire control party; and a detachment of the Australian New Guinea Administrative Unit—or about a thousand men.

If the landing succeeded and the reconnaissance force stayed, the BREWER support force, under Col. Hugh T. Hoffman, was to land on D plus 2. Hoffman's command embraced the remainder of the 5th Cavalry and the 99th Field Artillery Battalion, in addition to C Battery (90-mm.), 168th Antiaircraft Artillery Battalion; A Battery (multiple .50-caliber mount), 211th Antiaircraft Artillery Battalion; medical, engineer, and signal units from the 1st Cavalry Division; and E Company, Shore Battalion, 592d Engineer Boat and Shore Regiment. The 40th Naval Construction Battalion and detachments from other elements of the 4th Construction Brigade, all from the South Pacific, were to accompany the Support Force.

The remainder of the BREWER Task Force, including the rest of the 1st Cavalry Brigade and the 2d Cavalry Brigade, was to follow if needed as soon as shipping became available. To shorten sailing time, Cape Cretin was to be used as a staging area for reinforcements.

Hyane Harbour, scene of the initial

---

[20] The 1st Cavalry Division, a Regular Army unit with a high percentage of Regular officers and enlisted men, was not organized until 1921, but its regiments had long and distinguished histories. The 5th Cavalry (originally the 2d Cavalry), organized in 1855, was commanded by Robert E. Lee, and the 7th Cavalry was George A. Custer's old regiment.

[21] Rad, MacArthur to Comdr ALAMO, CG AdVon Fifth AF, and Comdr VII Amphib Force, 25 Feb 44, in GHQ SWPA G–3 Jnl, 25 Feb 44.

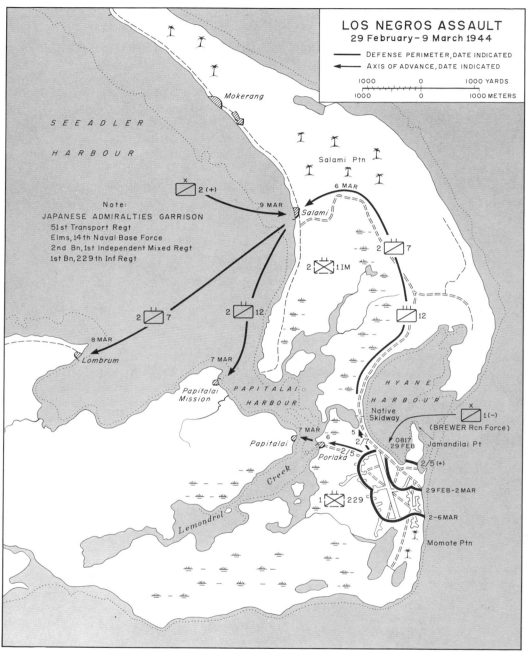

LOS NEGROS ASSAULT
29 February – 9 March 1944

⸺ DEFENSE PERIMETER, DATE INDICATED
◀⸺ AXIS OF ADVANCE, DATE INDICATED

1000   0   1000 YARDS
1000   0   1000 METERS

SEEADLER

HARBOUR

Mokerang

Salami Ptn

Note:
JAPANESE ADMIRALTIES GARRISON
51st Transport Regt
Elms, 14th Naval Base Force
2nd Bn, 1st Independent Mixed Regt
1st Bn, 229th Inf Regt

2 (+)

9 MAR

6 MAR

Salami

2   7

2   1 IM

2   12   2   7

8 MAR

Lombrum

2   7

7 MAR

12

Papitalai
Mission   PAPITALAI

HARBOUR

HYANE

HARBOUR

Native
Skidway

1 (–)

(BREWER Rcn Force)

7 MAR

Papitalai

6   5

2/7

0817
29 FEB

Jamandilai Pt

Porlaka

2/5

2/5 (+)

1   229

29 FEB–2 MAR

Creek

2–6 MAR

Lemondrol

Momote Ptn

MAP 20

F. Temple

ABOARD THE CRUISER PHOENIX, *28 February 1944. Left, gunfire directed at Japanese heavy guns; right, Admiral Kinkaid and General MacArthur viewing the bombardment.*

landing, was indeed an unlikely place. Two small points of land about 750 yards apart flanked the entrance; from them the enemy could put cross fire against landing craft sailing through the narrow gap in the barrier reef. Much of the shore line inside the harbor was covered by mangroves, but on the south, 150 yards behind Momote airfield, a 1,200-yard sandy beach with three jetties offered passage to troops and vehicles. (*Map 20*)

With H Hour set for 0815 to give bombers time to deliver heavy strikes in support of the landing, the APD's were to anchor five thousand yards off Hyane Harbour. The destroyers carrying troops would enter the transport area to unload their passengers, then return to their fire support stations. Twelve LCP(R)'s were

to carry the reconnaissance force ashore. The first three waves of four craft each would go in at five-minute intervals, unload, return forty minutes later, and depart again in three waves five minutes apart until the troops were ashore.

To join the expedition, MacArthur and Kinkaid flew to Milne Bay and boarded the cruiser *Phoenix* in the afternoon of 27 February. The same afternoon at Oro Bay, where the 1st Cavalry Division had been unloading ships and receiving amphibious training, the BREWER reconnaissance force boarded Admiral Fechteler's ships, 170 men per APD and about 57 men per destroyer. The ships departed Oro Bay in late afternoon and early evening of 28 February, rendezvoused with Berkey's cruisers and destroyers early next morning just south of

Cape Cretin, and followed eleven miles behind Berkey through Vitiaz Strait and the Bismarck Sea. No enemy ship or plane made an appearance. The sea was calm, the sky heavily overcast, as the ships neared Hyane Harbour.

The Landings

Fechteler ordered his ships to deploy at 0723, 29 February. Cruisers and destroyers took their support stations and commenced firing at 0740. APD's in the transport area lowered landing craft which proceeded toward their line of departure 3,700 yards from the beach.

The heavy overcast and generally bad flying weather prevented all but a handful of Allied B–24's from reaching the Admiralties before H Hour. P–38's, B–25's, and smoke-laying reconnaissance planes arrived later, but before they could attack the overcast closed in so tightly that they could do nothing. "The Fifth Air Force had made its chief contribution in pointing out the opportunity." [22]

The first sign of the Japanese came at H minus 20 minutes when the first wave of landing craft reached the line of departure. As it passed through the entrance, enemy 20-mm. machine guns on either side opened fire while heavier guns directed their fire against the *Phoenix* and the destroyers. The cruiser and the destroyer *Mahan* promptly silenced a gun on Southeast Point, and other vessels silenced the machine guns. According to Admiral Kinkaid this performance so thoroughly converted Gen-

eral MacArthur into a naval gunfire enthusiast that he became more royalist than the king, and thereafter Kinkaid frequently had to point out the limitations of naval gunfire to the general. [23]

Support plans called for naval gunfire to stop at 0755 (H minus 20 minutes) so that B–25's could bomb and strafe at low altitudes, but at 0755 no B–25's could be seen nor could any be reached by radio. The ships fired, therefore, until 0810, and then fired star shells as a signal that strafers could attack in safety. Soon afterward three B–25's bombed the gun positions at the entrance to the harbor. [24]

Thus supported by air and naval bombardment, the leading wave of landing craft, carrying G Troop, 2d Squadron, 5th Cavalry, met little fire as it passed through the entrance and turned left (south) toward the beach. It touched down at 0817, whereupon an enemy machine gun crew on the beach scrambled back for cover. The first man ashore, 2d Lt. Marvin J. Henshaw, led his platoon across the narrow beach to take a semicircular position on the edge of a coconut plantation. There were no American casualties, but several Japanese were killed as they hastily made off in the direction of the airstrip.

The Japanese resumed their positions at the harbor entrance when the naval shelling ceased and fired at the LCP(R)'s as they returned to the APD's. The *Mahan* steamed to within a mile of shore and fired 20-mm. and 40-mm. guns at the southern point. She could not put fire on the point opposite because the LCP(R)'s

---

[22] Craven and Cate, *The Pacific: Guadalcanal to Saipan,* p. 564.

[23] Oral statement of Adm Kinkaid to the author et al., 16 Nov 53.

[24] Craven and Cate, *The Pacific: Guadalcanal to Saipan,* p. 564.

First Wave of Landing Craft Unloading *men of G Troop, 2d Squadron, 5th Cavalry, 29 February 1944.*

were in the way. As the second wave started through the entrance so much enemy fire came from the skidway and from the northern point that it turned back. The destroyers *Flusser* and *Drayton* then put their fire on the north point while the *Mahan* pounded the southern. When the enemy fire ceased, the landing craft re-formed, went through the passage, fired their machine guns at the skidway, and landed 150 men of the second wave at H plus 8 minutes.

The second wave then passed through the first about a hundred yards inland. The third wave, which with the fourth received enemy fire on the way in, landed at H plus 30 minutes, pushed southwest, and established a line just short of the airstrip that included most of the eastern

revetment area. So far, except for firing at the boats, the Japanese had not fought. At 0900 General Chase radioed Krueger that a line had been established three hundred yards inland, and "enemy situation undetermined." [25] By 0950 the squadron, commanded by Lt. Col. William E. Lobit, had overrun Momote airfield. The troopers found it covered with weeds, littered with rusty fuselages, and pitted with water-filled bomb craters.

While the beachhead was relatively peaceful, the landing craft continued to receive fire on the way in and out. The destroyers continued intermittent bom-

---

[25] Serial 7, 0900, 1st Cav Brigade Unit Jnl, 29 Feb 44, Vol. III of 1st Cav Brigade Hist Rpt Admiralty Islands Campaign.

2D LT. MARVIN J. HENSHAW *receiving the congratulations of General MacArthur, who awarded him the Distinguished Service Cross, 29 February 1944.*

bardment of the harbor entrance for about six hours. By the time the LCP(R)'s of the third wave had returned to the APD's, four of the total twelve had been damaged by the enemy gunfire. Because the landing force probably could not be evacuated without the LCP(R)'s (although emergency plans called for an APD to penetrate the harbor and evacuate the 2d Squadron), the landing craft abandoned their schedule and entered the harbor only when the destroyers had forced the enemy to cease fire. A heavy rainstorm, which prevented the few

Allied planes over the target from bombing, soon reduced visibility so much that the Japanese fire became ineffective.

The entire reconnaissance force was unloaded by 1250 (H plus 4 hours, 35 minutes). Caliber .50 antiaircraft guns and the two 75-mm. pack howitzers had been manhandled ashore. Two cavalrymen had been killed, three wounded. Five Japanese were reported slain. Two sailors of the landing craft crews were dead, three wounded.

"Remain Here"

By afternoon Lobit's squadron had advanced over the entire airfield including the western dispersal area, an advance of thirteen hundred yards on the longest axis, without encountering any more Japanese. Patrols moved across the island to Porlaka and north to the skidway without seeing an enemy. But it was clear that the Japanese had not evacuated. Other patrols advancing to the south had found signs of recent occupancy, such as three kitchens and a warehouse full of rations, and a captured document indicated that some two hundred antiaircraft artillerymen were camped nearby.

General MacArthur and Admiral Kinkaid came ashore about 1600. MacArthur awarded the Distinguished Service Cross to Lieutenant Henshaw, inspected the lines, received reports, and made his decision. He directed General Chase "to remain here and hold the airstrip at any cost." [26] Having "ignored sniper fire . . . wet, cold, and dirty

---

[26] Quoted in 1st Cav Brigade Hist Rpt Admiralty Islands Campaign, I, 3. There are other versions of MacArthur's statement in existence.

with mud up to the ears," he and Kinkaid returned to the *Phoenix*, whence MacArthur radioed orders to send more troops, equipment, and supplies to the Admiralties at the earliest possible moment.[27] The cruisers and most of the destroyers departed for New Guinea at 1729, leaving behind the destroyers *Bush* and *Stockton* to support the cavalrymen.

Chase and Lobit had obviously concluded that the larger estimate of enemy strength, rather than the airmen's, was the right one. If all the Japanese they estimated to be on Los Negros should counterattack, the one thousand men of the reconnaissance force would find it very difficult to hold both the airfield and the dispersal area. An inland defense line, about three thousand yards long exclusive of the shore, would have been required to defend them. Because such a line could not safely be held by one thousand men, Chase decided to pull back east of the airstrip. He set up a line about fifteen hundred yards long which ran from the beach southward for about nine hundred yards, then swung sharply east to the sea. The troops did not occupy Jamandilai Point in their rear, but blocked its base that night and cleared it the next morning. The position selected on the edge of the strip provided a ready-made field of fire to the west.

In late afternoon the troopers organized their defenses. The beachhead was too small to permit the 75-mm. pack howitzers to cover the area immediately in front of the lines. Consequently the

DIGGING A FOXHOLE THROUGH CORAL ROCK *near the airstrip, 29 February 1944.*

field artillerymen were turned into riflemen. The .50-caliber antiaircraft guns were set up on the front line. Outposts were established in the dispersal area on the other side of the airstrip. The soldiers found digging foxholes even more arduous than usual, for the soil was full of coral rock. The Americans' defenses suffered from two weaknesses: the impossibility of field artillery support immediately in front of the line, and the lack of barbed wire.

To remedy the latter, Chase urgently requested Krueger to arrange for an airdrop of barbed wire and stakes, as well as mortar and small arms ammunition, on the north end of Momote drome as soon as possible.[28]

---

[27] Comment by Lt Col Julio Chiaramonte, attached to Ltr, Gen Chase to Gen Smith, Chief of Mil Hist, 6 Nov 53, no sub, OCMH; Rad, CINCSWPA to CTF 76, and CG's ALAMO and Fifth AF, 29 Feb 44, in GHQ SWPA G–3 Jnl, 1 Mar 44.

[28] Item 25, 1st Cav Brigade Unit Jnl, 29 Feb 44.

Careful preparations for defense were more than justified, because except for the air force ground crews the Japanese had not been evacuating either Los Negros or the island group. The larger intelligence estimates had been correct. And the Japanese, warned by American submarines that sent "frequently lengthy operational messages" from south of the Admiralties in late February, had been on the alert for an attack.[29] Most of the Admiralty garrison was stationed on Los Negros, with the *1st Battalion, 229th Infantry* responsible for the defense of the airfield and Hyane Harbour. One battalion defended Lorengau. The Japanese, expecting attack through Seeadler Harbour, had let the Americans slip in through the back door, but now they planned to take action. When General Imamura found out about the invasion, he ordered Colonel Ezaki to attack with his entire strength.[30] Ezaki did not immediately use the *2d Battalion, 1st Independent Mixed Regiment,* but left it at Salami Plantation north of the skidway. He directed the *1st Battalion, 229th*, commanded by a Captain Baba, to attack that night and "annihilate the enemy who have landed. This is not a delaying action. Be resolute to sacrifice your life for the Emperor and commit suicide in case capture is imminent."[31]

As dusk fell Japanese riflemen and the American outposts began a fire fight, whereupon the outposts were recalled. Shortly afterward small groups of enemy began moving up against the 2d Squadron's line in a series of un-co-ordinated attacks. Relying chiefly on grenades, the enemy groups attacked in darkness. Some managed to infiltrate through the line and cut nearly all the telephone wires.

Baba's battalion delivered its heaviest attack against the southern part of the perimeter. Some Japanese, using life preservers, swam in behind the American lines and landed. Another group broke through along the shore at the point of contact of the left (east) flank of E Troop and the right (south) flank of the field artillery unit, which was holding the beach. The Americans defended by staying in their foxholes and firing at every visible target and at everything that moved.

Two Japanese soldiers moved through the darkness and penetrated to the vicinity of General Chase's command post. Before they could do any damage Maj. Julio Chiaramonte, force S-2, killed one and wounded the other with a submachine gun.

By daylight of 1 March most of the enemy attackers had withdrawn. During the morning the infiltrators who had hidden themselves were hunted down and killed. Seven Americans were dead, fifteen wounded, as compared with sixty-six enemy corpses within the perimeter.

So far the reconnaissance force had held its own. But because the support force would not arrive until the next day patrols pushed westward and northward to determine just what Japanese opposition was to be expected. After moving an average distance of four hundred yards they encountered the enemy in some strength. Clearly, another attack was probable.

---

[29] Southeast Area Naval Operations, III, Japanese Monogr No. 50 (OCMH), 66.

[30] 8th Area Army Operations, Japanese Monogr No. 110 (OCMH), p. 135.

[31] This order, a copy of which was captured, is quoted in part in [Frierson] *The Admiralties*, p. 33.

Chase's situation was improved during 1 March by the arrival of more ammunition. As the weather had cleared, three B-25's dropped supplies at 0830. Later in the day a B-17 of the 39th Troop Carrier Squadron made two supply runs, and four B-17's of the 375th Troop Carrier Group each dropped three tons of blood plasma, ammunition, mines, and grenades. The reconnaissance force received no barbed wire.[32]

Captured documents had indicated the location of many enemy defensive positions, and the patrols that went out in the morning brought back more data. By now the Americans knew that Los Negros' south coast possessed prepared positions, and that the western dispersal area, Porlaka, and the coast of Hyane Harbour from the 2d Squadron's perimeter north to the skidway were fortified. In consequence the two supporting destroyers and the 75-mm. pack howitzers bombarded these areas. Starting at 1600 Fifth Air Force planes bombed the dispersal area, and at 1715, when antiaircraft guns near the south end of the airstrip fired on the planes, the *Bush* and *Stockton* pulled to within a thousand yards of the shore and shelled them. Several *4th Air Army* fighter planes from Wewak appeared but failed in their effort to drive off the American planes. The air bombardment flushed a body of Japanese, estimated one hundred strong, from cover in the dispersal area. When these men rushed east across the strip in an effort to escape the bombs, most were cut down by the cavalrymen's fire.

Otherwise enemy ground forces remained quiescent during most of the afternoon except for a seventeen-man patrol of officers and sergeants, led by Captain Baba, which had apparently infiltrated the lines on the previous night. Baba's patrol came through heavy underbrush to within thirty-five yards of General Chase's command post. When the Americans sighted the patrol, Chase and his executive officer, Col. Earl F. Thompson, directed the movements of Major Chiaramonte and four enlisted men who moved out to the attack. After Chiaramonte's party had killed several Japanese, the others committed suicide with grenades and swords.

The Japanese varied their pattern by striking at the perimeter at 1700 instead of after dark in an attack that was weaker than the one of the night before. Daylight simplified the defenders' task in repelling the attack, which ceased at 2000. Thereafter throughout the night small groups harried and infiltrated the lines. About fifty Japanese used life belts to cross the harbor entrance and attack the position at the base of Jamandilai. In the course of the action the field artillerymen fired three hundred 75-mm. rounds at the enemy and also killed 47 Japanese within the artillery positions with small arms fire. All together, 147 Japanese were killed within the perimeter during the two night battles.

Actually, the Japanese, though possessing numerical superiority, had never used their full strength and had not seriously threatened Chase's force, which still held its lines intact on the morning of 2 March. Recklessness, coupled with the skill and tenacity of the cavalrymen, had cost the Japanese their best chance.

---

[32] Craven and Cate, *The Pacific: Guadalcanal to Saipan*, p. 565, state that barbed wire was dropped, but several days later Chase was still protesting that he had not received any.

To the Shores of Seeadler Harbour

Seizure of Momote Airfield

Meanwhile, at Oro Bay and Cape Cretin Colonel Hoffman's support force, numbering about 1,500 ground combat troops and 428 Seabees, had loaded aboard six LST's and an equal number of 2d Engineer Special Brigade LCM's that were towed by the LST's. These vessels, escorted by Australian and American destroyers and two minesweepers under Capt. E. F. V. Dechaineux of the Australian Navy, made a quiet voyage and stood into Hyane Harbour shortly after 0900 on 2 March.

The two minesweepers and one destroyer steamed to the north of Los Negros in an attempt to force the 1,500-yard-wide entrance to Seeadler Harbour. They encountered such heavy fire from Japanese coastal guns on the guardian islands of Hauwei and Ndrilo that they retired. Captain Dechaineux then brought three more destroyers, which fired at the Japanese while the first three ships again unsuccessfully attempted to force the passage. Minesweeping would obviously have to await ships with heavier guns than those of destroyers and minesweepers.

The LST's and LCM's made their way through the entrance to Hyane Harbour and beached, whereupon Japanese mortars and machine guns north of the skidway opened up. The landing craft replied with their machine guns, and at the same time B–25's attacked the Japanese positions.

In the midst of the din the combat troops walked ashore. Then bulldozers left the LST's and began building ramps to get the other vehicles ashore. Unloading was finished by 1700, and the LST's departed; the LCM's remained in Hyane Harbour.

Before the LST's left for New Guinea Chase requested that the destroyers put fire in the northern point of land at Hyane Harbour. Four ships each fired fifty 5-inch rounds from close range, but when the LST's started out of the harbor they met machine gun fire. They replied and made the open sea in safety. One destroyer and the two minesweepers took the LST's to New Guinea while four destroyers stayed in the vicinity of the Admiralties to intercept any Japanese seaborne attacks.

Since Momote airfield was not yet in American hands, Chase assigned part of the 40th Construction Battalion to a defensive sector on the right (north) flank of the beachhead. The Seabees, meeting some rifle fire while moving into position, used their ditch-digger to scoop out a 300-yard-long trench.

As men, weapons, ammunition, supplies, and equipment came ashore during the day the beachhead became crowded. Chase decided to attack and enlarge his perimeter to include all the airfield, dispersal area, and revetments, and the roads immediately around the airfield. When Hoffman came ashore in the morning he was met by Colonel Thompson, who took him to Chase's headquarters where the three officers completed plans for an attack by the 5th Cavalry that afternoon.

At 1415, B–25's, P–38's, and P–47's began bombing and strafing the west half of the airfield, the dispersal area, the skidway, and the northern part of Los Negros. This attack lasted until 1530.

The 1st and 2d Squadrons of the 5th

Cavalry, on the left (south) and right respectively, had attacked at 1500. There was no opposition from the enemy; within the hour Hoffman's regiment was in possession of the entire airfield and had begun to dig in along the line of the western and southern dispersal bays. The day's sole casualties, two men killed and four wounded, were caused by three American bombs that fell on positions held by E Troop and antiaircraft artillerymen.

It was clear to the Americans that the Japanese garrison had not yet made its maximum effort, for papers found in the advance over the airfield indicated that Baba's battalion was still south and west of the airfield. And earlier estimates had placed two thousand troops in the west half of Los Negros and Lorengau. Major Chiaramonte therefore warned the invasion force to expect attacks from the south, from Porlaka in the west, and southward from the skidway.[33]

The invading Americans carefully prepared their defense positions. The front lines, still without barbed wire, included nearly all the dispersal area. Two antiaircraft batteries and E Company, 592d Engineer Boat and Shore Regiment, were assigned to beach defense. Seabees established an inner defense line west and northwest of Chase's command post. The three 75-mm. batteries of the 99th Field Artillery Battalion set up in revetments some five hundred yards behind the front in a semicircle with overlapping sectors of fire. Because it was next to impossible to prevent the Japanese from infiltrating the front lines, all units inside the perimeter prepared all-round local defenses.[34]

Ezaki Attacks Again

Colonel Ezaki now was preparing for a larger effort. He planned a co-ordinated attack, with the 2d Battalion, 1st Independent Mixed Regiment, driving south from Salami across the skidway, while one company, having moved from western Los Negros to Porlaka, struck eastward. Meanwhile, other detachments from the outlying islands and from inland regions of Manus were to concentrate at Lorengau. His forces were slow in concentrating, and Ezaki postponed the attack until the night of 3–4 March. As a result the 5th Cavalry was merely harassed in its new positions on the night of 2–3 March.

The Americans used the daylight hours to strengthen their defenses.[35] Bulldozers cleared fields of fire in front of the cavalry squadrons' lines. To keep infiltration to a minimum, each cavalry troop posted three rifle platoons in line with troop heavy weapons attached to each platoon. Japanese revetments were used as much as possible. Riflemen dug foxholes on the reverse slopes of the mounds, mines were laid in front, and the approaches to all positions were rigged with empty C-ration cans that

[33] Brewer Rcn TF S–2 Periodic Rpts 1–3, 1, 2, and 3 Mar 44, in Vol. II, 1st Cav Brigade Hist Rpt, 27 Feb–18 May 44.

[34] General Chase again requested barbed wire by air but reported that he never received it.

[35] [Frierson] The Admiralties, pp. 43–44, asserts that when a group of Japanese officers attempted to land on the beachhead from a boat on the morning of 3 March they were all killed, and that a document carried by one of them warned the Americans to expect attack that night. No contemporary evidence to support this statement has been found.

contained lumps of coral and were hung close to the ground so they would rattle when struck by a shoe. The 60-mm. mortars were situated to deliver close support fire directly in front of the cavalry squadrons, while the 81's were massed near the center of the perimeter in front of the field artillery to deliver deeper supporting fire. Most of the antiaircraft .50-caliber machine guns were returned to their normal missions, but since the main attacks were expected from the north and west the guns posted on the north end of Momote field facing the skidway remained at the front.

While the riflemen made ready, the artillery and the offshore destroyers fired at every evidence of the Japanese. They put concentrations on enemy groups north of the skidway. At 1600 field and antiaircraft artillery shot up several enemy barges that were observed behind overhanging vegetation on the north shore of Hyane Harbour.

After dusk Japanese patrols began probing the lines, and at 2100 a lone plane dropped eight bombs which cut the telephone wires between the 1st Squadron and the 5th Cavalry command post.

When the plane departed, flares and tracers heralded an attack by the remnants of the late Baba's battalion against the southwest portion of the perimeter, held by the 1st Squadron under Lt. Col. Charles E. Brady. Mortar and machine gun fire supported the attack, but it was weak. American mortars and machine guns beat off the attackers, although some infiltrated the lines, concealed themselves, and had to be flushed out and killed after daylight.

The *2d Battalion, 1st Independent Mixed Regiment,* delivered the main assault from the skidway, which was coupled with a drive east from Porlaka by other detachments. F Troop, which held the north-south portion of the line in the western dispersal area, and G Troop, defending the line from F Troop's right flank to the beach, received the brunt of the attacks. E Troop suffered only harassing attacks and infiltration. By now the 2d Squadron, having landed on 29 February, had had more than enough experience in repelling night attacks, but this one differed from earlier ones in which the enemy had moved quietly and concealed himself as much as possible. On this night the Japanese advanced in the open in frontal assault with a good deal of talking, shouting, and even singing. Artillery and mortars opened fire at once.

As they approached F and G Troops, the leading enemy waves hurled grenades, but they fell short of the cavalry lines. The Japanese pushed through the mine fields, taking casualties but not stopping, and drove into the interlocking bands of fire from the machine guns, which promptly cut them down. More kept coming; the cavalry lines held, but some Japanese managed to infiltrate and cut telephone lines. G Troop's three platoons stayed down in their positions and fired or hurled grenades at all possible targets. Just before dawn some Japanese soldiers penetrated G Troop's positions and Capt. Frank G. Mayfield organized a quick counterattack and drove them out. A few minutes later the Japanese assaulted again. This time, as two of Mayfield's platoons had exhausted their machine gun ammunition, the Japanese nearly succeeded in breaking through. But the Japanese were killed or driven off by a platoon of H Troop heavy machine guns under S/Sgt. Edwin C. Terry.

During these attacks Sgt. Troy A. McGill, of G Troop, was holding a revetment with his squad of eight men. When all but McGill and one other man had been killed or wounded, McGill ordered the other survivor to retire, fired his rifle until it jammed, then fought in front of his position with clubbed rifle until he was slain. McGill's gallantry won him the Medal of Honor.[36]

The attacks had been delivered with frequency and resolution throughout the night, but there was little evidence of skill or co-ordination. For example, about an hour before daylight a column of soldiers advanced down the road from Porlaka, singing, the cavalrymen later reported, "Deep in the Heart of Texas." [37] Mines, machine guns, rifles, and grenades killed nearly all of them.

Reports of the night's action also relate instances of Japanese shouting false commands in English and tapping telephone lines. One H Troop mortar section thought it heard an order to retreat and abandoned its position with the result that the 2d Squadron lost its 81-mm. mortar support.

During the night the 99th Field Artillery Battalion fired almost continuously, as did all mortars except those that were

abandoned. This fire was delivered in spite of harassing attacks from Japanese who had slipped through the front lines. Three field artillerymen were killed by infiltrators, and one antiaircraft crew abandoned its gun under pressure from the Japanese. Five Japanese, one with a grenade discharger, actually posted themselves on the roof of the dugout containing Colonel Lobit's command post, but Capt. Bruce Merritt killed them from his nearby foxhole. The Seabees, in their secondary line behind G Troop, passed ammunition to the hard-pressed cavalrymen and toward dawn some moved up to help G Troop hold its line. Other Seabees met a group of Japanese attacking two antiaircraft gun positions and killed them.

By daylight of 4 March the Japanese had pulled back and the close fighting was over, but enemy mortars and field pieces hit the American positions until about 0730. The intensity of the night's action is indicated by the fact that two of the machine guns in G Troop's sector had fired a total of 8,770 rounds, and 168 enemy corpses lay directly to the troop's front. There were no prisoners. Sixty-one Americans were killed, 244 wounded, of whom 9 dead and 38 wounded were Seabees. Ezaki had made his greatest offensive effort and failed. With more Americans due soon, the shattered Japanese units would be capable of defensive action only.

The Advance

On 1 March, meanwhile, at ALAMO headquarters on Cape Cretin General Krueger had completed plans for reinforcement of Chase's men and for seiz-

---

[36] WD GO 35, 9 May 45.

[37] The Japanese may have been singing, but it seems improbable that they sang this song, which was a favorite of the 1st Cavalry Division. The 2d Squadron had been on Los Negros for four days, and this was its third night in close combat. One may guess that nerves were strained, imaginations overactive.

ure of the entire Admiralties group.[38] Krueger ordered Swift to strengthen the reconnaissance force, seize Seeadler Harbour, extend control over the entire Admiralties, and start building airdromes and a naval base.[39] On the 2d, the day Hoffman's support force landed, Krueger received an urgent request from Chase, who asked for his other regiment, the 12th Cavalry. Krueger, Swift, and Barbey then arranged to speed up the movement to the Admiralties and land the 12th Cavalry and other units on 6 March, the 2d Cavalry Brigade on 9 March instead of on 9 and 16 March, as they had originally planned.[40] They also arranged to rush the 2d Squadron and the Weapons Troop, 7th Cavalry, and the 82d Field Artillery Battalion on three APD's, to arrive on the morning of 4 March.[41]

General Krueger desired that Seeadler Harbour be opened up. Two factors, besides the obvious one that Allied forces were eventually to use the harbor as a major naval base, motivated him. Hyane

Harbour and the initial beachhead were becoming too congested to receive the 2d Brigade, but Salami Plantation on the west shore of the northwest peninsula of Los Negros offered a good landing place. Clearing the harbor would also make possible a shore-to-shore movement from Los Negros against Manus. Therefore air and naval bombardments of enemy positions on the northwest tip of Los Negros, and on the guardian islands of Koruniat, Ndrilo, and Hauwei were arranged.[42] Krueger, on 3 March, ordered Swift to proceed to Los Negros at once, to survey the situation, and to take command ashore.

On the morning of 4 March, shortly after Ezaki's attack subsided and after supporting Allied destroyers had shelled the skidway and the region to the north, the 2d Squadron, 7th Cavalry, and the 82d Field Artillery Battalion (75-mm. pack howitzers) landed at Hyane Harbour. Chase decided to wait for more troops before attacking, and put the 2d Squadron, 7th, under Lt. Col. Robert P. Kirk, in the line to replace the weary men of the 2d Squadron, 5th Cavalry. Except for minor harassing attacks, infiltrations, and a one-plane bombing attack, the night of 4–5 March was quiet.

General Swift, accompanied by the 1st Cavalry Division's chief of staff, Col. Charles A. Sheldon, and the intelligence and operations officers, reached Hyane Harbour aboard the destroyer *Bush* on the morning of 5 March. He assumed command of the troops ashore at 1100, but since the *Bush* was busy executing fire support missions he stayed aboard

---

[38] The total forces involved included the rest of the 1st Cavalry Division; Headquarters and Headquarters Battery, 15th Antiaircraft Artillery Group; C Battery, 237th Antiaircraft Artillery Battalion (Searchlight); the 211th Coast Artillery Battalion (Antiaircraft); the 2d Battalion, 50th Coast Artillery Regiment; the Shore Battalion and A Company, Boat Battalion, 592d Engineer Boat and Shore Regiment; and a large array of signal, medical, quartermaster, and engineer units.

[39] ALAMO FO 11, 1 Mar 44, in ALAMO ANCHORAGE Jnl 7, 1–3 Mar 44.

[40] Rad, CG ALAMO to GHQ SWPA, 1 Mar 44, in GHQ SWPA G–3 Jnl, 1 Mar 44.

[41] [Frierson] *The Admiralties*, p. 43; Rad, Chase to CG ALAMO, 2 Mar 44, in ALAMO ANCHORAGE Jnl 7; Rad, ALAMO to GHQ SWPA, 2 Mar 44, and Rad, CTF 76 to Comdr Seventh Flt, 2 Mar 44, both in GHQ SWPA G–3 Jnl, 2 Mar 44. Barbey proposed using LST's for the 4 March reinforcements, but Krueger persuaded him to send them on APD's.

[42] ALAMO Force Rpt, BREWER Opns, p. 11; Rad, CG ALAMO to GHQ SWPA, 4 Mar 44, in GHQ SWPA G–3 Jnl, 4 Mar 44.

LT. GEN. WALTER KRUEGER *(front seat) with Brig. Gen. William C. Chase and Maj. Gen. Innis P. Swift on an inspection tour, Los Negros Island.*

until 1600 so as not to interrupt the firing.

Swift directed Chase's reconnaissance force to clear the major part of Los Negros from Momote to the north and west, and to be prepared to extend over the entire island. He instructed the 2d Cavalry Brigade, due to arrive on 9 March, to land at Salami Plantation, to be prepared to move to a point on Manus west of Lorengau, and to attack eastward against that airfield and secure the eastern half of Manus.[43]

To carry out the instructions for seizing all of Los Negros, the 2d Squadron,

7th Cavalry, was ordered to attack north across the skidway on the afternoon of the 5th. Accordingly the 2d Squadron, 5th, began relieving Colonel Kirk's squadron in the perimeter late in the morning. At 1120, while the relief was being effected, the Japanese began a series of harassing attacks, followed after noon by a resolute attack from Porlaka and the skidway. The enemy soldiers who broke into the front lines were all killed while field artillery and mortars broke up the attacks. Twenty-five dead Japanese bodies were counted, but twelve cavalrymen were wounded and it was 1630 before the 2d Squadron, 7th, was reorganized and ready to attack.

Once it had moved beyond the perim-

---

[43] BREWER TF FO 3, 5 Mar 44, in ALAMO ANCHORAGE Jnl 8, 4–6 Mar 44.

eter, Kirk's squadron found that the Japanese had mined the approaches to the skidway. The mines caused some casualties at first but thereafter were successfully detected and removed. The squadron advanced slowly past enemy corpses that littered the road, but by darkness had reached the skidway, where it halted for the night.

Kirk resumed his advance early on 6 March. Later in the morning the 12th Cavalry Regimental Combat Team, commanded by Col. John H. Stadler, Jr., came ashore. Transported to Hyane Harbour aboard four LST's, the combat team, 2,837 men strong, consisted of the 12th Cavalry; the 271st Field Artillery Battalion (105-mm. howitzers); three light tanks of the 603d Tank Company; five LVT's of A Company, 592d Engineer Boat and Shore Regiment; and engineer, medical, and signal troops.[44] When it reached shore, the 12th Cavalry, accompanied by the tanks, began moving north across the skidway to join Kirk in the advance, while the 271st Field Artillery Battalion moved into position near the airstrip. The Japanese, obviously in retreat, offered only minor resistance. The advance was slowed chiefly by mud and trees they had felled across the roads and trails to Salami. Near the beach at Salami some Japanese in bunkers and buildings offered fight but were blasted out by tanks and 75-mm. howitzers. By 1630 all three cavalry squadrons were established at Salami. The surviving Japanese had escaped by boat and canoe to the west. Thus by the day's end the 1st Cavalry

Brigade held the beachhead where the 2d Brigade was to land.

Meanwhile air and naval surface forces had been at work on the Japanese positions guarding the entrance to Seeadler Harbour. Two days after the minesweepers were driven off, cruisers and destroyers of Admiral Crutchley's Task Force 74 bombarded suspected enemy gun positions on orders from Admiral Kinkaid, and on 5 March they fired eighty 8-inch, three hundred 6-inch, and one hundred 5-inch rounds without meeting any return fire.[45] Next morning, the lone destroyer Nicholson approached the harbor entrance to draw enemy fire. The Japanese opened up at 850 yards range, whereupon Task Force 74 and Allied bombers struck at the enemy positions thus disclosed. They were bombed again on 7 March by seven B–24's, and on 8 March by seventeen B–24's and eleven B–25's. Thereafter LCM's, destroyers, and other craft entered the harbor freely without encountering enemy fire.

From 6 through 8 March the 5th Cavalry extended its holdings around the airstrip. The 2d Squadron took Porlaka on 6 March, then crossed Lemondrol Creek in canvas and rubber boats and amphibian tractors to seize Papitalai village on 7 March.

American control over Seeadler Harbour was furthered on 7 and 8 March by the seizure of two promontories northwest of Papitalai. The 2d Squadron, 12th Cavalry, using amphibian tractors, shuttled from Salami to Papitalai Mission and captured it against

---

[44] 12th Cav, Hist of 12th Cav During the Admiralty Islands Campaign, 27 May 44, p. 3.

[45] Rad, Comdr Seventh Flt to CTF 74, 4 Mar 44, and Rad, CTF 76 to CG ALAMO, 5 Mar 44, both in ALAMO ANCHORAGE Jnl 8, 4–6 Mar 44.

LST's LOADED WITH TROOPS AND EQUIPMENT *landing at Salami Plantation.*

sharp opposition. The 2d Squadron, 7th, using LCM's, took Lombrum Plantation.

The 12th Cavalry and the tanks patrolled to the northwest tip of Los Negros to cover the 2d Brigade's landing, releasing, in the process, sixty-nine Sikh soldiers that the Japanese had been using as laborers.

On the morning of 9 March destroyers shelled Lorengau and minesweepers checked Seeadler Harbour. Then six LST's and one cargo ship entered the harbor to land Brig. Gen. Verne D. Mudge's 2d Cavalry Brigade and attached units at Salami Plantation.[46]

[46] This force consisted of: the 2d Cavalry Brigade (less the 2d Squadron and Weapons Troop, 7th Cavalry); the 61st Field Artillery Battalion (105-mm. howitzers); various divisional and nondivisional engineer, medical, quartermaster, and ordnance units; B Battery, 168th Antiaircraft Artillery Battalion

Los Negros was now firmly in Allied hands. The next task facing the combat troops was the seizure of Lorengau.

Lorengau

Plans and Preparations

General Swift had assigned responsibility for capturing Manus to the 2d Cavalry Brigade. General Mudge accordingly had his plans ready the day after his brigade landed at Salami Plantation.[47] Not much was known about Jap-

(Gun); B Battery, 211th Coast Artillery Battalion; F Company, 592d Engineer Boat and Shore Regiment; an Australian New Guinea Administrative Unit detachment; and a detachment of No. 62 Works Wing, RAAF.

[47] 2d Cav Brigade FO 2, 10 Mar 44, in Hist of Hq Troop, 2d Cav Brigade, Admiralty Islands Campaign, 9 Mar–18 May 44 (actually the 2d Brigade's report); 8th Cav FO 2, 13 Mar 44, in 8th Cav Hist Rpt, Admiralty Campaign, 6 Mar–20 May 44, Sec 11.

anese strength on Manus, but reconnaissance had shown that Lorengau airdrome and Lorengau village east of it
were fortified. As Lugos Mission was
practically undefended, Mudge decided
to land there—about 3,000 yards west of
the airdrome. (*Map 21*) The beaches
selected, Yellow 1 and Yellow 2, lay
west and east of the Liei River. Yellow
1, of coral sand, was 700 yards long, 14
to 26 yards wide, with swamps immediately behind it. Yellow 2, 100 yards
long, gave access to Number 3 Road
which led along the coast to Lorengau.

Mudge assigned the assault to the 8th
Cavalry, commanded by Col. William
J. Bradley. It was to land in column
of squadrons, the 1st Squadron in the
lead. Troop A was to land in LVT's on
Yellow 2 east of the Liei, C Troop from
LCV's on Yellow 1 to the west. The
7th Cavalry, less the 2d Squadron, would
follow the 8th ashore. The 2d Squadron, 7th, would constitute the brigade
reserve. C Troop, 8th Engineer Squadron, was to land on Yellow 1, improve
the beaches, and bridge the Liei to
connect the beaches. Once ashore the
8th Cavalry was to send the 1st Squadron east along Number 3 Road against
Lorengau airfield while the other moved
inland to Number 1 Road, and then
moved east against Lorengau village to
keep the Japanese from escaping inland
to the jungled mountains where they
would have a great defensive advantage.[48]

The cavalry generals arranged with
naval officers and with Capt. George F.
Frederick of the 12th Air Liaison Party
for ample air and fleet support of the
landing, in addition to support by field
artillery. The islets north of Los Negros
would provide positions from which field
artillery could support the 2d Brigade's
advance east by firing across its front at
right angles to the axis of advance, as
had been done in New Georgia during
the advance on Munda airfield. Therefore plans were prepared for sending
patrols to Hauwei, the Butjo Luo group,
and Bear Point on Manus, just west of
Loniu Passage, to determine enemy
strength and look for artillery positions.
D Day for Manus was first set for 13
March.

The island patrols, consisting of detachments from the 302d Cavalry Reconnaissance Troop plus artillery officers, left Salami on 11 March. Bear
Point, though not occupied by the enemy, had so poor a beach that artillery
could not be landed. Butjo Mokau, the
most northern of the Butjo Luo group,
offered good artillery positions and bore
no signs of enemy occupation. In late
afternoon F Troop, 7th Cavalry, occupied both islands of the group.

The Hauwei patrol, a platoon strong,
left Salami aboard an LCV and a PT
boat and landed on the western part of
Hauwei.[49] After the patrol had moved
a short distance inland, machine gun,
mortar, and rifle fire struck it from the

---

[48] The landing force consisted of: the 2d Cavalry
Brigade; C Troop, 8th Engineer Squadron; a de-
tachment of the Shore Battalion, 592d Engineer
Boat and Shore Regiment; detachments of the 1st
Medical Squadron and the 1st Signal Troop; two
medium and three light tanks.

[49] Motor Torpedo Boat Squadrons 18 and 21 had
arrived in Seeadler Harbour with their tender
Oyster Bay. They served as a "sneak and peak" and
general utility organization. Morison, *Breaking the
Bismarcks Barrier*, p. 446.

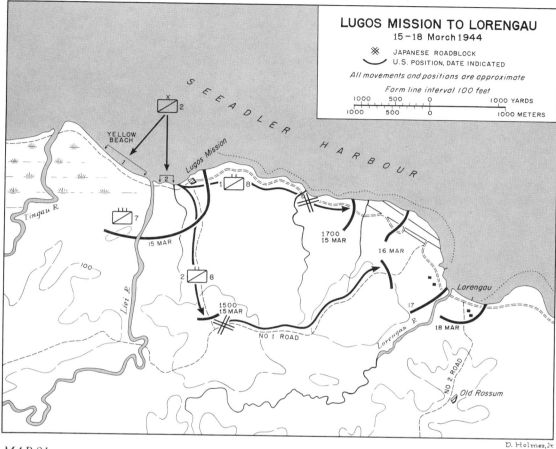

MAP 21

D. Holmes, Jr

front and both sides. The patrol made a fighting withdrawal to the beach, supported by fire from the PT boat and the LCV. But by the time the cavalrymen made the beach, the PT, whose skipper had been wounded, had returned to its tender. Five men boarded the LCV, but the remainder were still embroiled with the enemy. Mortar shells and machine gun bullets wounded most of the men aboard the LCV, which struck a submerged coral reef two hun-

dred yards from shore and sank, leaving the survivors floating in the water. When about six Japanese started to set up a machine gun on the beach, the cavalrymen still on shore shot them with submachine guns, then took to the water and joined the survivors from the LCV. After three hours in the water, the eighteen men, suffering from exposure to the sun and water, were picked up by a PT boat while a destroyer shelled Hauwei. An LCM later picked up one more man.

Six men of the reconnaissance troop and two artillerymen had been killed, three were missing, and every survivor was wounded as well as burned.[50]

A larger force was obviously needed for Hauwei, and the landing on Manus would have to be delayed if the artillery was to get into position in time to support the landing. Further, naval officers had already counseled delay in order to provide more time to clear the sea lanes to Lugos Mission.

Accordingly the 2d Squadron (less F Troop), 7th Cavalry, was selected to seize Hauwei. Supporting its attack would be destroyers, rockets, 105-mm. fire from the 61st Field Artillery Battalion at Mokerang Plantation north of Salami, and P–40's of No. 77 Fighter Squadron, RAAF, which had reached Momote on 9 March. The squadron boarded LCM's at noon, 12 March, set out for Hauwei, and landed under cover of the supporting bombardment at 1400. The squadron later reported that "the covering fire was not accurate and most missiles fell short in the sea." [51]

E Troop landed on the west shore under small arms fire while G Troop, debarking on the south, met machine gun fire. The Japanese had rigged trip wires to activate mines, but the soldiers detected and avoided them. Kirk's squadron then drove inland against rifle fire and by 1500 held a north-south line across Hauwei about three hundred yards from the western tip and one thousand yards from the eastern end. By now

the whole squadron was ashore, and H Troop's 81-mm. mortars were ready to fire. E Troop continued its advance but G stayed in place. As contact broke between the two troops, Colonel Kirk pulled E Troop back and dug in for the night.

General Mudge arrived at 1600 and after receiving Kirk's report ordered C Troop from Salami to Hauwei, and alerted one medium tank to move to Hauwei next day. C Troop arrived by LCM at 1800 and took up a support position. During the night Japanese on Pityilu fired 20-mm. guns at the 2d Squadron but hit no one. The 61st Field Artillery Battalion put one thousand rounds of harassing fire on the enemy's section of Hauwei.

Next morning, at 0900, the tank arrived and Kirk assigned his reconnaissance platoon as close support. The attack began at 1000 with C, E, and G Troops abreast from left (north) to right. On the right a bunker, manned by eight Japanese with two 7.7-mm. machine guns, grenade discharges, and rifles, withstood four direct mortar bursts and four 75-mm. shells before it crumbled. In the center E Troop enveloped a short trench equipped with machine guns, grenade dischargers, and rifles. With these positions reduced the troops moved rapidly. By noon the 2d Squadron had covered the whole island. Eight Americans had been killed, forty-six were wounded. Forty-three dead Japanese, all sailors, were counted. Captured booty included two 5-inch naval guns and a range-finder. One gun had been hit by the earlier bombardments; the other was in firing condition.

---

[50] Maj. B. C. Wright, *The 1st Cavalry Division in World War II* (Tokyo: Toppan Printing Company, 1947), p. 27.

[51] 7th Cav, Hist Rpt 7th Cav, 2 Mar–18 May 44, Pt. B, p. 5.

That afternoon the 61st Field Artillery Battalion unloaded its 105-mm. howitzers from LCM's and next day set them up on the southwest side while the 271st Field Artillery Battalion emplaced its 105-mm. howitzers on the west. The 99th Field Artillery Battalion, meanwhile, had emplaced twelve 75-mm. pack howitzers and six 37-mm. anti-tank guns on Butjo Mokau on 13 March.

The Landing at Lugos

With the artillery now in position, embarkation of the 2d Cavalry Brigade aboard twelve LCM's, seven LCV's, and one LST began shortly after 0400 on 15 March. The LST and the smaller craft proceeded separately to the rendezvous area off Lugos Mission and assembled about 0800.

The three supporting artillery battalions had begun firing intermittently at Lorengau village at 2100 the previous evening, and at 0830 they shifted their fire to Lugos Mission. Four destroyers lying offshore fired at the shore line between the Tingau River, west of Lugos, and Lorengau until 0900. At 0900 eighteen B–25's from Nadzab arrived overhead and from 0907 to 0925 put eighty-one 500-pound bombs and fired more than 44,000 machine gun bullets on the beaches. At 0925, when the bombers cleared the area, three engineer rocket boats covered the first wave's landing.

The LST had previously disgorged seven LVT's, and six of them (the seventh was a rocket boat) bore A Troop toward Beach Yellow 2 while LCV's carried C Troop toward Yellow 1. When the craft were close to shore, a machine

gun east of the beaches opened fire. LVT's, and engineer support craft, and two PT boats replied and the gun fell silent. LVT's and LCV's landed their troops without casualties, and almost exactly on schedule.[52]

The soldiers of A Troop left the LVT's and drove through Lugos Mission toward Number 3 Road. The few Japanese in the area, mostly sailors, did not offer determined resistance and were killed by A Troop and by later mop-up squads. C Troop, to the west, met no opposition as it advanced to a ridge some eight hundred yards inland where it established defenses to cover the landing of the 2d Brigade.

Colonel Bradley had ordered the bulk of the 8th Cavalry to land at Yellow 2 if it proved suitable for LCM's and LST's, and succeeding waves landed so quickly that Yellow 2 quickly became congested. The LST, which carried troops, weapons, and vehicles but no bulk cargo, was unloaded in forty-five minutes. It retracted to return to Salami for the 7th Cavalry.[53] This regiment, commanded by Col. Glenn S. Finley, landed from the LST and LCM's in the afternoon and took over defense of the beachhead.

Meanwhile the 8th Cavalry had begun its two-squadron advance against Lorengau airdrome and Lorengau village over Roads 1 and 3.

[52] General Swift, who observed the landing from the deck of a PT boat, is reported to have noted that timing was off by one and one-half minutes because a heavy sea slowed the landing craft. Wright, *The 1st Cavalry Division in World War II*, p. 28.
[53] 8th Cav Hist Rpt, Admiralty Campaign, Narrative of Events, p. 6.

The Advance East:
The Airfield and the Village

During the day the 2d Squadron, 8th, under Maj. Haskett L. Connor, made its way southward along a native track toward Number 1 Road. Tractors borrowed from the artillery towed supplies and ammunition. Japanese riflemen harassed the soldiers as they toiled slowly upward over a continuous succession of ridges. It was 1500 before F Troop, in the lead, reached Number 1 Road, where it ran into fire from three Japanese positions which covered the track's junction with the road. Enemy mortars to the south added their fire, and Connor decided to dig in for the night. At his request the 61st Field Artillery Battalion silenced the enemy temporarily while the squadron established night defenses about six hundred yards from the road.

The next morning, 16 March, General Mudge and Colonel Bradley visited the squadron and observed its attack which, supported by one light and two medium tanks, overran the positions and enabled Connor's squadron to move east along Number 1 Road. The tanks had been hauled through the jungle with the aid of a D–7 bulldozer which cut down grades, cleared undergrowth, and towed the tanks when they stuck. One tank and the bulldozer remained attached to the 2d Squadron on its advance along the road. By late afternoon it had reached a position on the road about a thousand yards west-northwest of Lorengau village and eight hundred yards south of the airstrip.

The chief obstacle to the 2d Squadron's advance was terrain. The 1st Squadron (less C Troop) had had to fight

its way along the coast on Number 3 Road. After landing on the morning of 15 March, the 1st, under Maj. Moyers S. Shore, had started east along the road behind A Troop. The road led through heavy rain forest interspersed with mangrove swamp on low ground. "The recent rains had softened the red clay until it assumed a glue-like consistence which made the footing difficult and slowed . . . leading elements." [54]

About one mile out of Lugos A Troop was halted by three pillboxes. [55] With the beach on one side and mangrove swamp on the other, there was no space for maneuver. Without orders from the troop commander one squad attempted an unsupported frontal assault which failed. Major Shore then alerted B Troop to pass through A and assault upon completion of an artillery preparation. From Hauwei 105's of the 271st Field Artillery Battalion swept the enemy area with shells that burst as close as a hundred yards from the cavalrymen. B Troop attacked but was quickly halted.

Shore then asked for a tank, more artillery fire, and a strike by RAAF P–40's (armed with 500-pound bombs), which had been on station since before H Hour, and arranged for 81-mm. mortar support. "The combination of fire and bombs" turned the trick. They "plowed the position into a mass of craters," and B Troop advanced past "the blasted

---

[54] *Ibid.,* p. 6.
[55] 1st Cavalry Division reports and journals use the word "bunker" for almost every enemy position encountered. Japanese positions along the road and at Lorengau appear to have been, according to World War II terminology, earth-and-log pillboxes.

remains of the pillboxes and scattered parts of their tenacious occupants. . . .''[56]

The three pillboxes had apparently constituted the airstrip's western defenses, for when they crumbled the 1st Squadron moved freely down the road. By 1700 it had advanced out of the jungle and held a ridge among the palms overlooking the southwest corner of the airstrip. Two of the squadron had been killed, eleven wounded, in the course of the action. Forty Japanese were reported killed. During the night of 15–16 March Shore's squadron, which C Troop rejoined at 1800 after its relief at the beachhead by the 7th Cavalry, received rifle fire from Japanese in a palm grove between the airfield and the sea.

Next morning, 16 March, Shore decided to hold up his attack while an A Troop platoon went north of the strip to clear out the enemy riflemen and C Troop moved along the south edge of the airdrome to reconnoiter enemy positions there. It was noon before the A Troop platoon accomplished its mission and the 1st Squadron could move.

Meanwhile C Troop, after advancing 200 yards over a series of rolling coconut-studded ridges which lay at right angles to the axis of advance, was halted by machine gun fire from a ridge about 150 yards to its front. The troop commander, Capt. Winthrop B. Avery, emplaced the heavy machine guns and 81-mm. mortars which had been attached from the Weapons Troop and attempted a coordinated attack. One platoon was to make a frontal assault while a second platoon worked around the south flank. The frontal attack failed, but the flank-

ing platoon, commanded by S/Sgt. Ervin M. Gauthreaux. literally gained the top of the enemy positions, threw grenades into two pillboxes, and flushed several Japanese.[57]

But at this point things went wrong. With the enemy threat removed from his left (north) flank, and aware that C Troop was held up, Shore decided to leave C Troop in place to hold the enemy while the remainder of A Troop followed its other platoon through the palms and squadron Headquarters Troop, B Troop, and elements of D Troop drove down the airdrome on C's left. As B Troop advanced in the open it was struck by fire from the very positions that Gauthreaux' platoon was straddling, whereupon it halted, withdrew, and as it carried its casualties back to safety returned the enemy's fire. But the fire hit Gauthreaux's platoon, and Avery was forced to order him off the Japanese positions.[58]

After four hundred 105-mm. rounds had pounded the enemy position, C Troop attacked frontally while B Troop completed its retirement. But the Japanese still remained in their positions on the ridge and broke up C Troop's attack. By now all elements of the squadron had been committed and the Americans had advanced to about the center of the airstrip.

General Mudge arrived on the scene, inspected the squadron, reconnoitered the front, and decided to relieve the 1st Squadron, 8th, with the 7th Cavalry. During the relief, which was effected

---

[56] 8th Cav Hist Rpt, Admiralty Campaign, Narrative of Events, p. 7.

[57] Gauthreaux received the Silver Star and a commission as 2d lieutenant.

[58] Tanks had advanced along the north side of the strip but did not fire on the C Troop platoon.

MEN OF THE 8TH CAVALRY *moving a 37-mm. antitank gun to a firing position near Lorengau Village, 18 March 1944.*

about 1600, the 7th Cavalry lost five men killed and fifteen wounded.

With the previous day's experience as a guide, General Mudge and Colonel Finley planned a co-ordinated attack for 17 March. The 7th Cavalry and the 2d Squadron, 8th, were to take the remainder of the airstrip and push on over the Lorengau River to the village. The 1st Squadron, 7th, with squads from the 8th Engineer Squadron attached, was to seize the eastern end of the airdrome while the 2d Squadron, 7th, moved south of the strip to make contact with the 2d Squadron, 8th, and advance to the river on Number 1 Road.

During the night of 16–17 March destroyers and field artillery battalions shelled the Japanese positions, and in the early morning twenty-four 81-mm. mortars, two light tanks, and two 37-mm. antitank guns put their fire on the pillboxes. An 81-mm. mortar of D Troop, 8th, attached to the 7th Cavalry, demolished one pillbox and its .50-caliber and .30-caliber machine guns and crew of fifteen men with a direct hit. When the mortars ceased fire automatic weapons opened up, and the 1st Squadron, 7th, assaulted. "At 1033 when our troops came out of their fox-holes there were numerous cries of 'Garry Owen' as the 1st Squadron went into its first action against the Japanese." [59]

There was little resistance, since the

[59] 7th Cav, Hist Rpt 7th Cav, 2 Mar–18 May 44, Pt. B, p. 11. "Garry Owen" is the 7th's regimental song.

supporting fires had "practically wiped out all enemy resistance except for necessary mopping up of a few bunkers still remaining intact." [60] The 1st Squadron, under Maj. James A. Godwin, quickly seized the ridge that had held up Shore's squadron the day before, then encountered another ridge position slightly to the east. After artillery and mortars had pounded it, cavalrymen moved in and occupied it. Flame throwers destroyed the pillboxes that remained in action.

Meanwhile noon found the two inland squadrons in contact with each other. By 1300 all three squadrons were in contact and had resumed the eastward advance. Only a few scattered Japanese opposed the move from the airstrip to the river, but emplaced mines caused some casualties and slowed the advance, so that it was 1500 before the three squadrons pulled up on a ridge on the west bank that overlooked the village. It was too late in the day to attack Lorengau, which the Americans had reason to believe was strongly defended. The 7th Cavalry's reconnaissance platoon had immediately crossed the river over the sandbar at its mouth, met fire from Japanese positions west of Lorengau, and withdrawn. Landing craft bringing in supplies received fire from the hills above the village. And, on the person of a Japanese officer who died defending the airdrome, the Americans had discovered maps of the defenses of Manus which showed that Lorengau and the road leading overland through the villages of Old Rossum and Rossum were fortified.

Lorengau lies in a cup-shaped valley surrounded by 400-foot-high hills. Most of the Japanese defenses faced seaward, although positions also covered the roads leading east, west, and south. As the Lorengau River was about sixty feet wide and ten to twenty feet deep in most places, the 2d Brigade's best approach route led over the alluvial sandbar at the mouth. The enemy had planted mines, controlled by a master switch in a pillbox on the hillside, on the stretch of beach between the sandbar and the hills. They had put foxholes and machine gun emplacements about a hundred yards inland from the shore, and had built about twelve pillboxes in the hills. The attackers would have to cross the river and the beach in full view of the enemy positions, but two factors favored an assault: repeated bombings and shellings had uncovered several Japanese positions so that they were visible, and the ridge taken in the 17 March attack provided good observation over Lorengau.

The 2d Squadron, 8th Cavalry, was designated to make the attack with mortar and artillery support. At 1000, 18 March, the reconnaissance platoon led out in single file followed by E, F, and G Troops. The move was unexpectedly easy; only scattered machine gun fire was directed at the reconnaissance platoon, which quickly cleared the beach and the rifle pits. It cut the master cable leading to the mines. Later a dead Japanese was found in a small pillbox with the detonator switch clutched in his hand.

The rifle troops received fire and some casualties while crossing the river, but got over rapidly. On the east shore they

[60] 7th Cav, Hist Rpt 7th Cav, 2 Mar–18 May 44, Pt. B, p. 11.

CROSSING THE LORENGAU RIVER *over the sandbar at the mouth of the river, 18 March 1944.*

deployed and prepared to attack. E Troop was to assault the enemy center in Lorengau with F Troop echeloned to the right rear; G Troop was to take the hills beside the river. Artillery and 81-mm. mortars hit the enemy once more, and when their fire ceased 60-mm.'s and machine guns opened up, whereupon the cavalry troops assaulted the bunkers with grenade, submachine gun, rifle, and flame thrower. Again, it was unexpectedly easy, for the Japanese apparently retreated inland over Number 2 Road.[61] Eighty-seven Japanese were killed defending Lorengau, while

the 2d Squadron, 8th Cavalry, captured it at a cost of seven wounded.

Fighting in the Admiralties was not yet over; it was 18 May before General Krueger officially terminated the operation. Los Negros was not cleared of the enemy until the end of March, and it took two squadrons, several tanks, P–40 strikes, and a good deal of artillery fire before the 2d Brigade cleared Number 2 Road to Rossum on 25 March. But the capture of Lorengau airfield, following the seizure of Momote, placed in Allied hands the main strategic objectives of the operation. During the entire operation (including the seizure of more outlying islands in April) the 1st Cavalry Division lost 326 men killed, 1,189 wounded, and 4 missing. It reported burying 3,280 and capturing 75

---

[61] Little is known about Japanese decisions and movements, as no Japanese survived to report to Rabaul. 8th Area Army Operations, Japanese Monogr No. 110 (OCMH), p. 134.

TROOP G, 8TH CAVALRY, NEAR NUMBER 1 ROAD *on the west side of the Lorengau River, 18 March 1944.*

of the enemy, and General Krueger estimated that the Japanese had disposed of 1,100 more bodies.[62]

Base Development

Meanwhile several battalions of Seabees, plus Army engineer units, were building airfields and a naval base. MacArthur, Nimitz, and the Joint Chiefs of Staff had intended that the naval base be used by all Allied fleets serving in the Pacific. In February Nimitz proposed to Admiral King that Admiral Halsey, who furnished most of the service troops, be given responsibility, under Nimitz, for developing and controlling the base.[63] Nimitz' proposal was rejected by

the Joint Chiefs but not before MacArthur became so irate that he ordered work on the Admiralties "restricted to facilities for ships under his direct command—the Seventh Fleet and British units."[64] Halsey, whom MacArthur vainly requested as his commander of Allied Naval Forces, made a hurried trip to Brisbane in early March and found that MacArthur "lumped me, Nimitz, King, and the whole Navy in a vicious conspiracy to pare away his authority."[65] Halsey was in a difficult position. MacArthur was very angry; he was Halsey's superior, and was vastly senior

---

[62] ALAMO Force Rpt, BREWER Opns, p. 26.
[63] Rad, CINCPAC to COMINCH, 23 Feb 44, CM–IN 16947.

[64] Halsey and Bryan, *Admiral Halsey's Story,* p. 189; Rad, Marshall to MacArthur, 9 Mar 44, CM–OUT 3710.
[65] Halsey and Bryan, *Admiral Halsey's Story,* p. 189; Suppl Min, JCS mtg, 8 Feb 44; Rad, MacArthur to Marshall, 2 Feb 44, CM–IN 1443.

to him.[66] And it is probably gratuitous to say MacArthur was formidable in argument. The scene, as Halsey records it, was lively, with MacArthur expressing himself strongly. "Unlike myself," the Admiral wrote, "strong emotion did not make him profane. He did not need to be; profanity would have merely discolored his eloquence." But the ram-jawed Halsey could also be formidable. Supported by Kinkaid and Carney, he asked the General to rescind his order: ". . . 'if you stick to this order of yours, you'll be hampering the war effort!' " Halsey went on to say that "the command of Manus didn't matter a whit to me. What did matter was the quick construction of the base. Kenney or an Australian or an enlisted cavalryman could boss it for all I cared, as long as it was ready to handle the fleet when we moved up New Guinea and on toward the Philippines." After long argument, General MacArthur agreed to cancel his order and the work went forward under Admiral Kinkaid's direction.[67]

Momote airfield, first used in March, was seven thousand feet long by 18 May. When the Lorengau airstrip proved unsuitable, Seabees and the 836th Engineer Aviation Battalion, working under pressure, finished one at Mokerang Plantation by 21 April, then put in a parallel runway. Seabees installed two runways for carrier aircraft on the outlying islands, and also developed Seeadler Harbour into one of the largest naval bases in the Pacific, with repair facilities for all types of warships and transports.[68] As planned, the naval base serviced the Third, Fifth, and Seventh Fleets in later operations, and the airfields supported the drives along the New Guinea coast and through the Central Pacific. The gallant action of the 1st Cavalry Division in execution of MacArthur's bold decision thus paid rich dividends.

---

[66] During World War I MacArthur had commanded a brigade and then a division while Halsey commanded a destroyer.

[67] Halsey and Bryan, *Admiral Halsey's Story,* pp. 189–90; Oral statement of Adm Kinkaid to the author *et al.,* 16 Nov 53. General Kenney, in his comments, remarked that Halsey's statement sounds as though "he didn't like *me,* the *Australians,* or *enlisted cavalrymen.*" Actually Halsey was probably only listing people unlikely to be directing construction of a naval base.

[68] *Building the Navy's Bases in World War II,* II, 295–302; Off of Chief Engr, GHQ AFPAC, *Airfield and Base Development,* pp. 208–22, and *Critique,* pp. 145–53.

CHAPTER XVII

Bougainville Counterattack

By March 1944 the Japanese were clearly beaten in the Southeast Area. With air and naval strength gone, the ground troops were stranded, immobilized, incapable of affecting the course of the war. Only at Rabaul were the Japanese strong, and that strength could not be employed unless the Allies chose to attack. But among the characteristics that made the Japanese a formidable opponent was his refusal to accept defeat even in a hopeless situation. If beaten, he knew it not. Thus it was that Generals Imamura and Hyakutake designed the destruction, in March, of the XIV Corps at Empress Augusta Bay, Bougainville.[1]

Preparations

The Approach

When in late 1943 the Japanese commanders had finally concluded that the invasion of Empress Augusta Bay was actually the Allied main effort at Bougainville, they began making plans for their counterattack. Unfortunately for him, Hyakutake's intelligence estimate was as inaccurate as most other Japanese estimates during World War II. He placed Allied strength at Empress Augusta Bay at about 30,000 of whom 10,000 were supposed to be aircraft ground crews. His figure for General Griswold's total strength was too low by half. Against the XIV Corps he planned to use the main strength of the *17th Army*, which consisted principally of General Kanda's *6th Division* and several battalions of the *17th Division* that Imamura had sent down in November. Total Japanese strength involved is variously reported as 15,000 to 19,000 men.[2]

---

[1] This chapter is based on SOPACBACOM, The Bougainville Campaign, Chs. IV–IX, supplemented by rpts, jnls, and jnl files of XIV Corps, Americal Div, 37th Div, and the principal component units which participated; Maj Gen Oscar W. Griswold, Bougainville: An Experience in Jungle Warfare (typescript); ACofS G–2 XIV Corps, History of the "TA" Operation, Bougainville, March 1944 [21 Apr 44]; 8th Area Army Operations, Japanese Monogr No. 110 (OCMH), pp. 106–22; 17th Army Operations, II, Japanese Monogr No. 40 (OCMH), 105–29; Capt. Francis D. Cronin, *Under the Southern Cross: The Saga of the Americal Division* (Washington: Combat Forces Press, 1951), pp. 143–68; Frankel, *The 37th Infantry Division in World War II*, pp. 141–70; Answers (27 Jul 49) of Gen Kanda [former CG, *6th Div*] to questions by Hist Sec G–2 FEC, in Hist Div MIS GHQ FEC, Statements of Japanese Officials on World War II (English Translations), II, 19–31, OCMH.

[2] ACofS G–2 XIV Corps, History of the "TA" Operation, a careful, conservative study written after the counteroffensive from prisoner-of-war interrogations, captured documents, and G–2 periodic reports and summaries, gives 15,400 men as the total. In 1949 General Kanda, speaking from memory, said there were 19,000 men involved plus about 2,000 sailors. He may have included all troops in rear areas in his figure.

During the early part of 1944 Japanese engineers built or improved roads, trails, and bridges so that the *17th Army* could move from north and south Bougainville to assembly areas in the hills inland from the XIV Corps' perimeter. By mid-February the enemy soldiers were all on their way, and Hyakutake left Erventa to supervise the action himself.

The Japanese had hoped to launch an amphibious assault against the Americans, coupled with an attack from inland. A shortage of landing craft made the amphibious assault impossible, but barges, operating on moonless nights to avoid Allied aircraft and PT boats, transported heavy equipment, including artillery, to a point east of Cape Torokina from where it was laboriously hauled inland to the hills. Packhorses and trucks carried supplies part of the way on the overland routes.

The infantry regiments of the *6th Division* advanced along both coasts, the *13th* and *23d Infantry Regiments* on the west, the *45th Infantry* up the east coast to Numa Numa, thence southwest by the Numa Numa Trail. The *17th Division* battalions also marched along both coasts from their positions in the north.

Such a move could hardly go unnoticed. Coastwatchers, radio intercepts, long- and short-range ground patrols, interrogation of prisoners and even of a few deserters, Japanese activity near the Fiji outpost at Ibu, interpretation of aerial photographs, and air and naval searches told General Griswold that the Japanese were on the move all over the island, and that attack was imminent. Allied planes regularly bombed all suspected troop movements, bridges, and assembly areas. When the Japanese launched strong attacks at Ibu in mid-February, the corps commander ordered the Fijians back to the perimeter. Four hundred and fifty Fiji soldiers and two hundred Bougainville natives made their way to Cape Torokina. Two Fijians were slightly wounded during the withdrawal.

Patrol clashes and fire fights in the hills north and northeast of the XIV Corps' perimeter indicated that the Japanese were concentrating there. Further, Japanese carelessness in safeguarding important documents played into General Griswold's hands. Papers taken from enemy corpses gave him a precise idea of Hyakutake's plan of attack, told him exactly which Japanese units were about to attack him, and gave him the general location of the enemy artillery units. Information about the attack was posted on the American units' bulletin boards.

XIV Corps' Defenses

At the beginning of March the XIV Corps' perimeter was somewhat larger than it had been when Griswold took over. It included, in a horseshoe-shaped line on the inland side, some 23,000 yards of low hills and jungle. The beach frontage totaled 11,000 yards. Depth of the position was about 8,000 yards. (*Map 22*) The main ground combat elements of the corps were the Americal and 37th Divisions, which numbered about 27,000 men. All together, 62,000 men, including naval units, were attached or assigned to the XIV Corps.

All the infantry regiments were placed on the front lines. A total of twelve rifle

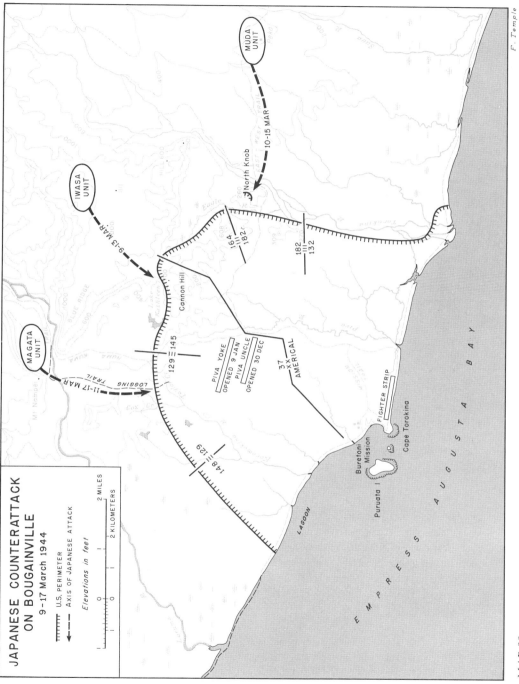

JAPANESE COUNTERATTACK
ON BOUGAINVILLE
9–17 March 1944

MAGATA UNIT

IWASA UNIT

MUDA UNIT

11–17 MAR

9–13 MAR

10–15 MAR

LOGGING TRAIL

Cannon Hill

North Knob

129 ≡ 145

148 ≡ 129

164
III
182

182
III
132

PIVA YOKE
OPENED 9 JAN

PIVA UNCLE
OPENED 30 DEC

37
XX
AMERICAL

FIGHTER STRIP

Cape Torokina

Buretoni
Mission

Puruata I

LAGOON

EMPRESS   AUGUSTA   BAY

BLUE RIDGE

F. Temple

MAP 22

470507 O–59—24

60-MM. MORTAR EMPLACEMENT *on Hill 700 held by 145th Infantry, 15 February 1944.*

battalions held frontages varying from 2,000 to 2,400 yards. Usually each regiment held one battalion in reserve. The 37th Division defended the left (northwest) sector from a point on the beach 5,500 yards northwest of Cape Torokina to the area of Hill 700, about 2,000 yards east of Lake Kathleen. The 148th Infantry, on the division left, and the 129th Infantry, in the center, held low ground. The 145th Infantry, on the right, held Hill 700, the highest ground possessed by the Americans. The Americal Division's line ran from just east of Hill 700, where the 164th Infantry's left flank tied in with the 145th's right, over Hills 608, 309, and 270, then along the west bank of the Torokina River. Near its mouth the line crossed over to the east

bank.[3] The 182d Infantry, in the division's center, held Hills 309 and 270 on the main perimeter line. The 132d Infantry on the right held low ground. In addition a detachment of the 182d Infantry, plus artillery and mortar observers, maintained an outpost on Hill 260, an eminence which was some distance east of the main line of resistance and overlooked the Torokina River. Griswold had ordered this hill held so that it could be used as an American artillery and mortar observation post, and so that the enemy could not use it to observe American positions.

---

[3] The 132d Infantry, Americal Division, had seized this area in an action in January wherein S/Sgt. Jessie R. Drowley fought so valiantly that he was awarded the Medal of Honor. WD GO 73, 6 Sep 44.

All units had been developing and strengthening positions on the main line of resistance, which now consisted of rifle pits and earth, log, and sandbag pillboxes, wired in behind double-apron or concertina barbed wire. In front of the wire were minefields. Various devices were employed to give illumination at night: searchlights, either shining directly or reflecting a spread beam off clouds; flares tied in trees and set off by pull wires; flashlights; thermite grenades; and cans full of sand and gasoline. Grenades, with wires attached, were set up as booby traps along obvious approach routes. Oil drums, each with scrap metal packed around a bangalore torpedo, were wired for electrical detonation. Fields of fire fifty yards or more deep, deep enough to prevent the enemy from throwing hand grenades at the American positions from cover and concealment, had been cleared. Almost all the infantry regiments possessed extra machine guns, and had issued two BAR's to each rifle squad. All regiments had constructed reserve positions. The naval construction battalions, the 3d Marine Defense Battalion, Army engineer units, and others maintained provisional infantry units as part of the corps reserve, which also included the 82d Chemical Battalion, the 754th Tank Battalion, and the 1st Battalion, 24th Infantry.[4]

Artillery support for the perimeter, though below American standards, was stronger than the enemy's supporting artillery. The XIV Corps still had neither organic artillery nor an artillery commander. Serving as corps artillery commander was General Kreber, artillery commander of the 37th Division. Under General Kreber's command were the eight (six 105-mm. and two 155-mm.) howitzer battalions organic to the two divisions, plus the provisional corps artillery. This consisted of two 155-mm. gun batteries of the 3d Marine Defense Battalion; four 90-mm. antiaircraft batteries of the 251st Antiaircraft Artillery Regiment; and four 90-mm. antiaircraft batteries of the 3d Marine Defense Battalion, of which one, D Battery, 70th Coast Artillery (Antiaircraft) Battalion, was attached from the Army. Gun power of the XIV Corps units was augmented on 3 March when six cannon companies, with 75-mm. pack howitzers, reached Bougainville and joined the infantry regiments.

The XIV Corps' positions were strong, and since he possessed interior lines General Griswold could easily switch his reserve units back and forth. But the positions were not ideal. The corps lacked enough men, by American standards, to hold all the high ground in the vicinity. Beyond the coastal plain the ground rises abruptly from ridge to ridge, each higher than the preceding one, up to the summits of the Crown Prince Range. Thus the Americans on Hills 608 and 700 held positions that were dominated by the higher ground in Japanese hands—Blue Ridge, three thousand yards north of Hill 700, and Hills 1000 and 1111, just southeast of Blue Ridge. These hills gave the enemy an excellent view over all the perimeter except the reverse slopes of the American-held hills. By 1 March, however,

---

[4] This unit had served on Bougainville since 30 January, chiefly as a labor battalion. See Ulysses G. Lee, Employment of Negro Troops, a volume in preparation for the series UNITED STATES ARMY IN WORLD WAR II.

General Griswold was sure that "the perimeter was as well organized as the personnel and the terrain would permit." [5]

The Japanese Plan of Attack

General Hyakutake organized most of his infantry into three forces, each named for its commander. The *Iwasa Unit,* under General Iwasa, consisted of the *2d Battalion, 13th Infantry;* the *23d Infantry;* and two batteries of field artillery, some mortars, and engineers and other supporting troops. The *Magata Unit,* led by Col. Isaoshi Magata of the *45th Infantry,* whom Kanda considered to be a crack regimental commander, included nearly all the *45th Infantry* plus mortars, field artillery, and engineers. The third unit, under Col. Toyoharei Muda, who had succeeded the late Tomonari in command of the *13th Infantry,* consisted of the remainder of the *13th* plus engineers. Supporting the attacks of the three infantry units was an artillery group commanded by a Colonel Saito. This consisted of four 150-mm. howitzers, two 105-mm. howitzers, and a number of smaller pieces. [6] Artillery ammunition supply totaled three hundred rounds per piece, of which one fifth was to be used for direct support of the infantry, the rest for interdicting the airfields.

Also present were elements of the *1st* and *3d Battalions, 53d Infantry,* and part of the *81st Infantry,* all from the *17th Division.* At first these were either placed in *17th Army* reserve or were assigned diversionary missions against the northwest part of the XIV Corps' beachhead.

The *Iwasa Unit* assembled behind Hill 1111, the *Magata Unit* behind Mount Nampei, a shoulder-shaped ridge extending outward from the Crown Prince Range just northwest of Blue Ridge. The *Muda Unit* assembled at Peko, a village on the East-West Trail about 5,400 yards east-northeast of Hill 260. The artillery group emplaced in the vicinity of Hill 600.

The plan of maneuver involved two thrusts from the north coupled with an attack from the northeast, all on a complicated schedule. Briefly, the *Iwasa Unit* was to attack and secure Hill 700 on Y Day (set, after some delays in moving into position, for 8 March), reorganize on 9 and 10 March, and advance to the Piva airfields. During this period the *Muda Unit* was to capture Hills 260 and 309, whereupon it and one battalion of the *Iwasa Unit* were supposed to attack Hill 608 from the southeast and northwest on 12 March. All these attacks were preliminary to an effort which was to be delivered, starting 11 March, by the *Magata Unit* against the 129th Infantry in its low ground west of Hill 700. Magata's men, after cracking the 129th's line, were to advance against the Piva airstrips in conjunction with Iwasa's advance. Then all units were to drive southward on a broad front to capture the Torokina fighter strip by 17 March. Haste was essential, since the *17th Army* had brought with it but two weeks' rations.

Hindsight indicates that the Japanese plan was unsound. Even had Hyaku-

---

[5] Griswold, Bougainville, p. 46.

[6] General Kanda specified 18 70-mm. battalion guns; ACofS G–2 XIV Corps, History of the "TA" Operation lists 168 75-mm. mountain guns. The Japanese 105 is often called a 10-cm. piece.

155-MM. GUNS OF THE 3D MARINE DEFENSE BATTALION *firing on enemy positions, 6 March 1944.*

take's estimate of American strength been correct, he still lacked enough strength in manpower and in artillery (he had no air support whatever) to attack prepared positions, and under the actual circumstances he was hopelessly outnumbered and outgunned. If his object had been to inflict maximum damage regardless of his own losses, he might have achieved a larger degree of success by concentrating his forces from the first in order to overwhelm a narrow portion of Griswold's front, break through, and spread destruction throughout the rear areas until Griswold could redeploy his infantry regiments. Of course, Hyakutake might have achieved more success had the American soldiers elected to turn

and run instead of standing their ground, but that was an imponderable that he could not count on. The Americal and 37th Divisions were veteran units.[7]

By 8 March almost everything was ready. The rhetorical manifestoes by which Japanese officers exhorted their troops were issued. General Hyakutake expressed himself along these lines:

The time has come to manifest our knighthood with the pure brilliance of the sword. It is our duty to erase the mortifica-

---

[7] Hyakutake, in 1942, had delivered a similar, unsuccessful, counterattack against Vandegrift's positions on Guadalcanal. See Miller, *Guadalcanal: The First Offensive,* Ch. VI.

tion of our brothers at Guadalcanal. Attack! Assault! Destroy everything! Cut, slash, and mow them down. May the color of the red emblem of our arms be deepened with the blood of the American rascals. Our cry of victory at Torokina Bay will be shouted resoundingly to our native land.

We are invincible! Always attack. Security is the greatest enemy. Always be alert. Execute silently.[8]

Not to be outdone, General Kanda had this to say:

We must fight to the end to avenge the shame of our country's humiliation on GUADALCANAL. . . . There can be no rest until our bastard foes are battered, and bowed in shame—till their . . . blood adds lustre . . . to the badge of the Sixth Division. Our battle cry will be heard afar. . . .[9]

Again, the most apt comment is in Proverbs XVI:18.

Hill 700

At 0545, shortly after daybreak of 8 March, Hyakutake's artillery heralded the opening of his counteroffensive by firing on all parts of the beachhead, with especial attention to the Piva airfields.

American observers on the ground, in artillery liaison planes, and on board destroyers, aided by information gained from documents, quickly determined the general location of the Japanese artillery, and counterbattery fire by the corps artillery and the organic division artillery battalions began at once. The Americal Division artillery put its fire on hills to the east and east-northeast, the 37th on

those to the northeast. Smoke shells were fired at suspected enemy observation posts to blind the enemy. In the 37th's sector the 6th Field Artillery Battalion, supporting the 129th Infantry, and the 129th Infantry Cannon Company were so situated that they could shoot directly at enemy gun flashes. The other battalions fired by forward observer.[10]

At 1045 twenty-four SBD's and twelve TBF's of the 1st Marine Air Wing dropped fourteen tons of bombs on Hills 250 and 600. A strike against Hill 1111 was planned for the late morning but was postponed when a sudden cloud screen obscured the hilltop. Finally, at 1600, fifty-six SBD's and thirty-six TBF's, guided by artillery smoke shells, dropped 100- and 1,000-pound bombs on Hill 1111 and environs.

In the course of the day's firing the Japanese destroyed one B–24 and three fighters, and damaged nineteen planes on Piva strips. Before nightfall all bombers except six TBF's which remained for local support left for New Georgia to escape destruction. The enemy also damaged one 155-mm. gun and several tanks. Early next morning, the 9th, the enemy guns turned their attention to the Torokina fighter strip and forced its planes to take to the air for safety. Almost no shells fell on the front lines except in the 145th Infantry's area, where shellfire and mortars caused several casualties.

The sector of the 145th, now commanded by Col. Cecil B. Whitcomb, extended from low ground in the vicinity of the Numa Numa Trail eastward past

---

[8] Quoted in Frankel, *The 37th Infantry Division in World War II*, pp. 142–43. The "red emblem" referred to was probably the shoulder patch of the *6th Division*.

[9] Quoted in Griswold, Bougainville, p. 81.

[10] Throughout the operation U.S. destroyers also fired counterbattery fire and against suspected enemy assembly areas and approach routes.

the south shore of Lake Kathleen and up along the military crest of Hill 700, a frontage of about 3,500 yards. The 3d Battalion, on the left (west), held the low ground just south of Lake Kathleen and Cannon Hill, an eminence slightly lower and to the west of Hill 700. On the right the 2d Battalion held Hill 700 with two rifle companies (E and G) and machine gun sections of H Company in line, F Company in reserve, and H Company's 81-mm. mortars grouped on the reverse (south) slope.

Hill 700, which commanded the entire beachhead, was steep, with slopes of 65 to 75 percent in all directions. American intelligence estimates, though not ruling out an enemy attack here, had tended to discount its probability. The steepness that increased the difficulty of attack also complicated the defense, for the forward (north) slope fell away too sharply to permit it to be completely covered with grazing fire. Thus the 2d Battalion had an extra allotment of machine guns. Its pillboxes housed 37-mm. antitank guns, light and heavy machine guns, BAR's, and rifles. The front was wired in, with some mines in front. In direct support were the 105-mm. howitzers of the 135th Field Artillery Battalion and, starting on 8 March, the 4.2-inch mortars of D Company, 82d Chemical Battalion.[11]

That the 145th Infantry was in danger of attack had become obvious on 6 March when patrols reported the presence of large numbers of Japanese about fourteen hundred yards north of Hill 700. Additional ammunition was made available to the troops, and two days' C

rations, ammunition, and a five-gallon can of water were stocked in each pillbox against a breakdown in supply. For nocturnal illumination each machine gun section was issued four incendiary grenades and a gallon can of flame thrower fuel.

On 7 March Japanese wire-cutting parties started work in front of the 145th. Next day patrols in front of Hill 700, Cannon Hill, and along Lake Kathleen's shores kept running into enemy troops. At the same time 129th Infantry patrols reported many enemy contacts, and Americal Division patrols also observed enemy troops east of the Torokina River, along the East–West Trail, and around Hills 250 and 600. In front of the 145th fire fights and skirmishes went on all day. When patrols reported that the enemy was massing, the 37th Division artillery, the 145th's Cannon Company, and the 4.2-inch mortars fired a counterpreparation twelve hundred yards wide and two thousand yards deep in front of the 2d Battalion. Japanese orders had called for an attack on 8 March, but none developed. The *23d Infantry* had spent the day moving into position in front of the 145th; the *2d Battalion* reconnoitered Cannon Hill, the *3d, 700,* but for some reason the regiment did not assault.[12]

Rain fell throughout the night of 8–9 March. Shortly after midnight, concealed by darkness, rain, and mists, about two companies of the *23d Infantry* attacked up the north slope of Hill 700 against the 1st Platoon, G Company, 145th,

---

[11] This company also supported the 129th Infantry.

[12] In 1949 General Kanda said that as the *23d's* attack had not succeeded, and as the *13th* had taken Hill 260 on 8 March, he ordered the attack continued on the 9th. Either his recollection was faulty or his subordinate commanders deceived him.

37TH DIVISION TROOPS CARRYING 5-GALLON CANS OF WATER *up the steep slope of Hill 700. Foreground, from left: Pfc. Howard K. Stoneburner, Sgt. Brant A. Johnson, and Pfc. Thomas J. Householder. Background, from left: Pfc. Gerald C. Menken, Pfc. Taylor Maggard, and S/Sgt. Robert G. Dove.*

which held a level saddle between the topmost eminence of the hill and a rise to the left (west) dubbed Pat's Nose. Other elements of the 23d put pressure on E Company, 145th, on the highest point of 700. This attack was repulsed.

About 0230, 9 March, the *23d Infantry* attacked G Company's 1st Platoon again, this time in column of battalions. The *2d Battalion*, in the lead, blew up the barbed wire, knocked out a pillbox, and through the gap its forward elements moved onto the saddle and set up machine guns. American mortars and artillery opened up and appear to have severely punished the *3d Battalion*, which was following the *2d*.

When day broke the Americans were not sure of the extent of the enemy penetration, as mists and enemy fire hampered reconnaissance. Some local counterattacks, largely un-co-ordinated, were attempted but all failed. Soldiers of the 145th tried to attack northward up the south slopes of Hill 700, but the Japanese drove them back by rolling down grenades.

By noon the situation was clarified. The Japanese had made but a minor penetration; about one company held a salient on the saddle about one hundred yards from east to west and fifty yards deep. It had captured seven pillboxes, plus observation posts, in the 1st Platoon's line and had set up light and heavy machine guns.

General Beightler released the 1st Battalion, 145th, from division reserve to Colonel Whitcomb, who attached it to the 2d Battalion, and elements of the 117th Engineer Battalion took up positions in the 145th's regimental reserve lines south of Hill 700.

About noon C Company, 145th, started northward up Hill 700 toward the saddle in frontal assault while two F Company platoons attacked the saddle from the east and west. By 1530 the platoon attacking from the east had recovered some of the lost ground but C Company had been halted about two thirds of the way to its objective.

Two light tanks of the 754th Tank Battalion, released out of corps reserve by General Griswold, tried to support an attack later in the afternoon, but the hill proved too steep for them. The F Company platoons pressed their attack anyway and by 1735 had retaken five pillboxes. By nightfall a solid line had been established in front of the Japanese. It ran along Hill 700 south of the crest in the region of the penetration and joined its flanks with the original main line of resistance. B and C Companies and one platoon of D Company held the new line.

During the day the Japanese used their point of vantage on the saddle to put mortar and machine gun fire on Mc-Clelland Road, a lateral supply route south of the crests of the hills, roughly parallel to the main line of resistance. This fire halted the 3/4-ton trucks and half-tracks that were used to bring up ammunition and required the use of hand-carrying parties, which hauled ammunition forward and took out the wounded under Japanese fire.

Neither Japanese nor Americans made any aggressive moves on the night of 9–10 March, but it was a noisy night. The Japanese laid mortar and small arms fire on the American lines, while the 37th Division artillery and mortars put close-in and deep supporting fires in front of the 2d Battalion, 145th.

At 0645 the next day, 10 March, while the *Muda Unit* began its attack against the Americal Division troops on Hill 260, the *23d Infantry* troops on the saddle renewed their attack and other elements of the *Iwasa Unit* attempted to get through the curtain of American artillery and mortar fire to reinforce the saddle. The Americans on Hill 700 responded with fire and local counterattacks. There was no change in the location of the front lines.

During the morning Griswold released the Provisional Infantry Battalion, 251st Antiaircraft Artillery Regiment, from corps reserve; it proceeded to the 145th's regimental reserve line. Elements of the 117th Engineer Battalion thereupon made ready to destroy the Japanese positions with bangalore torpedoes and pole charges of TNT. But this came to naught when four engineers, trying to snake a torpedo into a pillbox, were killed outright by the torpedo, which either exploded prematurely or was detonated by a Japanese shell. A Japanese-speaking American soldier brought a loud-speaker up close to the enemy and urged immediate capitulation; the Japanese responded with a mortar shell which knocked the loud-speaker out of action.

By afternoon of this day of patternless and ineffective action (which also featured enemy fire on McClelland Road and a 36-plane strike against Japanese positions), the American units in contact with the enemy had become intermingled. Sorting and reorganizing them consumed much of the afternoon, so that it was 1700 before elements of the 1st

and 2d Battalions, 145th, after a ten-minute mortar preparation, delivered a co-ordinated attack. The Americans used bangalore torpedoes, rocket launchers, and pole charges in the face of artillery, mortar, machine gun, and rifle fire. The fighting was close work; several pillboxes were recaptured and then lost. As darkness fell, however, the Americans had achieved some success. The Japanese penetration was now reduced by more than half. By 1930, G, F, A, C, B, and E Companies held the line; the 37th Reconnaissance Troop, which General Beightler attached to the 145th at 1815, was in reserve.

During the night, as Colonel Magata prepared to deliver his attack against the 129th Infantry, General Iwasa sent the rest of his command against the 145th's front from Cannon Hill to the crest of 700. The Japanese came in closely packed waves, shouting, the 37th Division reported, imprecations in Japanese. The fields of fire at Cannon Hill and Pat's Nose were better than at 700, and the 145th, heavily supported by artillery and mortars, handily repulsed Iwasa everywhere except on the saddle, where the Japanese captured one more pillbox.

As dawn broke on 11 March, a day on which Muda was active at Hill 260 and the *Magata Unit* began its attack against the 129th Infantry, General Beightler was obviously concerned over the 145th's failure to reduce the enemy salient. The night before he had ordered the 2d Battalion, 148th Infantry, to move from its regimental reserve positions to the 145th's sector. To replace it General Griswold placed the 1st Battalion, 24th Infantry, at Beightler's disposal. Beight-

Two Light Tanks M3 of the 754th Tank Battalion *heading up Hill 700 during the afternoon of 9 March.*

ler also dispatched his assistant division commander, Brig. Gen. Charles F. Craig, to the 145th's sector to observe operations and keep him informed. The regimental commander was suffering, Craig reported later, from extreme battle fatigue and was relieved. Colonel Freer, who had been serving as executive of the 145th, took his place.[13]

In the meantime the Japanese made valorous efforts to put more troops onto the saddle. The Americans resisted with vigor and with all the fire power at their disposal. Charging, literally, over the piled heaps of their dead comrades, the

enemy soldiers fought hard but vainly, and failed either to budge the Americans or to strengthen the saddle.

The 2d Battalion, 148th, reached its assembly area behind the 145th at 1115. Colonel Radcliffe, its commander, reconnoitered in preparation for an afternoon attack.

Three 105-mm. howitzer battalions, the 145th Infantry Cannon Company, 4.2-inch chemical mortars, the 81-mm. mortars of D, H, and M Companies of the 145th, and the 60-mm. mortars of all the rifle companies of the 2d Battalion, 148th, fired a preparation from 1320 to 1330. Then elements of the 148th attacked. Two platoons from E Company

[13] Ltr, Gen Craig to Gen Smith, Chief of Mil Hist, 30 Oct 53, no sub, OCMH.

moved east from Pat's Nose in an effort to envelop the saddle from north and south while a third platoon delivered a holding attack westward from the crest of Hill 700. The whole target was blanketed by artillery smoke shells. The 145th supported the attack with overhead fire. The platoon making the envelopment from the north gained the crest, losing eight dead, whereupon the platoon leader and four enlisted men seized a communication trench, then a pillbox. But the Japanese killed the five men and the attack halted about 1900. The troops dug in on the ground they had gained. During the night the Japanese harried the Americans but failed to penetrate the line.

The attack on 12 March followed the previous day's pattern. While intense local battles raged in the 129th Infantry sector and on Hill 260, E Company continued its attack and F Company attacked northwestward from the top of 700. Using grenades, rifles, flame throwers, and rocket launchers, the 148th soldiers methodically reduced the pillboxes one by one. When nearly all the officers in both companies were wounded, sergeants took over command. By 1300 the Japanese held but one pillbox; by 1317 they had lost it, and by 1530 mopping up was completed, all the Japanese save two wounded prisoners were dead, the 145th's line was restored. Three hundred and nine enemy corpses were counted in the immediate area. During the next day the *Iwasa Unit,* which had suffered heavily in its unsuccessful attack, withdrew behind a screen of combat patrols and fire.

During the period 8–13 March the 37th Division lost five officers and sev-

enty-three enlisted men killed.[14] The artillery expended a considerable amount of ammunition in defense of Hill 700: 20,802 105-mm. rounds; about 10,000 75-mm. rounds; 13,000 81-mm. and 811 4.2-inch mortar shells.[15]

Hill 260

While General Iwasa was meeting defeat at Hill 700, Colonel Muda was attacking the American outpost on Hill 260 in preparation for operations against Hills 309 and 608 in the Americal Division's sector. The *Muda Unit*—principally one battalion and two companies of the *13th Infantry*—completed its assembly at Peko and moved forward. On the night of 9–10 March small enemy forces infiltrated between Hill 260 and the main line of resistance, while an assault force assembled east of 260 and made ready to attack.[16]

Some 800 yards east of the main perimeter line and 7,500 yards north of the Torokina's mouth, Hill 260 is shaped like an hourglass. Its long axis runs from northwest to southeast. The two ends of the hourglass are rises called North Knob and South Knob. Each knob is about half the size of a football field. The handle between them is slightly

---

[14] Memo, G–1 37th Div for G–2 and G–3, 14 Mar 44, no sub, in 37th Div G–3 Jnl File, Vol. 13, Serials 4601–5400.

[15] On 14 March General Kreber ordered 90-mm. antiaircraft guns to supplement certain 40-mm. guns already in use on the front lines. Thereafter these flat-trajectory weapons sniped at enemy guns emplaced on the forward slopes of the hills to the north and northeast.

[16] In addition to sources cited above, this account of the Hill 260 action is based on comments of Col. William D. Long on draft MS of this volume, attached to his Ltr to Gen Smith, Chief of Mil Hist, 21 Mar 54, no sub, OCMH.

lower and so narrow that there was room for only a trail. North and South Knobs lie so close together—less than 150 yards apart—that to hit one knob with artillery or mortar fire inevitably showered the other with fragments. The slopes to the east and west are very steep.

The East–West Trail crossed the Torokina just east of 260 and, bending south of South Knob, entered the main perimeter line between Hills 309 and 608. A small north–south stream, called the Eagle River by the Americans, flowed between 260 and the main perimeter before running into the Torokina River. In the early part of March only one trail led from the main line to South Knob. The last hundred yards to the top consisted of a steep stairway revetted into the southwest slope. A small vehicular bridge had been built over the Eagle. The entire area, including the east and west slopes of 260, was heavily jungled.

From a platform on a 150-foot-high tree ("OP Tree") on South Knob, American mortar and artillery forward observers could view the banks of the Torokina below, the East–West Trail, and Hills 250 and 600 to the northeast. Conversely, in Japanese hands Hill 260 would have provided good observation of Hills 608 and 309 and of the corps' rear area between them. On 10 March the American garrison on 260 consisted of about eighty men including forward observers and a reinforced platoon from G Company, 182d Infantry, which regiment held the main perimeter west of 260. It was "a sore thumb stuck out into the poison ivy." [17] Defenses, all on South Knob, consisted of pillboxes and

"OP TREE" ON HILL 260

bunkers inside barbed wire and defensive warning devices arranged in a triangle around OP Tree. Fire lanes faced northeast, east, and southeast.

The Americans had been maintaining ambushes on the northeast and southeast approaches to South Knob but on 9 March withdrew them to put harassing and interdictory fires over the whole area from 1830 to 2330, 9 March, and again from 0415 to 0500, 10 March. A few minutes after 0600 on 10 March, during the 182d's normal stand to for the two hours before daylight, fire from Japanese mortars, machine guns, and

---

[17] Ibid.

rifles began striking the American positions on 260. At 0638 an officer of the 246th Field Artillery Battalion, Americal Division, reported from his post in OP Tree that the Japanese had attacked and were all around the base of his tree. He was not heard from again. The attack, which the Americans estimated was made by one company, was actually delivered by all or part of the *3d Battalion, 13th Infantry.* It overran most of the American positions, captured OP Tree, and drove the survivors of the American garrison to North Knob. One six-man group from the mortar and artillery observation teams took refuge in two pillboxes and put up such stout-hearted resistance that they held their positions in spite of the fact that the Japanese had surrounded them.[18]

When the enemy attack was reported to General Griswold, he ordered General Hodge, the Americal Division's commander, to hold 260 at all costs. This order came as a surprise to the Americal's officers, who had not expected to be required to hold 260 in the face of a strong enemy attack.[19] Col. William D. Long, commanding the 182d, promptly released two companies—E and F—of his 2d Battalion from regimental reserve and placed Lt. Col. Dexter Lowry, commander of the 2d Battalion, in charge of

operations.[20] F Company left the perimeter, crossed the Eagle River and pushed northward through virgin jungle to North Knob, made contact with the G Company soldiers who had made their way there, and established a perimeter defense. At 0845 E Company was ordered to advance east over the trail to attack the South Knob from the southwest in conjunction with a southward move by one platoon of F Company.

By 1045, when E Company reached the base of Hill 260's southwest slope, the troops on North Knob had become aware that some Americans on South Knob were still alive.[21] The attack began immediately after E Company's arrival. One E Company platoon started up the steep slope as the F Company platoon attempted to move south, but after a gain of about thirty-five yards both platoons, now coming into the cleared areas, halted under enemy fire. Shortly after 1300 Long authorized Lowry to contain the Japanese at the base of OP Tree until he could send flame throwers forward.

Lowry therefore held up the attack, received the flame throwers, and by 1420 was ready to go again. This time he planned a double envelopment from 260's southwest spur. One platoon of E Company was to move left (north) to make contact with the F Company platoon advancing south while a second E Company platoon moved right to attack from the south and southeast. The platoons moved out and began their at-

---

[18] For a stirring, well-told account by one of the observers, see Griswold, Bougainville, pp. 103–09, or SOPACBACOM, The Bougainville Campaign, Ch. VIII, pp. 368–75, OCMH. Colonel Long, in his comments on the draft MS of this volume, expressed his admiration for the skill of the Japanese who delivered the attack "from the most difficult direction with complete surprise."

[19] Comments on draft MS of this volume by Lt Col Carl D. McFerren, formerly ACofS, G–2, Americal Div, on Bougainville, in OCMH.

[20] Long had served as ACofS, G–2, Americal Division, during the Guadalcanal Campaign.

[21] They apparently based this conclusion on fire fights between the Japanese and the trapped observers.

tack at 1445. The Japanese quickly halted the northern attack. The southern platoon started up South Knob, met grazing fire, retired, moved to the right, and assaulted again. This time, using flame throwers and grenades, the platoon drove up onto a shelf on the southern edge of South Knob that protected it from small arms fire. It was within earshot of the trapped Americans. Colonel Lowry, now estimating that at least two enemy companies held South Knob, reported that his and the enemy's forces were too close for him to use 60-mm. mortars safely. The attack was renewed at 1800, but by then battle casualties and exhaustion had reduced E Company's strength by one half. Lowry and Colonel Long, who had arrived at South Knob at 1715, decided to hold their present positions. The six Americans in the pillboxes thought E Company had secured the hill, and stayed where they were. Active operations for the day were concluded by an enemy bayonet assault which F Company repulsed by fire.

Early next morning the Japanese, apparently strengthened during the night, struck at E Company in a quick attack. The company turned back the attackers, but of its 7 officers and 143 enlisted men who had left the perimeter the day before, only 1 wounded officer and 24 enlisted men remained at the front. Colonel Long therefore ordered G Company (less its original outpost platoon) out of the main perimeter to relieve E.

As G Company advanced up the west slope of South Knob it ran into enemy troops attacking from the east, southeast, and south. Colonel Lowry reported his troops in distress as the enemy threatened to encircle his position on South

Knob and began driving E Company off. But there was almost no way to strengthen him. General Hodge was required to hold one battalion available for service in corps reserve, and there were few other troops that could be committed without weakening the main line of resistance, which was now under attack on Hill 700 and in the 129th's sector. With the foothold on South Knob practically lost, and because South Knob could be neutralized from North Knob, Hodge and Long decided to pull E and G Companies off South Knob and send them to North Knob, and to send B Company forward to assist them in breaking contact.[22] The Japanese, failing to follow up their advantage, did not pursue E and G Companies as they retired toward the Eagle River, where they were joined by B Company. All companies proceeded to North Knob. B Company, cutting a trail from the old trail northward parallel to the north–south axis of 260, led the way. When a larger perimeter on North Knob was completed, G Company went back to the main line of resistance.

In midafternoon, Brig. Gen. William A. McCulloch, the Americal's assistant commander, arrived at the 182d Infantry command post and assumed command of operations at Hill 260.[23] In late afternoon B and F Companies, reinforced by a provisional flame thrower platoon from the 132d Infantry, attacked again. F Company pushed front-

---

[22] B Company's sector was taken over first by B Company, 57th Engineer Battalion, and then by G Company, 164th Infantry.

[23] McCulloch, then a colonel, had commanded the 27th Infantry of the 25th Division during the Guadalcanal Campaign.

ally while B Company attempted a flanking movement around OP Tree. This time flame throwers burned out two Japanese positions, and B Company managed to drive onto South Knob. The six trapped Americans successfully sprang for safety, but at 1915 both companies withdrew to North Knob. B Company established a trail block on East–West Trail, but unlike Magata and Iwasa in the 37th Division's sector, Muda attempted neither night attacks nor harassing infiltration.

The next day, 12 March, was subsequently referred to by the 182d Infantry as "Bloody Sunday." By now all combat elements of the *Muda Unit* were emplaced on South Knob. Operations on Bloody Sunday opened about 0700 when the Japanese put artillery and mortar fire on the America's main perimeter and the rear areas. Before 12 March the presence of American troops on both knobs had inhibited the employment of American artillery and mortars, but now that the Americans were off South Knob the supporting weapons could shoot with a little more freedom. The Americal Division, using OP Tree as a registration point, replied therefore to the Japanese with artillery and mortar fire on targets of opportunity, especially on South Knob and the approaches to Hill 260. This fire, like all similar fire, forced the Americans on North Knob to move back to avoid being hit by fragments from the shells landing on South Knob.

Meanwhile supplies on North Knob were running low, and getting more food, ammunition, and water to the companies there was proving difficult.

The only supply route was the trail B Company had cut northward from the old trail, and it was a footpath too narrow for vehicles. Carrying parties on the north leg of the trip encountered so much fire from the Japanese on South Knob and on the west slopes that they made the trip by running in spurts while covered by riflemen. This, to phrase it mildly, was tiring. But by noon these methods had succeeded in amassing enough ammunition to mount an attack, and the American commanders decided to deliver one and so capitalize on the advantages they presumed the morning bombardment had given them.[24]

The plan of attack called for F Company, 182d, to provide a base of fire from the perimeter on North Knob while B Company, with six flame throwers attached, moved south and west to attack South Knob from the west and northwest.[25]

In column of platoons, B Company started off North Knob at 1300. The 2d Platoon, in the lead, tried to storm the crest of South Knob from the northwest, but as it moved across a small gully two new Japanese pillboxes on the west slope opened fire and it halted. The enemy had revealed his positions, and 81-mm. mortars and machine guns opened up on the pillboxes. Under cover of this fire, and freely using flame throwers, the next platoon in column (the 3d) crossed the gully and moved as far as the top

---

[24] Later, when more troops became available, a trail wide enough for jeeps was built from the perimeter directly to North Knob.

[25] Colonel Lowry, lightly wounded and weary, had by this time been temporarily replaced in command of the 2d Battalion by Lt. Col. William Mahoney, until then the regimental executive officer.

of South Knob without losing a man. It had reached a point southwest of OP Tree when fire from Japanese positions on the east slope struck and the soldiers hit the ground. Every attempt to maneuver brought down enemy fire, but when American mortars struck the Japanese positions the 3d Platoon renewed the assault with grenades and flame throwers, with the latter protected by BAR men who blazed away almost continuously at the enemy. The fearsome sight of the flame is reported to have caused some Japanese soldiers to throw down their arms and flee.

At this point, when victory seemed almost won, the 3d Platoon was struck by machine gun fire from the east of OP Tree and from a machine gun at the base of the tree itself. The day was nearly gone; it was 1620, and the attackers' ammunition was running low. No fresh troops were immediately available on Hill 260. The 1st Battalion (less C and D companies), 132d, had been attached to the 182d and A Company was alerted for movement at 1515, but it was 1600 before A Company reached the 182d's main line of resistance. Hoping to hold the ground gained, McCulloch and Long decided to send A Company, 132d, along the old trail to attack the South Knob from the southwest, make physical contact with B Company, 182d, and establish a defensive position on the crest of South Knob. Time was running out. Another hour went by before A Company began its move, and as it neared Hill 260 it received enemy gunfire which killed the company commander. There was confusion and further delay until order was restored. By now it was obvi-

ous that A Company would not reach B before dark. Thus, because there were not enough men to hold the ground B Company had gained, the American commanders reluctantly made the "painful decision" to order B Company to return to North Knob, A Company to the main perimeter.[26]

The fight for Hill 260 had gone on for three days. Continued bombardments and attacks had failed to dislodge the Japanese. No reinforcements were available. The supply line to Hill 260 was tenuous, and it seemed that a resolute attack from the north might cut off the two-company garrison. In view of these factors, and perhaps because the cost of holding a small hill a half-mile in front of the main perimeter seemed disproportionately high, the Americal Division asked permission to pull off the hill. Corps headquarters refused.[27]

The 13th of March was largely a repetition of the previous day's action, except that different companies were involved. To improve the supply situation and prevent the Japanese from severing the old trail by attacks from South Knob, a more direct trail from the main perimeter was cut to North Knob. At 1000 A Company, 132d, relieved E Company, 182d, on North Knob. Additional flame throwers, this time a provisional platoon from the 164th Infantry, were attached to the 182d. During the morning about one thousand 105-mm. and

---

[26] Americal Div Rpt of Bougainville Opns, p. 4.

[27] It is not clear where the request originated. On 11 March there was talk of withdrawal, but Colonel Long forbade it as authority to withdraw could come only from headquarters higher than his.

SOUTH KNOB, HILL 260, *19 March 1944.*

another thousand 4.2-inch mortar rounds hit the enemy on South Knob.[28]

At 1400, B Company, 132d, having moved out from the main perimeter, attacked up the southwest slope toward OP Tree after an artillery and mortar preparation. On North Knob A Com-

pany, 132d, provided a base of fire; B Company, 182d, was in reserve. The uphill attack succeeded in getting two platoons abreast on the southwest and west slopes of South Knob but halted in the face of grenades and rifle fire. The Japanese then retaliated with a counterattack against the left flank of B Company. A Company pushed one platoon toward OP Tree to relieve the pressure on B but it too was quickly stopped. B Company's reserve platoon drove off the attacking Japanese, whereupon the American units withdrew.

Next day the American commanders considered using tanks against the Japanese but decided against it because the vehicles could not ford the Eagle

---

[28] As Colonel Long put it in his comments, "Artillery with its dispersion and range had to be used on South Knob carefully. Artillerymen were strong for an impact fuse which gave a treetop burst of help to the observer in adjusting fire. I wanted the artillery to dig after the Japanese with delayed action fuses. I think we finally compromised on 50–50." And "you can work up a healthy argument on the type of fuse to be employed in any Officers' Club throughout the world. The Artillery like to get it in the air where their FO's can see it, and the Infantry likes to get it down into the ground where the enemy can feel it."

NORTH KNOB, HILL 260. *Note effects of artillery and mortar fire.*

River over the new trail and the hill was too steep for them to climb. After one more unsuccessful effort to capture OP Tree, the American commanders changed their plans. Patrols to the northeast of 260 had failed to find any large bodies of the enemy. Since the Japanese apparently had no more reserves to commit in that sector, and were obviously incapable of driving beyond Hill 260 against the main perimeter, the Americans decided to reduce their casualties by halting general attacks against South Knob, but to harry the enemy and reduce his strength by raids and combat patrols, by sapping forward from North Knob, and by extensive artillery and mortar fire.

Ironically enough, on 15 March, after the Americans had made their decision, the Japanese commanders made a similar one. As Colonel Magata's main attack against the 129th Infantry had gone badly, Hyakutake and Kanda decided to send Muda's main strength to reinforce Magata, leaving only a screening force on South Knob.

From then until 18 March, when General McCulloch launched a series of coordinated attacks, the Americans shelled South Knob heavily and made several ingenious attempts to burn out the Japanese with gasoline. They threw gallon cans of gas by hand and tried to ignite them with white phosphorous grenades. They jury-rigged a 60-mm. mortar for throwing cans. Finally they took two hundred feet of flexible pipe and snaked it to within nine feet of an enemy emplacement; with oxygen pressure they pumped gasoline from a drum through the pipe and over the enemy, and ignited it with a white phosphorous grenade. All the while mortars and artillery hammered away, the artillery firing at the reverse slopes while the mortars covered the hilltop. The 182d Infantry's Cannon Company emplaced its 75-mm. pack howitzers on Hill 309 for direct fire and did its best to knock down OP Tree. By 14 March South Knob, jungled no longer, was a bare, blasted slope. At 1900, 17 March, OP Tree fell to the ground. During the action more then ten thousand 105-mm. rounds struck South Knob. When all was over, the Americans reported counting 560 enemy dead. American casualties totaled 98 killed, 24 missing, and 581 wounded.[29]

Action by the Creeks

The sector of the 37th Division's 129th Infantry, where Colonel Magata delivered his attack, was generally flat and low. In contrast with the *Iwasa Unit,* which assaulted up very steep slopes, Magata's soldiers possessed easy routes of approach along Numa Numa Trail and various streams. The 129th, in the center of the 37th Division's line, held about 3,900 yards of curving front from a point slightly east of the Numa Numa Trail west and southwest to the right

flank of the 148th Infantry. Several small streams, all tributaries of the Koromokina River, flowed through the area in a generally southerly direction. Taylor Creek cut through the 129th's lines less than 1,000 yards west of Numa Numa Trail. Cox Creek entered the line about 750 yards southwest of Taylor Creek's penetration. The Logging Trail, cut and used extensively by XIV Corps engineers in the relatively peaceful days before March, entered the main perimeter just west of Taylor Creek.

The 129th Infantry, commanded by Col. John D. Frederick, held its front with two battalions in line. The 2d Battalion, on the right, faced north, its left (west) flank joined to the right of the 3d Battalion between Cox Creek and another branch of the Koromokina River.

In general, the 129th's positions were stronger than the 145th's, since the terrain permitted grazing fire except in the numerous ravines and gullies that were scatttered throughout the area. Earth-and-log-pillboxes, mutually supporting and arranged in depth, formed the backbone of the main line of resistance, which was wired in behind single barbed wire and double-apron barbed wire fences. Antipersonnel mines had been laid in front of the wire. The entire front was covered by interlocking bands of machine gun fire. Additional rows of double-apron barbed wire extended diagonally from the main line of resistance to channel Japanese attacks into the machine gun fire lanes. In addition to division artillery, mortars, and the 75-mm. pack howitzers of the 129th's Cannon Company, the front was supported by 37-mm. antitank guns (firing canister) and 40-mm. antiaircraft guns.

---

[29] These figures come from Griswold, Bougainville, p. 120. The 182d Infantry's report gives figures which differ slightly from these. Colonel Long later wrote, in his comments, that the wounded-in-action figure was somewhat inflated because fatigue cases had been diagnosed with "unreasonable freedom" and counted among the wounded.

The 2d Battalion, under Lt. Col. Preston J. Hundley, had in line three rifle companies, F, G, and E from left to right. Cox Creek lay in F Company's sector, the Logging Trail and Taylor Creek in G's, and the Numa Numa Trail in E's.

During the early days of the *17th Army's* attack the 129th Infantry received mortar and artillery fire, engaged in fire fights and patrol clashes, and strengthened its positions, but was not heavily engaged in battle. But on 11 March Colonel Magata moved forward from his assembly area behind Mount Nampei to begin the attack that was designed to pierce the 129th Infantry and capture the Piva airfields not far away. Outposts and patrols reported increasing numbers of Japanese troops in front of the 129th, and the artillery fired on them off and on all day. When an antipersonnel mine in front of E Company was exploded about 1600, Colonel Frederick ordered in the outposts. Shortly afterward Japanese troops were reported advancing down the Logging Trail toward the perimeter. Starting at 1800, when all outposts and patrols had come in, division artillery and mortars laid a ten-minute concentration to the front of Colonel Hundley's battalion. A patrol from G Company went out to examine the impact area, now cleared of underbrush and foliage, but came under Japanese fire and returned to the perimeter to report that it had located no less than fourteen enemy machine guns.

In the gathering dusk Magata's troops —the *1st Battalion, 45th Infantry,* on the left (east) and the *3d Battalion* on the right—opened up on the 2d Battalion, 129th, with machine guns and rifles. The Americans replied with rifles, mortars,

machine guns, and a 40-mm. antiaircraft gun, which along with a .50-caliber machine gun put searching fire up the Logging Trail. Machine guns in the front-line pillboxes abstained from firing so as not to reveal their locations to the enemy. This fire fight continued until 1920, then died down to flare up sporadically throughout the night.

General Beightler, at 2100, ordered his regimental commanders to keep their troops alert, for documents captured that day (apparently on Hill 700) indicated that the Japanese planned to attack in strength the next day. At the same time, as Japanese soldiers began working their way through the American wire, C Company, 82d Chemical Battalion, was attached to the 129th Infantry, and at 0420 the next morning its 2d Platoon moved its 4.2-inch mortars into position behind the Antitank Company, 129th, which was supporting the rifle companies.

By dawn of 12 March, though the Japanese had made earnest efforts to get through the lines, they found they had been held for very small gains. As the coming of daylight clarified the situation, the 2d Battalion, 129th, found that the Japanese had succeeded in cutting through G Company's wire and effecting two minor penetrations. In the 2d Platoon sector, where Taylor Creek and the Logging Trail entered the perimeter, the Japanese had captured two pillboxes (one an alternate, unoccupied position), and to the right (east) they had seized five pillboxes.

The Japanese tried to exploit their penetrations and break out to the south but were held back by American artillery, mortar, machine gun, and rifle fire. Then the 129th prepared to counterattack and restore the line. Colonel Frederick ordered C Company out of regimental reserve and forward to support G Company at 0723. By 0810, when C Company moved into position behind the 2d Platoon of G Company, one platoon of the Antitank Company had attacked the western penetration and retaken one pillbox. During the rest of the morning another Antitank Company platoon moved in behind E Company; 81-mm. mortars of D Company, 129th, took up positions to support the 2d Battalion; and B Company moved forward behind C.

At 1255, after a mortar concentration, three rifle platoons (two from C and one from G), plus two flame throwers, attacked the western penetration and by 1405 had retaken the second pillbox. The Japanese retaliated with a counterattack that was promptly repulsed. By the end of the day the Japanese still held the five pillboxes, which the Americans had not attacked, in the 3d Platoon's sector. Two Americans had been killed, twenty-two wounded in the day's action as compared with one killed and six wounded the day before.

American artillery and mortars shelled the enemy during the night. Searchlights tried to illuminate him with direct beams, but failed as he took refuge in the ravines and draws. The searchlights then achieved more success by raising their beams so that they were reflected from the clouds.

The *1st* and *3d Battalions* of the *45th Infantry* struck again at G Company about 0400 of 13 March and gained one more pillbox before they were stopped. To eliminate this penetration, Colonel

Frederick requested tanks.[30] Corps headquarters, at 0815, released the 1st Platoon of C Company, 754th Tank Battalion, to the 129th. General Griswold released the tanks with the express proviso that they could not be used as stationary defenses, but must be employed in an attack to recapture the lost pillboxes. At 0812 General Beightler ordered the 129th not to deliver any piecemeal infantry attacks but to wait for the tanks and organize a co-ordinated tank-infantry assault. He issued this order just fifteen minutes after C Company, 129th, made a local counterattack which regained one pillbox.

Four tanks and elements of B, C, and G Companies attacked at 1000 after a ten-minute artillery preparation. Although the ground was generally level, the tanks had difficulty in bringing their guns to bear because the Japanese were down in ravines with steep slopes. After two pillboxes had fallen, the tanks withdrew. The attack was renewed at 1315. After another hour the tanks had almost exhausted their fuel and ammunition, and the attack was suspended while the 2d Platoon, C Company, 754th Tank Battalion, came up to replace them.[31] The new tanks and the same infantry units attacked at 1730. This time the tanks and infantry managed to demolish all the Japanese-held pillboxes. By 1930, at a cost of eighteen wounded, the original line was almost restored. Colonel Magata withdrew his battalions to rest, re-

---

[30] His request for tanks on 12 March had been turned down.

[31] During the afternoon XIV Corps headquarters assigned one battalion of the 131st Engineer Regiment to buttress the 1st Battalion, 24th Infantry, on the 129th regimental reserve line. A Company of the 131st had been assigned the day before.

organize, reconnoiter, and make ready for another attack.

On the 14th, a day that was quiet except for small arms fire and occasional shelling, the 2d Battalion repaired its positions, strung new wire, planted mines in the ravines that provided covered routes of approach, and fired its mortars. Patrols went out and reported the presence of strong bodies of the enemy not far from the perimeter. Thus the Americans were sure that the Japanese withdrawal was only temporary.

Temporary it was, for at 0400 of 15 March the *1st* and *3d Battalions* of the *45th Infantry* and the *2d Battalion, 81st Infantry,* renewed the assault. They again achieved a small local success in the Cox Creek sector held by the 2d Platoon of F Company. By dawn they had seized one pillbox and penetrated to a depth of about one hundred yards. F Company, supported by one platoon of C Company and aided by a 36-plane air strike in front of the battalion line, counterattacked with flame throwers and bazookas to recapture the pillbox by 1153. But the enemy, still holding a salient in the line, was digging positions in the roots of banyan trees and appeared to be pushing in reinforcements and more weapons.

General Craig, arriving in the sector to observe and inform General Beightler, as he had on Hill 700, asked for tanks. General Griswold sent a platoon. A tank-infantry attack, delivered at 1500 with artillery and mortar support, made small gains. A second, at 1635, killed or drove off all the enemy at a cost of seven killed, fifty-six wounded, and one tank damaged. One hundred and ninety Japanese corpses lay within the American lines,

and four enemy soldiers were captured. The Japanese suspended their assaults on 16 March but renewed them on the 17th and effected a small penetration in F Company's sector which tanks and infantry promptly eliminated.

This was the last attack for several days, for the Japanese overhauled their plans. They had decided to abandon the attacks on Hills 260 and 700 in favor of a massed attack by the depleted regiments of the *17th Army* against the 129th Infantry. While the survivors of the *Muda* and *Iwasa Units,* except for the screening forces on Hill 260, moved through the jungles to Magata's position, the front lines remained static. Artillery and mortar fire, patrol skirmishes, and fire fights continued, especially in the sector of the 2d Battalion, 129th Infantry. By 23 March the *13th* and *23d Regiments* had joined Magata and the attack was ready. But captured documents and reconnaissance enabled the Americans to divine Japanese intentions, so that in late afternoon of the 23d Beightler warned his troops to expect a general attack at dusk.

After dark the Japanese shelled the American positions. As before, sporadic fire fights went on all night and, concealed by the darkness, nearly all Hyakutake's remaining units attacked through the ravines.[32]

The 37th Division artillery and the various mortars promptly opened fire and largely broke up the Japanese assault before it got started. But the enemy

---

[32] In 1949 Kanda asserted that on his recommendation Hyakutake had called off this attack, but the validity of his assertion is belied by American experience and by contemporary Japanese documents.

MAJ. GEN. ROBERT S. BEIGHTLER, *Commanding General, 37th Division, directing tank-infantry attack, 16 March 1944.*

succeeded in again piercing the 1st Platoon of F Company in the Cox Creek area, this time a little to the west of the earlier penetration.[33] About one hundred Japanese soldiers captured four pillboxes and pushed to a low ridge about twenty-five yards from the battalion command post. When dawn broke a fire fight was raging throughout the entire area as the Japanese unsuccessfully attempted to enlarge their holdings.

The American commanders responded promptly. Two platoons of the Antitank Company and one platoon of K Company, 129th, assembled near the 2d Battalion command post, and General

Beightler dispatched two companies of the 148th Infantry to positions behind Colonel Hundley's battalion. The Antitank and K Company platoons, plus the 3d Platoon, A Company, 754th Tank Battalion, attacked northwest from the command post at 0725 and within twenty minutes had gained possession of the ridge. At 0930 the attackers reorganized and drove in again, supported this time by 37th Division artillery, three battalions of the Americal Division artillery, the 129th Infantry Cannon Company, and twenty-four 4.2-inch mortars, which fired into the ravines.[34] The Americans burned, dug, and blasted the Japanese

---

[33] Also defending this sector, in supporting positions, were platoons of B and C Companies.

[34] The fire was repeated twice during the afternoon.

TANK-INFANTRY ATTACK, *16 March 1944. Men following the medium M4 tank are from the 129th Infantry.*

out of their ravines, trenches, foxholes, and pillboxes while the seven artillery battalions, their fire directed by General Kreber and augmented by the heavy mortars, shelled the concentrated enemy troops in front of the American lines. By 1400 General Griswold had dispatched more reserves to the area but they were not needed. The Japanese were dead or dispersed, the line restored. Hyakutake's counteroffensive was over.

His troops withdrew from the 129th's front pursued by the Fijians and two American battalions from the corps reserve, and on the same day he told Imamura that further attacks would be fruitless. Imamura left the next move to Hyakutake but ordered him to resort to guerrilla warfare and raise as much of his own food as possible. Hyakutake, though not abandoning his desire to counterattack, elected to withdraw to the posts whence he had come. The *6th Cavalry* and the *2d Battalion, 4th South Seas Garrison Unit,* came north to cover the retreat which began on 27 March. South Knob of Hill 260 was evacuated; the Americans reoccupied it on 28 March. The withdrawal was an orderly affair, although wounded men and heavy equipment were abandoned along the way.

In the attack the Japanese had lost over 5,000 men killed, more than 3,000 wounded. The XIV Corps lost 263 dead

JAPANESE PILLBOX ON FIRE

in its successful defense.[35] The *17th Army*, in spite of its serious losses, was still an effective fighting force; late March and early April saw several sharp fights when the XIV Corps fanned out to pursue the enemy and enlarge the perimeter.[36]

So ended the last Japanese offensive effort in the Solomons. Had it succeeded, it would have seriously affected the course of the war in the Solomons by requiring the commitment of more men, ships, and planes to recapture Empress Augusta Bay. But it is unlikely that it would have had any real effect on the final outcome of the war.

---

[35] Griswold, Bougainville, p. 139; 8th Area Army Operations, Japanese Monogr No. 110 (OCMH), p. 111. By 29 April twenty-eight 75-mm., one 105-mm., and four 150-mm. field pieces had fallen into Allied hands.

[36] This was done to gain commanding ground, to establish trail blocks, and, at the behest of the War

Department, to give combat experience to the 1st Battalion, 24th Infantry, and the 25th Regimental Combat Team of the 93d Division, which arrived in late March.

CHAPTER XVIII

Finale: Emirau

March was a busy month in the Admiralties and at Empress Augusta Bay, where battles raged almost simultaneously. It was also a month of important decisions that culminated in the last Allied offensive move directed against Rabaul and Kavieng.

General MacArthur and his staff for some time had been convinced that the invasion of Hansa Bay in New Guinea was not a worthwhile move. On 3 March, just after the reconnaissance force landed in the Admiralties, General Chamberlin suggested to other members of the staff that since Rabaul and Kavieng were now so much weaker than when operations were planned it might be possible, if carrier-based aviation was provided, to bypass Hansa Bay and advance beyond Wewak in a long leap forward.[1] Two days later, by radio, MacArthur took up the question with the Joint Chiefs of Staff. Explaining that complete occupation of the Admiralties would soon follow, he argued that the success of the reconnaissance party presented an excellent opportunity to move west along the north coast of New Guinea. He suggested that his forces seize Kavieng at once, bypass Hansa Bay, and advance all the way to Hollandia in Netherlands New Guinea, if Admiral Nimitz could provide the carriers for a short time. Carriers would be required for fighter cover, for Hollandia lay beyond effective fighter-plane range of the most westerly Southwest Pacific bases. Such a move, he pointed out, would bypass the main strength of Adachi's *18th Army* (then at Madang and Wewak) and speed the advance to the Vogelkop by several months.[2]

The Joint Chiefs of Staff were undoubtedly influenced by Halsey's arguments against Kavieng and in favor of Emirau, and by Nimitz' opposition to Kavieng, as well as by MacArthur's proposals. They ordered that the Kavieng plan be canceled, that Emirau be seized instead, and that Kavieng and Rabaul be isolated with minimum forces. They authorized the bypassing of Hansa Bay in favor of the invasion of Hollandia. The Hollandia invasion would be the

---

[1] See Min of Conf, 1700, 3 Mar 44, at GHQ SWPA, in GHQ SWPA G–3 Jnl, 3 Mar 44. See also Smith, *The Approach to the Philippines*, p. 9.

[2] Rad, MacArthur to CofS for JCS, 5 Mar 44, in GHQ SWPA G–3 Jnl, 5 Mar 44. On the same day MacArthur told Krueger of the proposals he had made and ordered him to prepare plans for both Hollandia and Hansa Bay so as to be ready for any contingency. Rad, MacArthur to Comdr ALAMO, 5 Mar 44, in GHQ SWPA G–3 Jnl, 5 Mar 44.

first direct move in MacArthur's advance to the Philippines.[3]

MacArthur forwarded the relevant provisions of the orders to Halsey, directing him to revoke plans for Kavieng and to seize, occupy, and defend Emirau with minimum forces at the earliest possible moment. At Emirau a light air and naval base was to be established from which to blockade the Bismarck Archipelago and neutralize Truk. Meanwhile operations to neutralize Rabaul and Kavieng would continue.[4]

Admiral Halsey has written that when he received these orders at Nouméa he was surprised, but that no special problems were raised. "This entailed no more than dusting off our original plan, picking the landing force, and notifying Ping Wilkinson and Roy Geiger to load them in."[5]

Commodore Reifsnider was given command of the amphibious force. The landing force Halsey selected was a new regiment, the 4th Marines, which had been created out of the recently disbanded raider battalions.[6] Landing force command was entrusted to General Noble of the Marine Corps. Carried aboard nine APD's and one APA and escorted by nine destroyers and two tugs, the landing force sailed from Guadalcanal on 18 March and made a peaceful voyage past the Solomons and New Ireland to Emirau. On 20 March, while four old battleships fired 1,079 14-inch and 12,281 5-inch shells at Kavieng, the Marines went peacefully ashore. There were no Japanese; air bombardments and naval gunfire were unnecessary. This operation, wrote Admiral Halsey, established "a record of six days between 'Stand by to shove off!' and 'Well done!' "[7]

Within a month 18,000 men and 44,000 tons of supplies had been ferried to Emirau. The first airstrip was opened in May.[8] From here Allied planes and torpedo boats patrolled New Ireland, and when bomber strips were ready long-range bombers from Emirau and Nissan could reach Truk.

And so, peacefully and almost anticlimactically, the Emirau operation was concluded, and with it the long, hard-fought series of operations against Rabaul which had begun with the invasion of Guadalcanal almost two years before. Whereas the first of the operations, Guadalcanal and Papua, were agonizingly slow, the CARTWHEEL and Bismarck Archipelago campaigns had clicked off with speed and precision. In less than one year MacArthur's and Halsey's forces fought their way from Guadalcanal and Buna through Woodlark, Kiriwina, Nassau Bay, New Georgia, Lae, Salamaua, Nadzab, the Markham and Ramu Valleys, Finschhafen, the Treasuries, Empress Augusta Bay, Arawe, Cape Gloucester, Saidor, the Green Islands,

---

[3] JCS 713/4, 12 Mar 44, title: Future Opns in Pac; Rad, JCS to MacArthur, 12 Mar 44, in Marshall's OUT Log. For Hollandia and subsequent operations see Smith, *The Approach to the Philippines.*

[4] Rad, MacArthur to COMSOPAC, 13 Mar 44, in GHQ SWPA G–3 Jnl, 13 Mar 44.

[5] Halsey and Bryan, *Admiral Halsey's Story,* p. 190.

[6] It was numbered the 4th to commemorate the 4th Marine Regiment that was taken prisoner on Corregidor.

[7] Halsey and Bryan, *Admiral Halsey's Story,* p. 191.

[8] See Morison, *Breaking the Bismarcks Barrier,* pp. 423–24; Rentz, *Bougainville and the Northern Solomons,* pp. 117–19.

Emirau, and the Admiralties. They gained control of all the seas and straits, as well as the air, in the whole vast region of the Japanese Southeast Area. Using carrier aircraft and planes based on airfields captured by ground forces that had been transported and protected by air and naval surface forces, they reduced Rabaul to impotence. They destroyed hundreds of Japanese planes, seriously diminished the dwindling force of trained pilots, sank or damaged precious warships, chewed up three Japanese divisions and several brigades, and safely bypassed some 100,000 Japanese who, for practical purposes, were now out of the war. Together with Admiral Nimitz' forces, they forced Japanese air and naval surface forces to evacuate the Southeast Area. In taking these strides, the Allied forces of the South and Southwest Pacific Areas accomplished their assigned mission of defending the U.S.–Australian line of communications. They also placed MacArthur's forces in position to start the drive along the New Guinea coast to the Philippines.

This great advance from Guadalcanal and Buna employed elements of the armed forces of three nations and called for the most careful co-ordination and timing of a complex variety of operations. With the exception of large armored battles, true close air support, and struggles between aircraft carrier task forces, CARTWHEEL and the Bismarck operations boasted about every important type of action, singly and in combination, that, characterized World War II. There were bitter struggles for a few yards of swampy jungles; land marches; assaults against fortified positions; gallant defenses; parachute jumps and air-

lifts; amphibious invasions, both ship-to-shore and shore-to-shore; air and naval support bombardments; fighter sweeps; large bombing raids; strikes by land- and carrier-based planes against ships; and gun and torpedo actions between surface warships. Throughout the series of battles an improvement in technique, especially in amphibious operations, is apparent.

All the invasions shared a dominant feature; in each case the range of the fighter plane was a vital factor in determining the objective, setting the timetable, and fixing the limits of the advance. Aircraft carriers might have made longer advances possible, but during much of the time they were not available and doctrines then current warned against using carriers to support the invasion of air and naval bases.

Planning and executing these forward moves were military accomplishments of a high order, and the credit must be shared by all participants from the area commanders to the men in the ranks. But stamped upon the whole series of operations is the imprint of the higher commanders. Although many of the staff officers and subordinate commanders stood out prominently and later won greater fame and rose to higher posts—Krueger, Collins, Harmon, Twining, Carney, Turner, Kenney, Kinkaid, Barbey, Sutherland, Fechteler, Chamberlin, Swift, Vandegrift, Geiger, Griswold, Hodge, Wilkinson, Beightler, and Turnage, to name a representative few—it is clear that General MacArthur and Admiral Halsey dominated and controlled the campaigns.

They were different men, and they worked differently: MacArthur, austere and aloof, insisting that his staff and subordinate commanders reach agreement on details; Halsey, with a salty façade of bluff humor and informality, working more closely with his generals and admirals. But both possessed and exhibited exceptional leadership and judgment. And they worked well together. With an easy, cordial relationship, they co-operated and assisted each other to further the Allied cause. They shuttled ships back and forth from area to area to bolster each other's forces, and they timed operations in such a way that, as General Marshall predicted, forward moves in each area supported the other, thwarted the enemy strategy, and gained a significant victory. This victory was won at the cost of fewer casualties than the Japanese sustained in defeat. Both MacArthur and Halsey were obviously deeply conscious of their responsibility for conserving the lives of the men entrusted to their leadership, and considered each objective, not only in terms of its strategic value, but also in terms of human life.

In opposing the Allies, the Japanese had fought with characteristic resolution and often with great skill, but to little avail. Except for their delaying tactics in New Georgia, which slowed the campaign and required the commitment of far more Allied troops than had been planned, they were uniformly unsuccessful. General Imamura and Admiral Kusaka were, as far as the evidence indicates, experienced and skillful. Close analysis fails to show many overt errors in their strategy or in its execution. The flaw in their conduct of operations was fundamental, and was imposed on them by *Imperial General Headquarters;* they had to try too much with too little. Attempting to hold almost the entire Southeast Area with inferior numbers of men, ships, planes, and guns, they lost it all except the parts the Allies neither needed nor wanted. They had possessed, strategically speaking, interior lines which enabled them to switch reserves back and forth and to reinforce their forward units as long as they controlled the air and the sea. But they were so badly outnumbered that the advantages of interior lines were vitiated from the start, and when they lost control of the air and the sea the interior lines became valueless. Having lost the initiative, they never knew exactly where and when the next blow would fall and were never able to dispose their forces properly to meet it.

The Allied forces operated, strategically, on exterior lines—which as has often been pointed out present to the attacker greater difficulties but also greater promise of decisive results. Because of their superior strength the Allies could select targets so as to avoid strong points and seize lightly held, strategically valuable areas. In short, the Allies were able to use the bypass technique with its concomitant savings in lives and time.

So it was that March 1944 saw the Allies as far forward as Emirau, the Admiralties, and Saidor, with the Southwest Pacific forces making ready to drive toward the Philippines.

Bibliographical Note

This volume is based upon three general types of sources of information: official records, chiefly of the U.S. Army; manuscript histories or first narratives prepared during the war by Army historians in the field and now in the custody of the Office of the Chief of Military History (OCMH); and published works, especially the air and naval histories cited so frequently.

Official Records

Papers of the Combined and Joint Chiefs of Staff

These papers, which are basic to an understanding of strategy, were, when consulted, under the control of the Office of the Assistant Chief of Staff, G–3 Operations, General Staff, U.S. Army. Principal files consulted were: Combined Chiefs of Staff (CCS), Joint Chiefs of Staff (JCS), and Joint Staff Planners (JPS) minutes of meetings, including the bound volumes containing the minutes and papers of the various international conferences, from mid-1942 through March 1944; all CCS, JCS, and JPS papers dealing with Pacific strategy and command for the same period; and the Notes on Pacific Conference Held in March 1943.

Army Records

The bulk of the research for this volume was performed in Army records. They are voluminous in quantity, inconsistent in quality. Unless otherwise indicated, when consulted they were in the custody of the Army Records Section, Departmental Records Branch, Office of The Adjutant General (DRB AGO), now designated as the Military Records Branch, Federal Records Center, Region 3.

General George C. Marshall's Log for the period covered contains radiograms exchanged by Marshall and the theater and subordinate Army commanders in Marshall's capacities as Chief of Staff and as an Executive Officer for the JCS. It is filed in the Staff Communications Office, Secretary of the General Staff, U.S. Army.

The most useful body of records from General Headquarters, Southwest Pacific Area (GHQ SWPA), and successor commands, is the G–3 Journal and Journal File. It is an absolutely essential source for the period and region covered by this volume. It contains all the important planning papers, memoranda, letters, radiograms, orders, estimates, periodic operations and intelligence reports from immediately subordinate headquarters, and many action reports. Other useful papers from GHQ are: The ELKTON Plans of 12 February 1943 and 26 April, photostats of which are in OCMH files; Military Intelligence Section, General Headquarters, Far East Command, The Intelligence Series, Vol. III, Operations of the Military Intelligence Section, GHQ SWPA/FEC/SCAP (in six parts), Tokyo, 1950, and Vol. IV, Operations of the Allied Intelligence Bureau, GHQ SWPA, Tokyo, 1948 (both edited by Maj. Gen. Charles A. Willoughby, copies of OCMH files). Copies of the three volumes of the history prepared for General Douglas MacArthur by his historical section in Tokyo were received by the OCMH shortly before completion of the research and writing of this book. These volumes are works of some merit, but the first two, which deal with the war, do not add to the information that was already available in other sources. Volume I, tentatively entitled Allied Operations in the Southwest Pacific Area, contains little on Allied plans and operations that is not already available in published works; Volume II, tentatively entitled Japanese Operations in the Southwest Pacific Area, is largely based on the Japanese monographs discussed below but is not as detailed.

Since Headquarters, U.S. Army Forces in the South Pacific Area (USAFISPA), was not a tactical headquarters, its most valuable records are those dealing with planning. USAFISPA File No. 381, Preliminary Planning COMSOPAC and COMGENSOPAC (in the Kansas City Records Center, Office of the Adjutant General, Kansas City, Missouri), is a good source as are three files from the Historical Section, G–2, South Pacific Base Command (which succeeded USAFISPA): SOPAC Notes, a documented narrative on the preliminaries to Munda; Planning for New Georgia Operation, which contains 105 pages of copies of radios, letters, memoranda, and plans; and Supplementary New Georgia Material. The

last three are in the custody of the OCMH.

Records of the various tactical headquarters which conducted the invasions or battles described in this volume are, on the average, good.

For Woodlark and Kiriwina, the Sixth Army [ALAMO Force] prepared an excellent report. The operations reports and journals of the 112th Cavalry and the 158th Infantry are good.

Documents on New Georgia are uneven. The report of the New Georgia Occupation Force provides only a sketchy outline, but the G–2 and G–3 Journals and Files of the XIV Corps are satisfyingly complete. The XIV Corps and its principal subordinate headquarters also prepared the Informal Report on Combat Operations in the New Georgia Campaign. A report on lessons learned rather than an operations narrative, it is very valuable. The 43d Division's report is about the same as the Occupation Force report, and its journals and files are not always complete. Those of its regiments vary. The 37th Division, whose journals and files are complete, prepared a fine, crisp, day-by-day action report. The report of the 25th Division, which includes regimental and battalion reports, is a model of brevity, honesty, and clarity.

Pending publication of the Australian Army's official histories, Australian records must be studied for the complete story of the Nassau Bay–Lae–Salamaua–Nadzab–Finschhafen–Markham Valley–Ramu Valley operations. The following American records relate to U.S. Army participation: 41st Division Artillery, History of the Salamaua Campaign, 23 April–4 October 1943; 2d Engineer Special Brigade, Report of Combat Operations, 30 June 1943–30 June 1944; the 162d Infantry reports and journals, which are very full; the 503d Parachute Infantry Report of Operations, Markham Valley, 5–19 September 1943; and several of the published works listed below.

U.S. Army operations on Bougainville are excellently covered by the reports, journals, and files of the XIV Corps, 37th Division, Americal Division, and component units, all of which are good and complete. In addition Maj. Gen. Oscar W. Griswold's typewritten Bougainville: An Experience in Jungle Warfare, and the History of the "TA" Operation by the Assistant Chief of Staff, G–2, XIV Corps, are useful.

The Army side of the Arawe–Cape Gloucester–Saidor invasions is well covered by: the ALAMO Force reports, journals, and files which, like all papers from Lt. Gen. Walter Krueger's headquarters, are first-rate; the DIRECTOR Task Force and 112th Cavalry reports and journals; and the MICHAELMAS Task Force's reports and war diary. In addition a number of reports from observers at Arawe are in the GHQ SWPA and ALAMO Force G–3 Journals.

Similarly, the ALAMO Force records for the Admiralties are excellent, as are those of the 1st Cavalry Division which include reports and journals of the division, the two brigades, and all principal subordinate units.

Navy Records

The publication of Samuel Eliot Morison's excellent *Breaking the Bismarcks Barrier* in 1950 made extensive research in Navy records quite unnecessary. However the following, all filed in the Classified Operations Records Branch, Division of Naval History, Office of the Deputy Chief of Naval Operations for Administration (formerly the Office of Naval Records and Library), were consulted: Commander, South Pacific Area and South Pacific Force, War Diary: 1 January 1943–30 June 1944; Commander, Amphibious Force, South Pacific Force (Task Force 31), War Diary: 1–31 July 1943; Commander, Aircraft, South Pacific Force (Task Force 33), War Diary: 1 April 1943–31 March 1944. In addition several orders and reports from the Seventh Fleet and the VII Amphibious Force are also to be found the Operations Reports Collection (GHQ, SWPA) of The Adjutant General's Office, Department of the Army. At the time of this writing, this collection was in the custody of the Military Records Branch, Region 3, GSA.

Marine Corps Records

The existence of very good published works obviated the necessity for extensive research. Marine Corps documents, filed in the Historical Branch, G–3, Headquarters, U.S. Marine Corps, that were consulted include: I Marine Amphibious Corps, Bougainville Beachhead; Headquarters, New Georgia Air Force [Forward Echelon, 2d Marine Air Wing], Special Action Reports, 1st Phase, New Georgia, 29 June–13 August 1943, and 2d Phase, New Georgia, 14 August–20 October 1943, with annexes; and 1st Marine Raider Regiment, Special Action Report, New Georgia, and its War Diary, 15 March–30 September 1943.

Japanese Records

The best sources of enemy information, besides the innumerable documents captured in the field during World War II and employed extensively in the preparation of the first narratives, are contained in the series of monographs entitled Japanese Studies in World War II. These were prepared in Tokyo, after the conclusion of hostilities, by former Japanese Army and Navy officers and under the supervision of the Historical Section, G-2, GHQ Far East Command, and translated by the Allied Translator and Interpreter Section, Supreme Commander for the Allied Powers. Copies of the original Japanese and the translated versions are filed in OCMH, where dubious passages in the English versions were retranslated by Messers. Stanley L. Falk, Brewster Hurwitz, Burke C. Peterson, Thomas G. Wilds, and Robert J. C. Butow.

Miscellaneous

Admiral William F. Halsey, Jr.'s brief but explicit report, Narrative Account of the South Pacific Campaign, 29 April 1942–15 June 1944, is useful, as is Lt. Gen. Millard F. Harmon's similar The Army in the South Pacific. Australian activities are covered by Allied Land Forces' Report on New Guinea Operations, 23 September 1942–22 January 1944, a copy of which the Australian Army generously furnished to the OCMH. For geography and terrain the War Department's secret Survey of the Solomon Islands, and the Terrain Studies and Terrain Handbooks prepared by the Alllied Geographical Section, GHQ SWPA, are best.

Prior to publication of this volume draft copies of the manuscript were sent to over fifty surviving senior commanders and staff officers in an effort to elicit helpful criticisms, corrections, suggestions, and, particularly, additional information. The following officers responded most generously with letters, notes, and marked manuscript pages, which are filed in the OCMH: Vice Adm. Daniel E. Barbey (Ret.); Maj. Gen. Allison J. Barnett (Ret.); Maj. Gen. Robert S. Beightler (Ret.); Brig. Gen. William J. Bradley (Ret.); Rear Adm. Miles R. Browning (Ret.); Admiral Arthur S. Carpender (Ret.); Maj. Gen. William C. Chase (Ret.); Lt. Col. Julio Chiaramonte; Maj. Gen. Kenneth Cooper; Brig. Gen. Charles F. Craig (Ret.); Admiral D. B. Duncan (Ret.) (who answered for Admiral Robert B. Carney (Ret.), Vice Adm. Harry R. Thurber (Ret.), and Vice Adm. Ralph E. Wilson [Ret.]); Lt. Gen. Clyde D. Eddleman; Col. Glenn S. Finlay (Ret.); Maj. Gen. William H. Gill (Ret.); Lt. Gen. Oscar W. Griswold (Ret.); Col. J. Prugh Herndon (Ret.); Maj. Gen. John H. Hester (Ret.); General John R. Hodge (Ret.); Col. Temple G. Holland (Ret.); the late Lt. Col. Frank O. Hough; Col. Daniel H. Hundley (Ret.); General George C. Kenney (Ret.); the late Fleet Admiral Ernest J. King; General Walter Krueger (Ret.); Fleet Admiral William D. Leahy; Col. William D. Long (Ret.); Col. Archibald R. MacKechnie (Ret.); Maj. Gen. Robert B. McClure (Ret.); Brig. Gen. William A. McCulloch (Ret.); Maj. Gen. Clarence A. Martin (Ret.); Col. Alexander M. Miller, III (Ret.); Hon. Hugh M. Milton, II; the late Maj. Gen. Verne D. Mudge; Maj. Gen. Dewitt Peck, USMC

(Ret.); Lt. Col. David M. N. Ross (Ret.); Col. Douglas Sugg (Ret.); General Gerald C. Thomas (Ret.); General Allen H. Turnage, USMC (Ret.); General Nathan F. Twining.

Manuscript Histories

For all operations in the South Pacific Area, The History of the United States Army Forces in the South Pacific Area During World War II, 30 March 1942–1 August 1944, contains essential background information. It was prepared by, and under the supervision of, Maj. Frederick P. Todd, USAFISPA Historical Section, and Capt. Louis Morton, G–2 Historical Section, South Pacific Base Command.

The G–2 Historical Section of the South Pacific Base Command also prepared the History of the New Georgia Campaign and The Bougainville Campaign. The first consists of text, colored maps showing movements and dispositions, and photographs. Of nine chapters of text, which cover the New Georgia operation in great detail, the first was written by Todd, the other eight by WOJG Joseph J. Rubin. The Bougainville Campaign, which was written by Lt. Col. Edwin Cates, Cpl. Stanley L. Jones, and T/4 Francis A. Saunders, Jr., is a methodical, detailed discussion of the operation. It contains no maps except a dimly photostated version of a Marine Corps Hasty Terrain Map. No positions or movements are shown.

General MacArthur's headquarters wrote no similar campaign histories, but the Historical Section, G–3, GHQ SWPA, prepared a series called Studies in the History of the Southwest Pacific Area, of which Volume II, New Guinea and Bismarcks Campaign, 22 January 1943–20 October 1944, summarizes the planning and operations described in this volume. It was used extensively in preparing Allied Operations in the Southwest Pacific Area.

Published Works

The number of books relating to the subject matter of this volume grows with the years. Some of the volumes listed below bear directly on the CARTWHEEL operations. Others, not necessarily cited in this book, provide essential background information.

[Frierson, Maj. William C.] *The Admiralties: Operations of the 1st Cavalry Division (29 February–18 May 1944),* AMERICAN FORCES IN ACTION. This pamphlet is the definitive account.

Arnold, Henry H. *Global Mission.* New York: Harper & Brothers, 1949.

DeChant, John A. *Devilbirds: The Story of United States Marine Corps Aviation in World War II.* New York: Harper & Brothers, 1947.

Cline, Ray S. *Washington Command Post: The Operations Division,* UNITED STATES ARMY IN WORLD WAR II. Washington: U.S. Government Printing Office, 1951.

Craven, Wesley Frank, and James Lea Cate (eds.). *The Army Air Forces in World War II,* Vol. IV, *The Pacific: Guadalcanal to Saipan—August 1942 to July 1944.* Chicago: The University of Chicago Press, 1950. This fine book obviated the need for research in Army Air Forces records.

Feldt, Comdr. Eric A., RAN. *The Coastwatchers.* Melbourne, Australia, and New York: Oxford University Press,

1946. The American edition is shorter than the Australian.

Frankel, Stanley A. *The 37th Infantry Division in World War II*. Washington: Infantry Journal Press, 1948.

Gillespie, Oliver A. *The Pacific*. "The Official History of New Zealand in the Second World War, 1939–1945." War History Branch, Department of Internal Affairs. Wellington, New Zealand, 1952.

Halsey, Fleet Admiral William F., and Lt. Comdr. J. Bryan, III. *Admiral Halsey's Story*. New York: Whittlesey House, 1947.

Heavey, Brig. Gen. William F. *Down Ramp! The Story of the Army Amphibian Engineers*. Washington: Infantry Journal Press, 1947.

Hough, Lt. Col. Frank O., USMCR, and Maj. John A. Crown, USMCR. *The Campaign on New Britain*. Historical Branch, Headquarters, U.S. Marine Corps. Washington: U.S. Government Printing Office, 1952.

Karolevitz, Capt. Robert F. (ed.). *The 25th Division and World War II*. Baton Rouge, La.: Army and Navy Publishing Company, 1946.

Kenney, George C. *General Kenney Reports: A Personal History of the Pacific War*. New York: Duell, Sloan and Pearce, 1949.

King, Admiral Ernest J. *Our Navy at War: A Report to the Secretary of the Navy Covering Our Peacetime Navy and Our Wartime Navy and Including Combat Operations up to March 1, 1944*. Washington: U.S. News, 1944.

King, Ernest J., and Walter Muir Whitehill. *Fleet Admiral King: A Naval Record*. New York: W. W. Norton & Company, Inc., 1952.

Krueger, General Walter. *From Down Under to Nippon: The Story of the Sixth Army in World War II*. Washington: Combat Forces Press, 1953.

Leahy, Fleet Admiral William D. *I Was There: The Personal Story of the Chief of Staff to Presidents Roosevelt and Truman Based on His Notes and Diaries Made at the Time*. New York: Whittlesey House, 1950.

McCartney, William F. *The Jungleers: A History of the 41st Infantry Division*. Washington: Infantry Journal Press, 1948.

Marshall, General of the Army George C. *Biennial Report of the Chief of Staff of the United States Army, July 1, 1943, to June 30, 1945, to the Secretary of War*. Washington: U.S. Government Printing Office, 1945.

Matloff, Maurice, and Edwin M. Snell, *Strategic Planning for Coalition Warfare: 1941–1942*, UNITED STATES ARMY IN WORLD WAR II. Washington: U.S. Government Printing Office, 1953.

Morison, Samuel Eliot. *History of United States Naval Operations in World War II*, Vol. VI, *Breaking the Bismarcks Barrier: 22 July 1942–1 May 1944*. Boston: Little, Brown and Company, 1950.

Office of the Chief Engineer, General Headquarters, Army Forces Pacific. *Engineers of the Southwest Pacific: 1941–1945*. Vol. I, *Engineers in Theater Operations*. Vol. VI, *Airfield and Base Development*. Vol. VIII, *Critique*. Washington: U.S. Government Printing Office 1947, 1951, 1951.

Rentz, Maj. John N., USMCR. *Bougainville and the Northern Solomons*. Historical Section, Division of Public Information, Headquarters, U.S. Marine Corps. Washington: U.S. Government Printing Office, 1948.

———. *Marines in the Central Solomons.* Historical Branch, Headquarters, U.S. Marine Corps. Washington: U.S. Government Printing Office, 1952.

Robson, R. W. (ed.). *The Pacific Islands Handbook, 1944* (North American ed.). New York: The Macmillan Company, 1946.

Sherrod, Robert. *History of Marine Corps Aviation in World War II.* Washington: Combat Forces Press, 1952.

Sherwood, Robert E. *Roosevelt and Hopkins: An Intimate History.* New York: Harper & Brothers, 1948.

United States Strategic Bombing Survey. *The Thirteenth Air Force in the War Against Japan.* Washington: U.S. Government Printing Office, 1946.

———. *The Employment of Forces Under the Southwest Pacific Command.* Washington: U.S. Government Printing Office, 1947. This is a slightly rearranged version of the Studies in the History of the Southwest Pacific Area.

———. *Interrogations of Japanese Officials.* 2 Vols. Washington: U.S. Government Printing Office, 1946.

———. *The Allied Campaign Against Rabaul.* Washington: U. S. Government Printing Office, 1946.

Wright, Maj. B. C. *The 1st Cavalry Division in World War II.* Tokyo, Japan: Toppan Printing Company, 1947.

Zimmer, Col. Joseph E. *The History of the 43d Infantry Division, 1941–1945.* Baton Rouge, La.: Army and Navy Publishing Company, n.d.

Glossary

AA	Antiaircraft
AAF	Army Air Forces
ACofS	Assistant Chief of Staff
AdVon	Advance Echelon
AF	Air Force
AFPAC	Army Forces, Pacific
AGC	Combined operations communications headquarters ship. In Pacific most frequently used as flagships of amphibious force or group commanders.
AGO	Office of The Adjutant General
AKA	Cargo ship, attack
ALF	Allied Land Forces
ANF	Allied Naval Forces
AP	Transport
APA	Transport, attack
APC	Coastal transport
APD	High-speed destroyer-transport
ATIS SCAP	Allied Translator and Interpreter Section, Supreme Commander for the Allied Powers
AW	Automatic weapons
BAR	Browning automatic rifle
Bazooka	Rocket launcher, hand-carried
BB	Battleship
BYPRODUCT	Code name for Trobriand Islands (Kiriwina)
CA	Coast Artillery
CCS	Combined Chiefs of Staff
CG	Commanding General
CHRONICLE	Code name for plan for seizure of Woodlark and Kiriwina
CINCPAC	Commander in Chief, U.S. Pacific Fleet
CINCPOA	Commander in Chief, Pacific Ocean Area
CINCSWPA	[Commander in Chief] Supreme Commander, Southwest Pacific Area
CM–IN	Classified Message, In
CM–OUT	Classified Message, Out
CNO	Chief of Naval Operations
CO	Commanding Officer
C (s)ofS	Chief (s) of Staff
Com	Committee

COMAIRSOPAC	Commander [land-based], Aircraft, South Pacific Force
COMAMPHIBFORSOPAC	Commander, Amphibious Force, South Pacific Force
Comd	Command
Comdr	Commander
COMGEN	Commanding General
COMGENSOPAC	Commanding General, U.S. Army Forces in the South Pacific Area
COMINCH	Commander in Chief, U.S. Fleet
COMSOPAC	Commander, South Pacific Area and South Pacific Force
COMSOWESPAC	Commander, Southwest Pacific (also CINCSWPA)
Cons	Construction
CRU	Cruiser
CTF	Commander, Task Force
CTG	Commander, Task Group
CV	Aircraft carrier
CVE	Aircraft carrier, escort
DD	Destroyer
DEXTERITY	Code name for western New Britain–Saidor operation
DMS	Destroyer-minesweeper
DRYGOODS	Code name for assembly of supplies at Guadalcanal–Tulagi area for offensive in New Georgia, February 1943
DUKW	2½-ton, 6 x 6 amphibious truck
ELKTON	Code name for MacArthur's plan for recapture of Rabaul
ESB	Engineer special brigade
FA	Field Artillery
FEC	Far East Command
FM	Field Manual
FO	Field Orders
G–1	Personnel officer or section of a general staff, down through divisional level
G–2	Intelligence officer or section of general staff, down through divisional level
G–3	Operations officer or section of a general staff, down through divisional level
G–4	Supply officer or section of a general staff, down through divisional level
GHQ	General headquarters
GO	General Orders
Incl (s)	Inclosure (s)
Ind	Indorsement
Instal	Installation
JCS	Joint Chiefs of Staff
Jnl (s)	Journal (s)
JPS	Joint Staff Planners

Jt	Joint
JUSSC	Joint U.S. Strategic Committee
KCRC	Kansas City Records Center, Office of the Adjutant General, Kansas City, Missouri
LCI	Landing craft, infantry
LCM	Landing craft, mechanized
LCP (R)	Landing craft, personnel (ramp)
LCT	Landing craft, tank
LCV	Landing craft, vehicle
LCVP	Landing craft, vehicle, personnel
LEATHERBACK	Code name for Woodlark Island
LHQ	Land Headquarters (also ALF)
LST	Landing ship, tank
MAC	Marine Amphibious Corps
MAINYARD	Code name for Guadalcanal Island
Min	Minutes
MIS	Military Intelligence Section
MTB	Motor torpedo boat
NCB	Naval construction battalion
NGF	New Guinea Force
NGOF	New Georgia Occupation Force
NLG	Northern landing group
OCMH	Office of the Chief of Military History
OI	Operations Instructions
ONI	Office of Naval Intelligence
OPD	Operations Division, War Department General Staff
PB4Y4	Naval designation of B–24
PBY	Twin-engine U.S. Navy patrol bomber (Black Cat)
Plng	Planning
POA	Pacific Ocean Area
POSTERN	Code name for Lae–Finschhafen–Madang operations
PT	Motor torpedo boat
PTO	Pacific Theater of Operations
PV–1	Twin-engined Navy patrol plane, also used as a night fighter
RAAF	Royal Australian Air Force
RAAFCAAF	Royal Australian Air Force Comand, Allied Air Forces
RAF	Royal Air Force
RAN	Royal Australian Navy
Rcn	Reconnaissance
RCT	Regimental combat team
RENO	Code name for MacArthur's plan for advancing along north coast of New Guinea and thence to Mindano
RN	Royal Navy

S–3	Operations officer or section of a regimental or battalion headquarters
SBD	Scout bomber (Douglas)—a Navy dive-bomber
SC	Submarine chaser
SCR	Signal Corps radio
SL	Searchlight
SNLF	Special naval landing force (Japanese)
SOPAC	South Pacific Area, South Pacific Force
SOPACBACOM	South Pacific Base Command
SR	Special Regulations
SWPA	Southwest Pacific Area
SYMBOL	Code name for Casablanca Conference 14–23 January 1943
TBF	Single-engine U.S. Navy torpedo bomber
TF	Task Force
TM	Technical Manual
TOENAILS	Code name for New Georgia operation
TU	Task Unit
USA	U.S. Army
USAFFE	U.S. Army Forces in the Far East
USAFISPA	U.S. Army Forces in the South Pacific Area
USASOS SWPA	U.S. Army Services of Supply, Southwest Pacific Area
USMC (R)	U.S. Marine Corps (Reserve)
USN	U.S. Navy
USSBS	U.S. Strategic Bombing Survey
WD	War Department
WDGS	War Department General Staff
YMS	Motor minesweeper

Basic Military Map Symbols*

Symbols within a rectangle indicate a military unit, within a triangle an observation post, and within a circle a supply point.

Military Units—Identification

Antiaircraft Artillery . . . .

Armored Command . . . .

Army Air Forces . . . .

Artillery, except Antiaircraft and Coast Artillery . . . .

Cavalry, Horse . . . .

Cavalry, Mechanized . . . .

Chemical Warfare Service . . . .

Coast Artillery . . . .

Engineers . . . .

Infantry . . . .

Medical Corps . . . .

Ordnance Department . . . .

Quartermaster Corps . . . .

Signal Corps . . . .

Tank Destroyer . . . .

Transportation Corps . . . .

Veterinary Corps . . . .

Airborne units are designated by combining a gull wing symbol with the arm or service symbol:

Airborne Artillery . . . .

Airborne Infantry . . . .

*For complete listing of symbols in use during the World War II period, see FM 21–30, dated October 1943, from which these are taken.

Size Symbols

The following symbols placed either in boundary lines or above the rectangle, triangle, or circle inclosing the identifying arm or service symbol indicate the size of military organization:

Squad	●
Section	●●
Platoon	●●●
Company, troop, battery, Air Force flight	I
Battalion, cavalry squadron, or Air Force squadron	II
Regiment or group; combat team (with abbreviation CT following identifying numeral)	III
Brigade, Combat Command of Armored Division, or Air Force Wing	X
Division or Command of an Air Force	XX
Corps or Air Force	XXX
Army	XXXX
Group of Armies	XXXXX

EXAMPLES

The letter or number to the left of the symbol indicates the unit designation; that to the right, the designation of the parent unit to which it belongs. Letters or numbers above or below boundary lines designate the units separated by the lines:

Company A, 137th Infantry . . . . A⊠137

8th Field Artillery Battalion . . . . ·8

Combat Command A, 1st Armored Division . . . . A⬯I

Observation Post, 23d Infantry . . . . △23

Command Post, 5th Infantry Division . . . . ⊠5

Boundary between 137th and 138th Infantry . . . . —|||— 137 / 138

Weapons

Machine gun	●→
Gun	●
Gun battery	⊥⊥⊥⊥
Howitzer or Mortar	●+
Tank	◇
Self-propelled gun	◨

UNITED STATES ARMY IN WORLD WAR II

The multivolume series, UNITED STATES ARMY IN WORLD WAR II, consists of a number of subseries which are tentatively planned as follows: The War Department, The Army Air Forces, The Army Ground Forces, The Army Service Forces, Defense of the Western Hemisphere, The War in the Pacific, European Theater of Operations, Mediterranean Theater of Operations, The Middle East Theater, The China-Burma-India Theater, The Technical Services, Special Studies, and Pictorial Record.

The following volumes have been published or are in press: *

The War Department
> *Chief of Staff: Prewar Plans and Preparation*
> *Washington Command Post: The Operations Division*
> *Strategic Planning for Coalition Warfare: 1941–1942*
> *Strategic Planning for Coalition Warfare: 1943–1944*
> *Global Logistics and Strategy: 1940–1943*
> *The Army and Economic Mobilization*
> *The Army and Industrial Manpower*

The Army Ground Forces
> *The Organization of Ground Combat Troops*
> *The Procurement and Training of Ground Combat Troops*

The Army Service Forces
> *The Organization and Role of the Army Service Forces*

Defense of the Western Hemisphere
> *The Framework of Hemisphere Defense*

The War in the Pacific
> *Okinawa: The Last Battle*
> *Guadalcanal: The First Offensive*
> *The Approach to the Philippines*
> *The Fall of the Philippines*
> *Seizure of the Gilberts and Marshalls*
> *Victory in Papua*
> *CARTWHEEL: The Reduction of Rabaul*

European Theater of Operations
> *The Lorraine Campaign*
> *Cross-Channel Attack*
> *Logistical Support of the Armies, Volume I*
> *Logistical Support of the Armies, Volume II*
> *The Supreme Command*

Mediterranean Theater of Operations
> *Northwest Africa: Seizing the Initiative in the West*

---

* The volumes on the Army Air Forces, published by the University of Chicago Press, are not included in this list.

The Middle East Theater
The Persian Corridor and Aid to Russia
The China-Burma-India Theater
Stilwell's Mission to China
Stilwell's Command Problems
Time Runs Out in CBI
The Technical Services
The Transportation Corps: Responsibilities, Organization, and Operations
The Transportation Corps: Movements, Training, and Supply
The Transportation Corps: Operations Overseas
The Quartermaster Corps: Organization, Supply, and Services, Volume I
The Quartermaster Corps: Organization, Supply, and Services, Volume II
The Quartermaster Corps: Operations in the War Against Japan
The Ordnance Department: Planning Munitions for War
The Signal Corps: The Emergency
The Signal Corps: The Test
The Medical Department: Hospitalization and Evacuation, Zone of Interior
The Corps of Engineers: Troops and Equipment
The Chemical Warfare Service: Organizing for War
Special Studies
Three Battles: Arnaville, Altuzzo, and Schmidt
The Women's Army Corps
Rearming the French
Chronology: 1941–1945
Military Relations Between the United States and Canada: 1939–1945
Pictorial Record
The War Against Germany and Italy: Mediterranean and Adjacent Areas
The War Against Germany: Europe and Adjacent Areas
The War Against Japan

Index